Prioritizing Development

This book is a unique guide to making the world a
better place. Experts apply a critical eye to the United
Nations' Sustainable Development agenda, also
known as the Global Goals, which will affect
the flow of $2.5 trillion of development aid up
until 2030.

Renowned economists, led by Bjorn Lomborg,
determine what pursuing different targets will cost
and achieve in social, environmental, and economic
benefits. There are 169 targets, covering every area of
international development – from health to education,
and from a sanitation to conflict.

Together, these analyses make the case for
prioritizing the most effective development
investments. A panel of Nobel Laureate economists
identify a set of nineteen phenomenal development
targets and argue that this would achieve as much as
quadrupling the global aid budget.

BJORN LOMBORG is the President of the
Copenhagen Consensus Center and a visiting
professor at the Copenhagen Business School. He
researches the smartest ways to do good, for which he
was named one of *Time* magazine's 100 most
influential people in the world. His numerous books
include *The Skeptical Environmentalist* (Cambridge,
1998), *Cool It* (2010), *How to Spend $75 Billion to
Make the World a Better Place* (2014), and *The Nobel
Laureates' Guide to the Smartest Targets for the
World 2016–2030* (2015).

Prioritizing Development

A Cost Benefit Analysis of the United Nations' Sustainable Development Goals

Edited by

BJORN LOMBORG
Copenhagen Business School

CAMBRIDGE
UNIVERSITY PRESS

University Printing House, Cambridge CB2 8BS, United Kingdom

One Liberty Plaza, 20th Floor, New York, NY 10006, USA

477 Williamstown Road, Port Melbourne, VIC 3207, Australia

314–321, 3rd Floor, Plot 3, Splendor Forum, Jasola District Centre, New Delhi – 110025, India

79 Anson Road, #06–04/06, Singapore 079906

Cambridge University Press is part of the University of Cambridge.

It furthers the University's mission by disseminating knowledge in the pursuit of education, learning, and research at the highest international levels of excellence.

www.cambridge.org
Information on this title: www.cambridge.org/9781108415453
DOI: 10.1017/9781108233767

© Copenhagen Consensus Center 2018

First published 2018

Printed in the United Kingdom by TJ International Ltd. Padstow Cornwall

A catalogue record for this publication is available from the British Library.

ISBN 978-1-108-41545-3 Hardback
ISBN 978-1-108-40145-6 Paperback

Contents

List of Figures   x

List of Tables   xiii

List of Boxes   xix

List of Contributors   xx

Foreword: Why Measurement of
Costs and Benefits Matters for the SDG
Campaign   xxiv
Stefan Dercon and Stephen A. O'Connell

Introduction   1
Bjorn Lomborg

1   Benefits and Costs of Air Pollution Targets
for the Post-2015 Development
Agenda   13
Bjorn Larsen
1.1   ALTERNATIVE PERSPECTIVE
Mike Holland   35
1.2   ALTERNATIVE PERSPECTIVE
Marc Jeuland   37

2   Targets for Biodiversity and Deforestation   38
Anil Markandya
2.1   ALTERNATIVE PERSPECTIVE
Luke Brander   50
2.2   ALTERNATIVE PERSPECTIVE
Alistair McVittie   52

3   Benefits and Costs of the Climate Change
Targets for the Post-2015 Development
Agenda   54
Isabel Galiana
3.1   ALTERNATIVE PERSPECTIVE
Robert Mendelsohn   64
3.2   ALTERNATIVE PERSPECTIVE
Carolyn Fischer   66

4   Beyond Civil War: The Costs of Interpersonal
    Violence   67
    James Fearon and Anke Hoeffler
    4.1   ALTERNATIVE PERSPECTIVE
    S. Brock Blomberg   89
    4.2   ALTERNATIVE PERSPECTIVE
    Rodrigo R. Soares   90

5   Data Revolution: The Cost and Benefit of Data
    Needed to Monitor the Post-2015 Development
    Agenda   91
    Morten Jerven
    5.1   ALTERNATIVE PERSPECTIVE
    Deborah Johnston   117
    5.2   ALTERNATIVE PERSPECTIVE
    Gabriel Demombynes and Justin Sandefur   118

6   Benefits and Costs of the Education Targets
    for the Post-2015 Development Agenda   119
    George Psacharopoulos
    6.1   ALTERNATIVE PERSPECTIVE
    Caroline Krafft and Paul Glewwe   141
    6.2   ALTERNATIVE PERSPECTIVE
    Peter F. Orazem   142

7   Benefits and Costs of the Energy Targets for the
    Post-2015 Development Agenda   143
    Isabel Galiana
    7.1   ALTERNATIVE PERSPECTIVE
    Adele Morris   168
    7.2   ALTERNATIVE PERSPECTIVE
    Madeleine Gleave and Todd Moss   170

8   Benefits and Costs of the IFF Targets for the
    Post-2015 Development Agenda   171
    Alex Cobham
    8.1   ALTERNATIVE PERSPECTIVE
    Peter Reuter   189
    8.2   ALTERNATIVE PERSPECTIVE
    Dev Kar and Tom Cardamone   191

9   Benefits and Costs of the Trade Targets for the
    Post-2015 Development Agenda   192
    Kym Anderson
    9.1   ALTERNATIVE PERSPECTIVE
    Bernard Hoekman   216
    9.2   ALTERNATIVE PERSPECTIVE
    Patrick Low   217

10 Benefits and Costs of the Health Targets for the
    Post-2015 Development Agenda   219
    *Prabhat Jha, Ryan Hum, Cindy L. Gauvreau,
    and Keely Jordan*

11 Benefits and Costs of the Noncommunicable
    Disease Targets for the Post-2015 Development
    Agenda   231
    Rachel Nugent and Elizabeth Brouwer

12 Benefits and Costs of the Women's Health Targets
    for the Post-2015 Development Agenda   244
    *Dara Lee Luca, Johanne Helene Iversen,
    Alyssa Shiraishi Lubet, Elizabeth Mitgang,
    Kristine Husøy Onarheim, Klaus Prettner,
    and David E. Bloom*

13 Benefits and Costs of TB Control for the Post-2015
    Development Agenda   255
    Anna Vassall

14 Benefits and Costs of the Infant Mortality Targets
    for the Post-2015 Development Agenda   266
    Günther Fink

15 Benefits and Costs of the HIV/AIDS Targets for
    the Post-2015 Development Agenda   277
    *Pascal Geldsetzer, David E. Bloom,
    Salal Humair, and Till Bärnighausen*

16 Benefits and Costs of the Malaria Targets for the
    Post-2015 Consensus Project   287
    Neha Raykar

17 Benefits and Costs of Digital Technology:
    Infrastructure Targets for the Post-2015
    Development Agenda   295
    *Emmanuelle Auriol and Alexia Lee González
    Fanfalone*
    17.1 ALTERNATIVE PERSPECTIVE
    Pantelis Koutroumpis   320

18 Returns to Investment in Reducing Postharvest
    Food Losses and Increasing Agricultural
    Productivity Growth   322
    *Mark W. Rosegrant, Eduardo Magalhaes, Rowena
    A. Valmonte-Santos, and Daniel Mason-D'Croz*
    18.1 ALTERNATIVE PERSPECTIVE
    Christopher B. Barrett   337

19   Benefits and Costs of the Gender Equality Targets
      for the Post-2015 Development Agenda   339
      Irma Clots-Figueras
      19.1   ALTERNATIVE PERSPECTIVE
      Elissa Braunstein   364
      19.2   ALTERNATIVE PERSPECTIVE
      Joyce P. Jacobsen   366

20   Benefits and Costs of the Food and Nutrition
      Targets for the Post-2015 Development
      Agenda   367
      Susan Horton and John Hoddinott

21   Benefits and Costs of the Population and
      Demography Targets for the Post-2015
      Development Agenda   375
      Hans-Peter Kohler and Jere R. Behrman
      21.1   ALTERNATIVE PERSPECTIVE
      David Canning   395
      21.2   ALTERNATIVE PERSPECTIVE
      Gregory Casey and Oded Galor   397

22   Benefits and Costs of Two Science and
      Technology Targets for the Post-2015
      Development Agenda   399
      Keith E. Maskus
      22.1   ALTERNATIVE PERSPECTIVE
      Kamal Saggi   419
      22.2   ALTERNATIVE PERSPECTIVE
      Pamela Smith   420

23   Global Benefits and Costs of Achieving
      Universal Coverage of Basic Water and
      Sanitation Services as part of the 2030 Agenda
      for Sustainable Development   422
      Guy Hutton
      23.1   ALTERNATIVE PERSPECTIVE
      Dale Whittington   443
      23.2   ALTERNATIVE PERSPECTIVE
      Dale Whittington   444

24   Benefits and Costs of the Poverty Targets for the
      Post-2015 Development Agenda   446
      John Gibson
      24.1   ALTERNATIVE PERSPECTIVE
      Guarav Datt   473
      24.2   ALTERNATIVE PERSPECTIVE
      Valerie Kozel   474

25 Good Governance and the Sustainable
    Development Goals: Assessing Governance
    Targets   475
    Mary E. Hilderbrand
    25.1 ALTERNATIVE PERSPECTIVE
    Aart Kraay   497
    25.2 ALTERNATIVE PERSPECTIVE
    Matt Andrews   499

    Conclusion   501
    Identifying Phenomenal Development
    Targets   501
    Finn Kydland, Tom Schelling, and Nancy Stokey
    How to Implement the Global Goals, Knowing
    What Does a Lot of Good and What
    Doesn't   504
    Bjorn Lomborg

    Index   508

Figures

I.1 Social, economic, and environmental benefits for every dollar spent   *page* 10

1.1 Health effects of long-term PM2.5 exposure   18

3.1 Cost distributions for six cases with varying future availability of specific mitigation technologies   59

4.1 Homicides in low- and middle-income countries   68

4.2 Violence in low- and middle-income countries   68

4.3 Global child and young adult homicide rates   71

4.4 Child homicides (0–14 years) as a percentage of total homicides   71

4.5 Percent of primary caregivers using severe physical punishment   72

4.6 Percentage of women married at 18   74

4.7 Percentage of women married at 15   74

4.8 Prevalence rates of IP assault   76

4.9 Prevalence of female genital mutilation   77

4.10 Crime prevention aid and homicide rates   79

4.11 Prevalence of FGM by age   81

4.12 Civil war trends   82

6.1 Typical age–earnings profiles by level of education   120

6.2 Flat age–earnings profiles   121

6.3 A grand summary of education investment returns   126

6.4 Net primary enrollment ratio trend by region   126

6.5 Net secondary enrollment ratio (%)   127

6.6 Out-of-school children of lower secondary age   127

6.7 Tertiary education gross enrollment ratio by region   128

6.8 Moving toward the zero-target of primary school coverage   129

6.9 The marginal cost of schooling increases with enrollment   129

6.10 Benefit-cost ratio, discount rate, and rate-of-return relationship   136

7.1 Non-OECD energy consumption (quadrillion Btu) by country grouping   145

7.2 World energy consumption (quadrillion Btu)   146

7.3 Estimates of universal electrification costs   149

7.4 Energy efficiency outlook   152

7.5 Cumulative global energy efficiency investment by end-use sector in the new policies scenario 2014–2035   153

7.6 Cost curves of improving access to modern cooking fuels under differing levels of fuel price support and microfinance loans   160

8.1 Stylized representation of major IFF types   172

8.2 Ratio of average IFF to GDP, 1980–2009   176

12.1 The HPV virus family, comprised of more than 100 related viruses, and the health complications specific to oncogenic and nononcogenic types, respectively   246

14.1 Causes of under-five mortality   267

14.2 Changes in infant mortality, 1990–2013   268

14.3 Annual rates of improvements in infant mortality, 1990–2013, versus infant mortality in 1990   269

14.4 Physician density and infant mortality rates in low and middle income   272

15.1   Diagrammatic summary of
       the model   279
17.1   Mobile-cellular subscriptions per
       100 inhabitants (mobile voice
       penetration)   296
17.2   Analytical framework to assess the
       impact of broadband on the
       economy   297
17.3   Broadband penetration rates by
       speed tiers, 2012   298
17.4   Percentage of households with
       Internet access at home   299
17.5   Mobile broadband subscriptions
       per 100 inhabitants   299
17.6   Percentage increase of GDP for each
       10 percent increase in broadband
       penetration   301
17.7   Elements of a broadband
       network, access, and core/backhaul
       network   302
18.1   Mean losses by region and type
       of loss   327
18.2   Box plots of postharvest losses by
       type of loss and region   328
18.3   Mean losses by type of loss and
       commodity   329
19.1   Female-to-male ratio in primary
       education enrollment   340
19.2   Female-to-male ratio in secondary
       education enrollment   340
19.3   Female-to-male ratio in tertiary
       education enrollment   341
19.4   Ratio of female-to-male labor force
       participation rate (ILO)   341
19.5   Maternal mortality rates (per 100,000
       live births)   342
19.6   Percentage of the population with
       access to an improved water
       source   342
19.7   Adolescent fertility rate (births per
       1,000 women ages 15–19)   346
19.8   Percentage of women in national
       parliaments   352
19.9   Labor force participation rate for
       ages 15–24, female (%) (modeled
       ILO estimate)   355
19.10 Adolescent fertility rate (births
       per 1,000 women ages 15–19)   355

20.1   Trends in adult male height (in cm),
       representative countries from
       North America and Northern,
       Southern, and Eastern Europe,
       1900–2000   369
20.2   Trends in adult male height (in cm),
       representative countries from South
       America, 1900–2000   369
20.3   Trends in adult male height (in cm),
       representative countries from Asia,
       1900–2000   370
20.4   Wage path for children born in 2010
       who are not stunted, compared to
       those stunted   371
20.5   Benefit-cost ratio for nutrition
       investments, 17 countries   372
21.1   Percentage of women with an
       unmet need for family planning
       (any method) among those ages
       15–49 who are married or in a
       union: Most recent
       data available   378
21.2   Migration stock and flow across
       regions defined by economic
       development, late 2000s   384
23.1   Benefit breakdown for delivering
       universal access to basic water
       supply in urban areas   435
23.2   Benefit breakdown for delivering
       universal access to basic sanitation
       in urban areas   437
24.1   The uneven escape from extreme
       poverty around the world: Africa
       lagging   449
24.2   Overstated hunger from short
       reference period surveys   451
24.3   Declining effectiveness of growth in
       reducing poverty as poverty falls,
       Vietnam, 2002–2010   453
24.4   Changing importance of ingredients
       and eating out in household food
       consumption   454
24.5   Overstated spatial inequality
       in China's GDP per capita,
       2010   455
24.6   Agricultural productivity jumps after
       household responsibility system
       reforms in China   457

24.7   Falling inequality as China
        abandoned collective
        farming   458
24.8   Changing composition of poverty
        as countries escape mass poverty,
        Vietnam, 1993–2010   460

24.9   Lifetime labor income by gender and
        poverty status, 2012 (million VN
        dong, in December 2012 prices)   462
C.1   Efficiency of prioritizing targets   505
C.2   Social, economic, and environmental
        benefits for every dollar spent   506

Tables

I.1   Millennium development goals:
The seven key targets   *page* 4

1.1   Population exposure to ambient
PM2.5 air pollution   14

1.2   Populations using solid fuels   15

1.3   Urban and rural solid fuel use, 2012   15

1.4   Household air pollution control
targets   17

1.5   Long-term personal exposure to
PM2.5 from household fuel use
($\mu g/m^3$)   17

1.6   Levels of long-term personal
exposure to PM2.5 from household
fuel use ($\mu g/m^3$)   18

1.7   Health effects of long-term PM2.5
exposure   18

1.8   Estimated annual health effects of
household air pollution exposure   19

1.9   Valuation of mortality, 2012 (US$)   19

1.10   Valuation of morbidity, 2012 (US$)   19

1.11   Annual cost of health effects of
household air pollution exposure,
2012 (US$ billion)   20

1.12   Value of solid fuel savings of
switching to improved cookstove or
LPG, 2012 (US$/household/year)   20

1.13   Value of cooking time savings,
2012 (US$/household/year)   20

1.14   Estimates of unit costs, 2012   21

1.15   Global benefit-cost ratios of household
air pollution control targets   22

1.16   Benefit-cost ratios of household air
pollution control targets using VSL
for health valuation   23

1.17   Benefit-cost ratios of household air
pollution control targets using
DALY = US$1,000 for health
valuation   23

1.18   Benefit-cost ratios of household air
pollution control targets using
DALY = US$5,000 for health
valuation   24

1.19   Regional PM2.5 ambient air
pollution targets (annual maximum)   25

1.20   Health benefits of meeting PM2.5
ambient air quality targets
(% reduction in current health
effects)   25

1.21   Estimated annual health effects
of PM2.5 ambient air pollution
exposure   25

1.22   Valuation of mortality and
morbidity, 2012 (US$)   26

1.23   Annual cost of health effects of
outdoor ambient PM2.5 exposure,
2012 (US$ billion)   27

1.24   Cost of PM2.5 abatement from
household energy (US$/ton of
PM2.5)   28

1.25   Cost of PM2.5 abatement
from improved solid waste
management   28

1.26   Cost of PM2.5 abatement from
using ultra-low sulfur diesel
(50 ppm) for road vehicles   28

1.27   Cost of PM2.5 abatement from
DPF retrofitting of in-use diesel
vehicles (US$/ton)   29

1.28   Annual global benefits of reaching
the PM2.5 targets, 2012
(billion US$)   29

1.29   Benefits of PM2.5 emissions
reductions (US$/ton)   30

1.30   Benefit-cost ratios of household
use of improved biomass cookstoves
(ICS) and LPG, 2012   30

1.31   Benefit-cost ratios of household use of improved coal cookstoves (ICS) and LPG in East Asia, 2012   31

1.32   Benefit-cost ratios of improved solid waste management, 2012   31

1.33   Benefit-cost ratios of ultra-low sulfur diesel fuel (ULSD) for road vehicles, 2012   31

1.34   Benefit-cost ratios of DPF retrofitting of in-use vehicles, 2012   32

2.1   Aichi Targets: Qualitative assessment of benefits and costs   39

2.2   Aichi strategic goals and targets and associated investment costs   42

2.3   Net benefits from Target 5: 50 percent reduction in global forest loss   43

2.4   Net benefits from Target 5: 50 percent reduction in global wetland loss   44

2.5   Net benefits from Target 10: 50 percent reduction in global coral loss   45

2.6   Net benefits from Target 10: Increase in protected areas   46

2.7   Costs and benefits of biodiversity goals ($ billion 2012 prices)   47

2.8   Net benefits from Aichi Target 5: 50 percent reduction in rate of wetland loss   50

2.9   Net benefits from Aichi Target 10: 50 percent reduction in rate of coral loss   50

3.1   Benefit-cost summary   61

4.1   Homicide costs as a share of GDP, by World Bank region   69

4.2   Estimates of welfare costs of interpersonal and collective violence as a share of regional and global GDP for 2013   70

4.3   Estimates of welfare costs of interpersonal and collective violence as a share of country GDP for 2013, by region   70

4.4   Cost of nonfatal domestic child abuse   72

4.5   Cost of reported sexual abuse of children   73

4.6   Cost of female homicide   75

4.7   Cost of female homicides by intimate partners   75

4.8   Cost of intimate partner assault   76

4.9   Cost of reported cases of sexual violence   76

4.10   Sectoral shares of development assistance (% of total aid)   78

4.11   Aid shares (percentages) within the "Government and Civil Society" category, 2000–2010   79

4.12   Annual change in percent with war, 1990–2012   82

4.13   Percentage of countries with war, actual 2012 and 2030 by trend   82

4.14   Percentage of countries with war, actual 2012 and 2030 target   83

4.15   Number of countries with war, actual 2012 and 2030 target   83

5.1   Indicator list by information access type   95

5.2   Population survey estimated costs   97

5.3 $1 billion per target rule   101

5.4   DHS Survey question topic examples   106

5.5   Summary of the DHS Survey's general logistics   106

5.6   CWIQ Survey question topic examples   106

5.7   Summary of CWIQ Survey's general logistics   107

5.8   LSMS Survey question topic examples   107

5.9   Summary of LSMS Survey's general logistics   107

5.10   MICS Survey question topic examples   107

5.11   Summary of MICS Survey's general logistics   107

5.12   MDG time period (1990–2015) overall costs, small country (0–5 m)   108

5.13   MDG time period (1990–2015) overall costs, medium country (5–20 m)   108

5.14   MDG time period (1990–2015) overall costs, large country (20+ m)   109

5.15   CWIQ known samples   110

5.16   LSMS known surveys   110
5.17   Known censuses   112
5.18   Known DHS surveys   114
6.1   Rate of return and benefit-cost ratios
       of preschool programs in the
       United States   123
6.2   Benefit-cost ratios of preschool
       programs in developing
       countries   123
6.3   Social and private returns to
       investment in education by level
       and region (%)   124
6.4   Private returns to investment in
       education by region (%)   124
6.5   Average returns to education in
       29 OECD countries (%)   124
6.6   Social returns to investment in
       upper secondary school streams,
       Tanzania   125
6.7   Primary school enrollment ratio,
       latest data (%)   126
6.8   Preprimary gross enrollment
       ratio (%)   127
6.9   Secondary enrollment indicators,
       2011 or latest year   127
6.10   Countries at the top and bottom of
       the 2012 PISA score   128
6.11   Benefit-cost ratios by level of
       schooling and region – base
       scenario   129
6.12   Benefit-cost ratios of meeting the
       100 percent net primary enrollment
       target in sub-Saharan Africa
       by 2030   130
6.13   Benefit-cost ratios of meeting the
       100 percent net primary enrollment
       target in world by 2030   130
6.14   Preschool enrollment ratio
       2010 and target year (%)   131
6.15   Benefit-cost ratios of meeting the
       50 percent reduction of children
       who are not attending preschool in
       sub-Saharan Africa by 2030   131
6.16   Testing the sensitivity of the internal
       rate of return to B/C ratio
       conversion   136
7.1   Cost estimates for global modern
       cooking facilities   150

7.2   Benefits and costs of energy
       targets   151
7.3   Benefit-cost summary – universal
       energy access goals   161
8.1   Cost estimates for public register
       of UK company beneficial
       ownership, US$ 181
8.2   Range of benefit-cost ratios for
       proposed target (i), UK–global
       extrapolation   182
8.3   Range of benefit-cost ratios for
       proposed target (i), UK–EU–global
       extrapolation   183
8.4   Range of benefit-cost ratios for
       proposed targets   185
9.1   Comparative static effects on
       economic welfare of trade
       reform under three different
       prospective Asia–Pacific
       preferential free-trade agreements,
       2025   200
9.2   Assumptions used in the benefit-
       to-cost calculus   201
9.3   Net present value of benefits and
       costs to 2100, and benefit-to-cost
       ratios, from reducing trade barriers
       and farm subsidies globally under
       the WTO's Doha Development
       Agenda   204
9.4   Net present value of benefits and
       costs to 2100, and benefit-to-cost
       ratios, from reducing trade barriers
       and subsidies under three alternative
       Asia–Pacific regional trade
       agreements   205
10.1   Premature deaths in 2030 (millions):
       Unaltered and targeted
       reductions, by age, specific disease,
       and World Bank income
       groupings   223
10.2   Benefit-to-cost ratio for overarching
       goal: Avoiding 40 percent reduction
       in premature death   224
10.3   Benefit to cost ratio sensitivity
       analysis using a variety of
       methods   225
10.4   Benefit-to-cost ratio for proposed
       targets   226

10.5 Estimating the ratio of "disability adjusted life years" (DALY) to total "all-cause deaths," by age group, below age 70 years in the year 2012 229

11.1 Health and NCD goals, targets, and indicators 232

11.2 Projected deaths from noncommunicable diseases in 2030 235

11.3 Tobacco taxation, calculation inputs 235

11.4 Aspirin therapy, calculation inputs 236

11.5 Population salt reduction, calculation inputs 237

11.6 Hypertension management, calculation inputs 238

11.7 Secondary prevention of CVD with polydrug, calculation inputs 238

11.8 Selected interventions to achieve post-2015 NCD target: benefits and costs, BCR (3% discounting) 239

12.1 Comparison of benefit-cost ratios 249

13.1 Summary of recent studies on intensified and active case finding, screening, and the treatment of latent TB 257

13.2 Summary of key recent studies in the diagnosis and treatment of drug-susceptible TB 258

13.3 Summary of benefit-cost ratios for key TB strategies 259

13.4 Benefit for every dollar spent on reducing incidence of tuberculosis 259

14.1 Global trends in neonatal, infant, and under-five mortality 267

14.2 Regional distribution of child death by age group 268

14.3 Income per capita and distribution of infant mortality rates 270

14.4 Country-specific estimates of main causes of neonatal mortality 271

14.5 Estimated cost of scaling up essential maternal and neonatal child health services 272

14.6 Benefit-cost ratios for a comprehensive intervention package to reduce neonatal mortality by 70 percent 273

14.7 Neonatal mortality by country 275

15.1 Life years gained and cost of each goal 280

15.2 Benefit, cost, and benefit-to-cost ratio at US$1,000 per life year gained 280

15.3 Benefit, cost, and benefit-to-cost ratio at US$5,000 per life year gained 280

16.1 Western Africa: at-risk population 289

16.2 Southern and Eastern Africa: at-risk population 289

16.3 Benefit, cost, and benefit-to-cost ratio at US$1,000 per life year gained 290

16.4 Benefit, cost, and benefit-to-cost ratio at US$5,000 per life year gained 290

17.1 Targets to be analyzed in the CBA 303

17.2 Mapping penetration targets to change in lines needed for each target 304

17.3 Cost per line assumptions used for the cost-benefit analysis 305

17.4 Cost-benefit ratios depending on three scenarios 306

17.5 Net present value (NPV) of benefits and costs of conservative scenario, USD millions 306

17.6 Main parameter assumptions by scenario 308

17.7 CBA using different methodology to assess the benefits 309

17.8 Compound annual growth rate due to increase in broadband penetration, by broadband penetration target 313

17.9 Main parameters of CBA 314

17.10 Examples of broadband state aids in the European Union, 2013–2014 315

18.1 Average annual growth rates (%) to 2050 for GDP, population, and per capita GDP by region under SSP2 325

18.2 Scenario summary 325

18.3 Selected infrastructural variables and rationale 328

18.4 Econometric results 330

18.5 Investment (US$) requirements in infrastructure to reduce PHL by five percentage points 331

18.6 World prices in 2050 (% change from baseline) 331

18.7 Population at risk of hunger in 2050 332

18.8 Number of malnourished children in 2050 332

18.9 Global change in producer surplus, consumer surplus, and welfare by 2050 between baseline and investment scenarios, using a discount rate of 5 percent 333

18.10 Investment scenarios 334

18.11 Benefit-cost analysis under 100 percent cost allocation and a 5 percent discount rate 334

19.1 Violence against women 344

19.2 Violence against women, cost-effectiveness estimates 344

19.3 Percentage of 15- to 19-year-old girls married or in a consensual union by country and year 345

19.4 Reducing early marriage 347

19.5 Women's rights by country's income 350

19.6 Economic opportunities for women 354

19.7 Education for women 358

19.8 Summary of recommendations 359

19.9 Summary of BCRs 360

20.1 Benefit-cost ratio per child for nutrition investment in 17 countries 371

20.2 Benefit-cost ratio per child for nutrition investments in 17 countries for individuals working to age 50 or 60 373

21.1 Summary of costs, benefits, and benefit-cost ratios for voluntary family planning programs 377

21.2 International migrant stock as percentage of total population, by age range, 2010 384

21.3 Approximate benefit-cost ratios for key policy priorities in the area of population and demography 390

22.1 Basic figures on R&D ratios 401

22.2 Computations of discounted benefit-cost ratios for incremental R&D targets in developing countries: Raise RD/GDP ratio to 0.5 percent by 2030 (benefits and costs in $b) 404

22.3 Computations of discounted benefit-cost ratios for incremental R&D targets in emerging countries: Raise RD/GDP ratio to 1.5 percent by 2030 (benefits and costs in $b) 405

22.4 Estimates of intra-Americas bilateral migrant stocks of managerial and technical workers, 2010 408

22.5 Computations of discounted benefit-cost ratios for North–South Western Hemisphere Innovation Zone: 5 percent increase in visas for managerial and technical workers, 10-year duration (medium parameter values) 412

22.6 Computations of discounted benefit-cost ratios for North-South Western Hemisphere innovation zone: 20 percent increase in visas for managerial and technical workers phased in over five years, ten-year duration (high parameter values) 414

23.1 Population (000s) included in study by world region (years 2015 and 2030) 424

23.2 High- and low-cost scenarios for technology options for unserved populations 427

23.3 Benefits of drinking water supply, sanitation, and handwashing 428

23.4 Relative risk reductions in health impacts for WASH interventions 429

23.5 Variables, data sources, and values for health economic benefits, for the example of diarrheal diseases 431

23.6 Variables, data sources, and values for "convenience" time savings 431

23.7 Total population to serve from 2015 to 2030 to reach universal access to basic services (million) 432

23.8   Annual costs and benefits to meet
        and sustain universal access (100
        percent coverage), focusing on the
        projected unserved population in
        2015 (US$ billions)   433
23.9   Benefit-cost ratios for basic water
        supply in urban areas, by income
        quintile (3 percent discount rate)   434
23.10   Benefit-cost ratios for basic water
        supply in rural areas, by income
        quintile (3 percent discount rate)   434
23.11   Benefit-cost ratios for basic
        sanitation in urban areas, by income
        quintile (3 percent discount rate)   436
23.12   Benefit-cost ratios for basic sanitation
        in rural areas, by income quintile
        (3 percent discount rate)   436
23.13   Benefit-cost ratios for eliminating
        open defecation in rural areas, by
        income quintile (3 percent
        discount rate)   437
23.14   Benefit-cost ratios when premature
        mortality is valued at US$1,000

per DALY averted (3 percent
        discount rate)   438
23.15   Benefit-cost ratios when premature
        mortality is valued at US$5,000 per
        DALY averted (3 percent
        discount rate)   438
23.16   Countries included and excluded in
        study, by MDG region   440
23.17   Benefit-cost ratios when premature
        mortality is valued at US$1,000 per
        DALY averted (5 percent
        discount rate)   441
23.18   Benefit-cost ratios when premature
        mortality is valued at US$5,000
        per DALY averted (5 percent
        discount rate)   441
24.1   Comparison of monetary costs and
        benefits of eradicating extreme
        poverty in Vietnam (with benefits
        measured in terms of human
        capital)   463
25.1   Assessment of proposed governance
        targets   489

Boxes

25.1 Open working group proposals
for sustainable development goals:
Goal 16   476
C.1 The phenomenal development
targets   502

Contributors

Kym Anderson, George Gollin Professor of Economics, School of Economics, University of Adelaide, and Professor of Economics, Arndt-Corden Department of Economics, Australian National University, Canberra, Australia

Emmanuelle Auriol, Professor, Toulouse School of Economics, University of Toulouse, France

Till Bärnighausen, Alexander von Humboldt University Professor of Global Health, Heidelberg University, Germany and Adjunct Professor of Global Health, Harvard T.H. Chan School of Public Health, Massachusetts, USA and Lead for health systems research and impact evaluation, Africa Health Research Institute, Mtubatuba, KwaZulu-Natal, South Africa

Jere R. Behrman, W. R. Kenan, Jr. Professor of Economics and Director of Population Studies Center, University of Pennsylvania, USA

David E. Bloom, Clarence James Gamble Professor of Economics and Demography, Harvard T.H. Chan School of Public Health, Massachusetts, USA

Elizabeth Brouwer, Pharmaceutical Outcomes Research and Policy Program, University of Washington, USA

Alex Cobham, Chief Executive, Tax Justice Network

Irma Clots-Figueras, Associate Professor of Economics, Carlos III University, Madrid, Spain

Stefan Dercon, former Chief Economist, Department for International Development (DFID), UK; Professor of Economic Policy, Oxford University, UK

James Fearon, Professor in School of Humanities and Sciences and Professor of Political Science, Stanford University, California, USA

Günther Fink, University of Basel and Head of the Household Economics and Health Systems Research Unit, Swiss Tropical and Public Health Institute, Basel, Switzerland

Isabel Galiana, Lecturer, Department of Economics, McGill School of Environment, Montreal, Canada

Cindy L. Gauvreau, Post-Doctoral Fellow/Economist, Centre for Global Health Research, St. Michael's Hospital, Toronto, Canada

Pascal Geldsetzer, Research Fellow, Harvard T.H. Chan School of Public Health, Massachusetts, USA

John Gibson, Professor of Economics, University of Waikato, Hamilton, New Zealand

Alexia Lee González Fanfalone, OECD Economist/Policy Analyst and PhD Candidate Toulouse School of Economics, France

Mary E. Hilderbrand, Associate Professor of the Practice, George H. W. Bush School of Government and Public Service, Texas A&M University, USA and Faculty Affiliate, Center for International Development, Harvard University, Massachusetts, USA

John Hoddinott, H. E. Babcock Professor of Food & Nutrition Economics and Policy, Cornell University, Ithaca, New York, USA

Anke Hoeffler, Research Officer at the Centre for the Study of African Economies, University of Oxford, UK

Susan Horton, CIGI Chair in Global Health Economics, University of Waterloo, Canada

Ryan Hum, Special Lecturer, Faculty of Applied Science and Engineering, University of Toronto, Canada

Salal Humair, Senior Principal Research Scientist, Amazon.com, Inc.

Kristine Husøy Onarheim, University of Bergen, Norway

Guy Hutton, Senior Advisor, WASH, UNICEF

Johanne Helene Iversen, Medical Doctor, Advisor for Coalition for Epidemic Preparedness Innovations, University of Bergen, Norway

Morten Jerven, Associate Professor in School of International Studies, Simon Fraser University, Burnaby, British Columbia, Canada

Prabhat Jha, Professor of Economics, Canada Research Chair of Health and Development at the University of Toronto, Canada and Founding Director of the Centre for Global Health Research, St. Michael's Hospital, Toronto, Canada

Keely Jordan, Health Policy Analyst, University of California, San Francisco, USA

Hans-Peter Kohler, Frederick J. Warren Professor of Demography, University of Pennsylvania, USA

Finn Kydland, Nobel Laureate in Economic Science, Henley Professor of Economics, University of California, Santa Barbara, USA

Bjorn Larsen, Economist and Consultant

Dara Lee Luca, Economist, Mathematica Policy Research, Massachusetts, USA

Eduardo Magalhaes, Consultant, EPTD, IFPRI

Anil Markandya, Honorary Professor of Economics, University of Bath, UK and Distinguished

Ikerbasque Professor of the Basque Centre for Climate Change in the Basque Country, Spain

Keith E. Maskus, Professor of Economics, University of Colorado, Boulder, USA

Daniel Mason-D'Croz, Research Analyst, EPTD, IFPRI

Elizabeth Mitgang, Research Specialist, Georgetown University Center on Medical Product Access, Safety, and Stewardship, Washington, DC, USA

Rachel Nugent, Vice President, Global NCDs RTI International, Seattle WA, USA and Affiliate Faculty, Department of Global Health, University of Washington, Seattle, WA, USA.

Stephen A. O'Connell, former Chief Economist, United States Agency for International Development (USAID); Gil and Frank Mustin Professor of Economics, Swarthmore College, Pennsylvania, USA

Klaus Prettner, Professor of Economics, University of Hohenheim, Germany

George Psacharopoulos, Economics Expert, former London School of Economics and Political Science and the World Bank, UK

Neha Raykar, Nutrition Lead, Oxford Policy Management India

Mark W. Rosegrant, Director of the Environment and Production Technology Division, International Food Policy Research Institute (IFPRI), Washington, DC, USA

Tom Schelling, Nobel Laureate in Economic Science

Alyssa Shiraishi Lubet, School of Public Health, Harvard University, Massachusetts, USA

Nancy Stokey, Frederick Henry Prince Distinguished Service Professor in Economics, University of Chicago, Illinois, USA

Rowena A. Valmonte-Santos, Senior Research Analyst, EPTD, IFPRI

Anna Vassall, Senior Lecturer in Health Economics, London School of Hygiene and Tropical Medicine, UK

Alternative Perspective Contributors

Matt Andrews, Edward S. Mason Senior Lecturer in International Development, Harvard Kennedy School, Massachusetts, USA

Christopher B. Barrett, Stephen B. and Janice G. Ashley Professor of Applied Economics, Charles H. Dyson School of Applied Economics and Management, and Professor, Department of Economics, Cornell University, New York, USA

S. Brock Blomberg, Professor of Economics, Claremont McKenna College, California, USA

Luke Brander, Environmental Economist, Consultant

Elissa Braunstein, Associate Professor, Department of Economics, Colorado State University, USA

David Canning, Professor of Population Sciences and Professor of Economics and International Health, School of Public Health, Harvard University, Massachusetts, USA

Tom Cardamone, Managing Director, Global Financial Integrity, USA

Gregory Casey, Doctoral Candidate, Brown University, Rhode Island, USA

Guarav Datt, Associate Professor of Economics, Monash University, Australia

Gabriel Demombynes, Senior Economist, World Bank

Carolyn Fischer, Senior Fellow and Associate Director, Resources for the Future

Oded Galor, Herbert H. Goldberger Professor of Economics, Core Faculty, Population and Training

Center, Brown University, Rhode Island, USA and Fellow, Department of Economics, Hebrew University, Israel

Madeleine Gleave, Advanced Implementation Specialist, Dharma Platform, USA

Paul Glewwe, Professor of Economics, Department of Applied Economics, University of Minnesota, USA

Bernard Hoekman, Robert Schuman Chair and Research Area Director of Global Economics, European University Institute, Italy

Mike Holland, Independent Consultant, Ecometrics Research and Consulting

Joyce P. Jacobsen, Professor of Economics, Wesleyan University, Connecticut, USA

Marc Jeuland, Associate Professor, Duke University, North Carolina, USA

Deborah Johnston, Reader in Development Economics, School of Oriental and African Studies, University of London, UK

Dev Kar, Chief Economist, Global Financial Integrity, USA

Pantelis Koutroumpis, Research Fellow, Imperial College London, UK

Valerie Kozel, Associate Adjunct Professor, University of Wisconsin–Madison, USA

Aart Kraay, Economist in Development Research Group, World Bank

Caroline Krafft, Assistant Professor of Economics, St. Catherine University, Minnesota, USA

Patrick Low, Vice President for Research and Senior Fellow, Fung Global Institute, Hong Kong

Alistair McVittie, Resource Economist, Scottish Agricultural College, UK

Robert Mendelsohn, Edwin Weyerhaeuser Davis Professor of Forest Policy, Professor of Economics, and Professor, School of Management, Yale University, Connecticut, USA

Adele Morris, Fellow and Policy Director for Climate and Energy Economics Project, Brookings Institution, Washington, DC, USA

Todd Moss, Chief Operating Officer and Senior Fellow, Center for Global Development

Peter F. Orazem, Professor of Economics, Department of Economics, Iowa State University, USA

Peter Reuter, Professor in School of Public Policy and Department of Criminology, University of Maryland, USA

Kamal Saggi, Professor of Economics, Vanderbilt University, Tennessee, USA

Justin Sandefur, Research Fellow, Center for Global Development

Pamela Smith, Associate Professor of Applied Economics, University of Minnesota, USA

Rodrigo R. Soares, Professor of Economics, Sao Paulo School of Economics, Brazil

Dale Whittington, Professor, Departments of Environmental Sciences & Engineering, and City & Regional Planning, University of North Carolina at Chapel Hill, USA, and Manchester Business School, UK

Foreword

Why Measurement of Costs and Benefits Matters for the SDG Campaign

The Sustainable Development Goals (SDGs) provide an extraordinary vision of what global development should look like between now and 2030. Starting with the concept of sustainability, the SDGs go far beyond the Millennium Development Goals (MDGs) to incorporate a set of environmental and social-justice priorities that require national action at all levels of income. As agreed by 193 signatory nations at the September 2015 United Nations General Assembly, the 2030 Agenda for Sustainable Development (https://sustainabledevelopment.un.org/post2015/transformingourworld) is meant to be *universal, indivisible*, and *interlinked*. In conventional development arenas like extreme poverty and hunger the SDGs also inspire, doubling down on the MDGs by defining success in absolute rather than relative terms. Global partners target an end to poverty in all its forms, for example, rather than a 50 percent reduction in extreme-poverty headcount ratios.

The UN's drive for universal norms and targets involved widespread public debate and painstaking negotiations and compromises between national governments. The process was simultaneously more transparent and much more difficult and convoluted than when the MDGs emerged from behind closed doors a decade and a half ago. Some widening in the scope of commitments was inevitable and also desirable, to accommodate sustainability goals and build a truly global coalition. But there was also widespread awareness as negotiations proceeded that fewer goals might allow for greater success. By the latter standard, the 2030 Agenda is daunting. With 17 global goals and 169 highly ambitious targets, the Agenda seems in danger of departing not just in scope but also in coherence from the elegant eight goals and 17 targets of the MDGs.

In practice, therefore, a great deal remains on the table in terms of shaping global action. This is true not just in the conventional sense of identifying cost-effective approaches to individual targets but also in the deeper sense of operationalizing – and unavoidably, prioritizing – targets at the national and global levels. This book makes a vital contribution to what should be a collective effort to prioritize.

Cost-benefit analysis (CBA) is a well-established method for prioritizing spending in a world of limited budgets, not least in some of the poorest settings of the world. When done carefully, CBA and its cousin, cost-effectiveness analysis (which evaluates alternative approaches to achieving a given result), provide a transparent and evidence-based approach to identifying cost-effective uses of public money. Working together with ex-post evaluation and careful monitoring during program delivery, CBA can increase both the quality and the quantity of public spending, by shifting funds toward high-value projects and convincing funders (ultimately, taxpayers) that they are getting value for their money.

The Copenhagen Consensus should be applauded for its campaign to bring rigorous CBA evidence to bear in public debates on the scope of the SDGs. The papers collected here informed a comprehensive scorecard that covered the majority of the proposed targets and was available during the final year of negotiations. The analysis suggested what was at stake: assuming best-practice interventions, a failure to prioritize across goals could reduce a comprehensive measure of total benefits by 75 percent or more per dollar of costs. Losses of similar magnitude could accompany the pursuit of overambitious target levels or suboptimal interventions.

To date, this analysis has had less traction than the Copenhagen Consensus hoped, a result familiar to any practitioner of cost-benefit analysis within governments and development agencies. The hope that the analysis would guide a winnowing of the goals did not materialize. But these studies remain crucial, as inputs into the debates that will now be required to operationalize the SDGs.

We focus on two questions in this foreword. First, why prioritize? We will discuss what the MDGs accomplished and how these lessons should inform the SDG process looking forward. Second, how should development actors – governments, development agencies, and nongovernmental and civil-society organizations – use the cost-benefit evidence collected here?

We should be candid at the outset on two matters. First, neither of us is convinced that top-down goal setting within international organizations represents the best route to development success. Development efforts require local and national political buy-in to be successful. Achieving growth and development in a society is complicated, messy, and context-specific and is about more than allocating resources. Outside of narrow corridors within which best practices are known and the links between inputs and outcomes are tight (as with some public health and humanitarian interventions), the allure of "buying" development – reducing development to spending a particular sum of money – is an illusion. Second, cost-benefit analysis has its own methodological limitations. Almost by definition, the clarity of a benefit-to-cost ratio is greater than what the data and modeling apparatus can support. Used uncritically, the method can support overconfident rankings between outcomes that are not easily compared and invite generalization across contexts that differ in unmeasured ways. Despite these observations, however, we strongly believe that cost-benefit exercises as conducted in this book should get more attention and should be used in debates on the allocation of resources across the world.

From MDGs to SDGs

The SDG process was spurred on by global successes during the MDG period, including a spectacular outcome for the extreme-poverty headcount ratio that was confidently predictable well before the SDG consultations began in earnest. The argument for doubling down, however, rested on a claim that observed outcomes were the *result* of the MDGs, implying that they would not have occurred without the goals, targets, and institution building of the campaign. That claim remains controversial, for the simple reason that the counterfactual – the outcome that would have emerged without the MDGs – is not observable. Still, a few facts stand out that may well be attributable to some extent to the presence of the MDGs.

The global aid envelope expanded dramatically in the period since the MDGs were agreed, from US$80bn in 2000 to US$147bn in 2015 and after a period of stagnation in aid volumes during the 1990s. The clarity of the narrative around the MDGs may have helped to revive political interest in aid, amid fairly widespread disillusion among rich countries in the 1990s. The chosen goals were modest in number, and they were sufficiently non-controversial to mitigate conflicts of interest between donors and recipients. Their collective adoption was consistent with ongoing efforts to enhance donor coordination and avoid costly duplication of activity. Numerical targets were a key innovation of the MDG campaign: they promised an increase in two-way accountability, underpinned by credible and transparent mechanisms to monitor progress.

The discourse of *what gets measured gets done* acquired impetus late in the MDG campaign, reflecting a growing perception that the adoption of numerical targets did succeed in increasing accountability throughout the development cooperation system. By this argument, sending countries acquired leverage for holding recipients to account in the use of their funding, while recipient countries and other stakeholders were able to assess the alignment of donor portfolios – the countries and programs donors were willing to fund – with MDG priorities. Both sides plausibly faced new costs of reneging on MDG-related commitments, as no stakeholder could publicly repudiate a target like cutting poverty in half.

The Department for International Development (DFID) and the United States Agency for International Development (USAID) both made major efforts to bolster accountability during the 2000s, tied in some cases directly to MDG targets. USAID's Feed the Future program, for example, adopted the headcount ratio as a program target within its zones of influence, while DFID increasingly concentrated its spending in countries failing in income poverty reduction and the other MDGs. Late in the process both the World Bank (2013) and USAID (2014) appropriated extreme-poverty targets directly into their mission statements. The World Bank and UN system invested heavily from the outset in publicly available data and monitoring around the MDGs, an activity that undoubtedly spurred new research and may have facilitated watchdog innovations, including the Center for Global Development's aid-quality measures.

Formal attempts to construct a convincing counterfactual will continue. To date, the research has been limited to controlling for preexisting trajectories by looking for improvements in indicator trends among aid-receiving countries around the time the MDGs were adopted. Timing may of course be a weak proxy for the intensity of treatment, given that countries differed sharply in their exposure to MDG-related aid flows and that donor priorities had already moved decidedly in favor of poverty-reduction goals during the Highly Indebted Poor Countries Initiative of the late 1990s. These concerns notwithstanding, the research to date suggests a decidedly mixed picture: some indicators are consistent with a new departure around 2000, and others are not (see, for example, World Bank, Global Monitoring Report (GMR) 2016/2016). They also carry a sobering message looking forward because if preexisting trends represent a legitimate counterfactual, then the successes of the MDGs have made the remaining task considerably more difficult. The countries with the biggest indicator deficits in 2015 are, in many cases, those with the most adverse indicator trends over the past decade. This is in sharp contrast with China and India, which had the largest poverty deficits in 2000 but were already achieving spectacularly favorable (China) or at least modestly favorable (India) indicator trends before 2000. China, of course, received almost no development assistance

after 2000, and India received very little on a per capita basis.

Our own view is that whatever else the MDGs achieved, the campaign revitalized global development efforts by expanding aid flows and increasing accountability and coordination among donors. The troubling question is whether the sprawling scope of the SDGs puts these achievements at risk, especially against the headwinds of slower global growth. An agenda that is too broad to galvanize focused action may fail to sustain overall aid flows, misdirect such flows as are available, and risk returning the development community to a low-accountability mode of business as usual.

The SDG agreement shows clear if indirect awareness of this concern, pushing back vigorously with its characterization of the goals as universal, indivisible, and interlinked. From this perspective, the SDGs are less a set of competing goals than a comprehensive checklist for achieving the one great objective of ending global poverty on a sustainable basis. This interpretation is broadly consistent with the World Bank's interpretation of its own extreme-poverty mission (see World Bank, GMR 2015/2016, referenced earlier), and with USAID's *Vision for Ending Extreme Poverty*. These interpretations give targets for the extreme-poverty headcount ratio pride of place, but they define poverty as a multidimensional and contextualized phenomenon and lay out a theory of change that is broad enough to validate a very wide list of complementary targets.

But this returns us to prioritization. A central contribution of the MDG campaign was to elevate a plausibly universal concept of development itself – not as economic growth or progress, as crucial as those might be on instrumental grounds, but as elimination of human deprivation. The SDGs double down here as well, by incorporating sustainability and an insistence on *leaving nobody behind*. But characterizing a set of 169 targets as indivisible and interlinked comes close to repudiating any attempt to prioritize or assign responsibility. Accountability may lose its foothold if most forms of development spending can be validated in terms of their direct objectives while weak impacts can be explained away through appeals to inadequate efforts by other actors or failures elsewhere in the system. And even where lines of responsibility are clear – as in the data-collection arena where the public-good aspect demands public provision – the magnitude of the task overwhelms available resources. In short, the leverage implied by *what gets measured gets done* strains credulity when stretched so far. We cannot credibly claim that *whatever* gets measured gets done.

Finally, we worry that a proliferation of targets may run afoul of some well-defined perils of scale. Numerical targets risk extending a gap-filling mentality beyond its appropriate domain. They perpetuate the impression that development outcomes can be purchased at a unit cost that is invariant across countries. They can enforce over-uniformity, favoring large-scale commitments that may stifle experimentation and fail to exploit individual-country or individual-donor opportunities. If these concerns vary in systematic ways across goals, the implication is that some goals lend themselves more readily to such targets than others.

How Should Development Stakeholders Use These CBAs?

The need for prioritization is clear in our view, and therefore the drive for sensible criteria to inform global debates. The chapters collected here provide benefit-to-cost ratios for a wide range of targets, assuming best-practice interventions. To interpret these ratios, consider an intervention that incurs an up-front cost of c to deliver a perpetual stream of benefits equal to b dollars each year (adjusted for inflation). Suppose that future costs and benefits are discounted at rate $r > 0$; the studies collected here compare 3 and 5 percent ($r = 0.03$ and $r = 0.05$). Then the ratio of discounted benefits to discounted costs – or *benefit-to-cost ratio* – for this intervention is given by BCR = $(1/r)*(b/c)$. This calculation illustrates the standard result that higher discount rates (embodying greater societal impatience) discourage interventions whose benefits are deferred relative to costs. At bottom, however, the intervention caricatured here provides discounted benefits of BCR dollars for every discounted dollar of cost. If a private firm could

recoup its costs by collecting a revenue stream equal to b each year, any intervention with a BCR exceeding one would be privately profitable. But in a social cost-benefit analysis the costs and benefits include environmental and third-party impacts that are not priced in markets, along with indirect impacts that may include synergies with other targets. Interventions that are socially profitable by a BCR criterion – even hugely so – typically require public intervention precisely because they are not privately profitable.

The difference between a target's *BCR* and 1, multiplied by the scale of the intervention, summarizes what happens to the total economic pie, including the valuation of goods and services that are not priced in markets, as a result of achieving the target (we emphasize scale effects later). The calculation is meant to be comprehensive, including all direct and indirect impacts. A BCR above 1 therefore means that the overall pie is bigger, and by a larger amount per dollar of cost the bigger is the BCR. In the absence of distributional weights (see later), an intervention with a BCR above 1 delivers enough dollar-equivalent gains per dollar of cost that nobody has to lose, at least in the hypothetical sense that a set of costless side payments would make it possible to fully compensate any losers while leaving at least one person better off.

Three key features shape these chapters and the resulting rankings sufficiently to warrant some general observations for nonspecialist readers. The first is the curse of diminishing returns. At the level of ambition embodied by the SDGs, a number of global targets (including those for global average temperature, primary and secondary enrollment, and maternal mortality) are subject to sharply increasing marginal costs. The cost of reducing projected global temperatures by 2 degrees over a given horizon, for example, is much more than twice the cost of reducing projected temperatures by 1 degree. In the presence of rising marginal costs, the best becomes the enemy of the good, and CBA has a natural tendency to produce moderation. BCRs that are high at modest target levels start to fall as targets become more inspiring, and can go well below 1. The extreme-poverty headcount ratio falls to this argument – getting to zero is too costly. This effect is even stronger if benefits are declining on the margin, but the curse discourages extreme targets even when goals are viewed as intrinsic rights that must ultimately be satisfied in full as rapidly as feasible.

In a world of diminishing returns, smaller interventions will tend (other things equal) to produce larger BCRs. The optimal set of interventions over any fixed overall budget and time horizon will therefore tend to involve the partial fulfillment of multiple targets. The argument for focusing on a few big efforts has to come from somewhere else – in short, either from a prioritization of rights that classifies selected targets as nonnegotiable, or from some form of increasing returns to individual targets. Our arguments about accountability fall into the latter category. They embody a form of increasing returns, where the cost of effective action includes a large fixed component that may involve data provision, coalition- and institution-building, or development of target-specific supply chains. These costs are implicit in the book, in the sense that all of the chapters take ambitious goals and large-scale efforts as a starting point. Other sources of increasing returns, including network effects (e.g., in stopping epidemics) and irreversibilities (e.g., in environmental preservation), play an important role in some of the relevant chapters. But the curse of decreasing returns inevitably pushes a number of authors to embrace more moderate target levels than the SDGs propose.

The second feature relates to the valuation of benefits. Within development agencies and governments, it is often sufficient to treat in-kind targets as given and focus on the search for cost-effective interventions. The chapters collected here perform a similar (and invaluable) task on the cost side – a task that is heroic enough on its own, given the unavoidable distortions of having to assume, first, that interventions at a given global scale encounter the same unit costs everywhere in the world and, second, that these costs can be reasonably estimated using one or two well-designed impact assessments from particular times and places.

But authors were also asked to place dollar-equivalent values on all benefits, so that users could compare global temperature targets with completion of the Doha round and coral reef preservation with reductions in maternal mortality. Although expressing all benefits in dollar-equivalent values remains controversial, the appeal of this approach is obvious: if the analysis is even reasonably robust, it is hard to argue that projects with *phenomenal* BCRs (to use the Copenhagen Consensus's term for BCRs of 15 or above) should not receive priority relative to those with BCRs below 1. But the chapters vary widely in the comprehensiveness and robustness of their benefit estimates. Calculations of the social return to schooling, for example, are often famously modest in the sense of including only the social costs of schooling and none of the spillover benefits that a vast and admittedly contentious literature has emphasized over the years – spillovers that range from lower fertility to higher civic engagement and from improvements in institutional quality to women's empowerment and economy-wide innovation. Our own view is that these spillovers are of the essence. But Chapter 6 by Psacharopoulos is in this modest tradition – no spillover benefits, no synergies with other SDGs.

There may, in fact, be a general case for staying modest, given how contentious the assessment of these effects can be. And one does not need spillovers, for example, to favor a shift toward early-age interventions in education and health, given the increasing evidence of lifelong impacts on productivity and well-being. But the main point is caveat emptor: some chapters are braver (or more foolhardy) in this respect, and a more uniform treatment of benefits might substantially alter the rankings. The lesson is a general one when comparing CBAs across disparate sectors: users need to be attentive not only to how benefits are valued but also to what benefits are included.

The final feature relates to distributional objectives, which are central to the MDG and SDG campaigns but curiously absent in the cost-benefit calculation we described earlier. A thought experiment brings out the issue. Suppose for a moment that costless transfers were indeed possible and that the most cost-effective way to end extreme poverty was simply to guarantee each person on earth $1.90 a day. This would be done through targeted transfers to make up any difference relative to each person's market-related outcome. What BCR would this intervention generate? The answer is that unless the intervention altered the behavior of the household in some fundamentally favorable way – rather than just scaling up its consumption – the BCR could not exceed 1. The program benefit would be the discounted global consumption shortfall of the poor in the presence of the program – call this S – and the cost would be S as well. Any realistic accounting for administrative costs would in fact drive the BCR below 1.

Any outright efficiency gains from poverty reduction would help to push the BCR above 1. But some form of distributional weighting is arguably central to justifying any global poverty target. In the welfarist tradition within economics, this is done by making the social utility of an income-equivalent benefit depend on the household's income. A dollar of purchasing power is viewed as being worth more in the hands of a poor household than in the hands of a rich household. A rights-based approach has a similar feel: if $1.90 is an absolute right, then only another right can be in tension with it, not a cost that may happen to exceed $1.90.

Distributional concerns are handled in subtle ways in these chapters and readers should be prepared to query the individual chapters. In Chapter 24, on poverty, Gibson uses a modified version of S to measure costs. He assesses benefits, however, based on microeconomic evidence on the difference in lifetime earnings between individuals who grew up above and below the poverty line. This raises the BCR above 1, under the implicit assumption that some plausible combination of credit-market and information imperfections prevents the poor from borrowing to secure these efficiency gains themselves. But a simple distributional-weighting scheme could easily have raised the BCR of higher. Using log utility, for example, the value of transferring a dollar from a rich household to a poor household is not 1 but y_{Rich} / y_{Poor}. Logarithmic weights would therefore immediately translate an ambitious consumption-poverty target like 3 percent into phenomenal range because of its highly targeted beneficiary population (by implication, of course, the overall size of the pie is no longer the optimality criterion).

An implicit form of distributional weighting is embedded in some of these chapters, as when researchers apply an economy-wide value for disability-adjusted life years in evaluating health interventions that disproportionately favor poor communities. In these cases, as with distributional weights, the analyst places greater value on the well-being of the poor than their own willingness to pay would be able to reveal.

With these observations in mind, these chapters and the resulting rankings deserve a broad readership among development stakeholders and will raise the equality of public debates on priorities.

There are challenges and debates here for researchers as well. How far can a CBA platform take us in comparing health interventions with education interventions, let alone in accommodating improvements in accountability or sustainability? Can increasing returns and distributional impacts be handled more systematically? Is there external validity in the cost and benefit data, so that BCRs based on exemplary microeconomic evidence from individual countries can be appropriated for global calculations? Or do we actually have enough data to disaggregate in some cases – for example, to settle the costs of delivering a nutrition program in South Sudan, versus in Peru or India, all places with considerable stunting? How about synergies and general-equilibrium impacts; in some cases these are intrinsic to the calculation, as in the case of trade-policy reforms, while in others they are brought in selectively, as in the case of family-planning interventions that generate positive externalities through slower population growth. In still other cases they are excluded as too speculative. How important are these differences, and are there ways to formally incorporate successively more speculative elements of the analysis? Finally, how should the empirical methods employed to estimate treatment effects affect the interpretation of results? Should estimates based largely on randomized controlled trials, for example, be viewed as inherently conservative, while those that rely mainly on cross-country empirics or simulation modeling are viewed as decidedly less so?

Caveats are easy – too easy, because those who find these calculations uncomfortable will want to dismiss them. We ourselves would not recommend spending the global development budget, or even the portion allocated by foreign aid agencies, simply based on the benefit-cost ratios in this book. But the contributions here are nonetheless invaluable. By providing a rigorous examination of the cost and benefit evidence, they are a crucial buttress to the morally urgent work ahead. They ask an unavoidable question: when resources to improve the lives of the poor are scarce, how can we get these resources to go further – much further? The question is difficult, but cost-benefit analysis provides a set of answers that are transparent and evidence based. Their transparency favors debate and can serve as a check on those with the power to allocate resources. Good answers, in turn, will call forth more resources, by empowering the supporters of projects that contribute substantially to the overall public interest. There is a vast ongoing expansion of data, micro, and macroevidence that can be used to calibrate this analysis and improve it over time.

So we should see this work as a first step and invite those that care about how efficiently global resources are spent in development to reflect on this evidence. We should work to improve the global evidence base and replicate it in different settings, acknowledging that context will matter both for benefits and for costs. And while being impatient for further evidence, we should first and foremost insist on using what is in front of us. We should use this analysis to ask hard questions of those who would propose to spend resources at odds with the best available evidence on likely costs and benefits.

Stefan Dercon and Stephen A. O'Connell

Introduction

BJORN LOMBORG

We often think of efficiency gains in terms of an increase of a few percent here or there. Finessing at the edges. That is not the topic of this book. Rather, it is about making phenomenal strides to make the world better. This book shows us where we can spend money to do the most good, whether we are looking at aid money, philanthropic donations, or funds from developing country budgets.

What this book reveals is that the best polices are hundreds of percent better than an average policy, and the difference between the best and the poorest is thousands of percent.

As will be shown in the Conclusion, it is possible for us to do four times more good with every dollar, euro, or peso spent on development. This is not just about abstract efficiency: it means we can save four people from dying instead of one. It means we can help four children out of poverty instead of one, clean the air for four families instead of one, or teach four girls instead of one.

Being efficient isn't just an arcane concept. It is the difference between leaving the world better and making it four times better.

The UN Global Goals

In 2015, the United Nations negotiated one of the world's most powerful policy documents. Over 15 years, it will influence more than $2.5 trillion of development aid along with trillions from national budgets. It is aimed at helping pull hundreds of millions of people out of poverty, reduce hunger and disease, improve the environment, target the causes of violence, and improve education. Much depends on this being done well.

Tremendous progress has already been made in the fight against humanity's biggest challenges. In 1820 – nearly 200 years ago – around 94 percent of the planet was impoverished.[1] Even in 1990, poverty sat around 52 percent.[2] Recently, the World Bank has found that for the first time ever, in 2015, less than 10 percent of the globe is living in absolute poverty.[3]

Since the 1980s, a global middle class has emerged and more than doubled,[4] growing from around one billion people in 1985 to 2.3 billion today. Around 100 million people moved out of extreme poverty just from 2012 to 2013.[5]

Although there is definitely cause for concern about increasing income inequality in some developed nations like the United States and the UK, this is one of the reasons that *global* inequality has not increased and has likely decreased over the past three decades, with a significant decline over the past 15 years.[6]

Humans are living much longer, healthier lives:[7] in 1900, we lived to 30 on average; even in 2000, life expectancy was five years lower than the 71 years of today.[8] Inequality in life span today is likely lower than it has been for two centuries.[9]

[1] This finding is based on the paper by Bourguignon and Morrison (2002) in which the authors reconstructed measures of poverty; they used the measure of $1 per day that was then current.

[2] Bourguignon and Morrison (2002). To see the data graphed, see: https://ourworldindata.org/world-poverty/.

[3] Bourguignon and Morrison (2002). See also World Bank (2015). In 2013, the year for which the most comprehensive data on global poverty is available, 10.7 percent of the population was estimated to be living below the international poverty line of $1.90 per person per day.

[4] Brookings Institute (2012).   [5] World Bank (2016).

[6] Globalinequality (2015) and Paolo Liberati (2013).

[7] American Economic Association (2005).

[8] World Health Organization (2015).

[9] Bourguignon and Morrisson (2002).

In 1870, more than three-quarters of the world was illiterate.[10] In 1990, this had dropped to 32 percent, and today it is down to 15 percent.[11]

There is indeed much to celebrate. But there is also still a lot to do, to ensure that everyone on the planet has access to education, protected human rights, nutritious diets, security, and economic opportunities.

The challenge is acute when it comes to the world's poorest countries. More than 10 percent of the world's population lives in the nations designated as the least developed countries (LDCs).[12] Just over half of the population in these nations survive on less than $1.25 per day, and it is estimated that 24 percent – 210 million people – live with hunger. The vast majority (45 of 48) of LDCs have had the label for more than 20 years – 22 of them since the category was formally endorsed by the United Nations (UN) in 1971.[13]

Helping the world's poorest to close these massive gaps is one of the ambitions behind the UN's Global Goals, also known as the Sustainable Development Goals.

In general, there are many unfinished agendas. In education, for example, although almost all children are now in school,[14] there is still a huge problem with the quality of education. Research shows that more than one-third of all school-age children – a quarter-billion in all – currently fail to learn even the fundamentals of reading and mathematics.[15] Despite the huge progress against poverty noted earlier, the 10 percent remaining poor still translates into nearly 800 million people living on less than $1.90 a day.[16] Some 795 million people in the world go hungry, not receiving the minimum level of calories each day.[17] Around 1.1 billion people still live without access to electricity, and another 2.8 billion rely on wood or other biomass for cooking and heating, resulting in indoor air pollution that causes 4.3 million deaths each year.[18]

And the question is – which of these many issues should get our attention first?

The Millennium Development Goals

Over the years, UN has set many, many targets. The international community has pledged to achieve universal education in at least 12 UN-sponsored declarations since 1950.[19] For example, UNESCO promised in 1961 that, by 1980, primary education in Africa would be "universal, compulsory, and free."[20] Yet, when the time came, about half of primary-school-age children in Africa were still not attending school.[21]

Even today, the UN has a lot of well-meaning targets, goals, and declarations that have been overlooked or that receive little attention. Many readers probably didn't know that 2016 was the International Year of Pulses,[22] or that 2015 was the International Year of Soils as well as the Year of Light and Light-Based Technologies.[23] All these gestures and actions are well meaning, but not all are equally important or efficient.

In the long story of glittering promises and waylaid targets, one thing has stood out: the Millennium Development Goals (MDGs).

In September 2000 at the Millennium Summit, then the largest gathering of world leaders in history, heads of state agreed they held "a collective responsibility to uphold the principles of human dignity, equality and equity at the global level."[24]

As is customary, the politicians made lots of promises ranging from the aspirational "just and lasting peace all over the world" to specifics like

[10] Our World in Data. Literacy. https://ourworldindata.org/literacy/.
[11] Our World in Data. Literacy. https://ourworldindata.org/literacy/.
[12] UNFPA Fact Sheet, accessed at: www.unfpa.org/publications/fact-sheet-ldcs.
[13] The Guardian (2016).
[14] UNICEF. Rapid acceleration of progress is needed to achieve universal primary education. http://data.unicef.org/topic/education/primary-education/.
[15] UNESCO (2012).   [16] World Bank (2016).
[17] Food and Agriculture Organization of the United Nations (2015).
[18] World Bank (2017).
[19] Birdsall, Levine, and Ibrahim (2005),
[20] United Nations Economic Commission for Africa and United Nations Educational, Scientific and Cultural Organization (1961).
[21] UNESCO (2016).
[22] Global Pulse Confederation (2016).
[23] United Nations. International Years. www.un.org/en/sections/observances/international-years/.
[24] United Nations (2000).

urging the passing of the Kyoto Protocol and arguing for better safety for UN personnel.

But they also made a number of very specific promises, which later transformed into the Millennium Development Goals.

These covered the eight key areas of poverty, education, gender equality, child mortality, maternal health, disease, the environment, and global partnership.

Eight high-level goals (i.e., "Goal 3: Promote gender equality and empower women") were underpinned by 18 more specific targets (i.e., "Target 3A: Eliminate gender disparity in primary and secondary education preferably by 2005, and at all levels by 2015") and 60 indicators. UN member states agreed to achieve these objectives by the year 2015.[25] Often very broad and aspirational, the MDGs specified a destination but did not chart the journey.

Crucially, the specific targets are what resonated and are what we remember – not the goals or the indicators. We think of and reference the target, "halve the proportion of hungry," not the much more radical goal of "Eradicate hunger," which was never considered feasible by 2015. Nor do we remember the MDGs by their much more specific, technical indicators like "Proportion of population below minimum level of dietary energy consumption."

As a UN panel comprising senior experts from more than 50 UN entities and international organizations declared 12 years later, "The MDGs are simple, catchy and acceptable, and, in part they focus on ends with which no one would disagree."[26]

These were concise, specific, and obvious development targets that everyone could relate to – and they had a clear deadline of 2015. In short, world leaders had staked out real and verifiable promises.

Moreover, most of the MDG conversation boiled down to discussion of the seven most important promises: lift people out of poverty, out of hunger, ensure all children are in school, reduce child mortality, reduce maternal mortality, and provide water and sanitation to more people. In reality, it was a very short list.

This winnowing process was entirely sensible. A promise like "halve the proportion of people in poverty from 1990 to 2015" seems worthy of a global goal. This is perhaps less true of target 8C, which states, "Address the special needs of landlocked developing countries and small island developing states (through the Program of Action for the Sustainable Development of Small Island Developing States and the outcome of the twenty-second special session of the General Assembly)."

The progress on these seven targets has been remarkable. On hunger, almost 24 percent of all people in the developing world were starving in 1990. The latest figures show "only" 10.9 percent of people on the planet are undernourished.[27]

Indeed, as the period of the MDGs came to a close on January 1, 2016, on this and other measures the targets were broadly seen as a success:[28]

- The number of people living on less than USD $1.25 a day was reduced from 1.9 billion in 1990 to 836 million in 2015.
- Primary school enrollment figures showed an impressive rise, but the goal of achieving universal primary education was missed, with the net enrollment rate increasing from 83 percent in 2000 to 91 percent in 2015.
- About two-thirds of developing countries achieved gender parity in primary education.
- The child mortality rate was reduced by more than half but failed to meet the MDG target of a drop by two-thirds.

[25] Initially there were 18 targets. At the World Summit in 2006, three targets were added, and one was revised. A target to achieve universal access to reproductive health was added under Goal 5 for maternal mortality. A target to achieve universal access to HIV/AIDS treatment by 2010 was added under Goal 6 for infectious diseases. A target to reduce the rate of biodiversity loss by 2010 was added under Goal 7 for the environment. The original target relating to employment was tweaked to include the World Summit agreement to "achieve full and productive employment and decent work for all, including women and young people" and was relocated from Goal 8 on global partnership to Goal 1 for ending extreme poverty. The number of indicators increased from 48 to 60.
[26] Nayyar (2012).
[27] Food and Agricultural Organization of the United Nations (2015).
[28] World Vision International (2015).

Table I.1 Millennium development goals: The seven key targets

Goal	Promise by 2015	Improvement?	Faster progress?	On Track?
Poverty	Halve the proportion of poor	Y	Y	Y
Hunger	Halve the proportion hungry	Y	N	N
Education	Full course of primary schooling	Y	Y	N
Gender	Gender equality in school	Y	N	Y
Child mortality	Reduce under-5 mortality by two-thirds	Y	Y	N
Maternal mortality	Reduce maternal death by three-quarters	Y	Y	N
Environment	Halve the proportion without clean drinking water	Y	N	Y

- The global maternal mortality ratio fell by nearly half – short of the two-thirds reduction the MDGs aimed for.
- The target of halting and beginning to reverse the spread of HIV/AIDS by 2015 was not met, although the number of new HIV infections fell by around 40 percent between 2000 and 2013.
- Around 2.6 billion people gained access to improved drinking water between 1990 and 2015, so the target of halving the proportion of people without access to improved sources of water was achieved in 2010 – five years ahead of schedule.

Of course, some of the improvement would likely have happened anyway. Access to clean drinking water has been slowly and steadily increasing, with no apparent break around the time of the Millennium Summit.[29] On this account, the MDGs probably deserve no extra credit.

China and India's furious economic growth played a large role in poverty reduction–although, a quarter of a billion people were lifted out of poverty outside China and India, with 125 million in Africa.

Analysis shows that progress in education, child and maternal health sped up after 2000 and credit is at least partly due to the focus and energy inspired by the UN goals.

Also, the enthusiasm stemming from the MGDs helped recover OECD development aid from a slump in the 1990s and saw a two-thirds increase from $82 billion in 2000 to $135 billion in 2013 (both in 2012 dollars).

In short, the MDGs fired up the global imagination: With just seven simple targets, world leaders promised to help the poorest, and although not all objectives were met, they helped push us to a much, much better place.

Prioritizing

Yet, for all of this, were the MDGs the right targets? Because we didn't have money for all the targets – some were missed – how should we have traded them off? Should we have spent less on water and sanitation, and more on malaria and HIV? The MDGs gave us no sense of how to prioritize.

Providing such a framework for major global spending decisions was the reason that I set up the think tank the Copenhagen Consensus Center. The Copenhagen Consensus approach has always been to look at important issues and to ask: how can economic analysis help us do the most good here?

Most nations spend the vast bulk of their resources on themselves. In a well-functioning political system, this internal spending is prioritized through a democratic process and shaped by a solid framework of interest representation, as well as by social and ethical discussions in the national conversation.

However, the portion of spending that predominantly goes outside a nation's borders has traditionally been prioritized less because there is no obvious interest representation and little or no feedback from a development conversation.

[29] UNICEF (2015).

This is the spending that Copenhagen Consensus projects have generally focused on.

This covers official development assistance (ODA), spending on peacekeeping forces, research into vaccines and agricultural research for foreign food staples, efforts to reduce regional and global environmental issues, like global warming, and attempts to create more efficient trading systems, tackling terrorism, tax avoidance, and corruption on a global scale.

Each day, decisions are made about these global priorities. Governments, philanthropists, and international bodies choose to support some worthy causes while others are disregarded. Unfortunately, these decisions do not always fully take into account a comprehensive view of the effects, benefits, and costs of solving one problem instead of another.

Some global concerns receive a lot more media coverage than others. We focus on some issues because they get a lot of attention; they make the press because they offer good narratives, with clear and photogenic victims that we rally to help. This process is assisted by lobby groups and advocates who fight to ensure that certain causes are never far from the public eye. In contrast, some very good causes receive relatively little attention – and hence a lot less money.

Within the national context, society is typically presented with a menu of choices, debated by informed interest groups at least implicitly recognizing the trade-offs (if one gets funded more, others can't). In essence, the national conversation is over a menu of choices with some sense of price and size. But this is much less true for global spending. We get little sense of the trade-offs, of the costs, and of benefits from individual choices. Hence, we often rely on the media process – which can favor cute animals, photogenic victims, and clear-cut narratives – to inform us.

The Copenhagen Consensus process aims to put prices and sizes on the menu. The idea behind the Copenhagen Consensus is to render this process less arbitrary and to provide evidence on which informed decisions can be made by politicians and others, making choices better informed.

In 2004, 2008, and 2012, the Copenhagen Consensus Center gathered research on global challenges – from malnutrition and sanitation to terrorism - and commissioned panels of eminent economists, including in total seven recipients of the Nobel Memorial Prize in Economic Science, to rank different investments.

The research from these projects is available in the Cambridge University Press books *Global Crises, Global Solutions* (Lomborg, 2005); *Global Crises, Global Solutions* (2nd ed.; Lomborg, 2009), and *Global Problems, Smart Solutions* (Lomborg, 2013).

Copenhagen Consensus projects have brought the focus of benefit-cost analysis to diverse geographic regions and topics. In 2006, the Copenhagen Consensus United Nations brought together 24 UN ambassadors, including those from China, India, and the United States, and set them the task of prioritizing limited resources to mitigate the negative consequences of global challenges.

We have also looked at regional priorities: Consulta de San Jose in 2007 (the Copenhagen Consensus for Latin America and the Caribbean) was a collaboration with the Inter-American Development Bank (IADB). This project gathered highly esteemed economists to identify the projects that would best improve welfare in Latin America and the Caribbean. The research is available as *Latin American Development Priorities* (Lomborg, 2009).

And the approach has been used for individual policy areas: In 2009, the approach was applied to climate change. The Copenhagen Consensus on Climate assembled an Eminent Panel of five world-class economists, including three Nobel Prize recipients, to evaluate research on different responses to global warming and to deliberate on which solutions would be most effective; this project was published in *Smart Solutions to Climate Change* (Lomborg, 2010).

In 2011, RethinkHIV saw the Copenhagen Consensus Center gather teams of economists and medical scientists to perform the first comprehensive cost-benefit analysis of HIV/AIDS investment opportunities in sub-Saharan Africa. This research was published by Cambridge University Press as *RethinkHIV* (Lomborg, 2012).

These projects generated considerable attention and discussion – and measurably improved spending on some major challenges. Denmark's government spent millions more on HIV/AIDS projects, which topped the economists' "to-do" list in 2004. Micronutrient delivery programs in Africa and elsewhere received significant attention and greater resources after they topped the list in 2008. Copenhagen Consensus research was "one of the main drivers" that led to the International Zinc Association and UNICEF launching the Zinc Saves Kids initiative, with the Association investing $3 million to help save children dying from zinc deficiency–related issues. The World Bank quoted Copenhagen Consensus in 2006 when it created its new strategy on combatting malnutrition. Copenhagen Consensus findings on the benefits of investing in nutrition were cited by Prime Minister David Cameron when $4,150 million was pledged by governments at G8 meetings for Global Nutrition for Growth. In addition, the NGO alliance InterAction referred to Copenhagen Consensus analysis when it pledged $750 million on nutrition.

These Copenhagen Consensus projects showed that an informed ranking of solutions to the world's big problems is possible, and that cost-benefit analysis – much maligned by some – can lead to a clear focus on the most effective ways to respond to the real problems of the world's most afflicted people.

Therefore, in 2013, as the United Nations embarked on its process to replace the MDGs with what would become the Global Goals, the Copenhagen Consensus Center decided to apply its approach to help improve the outcome and to commission sorely needed economic evidence.

Best Targets for 2016–2030?

Many argued that the best approach was to continue to focus on the simple, sharp goals – an "MDG II." After all, there are still far too many poor and hungry and still many easily preventable deaths. The solutions to major challenges are often cheap and simple. We know how to tackle malaria deaths (ensure access to mosquito nets and Artemisinin treatment)[30] and undernutrition (more

fertilizer, promotion of better-yielding varieties,[31] and less food diverted to biofuels[32]).

But others argued that there were obvious gaps in the MDGs. They had no recognition of the world's biggest environmental challenge: indoor air pollution, which causes 4.3 million deaths annually.[33] These deaths happen because almost 3 billion people cook and keep warm by burning solid fuels such as charcoal, twigs, and dung. The solution is to increase access to electricity to power a stove and a heater. More electricity will also boost productivity in agriculture and industry and pull millions out of poverty, as we have seen in China.

Likewise, the MDGs skirted the question of free trade, although this is possibly the most important factor in pulling hundreds of millions out of poverty. World Bank models have indicated that even a moderately successful Doha round (which still has not been successfully concluded) could do amazing good. As we will see in Chapter 9, by 2020, such an agreement could add about $5 trillion to global GDP, with $3 trillion going to the developing world.

Toward the end of the century, such a free trade agreement would likely lead to an increase in annual GDP of more than $100 trillion annually. Most would go to the developing world, adding about 20 percent to their annual GDP. In comparison, the total costs, mostly to wean developed-world farmers from subsidies, are more than 10,000 times smaller, at approximately $50 billion per year for a decade or two.

However, there was another consideration that turned out to be even more important. The MDGs were perceived as having been drafted with no consultation – that a "small group wrote up the MDGs in the basement of the UN office in

[30] GiveWell. Against Malaria Foundation. 2017. www.givewell.org/charities/against-malaria-foundation.

[31] G. S. Khush, S. Lee, J. Cho, et al., "Biofortification of crops for reducing malnutrition," *Plant Biotechnology Reports* (2012) 6: 195–202. doi:10.1007/s11816-012-0216-5

[32] D. J. Tenenbaum, "Food vs. fuel: Diversion of crops could cause more hunger, *Environmental Health Perspectives* (2008); 116(6): A254-A257.

[33] World Health Organization. Household air pollution and health. 2016. www.who.int/mediacentre/factsheets/fs292/en/.

New York."[34] Although this led to a sharp set of goals, it was also seen as unacceptably undemocratic. Hence, the UN decided to focus on inclusion. In September 2013, at a UN session in New York, Secretary General Ban Ki-Moon announced that the goals to replace the MDGs would be finalized at a UN meeting in September 2015, based on a period of gathering a broad range of inputs, and intergovernmental discussions.

But inclusion clearly led to a rapidly multiplying list of targets. Everyone wanted to make sure their favored issues were included on the list. A High Level Panel suggested 12 goals and 54 targets. A tracker compiled by the North-South Institute revealed that in September 2013, almost 1,400 targets had been suggested by 120 organizations.[35] The Open Working Group, which drove the SDGs, had in its penultimate draft 212 targets.[36] In the final draft that became the official SDGs, this was reduced to 169 targets, but almost entirely through concatenating targets, rather than eliminating them.

Although international engagement and inclusion is to be applauded, too many goals and targets sharply increase the risk of losing focus. Having 169 priorities means having no priorities. People often tell me that their favorite topic matter is now officially in the SDGs, and I have to disappoint them by sharing that so too is almost everything else.

How Can We Focus When There Are 169 Targets?

We can't do it all. The cost of meeting all of the Sustainable Development Goals would be between USD$3.3 and $4.5 trillion annually according to the OECD,[37] while an intergovernmental committee reported to the UN that eradicating poverty alone would require annual investments "in infrastructure – water, agriculture, telecoms, power, transport, buildings, industrial and forestry sectors – [that] amount to $5 trillion to $7 trillion globally."[38]

To put these figures into context, only $132bn was spent globally on overseas development in 2015.[39] If we can't do everything, where should we start? This is the question that this book aims to help answer.

The research here explores how much social benefit each of the targets would achieve. It is clear that focusing on some targets would achieve a huge deal, and others very little. Spreading money and energy thinly among them reduces the overall good that we do.

As with the MDGs and with so many of the spending areas examined in the past by Copenhagen Consensus, the Global Goals consist of options without any identified costs or benefits. As it has done elsewhere, the Copenhagen Consensus process puts prices and sizes on this global menu.

When faced with too many choices, decision makers could be well served by first focusing on those targets that will do the most good. This, however, will require an information base.

Indeed, as the Conclusion, written by an Eminent Panel including Nobel laureate economists, reveals, the UN could achieve four times more good if it sharpened the 169 targets to a list of just 19 "phenomenal" investments. Achieving four times as much with every dollar of aid spending or government spending in developing countries will make a world of difference. There is a compelling moral case for donors to focus first on the areas where the most good can be achieved.

[34] The Guardian. Mark Malloch-Brown: developing the MDGs was a bit like nuclear fusion. www.theguardian.com/global-development/2012/nov/16/mark-malloch-brown-mdgs-nuclear.

[35] Canadian International Development Platform. Tracking Post-2015. http://cidpnsi.ca/tracking-post-2015/.

[36] International Institute for Sustainable Development. Summary of the Thirteenth Session of the UN General Assembly Open Working Group on Sustainable Development Goals. 2014. www.iisd.ca/vol32/enb3213e.html.

[37] The Organisation for Economic Co-operation and Development. Development Co-operation Report 2017. www.oecd.org/dac/development-co-operation-report-20747721.htm?utm_source=Adestra&utm_medium=email&utm_content=&utm_campaign=Copy of DACews July 2016&utm_term=demov.

[38] United Nations General Assembly. Report of the Intergovernmental Committee of Experts on Sustainable Development Financing. 2014. www.un.org/ga/search/view_doc.asp?symbol=A/69/315&Lang=E.

[39] The Organisation for Economic Co-operation and Development (2016).

Prioritization is also needed to ensure that monitoring and evaluation is possible. As Morten Jerven notes in research in Chapter 5, properly monitoring all the targets of the Millennium Development Goals would have cost around $27bn. (This is based on survey costs: it is the estimate of what it *would have cost* for proper monitoring and evaluation). That is a significant sum, but given that the world spent about $1.9tn on development aid over the same period, it is perhaps not unreasonable to suggest that 1.4 percent of this spending should have gone toward evaluation.

For the 169 Global Goal targets, Jerven estimates that even minimum data collection would cost at least $254bn, or almost twice the entire global annual development budget.

Also of note is the problematic fact that many targets aim for absolute goals – e.g., *eradication* of extreme poverty, *universal* access to education, and *the end* to hunger.

These are noble aspirations, but unfortunately, the evidence suggests these will be very hard to reach in just 15 years, by 2030. For example, reports by the Brookings Institute,[40] the Center for Global Development,[41] and the World Bank[42] agree that reducing extreme poverty to zero by 2030 is unlikely. Similarly, the Food and Agriculture Organization of the United Nations (FAO) predicts there will be 540 million hungry by 2030.[43]

Similarly, the target to achieve "full and productive employment and decent work for all women and men"[44] appears admirable – but making zero unemployment a global policy is foolish. Every economy needs some unemployment to allow workers to change jobs. All governments are already focused on getting more people into work. Moreover, studies show that such language is often used by interest groups to create comfortable jobs for a subset of workers, while leaving the rest out in the cold, often pushing vulnerable workers back into the informal economy and increasing poverty.[45] The costs of this target will likely outweigh the benefits.[46]

Standard economic theory tells us to be wary of zero and 100 percent targets. Saving the very last person from poverty or hunger is much more expensive than saving each of the first 30, 50, or 80 percent. So, continuing further toward zero or 100 percent is likely to lead to resources being spent that could have been used much better elsewhere. We need to know where the right cutoff is, even if that makes us feel uncomfortable.

In general, it pays to be wary of unrealistic, absolute aspirations and instead focus on achievable goals. Although such an approach might feel less rousing, it is *more* moral because it focuses on actually accomplishing the most good – and acknowledging what is and is not possible.

That's why researchers in this book were asked, for such targets, to attempt to identify the *nonabsolute* value that would provide the best benefit-cost ratio over the next 15 years. In the case of the extreme poverty target discussed earlier (Target 1.1, which reads, "by 2030, eradicate extreme poverty for all people everywhere, currently measured as people living on less than $1.25 a day"), it is unachievable and unrealistic. But as John Gibson advocates in Chapter 24, if amended to an achievable, realistic stretch target then it could be a good target.

He provides evidence to suggest that the alleviation of extreme poverty will not proceed as successfully as it did from 1990 to present. Previous policies have tended to lift those at the margin of extreme poverty. It will become more challenging to lift the remaining extreme poor. Residual poverty is often found in geographic pockets or along ethnic lines, making poverty alleviation not only an economic question, but a complex socioeconomic and political issue. As Gibson recommends, better wording for this target would be: "by 2030, reduce the proportion of people living on less than $1.25 a day (PPP) to 3 percent." This would be difficult but potentially achievable.

It is also important to be careful of language that is near impossible to parse. Consider this target:

---

[40] Chandy, Ledlie, and Penciakova (2013).
[41] Center for Global Development (2012).
[42] World Bank (2014).
[43] Food and Agriculture Organization of the United Nations (2012).
[44] United Nations (2012).
[45] Copenhagen Consensus Center (2015a).
[46] Copenhagen Consensus Center (2015b).

By 2030 ensure all learners acquire knowledge and skills needed to promote sustainable development, including among others through education for sustainable development and sustainable lifestyles, human rights, gender equality, promotion of a culture of peace and nonviolence, global citizenship, and appreciation of cultural diversity and of culture's contribution to sustainable development.

It is very difficult to know what exactly is promised, how governments should interpret it, let alone how it will be monitored or evaluated.

Prioritization on economic grounds will make some people uncomfortable, which is understandable. Of course, in principle we ought to deal with all of the world's woes. We should win the war against hunger, end conflicts, stop communicable diseases, provide clean drinking water to all, reach everyone with education, and halt climate change. But we will not and cannot achieve all of this at once. We live in a world with limited resources and even more limited attention for the biggest problems. This means there is a need to ask the crucial question: If we don't do it all, what should we do first?

Relying on costs and benefits, as the research in this book does, is a transparent and practical way to help establish whether or not spending is worthwhile – and to establish the areas that we should focus on first. It allows us to avoid the fear and media hype that often dictate the way that we see the world. Carefully examining where an investment would have the biggest rewards provides a principled basis on which important decisions can be made. Assigning a monetary value is the best way we have of introducing a common frame for comparison.

Some will argue that it is impossible or distasteful to put a value on a human life. But refusing to do so likely ends up costing more lives. In practice, prioritization occurs every day in areas as disparate as health policy and infrastructure. When we decide on a national speed limit, we are implicitly putting a price on human life, weighing the benefits of fewer lives lost with a slower speed limit against the dispersed costs of higher transport times. Making such trade-offs explicit allows us to better evaluate our choices.

In this book, researchers use tools including the "disability adjusted life year" (DALY). This allows economists and policy makers to add up the years of life that are lost, establish the impact of disability, and weigh these factors with other benefits and costs of different policies. Specifically, we have set low and high values of a DALY at $1,000 and $5,000, respectively, to ensure comparability across areas. Which DALY the reader chooses is a moral choice. But of course, it is necessary to set it equally across all areas.

Another economic tool that informs this project is discounting, which makes it possible to balance our own needs against those of future generations and to ensure a consistent approach across all the challenges presented in the book.

Commercial projects typically discount at the rate of current or expected market interest rates, often at 7 percent or even 12 percent in developing countries.[47] In this project, we have used 3 percent and 5 percent.

The former means that the future is more important, while 5 percent is closer to what most countries often do. Which one the reader chooses is again a moral choice – but again it is necessary to be consistent across all areas.

Figure I.1 is the result of taking the median of the four estimates from the two DALY values and the two discount rates.

Using these economic tools, we can gauge how the relative benefits and costs change as we alter discount rates, the value of DALYs, or change our assumptions about the relative likelihood of outcomes.

How to Use This Book

The Global Goals were signed into force in 2016. The research in this book is now more relevant than ever.

First, this is because it highlights the areas where more research and focus is needed to establish how to achieve laudable development objectives.

[47] Board of Governors of the Federal Reserve System (2014).

SOCIAL, ECONOMIC, AND ENVIRONMENTAL BENEFITS FOR EVERY DOLLAR SPENT

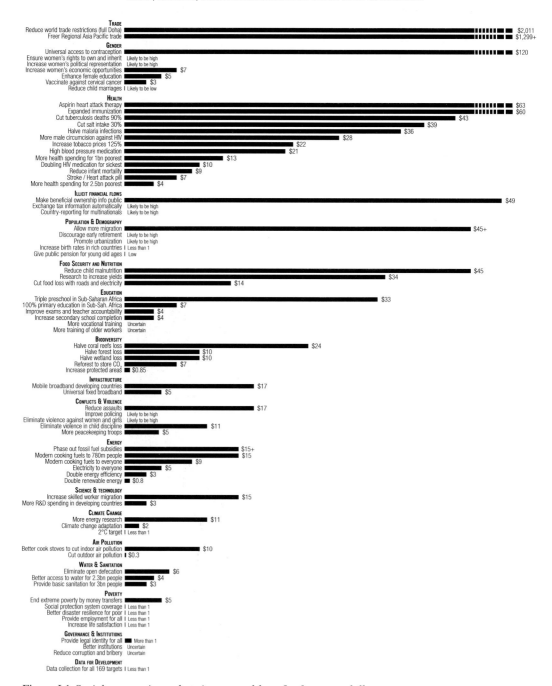

Figure I.1 *Social, economic, and environmental benefits for every dollar spent*

An example is target 5.3, "Eliminate all harmful practices, such as child, early and forced marriage and female genital mutilation (FGM)."

As Irma Clots-Figueras writes in Chapter 19, the benefits of later marriage are high, and different studies suggest a variety of ways to achieve this. Benefits, which include better health, are quite high compared to the costs. However, it is difficult to prove a causal link between specific programs and outcomes, and improving girls' education is probably the best-known approach right now.

When it comes to ending FGM, Clots-Figueras points out, in what will become a common theme for readers, that achieving an absolute target of "eliminating" this practice is infeasible. Furthermore, her research suggests that legislation is an ineffective solution: FGM is already outlawed in 26 of 29 countries where it is prevalent. Interventions to end FGM will need to change cultural norms, which is very difficult to accomplish. And the low quality of study designs that assess interventions raises further doubts. This is an area where more, and higher-quality, research and trials are sorely needed.

Second, governments and international organizations are only now beginning to focus on how they are going to implement the Global Goals. As described earlier, monitoring and evaluation is near impossible. With 169 targets, prioritization needs to happen. Regardless of their rhetoric, major donors are going to prioritize between targets. Some will be neglected, others will be pursued aggressively. This book provides policy makers – and readers – with evidence that cannot be found anywhere else on more than 100 of the targets considered by the United Nations and a foundation for making those decisions.[48]

The cost-benefit analyses in this book can help practitioners, politicians, and others to focus on the targets that can actually work and chose the ones that will do the most good first.

Of course, anyone reading this book may themselves make different choices in DALYs, discount rate, and estimates of plausibility.

But when presented with the strong findings of the economists' analyses, it is hard not to be persuaded by very high benefit-cost ratios or to be concerned by very low ones.

In the Conclusion, the reader can see the outcome from three eminent economists who considered the research and the targets they believe deserve the most urgent attention. I also outline what needs to happen next, as we turn to implementation.

I invite readers to form their own opinions on which of the many global targets should be our initial focus. Focusing on the best targets first will allow us to do much more good over the next 15 years.

Bjorn Lomborg
Prague, 2018

References

American Economic Association (2005). The Quantity and Quality of Life and the Evolution of World Inequality. Available at: www.aeaweb.org/articles.php?doi=10.1257/0002828053828563.

Birdsall, Nancy, Ruth Levine, and Amina Ibrahim (2005), "Toward Universal Primary Education: Investments, Incentives and Institutions," *European Journal of Education*, 40 (3): 337–49.

Board of Governors of the Federal Reserve System (2014). The Social Discount Rate in Developing Countries. www.federalreserve.gov/econresdata/notes/feds-notes/2014/the-social-discount-rate-in-developing-countries-20141009.html.

Bourguignon, François and Christian Morrisson (2002). "Inequality among World Citizens: 1820–1992," *American Economic Review*, 92 (4): 727–44.

Brookings Institute (2012). Development, Aid and Governance Indicators (DAGI). www.brookings.edu/research/interactives/development-aid-governance-indicators.

Center for Global Development (2012). MDGs 2.0: What Goals, Targets, and Timeframe? www.cgdev.org/files/1426271_file_Kenny_Karver_MDGs_FINAL.pdf.

Chandy, Laurence, Natasha Ledlie, and Veronika Penciakova (2013). The Final Countdown:

---

[48] It should be noted that some final versions of the UN's Global Goals targets differ slightly from those analyzed here.

Prospects for Ending Extreme Poverty by 2030. Policy Paper *2013–14*. The Brookings Institution. www.brookings.edu/wp-content/uploads/2016/06/The_Final_Countdown.pdf.

Copenhagen Consensus Center (2015a). Post-2015 Consensus: Poverty Assessment, Gibson. www.copenhagenconsensus.com/publication/post-2015-consensus-poverty-assessment-gibson.

(2015b). Poverty: What's the Smartest Post-2015 Target? www.copenhagenconsensus.com/post-2015-consensus/poverty-whats-smartest-post-2015-target.

FAO (2012). World Agriculture towards 2030/2050: The 2012 Revision. www.fao.org/docrep/016/ap106e/ap106e.pdf.

(2015). *The State of Food Insecurity in the World, 2015* (Rome: Author).

globalinequality (2015). The Ambivalent Role of China in Global Income Distribution. http://glineq.blogspot.cl/2015/12/the-ambivalent-role-of-china-in-global_89.html.

Global Pulse Confederation (2016). IYP 2016 Committee. http://iyp2016.org/about-us/iyop-committee.

The Guardian (2016). New Deal, Old Mess? Making the Global Goals Work for the Most Fragile Countries. www.theguardian.com/global-development-professionals-network/2016/feb/29/least-developed-countries-sustainable-development-goals-sudan-zambia-uganda.

Liberati, Paolo (2013). The World Distribution of Income and Its Inequality, 1970–2009. http://onlinelibrary.wiley.com/doi/10.1111/roiw.12088/abstract.

Nayyar, Deepak (2012). "The MDGs after 2015: Some reflections on the possibilities," United Nations System Task Team on the Post-2015 Development Agenda.

The Organisation for Economic Co-operation and Development (2016). Development Aid Rises Again in 2015, Spending on Refugees Doubles. www.oecd.org/dac/development-aid-rises-again-in-2015-spending-on-refugees-doubles.htm.

UNESCO (1961). Final Report, Conference of African States on the Development of Education in Africa, Addis Ababa, 15–25 May. See: http://unesdoc.unesco.org/images/0007/000774/077416e.pdf.

(2012). Technical Note Prepared for the "Education for All Global Monitoring Report 2012: Youth and skills: Putting education to work." http://unesdoc.unesco.org/images/0021/002193/219349E.pdf.

(2016). Education, Out-of-School Children of Primary School Age, both sexes. http://data.uis.unesco.org/Index.aspx?queryid=120.

UNICEF (2015). Progress on Sanitation and Drinking Water, 2015 Update and MDG Assessment. http://files.unicef.org/publications/files/Progress_on_Sanitation_and_Drinking_Water_2015_Update_.pdf.

Accessed February 2018. Rapid Acceleration of Progress is Needed to Achieve Universal Primary Education. http://data.unicef.org/topic/education/primary-education/.

United Nations (2000). Millennium Summit (6–8 September). www.un.org/en/events/pastevents/millennium_summit.shtml.

(2012). Open Working Group Proposal for Sustainable Development Goals. https://sustainabledevelopment.un.org/focussdgs.html, Target 8.5.

Accessed February 2018. International Years. www.un.org/en/sections/observances/international-years/.

WHO (2015). See: www.who.int/gho/mortality_burden_disease/life_tables/situation_trends/en/.

World Bank (2014). Is Extreme Poverty Going to End? An Analytical Framework to Evaluate Progress in Ending Extreme Poverty. www-wds.worldbank.org/external/default/WDSContentServer/IW3P/IB/2014/01/06/000158349_20140106142540/Rendered/PDF/WPS6740.pdf.

(2015). www.worldbank.org/en/news/press-release/2015/10/04/world-bank-forecasts-global-poverty-to-fall-below-10-for-first-time-major-hurdles-remain-in-goal-to-end-poverty-by-2030.

(2016). Poverty and Shared Prosperity 2016. www.worldbank.org/en/publication/poverty-and-shared-prosperity.

(2017). Understanding Poverty, Energy, 2017. www.worldbank.org/en/topic/energy/overview#1.

World Vision International (2015). Were the Millennium Development Goals a success? Yes! Sort of. www.wvi.org/united-nations-and-global-engagement/article/were-mdgs-success.

Benefits and Costs of Air Pollution Targets for the Post-2015 Development Agenda

BJORN LARSEN

Introduction

The last two decades have seen a large body of evidence of substantial health effects for long-term exposure to air pollution – especially fine particulate matter – be it in the form of outdoor ambient air pollution (AAP) or household air pollution (HAP) from the use of solid fuels. There are compelling arguments that air pollution should feature in a new set of post-2015 development goals.

Global Health Effects and Exposure to Air Pollution

Health Effects

Nearly six million deaths were attributed to AAP and HAP in 2010 according to the Global Burden of Disease (GBD) 2010 Project (Lim et al., 2012). This is more than from alcohol and drugs, about the same as from active and passive tobacco smoking, and four times more than from child and maternal undernutrition. Of 67 risk factors assessed, it is only surpassed by total dietary risk factors and high blood pressure, of which the latter is influenced by air pollution, tobacco smoking, and diet. The most recent estimates attribute 5.5 million (GBD 2013; Forouzanfar et al., 2015) to 6.5 million (WHO, 2016) deaths to air pollution.

The GBD 2010 Project developed an integrated PM2.5 exposure–response (IER) model to estimate these health effects by using relative risk (RR) information from studies of ambient PM2.5 air pollution, secondhand tobacco smoke, household solid fuel use, and active tobacco smoking (Burnett et al., 2014). The exposure–response relationships in the IER model are highly nonlinear with declining marginal relative risks of health outcomes at higher PM2.5 exposure levels.

Ambient Air Pollution Exposure

Nearly 90 percent of the world's population lived in areas with ambient outdoor PM2.5 concentrations exceeding WHO's AQG of 10 µg/m^3 (annual average) in 2005, and nearly one-third lived in areas with ambient PM2.5 exceeding WHO's Level 1 Interim Target of 35 µg/m^3 according to estimates by Brauer et al. (2012).

The highest annual average population weighted PM2.5 concentrations are found in a large belt extending from western sub-Saharan Africa (SSA-W) and the Middle East and North Africa (MNA) through South Asia (SA) to East Asia (EA) and the High Income Asia Pacific (HI AP) countries. Regional average population weighted exposures were below 10 µg/m^3 in most of South America, the southern part of Africa, and in Australia and the Pacific Islands (Table 1.1).

In South and East Asia, 99 percent of the population lived in areas with annual average ambient PM2.5 exceeding 10 µg/m^3, while 92 percent did so in Western Europe and 76 percent in North America according to Brauer et al. (2012) In South and East Asia, 26 percent and 76 percent of the population, respectively, was exposed to annual average PM2.5 exceeding 35 µg/m^3. Two-thirds of the global population is exposed to such ambient levels.

WHO has assembled an AAP database[1] that contains annual average PM2.5 concentrations in

[1] www.who.int/phe/health_topics/outdoorair/databases/cities/en/.

Table 1.1 Population exposure to ambient PM2.5 air pollution

Region	Population (millions), 2012	Population weighted PM2.5 ($\mu g/m^3$), 2005
East Asia (EA)	1,399	55
South Asia (SA)	1,629	28
Middle East and North Africa (MNA)	460	26
High-Income Asia Pacific (HI AP)	183	24
Western Sub-Saharan Africa (SSA-W)	357	24
Central Asia (CA)	85	19
Central Europe (CE)	115	17
South East Asia (SEA)	625	16
Western Europe (WE)	422	16
High-Income North America (HI NA)	349	13
Sub-Saharan Africa – other (SSA-O)	556	12
Eastern Europe (EE)	209	11
Latin America and the Caribbean (LAC)	604	9
Australasia(AA)	27	7
Oceania (OC)	9	6
World	7,044	27

Notes: Population weighted PM2.5 is from Brauer et al. (2012). Population is from World Bank (2014).
Source: Prepared by the author.

over 1,600 city locations in 91 countries.[2] Most of the locations in which Level 1 Interim Target was exceeded are in Asia. In HI countries, PM2.5 concentrations exceeded 10 $\mu g/m^3$ in 55 percent of locations. Level 1 Interim Target was exceeded in 2 percent of locations.

At ambient PM2.5 concentrations in the range of 35–100 $\mu g/m^3$, as found in many cities in low- and middle-income (LMI) countries in Asia, the exposure–response relationships are highly non-linear. Only moderate improvements in PM2.5 air quality will therefore give quite small health benefits.

Household Air Pollution Exposure

The predominant source of HAP, in terms of global health effects, is the use of solid fuels by households for cooking and other purposes. About 41 percent of the world's population – or 2.8 billion – used mainly solid fuels for cooking in 2010 (Bonjour et al., 2013).

An update for the purpose of this chapter finds that nearly 2.9 billion people used solid fuels in 2012 (Table 1.2). Over 95 percent of these people reside in China and India, sub-Saharan Africa (SSA), other countries in South Asia (SA) from Afghanistan to Bangladesh, and South East Asia (SEA).

Globally, about 15 percent of the urban population uses solid fuels while 67 percent of the rural population does so, according to analysis conducted in preparation of this chapter.[3] About 25 percent of the urban population and 79 percent of the rural population uses solid fuels in the main SFU regions (Table 1.3).

Wood is the most widely used solid cooking fuel in developing countries. Agricultural residues, straws, and dung are only widely used in a few countries, including rural China. Use of coal is quite widespread in China and Mongolia for both cooking and heating. Concentrations of PM2.5 in the household environment from cooking with wood or agricultural residues, straw, or dung on open fire or in a traditional, unimproved stove are often several hundred $\mu g/m^3$. Concentrations from use of coal are on average about half the levels of wood according to studies in China (Jin et al., 2005; Mestl et al., 2007;

[2] For a majority of cities in low- and middle-income countries the PM2.5 concentrations are conversions from PM10 measurements.

[3] A database of urban and rural solid fuel use for cooking was assembled from the most recent Demographic and Health Surveys (DHS) and Multiple Indicator Cluster Surveys (MICS), the India National Sample Survey, and for a few countries from www.cleancookstoves.org. Almost all the surveys are from the period 2008–2014. The database covers over 95 percent of global solid fuel users.

annex 2). Use of coal does, however, tend to be more carcinogenic than biomass.

Using an improved biomass cookstove with chimney or hood for venting of smoke often substantially reduces PM2.5 concentrations. Studies

Table 1.2 Populations using solid fuels

Region	Population (million), 2012	SFU population (million), 2012	SFU (%)
China	1,351	621	46
India	1,237	767	62
Sub-Saharan Africa (SSA)	913	752	82
South East Asia (SEA)[a]	629	304	48
South Asia (SA)[b]	412	306	74
Latin America and the Caribbean (LAC)	604	83	14
Others[c]	878	46	5
World	7,044	2,878	41

Notes: Estimates of SFU population are based on most recent DHS and MICS household surveys and Bonjour et al. (2013). Population is from World Bank (2014).
[a] Plus Korea DR.
[b] Excluding India.
[c] Countries in Central and Eastern Europe, Central Asia, Middle East and North Africa, and Oceania with populations using solid fuels.
Source: Prepared by the author.

have typically found that personal exposure declines from several hundred to 75–125 µg/m^3. Thus, exposure levels remain relatively high, and reductions in health effects of switching from an open fire or traditional stove to an improved cookstove may "only" be on the order of 20–30 percent due to the highly nonlinear exposure–response relationships for major health outcomes.

One should also bear in mind that household use of solid fuels has community effects. Smoke from fuel burning enters dwellings of other households as well as contributes to outdoor ambient air pollution. Only "smokeless" fuels and technologies prevent this problem of externalities.

Bottled LPG is by far the most common modern energy source used for cooking in LMI countries. Combustion of LPG results in very little PM emissions and is therefore considered a relatively clean cooking fuel. Studies have, however, found that household PM2.5 concentrations often remain as high as 40–60 µg/m^3, presumably mainly due to the community effects of neighboring households using solid fuels. If, however, all households in a community switch to LPG, reductions in health effects of PM pollution are likely greater than 65 percent, depending on the AAP levels from sources other than HAP.

While benefit-cost ratios of improved cookstoves may still be higher than those of switching to LPG, LPG or other clean energy is the time-tested option for effectively combatting health

Table 1.3 Urban and rural solid fuel use, 2012

Region	SFU prevalence			SFU distribution	
	Total (%)	Urban (%)	Rural (%)	Urban (%)	Rural (%)
China	46	22	71	25	75
India	62	19	82	10	90
SSA	82	63	93	27	73
SEA[a]	48	26	65	23	77
SA[b]	74	31	93	12	88
LAC	14	4	53	25	75
Subtotal	55	25	79	20	80

[a] Plus Korea DR.
[b] Excluding India.
Source: Prepared by the author from recent DHS, MICS, and other surveys.

effects of solid fuels, especially when achieved communitywide. In other words, improved cook-stoves may continue to be the efficient but not the most effective solution.

Targets

Domains of Targets

Three categories of target are considered next.

Reductions in Health Effects

The advantage of targeting a reduction in health effects of air pollution at regional or national levels is the flexibility this provides in how to achieve the targets. However, focusing on locations where reductions can be achieved at a lower cost may result in a socially unacceptable degree of inequity. Such targets are also difficult to monitor, and progress is therefore difficult to verify and subject to disagreements over evidence base and methodologies.

Improved Air Quality

Targets of this sort for AAP are easier to monitor and verify if good monitoring equipment is available, although this is currently not the case for the majority of cities in LMI countries. Air quality targets may also be economically inefficient if they are nationally or regionally uniform. Monitoring of improvements in households on any scale is costly and impractical.

Reductions in Sources of Pollution

The advantage of targeting sources of pollution is the relative ease with which many sources can be monitored and costs of achieving the targets be estimated. However, for AAP, the exposure and therefore health effects vary greatly between types of pollution source and location. Such targets are much more practical for households, where types of fuel and stoves can be easily monitored.

"Zero" Targets

"Zero" targets are targets that would eliminate outdoor and household air pollution (PM2.5), or at least bring anthropogenic PM2.5 concentrations outdoors and in the household environment below

the level known to cause health effects (about 5.8 $\mu g/m^3$). In practice, this is impossible to achieve everywhere because not all sources are anthropogenic (desert dust, for example). Achieving such a target where possible would mean the complete elimination of solid fuels in the home and other external sources of pollution. Currently, only a small number of locations, mainly in small, pristine areas of Australia, Canada, New Zealand, and the United States, meet PM2.5 of less than 5.8 $\mu g/m^3$.

Selected Targets

Targets for Ambient Air Pollution

As discussed earlier, air quality targets for AAP are easier to measure and verify, and these will be assessed in more detail in this chapter. A reasonable target for most high-income countries in the Americas, Europe, and Asia/Pacific would be the annual AQG of 10 $\mu g/m^3$. The interim target of 15–25 $\mu g/m^3$ may be the initial aim for Latin America and the Caribbean and much of Eastern Europe. The interim target of 25–35 $\mu g/m^3$ may initially be more realistic for many of the low- and middle-income countries in Western Africa and Asia.

Targets for Household Air Pollution

The most attractive targets for household air pollution center on stoves and cooking fuels, and these will be assessed in more detail in this chapter. To achieve the maximum benefits per dollar spent on household energy and stove interventions, all households would need to participate and thus achieve a "solid fuel use free" community or, alternatively, an "unimproved stove free" community.

Benefits and Costs of Household Air Pollution Control

Targets

Two interim (IT) and one final (FT) household air pollution control targets are selected for the purpose of assessing benefits and costs. The first and second interim targets (IT-1 and IT-2), are for a 50 percent adoption rate of improved cooking stoves and LPG stoves, respectively, among

Table 1.4 Household air pollution control targets

Control option	Target	Average PM2.5 exposure ($\mu g/m^3$)	
		Interim Target (IT) 50% adoption	Final Target (FT) 100% adoption
Improved cookstoves	Adoption of improved cookstoves by households currently using unimproved biomass or coal stoves	100	
LPG stoves	Adoption of LPG stoves by households currently using biomass or coal	50	<25

Source: Selected by the author.

households currently using biomass or coal. These interim targets can be pursued concurrently. There is also a longer-term final target (FT) of 100 percent adoption of LPG or other clean cooking (and heating) options.

The interim targets are expected to reduce personal PM2.5 exposure from an average of 250 to 100 $\mu g/m^3$ with adoption of improved stoves and to 50 $\mu g/m^3$ with adoption of LPG stoves. Achievement of the final target is expected to reduce PM2.5 exposure to less than 25 $\mu g/m^3$.

The difference in exposure from the use of LPG at interim (50 $\mu g/m^3$) and final (25 $\mu g/m^3$) target is due to community pollution from households using biomass or coal at the interim target (Table 1.4). PM2.5 exposure levels in relation to targets are discussed later.

Average levels of household members' long-term exposure to PM2.5 applied in the GBD 2010 project are presented in Table 1.5. Men's exposure levels are lower than women's due to different 24-hour activity patterns. The use of bio-mass – largely on open fire or in unimproved stoves – results in an average long-term PM2.5 exposure of 200–300 $\mu g/m^3$.

Levels of personal exposure to PM2.5 applied in this chapter to estimate health benefits of interventions are presented in Table 1.6. The exposure levels represent the type of stove or fuel used by a household living in a community in which other households may continue to use biomass fuels or in which air quality is affected by other sources of PM2.5 pollution, i.e., affected by community pollution or pollution originating outside the community. The levels are average exposures of men

Table 1.5 Long-term personal exposure to PM2.5 from household fuel use ($\mu g/m^3$)

	Women	Men
Biomass	300	200
Mix of gas and biomass in chimney stove	100	65
Gas	70	46

Source: Produced by the author from Burnett et al. (2014).

and women. Exposure levels of children are assumed to be the same as the average of men and women.[4]

For the purposes of this analysis, we can define a range of exposure levels as specified in Table 1.6.

Level 1 is the average current exposure level of the 2.8 billion people who use solid fuels for cooking and heating. The difference in exposure between levels 2 and 3 is assumed the same as between levels 3 and 4. The three targets selected for assessment of benefits and costs correspond to exposure levels 2, 4, and 5.

Health Effects

Health benefits are presented in Table 1.7 and Figure 1.1 relative to baseline PM2.5 exposure level of 250 $\mu g/m^3$ at which level health effects are indexed to 1.0. Because the response to reduced exposure is highly nonlinear, only one-third of the health benefit is realized by a

---

[4] Balakrishnan et al. (2012) report children's exposure level to be somewhere in the neighborhood of the average of exposure levels of men and women.

Table 1.6 Levels of long-term personal exposure to PM2.5 from household fuel use (μg/m³)

Exposure levels	PM2.5 (μg/m³)
1 Biomass largely used on open fire or in unimproved stove	250
2 Chimney stove or other improved biomass or coal stove with community pollution	100
3 Mix of gas and biomass or coal in chimney stove or other improved stove with community pollution	75
4 Gas (e.g., LPG) with community pollution	50
5 Gas (e.g., LPG) with limited community pollution	25
6 Gas (e.g., LPG) with very limited community pollution	<7.3

Source: The author.

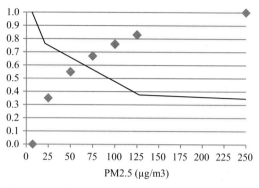

Figure 1.1 *Health effects of long-term PM2.5 exposure*

Source: The author.

Table 1.7 Health effects of long-term PM2.5 exposure

PM2.5 exposure (μg/m³)	Index of health effects	Health benefits of exposure reduction (%)
250	1.00	–
100	0.76	24
75	0.67	33
50	0.55	45
25	0.35	65
<7.3	0.00	100

Source: The author based on Burnett et al. (2014) and Shin et al. (2013).

reduction from 250 to 100 μg/m³, with two-thirds coming from the further reduction to 25 μg/m³. Even at this level, one-third of the baseline effects of household air pollution remain.[5]

An estimated 3.5 million people died and 19.7 billion disease days occurred globally in 2012 from household air pollution (Table 1.8). Almost 900,000 deaths and 4.8 billion disease days could be avoided annually if all households used an improved biomass or coal stove (exposure level 2; 100 μg/m³ of PM2.5). If all households used LPG or other clean fuels, over 2.3 million deaths and 12.8 million disease days could be

avoided annually (exposure level 5; 25 μg/m³ of PM2.5).

Monetized Values of Health Effects

Two alternative measures are used. The first uses the value of a statistical life (VSL), equivalent to fifty times GDP per capita (giving a value of a statistical life-year in the range $1,000 to $16,000[6]), and the second uses a uniform value of $1,000 or $5,000 per life-year (Table 1.8). Morbidity is valued either as 50 percent of daily wages or using the uniform values for a year of life (Table 1.9).

The global cost of household solid fuel use in 2012 is estimated at $646 billion, applying VSL for mortality and a fraction of wage rates for morbidity (Table 1.10). Using the uniform values for life-years or disability adjusted life-years (DALY), the cost is $111–555 billion (Table 1.11).

[5] Relative risk functions in Burnett et al. (2014) are mortality-cause specific. The exposure-reduction to health-benefit relation presented here therefore varies slightly across countries in relation to the structure of mortality.

[6] The number of years of life lost (YLL) per premature death from PM2.5 exposure in the household environment range from about 20 in China to about 54 in SSA. These figures are based on the Global Burden of Disease (GBD) 2010 Project results. YLL per death is high in countries and regions with high child mortality rates. No age-weighting or discounting is applied in the calculation of YLLs.

Table 1.8 Estimated annual health effects of household air pollution exposure

	PM2.5	China	India	SSA	SEA[a]	SA[b]	LAC	Other[c]	World
Deaths from PM2.5 (thousands)	Current levels	1,049	1,048	490	400	279	90	193	3,549
Avoided deaths (thousands) from PM2.5 reductions	100 μg/m³	263	254	118	96	67	22	46	865
	25 μg/m³	722	672	318	260	181	58	125	2,337
Disease days (millions) from PM2.5	Current levels	3,605	6,730	3,249	2,641	2,265	498	666	19,654
Avoided disease days (millions) from PM2.5 reductions	100 μg/m³	903	1,629	780	634	544	120	160	4,769
	25 μg/m³	2,481	4,314	2,112	1,717	1,472	324	433	12,852

[a] Plus Korea DR.
[b] Excluding India.
[c] Countries in Central and Eastern Europe, Central Asia, Middle East and North Africa, and Oceania.
Source: Author's estimates.

Table 1.9 Valuation of mortality, 2012 (US$)

	China	India	SSA	SEA[a]	SA[b]	LAC
Value of statistical life (VSL)	307,000	76,000	52,000	130,000	52,000	323,000
Value of statistical life-year (VSLY)	16,095	2,705	968	5,086	1,440	12,445
Value of a year of life lost (YLL) – lower	1,000	1,000	1,000	1,000	1,000	1,000
Value of a year of life lost (YLL) – upper	5,000	5,000	5,000	5,000	5,000	5,000

[a] Plus Korea DR.
[b] Excluding India.
Source: Author's estimates.

Table 1.10 Valuation of morbidity, 2012 (US$)

	China	India	SSA	SEA[a]	SA[b]	LAC
Value of a day of disease (50% of wage rates)	6.8	2.7	1.8	3.3	1.7	8.6
Value of a disability weighted year of disease (50% of wage rates)	16,657	6,455	4,377	8,040	4,156	21,038
Value of a year lost to disease (YLD) – lower	1,000	1,000	1,000	1,000	1,000	1,000
Value of a year lost to disease (YLD) – upper	5,000	5,000	5,000	5,000	5,000	5,000

[a] Plus Korea DR.
[b] Excluding India.
Source: Author's estimates.

Nonhealth Benefits

Nonhealth benefits of interventions included in this chapter are fuel and cooking time savings. Fuel savings are valued as the time that households spend on fuel collection, and time is valued at 50 percent of wage rates. Results are shown in Tables 1.12 and 1.13.

Table 1.11 Annual cost of health effects of household air pollution exposure, 2012 (US$ billion)

Valuation measure	China	India	SSA	SEA[a]	SA[b]	LAC	Other	World
VSL	347	98	31	61	18	33	58	646
DALY = US$1,000	21	32	28	11	11	3	5	111
DALY = US$5,000	107	161	138	57	55	13	24	555

[a] Plus Korea DR.
[b] Excluding India.
Source: Author's estimates.

Table 1.12 Value of solid fuel savings of switching to improved cookstove or LPG, 2012 (US$/household/year)

	China	India	SSA	SEA[a]	SA[b]	LAC
Improved cookstove (biomass/coal)	52	23	18	18	28	57
LPG (switching from unimproved stove)	175	77	59	60	94	189
LPG (switching from improved stove)	123	54	41	42	66	132

Notes:
[a] Plus Korea DR.
[b] Excluding India.
Source: Author's estimates.

Table 1.13 Value of cooking time savings, 2012 (US$/household/year)

	China	India	SSA	SEA[a]	SA[b]	LAC
Improved cookstove (biomass, coal)	42	16	11	20	10	53
LPG (switching from unimproved stove)	167	65	44	80	42	210
LPG (switching from improved stove)	125	49	33	60	32	157

Notes:
[a] Plus Korea DR.
[b] Excluding India.
Source: Author's estimates.

Costs of Pollution Control Options

Cost of improved biomass and coal cookstoves (ICS) varies tremendously depending on fuel and emission efficiency, durability, materials, and technology. Basic improved stoves cost in the range of US$2–10. Intermediate improved stoves cost US$25–35 and can provide up to 50 percent fuel savings and substantial emission reduction benefits. Advanced improved stoves such as natural or forced draft gasifier stoves cost US$20–75. LPG stoves typically cost US$30–100 depending on size and durability (Dalberg, 2013).

However, in China, heating is required for at least 3–5 months each year in the northern regions and 0–3 months in the southern regions (World Bank, 2013), and so improved or clean stoves and fuels are needed for both cooking and heating. Clean biomass and coal cookstoves are available for US$80–125 in China with a thermal efficiency of up to 35–45 percent. Clean combined cooking and heating stoves are available for US$ 100–160 with a thermal efficiency of as high as 70 percent (World Bank, 2013).

A price of an improved biomass stove of $30 is applied to most regions where heating is uncommon. This is the midpoint cost estimate of an intermediate improved cookstove. A price of $115 is applied to China reflecting an average of efficient cookstoves and combined cooking and heating stoves. The useful life of improved stoves is assumed to be three to five years. With such a short life the annualized cost is highly insensitive to discount rate.

A price of an LPG stove of $60 is applied to all regions and countries. The stove is for cooking only, and not heating. Useful life is assumed to be seven years. LPG fuel to replace solid fuels is applied at a rate of 30–40 kg per person per year, depending on average household size. A price of $1.3 per kg is applied as the economic cost of LPG to estimate the cost of switching to LPG for cooking.

All figures are summarized in Table 1.14.

Benefit-Cost Ratios

Four cases are considered. Cases 1 and 2 meet Interim Targets 1 and 2; Case 3 meets the Final Target. Case 4 is for comparison with Case 2, to demonstrate the effect of community pollution (Table 1.15).

Global Benefits

The global benefits of reaching the initial targets for ICSs and LPG are $120–270 billion per year, depending on the valuation method used. The global cost of ICS is estimated at nearly $20 billion, with an annualized cost of $5 billion. The global cost of LPG stoves is also estimated at about $20 billion. The global cost of LPG fuel is estimated at a little over $60 billion per year for the initial target.

The net benefits of the reaching the initial targets (Case 1 + 2) are $51–200 billion per year, depending on health valuation measure. Additional net benefits of progressing to the final target (Case 3) are $11–116 billion per year, bringing total net benefits to $62–316 billion per year.

Global Benefit-Cost Ratios

Globally, the benefit-cost ratio of improved biomass or coal stoves (ICS) is in the range of 6–18 (Case 1). The BCRs of LPG adoption (Cases 2 and 3) are much smaller than the BCR for

Table 1.14 Estimates of unit costs, 2012

	China	India	SSA	SEA[a]	SA[b]	LAC
Average household size (rural)	3	4.9	4.9	4.2	5.5	4.2
Cost of improved stove (US$)	115	30	30	30	30	60
Discount rate	5%	5%	5%	5%	5%	5%
Useful life of stove (years)	5	3	3	3	3	5
Annualized cost of stove (US$)	25.30	10.49	10.49	10.49	10.49	13.20
Cost of LPG cookstove (US$)	60	60	60	60	60	60
Discount rate	5%	5%	5%	5%	5%	5%
Useful life of stove (years)	7	7	7	7	7	7
Annualized cost of stove (US$)	9.88	9.88	9.88	9.88	9.88	9.88
LPG fuel (kg/person/year)	40	32	32	35	30	35
LPG fuel (kg/household/year)	120	157	157	147	165	147
LPG cost (US$/kg)	1.30	1.30	1.30	1.30	1.30	1.30
LPG fuel cost (US$/household/year)	156	204	204	191	215	191

Notes:
[a] Plus Korea DR.
[b] Excluding India.
Source: Author's estimates.

Table 1.15 Global benefit-cost ratios of household air pollution control targets

Case	(1)	(2)	(3)	(4)
Preadoption stove or fuel	UCS	UCS	ICS	UCS
Postadoption stove or fuel	ICS	LPG	LPG	LPG
Target	Initial target	Initial target	Final target	
Adoption rate	50%	50%	all in (a)	100%
PM2.5 ($\mu g/m^3$) preadoption	250	250	100	250
PM2.5 ($\mu g/m^3$) postadoption	100	50	25	25
Benefit-cost ratios:				
Using VSL	18	2.6	2.7	3.3
Using DALY = US$1,000	6	1.3	1.1	1.5
Using DALY = US$5,000	16	2.6	2.9	3.2
Net global benefits (US$ billion/year)				
Using VSL	87	113	116	316
Using DALY = US$1,000	28	23	11	62
Using DALY = US$5,000	76	110	124	310

Notes: UCS = unimproved biomass or coal cookstove. ICS = improved biomass or coal cookstove.
Source: The author.

ICS, but the net benefits are greater for LPG, suggesting that LPG should be promoted among those that can afford it. The BCR of switching to LPG from UCS (initial target) or from ICS (final target) are quite similar and all greater than 1. The BCR for case 4 is 15–25 percent higher than Case 2, reflecting the improvement from reduction of community pollution. More detail is given in Table 1.15.

Regional Benefit-Cost Ratios

Tables 1.16–1.18 present BCRs and net benefits for each major solid fuel using region by each valuation measure of health benefits. The overall picture is similar to the global one. However, valuing health benefits using either VSL or $1,000 per day gives BCRs slightly below 1 for sub-Saharan Africa.

Benefits and Costs of Outdoor Ambient Air Pollution Control

Targets

The air quality guideline (AQG) of WHO is an annual PM2.5 value of 10 $\mu g/m^3$, with interim targets of 35, 25, and 15 $\mu g/m^3$. Reflecting the large differences in regional ambient concentrations of fine particulates, three regional target groups are proposed, with all regions progressing toward the AQG over time. The initial regional targets are as follows:

1 East Asia (EA): IT-1 (35 $\mu g/m^3$)
2 South Asia (SA), Middle East and North Africa (MNA), High Income Asia Pacific (HI AP), Western sub-Saharan Africa (SSA-W), Central Asia (CA), Central Europe (CE), South East Asia (SEA): IT-2 (25 $\mu g/m^3$)
3 Western Europe (WE), High Income North America (HI NA), Other sub-Saharan Africa (SSA-O), Eastern Europe (EE), Latin America and Caribbean (LAC), Australasia (AA), Oceania (OC): IT-3 (15 $\mu g/m^3$)

These are summarized in Table 1.19.

Health Effects

Health benefits of reaching final target (AQG) are greatest in percentage terms for regions furthest away from the final target (Table 1.20). Reaching

Table 1.16 Benefit-cost ratios of household air pollution control targets using VSL for health valuation

Case	(1)	(2)	(3)	(4)
Preadoption stove or fuel	UCS	UCS	ICS	UCS
Postadoption stove or fuel	ICS	LPG	LPG	LPG
Target	Initial target	Initial target	Final target	
Adoption rate	50%	50%	all (a)	100%
PM2.5 ($\mu g/m^3$) preadoption	250	250	100	250
PM2.5 ($\mu g/m^3$) postadoption	100	50	25	25
Benefit-cost ratios:				
China	20	4.8	4.3	5.9
India	18	2.0	2.2	2.5
SSA	7	0.9	0.9	1.1
SEA[a]	23	2.6	3.1	3.4
SA[b]	11	1.3	1.3	1.6
LAC	39	5.8	6.6	7.5
Total	18	2.6	2.7	3.3
Net benefits (US$ billion)	87	113	116	316

Notes: [a] Plus Korea DR. [b] Excluding India. UCS = unimproved biomass or coal cookstove. ICS = improved biomass or coal cookstove.
Source: The author.

Table 1.17 Benefit-cost ratios of household air pollution control targets using DALY = US$1,000 for health valuation

Case	(1)	(2)	(3)	(4)
Preadoption stove or fuel	UCS	UCS	ICS	UCS
Postadoption stove or fuel	ICS	LPG	LPG	LPG
Target	Initial target	Initial target	Final target	
Adoption rate	50%	50%	all (a)	100%
PM2.5 ($\mu g/m^3$) preadoption	250	250	100	250
PM2.5 ($\mu g/m^3$) postadoption	100	50	25	25
Benefit-cost ratios:				
China	5	2.0	1.5	2
India	9	1.1	1.1	1.3
SSA	7	0.9	0.9	1.0
SEA[a]	7	1.1	1.0	1.2
SA[b]	8	1.0	1.0	1.2
LAC	11	2.3	1.8	2.4
Total	6	1.3	1.1	1.5
Net benefits (US$ billion)	28	23	11	62

Notes: [a] Plus Korea DR. [b] Excluding India. UCS = unimproved biomass or coal cookstove. ICS = improved biomass or coal cookstove.
Source: The author.

Table 1.18 Benefit-cost ratios of household air pollution control targets using DALY = US$5,000 for health valuation

Case	(1)	(2)	(3)	(4)
Preadoption stove or fuel	UCS	UCS	ICS	UCS
Postadoption stove or fuel	ICS	LPG	LPG	LPG
Target	Initial target	Initial target	Final target	
Adoption rate	50%	50%	all (a)	100%
PM2.5 (μg/m^3) preadoption	250	250	100	250
PM2.5 (μg/m^3) postadoption	100	50	25	25
Benefit-cost ratios:				
China	9	2.7	2.2	3.1
India	28	2.8	3.4	3.3
SSA	23	2.4	2.9	3.2
SEA[a]	22	2.4	2.9	3.2
SA[b]	26	2.6	3.1	3.5
LAC	20	3.4	3.4	4.1
Total	16	2.6	2.9	3.2
Net benefits (US$ billion)	76	110	124	310

Notes:
[a] Plus Korea DR.
[b] Excluding India.
UCS = unimproved biomass or coal cookstove. ICS = improved biomass or coal cookstove.
Source: The author.

the AQG target would give an 80 percent, 66 percent, and 39 percent reduction in health impacts for groups 1, 2, and 3, respectively, but as much as one-third of the global health effects remain after all regions have achieved the 10 μg/m^3 target.[7] An estimated 3.3 million people died and 9.4 billion disease days occurred globally in 2012 from PM2.5 ambient air pollution (AAP). Almost 2.2 million deaths and 6.3 billion disease days could be avoided annually if all regions reached the annual PM2.5 AQG of 10 μg/m^3. See Table 1.21 for more details.

Monetized Values of Health Effects

As for household air pollution, two alternative measures are applied to value the loss of a life or the benefit of avoiding a death associated with outdoor ambient PM2.5 air pollution. By the first measure using values of statistical life (VSL), a death is valued at 50 times GDP per capita in each of the countries and regions. The value of a statistical life-

year (VSLY) is found by dividing VSL by the number of years prematurely lost to death. VSLYs are thus in the range of $1.2–224 thousand.[8] By the second measure, a uniform value of $1,000 and $5,000 per year of life lost (YLL) is applied. The VSLYs are within this range for the lowest income

[7] The remaining health effects after reaching the AQG and the interim targets are likely to be lower than presented here. This is because it is assumed that air quality improvements only take place among the population with PM2.5 exposures exceeding the targets. In reality, air pollution control interventions aimed at areas with high PM2.5 concentrations will also benefit some of the areas with low concentrations and thus also reduce health effects in these areas.

[8] The number of years of life lost (YLL) per premature death from outdoor ambient PM2.5 range from about 14–16 in the high income regions to 48 in western sub-Saharan Africa (SSA-W). These figures are based on the Global Burden of Disease (GBD) 2010 Project results. YLL per death is high in countries and regions with high child mortality rates. No age-weighting or discounting is applied in the calculation of YLLs.

Table 1.19 Regional PM2.5 ambient air pollution targets (annual maximum)

	Target	IT-1	IT-2	IT-3	AQG
	max annual PM2.5	35 μg/m^3	25 μg/m^3	15 μg/m^3	10 μg/m^3
Regions	Regions				
Group 1	EA				
Group 2	SA, MNA, HI AP, SSA-W, CA, CE, SEA				
Group 3	WE, HI NA, SSA-O, EE, LAC, AA, OC				

Source: The author.

Table 1.20 Health benefits of meeting PM2.5 ambient air quality targets (% reduction in current health effects)

	Target	IT-1	IT-2	IT-3	AQG
	max annual PM2.5	35 μg/m^3	25 μg/m^3	15 μg/m^3	10 μg/m^3
Regions	Regions				
Group 1	EA	20%	34%	59%	80%
Group 2	SA, MNA, HI AP, SSA-W, CA, CE, SEA		13%	37%	66%
Group 3	WE, HI NA, SSA-O, EE, LAC, AA, OC			7%	39%
World	All	8%	19%	41%	67%

Source: Author's estimates.

Table 1.21 Estimated annual health effects of PM2.5 ambient air pollution exposure

	PM2.5	Group 1	Group 2	Group 3	World
Deaths from PM2.5 (000)	Current levels	1,276	1,452	542	3,269
Avoided deaths from reaching targets (000)	35 μg/m^3	261			261
	25 μg/m^3	439	182		621
	15 μg/m^3	755	539	38	1,331
	10 μg/m^3	1,022	962	212	2,196
Disease days from PM2.5 (million)	Current levels	3,270	4,481	1,621	9,372
Avoided disease days from reaching targets (million)	35 μg/m^3	670			670
	25 μg/m^3	1,125	571		1,696
	15 μg/m^3	1,936	1,694	127	3,757
	10 μg/m^3	2,620	2,998	662	6,280

Note: Groups are defined as in previous tables.
Source: Author's estimates.

Table 1.22 Valuation of mortality and morbidity, 2012 (US$)

	Value of statistical life (VSL)	Value of a statistical life-year (VSLY)	Value of a day of disease (50% of wage rates)	Value of YLD (50% of wage rates)	DALY lower value	DALY upper value
EA	309,000	15,912	8.0	19,378	1,000	5,000
SA	71,000	2,514	2.7	6,662	1,000	5,000
MNA	369,000	14,327	16.3	39,783	1,000	5,000
HI AP	2,042,000	149,253	89.6	218,093	1,000	5,000
SSA-W	58,000	1,211	2.4	5,893	1,000	5,000
CA	250,000	10,052	7.9	19,238	1,000	5,000
CE	544,000	32,467	22.7	55,203	1,000	5,000
SEA	166,000	7,131	4.7	11,517	1,000	5,000
WE	1,935,000	143,042	86.7	210,931	1,000	5,000
HI NA	2,609,000	164,705	113.6	276,415	1,000	5,000
SSA-O	69,000	1,791	2.5	6,138	1,000	5,000
EE	510,000	26,918	14.8	35,898	1,000	5,000
LAC	451,000	20,686	14.7	35,655	1,000	5,000
AA	3,161,000	223,794	140.8	342,582	1,000	5,000
Oceania	142,000	4,400	5.3	12,923	1,000	5,000

Source: Author's estimates.

regions of the world, but are much higher for middle- and high-income regions (Table 1.22).

Two alternative measures are also applied to value morbidity. By the first measure a day of avoided illness is valued as the equivalent of 50 percent of daily wages. This is converted to a value of disability weighted year of disease in the range of $6–343 thousand (Table 1.22).[9] The second measure values a year lost to disease (YLD) at $1,000 and $5,000 as for years lost to premature mortality.[10]

The global cost of outdoor ambient PM2.5 exposure in 2012 is estimated at $1.7 trillion, applying VSL for mortality and a fraction of wage rates for morbidity. About $0.9 trillion is in high-income regions, although they only account for 11 percent of global deaths.[11] About $637 billion of the cost is in developing regions in Asia, Africa, Latin America, and Oceania, which between them account for 81 percent of the deaths. The global cost of outdoor ambient PM2.5 is estimated at $78–388 billion in the same year when applying $1,000 to $5,000 per DALY (Table 1.23).

Pollution Control Options and Costs

There are many sources of outdoor air pollution, not all of which can be covered here. However, we look at two policy options and the costs of abatement from four sources of PM2.5.

Energy Subsidies

World energy subsidies contribute to energy waste and pollution. Energy consumption subsidies averaged over $400 billion per year during 2007–2010 and $520–540 billion per year during 2011–2012 according to the International Energy Agency (IEA). These subsidies are concentrated in thirty-nine countries responsible for over half of world fossil fuel consumption.[12]

[9] Applying an average disability weight of 0.15.
[10] YLD is a disability weighted measure of disease burden. If the disability weight is 0.15 then 2,433 days of disease is equivalent to one YLD.
[11] This disproportionately high share of cost is due to VSL being proportional to income level.
[12] www.worldenergyoutlook.org/resources/energysubsidies/.

Table 1.23 Annual cost of health effects of outdoor ambient PM2.5 exposure, 2012 (US$ billion)

Valuation measure	VSL	DALY = US $1,000	DALY= US $5,000
EA	420	26	131
SA	63	23	116
MNA	76	4.9	25
HI AP	213	1.4	6.8
SSA-W	5.4	4.0	20
CA	14	1.3	6.7
CE	54	1.6	8.1
SEA	30	4.1	21
WE	372	2.5	12
HI NA	346	2.0	10
SSA-O	3.9	2.0	10
EE	86	3.2	16
LAC	24	1.1	5.6
AA	6.7	0.03	0.14
Oceania	0.05	0.01	0.05
World	1,714	78	388

Source: Author's estimates.

Eliminating these subsidies would provide economic efficiency gains and thus PM2.5 emission reductions at a negative marginal cost (i.e., positive economic benefit). Additionally, OECD has identified over 550 measures that subsidize and support fossil fuel production and use in its thirty-four member countries, amounting to $55–90 billion per year from 2005 to 2011.[13] The majority of these subsidies and supports are to petroleum products, placing renewables and less-polluting energies at a disadvantage.

Taxation Policies

Although direct tax instruments for PM2.5 abatement are often difficult to design, indirect instruments can provide PM2.5 emission reductions at lower cost to society than regulatory, command-and-control options. These instruments include fuel taxes, vehicle taxes, and tax rebates on PM2.5 control technology.

Household Use of Solid Fuels

Household use of solid fuels does not only cause serious air pollution in the immediate household environment, but also contributes to outdoor pollution. Abatement could be via use of improved cooking stoves or switching to LPG. LPG is more expensive but also far more effective in reducing pollution. Taking into account fuel savings, moving to improved biomass stoves may actually save money, while the net cost of avoiding the emission of one ton of PM2.5 by switching to LPG can be up to $50,000 in East Asia. See Table 1.24 for more details.

Solid Waste Management

Uncontrolled burning of solid waste by households and scavengers contributes to urban ambient PM2.5 pollution. This is particularly the case in South Asia (SA) and sub-Saharan Africa (SSA), but also in poor neighborhoods in other parts of the world. Improved municipal solid waste management can reduce waste burning. The cost of improved management per ton of waste increases with GDP per capita, e.g., higher costs of labor and land, but declines as a percentage of GDP per capita (Table 1.25). The cost estimates are based on cost per ton of waste collection, city cleaning from littering, and sanitary disposal. The costs translate to $10–12 thousand per ton of PM2.5 abatement from avoided burning of waste in the lowest income regions of the world, somewhat higher in South East Asia (SEA) at $16–17 thousand, and $24–28 in East Asia (EA) and Latin America and the Caribbean (LAC; Table 1.25).

Fuel Quality

The majority of primary PM2.5 emissions from vehicle fuel combustion come from diesel vehicles, which accounted for 44 percent of global road transport fuel use in 2012. Fuel quality makes a big difference, and in recognition of the road transport sector's contribution to air pollution, there is

[13] www.oecd.org/site/tadffss/Fossil%20Fuels%20Inventory_Policy_Brief.pdf.

Table 1.24 Cost of PM2.5 abatement from household energy (US$/ton of PM2.5)

	FS not included			Including FS		
	EA	LAC	Other	EA	LAC	Other
Improved biomass cookstove	7,000	3,700	2,900	1,300	−2,100	−2,800
Improved coal cookstove	12,800			−1,500		
LPG instead of biomass for cooking	13,800	13,800	13,800	8,100	8,100	8,100
LPG instead of unimproved coal stove	27,700			13,400		
LPG instead of improved coal stove	64,500			50,300		

Note: FS = biomass or coal fuel savings from switching to improved stove or LPG.
Source: Estimates by the author.

Table 1.25 Cost of PM2.5 abatement from improved solid waste management

	SSA-W	SSA-O	SA	SEA	EA	LAC
GDP per capita, US$, 2012	1,153	1,367	1,414	3,299	6,128	8,936
Waste generation (kg/capita/day)	0.6	0.6	0.6	0.8	0.9	1.00
Waste generation (tons/capita/year)	0.22	0.22	0.22	0.29	0.33	0.37
Cost of waste management (% of GDP)	1.3%	1.3%	1.3%	1.0%	0.9%	0.8%
Cost of waste management (US$/ton)	68	81	84	113	168	196
PM2.5 per ton of waste burning (kg)	7	7	7	7	7	7
Cost of PM2.5 emission reductions (US$/ton)	9,800	11,600	12,000	16,100	24,000	28,000

Source: Estimates by the author.

Table 1.26 Cost of PM2.5 abatement from using ultra-low sulfur diesel (50 ppm) for road vehicles

	US$/bbl of diesel	US$/ton of PM2.5
Sulfur from 2000 ppm to 50 ppm	3	14,650
	6	29,300
Sulfur from 500 ppm to 50 ppm	1.5	14,000
	2	18,600

Source: Estimates by the author.

globally a major push for ultra-low sulfur (< 50 ppm) diesel for road vehicles. Depending on the starting level, reducing sulfur levels to 50 ppm gives abatement costs of $14–29,000 per ton of PM2.5 (Table 1.26). The upper bound reflects high refinery investment requirements in many refineries in SSA (ICF International, 2009). Lower costs may be achieved by importing ultra-low sulfur diesel, either from efficient refineries in SSA or elsewhere.

Road Vehicle Technologies

There are various ways to reduce road vehicle emissions. The option assessed here is retrofitting of in-use diesel vehicles with diesel particulate filters (DPFs). The cost per ton of PM2.5 abated is in the range $30–100,000 for relatively high usage vehicles used mainly in cities (Table 1.27). The cost of this abatement option is substantially higher than the previous options assessed, but highly effective.

Benefit-Cost Ratios

Global Benefits

Global benefits of reaching the final target, i.e., annual AQG of 10 μg/m^3 of PM2.5, are $52–971 billion per year (Table 1.28). The marginal or incremental benefits increase substantially as the world progresses from the interim targets to the AQG due to the nonlinear relationship between exposure and

Table 1.27 Cost of PM2.5 abatement from DPF retrofitting of in-use diesel vehicles (US$/ton)

	Low	High
Heavy-duty vehicles	32500	77500
Light-duty vehicles	57500	102500

Source: Estimates by the author.

Table 1.28 Annual global benefits of reaching the PM2.5 targets, 2012 (billion US$)

Interim and final targets (PM2.5)	Benefits by alternative health valuation measures		
	VSL	DALY = US $1,000	DALY = US $5,000
IT-1: 35 µg/m³	86	5	27
IT-2: 25 µg/m³	200	14	71
IT-3: 15 µg/m³	485	32	158
AQG: 10 µg/m³	971	52	262

Note: Groups are defined as in previous tables.
Source: Author's estimates.

health effects. About 87 percent of the avoided deaths are in low- and middle-income countries.

Benefits per Ton of PM2.5 Emissions

Health benefits must be estimated per ton of PM2.5 emission reductions to estimate benefit-cost ratios of PM2.5 pollution control. This is undertaken by using geographic-specific intake fractions. An intake fraction is a measure of how much of a ton of emissions in a geographic area is breathed in by the exposed population. The higher the intake fraction the larger are the health damages and thus the health benefits of emissions reductions.

Apte et al. (2012) estimate the intake fraction of distributed ground-level emission sources in over 3,600 cities of the world. Population weighted intake fractions by country range from less than 10 to over 100 ppm, and by major city from less than 5 to over 250.

Benefits per ton of PM2.5 emissions reductions are very location specific and are here estimated for cities with locations in which PM2.5 concentrations

exceed initial regional targets. Estimated benefits are presented in Table 1.29. These benefits per ton are applied to estimate benefit-cost ratios (BCRs) of PM2.5 emission control interventions.

Regional variations in benefits per ton are mainly explained by variations in intake fractions, initial PM2.5 concentrations, baseline health conditions, and valuation of health effects. Benefits per ton will increase intraregionally as regions progress from the interim targets to the AQG due to the nonlinear relationship between exposure and health effects.

Regional Benefit-Cost Ratios

As an estimated 81 percent of global deaths from outdoor ambient PM2.5 occur in low- and middle-income countries, the benefit-cost analysis in this chapter concentrates on these regions.

BCRs of controlling PM2.5 emissions to the outdoor environment from household use of solid fuels are larger than the BCRs of other abatement options assessed. This is mainly due to the biomass or coal fuel savings that the interventions provide. BCRs of improved solid waste management for minimization of uncontrolled burning and of ultra-low sulfur diesel for road vehicles are relatively similar, albeit with interregional variations.

Regional BCRs of improved biomass cookstoves range from 1.3 to 23.3. They are all greater than 1 even for health valuation of $1,000 per DALY. In East Asia (i.e., mainly China), BCRs of improved coal cookstoves are in the range of 1.4–5.2. Regional BCRs for using LPG instead of biomass cookstoves or unimproved coal cookstoves in East Asia are mostly greater or equal to one for health valuation using VSL or $5,000 per DALY (Tables 1.30–1.31). The BCRs are for households cooking outdoors or who vent the smoke out of the dwellings. They are conservative insofar as they do not include the benefits of household air pollution reduction.

Regional BCRs of improved municipal solid waste management to minimize uncontrolled burning of waste range from 0.13 to 2.88. They are mostly greater than 1 when using VSL or

Table 1.29 Benefits of PM2.5 emissions reductions (US$/ton)

				Benefits (US$/ton) by alternative valuation measures		
		Intake fraction (iF)	VSL	DALY = US$1,000	DALY = US$5,000	
Group 1 (IT-1: max 35 µg/m3)	EA	100	52,000	3,230	16,150	
Group 2 (IT-2: max 25 µg/m3)	SA	100	15,700	5,800	29,000	
	MNA	70	48,400	3,140	15,700	
	SSA-W	80	7,400	5,500	27,500	
	CA	30	30,100	2,920	14,600	
	SEA	90	40,500	5,510	27,550	
Group 3 (IT-3: max 15 µg/m3)	SSA-O	50	8,400	4,270	21,350	
	LAC	70	80,600	3,740	18,700	
	Oceania	15	5,800	1,230	6,150	
IT-2: max 25 µg/m3)	CE	30	99,000	2,970	14,850	
IT-3: max 15 µg/m3)	EE	40	288,400	10,620	53,100	
High-income regions	HI AP	60	361,300	2,310	11,550	
	WE	45	404,800	2,710	13,550	
	HI NA	40	533,000	3,030	15,150	
	AA	20	186,500	790	3,950	

Source: Author's estimates.

Table 1.30 Benefit-cost ratios of household use of improved biomass cookstoves (ICS) and LPG, 2012

	ICS (biomass)			LPG (from biomass)		
Region/valuation measure	VSL	DALY = US$1,000	DALY = US$5,000	VSL	DALY = US$1,000	DALY = US$5,000
EA	8.2	1.3	3.1	4.2	0.6	1.6
SA	7.4	4.0	12.0	1.6	0.8	2.5
SEA	15.9	3.9	11.5	3.3	0.8	2.4
SSA-W	4.5	3.9	11.5	1.0	0.8	2.4
SSA-O	4.9	3.4	9.3	1.0	0.7	2.0
LAC	23.3	2.6	6.6	6.3	0.7	1.8
Oceania	3.1	1.9	3.2	0.8	0.5	0.9

Note: ICS = improved cookstove.
Source: Author's estimates.

$5,000 per DALY for health valuation, but less than one in all regions for $1,000 per DALY. They are less than one in Oceania for all three health valuation measures, reflecting low intake fractions (Table 1.32). The BCRs do not, however, include cobenefits associated with a cleaner urban environment.

Regional BCRs of ultra-low sulfur diesel (ULSD) fuel for road vehicles range from 0.1 to 5.0. They are mostly greater than 1 when valuing health benefits using either VSL or $5,000 per DALY. They are less than one for $1,000 per DALY. They are quite similar for sulfur reduction from 2000+ to 50 ppm and from 500 to 50 ppm (Table 1.33).

Table 1.31 Benefit-cost ratios of household use of improved coal cookstoves (ICS) and LPG in East Asia, 2012

	VSL	DALY = US $1,000	DALY = US $5,000
ICS (coal)	5.2	1.4	2.4
LPG (from UCS with coal)	2.4	0.6	1.1
LPG (from ICS with coal)	1.0	0.3	0.5

Note: ICS = improved cookstove. UCS = unimproved cookstove.
Source: Author's estimates.

Table 1.32 Benefit-cost ratios of improved solid waste management, 2012

	VSL	DALY = US$1,000	DALY = US$5,000
EA	2.17	0.13	0.67
SA	1.31	0.48	2.42
SEA	2.52	0.34	1.71
SSA-W	0.76	0.56	2.81
SSA-O	0.72	0.37	1.84
LAC	2.88	0.13	0.67
Oceania	0.37	0.08	0.39

Source: Author's estimates.

The BCRs are for ULSD consumed primarily within the cities targeted for PM2.5 abatement. BRCs for nationwide use of ULSD are lower than presented in Table 1.33. However, as ULSD is a prerequisite for effective PM2.5 emission controls from diesel vehicles, there are indirect benefits not captured in the BCRs here.

Regional BCRs of retrofitting in-use diesel vehicles with diesel particulate filters (DPFs) range from 0.02 to 1.47. BCRs are less than one in most regions and for all three health valuation measures (Table 1.34). Cost of DPFs for vehicle retrofitting is declining, however, and installation of DPFs on new vehicles is cheaper than retrofitting of in-use vehicles.

The estimated BCRs suggest that outdoor PM2.5 abatement in especially low-income countries should be selective and well prioritized. They also suggest that a high priority is to control PM2.5 emissions from household use of solid fuel, be it for household and outdoor exposure reduction.

Only ground-level distributed PM2.5 abatement options have been assessed in this chapter. Options are also available to reduce PM2.5 emissions from power plants and industrial facilities. The PM2.5 intake fractions associated with these sources are often substantially lower than the fraction from ground-level sources, but abatement cost per ton

Table 1.33 Benefit-cost ratios of ultra-low sulfur diesel fuel (ULSD) for road vehicles, 2012

	ULSD (2000+ to 50 ppm)			ULSD (500 to 50 ppm)		
Region/valuation measure	VSL	DALY = US$1,000	DALY = US$5,000	VSL	DALY = US$1,000	DALY = US$5,000
EA	3.1	0.19	1.0	3.3	0.20	1.0
SA	0.9	0.35	1.7	1.0	0.36	1.8
SEA	2.4	0.33	1.6	2.5	0.34	1.7
SSA-W	0.3	0.23	1.2	0.5	0.34	1.7
SSA-O	0.4	0.18	0.9	0.5	0.27	1.3
LAC	4.8	0.22	1.1	5.0	0.23	1.2
Oceania	0.3	0.07	0.4	0.4	0.08	0.4
CA	1.8	0.17	0.9	1.9	0.18	0.9
MNA	2.9	0.19	0.9	3.0	0.20	1.0

Source: Author's estimates.

Table 1.34 Benefit-cost ratios of DPF retrofitting of in-use vehicles, 2012

Region/valuation measure	DPF for LDVs			DPF for HDVs		
	VSL	DALY = US$1,000	DALY = US$5,000	VSL	DALY = US$1,000	DALY = US$5,000
EA	0.65	0.04	0.20	0.95	0.06	0.29
SA	0.20	0.07	0.36	0.29	0.11	0.53
SEA	0.51	0.07	0.34	0.74	0.10	0.50
SSA-W	0.09	0.07	0.34	0.13	0.10	0.50
SSA-O	0.11	0.05	0.27	0.15	0.08	0.39
LAC	1.01	0.05	0.23	1.47	0.07	0.34
Oceania	0.07	0.02	0.08	0.11	0.02	0.11
CA	0.38	0.04	0.18	0.55	0.05	0.27
MNA	0.61	0.04	0.20	0.88	0.06	0.29

Note: DPF = diesel particulate filter. LDV = light duty vehicles. HDV = heavy duty vehicles.
Source: Author's estimates.

of PM2.5 is also often lower. Development of a least cost abatement strategy per unit of health benefit would need to include an assessment of these PM2.5 sources.

Conclusions

PM2.5 air pollution is a major cause of premature death and disease. The benefits of controlling household air pollution from solid fuel cooking are much greater than the costs, and reducing solid fuel use also improves outdoor air quality, particularly in Asia. The often low to moderate BCRs suggest that outdoor PM2.5 abatement in especially low-income countries should be selective and well-targeted. They also suggest that a high priority is to control PM2.5 emissions from household use of solid fuel, for both household and outdoor exposure reduction.

References

Apte, J., Bombrun, E., Marshall, J., and Nazaroff, W. 2012. Global intraurban intake fractions for primary air pollutants from vehicles and other distributed sources. *Environmental Science Technology*, 46: 3415–23.

Balakrishnan, K., Ghosh, S., Ganguli, B., et al. 2012. Modeling household concentrations and personal exposures for PM2.5 from solid fuel use on a national scale in India. Presentation at BAQ, Hong Kong, December 2012.

2013. State and national household concentrations of PM2.5 from solid cookfuel use: Results from measurements and modeling in India for estimation of the global burden of disease. *Environmental Health*, 12: 77–90.

Baumgartner, J., Schauer, J., Ezzati, M., et al. 2011. Indoor air pollution and blood pressure in adult women living in rural China. *Environmental Health Perspectives*, 119(10): 1390–5.

Bonjour, S., Adair-Rohani, H., Wolf, J., et al. 2013. Solid fuel use for household cooking: Country and regional estimates for 1980–2010. *Environmental Health Perspectives*, 121(7): 784–90.

Brauer, M., Amann, M., Burnett, R. T., et al. 2012. Exposure assessment for estimation of the global burden of disease attributable to outdoor air pollution. *Environmental Science Technology*, 46(2): 652–60.

Burnett, R. T., Pope, C. A. III., Ezzati, M., et al. 2014. An integrated risk function for estimating the global burden of disease attributable to ambient fine particulate matter exposure. *Environmental Health Perspectives*, 122: 397–403.

Clark, M., Peel, J., Burch, J., Nelson, T., Robinson, M., Conway, S., et al. 2009. Impact of improved cookstoves on indoor air pollution and adverse health effects among Honduran women. *International Journal of Environmental Health Research*, 19(5): 357–68.

Cynthia, A. A., Edwards, R. D., Johnson, M., et al. 2008. Reduction in personal exposures to particulate matter and carbon monoxide as a result of the installation of a Patsari improved cook stove in Michoacan Mexico. *Indoor Air*, 18(2): 93–105.

Dalberg Global Development Advisors. 2013. India Cookstoves and Fuels Market Assessment. www.cleancookstoves.org.

Desai, M. A., Mehta, S., and Smith, K. 2004. *Indoor Smoke from Solid Fuels: Assessing the Environmental Burden of Disease at National and Local Levels.* Environmental Burden of Disease Series, No. 4. Geneva: World Health Organization.

Dherani, M., Pope, D., Mascarenhas, M., Smith, K., Weber, M., and Bruce, N. 2008. Indoor air pollution from unprocessed solid fuel use and pneumonia risk in children aged under five years: A systematic review and meta-analysis. *Bulletin of the World Health Organization*, 86:390–8.

D'Sa, A. and Murthy, K. V. 2004. Report on the Use of LPG in as a Domestic Cooking Fuel Option in India. Bangalore: International Energy Initiative.

Edwards, R. D., Liu, Y., He, G., Yin, Z., Sinton, J., Peabody, J., et al. 2007. Household CO and PM measured as part of a review of China's national improved stove program. *Indoor Air*, 17(3): 189–203.

Forouzanfar, M. H., Alexander, L., Anderson, H. R., et al. 2015. Global, regional, and national comparative risk assessment of 79 behavioural, environmental and occupational, and metabolic risks or clusters of risks in 188 countries, 1990–2013: A systematic analysis for the Global Burden of Disease Study 2013. *Lancet*, 386: 2287–323.

Goldemberg, J., Johansson, T., Reddy, A., and Williams, R. 2004. A global clean cooking fuel initiative. *Energy for Sustainable Development*, 8(3): 5–12.

Habermehl, H. 2007. *Economic Evaluation of the Improved Household Cooking Stove Dissemination Programme in Uganda.* Eschborn: GTZ.

Hutton, G., Rehfuess, E., Tedioso, F., and Weiss, S. 2006. *Evaluation of the Costs and Benefits of*

Household Energy and Health Interventions at Global and Regional Levels. New York: World Health Organization.

ICF International. 2009. *Final Report Sub-Saharan Africa Refinery Project, Volume II-A: Refinery Study.* World Bank Refinery Report. New York: The World Bank and The African Refiners Association.

Jeuland, M. and Pattanayak, S. 2012. Benefits and costs of improved cookstoves: Assessing the implications of variability in health, forest and climate impacts. *PLoS ONE*, 7(2): e30338. doi:10.1371/journal.pone.0030338.

Jin, Y. L., Zhou, Z., He, G. L., et al. 2005. Geographical, spatial, and temporal distributions of multiple indoor air pollutants in four Chinese provinces. *Environmental Science & Technology*, 39(24): 9431–9.

Kojima, M., Bacon, R., and Zhou, X. 2011. Who Uses Bottled Gas? Evidence from Households in Developing Countries. Policy Research Working Paper 5731. New York: World Bank.

Kurmi, O. P., Semple, S., Simkhada, P., Smith, W. C., and Ayres, J. G. 2010. COPD and chronic bronchitis risk of indoor air pollution from solid fuel: A systematic review and meta-analysis. *Thorax*, 65: 221–8.

Lim, S. S., Vos, T., Flaxman, A. D., et al. 2012. A comparative risk assessment of burden of disease and injury attributable to 67 risk factors and risk factor clusters in 21 regions, 1990–2010: A systematic analysis for the Global Burden of Disease Study 2010. *Lancet*, 380: 2224–60.

Lindhjem, H., Narvud, S., Braathen, N. A., and Biausque, V. 2011. Valuing mortality risk reductions from environmental, transport, and health policies: A global meta-analysis of stated preference studies. *Risk Analysis*, 31(9): 1381–407.

Malla, S. and Timilsina, G. 2014. Household Cooking Fuel Choice and Adoption of Improved Cookstoves in Developing Countries: A Review. Policy Research Working Paper 6903. New York: World Bank.

McCracken, J. P., Smith, K. R., Díaz, A., Mittleman, M. A., and Schwartz, J. 2007. Chimney stove intervention to reduce long-term wood smoke exposure lowers blood pressure among Guatemalan women. *Environmental Health Perspectives*, 115(7): 996–1001.

Mehta, S., Shin, H., Burnett, R., North, T., and Cohen, A. 2013. Ambient particulate air pollution and acute lower respiratory infections: A systematic review and implications for estimating the global burden of disease. *Air Quality, Atmosphere, and Health*, 6: 69–83.

Mestl, H. E. S., Aunan, K., Seip, H. M, Wang, S., Zhao, Y., and Zhang, D. 2007. Urban and rural exposure to indoor air pollution from domestic biomass and coal burning across China. *Science of the Total Environment*, 377(1): 12–26.

Mrozek, J. and Taylor, L. 2002. What determines the value of life? A meta analysis. *Journal of Policy Analysis and Management*, 21(2): 253–70.

Navrud, S. and Lindhjem, H. 2010. Meta-Analysis of Stated Preference VSL Studies: Further Model Sensitivity and Benefit Transfer Issues. Prepared for the Environment Directorate. Paris: OECD.

Northcross, A., Chowdhury, Z., McCracken, J., Canuz, E., and Smith, K. 2010. Estimating personal PM2.5 exposures using CO measurements in Guatemalan households cooking with wood fuel. *Journal of Environmental Monitoring*, 12: 873–8.

Po, J. Y. T., FitzGerald, J. M., and Carlsten, C. 2011. Respiratory disease associated with solid biomass fuel exposure in rural women and children: Systematic review and meta-analysis. *Thorax*, 66: 232–9.

Pope, C. A. III, Burnett, R. T., Krewski, D., et al. 2009. Cardiovascular mortality and exposure to airborne fine particulate matter and cigarette smoke: Shape of the exposure–response relationship. *Circulation*, 120: 941–8.

Pope, C. A. III, Burnett, R. T., Turner, M., et al. 2011. Lung cancer and cardiovascular disease mortality associated with ambient air pollution and cigarette smoke: Shape of the exposure–response relationships. *Environmental Health Perspectives*, 119(11): 1616–21.

Pope, C. A. III, Burnett, R. T., Thun, M. J., Calle, E., Krewski, D., Ito, K., et al. 2002. Lung cancer, cardiopulmonary mortality, and long-term exposure to fine particulate air pollution. *Journal of the American Medical Association*, 287: 1132–41.

Shin, H., Cohen, A., Pope III, C., et al. 2013. Critical issues in combining disparate sources of information to estimate the global burden of disease attributable to ambient fine particulate matter exposure. Working Paper prepared for Methods for Research Synthesis: A Cross-Disciplinary Workshop. October 3, 2013. Harvard Center for Risk Analysis.

Siddiqui, A. R., Lee, K., Bennett, D., Yang, X., Brown, K. H., Bhutta, Z. A., et al. 2009. Indoor carbon monoxide and PM2.5 concentrations by cooking fuels in Pakistan. *Indoor Air*, 19:75–82.

Smith, K. R., Bruce, N., Balakrishnan, K., et al. 2014. Millions dead: How do we know and what does it mean? Methods used in the comparative risk assessment of household air pollution. *Annual Review of Public Health*, 35: 185–206.

Smith, K., Mehta, S., and Feuz, M. 2004. Indoor air pollution from household use of solid fuels. In: M. Ezzati et al., eds., *Comparative Quantification of Health Risks: Global and Regional Burden of Disease Attributable to Selected Major Risk Factors*. New York: World Health Organization.

Tennakoon, D. 2008. Estimating the level of energy poverty in Sri Lanka. Report submitted to Practical Action South Asia.

World Bank. 2013. *China: Accelerating household access to clean cooking and heating*. Washington, DC: World Bank.

2014. *World Development Indicators*. Washington, DC: World Bank.

World Bank and Institute for Healthy Metrics and Evaluation. 2016. *The Cost of Air Pollution: Strengthening the Economic Case for Action*. Washington, DC: World Bank.

World Health Organization (WHO). 2004. *Comparative Quantification of Health Risks: Global and Regional Burden of Disease Attributable to Selected Major Risk Factors*. Geneva: World Health Organization.

2009. *Estimated Deaths and DALYs Attributable to Selected Environmental Risk Factors, by WHO Member States, 2004*. Geneva: World Health Organization. *Downloadable at:* www.who.int/quantifying_ehimpacts/national/countryprofile/intro/en/index.html.

2016. *World Health Statistics*. Geneva: World Health Organization.

Zuk, M., Rojas, L., Blanco, S., et al. 2007. The impact of improved wood-burning stoves on fine particulate matter concentrations in rural Mexican homes. *Journal of Exposure Science and Environmental Epidemiology*, 17:224–32.

Alternative Perspective

1.1

MIKE HOLLAND

As realization has grown of the impact of air pollution, so too has it become clear that the effects of individual pollutants are linked and that they cannot be considered purely in isolation. Health has become the prime driver of air pollution policies in North America and Europe since the mid-1990s, following new analysis that found detectable effects at levels previously considered "safe" and no evidence for an exposure threshold for fine particulates.

Considering Larsen's chapter, the first point is that the focus is on epidemiology, which in isolation provides no proof of causality. However, the evidence in this case is considered to demonstrate causality, so the author's reliance on epidemiological data is not problematic. However, there is more problem with attribution of health impacts to fine particles because other pollutants such as ozone, SO_2, NO_2, and dioxins also have an effect. Ozone impacts may add 20 percent or more to the total damage quantified in European policy assessments for fine particles. NO_2 may cause greater impacts still, perhaps of a similar magnitude to fine particles. Larsen's analysis may therefore be an underestimate of impacts because he focuses on PM2.5 alone.

Another question is whether all particles have an equal impact on health. Although their different chemical and physical nature must make some difference, fine particles do generally appear to be harmful to health. Differentiating them is unlikely to make any significant changes to policy necessary.

An important issue is the actual impact of pollution, which is inferred to be the sole cause of death. In fact, it could also be one of a number of contributory factors that affect longevity or, alternatively, a final trigger for death. Such questions are of relevance for valuing mortality effects. Larsen states that there are four times as many deaths attributed to air pollution as to infant and maternal undernutrition. However, this comparison may not be valid because child and maternal mortality accounts for a much higher quantity of lost life expectancy.

Although mortality is clearly important, the effect on morbidity also warrants attention, for example, the impact of cancers, cardiovascular disease, and stroke. This adds to the health burden both directly and via the demands it places on the health system. We should also remember that the benefits of clean air policies are broader than health alone. Larsen covers reduced fuel costs and savings in time spent gathering biomass, and there are also impacts on ecosystems and cultural heritage (the effect of acid rain on stonework).

Larsen acknowledges that some options are not considered in his chapter. A notable omission is the use of emission ceilings, adopted most famously through the Kyoto Protocol on greenhouse gases, but also through legislation under the UNECE (United Nations Economic Commission for Europe) Convention on Long Range Transboundary Air Pollution.

There is, as Larsen notes, a tension between protecting individuals and maximizing the benefits to society, with an inherent conflict between equity and economics. Overall, when legislating for limits, there is no point in setting standards that cannot be achieved because this may prove a deterrent to taking action.

Moving beyond the scope of Larsen's chapter, there are a number of other factors to be considered, including the need to improve scientific knowledge of air pollution, prioritizing pollutants on the basis of those causing greatest harm rather than those of most public concern, the correct characterization of mortality, and the cobenefits of other policies such as CO_2 emissions control.

Finally, air pollution has impacts at the hemispheric scale rather than simply locally, making international collaboration important. A model for this already exists through the UN Economic Commission for Europe's Convention on Long Range Transboundary Air Pollution and related activities of the European Commission.

1.2 Alternative Perspective

MARC JEULAND

The assessment chapter provides an accessible entry into a problem of major global importance for both health and environmental sustainability.

As discussed in Larsen's chapter, there are a number of important challenges with setting targets related to HAP. Unfortunately, the technological solutions proposed do not properly address the issues because they may have undesirable side effects and because air quality and the costs and benefits of specific changes vary considerably across households and locations. Thus, it is puzzling that this important variation does not figure in the subsequent benefit-cost analysis of clean cooking interventions, which instead looks like an analysis based on hypothetical air quality (not technology-based) targets.

The most striking omission is a significant discussion of the role and implications of behavior. In practice, individual decisions to invest in preventive health or environmental improvements involve a rational trade-off with consumption of other goods and leisure. But people often make decisions that would seem to endanger their well-being, sometimes because they misunderstand the risks they face. Also, because of the nonlinear response to air pollution, a relatively large investment may not be enough to deliver substantial health benefits.

Existing work supports the idea that there is something households and individuals like about traditional stoves. The study also ignores the fact that strikingly few households who obtain a cleaner biomass stove end up using it exclusively. In fact, surprisingly little is known at this time about how to induce the behavior change that effectively delivers long-term benefits. As such, setting technology-based targets creates a risk that policies designed to reach them will repeat the hard failures of related domains (e.g., water and sanitation, and malaria prevention), which generally failed to incentivize the pursuit of locally responsive and desired solutions. Making prescriptive recommendations about the specific stoves that people should or should not own will likely result in dissemination of large numbers of stoves that households do not want or use.

Behavior may also change and reduce the cost-effectiveness of interventions. In the case of clean stove promotion, one example of this type of behavioral feedback would be if household members increase the amount of time spent and cooking done indoors, thereby offsetting anticipated reductions in harmful exposures.

The author is deeply skeptical of the meaning and usefulness of the deterministic benefit-cost calculations used to justify promotion of cleaner stoves. This is borne out by the history of failures in similar sectors and reinforced by the dramatic divergence between the implications of the analysis and actual behavior. Even the impressive demonstration of the large variation in benefit-cost ratio between countries does not properly cover the heterogeneity; for example, most solid fuel users have low incomes and hence low VSLs.

Actual behavior is often ignored. For example in India even among relatively wealthy rural households who own alternative stoves (mostly LPG), traditional stove use remains ubiquitous for cooking tasks such as making bread or simmering. On the other hand, some factors such as the broader environmental benefits of cleaner stoves are also ignored.

Despite the clear negative implications of household use of solid fuels, it has proven difficult for many to make the switch to cleaner technologies. A successful approach must allow for tailoring of policies and interventions to local realities, must engage local institutions, and must acknowledge the fact that traditional technologies generate a large set of benefits for users that are systematically mischaracterized or ignored.

Targets for Biodiversity and Deforestation

ANIL MARKANDYA

Background

The Millennium Development Goals (MDGs), set up in 2000, tracked a number of indicators for sustainable development to 2015. Some of the goals, such as halving the poverty rate, have been met, and considerable progress has been made on others. Overall they are seen as a successful way of focusing attention and mobilizing resources to address the major gaps in human development, including those relating to the environment. The post-2015 agenda seeks to replace the MDGs with new goals that "move beyond meeting basic human needs and promote dynamic, inclusive and sustainable development" (CIGI, 2012).

Biodiversity and deforestation are primarily covered in proposed Goals 14 and 15, dealing with marine and terrestrial resources, respectively. These targets draw significantly on the Aichi Targets that were adopted as part of the Convention of Biological Diversity's (CBD's) Strategic Plan for Biodiversity 2011–2020, in Nagoya, Japan, in 2010 (see Table 2.1). However, there are differences between the two sets: the Aichi Targets include more quantitative values than the Sustainable Development Goals, and the SDGs cover a broader range of topics. Because the SDGs in this area are not quantitative and so cannot be adequately costed, this chapter looks in detail at the Aichi Targets and estimates the net benefits of those that are able to be evaluated in monetary terms.[1]

The Aichi Targets

In this section the full set of 20 targets is discussed and a qualitative assessment made of the net benefits they provide (Table 2.1).

The CBD and the United Nations Environment Program (UNEP) have grouped the targets into five strategic goals:

A. Address the underlying causes of biodiversity loss be mainstreaming it across government and society (Targets 1–4)
B. Reduce the pressures on biodiversity and promote sustainable use (Targets 5–10)
C. Improve status of biodiversity by safeguarding ecosystems, species, and genetic diversity (Targets 11–13)
D. Enhance benefits to all from biodiversity and ecosystem services (Targets 11–16)
E. Enhance implementation through participatory planning, knowledge management, and capacity building (Targets 17–20)

---

[1] Looking at individual targets in terms of their costs and benefits has been criticized as having the shortcoming of not picking up on the synergies and interlinkages between the goals. There is merit in this criticism, and indeed the CBD report notes that "Some of the Targets are inter-related and will benefit from joint programmes of activity that contribute to more than one Target. Thus delivering some Targets will influence the resources required to deliver others and (though delivering Targets by 2020 requires simultaneous action across the Targets) sequencing delivery can be expected to enhance cost effectiveness." (CBD, 2012a). The problem is to convert this general statement into something more specific. If it can be shown that significant spillover benefits are being ignored by looking at the targets individually, then the analysis should attempt to take account of those. In what follows, we would argue that this is not generally the case, or at least no one has demonstrated that important benefits have been ignored. In future work, looking at sets of targets as a group may be possible, but it will require a higher level of modelling and quantification and the allocation of more resources than has been possible in this exercise.

Table 2.1 Aichi Targets: Qualitative assessment of benefits and costs

Target	Possibility of Estimating Net Benefits
1. By 2020, at the latest, people are aware of the values of biodiversity and the steps they can take to conserve and use it sustainably.	This is an important objective but it is not amenable to a benefit-cost assessment. A measure of degree of awareness and cost effectiveness indicators may be constructed.
2. By 2020, at the latest, biodiversity values have been integrated into national and local development and poverty reduction strategies and planning processes and are being incorporated into national accounting, as appropriate, and reporting systems.	Also a worthwhile objective. Estimating biodiversity values is a key part of it and can provide the data that will allow future benefit-cost assessments for different interventions to be made. The target itself, however, cannot be credibly evaluated in benefit-cost terms.
3. By 2020, at the latest, incentives, including subsidies, harmful to biodiversity are eliminated, phased out or reformed in order to minimize or avoid negative impacts, and positive incentives for the conservation and sustainable use of biodiversity are developed and applied, consistent and in harmony with the Convention and other relevant international obligations, taking into account national socioeconomic conditions.	In principle this is an area where benefit-cost methods can be used. Data on the subsidies and their negative effects need to be collected and estimates made of the benefits of removing them. The High Level Panel looking into the targets has, rightly, allowed a budget of between \$7.5 and \$15 million for these and a similar amount for studies on positive schemes. It will take two to three years to do these. The result will not be a single benefit cost figure but different numbers for different schemes.
4. By 2020, at the latest, governments, business, and stakeholders at all levels have taken steps to achieve or have implemented plans for sustainable production and consumption and have kept the impacts of use of natural resources well within safe ecological limits.	The target is multidimensional. The only component that I think can be evaluated in terms of monetary benefits and costs is the public procurement changes that would alter the use of natural resources. Even for these it would be a major task to get a benefit-cost evaluation at the national let alone the global level.
5. By 2020, the rate of loss of all natural habitats, including forests and wetlands, is at least halved and where feasible brought close to zero, and degradation and fragmentation is significantly reduced.	We have some estimates of rates of loss of several habitats, and we have some estimates of the value of services they provide. Hence we should be able to value a reduction in these rates of loss and compare it to the estimated costs. Separate estimates for wetlands and forests can be made.
6. By 2020, all fish and invertebrate stocks are managed and harvested sustainably, legally and applying ecosystem based approaches, so that overfishing is avoided, recovery plans and measures are in place for all depleted species, fisheries have no significant impacts on threatened species and vulnerable ecosystems and the impacts of fisheries on stocks, species and ecosystems are within safe limits.	The benefits of the program can be measured against the costs of inaction where total losses of some species are possible. Such losses can be valued, but it is a major task to do so as the background research on the subject is still relatively weak.
7. By 2020 areas under agriculture, aquaculture, and forestry are managed sustainably, ensuring conservation of biodiversity.	Degradation of agriculture (at the national level) and forestry (national and global levels) under business as usual have been estimated in some studies. Less is known globally about aquaculture. The problem is to know what share of degradation would be stopped by the program. There is also overlap and conflict with target 5.
8. By 2020, pollution, including from excess nutrients, has been brought to levels that are not detrimental to ecosystem function and biodiversity.	Estimates of damages done by pollutants and nutrients are available as are some figures for the benefits of marine debris cleanup. But they are not available globally, and to make global estimates would be a major task.
9. By 2020, invasive alien species and pathways are identified and prioritized, priority species are controlled or eradicated, and measures are in place to manage pathways to prevent their introduction and establishment.	Invasive species cause a lot of damages, which have been estimated for some regions. The problem is similar to above of not having figures for all regions. In addition it is not clear whether the program would eradicate key species. It is unlikely that it will.

(cont.)

Table 2.1 (*cont.*)

Target	Possibility of Estimating Net Benefits
10. By 2015, the multiple anthropogenic pressures on coral reefs, and other vulnerable ecosystems impacted by climate change or ocean acidification, are minimized so as to maintain their integrity and functioning.	We have estimates of rates of loss of coral and we have estimates of the value of coral in different locations. We have to put an interpretation on what they mean by minimized (reduced to zero?). Based on that, we could make some estimates of benefit-cost ratios.
11. By 2020, at least 17 percent of terrestrial and inland water areas and 10 percent of coastal and marine areas, especially areas of particular importance for biodiversity and ecosystem services are conserved through effectively and equitably managed, ecologically representative, and well-connected systems of protected areas and other effective area-based conservation measures and integrated into the wider lands.	Some estimates have been made of the benefits of an increase in terrestrial areas of importance for biodiversity. These can be used to make a preliminary cost-benefit assessment of the target. Coverage of conservation of coastal and marine areas is more problematic, as estimates of benefits of increasing coverage of conservation have not been made and would require considerable work. It can be done, however, given time.
12. By 2020 the extinction of known threatened species has been presented, and their conservation status, particularly of those most in decline, has been improved and sustained.	Although prevention of extinction has been valued for selected species, the data do not cover all such species. There is, however, no value for the reduced risk of extinction and no estimates of the amount by which risk is reduced, so benefit-cost estimation is not possible.
13. By 2020, the genetic diversity of cultivated plants and farmed and domesticated animals and of wild relatives, including other socioeconomically as well as culturally valuable species is maintained, and strategies have been developed and implemented for minimizing genetic erosion and safeguarding their genetic diversity.	This is an important target, and although there are some estimates of the loss of ecosystems across all biomes, the figures are particularly weak on the costs of loss of genetic diversity. It has also been noted that the target should include genetic diversity of trees and wild animals. Undertaking a benefit-cost assessment would need considerable further work.
14. By 2020, ecosystems that provide essential services, including services related to water, and contribute to health, livelihoods, and well–being, are restored and safeguarded, taking into account the needs of women, indigenous and local communities, and the poor and vulnerable.	If the program can stop all these losses, we can make a benefit-cost estimation, but coverage of the loss of biodiversity studies does not pick up all genetic losses.
15. By 2020, ecosystem resilience and the contribution of biodiversity to carbon stocks has been enhanced, through conservation and restoration, including restoration of at least 15 percent of degraded ecosystems, thereby contributing to climate change mitigation and adaptation and to combating desertification.	This mainly referrs to forests although other ecosystems also contribute to carbon stocks. We could estimate the extent to which degradation reduces carbon sequestration capacity and then value the increase in carbon sequestration achieved.
16. By 2015, the Nagoya Protocol on Access to Genetic Resources and the Fair and Equitable Sharing of Benefits Arising from their Utilization is in force and operational, consistent with national level legislation	Access to benefit sharing is first and foremost an issue of equity and not one of generating benefits. That said, more equitable systems are more likely to work in preserving genetic resources but information on the size of that effect is not available.
17. By 2015, each Party has developed, adopted as a policy instrument, and has commenced implementing an effective, participatory and updated national biodiversity strategy and action plan.	It is a desirable objective but not one that can be evaluated using benefit-cost methods.
18. By 2020, traditional knowledge, innovations and practices of indigenous and local communities relevant for the conservation and sustainable use of biodiversity, and their customary use of biological resources are respected, subject to national legislation and relevant international obligations, and fully integrated and reflected in the implementation of the Convention with the full and effective participation of indigenous and local communities, at all relevant levels.	The actions proposed to implement this target are largely to share knowledge and build capacity. Links to increased conservation are extremely difficult to estimate from the program, and a benefit-cost assessment is impossible.

(cont.)

Table 2.1 (cont.)

Target	Possibility of Estimating Net Benefits
19. By 2020, knowledge, the science base and technologies relating to biodiversity, its values, functioning, status and trends, and the consequences of its loss, are improved, widely shared and transferred, and applied.	Such knowledge is very useful and will help both evaluate future programs as well as making better use of existing biodiversity. It is not possible to estimate these gains in monetary terms.
20. By 2020, at the latest, the mobilization of financial resources for effectively implementing the Strategic Plan for Biodiversity 2011–2020 from all sources and in accordance with the consolidated and agreed process in the Strategy for Resource Mobilization should increase substantially from the current levels.	This target is important but is not amenable to a benefit-cost analysis.

Note: targets with a thick border are subject to quantitative cost-benefit analysis in this chapter.

As far as benefit-cost analysis is concerned, these targets can also be divided into three other groups: those where the benefit-cost method is not possible or appropriate, those where it could be applied if data were available but such data are not, and those where the method can be applied now, with some qualifications.

The first group where we cannot apply benefit-cost methods includes eight targets: 1, 2, 12, 16, 17, 18, 19, and 20. These are mostly the targets relating to enhancing implementation through participatory planning, knowledge management, and capacity building. In these cases the benefits are impossible to quantify in money terms, or so uncertain as to make the exercise noncredible.

The second group consists of nine targets: 3, 4, 6, 7, 8, 9, 11, 12, and 13. For these, work has to be carried out from the bottom up at the regional level and then aggregated to arrive at regional and global estimates.[2] It is not clear whether one should do the exercise regionally or globally – it is almost certain that the benefit-to-cost ratios will vary across regions. The amount of work involved in collecting the data is considerable; for example, for target 3 on the benefits of eliminating subsidies the Secretariat has allocated some $15–30 million for the underlying studies.

The third group consists of targets where an attempt can be made now to estimate the benefits relative to the costs. This consists of targets 5, 10, 11, and 15 as highlighted with a thicker border in Table 2.1. The exercise of evaluating these is necessarily approximate, and only a first attempt has been made with very limited resources. In some cases only a part of the target has been valued (e.g., for target 11 we can only make a stab at terrestrial areas; for target 12 we cover only some of the species under threat of extinction, and for target 15 we have to make many simplifying assumptions about the rate of sequestration.

Cost and Benefit Assessment

In the rest of the chapter the present value of the costs and benefits of four targets are presented. The rate of discount used here is 5 percent, to be consistent with the other studies in this series, but this is relatively low compared to rates applied for investment projects in developing countries. However, although a sensitivity analysis for different rates can be applied in further work, we do not consider that the relative benefit-to-cost ratios obtained here will be changed by such an analysis.

Our analysis gives us results in terms of benefit-cost ratio (BCR) and the internal rate of return (IRR). An IRR greater than a "test" rate (e.g., 7 percent in the U.S.) would indicate a project or policy is acceptable on this criterion.

As far as the costs are concerned, the assessment has used data collected by UNEP and summarized in Table 2.2. It is taken from CBD, 2012a. The costs are given separately for each of the 20 targets

---

[2] Indeed, this is exactly what the CBD is undertaking under its current work program. It recognizes the importance of estimating such benefits but has no figures at the present time (see Section 5.4, CBD, 2012a).

Table 2.2 Aichi strategic goals and targets and associated investment costs

Strategic Goal	Target	Investment Needs ($Mn.)	Annual Recurrent Exp. ($Mn.)
A: Address underlying causes of biodiversity loss by mainstreaming it across government and society	1. Awareness raising 2. Biodiversity values 3. Incentives 4. Sustainable consumption and production	54 450–610 1,300–2,000 55–107	440–1,400 70–130 8–15 8–15
B: Reduce the pressures on biodiversity and promote sustainable use	5. Reducing habitat loss 6. Fisheries 7. Sustainable agriculture 8. Pollution 9. Invasive alien species 10. Coral reefs	252,300–288,800 129,900–292,200 20,800–21,700 77,600–772,700 34,100–43,900 600–960	13,300–13,700 800–3,200 10,700–11,000 24,400–42,700 21,005–50,100 6–10
C: Improve status of biodiversity by safeguarding ecosystems, species, and genetic diversity	11. Protected areas (terrestrial and marine) 12. Species conservation 13. Genetic diversity	66,100–626,400 – 55–1,400	970–6,700 3,400–4,800 15–17
D: Enhance benefits to all from biodiversity and ecosystem services	14. Ecosystem restoration 15. Forest restoration 16. Nagoya protocol	30,000–299,900 100 55–313	– 6,400 –
E. Enhance implementation through participatory planning, knowledge management, and capacity building	17. National biodiversity strategy and action plan 18. Traditional Knowledge 19. Science Base 20. Mobilize financial resources	114–1,100 210–340 1,800–4,200 10–79	110–560 180–297 1,400–1,600 3–20

Source: http://www.cbd.int/financial/hlp/doc/communications/HLP%20on%20Resourcing%20the%20CBD%20Strategic%20Plan%202011-2020%20(summary).pdf. Accessed June 11, 2014.

and are stated to cover the period 2013–2020.[3] They are further separated into investment costs and annual recurrent costs, all in 2012 prices. The cost data is supplemented by considerable information on the elements of cost included and the reasons for the range of figures reported. In the analysis carried out, we have used as much of this information as possible.

In summary, we note, as do the authors of the data compiled, that these cost estimates have gaps and inconsistencies, and the range of estimates is wide. Nevertheless, they do provide a more or less coherent set of figures calculated on a common basis.

Costs and Benefits of Reducing the Rate of Loss of Forests and Wetlands (Aichi Target 5)

Target 5 states that "By 2020, the rate of loss of all natural habitats, including forests and wetlands, is at least halved and where feasible brought close to zero, and degradation and fragmentation is significantly reduced."

The emphasis of this target should be on preventing the loss of high-biodiversity value habitats, such as primary forests and many wetlands, and of ecosystems where continued loss risks passing "tipping points" that could lead to large-scale negative effects on human well-being. Reduction in the loss of natural habitats could be achieved through improvements in production efficiency and land-use planning, the use of degraded land for agricultural production, improved ecosystem connectivity, and enhanced mechanisms for natural resource governance combined with recognition of the economic and social value of ecosystem services provided by

---

[3] There is some uncertainty, however, about the exact period covered, as one source states 2013–2020 (8 years) but the main CBD document, which it purports to summarize states different periods for some targets.

natural habitats. In order to determine if the rate of habitat loss has been reduced, a baseline will need to be established against which to gauge progress toward this goal (CBD, 2012b).

The estimation of the loss of habitats is divided into two parts: one for forests and the other for wetlands.

Forests

Some analysis has already been conducted on the damage caused by forest losses, which are of course the mirror image of the benefits to be gained by preventing that loss. Markandya and Chiabai (2013) estimated the value of the physical losses of boreal, temperate, and tropical forests under a business-as-usual scenario. The physical data were taken from the extensive work of Aklemade et al., 2006, who calculated losses if no further actions were taken for the period 2000–2050. These physical losses are estimated at 9 percent of 2000 boreal forest stocks, 19 percent of temperate forest stocks, and 12 percent of tropical forest stocks.

The losses were then valued using studies of the commercial and fuel wood values of timber, recreational values for forests, passive values (i.e., the values of those who are willing to pay for forest to be conserved in addition to paying for those services they do use), and carbon storage values of forests. Taken together these give the total value for the whole period. As expected the study comes up with a range: the lower bound is US$334 billion per year while the upper bound is US$1,118 billion or over three times as much. In this chapter we have taken these estimates, assumed the losses are uniform over the time period 2000 to 2050, and then updated the figures to 2012 U.S. dollars. The corresponding costs are taken from the CBD (2013) study, which cover the period 2013–2020.[4]

It is further assumed that: (a) as per the target, 50 percent of the losses will be arrested as a result of the program, (b) the benefits in terms of reduced losses will only start appearing in 2021 when the program is complete, and (c) the benefits will continue to 2050.

The benefit-to-cost ratio at a 5 percent discount rate and the internal rate of return (IRR) for forest protection are shown in Table 2.3.[5]

Table 2.3 Net benefits from Target 5: 50 percent reduction in global forest loss

	Benefit-Cost Ratio	IRR%
Lower bound benefits	29.7	44%
Upper bound benefits	99.4	66%

The table shows very high benefit-to-cost ratios and IRRs well in excess of any possible test rates. This suggests, therefore, that if the program of forest protection described in the high-level CBD report can deliver the 50 percent reduction in forest loss it would be highly justified. Annualized benefits in terms of reduced forest loss amount to around $219 billion from 2021 onward, while costs in the period 2013–2020 run at only $10–14 billion. The issue of implementation, however, is a major factor here. The main funding requirement for the program is derived from World Bank (WB) estimates of lost revenue from uncollected forest fees and taxes. Problems of encroachment are difficult to address, and it is possible that the costs of attaining the targets are underestimated. Indeed, it may be impossible to prevent losses in some places for this reason. There are also difficulties relating to data on forest stocks that the CBD notes and that make the figures uncertain. Nevertheless, the ratios are so high that even a partial success would make a program such as this justified on cost-benefit grounds.

Wetlands

In the case of wetlands the calculation is more difficult. Current areas are even more uncertain than they are for forests, and services provided vary significantly by location. The present estimates are based on the following assumptions:

a. The current stock of wetlands is divided into inland and coastal with the latter including mangroves. Areas were taken from the wetland database World Wildlife Fund (WWF) and Center for Environmental Systems Research, University

---

[4] For this component of the target only a single set of figures is given, and there is no range of costs.
[5] Calculations can be obtained from the author. A 10 percent discount rate is only used as benchmark.

of Kassel, Germany. From their figures, which are global, we took lakes, rivers, freshwater marshes/ flood plains, and swamp forests as inland wetlands and those defined as coastal and saline wetlands (including mangroves) as coastal.[6] The respective areas in 2010 were 1,061 million ha for the former and 152 million ha for the latter.[7]

b. Estimates of rate of loss from a number of sources is put at around 0.7 percent per annum for both types of wetlands (Finlayson and Spiers, 1999).

c. The services provided by different wetlands have been synthesized in a number of studies, of which perhaps De Groot et al. (2012) is the most recent. Those included in the studies reviewed cover: provisioning (food, water, raw materials, etc.), regulating (climate regulation, water flow, erosion prevention, etc.), habitat (nursery and genetic diversity), and cultural (recreational use, spiritual experience, etc.). In total 139 studies of coastal wetlands and 168 studies of inland wetlands studies were carefully analyzed to provide a range of benefits in US$/ha/yr. The ranges are indeed wide: for freshwater wetlands the lower bound (in 2007 international dollars) is around $3,000/ha/yr, and the upper bound is $105,000/ha/yr. Likewise the ranges for coastal wetlands range from $37,000/ha/yr to $888,000/ha/yr.

d. The benefit figures were updated to 2012 prices so the cost and benefits could be compared. The target program that is valued is expected to reduce loss rates by 50 percent, starting from 2021.

The resulting net benefits are shown in Table 2.4. Four cases are considered, from highest cost/lowest benefits to lowest cost/highest benefits. The results are clearly more sensitive to the benefits than to the costs. If the lower bound of the benefits is right, the target is hard to justify on benefit-cost grounds. If, however, the upper bound is correct, the target is amply justified. In practice the true values are probably somewhere between the two and will depend on where the programs are implemented.

Costs and Benefits of Reducing Loss of Coral Reefs (Aichi Target 10)

Given the expected longer-term impact of climate change and ocean acidification, it is important

Table 2.4 Net benefits from Target 5: 50 percent reduction in global wetland loss

Case	Benefit to Cost Ratio	IRR%
Lower bound of benefits/ lower bound of costs	0.9	5
Upper bound of benefits/ lower bound of costs	72.7	63
Lower bound of benefits/ upper bound of costs	0.5	1
Upper bound of benefits/ upper bound of costs	37.4	50

to reduce other anthropogenic pressures on coral reefs and other vulnerable ecosystems. This would include, for example, reducing pollution and overexploitation, as well as harvesting systems with negative impacts. Indicators for this target include the extent of biomes ecosystems and habitats (percentage live coral and coral bleaching), Marine Trophic Index, the incidence of human-induced ecosystem failure, the health and well-being of communities who depend directly on local ecosystem goods and services, and the proportion of products derived from sustainable sources (CBD, 2012b).

Areas of coral were estimated to be around 25.5 million hectares (Spalding and Grenfell, 1997), and rates of loss are put at around 1–2 percent a year, depending on which region is considered.[8] A NOAA study estimates that loss rates are such that by 2050, 60 percent of the world's coral will be dead,[9] implying a loss rate of 2.2 percent. We take this rate and apply it to the estimated stock as of 2010, estimated to be around 19 million hectares (applying the loss rate of 2.2 percent from 1997 to 2010).

[6] http://www.worldwildlife.org/science/data/item1877.html. Accessed June 12, 2014.
[7] This still leaves a number of areas that are ambiguous but that would have some wetland function. Excluding them could underestimate the area of wetland by as much as 30 percent.
[8] http://news.nationalgeographic.com/news/2007/08/070807-coral-loss.html. Accessed June 13, 2014.
[9] http://www.coris.noaa.gov/about/hazards/. Accessed June 13, 2014.

According to De Groot et al., 2012, coral reefs provide very significant ecosystem services, in the forms of raw materials and genetic resources (habitats for fish), erosion prevention and disturbance moderation, and recreation. The 94 studies reviewed by the authors have a lower bound of benefits of $36,800/ha/yr, while the upper bound is $2.129 million/ha/yr.[10]

In making the cost-benefit estimate we use the lower bound of the benefits and apply it to a program that starts in 2013, and provides benefits starting in 2021. Two programs are envisaged: one that reduces losses by 50 percent and the other by 80 percent. The former has a capital cost of $684 million and a recurrent cost of $81 million, while the latter has a capital cost of $1,036 million and a recurrent cost of $130 million. Table 2.5 summarizes the results.

Instead of analyzing different ranges of costs and benefits, we consider here the two programs with a lower bound of the benefits. Even with this lower bound, the benefit-to-cost ratio is well above one for both programs, and the IRR is well in excess of the required rate. Hence in this case the target and associated program are well justified. Indeed, it would make sense to go for the more ambitious target of reducing losses by 80 percent. There is some concern, however, that the outlays of around $80 million a year are not enough to achieve the goal of a 50 percent reduction in loss rates. Thus one may conclude that the cost estimates may be on the low side, and more resources may be needed to achieve the goals, but there is ample scope to increase outlays and still achieve a benefit-to-cost ratio that is well over one.

Costs and Benefits of Increasing Protected Area Coverage (Aichi Target 11)

Target 11 aims to increase protected areas to 17 percent of terrestrial land area and 10 percent of coastal and marine areas by 2020. There are currently some 13 percent of terrestrial areas, 5 percent of coastal areas, and very little of the open oceans under protection. Major efforts would therefore be needed to expand marine protected areas. Protected areas should be established and managed in close collaboration with indigenous communities and

Table 2.5 Net benefits from Target 10: 50 percent reduction in global coral loss

	Benefit to Cost Ratio	IRR%
Net benefits with losses reduced by 50%	95.3	52%
Net benefits with losses reduced by 80%	98.5	53%

vulnerable populations. Relevant indicators to measure progress are numbers of sites of biodiversity significance covered by protected areas and the connectivity/fragmentation of ecosystems. Other possible indicators include the overlay of protected areas with ecoregions, and the governance and management effectiveness of protected areas.

The closest estimate of the benefits of the increase in terrestrial area is in the TEEB-related study of Hussain et al. (2011). They analyze a slightly different expansion: of 20 percent by 2030 but from annual benefits and costs of their program we can make an estimate of the corresponding costs and benefits for the target program. We assume, as they do, that currently 10 percent of all ecoregions of the world are protected, giving a total protected area of 13.2 million Km^2 in 2000 (i.e., the same as the CBD estimate).

The cost of converting land to protected areas is considerable. Hussain et al. carried out a detailed survey of the different components of the cost, which include transfer of property rights in some cases, establishing and maintaining networks of areas, transactions costs, and most important, opportunity costs of the alternative use of the land. Cost per

[10] It has been suggested that a benefit of ecosystem services from coral of $37,000/ha/yr is too high. If applied to the stock of coral, for example, it would imply an annual value of $703 billion, which is much greater, for example, than the estimated total annual value of fisheries of about $80 billion (http://edition.cnn.com/2008/WORLD/asiapcf/03/24/eco.aboutfishing/). Such a valuation of total stocks of coral, however, is not valid. The studies conducted have valued small changes and cannot be applied to the total stock. It is important to recall that coral ecosystems derive value from many services, especially erosion prevention and recreation, which are highly site dependent. Moreover, losses tend to be concentrated in locations where such values are high. Hence the programs to prevent loss need to focus on such locations.

hectare turn out to be in the range of $2,473 to $10,513.[11] On the other hand, the costs in the CBD (2013) study are even higher: in total they estimate costs of around $761 billion over the period 2011–2020 to attain the target increase (compared to a range of $46–196 billion by Hussain et al.). The CBD figure includes, however, not only the terrestrial increase of 17 percent in protected areas but also a target of 10 percent of all marine areas. Because it has not been possible to get the breakdown between the two, it has been necessary to only use the cost data from Hussain et al.

In terms of benefits, Hussain et al. estimate the biophysical changes resulting from the protection and value of the ecosystem services that such a change provides. The areas that increase in most parts of world include grassland and forest, but in some cases protected areas are created by reducing land from these biomes as well. They provide estimates of the services gained into two groups: those related to the capture of carbon and the rest. The reason is that the former has, in their view, much greater uncertainties and are global benefits, while the rest are, in large part, local benefits. The benefits are then reported as a lower bound (without carbon storage benefits) and an upper bound (with carbon storage benefits).[12]

The results are summarized in Table 2.6, in which we have taken per hectare benefits and costs from Hussain et al. and applied them to the increases in protected areas proposed by the Target, to be achieved over the period 2011–2020.

The target only comes up with a benefit-to-cost ratio of more than unity when we take the lower bound of the costs. With the upper bound of costs it is below one irrespective of the benefits. It is not possible to calculate the IRR because the stream of net benefits does not have a turning point.

Some important qualifications apply here. First, the method of estimating benefits does not account for some of the possible gains from protection, in the form of species protection and increase in biodiversity. Second, it is doubtful that such an increase in area can be achieved in a period as short as 2011 to 2020, at least not without a substantial increase in transactions costs. Third, the distribution of the costs of protection is important. If an area is heavily used by poor people, then the

Table 2.6 Net benefits from Target 10: Increase in protected areas

	NPV and Benefit Cost Ratios			
	Costs from Hussain et al.			
	LB LC	LB UC	UB LC	UB UC
Benefit-Cost Ratio	1.15	0.27	1.97	0.46

Note: LB: Lower bound of benefits. LC: Lower bound of costs. UB: Upper bound of benefits. UC: Upper bound of costs.

costs to them of restricting access has be taken into account. This has not been done in the present analysis.

Costs and Benefit of Conserving Carbon Stocks (Aichi Target 15)

The program for forest restoration assumes that 150 million hectares will be planted over the period 2013 to 2020. The carbon value depends critically on where these plantations will take place and what species will be planted. In the calculations made here, we assume that the carbon sequestered is between 2.4 and 16.9 metric tons of CO_2 per hectare per year (Gorte, 2009). The sequestration starts after year 1, reaches a maximum at year 10, and continues for another 30 or more years (Johnson and Coburn, 2010).[13] The value of carbon sequestered is valued using two methods. First, a global model economic (POLES) was used to estimate the marginal cost of reducing carbon emissions so as to achieve a given target reduction.

[11] Hussain et al., 2011 figures updated to 2012 prices.

[12] The carbon benefits are estimated on two bases: first, from models in which a carbon target has been set and in which one can calculate the cost per ton reduced, and second, from models that estimate the damage done per ton emitted via climate change. See Hussain et al., 2011 for details.

[13] Estimates of the rates of sequestration are different in this report from those in Gorte (2009), but it provides some guidance to the rate at which sequestration takes place. It also states that sequestration can go on for up to 100 years. I have stopped the calculations in 2050 (about 40 years at a maximum) partly because the very long periods are more speculative and partly because it makes little difference to extend the benefits after about 40 years.

Table 2.7 Costs and benefits of biodiversity goals ($ billion 2012 prices)

Target	3% Discount			5% Discount		
	Benefit	Cost	B:C Ratio	Benefit	Cost	B:C Ratio
Reduce global coral loss by 50%	130	1.2	112	105	1.1	95
Reduce global coral loss by 80%	207	1.8	115	167	1.7	98
Reduce global wetland loss by 50% Lower benefit estimate	164	127	1.3	111	227	0.5
Reduce global wetland loss by 50% Higher benefit estimate	12,527	247	51	8,502	227	37
Reduce global forest loss by 50% Lower benefit estimate	3,388	82	41	2,278	77	30
Reduce global forest loss by 50% Higher benefit estimate	11,339	82	137	7,625	77	99
Increase PAs to 17% of land area Low cost/low benefit	69	60	1.2	64	56	1.2
Increase PAs to 17% of land area High cost/low benefit	69	259	0.3	64	239	0.3
Increase PAs to 17% of land area Low cost/high benefit	119	60	2	109	56	2
Increase PAs to 17% of land area High cost/high benefit	119	259	0.5	109	239	0.5
Forest Restoration High carbon benefit	114	39	3	76	36	2
Forest Restoration Low carbon benefit	570	39	14	378	36	11

Second, integrated assessment models were used to estimate the damages done per tonne of CO_2 equivalent emitted. Details can be found in Hussain et al. (2011).

The costs of the program are taken from the CBD (2013) report, which estimates a one-off investment cost of $100 million and a recurrent cost of $6.4 billion per year for the years 2013 to 2020. It is assumed that the reforestation of the 150 million hectares takes place evenly over that period.

The net benefits of the program are positive, with both sets of carbon values and the whole range of sequestration referred to earlier. With the lower end of the sequestration range (2.4 tonnes/ CO_2/ha/yr) the net benefits (NPV) are $2 billion using the SCC estimate and $119 billion using the marginal cost of abatement method. The IRR is 11 percent in the first case and 25 percent in the second case, and the benefit-to-cost ratios are 2.1 in the first case and 10.5 in the second. With higher rates of sequestration the IRRs and the benefit-to-

cost ratios rise correspondingly, indicating that the program is well justified.[14,15]

Conclusions

A summary of costs and benefits is provided in Table 2.7.

Many of the Aichi targets are really difficult to evaluate in terms of costs and benefits. This is not a reason to reject them outright (not everything that is important can be so quantified), but it does suggest that we will need other indicators of cost effectiveness to be sure we get good value for money.

---

[14] Calculations are available from the author.
[15] It has been pointed out that the reforestation program may be in conflict with the target of maintaining biodiversity. If fast-growing exotic trees are planted where formerly slower-growing trees that provided habitat were present, there will be a cost in this respect. This has not been accounted for.

For Target 5 (to halve the rate of loss of forests and wetlands), it is necessary to divide it into the forests and wetlands components. The figures indicate that the forest component is justified at the global level, but the wetlands component depends on which of the wide range of possible benefits we take.

Target 10 relates to coral reefs, and the figures indicate that the benefits are well in excess of the costs, even with the lower bound of estimates being taken for the former. The costs, however, may be underestimated, and more work is needed to fully determine these.

Target 11 is analyzed only with respect to the terrestrial protected areas as data were not available for the marine areas. The figures here are more problematic as the range of costs is very wide and the benefits that can be quantified are limited. The analysis shows that if we include carbon benefits and take the lower end of the range of costs, the target is justified but it is not justified if the costs are at the upper end.

Finally, for Target 15 (forest restoration) the benefits are in excess of the costs based on current estimates of carbon values.

One important caveat is the need to look at who pays the costs and who benefits from these investments. We have hinted at some cases where such issues are likely to arise but a comprehensive coverage of the distributional issues is warranted.

A second caveat is the need to account for effects of one target on other targets through an integrated assessment. In one of the comments received, it was noted that International Institute for Environment and Development (IIED) is proposing a "modular" approach in which targets are evaluated as a group. This may represent a way forward, but if it is to generate measures of performance that are comparable to those used for other investments, considerable work will be needed to develop summary indicators of overall outcomes and to show how these outcomes change if one target is modified.

A key message, therefore, is that further work should be undertaken to confirm these results.

References

Alkemade R., M. Bakkenes, R. Bobbink, et al. (2006). GLOBIO 3: Framework for the assessment of global terrestrial biodiversity. In: A. F. Bouwman, T. Kram, and K. Klein Goldewijk (eds.), *Integrated modeling of environmental change. An overview of IMAGE 2.4. NEAA/MNP*, Bilthoven: Netherlands Environmental Assessment Agency (MNP), 171–186.

Centre for International Governance Innovation (CIGI). (2012). *Post 2015 Development Agenda: Goals, Targets, Indicators.* Special Report. Centre for International Governance Innovation (CIGI), Waterloo, Ontario, Canada.

Convention of Biological Diversity (CBD). (2012a). *Resourcing the AICHI Biodiversity Targets: A First Assessment of the Resources Required for Implementing the Strategic Plan for Biodiversity 2011–2020.* Secretariat for the Convention on Biological Diversity, Montreal. Retrieved from: http://www.cbd.int/doc/meetings/fin/hlpgar-sp-01/official/hlpgar-sp-01-01-report-en.pdf. Last accessed June 11, 2014.

(2012ab). *Strategic Plan for Biodiversity 2012–2020: Technical Rationale* (document COP/10/27/Add.1). Available at: http://www.cbd.int/sp/targets/rationale/default.shtml.

De Groot R. et al. (2012). Global estimates of the value of ecosystems and their services. *Ecosystem Services* 1, 50–61.

Environmental Protection Agency (EPA). (2010). Regulatory Impact Analysis. Available at: http://www.epa.gov/ttnecas1/ria.html. 47.

European Commission (EC). (2001). *Recommended interim values for the value of preventing a fatality in DG Environment Cost Benefit analysis 2001*. European Commission. Available at: ec.europa.eu/environment/enveco/others/pdf/recommended_interim_values.pdf.

Finlayson, C. M. and A. G. Spiers (1999). *Global Review of Wetland Resources and Priorities for Wetland Inventory*. Wetlands International. Available from http://www.wetlands.org/Portals/0/publications/Report/WI_GRoWI-Report_1999.pdf.

Gorte, R. W. (2009). *U.S. Tree Planting for Carbon Sequestration*. Washington, DC: Congressional Research Service.

Hussain, S., A. McVittie, L. Brander, et al. (2011). *The Economics of Ecosystems and Biodiversity: Quantitative Assessment.* Draft final report to the United Nations Environment Programme.

Johnson, I. and R. Coburn (2010). *Trees for Carbon Sequestration*. Primefact 981. Government of New South Wales, Australia.

Markandya, A. and A. Chiabai (2013). Economic loss of ecosystem services from 1900 to 2050, Chapter 4. In: B. Lomborg (ed.), *How Much Have Global Problems Cost the World?: A Scorecard from 1900 to 2050*. Cambridge: Cambridge University Press.

Spalding, M. D. and A. M. Grenfell (1997). New estimates of global and regional coral reef areas. *Coral Reefs*, 16: 225–30.

2.1 Alternative Perspective

LUKE BRANDER

This perspective makes a proposal for improved methodologies for conducting large-scale assessments of the costs and benefits of meeting targets for biodiversity and ecosystem change. This is driven by the recognition that currently applied approaches, such as those used by Markandya in the challenge chapter, do not produce sufficiently accurate information for use in cost-benefit analysis. For example, the enormous span of results for the wetland program implies that we cannot estimate even the order of magnitude of benefits.

There are several related methodological problems. First, values for ecosystem services are unlikely to be globally constant across an entire biome. Second, marginal values for ecosystem services are unlikely to remain constant as the stocks of ecosystems change. Third, assessing this expected variation in values by using minimum and maximum values in a sensitivity analysis will produce an enormous range of results that are of little help in decision making.

To address these problems we propose to use meta-analytic value transfer methods combined with spatial data on biophysical and socioeconomic determinants of ecosystem service values to produce spatially variable and more accurate estimates of benefits. We use this method to reestimate the benefits of meeting the target on wetland loss. Markandya also raises the issue of uncertainty and questionable credibility of cost estimates from the CBD study, and we evaluate the target on coral reef protection to examine the effect of cost uncertainty.

For wetlands, we do not include lakes and rivers and estimate the value of ecosystem services using a meta-analytic function, with upper and lower bounds calculated using 95 percent prediction intervals. Analytical results are given in Table 2.8. In contrast to the cost-benefit analysis results presented in Markandya, the present analysis produces very different results and more clear-cut decision rules.

A similar approach is taken for coral reefs, with costs being reestimated using comparable methodology. Results are shown in Table 2.9. Our analysis showed both costs and benefits to be higher, but the overall outcome was much the same.

Our analysis attempts to improve on the treatment of uncertainty in the value of ecosystem

Table 2.8 Net benefits from Aichi Target 5: 50 percent reduction in rate of wetland loss

Case	Benefit to Cost Ratio	IRR (%)
Lower bound of benefits/lower bound of costs	1.69	8
Upper bound of benefits/lower bound of costs	2.45	11
Lower bound of benefits/upper bound of costs	1.29	7
Upper bound of benefits/upper bound of costs	1.87	9

Table 2.9 Net benefits from Aichi Target 10: 50 percent reduction in rate of coral loss

Case	Benefit to Cost Ratio	IRR (%)
Lower Bound of benefits/lower bound of costs	24.21	37
Upper bound of benefits/lower bound of costs	33.15	41
Lower bound of benefits/upper bound of costs	17.58	33
Upper bound of benefits/upper bound of costs	24.07	37

services. As such it only deals with the uncertainty arising from transferring values from primary valuation studies to out-of-sample policy sites. In addition, it is necessary to systematically examine other sources of uncertainty (e.g., measurement errors in primary valuation estimates; biased sampling of available primary valuation studies; consistency and accuracy of spatial data on ecosystem type and extent), recognizing that this type of global analysis of costs and benefits of ecosystem change stacks multiple sources of uncertainty.

2.2 Alternative Perspective

ALISTAIR MCVITTIE

This perspective explores in greater depth part of the cost-benefit analysis undertaken by Markandya, particularly for Sustainable Development Goal 15.2: *By 2020, promote the implementation of sustainable management of all type of forests, halt deforestation, restore degraded forests, and increase afforestation and reforestation by x percent globally.*

Although the implementation costs of measures to achieve the Aichi targets have been estimated during a specific program of work, the same is not the case for the benefits. Looking at ecosystem services for both tropical and temperate forest biomes, we find that the largest category for tropical forest is provisioning services (43 percent of value), while for temperate forest 49 percent relates to cultural services (largely recreation).

The majority of tropical forest valuations use market value type estimates. By contrast, nearly 60 percent of the temperate forest values are from stated preference techniques (contingent valuation, choice experiments). This raises a number of important issues; arguably the key ones with respect to the use of these extant values are passive use values and nonmarginal values.

The estimates collected for valuation databases typically reflect marginal changes in the provision of ecosystem services. They are not appropriate for estimating the total value of an ecosystem. Put simply, can we defensibly use a $/ha value originally elicited for changing forest extent at one site by 10 ha to value changes totalling thousands of hectares on a global scale? Nevertheless, existing value estimates are likely to be the only reasonable source for global cost-benefit analysis.

We can estimate benefits on a regional basis by using spatial variables to account for differences.

Value functions can be used to allow for the impact of different variables. For example, smaller sites have higher values per hectare, consistent with diminishing marginal utility, and the extent of urban areas within 50 km also increases per ha values of forest. Values across regions also reflect variables such as income levels.

The total losses from deforestation from 2000 to 2050 reported by Markandya range from US\$334 billion to US\$1,118 billion, compared to a total undiscounted value of US\$1,322 billion implied by the value functions in this perspective. However, a key aspect of the current analysis is that by using regional estimates of value it is possible to explore the distributional aspects of policy intervention. For tropical forests the loss in the value of ecosystem benefits from deforestation reflects both the relative biome extent across regions and also the greater variability in per ha values, whereas losses in OECD countries are relatively high despite modest changes in forest extent.

There are 17 countries with forest extent greater than 40 million ha each (>1 percent of total global forest) accounting for a cumulative 76.6 percent of global area. An approach to allocating costs across regions would be to use the number of countries from that list of 17 in each region. It would be reasonable to assume that the incidence of costs, particularly where these are to create capacity not currently present, will fall disproportionately on some regions and most likely the least developed and those with large forest resources.

Using an equal allocation of costs across regions, BCRs range from 0.9 for the upper cost estimate in sub-Saharan Africa (the only case below unity) to 5.9 for lower costs in Russia and Central Asia. If legal and enabling costs are allocated across non-OECD countries, the BCRs for the OECD rise to over 200, but ratios for other regions fall only modestly. However, it can be argued that the analysis remains partial in that it does not explicitly consider spillover effects such as those due to carbon sequestration and passive use values. Consequently there is the potential for those OCED nations experiencing the highest benefits both from policy action within their nations and also from passive use and carbon spillovers to transfer resources to ensure those benefits are achieved.

Benefits and Costs of the Climate Change Targets for the Post-2015 Development Agenda

ISABEL GALIANA

Introduction

It has been argued that climate change is the greatest threat facing humanity and yet is not explicitly targeted in the UN Millennium Development Goals (MDGs) but falls rather under Goal 7's (Ensure Environmental Sustainability) target 1, "Integrate the principles of sustainable development into country policies and programs and reverse the loss of environmental resources," and less directly through Goal 8: "Global partnership for development." Since their implementation in 2000, the MDGs have been shown to be quite successful in mobilizing support for health, hunger, and education. The subprioritization of climate change recognizes an implicit conflict between development, with the energy use (and emissions) it entails, and climate policy. Climate change mitigation in emerging and developing countries could be harmful from a development perspective if it slows economic growth by requiring more costly, low-carbon energy sources (Jakob and Steckel, 2013).

This chapter discusses and evaluates common and innovative global climate policy targets and metrics within a benefit-cost framework appropriate for use as post-2015 goals. Moreover, it highlights the potential for the UN post-2015 Sustainable Development Goals to acknowledge current technological limitations and developmental objectives facing policy makers and thus identify policies that are regionally acceptable, appropriate, and most important, effective in slowing global warming.

International Climate Cooperation

The Intergovernmental Panel on Climate Change (IPCC) was created over a quarter century ago to assess the risks associated with anthropogenic climate change. In 1992 the United Nations Framework Convention on Climate Change (UNFCCC) was created to help establish enforceable treaties to "avoid dangerous climate change" through yearly Conferences of the Parties (COPs). The past 26 years of climate negotiations have shown that establishing such an agreement is a highly challenging task. In 1996 the goal of limiting climate change to a 2°C rise in average global temperature came on the scene and has become a key focus of the international climate debate. Despite much media attention and repeated negotiations within the UNFCCC framework, if measured by performance, global climate policy has failed. Since 1990 the globe has witnessed a steady rise in emissions, only halted by the global recession, with carbon dioxide emissions having increased by more than 46 percent.

> Despite the variety of existing policy efforts and the existence of the UNFCCC and the Kyoto Protocol, GHG emissions have grown at about twice the rate in the recent decade (2000–2010) than any other decade since 1970. (robust evidence, high agreement) [1.3.1].
> (IPCC, 2014, Chapter 1, p. 4)

Given this complete failure of the UNFCCC process to achieve emissions cuts, why does the world continue to pursue this framework? Studies have shown that international cooperation would significantly reduce the costs of climate policy and accelerate the transition to a low-carbon economy (Aldy, Barrett et al., 2003; Aldy and Stavins, 2007; Blanford, Kriegler, et al., 2013; Clarke, Edmonds, et al., 2009; Victor, 2006). Generally, the failure of international climate agreements, for example, the Kyoto Protocol, is attributed to strong incentives to free-ride and ineffective compliance mechanisms and sanctions. But this fails to acknowledge the fundamental nature of the climate change problem: the energy technology problem.

The IPCC has recently published its Fifth Assessment Working Group 3 Report (AR5 WG III) on the mitigation of climate change (IPCC, 2014). This latest report acknowledges the need for large-scale changes to energy systems at all levels and that these changes are inconsistent with current trends (Chapter 6, p. 6). Unfortunately the limitations (including scalability, sociopolitical, etc.) of technologies, such as carbon capture and storage (CCS), nuclear, and renewables, among others, are scarcely touched on. The lack of scalable, reliable, and cost-effective low-carbon energy sources is a leading cause of the failure of global efforts to curb greenhouse gas emissions. The UNFCCC's universal membership provides it with a high degree of global legitimacy (Karlsson-Vinkhuyzen, and McGee, 2013), and thus its lack of clarity about technological limitations is at best misguided and at worst a dangerous impediment to progress toward a low-carbon world. As Bullis (2014) points out, governments are unwilling to commit to emission reduction targets because the costs of developing and deploying low-carbon technologies is uncertain.

Recently there has been an increase in unilateral and multilateral action outside the UNFCCC process (IPCC WG3 AR5). In the case of "fragmented" action – in which OECD countries join a climate treaty immediately, the emerging economic (BRIC) in 2030, and other developing economies in 2050 – the increased costs to first movers (OECD countries) are found to be double those of the perfectly cooperative case.[1] In addition, fragmentation has contributed to carbon leakage, a growing transfer of carbon emissions from the developed world to the emerging economy/developing world (Davis and Caldeira, 2010; Peters, Minx, et al., 2011).[2] Although it is still unclear how much of the transfer is attributable to fragmented climate policy and how much to globalization and other cost advantages that would have occurred in the absence of climate policy, carbon leakage is a growing concern for policy makers.

The Energy Technology Problem

The UN Secretary-General's High-Level Panel (HLP) of eminent persons on the post-2015 development agenda strongly endorses the call to hold the increase in global average temperature to 2°C above preindustrial levels, in line with international agreements. The HLP (2013) report states that "tools are already available. We can reach large-scale, transformative solutions worldwide with more investment, collaboration, implementation and political will." These assertions pose the greatest threat to dealing with climate change effectively. Although free-riding and politics may be part of that climate challenge, they are not the major factor.

The HLP is not the only entity to misdiagnose the climate change problem as one of political will to generate price incentives to adopt existing tools. The IPCC has for years asserted the readiness of low-carbon alternatives, although it has recently acknowledged the need for "nearly all governments to promptly engage in international cooperation, adopt stringent national and international emission control policies, and deploy rapidly a wide array of low- and zero-emission technologies"(IPCC, 2014). The IPCC (2014) goes on to admit that real-world assumptions, including fragmented action and limited technologies, drastically increases policy costs. Moreover, low-concentration scenarios are rarely found in the literature given their higher costs or unrealistic technological assumptions (Tol, 2013). The assumptions about availability and scalability of low-carbon technologies determine the estimates of the world's ability to cost effectively achieve given atmospheric concentrations of GHGs (Kriegler, Weyant, et al., 2014). In a technology constrained world, estimated mitigation costs can be more than double those in a nonconstrained world (IPCC, 2014; Kriegler, Weyant, et al., 2014).

Stabilizing global greenhouse gas concentration (stock) requires stabilizing emissions (flow), followed by deep reductions beyond anything

---

[1] In NPV at 5 percent discount rate over 2015–2100 (IPCC, 2014, Chap. 6).

[2] Evaluated on production-based accounting.

experienced to date. Since 2010, coal-fired electricity generation growth has increased more rapidly than nonfossil sources combined. Moreover, the majority of this increase has been the least-efficient type of coal-fired generation, driving significant increases in emissions. It is widely recognized that climate models that reveal low to moderate abatement costs include some type of backstop technology to offset this use of coal. In the recent IPCC report, of particular significance is the clear importance of: (1) carbon capture and storage (CCS) and (2) bioenergy technologies and sources, to achieving low atmospheric carbon concentration goals at reasonable costs. Similarly in Redrawing the Energy-Climate Map (IEA, 2013) there is strong reliance on BECCS (bioenergy with carbon capture and storage) to achieve negative emissions in order to achieve the 2°C scenario. Alternatively they define a "4-for-2°C scenario"[3] to 2020 that does not require technological breakthroughs. Despite being potentially cost effective, this scenario does not expect to achieve significant emission reductions in the short term.

> The future of CCS is uncertain; at present, the technology is advancing slowly, due to high costs and lack of political and financial commitment. Near-term progress in CCS research, development and demonstration is needed to ensure long-term and cost-competitive deployment towards meeting climate goals.
>
> (IEA 2014)

CCS still remains untried and untested at large scales, and its political acceptability is weak because it suffers from the NIMBY phenomenon that has contributed to the cancellation of several plants.[4] Biomass and bioenergy not only compete with other important uses of land (e.g., food), but also the conversion of pasture and unused land to bioenergy production may release substantial carbon from the soil (Haberl, Erb, et al., 2013; Searchinger, Heimlich, et al., 2008). Further, second-generation bioenergy from algae and wastes may not prove scalable to the extent required. The potential limits on bioenergy have implications for scaling up other renewables, because without it, or some other low-carbon energy source, scaling up the currently nonstorable

intermittent and variable solar and wind energies would imply relying on fossil fuels (especially natural gas) for "spinning reserve" backup. This is not an insignificant concern as reliability is a serious concern for energy producers as well as governments.

There is a substantial literature addressing the limitations of current technologies directly and their use in emission scenarios as baselines. These have been shown to substantially understate the magnitude of the technology challenge and therefore do not provide a valid means for assessing whether current technologies are sufficient (Anadon, Bunn, et al., 2011; Constable, 2011; Edmonds, Calvin, et al., 2012; Galiana and Green, 2009, 2010; Hoffert, 2011; Hoffert, Caldeira, et al., 1998; Myhrvold and Caldeira, 2012; Nemet, 2009; Schilling and Esmundo, 2009).

According to Kriegler, Weyant, et al. (2014), "technology is a key element for reaching climate targets." Of course, as is clear from the IEA report Redrawing the Energy-Climate Map (among others), implementing cost-effective policies today can set the world on a cleaner path and limit lock-in to fossil-based energy. Most scenarios present modest emission cuts over the near term followed by deep emission cuts, or negative emissions, in the future. These policies present the potential for a time-inconsistency if cheaper, scalable, low-carbon technologies do not materialize in the future. Actively pursuing the development of such technologies in combination with currently cost-effective mitigation measures appears may be a way forward (Bullis, 2014; Galiana and Green, 2010).

The Post-2015 Process

Climate change is not simply an issue of environmental sustainability or sustainable development; it must be addressed as a distinct objective

---

[3] "4-for-2°C scenario" measures – energy efficiency, limit inefficient coal-fired plants, minimize methane emission, and further phase out of fossil-fuel subsidies.
[4] http://sequestration.mit.edu/tools/projects/index_cancelled.html.

because its consequences are so widespread and overarching. The HLP–P2015 report highlights 12 universal goals. Climate change policy falls primarily within the scope of goals 7, 9, and 11. Goal 7, "Secure Sustainable Energy," has the related subgoals of doubling the share of renewable energy in the global energy mix, ensuring universal access to modern energy services, and the phasing out of fossil fuel subsidies that encourage wasteful consumption. Goal 9 is to "Manage natural resource assets sustainably through the specific goal of reducing deforestation and increasing reforestation." Goal 12, "Create a global enabling environment and catalyze long-term finance," explicitly states the climate change goal of holding the increase in global average temperatures below 2°C above preindustrial levels. These are some potential targets, but the issue of how to achieve these is sidestepped by the HLP.

As part of the UN Post-2015 process the Open Working Group (OWG) on Sustainable Development Goals[5] published an Outcome Document in July 2014. As a result of multiple consultations with stakeholders, interested parties, governments, NGOs, etc., climate change has been assigned a specific goal: "Goal 13. Take urgent action to combat climate change and its impacts." The specific targets under Goal 13 appear to focus on adaptation, resilience, and planning, as well as the Green Climate Fund.[6] Although the energy goals and innovation goals within the latest OWG document do not explicitly mention greenhouse gas emissions, a number of them could be considered climate targets; namely, those targeting renewables, energy efficiency, and clean energy research/R&D spending.

To identify the mechanism though which each goal is targeting emissions, it is helpful to present the Kaya identity. Each goal targets one or more of the drivers of emissions (income, energy intensity of output, carbon intensity of energy) either directly or indirectly. Emission reduction targets are the only policy to focus on the left-hand side of the Kaya identity, growth in emissions, without necessarily addressing the means of achieving these reductions. Emission intensity, renewable standards, and energy R&D all target the means of reducing emissions without explicitly targeting an

emission level. Adaptation, on the other hand, sidesteps the issue of reducing emissions altogether. It is likely that some portfolio of complementary policies will be needed to address the environmental, technological and political limitations of each.

The   Kaya Identity

$$\widehat{C} = \widehat{GDP} + \left(\widehat{E/GDP}\right) + \left(\widehat{C/E}\right)$$

where

1) $\widehat{C}$ is the growth in carbon emissions

2) $\widehat{GDP}$ is the growth in global income

3) $\left(\widehat{E/GDP}\right)$ the growth in energy intensity of output

4) $\left(\widehat{C/E}\right)$ is the growth in carbon intensity of energy

Prominent Targets under Consideration: Benefit-Cost Analyses (BCAs)

1 Global Annual Carbon Emission Reduction Targets

The target of stabilizing global temperature rise at less than 2°C above preindustrial levels can be translated into atmospheric GHG concentrations and further into yearly emission allowances (Meinshausen, Meinshausen, et al., 2009). Targets of 450 and 550 ppm CO_2e require substantial reduction of CO_2 emissions from fossil fuel use and industry compared to baseline levels (Blanford, Kriegler, et al., 2013). This target is the most common metric used in international climate negotiations and is being addressed by policies that target the left-hand side of the Kaya identity, i.e., emissions growth. For example, the Kyoto Protocol called for fixed emissions reduction targets relative to 1990 levels. Copenhagen pledges have been based on both reductions relative to a historical base year, as well as reduction relative to a base year's business-as-usual trends.

---

[5] http://sustainabledevelopment.un.org/focussdgs.html.
[6] www.gcfund.org/home.html.

Interestingly, many if not all integrated assessment models that successfully achieve the 450, 500, or even 550 ppm targets allow for overshooting the target and then rely on negative emissions though either advanced CCS or bioenergy and carbon capture and storage (BECCS).[7] Lemoine and McJeon (2013) use the technology-rich GCAM integrated assessment model to assess the implications of 450 and 500 ppm carbon targets. They find that the 500 ppm target provides net benefits across some futures, but the 450 ppm target provides net benefits only when social costs of carbon are high, low-carbon technological breakthroughs abound, and discount rates are low. Blanford, Kriegler, et al. (2013) show that models that find a feasible solution for the 450 ppm CO_2e target have added a technological option for negative emissions, in most cases BECCS in the electric sector. This allows for atmospheric concentration overshoot followed by rapid reductions in the latter half of the century.

Rogelj, McCollum, et al. (2013) show that the 2°C target can be met with a >66 percent probability under central technology and energy demand assumptions only if there is immediate and globally coordinated action. These conditions are what are referred to in the IPCC AR5 as "idealized" situations. Figure 3.1 shows the consequences of deviations from these idealized conditions; the probability of achieving the 2°C target is greatly hindered by either a lack of technological availability, strong energy demand (also associated with economic development) or delayed and fragmented action.

Tol (2013), under more realistic conditions, finds that cost-effective emission reduction would set the world on a path to 625 ppm CO_2e and that targets such as the 2°C, 450 ppm, or 550 ppm would not be supported by benefit-cost analyses.

2 Emission Intensity Targets

Emission intensity targets can be reassuring if economic forecast are uncertain. These allow for continued growth by focusing on the per unit emissions rather that the level. Intensity targets

have been proposed by China and India: their pledge is a reduction of carbon intensity (i.e., emissions per unit of economic output) between 40 and 45 percent and 20 and 25 percent, respectively, by 2020 with respect to 2005 (Steckel et al., 2011; Yuan et al., 2012; Zhang, 2011; Zhu et al., 2014). Another carbon target linked to GDP was the one planned by Argentina in 1999 (Barros and Conte Grand, 2002).

Emission intensity targets focus on the right-hand side of the Kaya identity by encouraging energy-efficiency improvements and/or reductions in the fossil fuel content of energy. These goals are similar to the emission reduction targets with a business-as-usual baseline as opposed to a historical year baseline. Emerging economies in particular have strong economic growth forecasts that imply rapidly growing emissions. The majority of emissions growth over the past decade has been from emerging economies, and their share of emissions is expected to continue to increase (IPCC, 2014). Policies with strong development goals prefer this type of target as it allows flexibility should growth be strong. Emission intensity targets have been criticized as they do not explicitly limit the amount of CO_2 entering the atmosphere and do not necessarily provide strong incentives for innovation.

Alternative Targets (BCAs)

3 Invest 0.5 Percent of GDP in Energy Technology RD&D

There is growing awareness of the need for innovation in energy technologies to address the climate change problem. Energy Technology Perspectives (IEA, 2014) presents evidence that an additional global investment of $44 trillion could decarbonize the energy system sufficiently to meet the 2°C target by 2050. Moreover, this expenditure is more than offset by over $115 trillion in fuel savings – resulting in net savings of $71 trillion. Even with a 10 percent discount rate, the net savings are more than $5 trillion

---

[7] Bioenergy with carbon capture and storage.

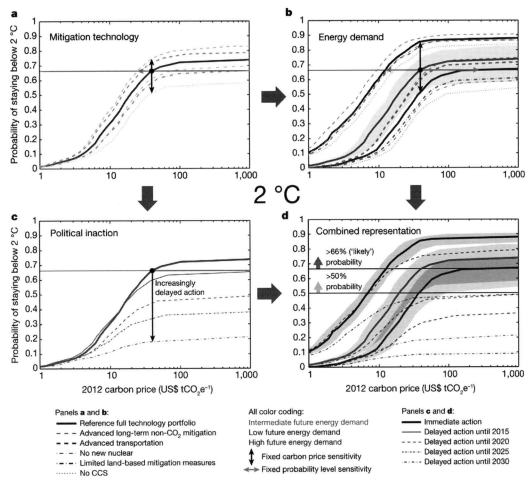

Figure 3.1 *Cost distributions for six cases with varying future availability of specific mitigation technologies (a) and three sensitivity cases for future energy demand (b, thick solid lines). Shaded areas and dashed lines in b represent technology-sensitivity cases comparable to those shown in a. Shaded areas and dashed lines in d represent technology- and politics-sensitivity cases comparable to those in b and c, respectively. c, Impact of delayed global mitigation action. d, Overview figure combining all sensitivity cases. The horizontal line in a–c is the 66 percent line (Rogelj, McCollum, et al., 2013).*

(IEA, 2014). This objective has also been raised at the sixth session of the Open Working Group on Sustainable Development Goals[8] and World Economic Forum (WEF, 2013).

The Green Investment Report calls for an acceleration of low-carbon innovation. In particular, it recommends using revenues from carbon pricing measures to increase support for research, development, demonstration, and precommercial deployment of low-carbon technologies by pooling international efforts (WEF, 2013). Galiana

and Green (2010) evaluated a proposal for a technology-led approach to climate policy funded by a low and slowly rising carbon tax and find that the BCAs are between 1.3 and 10. When comparing the Galiana–Green approach to the standard carbon pricing approach to policy, BCRs are in the range of 12–15.

---

[8] http://sustainabledevelopment.un.org/content/documents/3412Summary%20Cochairs%20OWG6.pdf.

Policies that advance low-carbon technologies have substantial value in making future reduction in CO_2 cost effective. Further, CO_2 targets and improved low-carbon technologies are probably correlated to some degree. Pricing carbon emissions can induce some innovation that reduces the cost of attaining the carbon target but will primarily drive the initial uptake of more costly innovations as they reach the market. According to modeling by (Lemoine and McJeon, 2013), the 450 ppm target is only likely to be welfare enhancing in a world with multiple breakthroughs in low-carbon technology.

4 Invest 0.05 Percent of GDP in Adaptation

Adaptation can be defined as purposeful adjustments in behavior to reduce society's vulnerability to climate change. Climate adaptation includes reducing existing vulnerabilities, building adaptive capacity, current and future risk management, and building long-term resilience to climate change. Adaptation tends to occur reactively, and there is a tremendous benefit to taking planned measures.

Adaptation has been seen as especially important in developing countries because those countries are predicted to bear the brunt of the effects of climate change and have lower adaptive capacity. In fact, much of the literature on reducing vulnerability to climate change conveys a well-defined relationship between adaptation and development (Jerneck and Olsson, 2008; Klein et al., 2005; Pouliotte et al., 2009; Schipper and Pelling, 2006). Contrary to most other responses to climate change, adaptation does not suffer from a free-rider problem, and consequently there are strong incentives to adapt even unilaterally (Bosello, Carraro et al. 2013). Most studies on costs and benefits of adaptation take a sectoral approach (Agrawal, 2010; Hunt and Watkiss, 2011). There is some concern that effective adaptation could lead to lesser mitigation[9] and thus higher atmospheric concentrations in the long run, with tragic consequences for countries (like small island nations) with limited means to adapt. de Bruin, Dellink, et al. (2009) show that adaptation reduces the benefit–cost ratio of mitigation.

Bosello (2004) shows that in 2050 a complete adaptation to the damage implied by the four climate change consequences (full coastal protection, space heating and cooling, resettlement and migration costs, and health) is roughly equal to 0.15 percent of world GDP. Depending on the study, adaptation covers some 7–25 percent of total damages for a doubling of the atmospheric concentration of carbon dioxide (Hallegatte, Shah, et al., 2012; Tol, 2005). Bosello, Carraro, et al. (2012) found that benefit-cost ratios of adaptation expenditure are larger than one (and up to three) for all considered scenarios, and BCRs are always greater when combined with mitigation. Adaptation, as with other climate policies, should be used as part of a portfolio that includes mitigation policies, both in the form of pricing and RD&D.

Ultimately, adaptation needs to be combined with mitigation policy because most adaptation analyses focus on 2–3°C climate change impacts; the costs beyond this are highly uncertain but undoubtedly significantly higher.

Target Recommendations for Post-2015 and Conclusion

Current emissions reduction targets under consideration are dangerously unlikely to produce results. They rely heavily on the assumption that climate policy failures to date are simply a matter of political ill will and that technologies are available. Studies that show strong benefit costs of emissions reduction targets rely heavily on negative emissions through CCS and bioenergy with carbon capture and storage (BECCS) in future decades (Table 3.1). The development of these and other burgeoning technologies is key to achieving significant cuts in GHG emissions. By setting goals that target low-carbon energy RD&D and adaptation, the UN post-2015 will be acknowledging current technological limitations and developmental objectives of emerging economies.

[9] Mitigation and adaptation policies can be viewed as substitutes.

Table 3.1 Benefit-cost summary[10]

	Benefit-Cost Ratios			
	3% discount	5% discount	Cobenefits	Criticism
Emission targets 450 ppm or 550 ppm	<1	<1	Certainty of emission if policy is effective. Induces innovation. Reduces conventional air pollutants.	Costs can be massive. Limits growth. Does not address long-term climate concerns.
Emission intensity targets	uncertain	uncertain	More palatable for countries with high growth uncertainty.	Emissions can vary. Does not address long-term climate concerns.
EU 20-20-20[11]	0.03–0.06	<0.03	First mover advantage. May incite other nations to follow suit.	Unnecessarily costly from a $/emission reduction perspective.
0.5% of GDP in low-carbon energy RD&D[12]	2–15	1–12	Spillovers to other sectors. Potential for significant mitigation at much lower cost.	No guarantee of emission reductions. Uptake will be limited in the absence of other mitigation policies.
Adaptation[13]	Project and region specific (>1)	Project and region specific (>1)	Resilience to all types of climate variability.	Potentially reduces the need for mitigation.

Moreover, these targets will not conflict with economic objectives and access to energy needs. It is likely that a portfolio of policies including RD&D funding, adaptation, and moderate carbon pricing would yield the most significant results; the complementarity of three approaches should not be overlooked. Last, this portfolio of approaches will address both short-term and long-term needs without burdening economic development and thus would be globally acceptable, realistic, and most important, effective.

References

Agrawal, A. (2010). "Local institutions and adaptation to climate change." *Social Dimensions of Climate Change: Equity and Vulnerability in a Warming World*. Washington, DC: World Bank: 173–98.

Aldy, J. E., et al. (2003). "Thirteen plus one: a comparison of global climate policy architectures." *Climate Policy* 3(4): 373–97.

Aldy, J. E. and R. N. Stavins (2007). *Architectures for Agreement*. Cambridge: Cambridge University Press.

Anadon, L. D., et al. (2011). *Transforming U.S. Energy Innovation*. Belfer Center for Science and International Affairs, Harvard Kennedy School.

Barros, V. and M. C. Grand (2002). Implications of a dynamic target of greenhouse gases emission reduction: the case of Argentina. *Environment and Development Economics* 7(3): 547–69.

Blanford, G. J., et al. (2013). "Harmonization vs. fragmentation: Overview of climate policy scenarios in EMF27." *Climatic Change*: 1–14.

Bosello, F. (2004). *Timing and Size of Adaptation, Mitigation and R&D investments in Climate Policy*. Venice: Fondazione Eni Enrico Mattei.

Bosello, F., et al. (2012). *An Analysis of Adaptation as a Response to Climate Change*. Tewksbury MA: Copenhagen Consensus.

Bullis, K. (2014). "A Plan B for climate agreements." *MIT Technology Review* 117(4): 84–86.

[10] Recommended targets. Estimates of the costs and the benefits of an intervention are never complete and rarely do justice to the complexity of the situation: the table provides approximations.

[11] Tol, R. S. (2012). "A cost–benefit analysis of the EU 20/20/2020 package." *Energy Policy* 49: 288–95.

[12] Recommended targets.   [13] Recommended targets.

Clarke, L., et al. (2009). "International climate policy architectures: overview of the EMF 22 International Scenarios." *Energy Economics* 31: S64–81.

Constable, J. (2011). *The Green Mirage: Why a Low-Carbon Economy May Be Further Off Than We Think*. London: Civitas.

Davis, S. J. and K. Caldeira (2010). "Consumption-based accounting of CO(2) emissions." *Proceedings of the National Academy of Sciences of the United States of America* 107(12): 5687–92.

de Bruin, K., et al. (2009). *Economic Aspects of Adaptation to Climate Change: Integrated Assessment Modelling of Adaptation Costs and Benefits*. Paris: OECD Publishing.

Edmonds, J., et al. (2012). "Energy and technology lessons since Rio." *Energy Economics* 34: S7–14.

Galiana, I. and C. Green (2009). "Let the global technology race begin." *Nature* 462(7273): 570–71.

    (2010). *An Analysis of a Technology-led Climate Policy as a Response to Climate Change. Smart solutions to climate change: Comparing costs and benefits*. Cambridge: Cambridge University Press.

Haberl, H., et al. (2013). "Bioenergy: how much can we expect for 2050?" *Environmental Research Letters* 8(3): 031004.

Hallegatte, S., et al. (2012). *Investment Decision Making under Deep Uncertainty: Application to Climate Change*. Washington, DC: World Bank.

High-Level Panel of Eminent Persons on the Post-2015 Development Agenda (HLP). (2013). *A New Global Partnership: Eradicate Poverty and Transform Economies through Sustainable Development*. New York: United Nations.

Hoffert, M. (2011). "Governments must pay for clean-energy innovation." *Nature* 472(7342): 137.

Hoffert, M. I., et al. (1998). "Energy implications of future stabilization of atmospheric CO_2 content." *Nature* 395(6705): 881–4.

Hunt, A. and P. Watkiss (2011). "Climate change impacts and adaptation in cities: a review of the literature." *Climatic Change* 104(1): 13–49.

International Energy Agency (IEA) (2013). *Redrawing the Energy-Climate Map*. World Energy Outlook Special Report. Paris: Author.

(2014). *Energy Technology Perspectives 2014 – Executive Summary*. Paris: Author.

Intergovernmental Panel on Climate Change (IPCC) (2014). *Climate Change 2014, Mitigation of Climate Change*. Working Group III Contribution to the Fifth Assessment Report of the Intergovernmental Panel of Climate Change. New York: Cambridge University Press.

Jakob, M. and J. C. Steckel (2013). "How climate change mitigation could harm development in poor countries." *Wiley Interdisciplinary Reviews: Climate Change*.

Jerneck, A. and L. Olsson (2008). Adaptation and the poor: development, resilience and transition. *Climate Policy* 8(2): 170–182.

Karlsson-Vinkhuyzen, S. I. and J. McGee (2013). Legitimacy in an era of fragmentation: The case of global climate governance. *Global Environmental Politics* 13(3): 56–78.

Klein, R. J., E. L. F. Schipper, and S. Dessai (2005). Integrating mitigation and adaptation into climate and development policy: three research questions. *Environmental Science & Policy* 8(6): 579–588.

Kriegler, E., et al. (2014). "The role of technology for achieving climate policy objectives: overview of the EMF 27 study on global technology and climate policy strategies." *Climatic Change*: 353–367.

Lemoine, D. and H. C. McJeon (2013). "Trapped between two tails: trading off scientific uncertainties via climate targets." *Environmental Research Letters* 8(3): 034019.

Meinshausen, M., et al. (2009). "Greenhouse-gas emission targets for limiting global warming to 2 C." *Nature* 458(7242): 1158–62.

Myhrvold, N. P. and K. Caldeira (2012). "Greenhouse gases, climate change and the transition from coal to low-carbon electricity." *Environmental Research Letters* 7(1): 014019.

Nemet, G. F. (2009). "Demand-pull, technology-push, and government-led incentives for non-incremental technical change." *Research Policy* 38(5): 700–9.

Peters, G. P., et al. (2011). "Growth in emission transfers via international trade from 1990 to 2008." *Proceedings of the National Academy of Sciences of the United States of America* 108(21): 8903–08.

Pouliotte, J., B. Smit, and L. Westerhoff (2009). Adaptation and development: livelihoods and climate change in Subarnabad, Bangladesh. *Climate and Development* 1(1): 31–46.

Rogelj, J., et al. (2013). "Probabilistic cost estimates for climate change mitigation." *Nature* 493(7430): 79–83.

Schilling, M. A. and M. Esmundo (2009). "Technology S-curves in renewable energy alternatives: Analysis and implications for industry and government." *Energy Policy* 37(5): 1767–81.

Schipper, L. and M. Pelling (2006). Disaster risk, climate change and international development: scope for, and challenges to, integration. *Disasters* 30(1): 19–38.

Searchinger, T., et al. (2008). "Use of US croplands for biofuels increases greenhouse gases through emissions from land-use change." *Science* 319(5867): 1238–40.

Steckel, J. C., M. Jakob, R. Marschinski, and G. Luderer (2011). From carbonization to decarbonization?—Past trends and future scenarios for China's CO2 emissions. *Energy Policy* 39(6): 3443–55.

Tol, R. S. (2005). "Adaptation and mitigation: trade-offs in substance and methods." *Environmental Science & Policy* 8(6): 572–8.

—— (2012). "A cost–benefit analysis of the EU 20/20/2020 package." *Energy Policy* 49: 288–95.

—— (2013). "Targets for global climate policy: an overview." *Journal of Economic Dynamics and Control* 37(5): 911–28.

Victor, D. G. (2006). "Toward effective international cooperation on climate change: Numbers, interests and institutions." *Global Environmental Politics* 6(3): 90–103.

World Economic Forum (WEF). (2013). *The Green investment Report: The Ways and Means to Unlock Private Finance for Green Growth.* Geneva: World Economic Forum.

Yuan, J., Y, Hou, and M. Xu (2012). China's 2020 carbon intensity target: Consistency, implementations, and policy implications. *Renewable and Sustainable Energy Reviews* 16(7): 4970–81.

Zhang, Z. (2011). Assessing China's carbon intensity pledge for 2020: stringency and credibility issues and their implications. *Environmental Economics and Policy Studies* 13(3): 219–35.

Zhu, Z. S., H. Liao, H. S. Cao, L., Wang, Y. M. Wei, and J. Yan (2014). The differences of carbon intensity reduction rate across 89 countries in recent three decades. *Applied Energy* 113: 808–15.

3.1 Alternative Perspective

ROBERT MENDELSOHN

The optimal solution to the greenhouse gas problem minimizes the sum of the climate damage and the cost of mitigation over the long run, but the current UN initiative is not even close to achieving this. There are three key insights that emerge. First, mitigation cost should be balanced against climate damage; second, as marginal damage increases with higher concentrations of greenhouse gases, so marginal cost should also rise; and third, the marginal cost of mitigation should be equated across all emitters.

However, there are serious political difficulties, as the objective for each country is not necessarily what is best for the world overall. Thus, without international cooperation, individual countries have very little incentive to reduce emissions. Damages and costs are very difficult to estimate, and lowest cost strategies call for long-term commitments, which are alien to most politicians and voters. The long delay between action and damage also raises questions about discounting.

Developed and emerging economies are each responsible for about 45 percent of emissions and must do most of the mitigation. But there is no silver bullet, and a portfolio of technologies is needed. Energy conservation, a move from coal to gas, renewable energy sources, bioenergy, and nuclear power can all make contributions. Carbon capture and storage is also an important part of the solution, but the feasibility of the technology on a large scale must still be assessed. Finally, using forests for sequestration is cost effective, but using woody biomass as part of a BECCS solution is expensive.

The most important insight from economics is that the cost of mitigation rises rapidly the more stringent the target. The cost of meeting a target of a maximum 5°C rise is about $10 trillion. Reducing this to 4° adds a further $10 trillion, but going down to 3°C would cost $40 trillion, and to 2°, $100 trillion. The world is not yet ready for a large-scale cost-effective mitigation program, and the more aggressive targets do not allow for such delays.

In practice, a large fraction of the potential damage from climate change can be avoided by adaptation. Indeed, this is hard to prevent because all sections of society have an incentive to do so.

However, there are still a number of types of damage that would occur, with reduction in global food production being the most feared. Coastal impacts – affecting areas where a large fraction of the world's population and infrastructure are found – could also be large, but coastal cities could be relatively easily protected. Forests, on the other hand, are expected to prosper in a warmer, wetter world with more CO_2, while the increased demand for cooling would be one of the biggest damages of global warming. On balance, ecosystem changes are likely to be modest, as are the overall health effects. However, there remains the possibility of a catastrophe, such as the melting of the Greenland and Antarctica ice sheets, which would take place slowly but double the cost of damage from sea level rise.

Summing all these effects, we see that small amounts of warming are unlikely to cause large damages. However, the net impact is likely to be harmful above a 2° rise, and the cost of this would reach $100 billion a year by the time 3° was reached and $1 trillion for a 4° rise.

This perspective argues that the present 2° limit is too stringent and does not justify the $100 trillion cost. The worst effects would only occur over 4°, and the present value of a program to keep to this limit would be $20 trillion. However, any mitigation program is unlikely to be equitable, and some compensation to poorer, low-latitude countries in the form of help to diversify their economies would also be needed.

Finally, an insurance program is needed in case the effect of warming does indeed turn out to be greater than we estimate. This would be in the form of a program of geoengineering, which could be implemented quickly if climate change turned out to be worse than expected.

3.2 Alternative Perspective

CAROLYN FISCHER

Although concurring with some of the broad conclusions of the challenge chapter, there is no scientific consensus that a limit of 450 ppm of CO_2 does not pass a cost-benefit test; in fact, broad political consensus implies that limiting temperature rise to 2°C is cost effective. Neither are annual emissions caps inherently costly, depending on the policy measures used to achieve them. Overall, bringing fossil fuel prices more in line with their social costs necessarily produces greater benefits, which suggests that negotiating higher and converging carbon prices may hold more promise than trying to agree on quantity targets.

Any policy portfolio that focuses primarily on R&D and/or renewable energy deployment is inherently more costly than one that incorporates a fundamental role for carbon pricing, which encourages the use of all abatement options. To avoid costly delay in taking action on mitigation while waiting for international agreement on emissions targets, we should immediately work toward aligning the prices of emitting energy sources with their social costs – removing fossil fuel subsidies, using market-based mechanisms to regulate conventional air pollutants, and pricing carbon.

Galiana cites a few studies, which find that even less-ambitious stabilization targets than 2° are unlikely to be cost effective in a conventional analysis. However, models are limited in their ability to estimate the full range of potential costs and do not necessarily take account of possible catastrophic damage caused by uncertain events. Neither can modeling address the ethical and distributional effects of climate change. Environmental justice argues for an even lower target, for example, to protect vulnerable small island states. In contrast to the challenge chapter, the IEA emphasizes the feasibility of meeting climate goals cost effectively with existing technologies.

Bringing down the cost of low-carbon technologies – or even finding breakthrough technologies – has many advantages, particularly in a world reluctant to take costly measures to reduce emissions. If low-carbon energy sources can become cost-competitive on their own, they will naturally displace fossil-based sources. This is particularly relevant for developing countries, which could then decarbonize without sacrificing growth.

However, a target of 0.5 percent of GDP spent on low-carbon technology R&D is highly ambitious, if not unrealistic, considering that OECD countries spend on average just 0.04 percent of GDP on *all* energy-related R&D. Relying too heavily on innovation as a mitigation policy also creates two main problems. The first is delay, which will raise overall costs substantially. The second is the lack of incentive for other abatement options, which may be ignored. On the other hand, developing backstop technologies – particularly for carbon capture and storage – would be very useful, but they would not be deployed without carbon pricing or regulation.

Overall, it is difficult to avoid making emissions pricing a central piece of mitigation policy because carbon pricing encourages all options. The first step would be to remove all fossil fuel subsidies, followed by aligning fossil fuel prices at least with the cost burdens they impose locally. The final step would be to add a price for carbon, either through a carbon tax or emissions trading mechanisms. Given that the national benefits of a green tax shift can be more transparent than those of an emissions target, finding agreement on prices may well be more feasible than an agreement on quantities.

Finally, for me, the challenge chapter's presentation of cost-benefit ratios is at best uninformative and at worst misleading. Broad political consensus has already been reached for limiting global temperature rise to 2.0°C. The much bigger question is how to get there. Economists have demonstrated time and again that the single most cost-effective policy for reducing emissions is to price them.

Beyond Civil War

The Costs of Interpersonal Violence

JAMES FEARON AND ANKE HOEFFLER[*]

Introduction

In the broad area of building stable and peaceful societies, the UN High-Level Panel (HLP) has identified several areas where the benefit-cost ratio may be very high and that have been relatively neglected by the development community to date. There are areas where the current economic and social costs are plausibly quite large, and where the amount of attention is very small in comparison to other areas such as health, education, and governance reform. We argue that there is a strong case for making societal violence reduction a priority in the post-2015 Sustainable Development Goals.

When thinking about the costs of violence, the international community has focused primarily on civil wars. However, for each battlefield death in civil war, about nine times as many people are killed in interpersonal disputes, including many killings related to drug trafficking, intimate partner violence (of all homicides, 7 percent female and 5 percent male), and killing of children (7 percent). About 43 percent of all female homicide victims were killed by a current or former intimate partner.

Beyond the 418,000 homicides, *reported* crime figures suggest that there are about 300,000 cases of sexual violence, of which almost one-third are committed against children. There are also more than 2 million cases of assault. In addition to these reported crime figures, survey estimates suggest that about 275 million children are subjected to violent physical discipline in their homes, that 100 million girls and women live with female genital mutilation, and that about 30 percent of all partnered women have been subjected to intimate partner violence during their lifetime. This corresponds to about 769 million women.

Thus, physical violence in societies is a much larger and more pervasive phenomenon than just

civil war violence. Figures for homicides and violence in low- and middle-income countries are summarized in Figures 4.1 and 4.2. As we discuss later, a number of studies suggest that the strictly economic consequences are very large and, of course, will be much larger if we try to factor in social damage and individual suffering, and yet a tiny fraction of aid funding goes toward reducing societal violence or improving criminal justice systems. Because the area receives so little attention, it is impossible to estimate a rate of return for projects aimed at reducing violence, but it is plausible that returns are substantially higher for this than for projects aimed to improve governance in developing countries (which usually means improving performance and accountability of local institutions that make decisions about local public goods).

Although the goal of eliminating violence against women and children by 2030 as advocated by the UN HLP must be seen as purely aspirational, substantial reductions can be made as falling homicide rates in high-income countries in general and also in Colombia have shown. Maintaining an annual reduction of 1.5 percent – half the average seen in these examples – would reduce the global homicide rate by 21 percent by 2030. Halving the current high level of intimate partner violence would dramatically improve the welfare of millions of women and help break ongoing cycles of violence.

Arguably this would be an ambitious target – it is greater, for example, than the World Health Organization (WHO) projection of a 13.5 percent decline in "interpersonal violence" globally from

[*] We would like to thank Giles Dickenson-Jones, Institute for Economics and Peace (IEP), for help with the data. Howard Friedman, Zahra Siddique, and three anonymous referees provided useful suggestions. All remaining errors are our own.

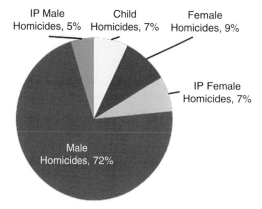

Figure 4.1 *Homicides in low- and middle-income countries*

Sources: WHO (2013b) for the age and sex of victims and Stöckl et al. (2013) for intimate partner violence.

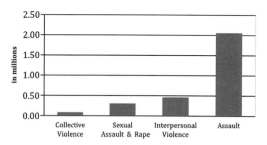

Figure 4.2 *Violence in low- and middle-income countries*

Sources: WHO (2013b) for collective and interpersonal violence and UNODC (2013) for sexual assault, rape, and assault.

2015 to 2030. But targets should be somewhat ambitious, and though we have little go on in terms of evidence about the responsiveness of homicide rates to social programs and policy reforms, the experience of Colombia and the United States suggests 21 percent over 16 years is feasible.

Interpersonal and Collective Violence

According to United Nations Office on Drugs and Crime (UNODC) figures, in 2008 there were just over 418,000 homicides in the 186 countries with data. In that same year, about 49,000 people are

estimated to have died in "battle deaths" in civil wars, slightly more than the average annual battle death estimate of 43,410 for the period 1998–2008. So by these measures total homicides run at about eight and a half times the rate of civil war battle deaths.[1]

Civil wars can cause wholesale destruction and displace communities, but recently only 20–25 countries have been affected each year, generally involving only a small part of the country. In contrast, about a third of countries had a homicide rate of over 10 per 100,000, considered to be an epidemic level by WHO.

A recent study estimated each homicide in the United States to cost $9.1 million, and this does not take account of effects on family and friends nor the dynamic economic effects of violent crime. Scaling this on the basis of each country's GDP and their murder rate, the total cost varies from 0.33 percent of GDP for high-income countries to 4.1 percent for Latin America and the Caribbean. Results are shown in Table 4.1. The table uses World Bank categories for low- and middle-income countries, showing the estimate for the "High-Income Countries" as a point of comparison. These are large costs – especially for Africa and Latin America and the Caribbean – given that this is a single category of violent crime and that the method here probably does not come close to counting the full social and economic cost of homicides.[2]

[1] We use 2008 because this is the year with the most complete set of homicide estimates, and it is also the last year for which the best source for estimates of civil war battle deaths exists (Lacina and Gleditsch, 2005). The reliability of the data for both battle deaths and homicides, at least the global level, is doubtful. The battle deaths data deliberately tries to count only intentional killing in war fighting and so leaves out what appears to be a great deal of mortality that is the indirect result of civil war. For homicide data, these appear to be fairly accurate for developed countries, but may be highly inaccurate (and understated) for many developing countries.

[2] In fact, to follow IEP as closely as possible (we use more of their data later in the chapter), the estimates for Table 4.1 used only the "intangible costs" of homicide as estimated by McCollister et al., thus a unit cost of 1.08 * $8,442,000 = $9,117,360, where the 1.08 is a CPI adjustment to express the 2008 McCollister et al. estimate in 2013 dollars. IEP count the "tangible costs" of homicide under a category for the criminal justice system; see footnote 3.

Table 4.1 Homicide costs as a share of GDP, by World Bank region

Region	As % of regional GDP	As % of country GDP (avg.)
Latin America and Caribbean	3.68	4.10
Sub-Saharan Africa	3.68	3.01
Europe and Central Asia	1.11	0.67
Middle East and North Africa	0.71	0.66
South Asia	0.68	0.61
High-Income Countries	0.42	0.33
East Asia and Pacific	0.26	1.03
World	0.82	1.71

Notes: Based on Institute for Economics and Peace (IEP, 2013) estimates. First column is total costs in region as % of total GDP of countries in region. Second column is average of country costs (as % of country GDP) in region. World Bank regions are for low- and middle-income countries; High-Income Countries can be anywhere.

Overall, this comes to 1.71 percent of global GDP for a single category of violent crime. These figures are an estimate of the benefits that could be achieved from a reduction in violence, not a current loss to the economy.

Other violent crimes, such as assault, are much more common, though less costly individually. A U.S. study estimated total costs of violent crime in 2012 to be 2 percent of GDP, while the British Home Office estimated 6.1 percent for England and Wales in 2003. The higher figure in the UK is due in part to an assumed underreporting of actual crime. Developing country estimates are of a similar magnitude, although figures are less common and more conjectural. Incorporating intangible costs, Londoño and Guerrero (1999) offer 14 percent of annual GDP per year for crime in Latin America. Other estimates are 7.5 percent for Latin America (and 3.7 percent for the U.S.) for 1995. Acevedo's (2008) study of costs of violence in Central America produced estimates of 10.8 percent per year for El Salvador, 10.0 percent for Nicaragua, 9.6 percent for Honduras, 7.8 percent for Guatemala, and 3.6 percent for Costa Rica. A study

of South Africa, which has very high crime rates, finds that 3.7 percent of GDP is spent on the criminal justice system *alone* (Altbeker, 2005).

Using 2013 figures from the Institute for Economics and Peace, interpersonal violence has a global welfare cost of 2.1 percent for an average country, or 1.44 percent if we weight by country population. In comparison, collective violence (dominated by civil war) has a cost of only 0.33 percent on average: less than one-sixth of the cost of interpersonal violence. The difference is actually even greater in most regions, but the civil conflicts arising from the Arab Spring raise the average collective violence estimates.

Tables 4.2 and 4.3 use the IEP's most recent estimates for 186 countries to calculate measures of the welfare cost of interpersonal and collective violence as a percentage of GDP circa 2013. In Table 4.2, costs are summed by region and divided by total GDP for the region. Table 4.3 provides country averages and country averages weighted by population. The estimates in Tables 4.2 and 4.3 are arguably quite conservative.[3] To summarize, these estimates suggest that both civil war and interpersonal violence impose large costs globally, with interpersonal violence being much more pervasive and much costlier than civil war violence.

Violence against Children

There is no universally accepted definition of what constitutes child abuse and neglect. For example, corporal punishment is common, but what is regarded as excessive is a cultural issue. In some societies, for example, Egypt, Somalia, and Ethiopia, the majority of girls still undergo female genital mutilation (FGM). Overall, the global prevalence of violence against children is difficult to estimate because much abuse is never reported. And despite

---

[3] See IEP, 2014 for further discussion of the conservatism of their estimates (in the categories we are using). The one highly consequential component of these estimates that one might argue overstates true costs is the value of human life based on the value per statistical life (VSL) approach (or that of other methodologies), and scaling this for developing countries by the ratio of GDP per capita to U.S. GDP per capita. Perhaps people put a proportionally high value on years of life at higher income levels, for example.

Table 4.2 Estimates of welfare costs of interpersonal and collective violence as a share of regional and global GDP for 2013

	Interpersonal violence		Collective violence	
	Cost ($ billions)	% of GDP	Cost ($ billions)	% of GDP
L. America/Carib.	334.52	4.43	40.86	0.54
Sub-Saharan Africa	85.55	3.90	14.6	0.67
Europe and Central Asia	86.79	1.58	53.47	0.98
High-Income Countries	592.87	1.33	1.41	0.00
M. East/N. Africa	25.62	0.95	40.20	1.48
South Asia	47.4	0.78	15.61	0.26
East Asia/Pacific	72.53	0.41	1.03	0.01
World	1245.27	1.44	167.19	0.19

Notes: Estimates based on IEP data for 2013. % of GDP refers to total GDP of region.

Table 4.3 Estimates of welfare costs of interpersonal and collective violence as a share of country GDP for 2013, by region

	Interpersonal violence cost as % of GDP		Collective violence cost as % of GDP	
	Avg.	Avg. (pop weighted)	Avg.	Avg. (pop weighted)
L. America/Caribbean	4.57	4.61	0.11	0.45
Sub-Saharan Africa	3.31	3.23	0.47	0.72
East Asia/Pacific	1.26	0.46	0.02	0.01
High-Income Countries	0.97	1.23	0.01	0.00
Europe and C. Asia	0.94	1.41	0.11	0.74
M. East/N. Africa	0.90	0.96	2.03	2.05
South Asia	0.74	0.76	0.4	0.27
World	2.10	1.44	0.33	0.34

Notes: Estimates based on IEP data for 2013.

the media attention on such issues as FGM and child prostitution, most of the violence happens at home: 80 percent of all perpetrators are the child's parents. We do not consider abuse and neglect in schools, care institutions, prison, at work, and in the community because no comparable figures are available across countries.

WHO provides global data for children up to age 14. Almost 34,000 deaths are attributed to interpersonal violence. The great majority of these occur in the first month of life, and girls are more at risk than boys (18 per 100,000 as against 14 per 100,000). Figure 4.3 shows global homicide rates per 100,000 of the population. However, the

highest rate is for newborn girls in the East Asia Pacific region: 46 per 100,000. Beyond that, the rate drops to around 2 per 100,000 for both genders. For comparison, the highest overall homicide rate is for boys and men ages 15 to 29, at 19 per 100,000 (mainly driven by high rates in Latin America and the Caribbean and sub-Saharan Africa). Child homicides as a percentage of the total vary from 2 in Europe and Central Asia to 14 in the Middle East and North Africa, and we use these figures to estimate total costs.

Data on child homicide, in particular neonatal homicide, are difficult to collect. If no signs of physical violence are present, is it difficult to

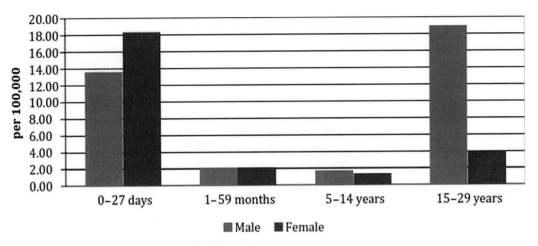

Figure 4.3 *Global child and young adult homicide rates*

Source: WHO, 2013b.

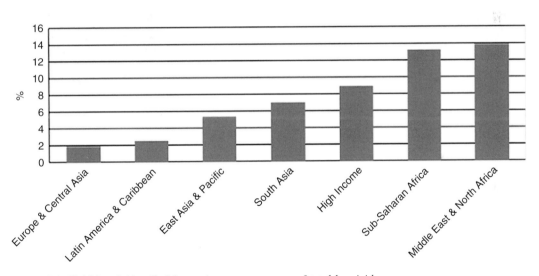

Figure 4.4 *Child homicides (0–14 years) as a percentage of total homicides*

Source: WHO, 2013b.

attribute the death to neglect rather than illness. Nevertheless, using WHO data, we calculate the percentage of child homicides (persons under 14 years of age) in total homicides. Figure 4.4 presents these child homicide figures by region.

Overall, using the same figure for a child homicide as that for an average homicide ($8.44 million) – corresponding to the intangible cost of the death – we estimate a total cost of $37.7 billion for child homicide, corresponding to 0.044 percent of world GDP.

Not all violence against children is fatal. We approximate the level of non-fatal child abuse through violent disciplinary practices from UNICEF data covering 34 countries (about 10 percent of children). Aggressive and violent punishment is

Table 4.4 Cost of nonfatal domestic child abuse

Region	(1) Total Cost (in UDS billions)	(2) Region Average (% of GDP)	(3) Country Average (% of GDP)
High Income	829	1.87	1.87
East Asia & Pacific	608	3.60	5.29
Europe & Central Asia	173	3.16	3.46
L. America & Caribbean	512	6.78	7.41
Middle East & N. Africa	437	16.13	17.52
South Asia	604	9.93	10.96
Sub-Saharan Africa	431	18.66	19.89
World	3,594	4.21	9.57

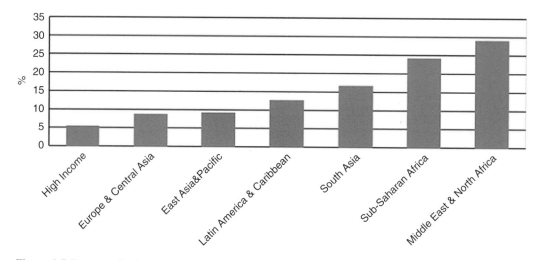

Figure 4.5 *Percent of primary caregivers using severe physical punishment*

Data Source: UNICEF (2014), no data available for South Asia (using sample average). Trinidad and Tobago is the only high-income country.

common and used by 73 percent of caregivers surveyed. Severe physical punishment is used by 28 percent of primary caregivers in the Middle East and North Africa and 24 percent in sub-Saharan Africa, but it is less common elsewhere. Figure 4.5 summarizes the regional situation.

Using average regional rates for severe physical punishment, a total of about 290 million children (15.5 percent of the total) are abused in this way. Our definition of child abuse includes slapping on the face, head, or ears, and/or beaten repeatedly with an implement. If someone outside the family received such treatment, this would be classified as assault. Thus, we suggest that figures for the unit cost of assault can be used to approximate the cost of child abuse. At a unit cost of $98,000, we estimate the total cost of child abuse as about $3.6 trillion, or 4.2 percent of global GDP. Although this is about 1.9 percent of GDP in high-income countries, it rises to nearly 19 percent in sub-Saharan Africa. A breakdown of the data is given in Table 4.4.

Table 4.5 Cost of reported sexual abuse of children

Region	(1) Total Cost (in UDS billions)	(2) Region Average (% of GDP)	(3) Country Average (% of GDP)
High Income	25.4	0.057	0.066
East Asia & Pacific	3.9	0.023	0.023
Europe & Central Asia	1.1	0.020	0.013
Latin America & Caribbean	4.9	0.065	0.079
Middle East & North Africa	0.2	0.008	0.008
South Asia	0.1	0.002	0.002
Sub-Saharan Africa	1.2	0.051	0.051
World	36.8	0.043	0.046

Sexual abuse is another facet of the overall problem. UNODC figures show 72,000 cases of child sexual assault and rape (almost a quarter of the total), but based on surveys of women, it seems that this is just the tip of the iceberg, with significant adults in children's lives most likely to be the abusers. Using a unit cost for all rape/sexual assault cases of $199,642 and considering only reported cases, the absolute minimum cost of child sex abuse is about $37 billion (0.043 percent of world GDP). For a breakdown of the costs, see Table 4.5.

In the context of violence against children, it is sensible to highlight the practice of early marriage in some cultures. Marriage of emotionally and physiologically immature girls to older men, often against their will, has a number of health implications as well as a higher risk of violence and sexual abuse. For girls under 16 in Nigeria, Cameroon, and Ethiopia, the maternal mortality rates were found to be about six times higher than for mothers ages 20–24. Fifteen percent of all deaths for girls and women ages 10–24 are due to maternal conditions, the leading cause of deaths in this age group.

Early marriage is most prevalent in South Asia; in 2000, 56 percent of all young women were married before they were 18. However, although 41 percent of women ages 45–49 were married by age 15, only 15 percent of women in the 20–24 age range were married this young. This declining trend is the same for all regions. In the countries surveyed, 47 percent of all women ages 45–49 were married by the age of 18 in 2000. If the trend continues, this figure should be 25 percent in 2030.

Figures 4.6 and 4.7 show the percentage of women married at a young age.

We have concentrated on violence against children in the home, but we should not forget that neglect and physical, sexual, and emotional abuse of children also happens in school, in care institutions, in prisons, at work, and in the community.

Violence against Women

Across the world there are a number of harmful traditional practices that constitute violence against women. Examples include female infanticide and prenatal sex selection, early marriage, dowry-related violence, female genital mutilation (FGM), "honor" crimes, and maltreatment of widows. However, there is limited information on many of these practices, with the exception of FGM.

The most common form of violence experienced by women globally is intimate partner violence (IPV), with about 30 percent of women experiencing this in some form during their lifetime. WHO studies conclude that women suffering IPV are 16 percent more likely to have a low-birth-weight child, and they also have a higher risk of contracting sexually transmitted diseases. There are also longer-term consequences for children of abused women: daughters are more likely to be abused by their partners, and sons are more likely to become abusers themselves.

About 16 percent of all homicide victims are women of 15 and over; 43 percent of all female victims are killed by a current or former intimate

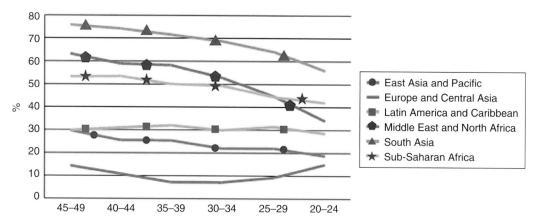

Figure 4.6 *Percentage of women married at 18*

Source: UNICEF (2005)

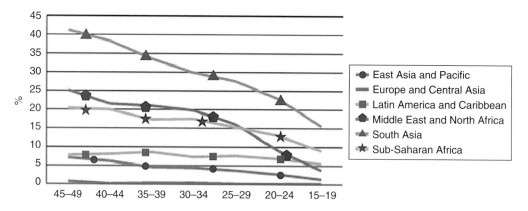

Figure 4.7 *Percentage of women married at 15*

Source: UNICEF (2005)

partner (Stöckel et al., 2013). Using the World Bank classification of regions, we find that the prevalence of intimate partner homicides among all female homicides was highest in high-income countries (56 percent) and lowest in Europe and Central Asia (20 percent).

Using a standard unit cost of $8.44 million per homicide (which may be too high because women's earnings are lower), the global cost of female homicides is estimated at around $105 billion, or 0.12 percent of GDP, as set out in Table 4.6.

Because we have data on the homicides due to IPV from Stöckl et al. (2013), we can also calculate

the cost estimates for female homicides committed by intimate partners: see Table 4.7.

Overall prevalence of nonfatal violence against women is difficult to estimate, but there are figures available for sexual assault and rape. However, reported sexual violence is likely to be only the "tip of the iceberg," most cases are never reported (Palermo et al., 2014). Thus, the figures on sexual violence should be regarded as a very conservative estimate of sexual violence. Much violence – sexual, physical, and emotional – is perpetrated by intimate partners. Revealingly, over half of women in sub-Saharan Africa think

Table 4.6 Cost of female homicide

Region	(1) Total Cost in USD billions	(2) Regional Averages % of GDP
High Income	34.7	0.078
East Asia & Pacific	12.8	0.076
Europe & Central Asia	15.2	0.277
Latin America & Caribbean	23.3	0.309
Middle East & North Africa	1.8	0.067
South Asia	5.7	0.094
Sub-Saharan Africa	11.8	0.511
World	105.3	0.123

Note: WHO (2013b) provides data on deaths due to interpersonal violence by sex and age. We use the ratio of deaths of females age 15 and over to total deaths and apply this ratio to the UNODC (2013) homicide rates to estimate the number of female homicide victims.

Table 4.7 Cost of female homicides by intimate partners

Region	(1) Total Cost in USD billions	(2) Regional Averages % of GDP
High Income	19.3	0.043
East Asia & Pacific	4.1	0.024
Europe & Central Asia	3.1	0.056
Latin America & Caribbean	6.6	0.087
Middle East & North Africa	0.1	0.004
South Asia	2.5	0.041
Sub-Saharan Africa	4.5	0.193
World	40.1	0.047

Note: WHO (2013b) provides data on deaths due to interpersonal violence by sex and age. We use the ratio of deaths of females age 15 and over to total deaths and apply this ratio to the UNODC (2013) homicide rates to estimate the number of female homicide victims and the information from Stöckl et al. (2013) to approximate homicides perpetrated by intimate partners.

their husbands are justified in beating them for such things as arguing or burning the food, while only 37 percent of men agreed that this would be acceptable.

The prevalence of IPV varies widely, as we can see from Figure 4.8. Only 4 percent of women over 15 in high-income countries report it, compared to a high of 28 percent in sub-Saharan Africa.

Assuming 90 percent of women have partners and using a cost of $95,023 for an assault (actually more than double this figure for rape and sexual assault), the total costs of IPV are $4.4 trillion, or 5.2 percent of global GDP, as shown in Table 4.8.

The figure for reported cases of sexual violence, whoever the perpetrator, is $67 billion, or 0.08 percent of global GDP, using a unit cost of $199,642. In both cases, the actual figure is likely to be much higher because of the high level of underreporting (see Table 4.9).

FGM is still widespread in Africa and the Middle East, as shown in Figure 4.9. Although it is outlawed in 26 of 29 countries surveyed, UNICEF estimates that about 100 million women worldwide have undergone FGM and that 30 million girls are at risk over the coming decade. Among women ages 15–49 FGM is almost universal (88 percent or

Table 4.8 Cost of intimate partner assault

Region	(1) Total cost of IPV, USD billions	(2) Regional Averages, % of GDP	(3) Country Averages, % of GDP
High Income	1,360	3.06	2.93
East Asia & Pacific	894	5.29	4.81
Europe & Central Asia	333	6.08	5.81
Latin America & Caribbean	605	8.01	7.65
Middle East & North Africa	286	10.55	10.15
South Asia	600	9.87	9.52
Sub-Saharan Africa	345	14.94	14.28
World	4,423	5.18	8.02

Table 4.9 Cost of reported cases of sexual violence

Region	(1) Total cost, USD billions	(2) Regional Averages, % of GDP	(3) Country Averages, % of GDP
High Income	49,3	0.111	0.112
East Asia & Pacific	5,5	0.033	0.033
Europe & Central Asia	0,8	0.014	0.012
Latin America & Caribbean	8,2	0.109	0.122
Middle East & North Africa	0,3	0.011	0.011
South Asia	1,3	0.022	0.022
Sub-Saharan Africa	1,3	0.056	0.057
World	66,7	0.078	0.066

Source: UNODC (2013).

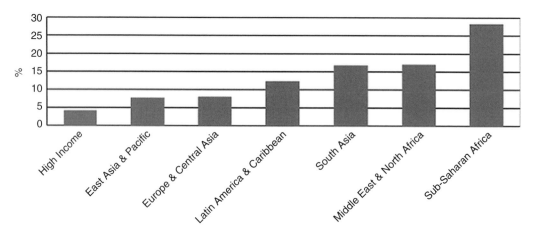

Figure 4.8 *Prevalence rates of IP assault*

Source: Devries et al. (2013).

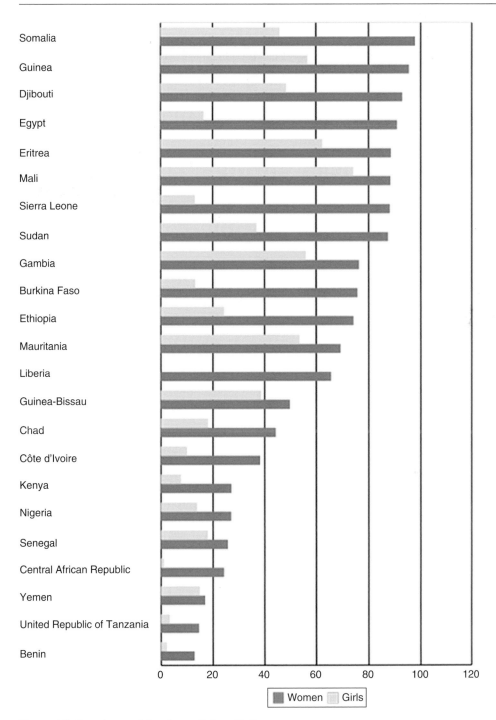

Figure 4.9 *Prevalence of female genital mutilation*
Source: UNICEF, 2013.

Table 4.10 Sectoral shares of development assistance (% of total aid)

Sector	1990–94	1995–99	2000–04	2005–09
Social health	3.26	3.75	4.81	7.70
Education	4.64	4.03	4.79	5.43
Water	5.37	4.67	3.83	4.55
Environment	1.66	1.79	1.47	2.36
Women	0.03	0.08	0.03	0.04
Government/civil society	4.35	7.46	10.59	13.63
Legal/judicial	0.06	0.24	0.52	1.04
Economic transport/communications	13.42	11.02	9.71	10.31
Energy	10.48	7.76	5.29	6.95
Production agriculture	9.82	6.10	4.45	4.47
Industry	8.16	6.41	3.00	2.94
Trade	3.60	1.41	1.18	1.25
Multisector	6.49	5.48	5.49	5.60
Budget support and finance				
Budget support	11.75	21.35	21.24	10.63
Finance, debt	14.62	13.51	15.33	13.60
Humanitarian emergency	1.87	3.68	4.70	5.50
Other	0.48	1.49	4.09	5.03
Total aid (billions current $)	437	612	766	1063

higher) in Somalia, Guinea, Djibouti, Egypt, Eritrea, Mali, Sierra Leone, and Sudan, although in all countries the prevalence rates among girls ages 0–15 are lower than for their mothers. A WHO study shows that women who have undergone FGM suffer more obstetric problems, including higher rates of perinatal death.

Aid Programs Targeted at Reducing Violent Crime or Improving Police and Judicial System Performance

Considerable amounts of aid are directed toward "fragile states" to help stop or prevent civil war and to emergency humanitarian aid, but violent crime, child abuse, and domestic violence are far more pervasive and costly in terms of human welfare. There is, however, great wariness about providing aid to police and other security forces. Tables 4.10 and 4.11 give shares of total development assistance spent in different sectors for five-year periods

from 1990, together with a closer look at the category "Government and Civil Society."

Aid for government and civil society projects has risen sharply to 13.63 percent of the total since the end of the Cold War; within this larger category, legal and judicial aid has increased, but still only to about 1 percent of the total. Projects that have "crime prevention" as one component receive in total only 0.27 percent of funding. The bulk of this goes to postconflict countries and is not directly related to preexisting levels of societal violence. Although it is very difficult to derive reliable figures for benefits of projects of this type, funding for peace-keeping operations and postconflict aid does seem to be modestly cost-effective.

Figure 4.10 plots average "crime prevention" aid for 2008–10 (for each country that received at least some such aid) against the 2008 homicide rate in that country. Both variables are logged to deal with extreme skew. It is evident that however these

Table 4.11 Aid shares (percentages) within the "Government and Civil Society" category, 2000–2010

Administration, policy	48.32	
Government administration		21.39
Economic and development policy/planning		18.66
Public-sector financial management		7.43
Decentralization and support to subnational govt.		0.84
Governance and civil society	25.67	
Government and civil society		22.38
Human rights		2.32
Women's equality organizations and institutions		0.85
Anticorruption organizations		0.12
Civil conflict-related	13.32	
Conflict prevention		5.11
Reintegration and small weapons control		2.18
Security system management and reform		2.54
Land mine clearance		1.71
Postconflict peace building (un)		1.71
Child soldiers (prevention and demobilization)		0.07
Legal and judicial development	10.84	
Legal and judicial development		10.84
Parties, elections, media	1.86	
Elections		1.35
Legislatures and political parties		0.13
Media and free flow of info		0.38

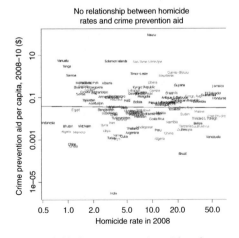

Figure 4.10 *Crime prevention aid and homicide rates*

projects are being allocated, the level of violent crime in the country is not an important consideration. There is no relationship at all between the two variables.

The Return on Investment in Reducing Civil War and Societal Violence

At the outset it has to be stressed that in both cases – civil war violence and societal violence – it is impossible to provide benefit-cost ratios (BCRs) for aid spending that are more than *extremely* conjectural.

For internal conflict, BCRs for a package of interventions that include UN Peacekeeping Operations are between 2 and 7 (depending on discount rates and general conflict prevention or postconflict stabilization). There is limited evidence that aid prevents conflict. Although there is no evidence that aid prevents civil war onset (Hoeffler, 2014), there is some evidence that development aid helps to stabilize postconflict situations. Aid has a positive effect on growth in postwar economies. However, the effect is moderate: an extra 1 percent of aid might increase growth by 0.05–0.1 percent per year.

There are alternative ways to use aid to reduce other forms of violence. Wealthier regions tend to be characterized by lower rates of societal violence, so development is likely to decrease violence with time. In addition to social programs, one of the commonly suggested measures is to criminalize certain forms of violence, but this appears to have a limited effect when it runs counter to social norms. Also, studies on policy interventions have mainly been in high-income countries, where police and the criminal justice system have the institutional capability to be effective. In contrast, in many low-income countries, police corruption, abuse, and simple poor performance appear to be a large part of the problem of societal violence.

In rich countries, targeting resources on "hot spots" and using "problem-oriented policing" appear to have a very low cost, and their BCRs are likely to be high. A similar approach could be very effective in developing countries where police and state authorities are interested in improving performance and where there is sufficient political will. Alcohol consumption is another contributory factor to violence, and a number of cost-effective interventions to make drinking more responsible seem to be possible. Changing permitted alcohol sales times, reducing the density of alcohol outlets, increasing alcohol prices, specific interventions targeted at problem drinkers, and improving drinking environments by encouraging/training service staff to serve alcohol responsibly all seem to be helpful.

The last intervention strategy is, for example, analyzed by Moore et al. (2012). They suggest that randomized controlled trials (RCTs) are feasible to assess the effectiveness of reducing alcohol-related violence. In the UK they matched pairs of 32 licensed premises (pubs, bars, and nightclubs) and in the treatment group they encouraged the enforcement of the existing laws, e.g., not supplying alcohol to already intoxicated customers. This trial study suggests that the incidence of violence decreases by about 10 percent in the control group. The BCR appear to be phenomenal; they cite a cost of the intervention of £600, which prevents roughly one assault, costed at £10,407. This provides a BCR of about 17.

Turning to specific interventions, a number of programs have been assessed to reduce the level of violence against children. Early response of trained social service and welfare officers appear to provide the best BCR, at about 13–14. Home nurse visits to at-risk mothers and newborns also offer a positive BCR, estimated at around 2.75. However, implementation could be difficult in low- and middle-income countries.

Programs to improve parenting skills can also be very cost effective. The best-known is the Positive Parenting Program, or "Triple P," applied in a number of high- and middle-income countries (Prinz et al., 2009). A two-year evaluation in the United States found that in a population of 100,000 children under 8 years of age there were 688 fewer cases of substantiated child maltreatment recorded by child protective services staff, 240 fewer out-of-home placements, and 60 fewer children with injuries requiring hospitalization or emergency room treatment. This has a calculated BCR of 8.74.

On the question of FGM, legal reform appears to have had little impact, and there is no reliable evidence of other specific interventions lowering the prevalence. However, the incidence of FGM has declined in a number of countries with medium to low prevalence rates over the last 15 years; in contrast there has been little reduction in countries with high prevalence of the practice. Prevalence by age is plotted for several countries in Figure 4.11.

Interventions to combat domestic abuse such as the DASH (Domestic Abuse, Stalking, and Honour-Based Violence) risk identification model in the UK and the Duluth model in the United States and elsewhere have not been properly evaluated in terms of their impact.

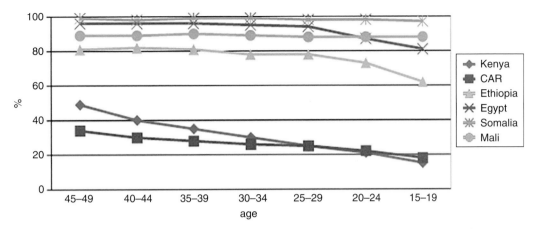

Figure 4.11 *Prevalence of FGM by age*

Source: UNICEF, 2013

Programs aimed at economic empowerment, such as (un)conditional cash transfers and micro-finance programs do not appear to systematically lower levels of violence, although a conditional cash transfer program in Ethiopia increased the chances of girls going to school threefold and reduced their chances of early marriage by 90 percent. Messages promoting the positive aspects of "doing the right thing" have also been successful, but no BCRs are available for any of these interventions.

Targets

As of 2012, there were about 30 active civil conflicts ongoing in 25 countries. Although they account for a relatively small proportion of violent deaths, they can have massive indirect effects. But civil war is probably far less amenable to "treatment" by international aid programs or other policy interventions than are obstacles to development in areas like health and education. So the idea of international targets for levels of civil war is necessarily going to be much more aspirational than operational.

Figure 4.12 shows the regional trends over time for our two types of war, at two levels of intensity for the period 1946 through 2012. The y-axis is the share of countries in the region that were experiencing the type of war in question in the year indicated on the x-axis. A first, encouraging observation is that high intensity wars of both types (center-seeking and autonomist) have been in significant decline in all regions except for Middle East/North Africa. Indeed, proposing a zero target for large separatist wars just means aiming to continue the current state affairs. Second, note that in a number of regions the other types and levels of civil conflict have been in significant decline for most of the post–Cold War period.[4]

We have developed targets for wars of different intensity ("small" being 25–999 killed in combat in a given year) and different objectives (taking over central government or gaining more autonomy for a region). Given the downward trend, we propose a 2030 target of a 20 percent reduction from 2012 levels or a 20 percent reduction in the current trend, if this is larger. Total wars would decline modestly to 17.1 from the 2012 level of 20, but large-scale civil violence would be rare, at only three ongoing conflicts. Tables 4.12–15 show

---

[4] The increase since 2001 in low-level center-seeking wars in Western Europe and North America is entirely due to Armed Conflict Dataset (ACD) coding an "internationalized civil war" between the U.S. and al Qaeda and locating this conflict in the U.S. ACD codes the start of the conflict with 9/11, and then presumably is coding U.S. attacks on al Qaeda abroad since then as part of the same conflict. So the location coding here is not right except for 2001.

Table 4.12 Annual change in percent with war, 1990–2012

Region	Small Aut.	Large Aut.	Small Cen.	Large Cen.
Asia	−0.29	−0.40	−0.40	0.03
SSA	0.05	−0.04	−0.06	−0.28
NA/ME	−0.33	−0.25	−0.01	0.28
LA/Ca	0	0	−0.41	−0.06
E Eur	−0.41	−0.36	−0.20	−0.06

Table 4.13 Percentage of countries with war, actual 2012 and 2030 by trend

	War type							
	Small Aut.		Large Aut.		Small Cen.		Large Cen.	
Region	2012	2030	2012	2030	2012	2030	2012	2030
Asia	16.2	11.3	0	0	5.4	0	5.4	5.9
SSA	6.1	7	0	0	12.2	11.2	4.1	0
MENA	10	4.4	0	0	10	9.8	10	14.8
LA/Ca	0	0	0	0	3	0	0	0
E Eur/FSU	6.9	0	0	0	0	0	0	0

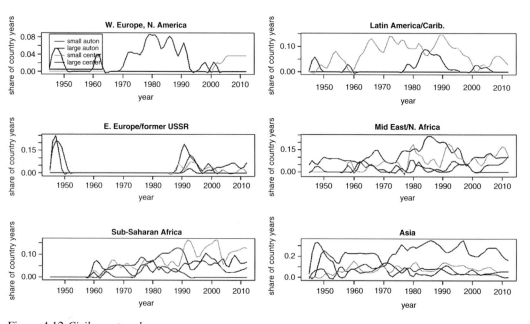

Figure 4.12 *Civil war trends*

Table 4.14 Percentage of countries with war, actual 2012 and 2030 target

| | War type | | | | | | | |
| | Small Aut. | | Large Aut. | | Small Cen. | | Large Cen. | |
Region	2012	2030	2012	2030	2012	2030	2012	2030
Asia	16.2	11.3	0	0	5.4	0	5.4	4.3
SSA	6.1	4.9	0	0	12.2	9.8	4.1	0
MENA	10	4.4	0	0	10	8	10	8
LA/Ca	0	0	0	0	3	0	0	0
E Eur/FSU	6.9	0	0	0	0	0	0	0

Table 4.15 Number of countries with war, actual 2012 and 2030 target

| | War type | | | | | | | |
| | Small Aut. | | Large Aut. | | Small Cen. | | Large Cen. | |
Region	2012	2030	2012	2030	2012	2030	2012	2030
Asia	6	4.2	0	0	2	0	2	1.6
SSA	3	2.4	0	0	6	4.8	2	0
MENA	2	0.9	0	0	2	1.6	2	1.6
LA/Ca	0	0	0	0	1	0	0	0
E Eur/FSU	2	0	0	0	0	0	0	0
total Eur/FSU	13	7.5	0	0	11	6.4	6	3.2

current trends and projected figures using our proposed target.

Moving away from civil conflict, evidence from the UK suggests that child homicides have been reduced by 40 percent over the last 10 years. With 75 percent of all children being murdered by a member of their family, a friend, or an acquaintance, interventions should be targeted mainly at the family. If a reduction of 43 percent could be achieved by 2030, the number of neonatal deaths could be reduced by 745 annually, and there would be 6,370 fewer deaths of children under 14. We propose a zero target for severe physical punishment, with the incidence of less violent punishment halving to 30 percent.

Given large reductions in the incidence of intimate partner violence in the United States, it is feasible to target a halving of the number of women experiencing this by 2030. We also suggest a target of no marriages before the age of 15. Because of the difficulties of reducing the number of young women suffering FGM in high-incidence countries, we suggest an aspirational target of a 50 percent reduction. In societies with lower incidence, an elimination of the practice seems feasible.

Conclusion

Civil war violence is too narrow a category when considering what the next set of international development goals concerned with violence should be. Interpersonal violence in its major forms – homicide and violent assaults, including intimate partner violence, child abuse, and FGM – are far more pervasive than civil war violence and almost surely far more costly in terms of human welfare. If it is the case that the benefit-cost ratio of interventions are at least comparable across these three areas (societal violence, civil war-related costs, and poor governance), then there is a strong case that much more aid should be flowing to programs to address violent crime and abuse.

Summary of Targets and Cost-Benefit Ratios

Target	Example interventions	Studies and context	Reported Cost-Benefit Ratio	Comments
By 2030, reduce the number of countries experiencing large scale wars (1000+ deaths) to 3 or fewer and the number of countries experiencing small scale wars (>1000 deaths) to 14	UN Peace Keeping Operations Increase aid in postconflict zones	Dunne (2012) Hoeffler (2014)	2–7 None reported	Only available as option in limited circumstances Does not prevent onset of civil war conflict
Reduce assaults	Enforcing laws on alcohol consumption	Moore et al. (2012) in UK	17	Small pilot study in the UK, high BCR because existing rules were enforced (i.e., intervention required few resources)
Improve policing	India, Rajasthan: program to improve perception of and actual police performance	Banerjee et al. (2012)	None reported	BRC likely to be high because the program required no additional resources
Improve policing	Bogotá, Columbia	Moncada (2009)	None reported, depending on cost of program BRC could be large	
Reduce infant homicide globally by 43%	UK policies	Time series evidence in this study	None reported	Difficult to establish why homicides of infants fell in the UK
Eliminate severe physical violence as a method of child discipline	Social services Triple P program	WSIPP (2013) in U.S. Prinz et al. (2009) in U.S.	13–14 8.7	Only measured in U.S. – unlikely that developing countries have the capacity to roll out early intervention programs Large RCT in Georgia, U.S., difficult to generalize to low- and middle-income countries
Eliminate all forms of violence against women and girls	DASH, Domestic Abuse, Stalking and Honour Based Violence Duluth Model SASA! Program against Domestic Violence in Uganda Use of TV and Radio Programs, for example Soul City in South Africa	Richards et al. (2008) in UK Corvo et al. (2008) in US World Bank (2014b) World Bank (2014b)	None reported None reported None reported, depending on cost of program BRC could be large None reported, depending on cost of program BRC could be large	No evaluation so far, but BCRs potentially large because DASH requires very few new resources No evaluation so far Rigorous evaluation, large significant impact Large significant impact

(cont.)

(cont.)

Target	Example interventions	Studies and context	Reported Cost-Benefit Ratio	Comments
	Conditional cash transfer program to prevent early marriage in Ethiopia	World Bank (2014a)	None reported, depending on cost of program BRC could be large	Large significant impact
	(Un)conditional cash transfer for female empowerment	World Bank (2014a)	None reported	BRCs likely to be very low or even negative, domestic violence increased after some interventions
	FGM	Meta study by Denison et al. (2009)	None reported, BRCs likely to be (very) low	Most programs are not rigorously evaluated but it appears that very few have any impact on prevalence rates

References

Acevedo, C. 2008. Los costos económicos de la violencia en Centroamérica. Consejo Nacional de Seguridad, San Salvador. Cited in: *Crime and Violence in Latin America: A Development Challenge*. Washington, DC: World Bank, 2011.

Aldy, J. E. and W. K. Viscusi. 2007. Age difference in the value of statistical life: revealed preference evidence. *Review of Environmental Economics and Policy* 1 (2): 241–60.

Altbeker, A. 2005. *The Dirty Work of Democracy: A Year on the Streets with the SAPs*. Johannesburg: Jonathan Ball Publishers.

Banerjee, A., R. Chattopadhyay, E. Duflo, D. Keniston, and N. Singh. 2012. Can Institutions Be Reformed from Within? Evidence from a Randomized Experiment with the Rajasthan Police. NBER Working Paper #17912.

Bhaskar, V and B. Gupta. 2007. India's missing girls: biology, customs, and economic development. *Oxford Review of Economic Policy* 23(2): 221–38.

Bishai, D., Y.-T. Bonnenfant, M. Darwish, et al. 2008. Estimating the obstetric costs of female genital mutilation in six African countries. *Bulletin of the World Health Organization* 88: 281–88.

Chalfin, A. 2014. The economic cost of crime. In: *The Encyclopedia of Crime and Punishment*. Thousand Oaks, CA: Sage Publications, 1–12.

Chauvet, L., P. Collier, and H. Hegre. 2008. The Challenge of Conflicts, Copenhagen Consensus 2008 Challenge Paper, Copenhagen.

Collier, P. and A. Hoeffler. 2004. Conflicts. In: B. Lomborg (ed.), *Global Crises: Global Solutions*, Cambridge University Press.

Corvo, K., D. Dutton, and W. Y. Chen. 2008. Toward evidence-based practice with domestic violence perpetrators. *Journal of Aggression, Maltreatment & Trauma* 16 (2): 111–30.

Das Gupta, M., W. Chung, and L. Shuzhuo. 2009. Evidence for an incipient decline in numbers of missing girls in China and India. *Population and Development Review* 35 (2): 401–16.

Deaton, A. 2010. Instruments, randomization, and learning about development. *Journal of Economic Literature* 48 (2): 424–55.

Denison, E., R. C. Berg, S. Lewin, and A. Fretheim. 2009. Effectiveness of interventions designed to reduce the prevalence of female genital mutilation/cutting Report from Kunnskapssenteret (Norwegian Knowledge Centre for the Health Services) No 25–2009 Systematic Review.

Devries, K.M., J. Y. T. Mak, C. García-Moreno, et al. 2013. The global prevalence of intimate partner violence against women. *Science* 340: 1527–28. Data available at www.sciencemag.org/cgi/content/full/science.1240937/DC1.

Doo-Sub, K. 2004, Missing girls in South Korea: trends, levels and regional variations, *Population* 59(6): 865–78.

Dunne, J. P. 2012. An Economic Analysis of the Challenge of Armed Conflicts. Tewksbury MA: Copenhagen Consensus.

Dutton, D. and K. Corvo. 2006. Transforming a flawed policy: A call to revive psychology and science in domestic violence research and practice. *Aggression and Violent Behavior* 11: 457–83.

Ebenstein, A. Y. 2010. The "missing girls" of China and the unintended consequences of the one child policy. *Journal of Human Resources* 45 (1): 87–115.

Ebenstein, A. Y. and E. J. Sharygin. 2009. The consequences of the "missing girls" of China. *World Bank Economic Review* 23 (3): 399–425.

Ellsberg, M., H. A. Jansen, L. Heise, C. H. Watts, C., and Garcia-Moreno (on behalf of the WHO Multi-country Study on Women's Health and Domestic Violence against Women Study Team). 2008. Intimate partner violence and women's physical and mental health in the WHO multi-country study on women's health and domestic violence: an observational study. *The Lancet* 371: 1165–72.

Fang, X., D. S. Brown, C. S. Florence, and J. A. Mercy. 2012. The economic burden of child maltreatment in the United States and implications for prevention. *Child Abuse & Neglect* 36: 156–65.

Fearon, J. 2008. The rise of emergency relief aid. In: M. Barnett and T. G. Weiss (eds.), *Humanitarianism in Question*. Ithaca, NY: Cornell University Press.

Garcia-Moreno, C., H. A. Jansen, M. Ellsberg, L. Heise, and C. Watts (on behalf of the WHO Multi-country Study on Women's Health and Domestic Violence against Women Study Team). 2006. Prevalence of intimate partner violence: findings from the WHO multi-country study on women's health and domestic violence. *The Lancet* 368: 1260–69.

Hindin, M. J., S. Kishor, and D. L. Ansara. 2008. *Intimate Partner Violence among Couples in 10 DHs countries: Predictors in Health Outcomes*. DHS Analytical Studies No. 18. Calverton, MD: Macro International Inc.

Hoeffler, A. 2014. Can international interventions secure the peace? *International Area Studies Review* 17(1): 75–94.

Human Security Report Project. 2012. *Human Security Report 2012: Sexual Violence, Education, and War: Beyond the Mainstream Narrative*. Vancouver, BC: Human Security Press.

2013. *Human Security Report 2013: The Decline in Global Violence, Evidence, Explanation, and Contestation*. Vancouver, BC: Human Security Press.

Institute for Economics and Peace (IEP). 2014. *The Economic Cost of Violence Containment*. Sydney: Author.

Krug, E. G., L. L. Dahlberg, J. A. Mercy, A. B. Zwi, and R. Lozano. 2002. *World Report on Violence and Health*. Geneva: World Health Organization.

Lacina, B. and N. P. Gleditsch. 2005. Monitoring trends in global combat: a new dataset of battle deaths. *European Journal of Population* 21(2–3): 145–66.

Leung, J. and J. Guria. 2006. Value of statistical life: adults versus children. *Accident Analysis and Prevention* 38 (6): 1208–17.

Londoño, J. L. and R. Guerrero. 1999. *Violencia en América Latina: Epidemiología y Costos*. IDB Working Paper R-375. Washington, DC: IDB.

Mathews, S, N. Abrahams, R. Jewkes, L. J. Martin, and C. Lombard. 2013. The epidemiology of child homicides in South Africa. *Bulletin of the World Health Organization*. 91: 562–68.

McCollister, K. E., M. T. French, and H. Fang. 2010. The cost of crime to society: new crime-specific estimates for policy and program evaluation. *Drug and Alcohol Dependence* 108: 98–109.

Moncada, E. 2009. Toward democratic policing in Colombia? Institutional accountability through lateral reform. *Comparative Politics* 41: 431–49.

Moore, S. C., S. Murphy, S. N. Moore, et al. 2012. *BMC Public Health* 12: 412–28.

National Research Council. 2012. *Deterrence and the Death Penalty*. Washington, DC: The National Academies Press.

Otoo-Oryortey, N. and S. Pobi, Early marriage and poverty: exploring links and key policy issues. *Gender and Development* 11(2): 42–51.

Palermo, T., J. Bleck, and A. Peterman. 2014. Tip of the iceberg: reporting and gender-based violence in developing countries. *American Journal of Epidemiology* 179(5): 602–12.

Patton, G.C., C Coffey, S M Sawyer, et al. 2009. Global patterns of mortality in young people: a systematic analysis of population health data. *The Lancet* 374: 881–92.

Pinheiro, P. S. 2006. *World Report on Violence against Children*. Geneva: WHO.

Pinker, S. (2012). *Better Angels of Our Nature: A History of Violence and Humanity*. London: Penguin Books.

Platteau, J. P. and Z. Wahhaj. 2014. Strategic interactions between modern law and custom. In: V. Ginsburgh and D. Throsby (eds.), *Handbook of the Economics of Art and Culture*, Vol. 2. Amsterdam: Elsevier, pp. 633–78.

Prinz, R. J., M. R. Sanders, C. J. Shapiro, D. J. Whitaker, and J. R. Lutzker. 2009. Population-based prevention of child maltreatment: The US Triple P system population trial. *Prevention Science* 10 (1): 1–12.

Richards, L., S. Letchford, and S. Stratton. 2008. *Policing Domestic Violence*. Oxford: Oxford University Press.

Roman, J. K., T. Dunworth, and K. Marsh. 2010. *Cost-Benefit Analysis and Crime Control*, Washington DC: Urban Institute Press.

Runyan, D. K., V. Shankar, F. Hassan, et al. 2010. International variations in harsh child discipline. *Pediatrics* 126(3): 701–11.

Shepherd, M. 2005. Twenty years of progress in addressing domestic violence: an agenda for the next 10. *Journal of Interpersonal Violence* 20(4): 436–41.

Skaperdas, S., R. Soares, A. Willman, and S. C. Miller. 2009. *The Cost of Violence. Social Development Department*. Washington, DC: The World Bank.

Skogan, W. and K. Frydl, eds. 2004. *Fairness and Effectiveness in Policing: The Evidence*. Washington, DC: National Research Council. National Academies Press.

Stöckl, H., K. Devries, A. Rotstein, et al. 2013. The global prevalence of intimate partner homicide: a systematic review. *Lancet* 382: 859–65.

Straus, M. A., S. L. Hamby, D. Finkelhor, D. W. Moore, and D. Runyan 1998. Identification of child maltreatment with the Parent-Child Conflict Tactics Scales. *Child Abuse & Neglect* 22(4): 249–70.

UN. 2006. *Ending Violence against Women: From Words to Action*. New York: United Nations.

2012. *World Population Prospects: The 2012 Revision*. Excel Tables – Population Data. http://esa.un.org/unpd/wpp/Excel-Data/ population.htm, last accessed 28 April 2014.

UNICEF. 2005. *Early Marriage: A Harmful Traditional Practice*. New York: Author.

2010. *Child Disciplinary Practices at Home: Evidence from a Range of Low- and Middle-Income Countries*. New York: Author.

2013. *Female Genital Mutilation/Cutting: A Statistical Overview and Exploration of the Dynamics of Change*. New York: Author.

2014. *The State of the World's Children 2014 in Numbers: Every Child Counts – Revealing Disparities, Advancing Children's Rights*. New York: Author.

UNODC, United Nations Office on Drugs and Crime. 2013. *Statistics on Homicide, Assault, Sexual Assault and Rape*. https://www.unodc.org/ unodc/en/data-and-analysis/statistics/data.html, last accessed 28 April 2014.

U.S. Department of Health and Human Services (USDHHS), Administration on Children, Youth and Families. 2012. *Child Maltreatment 2012*. Available at http://www.acf.hhs.gov/sites/ default/files/cb/cm2012.pdf, last accessed 10 April 2014.

Viner, R. M., C. Coffey, C. Mathers, et al. 2011. 50-year mortality trends in children and young people: a study of 50 low-income, middle-income, and high-income countries. *The Lancet* 377: 1162–74.

Washington State Institute for Public Policy (WSIPP). 2013. *Benefit-Cost Technical Manual: Methods and User Guide*. (Document No. 13–10–1201b). Olympia, WA: Author. BCR were downloaded from http://www.wsipp.wa .gov/BenefitCost, last accessed March 18, 2014.

WHO. 2009. *Violence Prevention: The Evidence*. Geneva: World Health Organization.

2013a. *Global and Regional Estimates of Violence against Women: Prevalence and Health Effects of Intimate Partner Violence and Non-Partner Violence*. Geneva: World Health Organization.

2013b. *Global Health Estimates (GEH)*.
www.who.int/healthinfo/global_burden_disease/
en/, last accessed April 10, 2014.

WHO Study Group on Female Genital Mutilation
and Obstetric Outcome. (2006). Female
genital mutilation and obstetric outcome: WHO
collaborative prospective study in six African
countries. *Lancet*, 367:1835–41.

World Bank. 2012. *The World Development Report
2012: Gender Equality and Development*.
Washington, DC: Author.

2014a. *The World Development Report 2014:
Risk and Opportunity - Managing Risk
for Development*. Washington, DC:
Author.

2014b. *Voice and Agency: Empowering Women
and Girls for Shared Prosperity*. Washington,
DC: Author.

Zabin, L. S. and K. Kiragu 1998. The health
consequences of adolescent sexual and fertility
behavior in sub-Saharan Africa. *Studies in
Family Planning* 29(2): 210–32.

4.1 Alternative Perspective

S. BROCK BLOMBERG

My purpose in this perspective is to estimate benefit-cost ratios for the various targets proposed by Fearon and Hoeffler. I estimate most of the targets to be in the Fair to Good range. The authors have done a remarkable job in cataloging various forms of violence, their costs, and the benefits of existing programs. However, one notable weakness is the inability to provide systematic BCRs.

If I could obtain estimates of the benefits of reduced violence, the cost of aid, and the elasticity of aid effectiveness on violence, I could estimate the various BCRs, but this is not a simple task. The authors' reluctance to follow this route is understandable because such an exercise may be highly speculative.

Fearon and Hoeffler's estimates of the benefits of a world without violence – 11.9 percent of GDP for low- and middle-income countries – are consistent with what one might expect. I assume that the elasticity of aid effectiveness is similar to that for other areas, reducing poverty and encouraging growth and development, for example. The typical estimate of elasticity is 0.01, but I use both this and a more recent, but still small, estimate of 0.03.

The costs of violence differ dramatically with its type and the region. The welfare costs are largest for child abuse and female violence by intimate partners. Latin America and the Caribbean, the Middle East and North Africa, and sub-Saharan Africa are the areas with the greatest potential for benefits.

The ratio of the cost of aid to the potential benefits is significantly large. Using the authors' measures, the ratio is greater than 30 on average and is as large as 110 in Europe and Central Asia. It is smaller in sub-Saharan Africa and other regions because there is such a significant commitment to aid in these regions. Using the elasticities from the literature, the BCRs fall below 1 for measures to curb violence on a global basis. However, individual regions fare better, particularly Europe and Central Asia and the Middle East and North Africa, where the estimates are between 1 and 3 (Fair).

Looking at each subcategory of violence, BCRs are again relatively small. However, both stemming child abuse and female violence have ratios in the range 3–5 for a conservative elasticity of 0.01 (Fair to Good). For the less-conservative assumption of an elasticity of 0.03, these rise to 10–16.

In the future, it would be valuable for policy makers to adopt the approach that the World Bank and others have taken with regard to certain policies. This approach has been to conduct experiments in targeted areas. If policy makers are really interested in best evaluating these issues, then they can only be really understood using such a methodology. This may be costly and challenging to implement, but it would go a long way to helping our understanding.

4.2 Alternative Perspective

RODRIGO R. SOARES

Because of the difficulties involved, I sympathize with Fearon and Hoeffler's general approach of trying to highlight certain relevant costs rather than coming up with specific cost-benefit ratios. However, I think the discussion would benefit from a slightly different perspective, taking a further step back to define specific issues of paramount importance together with promising interventions because any attempt to paint a broad picture inevitably becomes somewhat fragmented and superficial. Considering which issues could deliver potentially the highest benefits and be tackled by fairly standardized interventions, I believe the focus should be on common crime and violence.

The authors correctly stress that deaths from common crime in societies subject to chronically high levels of violence far outweigh mortality from civil and military conflicts. One point overlooked is the heterogeneous nature of both civil conflicts. In particular, because civil conflicts have political origins, it is difficult to conceive of standardized interventions that would be acceptable to all parties. Addressing common crime, on the other hand, would benefit virtually the entire population of affected countries.

What distinguishes societies subject to chronically high violence is an astonishingly high fatality rate for young men. High levels of common crime seem to be closely connected to socioeconomic conditions and state policy, whereas violence against women and children usually has more of a cultural nature.

We can think of an "equilibrium level" of crime set by balancing the potential supply of criminals with repressive state policies. Most public security policies focus on the latter side of the equation, but interventions with improved socioeconomic conditions and job prospects can also help. Overall costs of crime can be calculated, but from a policy perspective, we should be comparing marginal benefits to marginal costs, for example, the social value of spending an extra dollar to reduce the likelihood of homicides. To assess this, we can use either marginal willingness to pay or contingent valuation, but these methods can still miss some of the most harmful dimensions of the cost of crime, such as the reduction of the quantity and quality of investment in education. There is also a problem with trying to scale numbers from country to country for comparison, which may not be valid.

Against this background, target setting seems a hazardous business. For example, Fearon and Hoeffler's suggestion of a 20 percent reduction in various dimensions of violence seems rather arbitrary, and I would advocate a more focused and conservative approach. Focusing on those countries whose homicide rate is higher than the WHO criterion of 10 per 100,000 for an epidemic seems like a natural starting point. Some local governments in developing countries have substantially reduced levels of fatal violence through a combination of policy efforts, with an unmistakable improvement in citizen security. Bogotá and São Paulo are notable examples.

In summary, my take on this issue is probably much less ambitious than the Copenhagen Consensus would want. The priority, right now, should be the production of high-quality comparable data and the creation of knowledge related to program effectiveness in the area of public security in developing countries.

Data Revolution

The Cost and Benefit of Data Needed to Monitor the Post-2015 Development Agenda

MORTEN JERVEN

Introduction

The UN High-Level Panel (HLP) has called for a data revolution. The world's population should be counted, measured, weighed, and evaluated. This information should be collected, compiled, aggregated, and presented in such a form that it can usefully inform policy makers and citizens in aggregated forms and disaggregated according to region, village, gender, and population group.

There is no automatic connection between having correct information and making the right policy choice. It is tempting to conclude that we have been making wrong decisions because we have not had the right information, but it contains an unstated assumption that the chief constraint in policy making has been a lack of information. That may be a wrong assumption to make, but we will ignore that for a second, as this chapter's primary focus is on *the cost* of data revolution, rather than the benefits of a data revolution.

The simple starting point taken here is that data do have a cost. So, what are the proportions we are talking about? For a start, let us say it costs roughly 1 dollar per capita to conduct a population census. Without a population census there is no baseline estimate, and the statistical office does not have a sampling frame to conduct all other needed surveys and queries. Should we conduct a worldwide population census in 2015 that would cost about $7 billion? If the census were covered entirely by ODA, it would take a quarter of the USAID budget and eat up the combined budgets of Norway and Denmark.

But that may be a conservative estimate. The cost of censuses obviously varies – from 0.40 dollar per capita in India, and 1 dollar per capita in China to the United States' last census that cost $13 billion, or about $42 per head (The Economist, 2011). These censuses form the baseline for most kinds of sampled based surveys to measure per capita trends in social and economic development.

The data revolution will have a considerable cost – yet the cost of data has so far gone missing in the MDG debates. There is a *financial cost* of monitoring, but there is also *opportunity cost* in terms of the competing demands placed on survey capacity. Furthermore, particular indicators have the *behavioral effects* of skewing activities to the completion of a specific indicator and thus away from other nonquantified goals.

The first MDG agenda was an ambitious list of development targets. Arguably, the list was adopted foremost with a view to appease different political stakeholders involved in the policy dialogue. As a result, the initial list of eight goals and 18 targets was drawn up without a clear idea of where the data would come from. It was left to a technical group led by the World Bank to design the 48 indicators. Even today there has been no analysis into how much the provision of these data would have cost and, finally, whether the list that was adopted in 2000 was (a) feasible and (b) the best possible use of current resources.

This chapter aims to shift the discussion in this direction. The proposal put together by the HLP, the post-2015 list, contained 12 goals, 54 targets, and 85 indicators (United Nations, 2013a). At that point, one could have hoped that the list would be narrowed further, but the post-2015 list turned out to be bigger and costlier – the lists are getting longer instead of shorter.[1] A previous and preliminary list of the Open Working Group's Sustainable Development Goals had 16 "focus areas" with 160 targets, although the outcome document finally settled on 17 goals and 169 targets (UN, 2014).

If the call for a "data revolution" is met, it has to be accompanied by a realistic assessment of the costs and benefits of providing the data. The calculation presented here suggests that the additional survey cost of the previous MDG amounted to about $27 billion – or about $1 billion per target. Following that rule of thumb – $1 billion per target – the current suggested list would cost $169 billion. That is more than the annual total spent on ODA – unless the Open Working Group thinks it is a good idea that as much as 10 percent of the total ODA is spent on statistics, then the list of targets will need to be trimmed considerably.

The development community may be repeating a mistake by simply demanding more and better data. The monitoring of specific projects should be tempered by a realistic assessment of the capacity of the statistical office to deliver this information. Although in part the motivation behind the call for a "data revolution" may be about building up the capacity of national statistical offices, there may be unintended consequences. The MDGs agenda identified targets, but gave less thought to where the information should come from. This chapter turns this important development question upside down. Rather than asking: "What kind of development should we target?" the question should be: "What kind of development are we able to monitor?" If official statistics is considered a public good, then just demanding more data, without a clear idea of the cost of providing the good and the effect it may have on the quality of the public good may cause the well-known "tragedy of the commons." Everyone wants more data to measure their own development priority, but no one is willing to bear the cost and responsibility of valid and reliable measurement.

More data is only better data if it contains meaningful information and there are no opportunity

costs to its supply. But most data do have a cost. In particular, survey data are expensive to collect, disseminate, and analyze. How expensive? This chapter first goes through the eight goals and 48 targets that ran to 2015 and calculates the cost of supplying all those data on an annual basis for all measured countries.

Looking toward the future, it would seem prudent to conduct a costing of the second set of MDG goals for post-2015. With an increase in the number of survey measurements necessary, we can expect a larger costing estimate for post-2015 goal measurement (United Nations, 2013a). For the second round, a reassessment of each measurement type will be required, as will a recalculation of the cost estimates to incorporate the changes taking effect in both measurement and overall purpose.

The funding available for MDG measurement is very limited, and every effort must be taken to ensure that the available funding is spent responsibly. This chapter's purpose is to reconcile the existing measurement types within one body of literature, for further study and refinement where necessary. The conclusions reached are intended to be a reference for scholars concerned with MDG feasibility and operationalization.

How Much Would the Previous MDGs Cost?

So, the first question is how much would the first set of MDGs (1990–2015) have cost to measure *if* they actually had been measured? Although you are able to download MDG reports with country data in them, these are not "data" in the strict meaning of the word – it actually means something that is "given" – rather the contents in the MDG dataset are in fact more often projections and estimates. There are more gaps than real observations in the MDG indicator database, and many of those

---

[1] This exercise was conducted in 2014, when the final list of Sustainable Development Goals and the attached targets and indicators was not yet ready.

observations that are actually contained in the database are of dubious quality (Jerven, 2013).

The previous MDGs have been criticized for being scientifically and statistically flawed (Kenny and Sumner, 2011). They have been termed a "faulty yardstick" and considered to be biased because the use of absolute measures adopted by the MDGs did not take into account the relative gains many of these countries made (Vandemoortele, 2009, 356). The underlying reasons for the bias of the indicators themselves have also been called into question, and the apparently arbitrary nature of the indicators has been pointed out (Easterly, 2009).

The "constructive criticism" of the MDGs has tended to focus on calling for inclusion of the number of individuals not represented in the measurement, especially those often left out of surveying mechanisms – street children, institutionalized persons, and so forth (Attaran, 2005) – or more "appropriate" measurements, that, for instance, capture equity and the distribution of income (United Nations, 2013b). The desire to leave no one behind is clearly present, and one central UN document suggests that in the post-2015 agenda inequalities could be addressed through:

> Setting tailored targets and disaggregating data in order to address inequalities within all goals, targets and indicators: Disaggregation of data will help measure the gaps between social and economic groups and identify who is being left behind. Setting targets to reduce these gaps (e.g. in health and education outcomes, in incomes and employment) will ensure that the most deprived are not "left until last." This will further help to focus attention on and address direct and indirect discriminations between groups that underpin inequalities. Data should be disaggregated by at a minimum by age, sex, location, ethnicity, income quintiles and disability.
>
> (United Nations, 2013b, 7)

Seemingly, in the MDG debates only the imagination limits what should be measured. Here, on the contrary, it is suggested that the ambitions in the post-2015 measurement agenda should be tempered by moderation and an appreciation of the resources actually required to supply the data demanded.

How much would the previous MDG data have cost? In order to have any idea of whether infant mortality, access to clean water, or monetary poverty, or any other indicator has increased or decreased, you first need to a have a valid baseline measure. The instrument used for this purpose is a population census. With the subsidiary information collected in a population census you can not only draw direct information used for social and economic development indicators, but you also have a representative sampling frame that can be used to conduct smaller surveys in following years. Reporting on MDG indicators has been done on annual basis, so this means that you would have to have an update of the baseline (a census) every ten years, an annual smaller survey, and more sizeable surveys every five years or so to get reasonably accurate reporting on MDG progress.

According to the best estimates available, the total cost for solely supporting the MDG surveys from 1990 to 2015 would have been $27 billion. Or, just to provide survey data needed to fill the MDG database with annual observations would have cost more than the total amount Denmark spent on ODA from 1995 to 2010.[2]

It should be emphasized that the $27 billion estimate is a proxy costing of monitoring of the original MDG agenda, and not an actual record of the expenditures on MDG monitoring. MDG 1, for instance, requires monitoring of the poverty headcount typically through a Living Standard Measurement Survey.

Although we demand these data to be available, and generally assume that they are, they do not exist for many countries in sub-Saharan Africa. According to one report, 6 of the 49 countries in sub-Saharan Africa have never had a household survey, and only 28 countries have been surveyed in the past seven years. A similar gap in coverage persists in surveys for social indicators, such as

---

[2] According to OECD, QWIDS, Query Wizard for International Development Statistics.

Multiple Indicator Cluster Surveys and Demographic and Health Surveys, and only about 60 countries in the world have vital registrations systems required to monitor basic trends in social indicators (Jerven, 2014a). In other words, monitoring of all indicators in all countries did not take place – partly due to insufficient funds.

Currently, an even more ambitious agenda for data and development is being put forward. This agenda would either widen the gap between the ambitions and realistic achievements, or it will have to mean a dramatic increase in the allocation of development spending toward statistics. I will discuss the costs and benefits of "bad" and "good" data in the following section, but I will first lay out how we reached the estimate costs of the previous MDG and suggest how much the post-2015 data agenda may cost.

Methodology

The total figure was reached by estimating the costs of providing annual data from the most widely used survey methods, in addition to establishing benchmark data with a population census. The estimate has a number of caveats, including, but not limited to:

i. Cost information for surveys is sparse and hard to come by, and in many cases it is purposefully not made public. The costing suggested here relies heavily on guesswork and extrapolation from known costs.

ii. In reaching the estimate we made the crucial and unrealistic assumption that existing statistical capacity in these regions was sufficient to support this survey measurement, and thus:

iii. Administrative costs of running and expanding the statistical capacity would be in addition to this figure suggested here. The number proposed here is closer to a marginal cost of the MDGs. Note that the number also does not take into account the negative costs – such as when other statistical capacity (such as macroeconomic statistics, labor statistics, agricultural statistics) has been depleted, with resources being prioritized toward MDG measurement.

iv. The final estimate is conservative. I picked the lower end of all guesses, but there is also evidence that costs might be much higher. I think the conservative estimate is high enough to make a reconsideration of the data demands in the post-2015 debate necessary.

Broadly speaking, the post-2015 MDGs have more survey requirements in order to be measured properly, and this will result in an increased cost.

To systematically examine the MDGs indicator by indicator, it is first necessary to distinguish between *Administrative* and *Survey* data. In the case of Administrative data – which is defined as readily accessible information that are regularly collected by the governments due to its day-to-day operations – the cost burden is born solely by the governments' existing mechanisms, but collection, aggregation, reporting, and dissemination is still resource demanding. For the purposes of this exercise, the marginal cost of supplying administrative data has not been calculated.

One of the objectives of a data revolution might be to shift the balance in data collection from survey to administrative data – but that would require matching resources on the regular capacity of these offices to handle increased demand for collecting, harmonizing, and disseminating administrative data. By comparison, according to PARIS21 – the Organization for Economic Co-operation and Development (OECD)-based secretariat tasked with oversight on statistical development – $2.3 billion was allocated for statistical development worldwide during the period of 2010–2012 (PARIS21, 2012). If the same annual average amount would have been spent over the 25-year period (1990–2015), it would have amounted to about $19 billion.

In contrast, for the survey data – which is defined as an ad hoc data collection exercise done to fill a specific information demand that may or may not be recurring – there is an active and concerted effort (with a measurable cost) to collect the data for the indicators.

Table 5.1 summarizes these information access categories for each MDG indicator. Whether the

Table 5.1 Indicator list by information access type

Information Access Type	Indicators	Total
Administrative	1.4, 3.3, 7.1, 7.2, 7.3, 7.4, 7.5, 7.6, 7.7, 8.1, 8.2,	21
	8.3, 8.4, 8.5, 8.6, 8.7, 8.8, 8.9, 8.10, 8.11, 8.12	
Survey	1.1, 1.2, 1.3, 1.5, 1.6, 1.7, 1.8, 1.9, 2.1, 2.2, 2.3, 3.1, 3.2	49
	3.3, 4.1, 4.2, 4.3, 5.1, 5.2, 5.3, 5.4, 5.5, 5.6, 6.1, 6.2, 6.3,	
	6.4, 6.5, 6.6, 6.7, 6.8, 6.9, 6.10, 7.8, 7.9, 7.10, 8.13, 8.14,	
	8.15, 8.16	
		60

data is primarily or typically collected from administrative or survey systems does vary from country to country, and as a general rule, in countries with weaker capacity in state administration, data are necessarily drawn from survey sources rather than administrative sources. The objectivity of the data is generally believed to be higher in survey data. It has been well documented that in poor countries data on improvements in – for instance – agricultural production, health, and education tend to be overstated in the administrative data (Jerven, 2013).

In 2008, there were 60 MDG indicators in effect (United Nations, 2008), the majority of them being survey data. Some of them, like schooling (for instance, 2.1, 2.2, 2.3) or health indicators such as mortality and number of births (indicators through 4.1–4.3 and 5.1–5.6) are sometimes provided as administrative data, but they are classified as survey data here because they are phrased as "proportion of ...," which makes reference to a universal, valid population measure. In practice, administrative education, and health data and civil statistics are drawn from medical institutions, line ministries, and official registered births and deaths. When schooling and health has limited reach, only a marginal share of the population is registered in civil registries and only a small proportions of deaths and births are covered by vital statistics systems, these should be considered survey data for all practical purposes. In sum, this leaves

gross domestic product (GDP) growth, share of seats in parliament held by women, data on CO_2 emissions, environmental sustainability (indicators 7.1 through 7.7), and data on global partnerships for development under Goal 8 as administrative goals. The majority of the list's indicators are resource-intensive survey data, which countries in the bracket below $1500 GDP per capita will have a great difficulty in supplying without direct donor interest and funding.

The administrative costs are ignored, and instead the focus is on costing the required surveys and population censuses. These are the most common standardized surveys used to collect development data across the world (detailed descriptions in Appendix B):

1. *Population Census* – As every survey requires a sampling frame, the only way to achieve this is to take an initial census, which would precede the surveys indicated and would need to be updated every ten years.

2. *Living Standards Measurement Study – LSMS* – Created as a way of monitoring policy-based decisions and assessing their effects on a national scale, to better inform policy makers. Administered by the Development Research Group. The standard source of monetary poverty data.

3. *Demographic and Health Surveys – DHS* – The DHS household surveys, focusing on population,

health, and nutrition, is one of the most prolific global household surveys. They are funded by USAID and administered by Measuring DHS.

4. *Core Welfare Indicator Questionnaire – CWIQ* – A prepackaged survey administered by the World Bank that is designed to monitor social indicators globally, with a proven track record in Africa. The CWIQ is developed to show who is, and who is not, benefitting from actions designed to improve social and economic conditions.

5. *Multiple Indicator Cluster Surveys – MICS –* Developed by UNICEF, is meant to work in concert with other survey measurement types (e.g., DHS) to coordinate survey taking. Very adaptable, MICS has seen an increase in usage and awareness in recent years.

A suggestion for the minimum data requirements were as follows:

–   Population census every ten years
–   Demographic and Health Surveys every five years
–   Living Standards Measurement Study every five years
–   Core Welfare Indicator Questionnaire annually

In addition, we wanted to add an annual Multiple Indicator Cluster Survey, but as discussed later, cost data were not available on this survey instrument, and it was therefore not included in our analysis that gave the $27 billion estimate.

The final step was to provide a cost estimate for these surveys. This proved to be quite challenging. Apparently, there has been low demand for the cost of development data, and when attempting to get the financial figures for the different survey types we encountered, we found them to be largely unavailable or undisclosed, indicating an overall lack of transparency. The reasoning for this was generally one of the following:

1. The information is considered sensitive, and thus closely guarded by the survey administrators in

light of the bidding process in the tender for the data collection, and;

2. Financial records were never kept – estimates or exact figures – because of various "in-kind" contributions or the efforts of the domestic governments with whom the survey administrators partner to do their research.

I made full use of the data available to us, adding information from alternate sources and using different methods to help fill in the gaps. As a result, we have arrived at some estimates for the cost of the MDGs' measurement requirements for 1990–2015, and this may serve as a benchmark to project future costs. Although there are caveats to this research, I still maintain some confidence in these "back of the envelope" cost analyses. Of course, with full information on the costs of all the surveys needed, or even better, combined with a full record of funds committed to data collection, we could have had a complete picture of the funds needed versus the funds actually earmarked for data collection.

Results

Because the costs of censuses are based on talking to people and the cost of surveys are based on samples, population size is the key determinant – there are other costs, but these were ignored in the following.[3] Table 5.2 gives a summary of the costing for small, medium, and large countries for the different survey types. The full country list for all 138 countries is found in Appendix C.

The final total cost estimate we reached was approximately $27 billion.

A rule of thumb for census costs in developing countries has been $1 USD per enumerated person; more realistic figures today may be around $3 USD (Virtual Statistical System

---

[3] For example, a country with rugged terrain, with low literacy levels or weak infrastructure would be much more difficult to survey.

Table 5.2 Population survey estimated costs

	Estimated Costs		
	Small Population	Medium Population	Large Population
Population range: (WDI Database, 2014)	1–5 million	5–20 million	20+ million
Census (every 10 years) (VSS, 2014)	$1/person	$2/person	$3/person
LSMS (every 5 years) (Sette, 2008; United Nations, 2005, 534; Randriamamonjy, 2008, 1; United Nations, 2013c)	$0.4 million	$0.9 million	$1.5 million
DHS (every 5 years) (Yansanch, 2000, 771; Rommelmann et al., 2005, 20; WHO, 2009, 2)	$0.8 million	$1 million	$1.2 million
CWIQ (annually) (PARIS 21, 2000, 24; Sette, 2008)	$330,000/year	$500,000/year	$665,000/year
MICS (annually)	Financial data not disclosed. No estimates available.		

[VSS], 2014). As noted in the introduction, censuses may be more expensive for some countries. India and China have had relatively cheap censuses, at about 40 cents and a dollar per capita cost, respectively. By contrast, the censuses in Canada have cost from 16 to 20 dollars per capita since 1991, and in the United States the per capita cost has risen from about 5 dollars in 1970 to 10 in 1980, 13 in 1990, and 23 in 2000 (Yacyshyn and Swanson, 2011, 21). Larger countries, with the exception of India and China, do seem to have more expensive censuses (per capita) than the smaller ones. Presumably this is because in larger countries some parts on the population are harder to reach. In the cost estimation we used the actual costs – which were found for 67 of the countries (the details are available in Appendix B).

As noted, the estimates and the total measurement costs faced some information restrictions.

Measure DHS does not release budgetary information for fear of competitive bidding, despite repeated requests for such cost data.[4] Aside from the total costs of the organization in select years, cost extrapolations are only possible thanks to third-party information (Yansanch, 2000, 771; Rommelmann et al., 2005, 20; WHO, 2009, 2). I have used lower and upper of typical costs of a DHS on small and large countries and used the typical cost for a medium country. The costs of the LSMS are best documented. I have precise country data sometimes (United Nations, 2005, 534). CWIQ's official handbook (administered by the World Bank) lists a cost of $330,000 per study for a sampling of 10,000 households as being the

---

[4] As informed per correspondence by email with Susan McInturff and Martin Vaessen of Measure DHS, January 15, 2014, and January 27, respectively.

norm.[5] However, our research uncovered that the sampling range varied widely – between 3,600 and 77,400 households (International Household Survey Network [IHSN], 2014). Therefore, our adjustments for the CWIQ needed to take into account the uppermost limit of CWIQ sampling size. To do so, I developed an estimated real-world CWIQ cost using these extrapolated samples as guides, finding an upper limit to be $665,000/study (largest populations), a lower limit of the original figure of $330,000/study (smaller populations), and a "middle-of-the-road" estimate of $500,000/study (medium-sized countries). Further cost clarification was not provided after multiple World Bank information requests. Finally, MICS (administered by UNICEF), does not record either a per household cost or a total average cost, even on the level of rough estimates,[6] which makes estimation impossible – so it is excluded, and instead I assumed the cost of having an annual CWIQ would be sufficient.

As indicated in the source tables, I have strived to include known survey/census sampling and cost figures wherever possible. These included 9 CWIQ surveys, 38 LSMS surveys, 6 DHS surveys, and 68 censuses. Please see tables in Appendix D for a detailed breakdown, per country, of our cost estimates for total MDG measurement.

With this rough estimation the total amount overshoots what is currently being earmarked for statistics in development assistance by quite a distance.

The $27 billion amount would be an underestimate for a couple of reasons. First of all, we are inferring observed costs of running a DHS and LSMS in Ghana and Tanzania and projecting that to countries like Sudan and Democratic Republic of Congo which have not yet been measured. There is a reason why some countries are surveyed on a regular basis, although for other countries no data are available. Second, it does not take into account that some data would be missing. Administrative data are not included, and a range of statistics that needs to be collected for calculating GDP is not allowed for in this calculation. Third, and most important, there is no allowance for maintaining the statistical office, training and retaining personnel,

analyzing and disseminating the data, and so forth. There is ample evidence that the MDG agenda has already stretched statistical capacity and strained statistical offices in poor countries (Jerven, 2013). Or, as it was summarized by Richard Manning, formerly of DAC-OECD in a DIIS report (Manning, 2009, 38):

> It is not clear that the expanding number of surveys and data collection exercises has had a positive and sustainable impact on local capacity. It is quite possible that we are in fact seeing a growing mismatch between the multiple demands for monitoring and the ability of local systems to generate credible data. There is a danger that an "MDG Results Industry" could consume a lot of resources to rather little effect.

The new proposed items for the post-2015 list is likely to stretch this gap even further. The post-2015 debate has so far been dominated by what goals and targets are desired, and as of yet there has been less discussion about what can be realistically measured, what kind of indicators might be needed and even less consideration given to who should pay for the measurement. One could take the view that right now the concern should not be "how much does it cost," but rather first determine "what do we need," and then later on figure out "how do we pay for it." I strongly suspect that the latter will be the ad hoc approach taken, but I would not recommend such an approach. The cost of monitoring should be taken into account. It is not the case that all increases in measurement activities are improvements in overall statistical capacity. Provision of data has opportunity costs, and provision of data further has behavioral implications.

---

[5] With a special reference to the CWIQ study, although the World Bank CWIQ handbook listed a 10,000 household study and $330,000 yearly cost, we found household sample averages for medium- and large-sized population countries to be higher and have adjusted our costs accordingly to better represent the reality of the CWIQ surveys previously taken.

[6] As informed per email correspondence and telephone conversation with Tara Moayed of UNICEF, January 30, 2014.

The Benefits of Good Data and Costs of Bad Data

It is not feasible to address, much less quantify in dollars and cents, the potential upside and the potential costs of each and every of the targets in the different focus areas suggested by the Open Working Group. Instead I will suggest a broad typology for thinking through the potential benefits of good data and also the costs of providing bad data.

Benefits of Good Data

An example from fiscal spending in Uganda demonstrates this very clearly. Reinikka and Svensson report that surveys of central government expenditures on primary schools in Uganda between 1991 and 1995 showed that only 13 percent of the funds allocated actually reached the schools. In response, a campaign was started to advertise in local newspapers how much public funding was allocated to the schools, thus enabling local schools to compare these with actual funds received. It was estimated that this intervention reduced graft considerably, and that by 1999, 90 percent of the funds reached their destination (Reinikka and Svensson, 2001). Quality in the production and dissemination of data is crucial to the accountability policy process.

This is a good example of what good data can do. However, it is not really a demonstration of the value of the kind of data on outcomes that is likely to be the core of post-2015 monitoring. It is unlikely that the statistical office will get the necessary funds and political support needed to play this role in the Measurement Agenda in the MDGs. Most indicators are geared toward monitoring very specific progress. Governments need disaggregated, high frequency data linked to subnational units of administrative accountability. The emphasis in the MDG is on global standards and international comparability. An emphasis on monitoring progress toward an indicator that supports donor goals X, Y, and Z essentially lowers the fungibility of the statistics. That means that one may ask, and even fund a statistical office to monitor a specific indicator, but it is not certain that this indicator is useful for the line ministry of the country concerned.

A good example is poverty headcount data. These data are essential for the international discourse on the relationship between poverty, and economic growth and feeds into long-term strategic plans and documents. Day-to-day policy work at the Ministry of Finance and Central Banks, who do work that is essential for long-term trends in poverty, need monthly data on employment and inflation. Of course, the poverty data make important baselines and put short-term policy planning into a long-term perspective, but the danger is that donor preference for global comparable data comes at the expense of reliable high-frequency data needed at the local level.

I suggest that the list of indicators should be designed with the view of directly increasing accountability. One way of assessing indicators and the data needs is not only the costing of them, but also the likelihood that they can be provided in a timely fashion and in a form that makes the data useable for domestic policy making and that are digestible for media and civil society to further policy debates and accountability.

Costs of Bad Data

Increase in demand for data may also be met by a supply of inferior data. This is very likely if two things coincide: (1) if the demand for data overshoots supply of reliable data, and (2) if the data provision process is incentivized through rewards and punishments for meeting certain targets. Unfortunately, very often both of these conditions were met in the previous MDG agenda.

There is evidence showing that "results-based financing can have undesirable effects, including motivating unintended behaviors, distortions (ignoring important tasks that are not rewarded with incentives), gaming (improving or cheating on reporting rather than improving performance), widening the resource gap between rich and poor, and dependency on financial incentives" (Oxman and Fretheim, 2009, 70).

This is why one needs to be careful in responding to calls for increased "accountability" in measurement and "paying for results" to achieve the

MDGs. This will be harmful if one does not take into account the fundamental weaknesses of the evidence and the fragility of the statistical infrastructure that is tasked with providing proof of the targets being met or not (Jerven, 2013, 2014b).

Sandefur and Glassman (2013) present a very clear case of the potential pitfalls of incentivizing data. They look at Kenyan education data. The Ministry of Education's administrative data indicate a steady increase in primary enrollment rates, and furthermore that there is a big jump upward in 2003. In 2003 Kenya abolished all school fees in primary schools. They compare these administrative data with survey data that paint a very different picture. Figures from the Kenyan National Bureau of Statistics (KNBS) and the Demographic and Health Survey (DHS) show enrollment rates that are completely flat over the same time period.

Why did administrative data differ so much from survey data? The key difference is administrative data are collected from school administrators, whereas the survey data is collected from heads of households in surveys. Sandefur and Glassman argue that when the Ministry of Education abolished primary school fees, it changed the incentives for truthful reporting by head teachers. Schools get allocated more teachers and more funding if they report more pupils, and therefore schools have an incentive to exaggerate their numbers.

The same problem applies to vaccination programs and fertilizer projects (Jerven, 2013).

The Cost and Benefit of the Post-2015 Agenda

It has been challenging to come up with a cost of the MDGs *if* they would have been properly measured with valid baselines and reliable annual data updates. It is even more hazardous to venture a guess of what the potential cost of data for the post 2015 list would be. The rule of thumb suggested here would be about $1 billion per target.

The best guess, judging from the list currently being discussed by the Open Working Group (OWG), would be about 169 targets – compared to 28 targets in the previous MDG agenda. The roughest way of estimating a cost is to assume a proportional increase in costs. In some areas

providing more indicators may have lower marginal costs once a baseline and annual survey capacity has been set up. On the other hand, surveying in completely new areas – such as to generate data for governance indicators or providing regionally disaggregated data – may result in higher-than-proportional costs.

In the costing of the 28 MDG targets it was assumed that you only needed a population census, a household budget survey every five years, a demographic health survey every five years, and an annual survey to update on basic health, education, and living standard metrics. The 169 new targets also include areas such as agriculture, industry, and employment (UN, 2014). To ensure validity and reliability in measurement, one would need agricultural censuses and economic censuses with annual surveys of the labor force, industrial, and agricultural sectors. There are furthermore indicators that mention industrial share in GDP and the pace of economic growth (7 percent) – with the well-known measurement problems of GDP (Jerven, 2013) – and in particular the largely unmeasured informal economy, such as unrecorded activities in construction, transport, and trade sectors. There are very expensive and time-consuming data requirements that need to be fulfilled for the post-2015 agenda.

Assuming constant marginal cost may indeed be an understatement, as the basic capacity of the statistical offices would have to be greatly expanded to collect, collate, aggregate, disaggregate, analyze, and disseminate all these new statistical priorities.

Part of the attractiveness of the data revolution is, of course, that it is believed and hoped that technological innovation may enable cheaper, more frequent, and more refined data. I think that this is true for some very specific areas. But typically big data innovations benefit from already existing information structures and makes use of algorithms to analyze patterns in passive data exhaust. Google Flue Trends is the prime example, and although their data have been cheaper and timelier, the data have also been off and incompatible with administrative structures (Harford, 2014). Therefore it is currently unclear what direct benefits big data can have for MGD monitoring – and

Table 5.3 $1 billion per target rule

# Targets	% Share of ODA	# Danish ODA Budgets
5	0.2	2
10	0.5	4
20	1.0	7
50	2.5	18
100	4.9	36
150	7.4	54
200	9.9	71
250	12.3	89

more important for this exercise. For most low-income countries to benefit, it would require substantial investment in data infrastructure and human capital to make such a change. In sum, it seems most prudent to assume similar costs for the future.

If 28 targets from MDGs cost $27 billion, 169 targets would roughly amount to $170 billion for the 2015–2030 MDG round. That is a fairly big number. It is close to the annual global total spent on ODA in any recent year. It thus seems that the emphasis on measurement in the post-2015 agenda needs a radical change. Are development donors prepared to commit more than one annual ODA budget to measure the effect of development efforts? In 2013 the ODA, as reported by OECD, was $135 billon, and the Danish ODA was $2.8 billion. Table 5.3 uses the $1 billion per target rule and works out some ratios to be spent on measurement under different scenarios.

The real question is – if we are serious about actually measuring the targets – how much do we want to spend on data? At 169 targets, we are looking at spending about 8 percent of all the ODA in the period 2015–2030 on getting data – or 60 times what Denmark spends on aid annually.

To put this in perspective, one could consider what other operations normally spend on statistics or measuring the effect of their activities. Small volunteer charity organizations, like a soup kitchen, will in all likelihood have no impact measurement budget. The organization would contend that giving out soup is a good thing, but it does not have the mandate or capacity to measure how many hungry people there were before the soup kitchen, or even how many of these hungry people the soup kitchen feeds. Nation-states have different measurement requirements because there need to be decisions not only on decreasing or reducing capacity, but also some idea of what total desirable capacity is needed for schools, hospitals, and food production. Countries like the centrally planned economies probably spent a large share on statistics – we do not have complete information on budgets for these statistical offices, but for a comparison Statistics Norway had a budget of 733 million NOK in 2013. This compares to a total government budget of 324 billion NOK – or about 0.2 percentage. Thus, if the post-2015 measurement agenda is about as willing as the Norwegian state to spend on statistics, it should recommend and prioritize 5 targets, not 169.

It is simply not realistic nor desirable that such a large share of the aid budget be spent on measurement. An improvement in measurement would have to go through a gradual expansion in the capacity of national institutions, although large funds for ad hoc measurement is unlikely to have lasting long-term benefits, but very likely to have immediate negative trade-offs. It is absolutely certain that 169 targets would not be measured appropriately. It is very likely that success and failure in the post-2015 agenda will be measured with deficient and bad data unless the list of targets is radically shortened.

Conclusions

In the 1990–2015 MDG database there were more gaps than observations. The previous agenda suffered from a mismatch between ambition in monitoring and ability in measurement. I have suggested that the previous MDG agenda could have cost something in the vicinity of $27 billion just in marginal survey cost. It does not take into account the needs for statistical capacity building or the cost of providing administrative data. The post-2015 agenda might be end up being much more expensive.

The potential benefits of more data and better data should be weighed against the very real cost of providing statistics. This is not only a question of sheer financial cost. There are also important opportunity costs. If resources at a statistical office are pulled from regular reporting to government institutions toward filling gaps in the global monitoring database, increases in financial funds available for specific measurement projects may actually have unintended negative consequences for the country-level capacity to formulate and monitor independent policy.

What would be the benefit if they used an extra $27 billion to get good data in the previous agenda? Or would the benefits of revolutionizing the data supply for the post 2015 period outweigh an allocation of $75 billion? I hazard the guess that the cost-to-benefit ratio is below 1, and that therefore the data revolution as currently envisaged is a bad idea.

Appendix A

Official list of MDG indicators
(United Nations 2008)

Millennium Development Goals (MDGs)	
Goals and Targets (from the Millennium Declaration)	Indicators for Monitoring Progress
Goal 1: Eradicate extreme poverty and hunger	
Target 1.A: Halve, between 1990 and 2015, the proportion of people whose income is less than one dollar a day	1.1 Proportion of population below $1 (PPP) per day[a] 1.2 Poverty gap ratio 1.3 Share of poorest quintile in national consumption
Target 1.B: Achieve full and productive employment and decent work for all, including women and young people	1.4 Growth rate of GDP per person employed 1.5 Employment-to-population ratio 1.6 Proportion of employed people living below $1 (PPP) per day 1.7 Proportion of own-account and contributing family workers in total employment
Target 1.C: Halve, between 1990 and 2015, the proportion of people who suffer from hunger	1.8 Prevalence of underweight children under five years of age 1.9 Proportion of population below minimum level of dietary energy consumption
Goal 2: Achieve universal primary education	
Target 2.A: Ensure that, by 2015, children everywhere, boys and girls alike, will be able to complete a full course of primary schooling	2.1 Net enrollment ratio in primary education 2.2 Proportion of pupils starting grade 1 who reach last grade of primary 2.3 Literacy rate of 15- to 24 year-olds, women and men
Goal 3: Promote gender equality and empower women	
Target 3.A: Eliminate gender disparity in primary and secondary education, preferably by 2005, and in all levels of education no later than 2015	3.1 Ratios of girls to boys in primary, secondary, and tertiary education 3.2 Share of women in wage employment in the nonagricultural sector 3.3 Proportion of seats held by women in national parliament
Goal 4: Reduce child mortality	
Target 4.A: Reduce by two-thirds, between 1990 and 2015, the under-five mortality rate	4.1 Under-five mortality rate 4.2 Infant mortality rate 4.3 Proportion of 1-year-old children immunized against measles
Goal 5: Improve maternal health	
Target 5.A: Reduce by three-quarters, between 1990 and 2015, the maternal mortality ratio	5.1 Maternal mortality ratio 5.2 Proportion of births attended by skilled health personnel
Target 5.B: Achieve, by 2015, universal access to reproductive health	5.3 Contraceptive prevalence rate 5.4 Adolescent birthrate 5.5 Antenatal care coverage (at least one visit and at least four visits) 5.6 Unmet need for family planning
Goal 6: Combat HIV/AIDS, malaria, and other diseases	
Target 6.A: Have halted by 2015 and begun to reverse the spread of HIV/AIDS	6.1 HIV prevalence among population aged 15–24 years 6.2 Condom use at last high-risk sex

(cont.)

(cont.)

Millennium Development Goals (MDGs)	
Goals and Targets (from the Millennium Declaration)	Indicators for Monitoring Progress
	6.3 Proportion of population ages 15–24 years with comprehensive correct knowledge of HIV/AIDS
	6.4 Ratio of school attendance of orphans to school attendance of nonorphans ages 10–14 years
Target 6.B: Achieve, by 2010, universal access to treatment for HIV/AIDS for all those who need it	6.5 Proportion of population with advanced HIV infection with access to antiretroviral drugs
Target 6.C: Have halted by 2015 and begun to reverse the incidence of malaria and other major diseases	6.6 Incidence and death rates associated with malaria
	6.7 Proportion of children under 5 sleeping under insecticide-treated bednets
	6.8 Proportion of children under 5 with fever who are treated with appropriate antimalarial drugs
	6.9 Incidence, prevalence, and death rates associated with tuberculosis
	6.10 Proportion of tuberculosis cases detected and cured under directly observed treatment short course
Goal 7: Ensure environmental sustainability	
Target 7.A: Integrate the principles of sustainable development into country policies and programs and reverse the loss of environmental resources	7.1 Proportion of land area covered by forest
	7.2 CO_2 emissions, total, per capita and per \$1 GDP (PPP)
	7.3 Consumption of ozone-depleting substances
Target 7.B: Reduce biodiversity loss, achieving, by 2010, a significant reduction in the rate of loss	7.4 Proportion of fish stocks within safe biological limits
	7.5 Proportion of total water resources used
	7.6 Proportion of terrestrial and marine areas protected
	7.7 Proportion of species threatened with extinction
Target 7.C: Halve, by 2015, the proportion of people without sustainable access to safe drinking water and basic sanitation	7.8 Proportion of population using an improved drinking water source
	7.9 Proportion of population using an improved sanitation facility
Target 7.D: By 2020, to have achieved a significant improvement in the lives of at least 100 million slum dwellers	7.10 Proportion of urban population living in slums[b]
Goal 8: Develop a global partnership for development	
Target 8.A: Develop further an open, rule-based, predictable, nondiscriminatory trading and financial system Includes a commitment to good governance, development, and poverty reduction – both nationally and internationally	*Some of the indicators listed below are monitored separately for the least developed countries (LDCs), Africa, landlocked developing countries and small island developing states.*
Target 8.B: Address the special needs of the least developed countries Includes: tariff and quota free access for the least developed countries' exports; enhanced program of debt relief for heavily indebted poor countries (HIPCs) and cancellation of official bilateral debt; and more generous ODA for countries committed to poverty reduction	Official development assistance (ODA) 8.1 Net ODA, total and to the least developed countries, as percentage of OECD/DAC donors' gross national income
	8.2 Proportion of total bilateral, sector-allocable ODA of OECD/DAC donors to basic social services (basic education, primary health care, nutrition, safe water, and sanitation)
Target 8.C: Address the special needs of landlocked developing countries and small island developing states (through the Programme of Action for the Sustainable Development of Small Island Developing States and the outcome of the twenty-second special session of the General Assembly)	8.3 Proportion of bilateral official development assistance of OECD/DAC donors that is untied
	8.4 ODA received in landlocked developing countries as a proportion of their gross national incomes
	8.5 ODA received in small island developing states as a proportion of their gross national incomes

(cont.)

(cont.)

Millennium Development Goals (MDGs)	
Goals and Targets (from the Millennium Declaration)	Indicators for Monitoring Progress
Target 8.D: Deal comprehensively with the debt problems of developing countries through national and international measures in order to make debt sustainable in the long term	**Market access** 8.6 Proportion of total developed country imports (by value and excluding arms) from developing countries and least developed countries, admitted free of duty 8.7 Average tariffs imposed by developed countries on agricultural products and textiles and clothing from developing countries 8.8 Agricultural support estimate for OECD countries as a percentage of their gross domestic product 8.9 Proportion of ODA provided to help build trade capacity **Debt sustainability** 8.10 Total number of countries that have reached their HIPC decision points and number that have reached their HIPC completion points (cumulative) 8.11 Debt relief committed under HIPC and MDRI Initiatives 8.12 Debt service as a percentage of exports of goods and services
Target 8.E: In cooperation with pharmaceutical companies, provide access to affordable essential drugs in developing countries	8.13 Proportion of population with access to affordable essential drugs on a sustainable basis
Target 8.F: In cooperation with the private sector, make available the benefits of new technologies, especially information and communications	8.14 Fixed-telephone subscriptions per 100 inhabitants 8.15 Mobile-cellular subscriptions per 100 inhabitants 8.16 Internet users per 100 inhabitants

The Millennium Development Goals and targets come from the Millennium Declaration, signed by 189 countries, including 147 heads of State and Government, in September 2000 (http://www.un.org/millennium/declaration/ares552e.htm) and from further agreement by member states at the 2005 World Summit (Resolution adopted by the General Assembly – A/RES/60/1, http://www.un.org/Docs/journal/asp/ws.asp?m=A/RES/60/1). The goals and targets are interrelated and should be seen as a whole. They represent a partnership between the developed countries and the developing countries "to create an environment – at the national and global levels alike – which is conducive to development and the elimination of poverty."

[a] For monitoring country poverty trends, indicators based on national poverty lines should be used, where available.

[b] The actual proportion of people living in slums is measured by a proxy, represented by the urban population living in households with at least one of the four characteristics: (a) lack of access to improved water supply; (b) lack of access to improved sanitation; (c) overcrowding (three or more persons per room); and (d) dwellings made of nondurable material.

Appendix B

This Appendix presents a summary of the principal survey types encountered, a brief description of their origins and administration, and a selection of some of the questions typically asked of respondents. Additionally, costing and logistical information (where possible) is included, as well as admissions of estimation where it was deemed both necessary and practical – for example, our extrapolation of CWIQ costs is based on known sampling sizes of past CWIQ surveys.

Demographic and Health Surveys – DHS

The Demographic and Health Surveys (DHS) are nationally representative household surveys that provide data for a wide range of monitoring and impact evaluation indicators in the areas of population, health, and nutrition (Tables 5.4 and 5.5). They are funded by USAID and administered by Measuring DHS. They are performed in one of two varieties:

1.) *Standard:* Have a large sample size (5,000–30,000 household units) and are performed every five years to allow data comparison.
2.) *Interim:* A much smaller, varying sample of households and is meant to be supplemental to the standard survey. Performed at the discretion of Measuring DHS/USAID (Measure DHS 2014).

Core Welfare Indicator Questionnaire – CWIQ

An "off-the-shelf" survey set administered by the World Bank, the CWIQ uses a structured questionnaire and probability-based samples (Tables 5.6

Table 5.4 DHS Survey question topic examples

Anemia	Infant/Child Mortality
Child Health	Malaria
Domestic Violence	Maternal Health
Education	Fertility and Fertility Preferences
Environmental Health	Gender/Domestic Violence
Family Planning	HIV Knowledge/Attitudes
Female Genital Cutting	HIV Prevalence

and 5.7). Developed jointly by the World Bank with UNDP and UNICEF, the CWIQ is designed to monitor social indicators in Africa on an annual basis. The CWIQ is developed to show who is, and who is not, benefitting from actions designed to improve social and economic conditions. The CWIQ collects (1) indicators of household well-being, and (2) indicators of access, usage, and satisfaction with community and other basic services. It draws extensively from market research methodologies to monitor development objectives. Leading indicators play a major role in the CWIQ measurement style, especially in regard to economic factors (World Bank, 2014a).

Living Standards Measurement Study – LSMS (Table 5.8 and 5.9)

The Living Standards Measurement Study (LSMS) and the Living Standards Measurement Study-Integrated Surveys on Agriculture (LSMS-ISA) were

Table 5.5 Summary of the DHS Survey's general logistics

	Demographic & Health Surveys DHS
Number of households surveyed	Between 5,000 and 30,000
Cost per household	Per Participant, as only women of a certain age are targeted in this survey = $19.57
Total cost	Between $0.8 and $1.2 million (best estimate, as DHS costs are not released on a country-to-country basis)[a]
Survey time	18–20 months

Sources: (Rommelmann et al., 2005, 20; WHO, 2009, 2; Yansanch, 2000, 771).

[a] As informed per correspondence by email with Susan McInturff and Martin Vaessen of Measure DHS, January 15, 2014, and January 27, respectively.

Table 5.6 CWIQ Survey question topic examples

Household roster (all de jure household members)
Children roster (less than or equal to 5 years old)
Household and other amenities
Assets
Consumption correlates

Table 5.7 Summary of CWIQ Survey's general logistics

Core Welfare indicator Questionnaires	
CWIQ	
Number of households surveyed	1000 (Pilot) –> 10,000 (2nd Year)
Cost per household	$54 (Pilot) –> $33 (2nd Year)
Total cost	$54,000 (Pilot) –>$330,000 to $665,000 (estimated maximum, further information not available)
Survey Time	2–3 months

Source: PARIS 21, 2000, 24; Sette, 2008.

Table 5.8 LSMS Survey question topic examples

Household Residents	Monetary Assets
Head of household information	Land Ownership
Dwelling information	Animals Owned
Rent and other household costs	Farming Equipment owned
Nutrition	Businesses invested in/started
Sources of Income	Appliances owned/ rented
Employment	Vehicles owned/rented

Table 5.9 Summary of LSMS Survey's general logistics

Living Standards & Measurement Surveys	
LSMS	
Number of households surveyed	3,200
Cost per household	$170
Total cost	Between $0.4 and $1.5 million
Survey Time	2 Years

Source: Randriamamonjy, 2008, 1; Sette, 2008; United Nations, 2005; United Nations 2013c.

established by the Development Research Group (DECRG) to explore ways of improving the type and quality of household data collected by statistical offices in developing countries. The goal is to foster increased use of household data as a basis for policy decision making. The program is designed to assist policy makers in their efforts to identify how policies could be designed and improved to positively affect outcomes in health, education, economic activities, housing, and utilities (World Bank, 2014b).

Table 5.10 MICS Survey question topic examples

Births/Deaths	Sanitation Facilities
Primary school enrollment	Fresh/safe water access
HIV prevalence/infection rate	Dehydration issues
Learning support/funding	Vaccination data
Breastfeeding information	Pneumonia rates
Child growth rates	Malaria Rates
Weight related information	Polio Rates

Table 5.11 Summary of MICS Survey's general logistics

Multiple Indicator Cluster Surveys	
MICS	
Number of households surveyed	10,000[a]
Cost per household	Data not calculated by UNICEF
Total cost	Data not calculated by UNICEF
Survey Time	One year per survey

Source: ChildInfo, 2014; UNICEF, 2014.

[a] As informed per email correspondence and telephone conversation with Tara Moayed of UNICEF, January 30, 2014.

Multiple Indicator Cluster Surveys – MICS (Table 5.10 and 5.11)

The MICS survey tools were developed by UNICEF after consultations with relevant experts from various UN organizations as well as with interagency monitoring groups. UNICEF works closely with other household survey programs, in particular the Demographic and Health Surveys (DHS), to harmonize survey questions and modules and to ensure a coordinated approach to survey implementation, with the objective to provide comparability across surveys and to avoid duplication of efforts. The survey questionnaires are modular tools that can be adapted to the needs of the country. MICS surveys are typically carried out by governments, with the support and assistance of UNICEF and other partners, the makeup of which varies depending on which country is being surveyed. Technical assistance and training for the surveys is provided through a series of regional workshops where experts from developing countries are trained on various aspects of MICS (UNICEF, 2014).

Appendix C

Table 5.12 MDG time period (1990–2015) overall costs, small country (0–5 m)

São Tomé and Príncipe	$14.63 M
Albania	$56.25 M
Armenia	$16.43 M
Bahrain	$17.45 M
Barbados	$14.82 M
Belize	$14.9 M
Bhutan	$15.73 M
Bosnia and Herzegovina	$71.28 M
Botswana	$84.85 M
Cape Verde	$15.24 M
Central African Republic	$23.3 M
Comoros	$15.69 M
Congo, Rep.	$22.92 M
Costa Rica	$21.45 M
Croatia	$45.75 M
Djibouti	$22.01 M
East Timor	$22.18 M
Equatorial Guinea	$15.72 M
Fiji	$28.25 M
Gabon	$17.52 M
Gambia	$26.25 M
Georgia	$23.27 M
Guinea-Bissau	$17.58 M
Guyana	$24.79 M
Jamaica	$2814.48 M
Kosovo	$44.7 M
Kuwait	$20.75 M
Latvia	$24.25 M
Lebanon	$23.1 M
Lesotho	$14.38 M
Liberia	$20.15 M
Lithuania	$20.22 M
Macedonia, FYR	$52.25 M
Maldives	$14.93 M
Mauritania	$21.84 M
Mauritius	$16.83 M
Moldova	$20.15 M
Mongolia	$19.84 M
Montenegro	$15.49 M
Namibia	$206.25 M
Panama	$50.91 M
Samoa	$14.63 M
Suriname	$21.65 M
Swaziland	$18.13 M
Trinidad and Tobago	$180.25 M
Uruguay	$21.04 M
West Bank and Gaza	$31.45 M

Table 5.13 MDG time period (1990–2015) overall costs, medium country (5–20 m)

Azerbaijan	$26.21 M
Belarus	$60.11 M
Benin	$41.05 M
Bolivia	$122.25 M
Bulgaria	$49.21 M
Burkina Faso	$86.34 M
Burundi	$61.65 M
Cambodia	$37.75 M
Chad	$82.25 M
Chile	$86.25 M
Côte d'Ivoire	$98.22 M
Cuba	$67.33 M
Dominican Republic	$63.36 M
Ecuador	$83.95 M
El Salvador	$47.44 M
Eritrea	$46.77 M
Guatemala	$68.25 M
Guinea	$68.06 M
Haiti	$38.25 M
Honduras	$53.99 M
Jordan	$47.52 M
Kazakhstan	$34.4 M
Kyrgyz Republic	$44.58 M
Lao PDR	$48.83 M

Libya	$46.87 M
Malawi	$47.68 M
Mali	$28.55 M
Nicaragua	$45.64 M
Niger	$89.5 M
Papua New Guinea	$47.35 M
Paraguay	$42.25 M
Rwanda	$64.85 M
Senegal	$77.15 M
Serbia	$53.61 M
Sierra Leone	$36.85 M
Somalia	$63.03 M
South Sudan	$220.25 M
Tajikistan	$50.17 M
Togo	$48.82 M
Tunisia	$65.36 M
Turkmenistan	$42.94 M
United Arab Emirates	$58.25 M
Zambia	$78.55 M
Zimbabwe	$54.25 M

Table 5.14 MDG time period (1990–2015) overall costs, large country (20+ m)

Afghanistan	$118.1 M
Algeria	$94.1 M
Angola	$430.1 M
Argentina	$276.62 M
Bangladesh	$114.1 M
Brazil	$1844.8 M
Cameroon	$160.3 M
China	$2037.26 M
Colombia	$316.33 M
Congo, Dem. Rep.	$424.33 M
Egypt, Arab Rep.	$78.1 M
Ethiopia	$576.35 M
Ghana	$134.04 M
India	$746.51 M
Indonesia	$1511.29 M
Iran, Islamic Rep.	$170.1 M

Iraq	$233.99 M
Kenya	$180.1 M
Korea, Dem. Rep.	$178.68 M
Korea, Rep.	$344.1 M
Madagascar	$163.86 M
Malaysia	$152.1 M
Mexico	$530.1 M
Morocco	$220.55 M
Mozambique	$189.66 M
Myanmar	$147.1 M
Nepal	$191.55 M
Nigeria	$1824.93 M
Pakistan	$1101.64 M
Peru	$206.88 M
Philippines	$610.34 M
Poland	$261.36 M
Romania	$177.2 M
Russian Federation	$889.32 M
Saudi Arabia	$199.83 M
South Africa	$398.25 M
Sri Lanka	$152.07 M
Sudan	$253.27 M
Syrian Arab Republic	$164.5 M
Tanzania	$162.96 M
Thailand	$430.81 M
Turkey	$474.08 M
Uganda	$149.02 M
Ukraine	$303.66 M
Uzbekistan	$208.76 M
Venezuela, RB	$176.1 M
Vietnam	$99.12 M
Yemen, Rep.	$166.1 M

Appendix D

Table 5.15 CWIQ known samples

Country	#Households surveyed*	Cost per Household	Cost (x25 for MDG)
	CWIQ Known Samples*		
Burkina Faso	9,000	Medium, ∴ $50/household	**$450,000**
Ghana	14,700	Large, ∴ $66.5/household	**$977,550**
Lesotho	5,200	Small, ∴ $33/household	**$171,000**
Liberia	3,600	Small, ∴ $33/household	**$118,800**
Malawi	10,593	Medium, ∴ $50/household	**$529,650**
Mozambique	15,500	Large, ∴ $66.5/household	**$997,500**
Nigeria	77,400	Large, ∴ $66.5/household	**$5,147,100**
* Largest CWIQ on Record			
Sierra Leone	7,800	Medium, ∴ $50/household	**$390,000**
Tanzania	13,500	Large, ∴ $66.5/household	**$897,750**

*Confirmed through the International Household Survey Network (ISHN).

http://catalog.ihsn.org/
index.php/catalog.

-> *Search Term "CWIQ"*

Table 5.16 LSMS known surveys

Country	#Households surveyed*	Cost per Household	Cost (x5 for MDG)
	LSMS Known Surveys*		
Armenia	4,920	$170	**$836,400**
Azerbaijan	2016	$170	**$342,720**
Bosnia and Herzegovina	3,562 (average of 4 surveys)	$170	**$605,540**
Brazil	4,940	$170	**$839,800**
Bulgaria	2,928 (average of 5 surveys)	$170	**$497,760**
China	780	$170	**$132,600**
Côte d'Ivoire	1,597 (average of 4 surveys)	$170	**$271,490**
Ecuador	5,267 (average of 3 surveys)	$170	**$895,390**
Ethiopia	3,969	$170	**$674,730**
Ghana	4,240 (average of 4 surveys)	$170	**$720,800**
Guatemala	7,940	$170	**$1,349,800**
Guyana	5,340	$170	**$907,800**
India – Uttar Pradesh + Bihar	2,250	$170	**$382,500**
Iraq	18,144	$170	**$3,084,480**
Jamaica	2,623 (average of 14 surveys)	$170	**$445,910**
Kazakhstan	1,996	$170	**$339,320**

(cont.)

Table 5.16 (cont.)

Country	LSMS Known Surveys*		
	#Households surveyed*	Cost per Household	Cost (x5 for MDG)
Kosovo	2,880	$170	$489,600
Kyrgyz Republic	2,473 (average of 4 surveys)	$170	$420,410
Malawi	11,755 (average of 2 surveys)	$170	$1,988,350
Morocco	3,323	$170	$564,910
Nepal	4,828 (average of 3 surveys)	$170	$820,760
Nicaragua	4,915	$170	$835,550
Niger	3,968	$170	$674,560
Nigeria	5,000 (average of 2 samples)	$170	$850,000
Pakistan	4,800	$170	$816,000
Panama	6,663 (average of 3 samples)	$170	$1,132,710
Papua New Guinea	1,396	$170	$237,320
Peru	5,120	$170	$870,400
Romania	36,000	$170	$6,120,000
Russian Federation	6,500	$170	$1,105,000
Serbia	4,831 (average of 3 surveys)	$170	$821,270
South Africa	9,000	$170	$1,530,000
Tajikistan	3,141 (average of 4 surveys)	$170	$533,970
Tanzania	4,134 (average of 3 surveys)	$170	$702,780
Timor-Leste (East Timor)	1,800	$170	$306,000
Uganda	2,851 (average of 3 surveys)	$170	$484,670
Vietnam	12,378 (average of 4 surveys)	$170	$2,104,260

*Confirmed through the International Household Survey Network (ISHN) and World Bank Dataset Archive.

http://econ.worldbank.org/WBSITE/EXTERNAL/EXTDEC/EXTRESEARCH/EXTLSMS/0,,contentMDK:
21485765~menuPK:4196952~pagePK:64168445~piPK:64168309~theSitePK:3358997~isCURL:Y,00.html.

–> LSMS Datasets

Table 5.17 Known censuses

Country	Using our Estimate Formula (this figure later multiplied by 2 to indicate two censuses)	Census Reported Cost (this figure later multiplied by 2 to indicate two censuses)	Source
	Known Censuses*		
Afghanistan (2008)	$89.47 M	$44. M	http://tinyurl.com/qfxqhkk
Albania (2011)	$3.16 M	$21. M	http://tinyurl.com/oh26hbf
Algeria (2007)	$115.45 M	$32. M	http://tinyurl.com/pqo8lh3
Angola (2014)	$62.46 M	$200. M	http://tinyurl.com/oluy5du
Armenia (2011)	$2.97 M	$6.4 M	http://tinyurl.com/o4a86sc
Azerbaijan (2009)	$18.6 M	$3.5 M	http://tinyurl.com/pn7v9n6
Bahrain (2010)	$1.32 M	$1.6 M	http://tinyurl.com/nfhwgz3
Bangladesh (2011)	$464.09 M	$42. M	http://tinyurl.com/qjm2cqh
Benin (2013)	$19.7 M	$9.4 M	http://tinyurl.com/oxz5f7n
Bolivia (2012)	$20.99 M	$50. M	http://tinyurl.com/qyhj2ah
Bosnia and Herzegovina (2012)	$3.83 M	$28. M	http://tinyurl.com/pme3f94
Botswana (2011)	$2. M	$35.3 M	http://tinyurl.com/of2lxak
Brazil (2010)	$595.97 M	$909. M	http://tinyurl.com/nanf7om
Burma (2014)	$158.39 M	$58.5 M	http://tinyurl.com/qasm6xx
Cambodia (2008)	$29.73 M	$8. M	http://tinyurl.com/kkvcbtp
Chad (2011)	$24.9 M	$30. M	http://tinyurl.com/pgtx9ve
Chile (2012) *Later Annulled*	$34.93 M	$32. M	http://tinyurl.com/p5zbqx7
China	$4052.09 M	$1007. M	http://tinyurl.com/q82hnuz
Costa Rica (2011)	$4.81 M	$3.6 M	http://tinyurl.com/otco3ck
Croatia	$4.27 M	$31.5 M	http://tinyurl.com/o6vnq86
Djibouti (2009–2013 range)	$.86 M	$3.88 M	http://tinyurl.com/psqfqv5
East Timor (2010)	$1.21 M	$4.2 M	http://tinyurl.com/qffo8gk
Egypt (2006)	$242.17 M	$24. M	http://tinyurl.com/ox93oxx
Fiji (2007)	$.87 M	$7. M	http://tinyurl.com/ppewu3r
Gambia (2013)	$1.81 M	$6. M	http://tinyurl.com/q2n7fmt
Ghana (2010)	$76.1 M	$50. M	http://tinyurl.com/ngolhg7
Guatemala (2013)	$30.17 M	$22. M	http://tinyurl.com/py6gsgw
Guinea-Bissau (2007)	$1.66 M	$5. M	http://tinyurl.com/newmsw5
Guyana (2012)	$.8 M	$4. M	http://tinyurl.com/op9ws24
Haiti (2006)	$20.35 M	$8. M	http://tinyurl.com/pxg76lh
India (2011)	$3710.06 M	$361. M	http://tinyurl.com/omeakfj
Iran (2011)	$229.27 M	$70. M	http://tinyurl.com/nka94j7
Jamaica (2011)	$2.71 M	$1400. M	http://tinyurl.com/pqt5co3
Kazakhstan (2009)	$33.59 M	$7.6 M	http://tinyurl.com/oct2qhe

(cont.)

Table 5.17 (*cont.*)

Country	Known Censuses*		Source
	Using our Estimate Formula (this figure later multiplied by 2 to indicate two censuses)	Census Reported Cost (this figure later multiplied by 2 to indicate two censuses)	
Kenya (2009)	$129.53 M	$75. M	http://tinyurl.com/oe88ys9
Korea, Rep. (2010)	$150.01 M	$157. M	http://tinyurl.com/oh6b62q
Kosovo (2011)	$1.81 M	$15. M	http://tinyurl.com/pm9fgmf
Latvia (2010)	$2.03 M	$5. M	http://tinyurl.com/ou5suy6
Liberia (2010)	$4.19 M	$5.6 M	http://tinyurl.com/pmf6usu
Macedonia FYR (2011)	$2.11 M	$19. M	http://tinyurl.com/praqley
Malawi (1998)	$31.81 M	$10. M	http://tinyurl.com/kkvcbtp
Malaysia (2010)	$87.72 M	$61. M	http://tinyurl.com/o4qguj5
Mali (2012)	$29.71 M	$3.15 M	http://tinyurl.com/o92mw4v
Mexico (2000)	$362.54 M	$250. M	http://tinyurl.com/o8443zv
Moldova (2004)	$3.56 M	$2.7 M	http://tinyurl.com/kkvcbtp
Namibia (2011)	$2.26 M	$96. M	http://tinyurl.com/qcp9n6n
Nigeria (2006)	$506.5 M	$843. M	http://tinyurl.com/pdskmc4
Panama (2010)	$3.8 M	$16.5 M	http://tinyurl.com/peazatz
Paraguay (2002)	$13.37 M	$10. M	http://tinyurl.com/nvrlb56
Romania (2014)	$63.98 M	$62. M	http://tinyurl.com/on98j72
Rwanda (2012)	$22.92 M	$21.3 M	http://tinyurl.com/njoduuh
Serbia (2011)	$14.45 M	$32. M	http://tinyurl.com/oxm8dz7
Sierra Leone (2014)	$11.96 M	$10. M	http://tinyurl.com/nzumosb
South Africa (2011)	$153.57 M	$184. M	http://tinyurl.com/oo8q4dp
South Sudan (2014)	$21.68 M	$99. M	http://tinyurl.com/pwjcx5v
Suriname (2011)	$.53 M	$3.7 M	http://tinyurl.com/q4ap4ym
Swaziland (2007)	$1.23 M	$1.94 M	http://tinyurl.com/qffrtsg
Tajikistan (2010)	$16.02 M	$15. M	http://tinyurl.com/q99gaqs
Tanzania (2011)	$143.35 M	$66.6 M	http://tinyurl.com/o69seay
Trinidad and Tobago (2010–2013 *3-year census*)	$1.34 M	$83. M	http://tinyurl.com/oxovhsx
UAE (2010)	$18.41 M	$18. M	http://tinyurl.com/pp5rdp4
Uganda (2014)	$109.04 M	$62. M	http://tinyurl.com/nq327vw
Venezuela (2011)	$89.86 M	$123. M	http://tinyurl.com/43cpy5y
Vietnam (2009)	$266.33 M	$33. M	http://tinyurl.com/o8wmukk
West Bank and Gaza (2008)	$4.05 M	$8.6 M	http://tinyurl.com/pwldut6
Yemen (2014)	$71.56 M	$68. M	http://tinyurl.com/q2rjpeb
Zimbabwe (2014)	$27.45 M	$16. M	http://tinyurl.com/ogkqugo

Table 5.18 Known DHS surveys

Known DHS Surveys*			
Country	Year	Cost (later multiplied by 5 to indicate five surveys)	Source
Burkina Faso	2003	$0.9m	http://tinyurl.com/kkvcbtp
Cambodia	2000	$0.9m	http://tinyurl.com/kkvcbtp
Malawi	2002	$0.9m	http://tinyurl.com/kkvcbtp
Moldova	2000	$0.9m	http://tinyurl.com/kkvcbtp
Peru	2000	$1.20	http://tinyurl.com/kkvcbtp
Tanzania	Average of '91, '94, '96, '99	$0.8m	http://tinyurl.com/kkvcbtp

References

Attaran, Amir. 2005. "An immeasurable crisis? A criticism of the millennium development goals and why they cannot be measured." *PLoS Medicine* 2.10.

ChildInfo. 2014. "Multiple Indicator Cluster Survey/ MICS3," ChildInfo: Monitoring the Situation of Children and Women, subsection: MICS. http:// www.childinfo.org/mics3.html.

Easterly, William. 2009. "How the millennium development goals are unfair to Africa," *World Development* 37(1): 26–35.

Harford, Tim. 2014. "Big data: are we making a big mistake?" *Financial Times, March* 28, 2014.

International Household Survey Network (IHSN). Survey Database catalog. Search terms: "CWIQ," "LSMS," "DHS," "MICS," "Census." http://catalog.ihsn.org/index.php/catalog.

Jerven, Morten. 2013. *Poor Numbers: How We Are Misled by African Development Statistics and What to Do About It.* Ithaca, NY: Cornell University Press.

Jerven, Morten. 2014a. "Poor numbers and what to do about them," *The Lancet* 383(9917): 594–5.

2014b. "The political economy of agricultural statistics and input subsidies: evidence from India, Nigeria and Malawi," *Journal of Agrarian Change* 14(1): 129–45.

Kenny, Charles and Andy Sumner. 2011. *More Money or More Development: What Have the MDGs Achieved*, CGD Working Paper 278. Washington, DC: Center for Global Development.

Manning, Richard. 2009. "using indicators to encourage development: lessons from the millennium development goals," Danish Institute for International Studies (DIIS), *Report* 2009(1): 1–100.

Measure DHS. 2014. "What We Do/Survey Types: Demographic and Health Surveys (DHS)", ICF International, USAID. https://www.measuredhs .com/What-We-Do/Survey-Types/DHS.cfm.

Oxman, Andrew and Atle Fretheim. 2009. "Can paying for results help to achieve the Millennium Development Goals?: Overview of the effectiveness of results-based financing." *Journal of Evidence-Based Medicine* 2: 70–83.

PARIS21. 2012. "Partnership in Statistics for the 21st Century, PRESS release for the 2012 Round of statistics measurements," PARIS 21 Group. http://paris21.org/PRESS2012.

2000. "CWIQ Summary: 782–1," PowerPoint summary of CWIQ Questionnaire, sourced from The World Bank Group. www.google.ca/url?sa=t&rct=j&q=&esrc=s& source=web&cd=1&ved=0CCoQFjAA&url= http%3A%2F%2Fparis21.org%2Fsites% 2Fdefault%2Ffiles%2F782.ppt&ei= LIhUUomkGKXBiwLOjIGYCw&usg= AFQjCNEeScEC_ 8DnO4dNvMhOxDxpc0IDEg&sig2= P81yT2FWpPDvW1jM1l0t1A&bvm= bv.53760139,d.cGE.

Randriamamonjy, Josée. 2008. "Estimating Household Income to Monitor and Evaluate Public Investment Programs in Sub-Saharan Africa." *International Food Policy Research Institute*, Discussion Paper 00771, Consultative

Group on International *Agricultural Research:*
v-25.

Reinikka, Ritva and Jacob Svensson. 2001.
"Explaining leakage of public funds." Policy
research Working Paper Series no. 2709,
Development Research Group, World Bank.

Rommelmann, Vanessa et al. 2005. "Costs and results
of information systems for poverty monitoring,
health sector reform, and local government reform
in Tanzania: No.1 – Descriptions of Indicator
Coverage and Systems with Preliminary
Comparative Costing." USAID: ii-81.

Saith, Ashwani. 2006. "From Universal Values to
Millennium Development Goals: Lost in
Translation." *Development and Change* 37:
1167–99.

Sandefur, Justin and Amanda Glassman. 2013. "The
political economy of bad data: Evidence from
African survey & administrative statistics."
Paper presented at UNU-WIDER Development
Conference: Inclusive Growth in Africa
Measurement, Causes, and Consequences,
20–21 September 2013, United Nations.

Sette, Cristina. 2008. "Formal Surveys." Institutional
Learning and Change Initiative, *Consultative
Group on International Agricultural Research*,
sourced and summarized from World
Bank. 2004. "Monitoring and Evaluation: Some
Tools, Methods & Approaches," The World
Bank Group. www.cgiar-ilac.org/content/
formal-surveys.

The Economist. 2011. "Censuses. Costing the count."
June 2, 2011.

UNICEF. 2014. "The State of the World's Children
2014 in Numbers – Every Child Counts:
Revealing Disparities, Advancing Children's
Rights", United Nations Children's Fund:
1–111. www.unicef.org/sowc2014/numbers/
documents/english/EN-FINAL FULL
REPORT.pdf.

United Nations (UN). 2005. "Household surveys in
developing and transition countries." Statistical
Division, United Nations Department of
Economic and Social Affairs, no. 96, United
Nations: i-619.

2008. "Official list of millennium goal indicators."
United Nations Statistics Division, Department
of Economic and Social Affairs, United Nations.
http://mdgs.un.org/unsd/mdg/host.aspx?
Content=indicators/officiallist.htm.

2013a. "A new global partnership: eradicate
poverty and transform economies through

sustainable development." The Report of the
High-Level Panel of Eminent Persons on the
Post-2015 Development Agenda. www.un.org/
Sg/Management/Pdf/Hlp_P2015_Report.Pdf.

2013b. United Nations Research Institute for Social
Development. 2013. "Inequalities and the Post-
2015 Development Agenda: Brief 2", UNRISD,
United Nations.

2013c. "TST issues brief: Promoting equality,
including social equality." United Nations
Technical Support Team, United Nations: 1–10.
http://sustainabledevelopment.un.org/content/
documents/2406TST%20Issues%20Brief%20on
%20Promoting%20Equality_FINAL.pdf.

2014. "Outcome Document – Open Working Group
on Sustainable Development Goals." http://
sustainabledevelopment.un.org/focussdgs.html.

Vandemoortele, Jan. 2009. "The MDG conundrum:
meeting the targets without missing the point."
Development Policy Review 27(4): 355–71.

Virtual Statistical System (VSS). 2014. "Section 4 –
registers, frames censuses, sub-section 3:
"Censuses." VSS, World Bank.
www.virtualstatisticalsystem.org/activities/
activity/43censuses/?no_cache=1&seltab=132&
print=1.

WDI. 2014. "Filter: Population 2012." World
Development Indicator, Database Inquiry for
Global Populations 2012, World Bank. http://
databank.worldbank.org/data/views/
variableSelection/selectvariables.aspx?source=
world-development-indicators.

World Bank. 2014a. "Core Welfare Indicator
Questionnaire (CWIQ)." Questionnaire
Overview, The World Bank Group.
http://web.worldbank.org/WBSITE/
EXTERNAL/COUNTRIES/AFRICAEXT/
EXTPUBREP/EXTSTATINAFR/0,,
contentMDK:21104598~
menuPK:3091968~page
PK:64168445~piPK:64168309~
theSitePK:824043,00.html.

2014b. "About LSMS." The Living Standards
Measurement Study (LSMS), World Bank.
http://econ.worldbank.org/
WBSITE/EXTERNAL/EXTDEC/
EXTRESEARCH/EXTLSMS/
0,,contentMDK:21478196~menuPK:
3359066~pagePK:64168445~
piPK:64168309~theSitePK:3358997,00.html.

World Health Organization (WHO). 2009. "Biennial
report annex: technical note on the costs of

alternative approaches to collecting population and vital events data." *Health Metrics Network*: 1–7.

Yacyshyn, Allison M and David M. Swanson. 2011. *The Costs of Conducting a National Census: Rationale for Re-Designing Current Census Methodology in Canada and the United States.*

Center for Sustainable Suburban Development Working paper #11–05.

Yansanch, Ibrahim S. 2000. *Design Effect and Cost Issues for Surveys in Developing Countries.* Bureau of Labor Statistics, U.N. Statistics Division, New York: United Nations: 770–5.

Alternative Perspective

DEBORAH JOHNSTON

Summary

There is clearly an existing problem with development data provision. For example, even population figures may be uncertain because of undercounting of some groups in society, and changes to the statistical basis of GDP estimates can make large differences. Ghana became a middle-income country overnight when its estimated GDP doubled in this way.

Food and Agriculture Organization (FAO) data on undernutrition – on which many poorer countries rely in the absence of official national statistics – has also been shown to be prone to significant errors.

This matters because the post-2015 agenda is likely to have a far greater monitoring burden, and Jerven has shown convincingly that paying for a full set of development data is not feasible. The second issue is that, even if it was available, throwing money at the problem will not solve it. The problem of lack of statistical capacity is hard to solve, and the chapter also points out the opportunity cost. The Partnership in Statistics for Development in the Twenty-First Century (PARIS21) group estimates that there has been an increase in data-gathering exercises in Africa because of the MDGs, but a shift away from surveys not closely geared to them. As Jerven correctly argues, macroeconomic, labor, and agricultural statistics have suffered in particular.

This chapter is a groundbreaking attempt to delineate the issue, map the extent of the problem, and make recommendations; essentially it is a wake-up call to the development community. It makes several important contributions, the most important of which is its careful enumeration of the costs of monitoring the MDG indicators. This quantification is extremely powerful in showing the need for prioritization of

targets and indicators – and so is highly complementary to the Copenhagen Consensus exercise.

Because there is not yet a definitive list of targets and indicators, a precise costing is impossible, but the chapter usefully lays out the likely minimum data requirements. However, the cost of data analysis and utilization is excluded from these estimates, and this is, of course, a necessary requirement for the information to be debated by politicians and the public.

As the author points out, many data-gathering exercises are flawed. This may be due to methodological, conceptual, or political problems. The potential for misunderstanding and bias is rife, and poor quality data is a challenge for both academics and statisticians. Once the post-2015 list is formally agreed, Jerven's extremely useful overview of each of the major international survey types could be expanded to include quality issues.

The methodology of the chapter is innovative and important. I am not aware of any other exercise that has attempted to cost the MDG agenda or, of course, the post-2015 agenda. A key issue that is highlighted is the extent to which monitoring depends on surveys rather than administrative data. Also emphasized is the difficulty of getting data on the costs of surveys and, in particular, the complete lack of estimates for Multiple Indicator Cluster surveys. The impact of not doing these surveys is, of course, unknown.

The chapter has constructed a groundbreaking argument that raises to public attention a dangerous gap in the development debate. It convincingly shows that we risk repeating the mistakes of the past, in ignoring the costs of data collection in the post-MDG world. By providing a cost estimate of each of the crucial surveys and of the overall MDG exercise, the chapter also kick-starts a discussion about prioritization.

Alternative Perspective

GABRIEL DEMOMBYNES AND JUSTIN SANDEFUR

Summary

This perspective takes a look at three questions relating to the provision of more data via surveys. First, we ask whether surveys in poor countries have produced results, second, what types of users demand what types of data, and third, how much it would cost to close the remaining gaps in household survey provision.

The International Household Survey Network (IHSN) database provides the most comprehensive information on surveys and censuses in low- and middle-income countries. The pace of survey data collection has accelerated rapidly across all regions, as has the trend toward making data open. Poorer countries actually produce significantly more household surveys each year and are more likely to put their data into the public domain.

The demand for such data, and also for it to be openly available, is likely to come from citizens and international aid donors, and the evidence tends to support this. Countries receiving more foreign aid tend not to conduct more household surveys but are somewhat more likely to publish open data. More democratic countries are also more likely to publish their data.

Jerven estimates a figure of $1 billion a year to produce an adequate data package to cover the MDGs. This seems to us to be a reasonable approximation, but what it neglects is that many of the middle-income countries included are wealthy enough to fully fund their own statistical services. Countries such as Kuwait, South Korea, and Chile, for example, are included in the figure.

Recognizing the need for socioeconomic data, we would expect international development assistance to fund a substantial fraction of statistical costs for countries below a cutoff level and only a small share of costs above that level.

The cut-off point should be somewhere in the range of $2,000–5,000 GDP per capita. Total data package costs would be $275 million for the lower limit or $510 million for the upper one. Thirty-six out of 52 countries with GDP per capita below $2,000 are in sub-Saharan Africa, and total annual survey costs for this region would be $276 million. We therefore suggest that the total amount of international aid needed to support this basic survey program is about $300 million. We should note that IDA already provides a substantial proportion of the funds, so the $300 million does not represent a marginal increase in aid required, but a total figure including some current funding.

We argue that greater efforts to ensure data openness are as important as supporting data production. There are already a number of laudable data access models, including Afrobarometer and the International Integrated Public Use Microdata project.

International statistics must also have the right goals. The main value of data is not for monitoring international targets but to generate knowledge for policy decision making in each country. High-frequency, disaggregated data are needed for domestic users. Finally, although household survey data will be useful for monitoring the SDGs, actually achieving them will require greater focus on other types of data, including administrative systems.

Benefits and Costs of the Education Targets for the Post-2015 Development Agenda

GEORGE PSACHAROPOULOS

Introduction

The Post-2015 MDG discourse has generated an omnibus of education goals and targets to be fulfilled by 2030. The aim of this chapter is to have a closer look at such targets and identify the most concrete and prominent ones that are amenable to cost-benefit analysis. Based on existing research, the targets are evaluated according to findings in the economics of education literature. A short list of education targets that are likely to be most cost-effective if reached by 2030 is prioritized.

Historical Perspective

There is a long history of international organizations setting numerical targets for education. As of today, none of these targets has been achieved. For example, in 1961 UNESCO convened a high-level conference of African states in Addis Ababa on the development of education in Africa (UNESCO, 1961a). A goal was set that by 1980 primary enrollment in Africa should be 100 percent, relative to 40 percent in 1960 (UNESCO, 1961b). Yet, by 1980 the net primary enrollment ratio in sub-Saharan Africa stood at 56 percent (UNESCO, 1993).

More recently, in 2011, the World Bank issued its education strategy for 2020 pledging learning for all, meaning that "all students . . . acquire the knowledge and skills they need to live happy, productive lives" (World Bank, 2011). Although the target year of this noble goal is six years away, one wonders how it would be achieved given the huge gaps in educational achievement documented in the recent Organization for Economic Co-operation and Development (OECD, 2013b) PISA report.

But setting never-fulfilled education targets is not only a phenomenon in developing countries. At the 2000 European Council in Lisbon, the Union set a goal that "the proportion of early school leavers should be no more than 10 percent by 2010" (European Commission, 2000). According to the latest Eurostat (2013) data, 14 percent of those ages 18 to 24 are early leavers from education and training, with at most a lower secondary education.

It is a pity that no lessons were learned from past grandiose but unrealistic education target settings in the current post-2015 MDG discourse (Clemens et al., 2007; Psacharopoulos, 1989).

Lack of finance is the most cited reason for failing to meet targets, calling for increased foreign aid (Global Campaign for Education, 2003; Oxfam, 2002). However, even if plenty of finance were available, there are many reasons why parents may not want to send their children to school (Glewwe et al., 2006). Culture is one factor, e.g., in some countries parents not allowing girls to attend school beyond puberty. Poverty is another factor, when child labor is necessary to supplement family income. Another factor is high personal discount rates and lack of information on the lifetime benefits of education. Other reasons relate to the political climate in these countries or the high incidents of orphans and single parents. An additional reason is that the quality of schooling might be too low for parents to expect a value in return.

Education in the Post-2015 Agenda

An international call for defining post-2015 millennium goals and targets has generated an omnibus of proposals (North-South Institute,

2013). Appendix 1 to this chapter lists a consolidation of the proposals.

The dominant characteristic of the proposals is their very general nature. They express well-intended directions of educational systems, but with very few specifics (Center for International Governance Innovation [CIGI], 2012), e.g.:

- Establish sufficient education system accessible to all at all levels
- Lifelong learning
- Continued pursuit of lifelong learning
- Equal right to education
- Socioeconomic equality

Past MDG targets that are not likely to be achieved by 2015 are repeated with 2030 as a new target date (North-South Institute, 2013).

Many of the goals or targets are expressed in very general terms that defy rigorous economic analysis, e.g., calls for a "strong" or "sufficient" educational system. The keywords "all" or "every child" are used repeatedly, meaning zero target, i.e., elimination of the related problem by the target date (United Nations, 2013). In terms of indicators for monitoring the achievement of targets, the enrollment ratio is dominant, meaning that 100 percent of school-age children should be attending school by 2030.

Pulling the threads together, post-2015 MDG goals and targets could be grouped into the following major clusters for contrasting with findings in the economics of education literature:

- Preschool
- Primary
- Secondary
- Tertiary
- Education quality
- Vocational education
- Education finance

Cost-Benefit Analysis of Investment in Education

Before presenting the available evidence on cost-benefit analysis of the proposed goals, it is important to review the alternative methods that have been used in the empirical literature to arrive at such estimates.

Considering the typical age–earnings profiles of graduates from two adjacent levels of education, a comparison is made between the discounted annual costs and benefits of providing the higher level of education over the base one, say, university over secondary education, as illustrated in Figure 6.1.

The benefits of education amount to what the more educated individual earns above the control group of individuals with less education. The costs are measured by the expenses to keep a student in school, plus his/her foregone earnings while studying.

The stream of annual costs (C) and benefits (W) for the two educational levels, university (u) and secondary education (s) subscripts in our example, are discounted to a given point in time for comparison. The result of the comparison can be expressed as three metrics:

(a) **The internal rate of return** (r) of the investment is found by solving the following equation for r:

$$\sum_{t=1}^{43} \frac{(W_u - W_s)_t}{(1+r)^t} = \sum_{t=1}^{4} (W_s + C_u)_t (1+r)^t$$

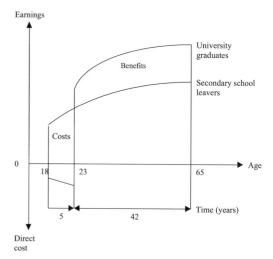

Figure 6.1 *Typical age–earnings profiles by level of education*

(b) **The net present value** (NPV) of the investment is found by subtracting the benefits from the costs that have been discounted at a given discount rate (i):

$$NPV = \sum_{t=1}^{43} \frac{(W_u - W_s)_t}{(1+r)^t} - \sum_{t=1}^{4} (W_s + C_u)_t (1+r)^t$$

(c) **The benefit-cost ratio** is found by dividing the benefits by the costs

$$B/C \text{ ratio} = \frac{\displaystyle\sum_{t=1}^{43} \frac{(W_u - W_s)_t}{(1+r)^t}}{\displaystyle\sum_{t=1}^{4} (W_s + C_u)_t (1+r)^t}$$

Given the costs of investment in education occur within a time span of four years and the benefits last over 40 years, the rate of return to such investment could be estimated by the so-called shortcut formula,

$$\text{private } r = \frac{\overline{W}_u - \overline{W}_s}{4(\overline{W}_u)}$$

where a bar over variables denotes mean annual values of earnings and cost. This method assumes that age–earnings profiles are flat, as depicted in Figure 6.2. The calculation is similar to putting $100 in a bank deposit account and getting $5 annual interest, implying a 5 percent return,

$$r = \frac{\text{Annual benefit}}{\text{Total cost}}$$

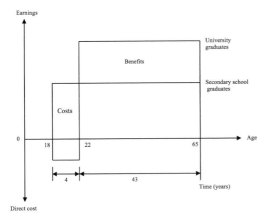

Figure 6.2 *Flat age–earnings profiles*

The Earnings Function Method. This method is also known as the "Mincerian" method and involves the fitting of a function of log-wages (LnW), using years of schooling (S), years of labor market experience (EX), and its square as independent variables (Mincer, 1974),

$$\ln W_i = \alpha + \beta S_i + \gamma_1 EX_i + \gamma_2 EX_i^2,$$

where S is the number of years of schooling of the worker, and *EX* stands for years of labor market experience, defined as (*Age − S − School starting age*). In this function, the β coefficient on years of schooling can be interpreted as the average rate of return to one additional year of schooling. Because $\beta = \frac{\partial \ln W}{\partial S}$, this is the relative increase in wages following an increase in S, or the rate of return to the marginal year of schooling. This method assumes that forgone earnings represent the only cost of education and so measures only the private rate of return. It assumes further that individuals have an infinite working horizon.

In addition, this function does not distinguish between different levels of schooling. To solve this problem, the extended earnings function substitutes a series of 0–1 dummy variables for S, corresponding to discrete educational levels,

$$\ln W_i = \alpha + \beta_p D_p + \beta_p D_p + \beta_u D_u + \gamma_1 EX_i + \gamma_2 EX_i^2$$

where D is the dummy variable for the subscripted level of schooling. To avoid matrix singularity, one of the mutually exclusive education categories is omitted, for example, the dummy corresponding to those with no schooling.

The private rates of return between levels of education can then be calculated from the extended earnings function by the following formulas:

$$r_p = \frac{\beta_p}{S_p},$$

$$r_s = \frac{\beta_s - \beta_p}{S_s - S_p},$$

$$r_u = \frac{\beta_u - \beta_s}{S_u - S_s},$$

where r_p is the rate of return to primary schooling, r_s is the rate of return to secondary, and r_u is the rate of return to university. This calculation resembles the shortcut method in that the rate of return is computed as a ratio of a constant annual benefits flow to the total education cost for attaining the next level of education.

The advantage of the Mincerian way of estimating the returns to education is that it can smooth out and handle low-count cells in an age–earnings profile matrix by level of education. Although convenient, this method is slightly inferior to the full discounting method presented earlier as it assumes flat age–earnings profiles for different levels of education (see Psacharopoulos and Layard, 1979).

Of course, there is a relationship between the preceding three alternative metrics, in the sense that if the rate of return found by the full discounting method exceeds the discount rate, the net present value must be positive, and the benefit-cost ratio must exceed 1. Given that the net benefit stream of an education investment is "well behaved." in the sense of not giving rise to multiple rate of return solutions (Hirshleifer, 1958), any one of the three metrics would give the same answer regarding the ranking of the profitability of the investment.

In the empirical literature the vast majority of education cost-benefit studies are in terms of rates of return. The reason for the rate of return popularity among researchers is that it compares easily across countries, exchanges, and discount rates.

Rate of Return Types. Two types of returns are usually estimated, each answering a different question: First, the private rate of return compares the costs and benefits of education as incurred by and realized by the individual student who undertakes the investment. And second, the social rate of return compares costs and benefits from the country as a whole or society's point of view.

The main computational difference between private and social rates of return is that, for a social rate of return calculation, the costs include the state's or society's at-large spending on education. Hence, in the preceding example, C_u would include the rental of buildings and professorial salaries. Gross earnings (that is, before taxes and other deductions) are used in a social rate of return calculation, and such earnings should also include income in kind where this information is available.

There exists some confusion in the literature regarding the "social" adjective attached to rates of return to investment in education. It has been the tradition in the mainstream economics of education literature to mean by a "social" rate, a private rate adjusted for the full cost of schooling, rather than just what the individual pays for his or her education.

However, in the economics literature at large, a "social" rate should include externalities, that is, benefits beyond those captured by the individual investor, e.g., lower fertility or lives saved because of improved sanitation conditions followed by a more educated woman who may never participate in the formal labor market (Summers, 1992). Given the scant empirical evidence on the external effects of education, social rate of return estimates are usually based on directly observable monetary costs and benefits of education.

Traditional social returns to education are called "narrow-social" and returns that include externalities "wide-social." The distinction between narrow and wide social returns is more than theoretical. By adding externalities to the narrow-social returns, one can reach diametrically opposite policy conclusions, e.g., if primary and tertiary education have differential externalities, by considering the latter the ranking of profitable education investments could be changed.

Because the costs are higher in a social rate of return calculation relative to the one from the private point of view, social returns are typically lower than a private rate of return. The difference between the private and the social rate of return reflects the degree of public subsidization of education.

Estimation Method Popularity. As individual age-earnings-education characteristics became available over the years in censuses and household surveys, the Mincerian method became more dominant. Net present values of education investments have not been popular because of the difficulty of comparing returns across countries and exchanges. Interestingly, benefit-cost ratios have been published for preschool education.

Cost-Benefit Evidence on the Proposals

Early Childhood Education

Very few studies on the effect of preschooling on eventual educational attainment, adult earnings, and other externalities include cost-benefit analysis, except in the United States.

Table 6.1 presents rates of return and benefit-cost ratios of four preschool programs. Experimentally induced changes in noncognitive skills at an early age explain a sizable portion of later education, employment, and earnings (Heckman 2000, 2008).

The importance of kindergarten on adult earnings has been documented in an experimental study in the United States (Project STAR) as shown in Chetty et al. (2011).

Table 6.2 presents benefit-cost ratios of preschool programs in developing countries. Preschool programs typically contain a health/nutrition element and affect lifetime earnings through better health, reduced grade repetition, increased cognitive skills, and adult earnings.

Evidence on the Main School System

Next we present three compilations of the returns to investment in education covering over 100 countries. Costs are defined as foregone earnings while in school plus the direct resource cost of keeping a student in school. Benefits are defined as the difference between earnings of graduates of one particular level of education relative to graduates of a lower level of education.

World Bank 2004 Compilation

The estimates in Table 6.3 are based on the full discounting method. Public subsidy of education

Table 6.1 Rate of return and benefit-cost ratios of preschool programs in the United States

Program	Target group	Rate of return (%)	B-C ratio (3% discount rate)
(1)	(2)	(3)	(4)
Chicago parent–child	3–4 years	18	6.9
High Scope Perry	3–4 years	10	7.2
Abecedarian	3 months–4 years	7	2.7

Source: Col. (3), Bialik (2013), p. A2.
Col. (4), Temple and Reynolds (2007).

Table 6.2 Benefit-cost ratios of preschool programs in developing countries

Country	Discount rate		
	3%	6%	Unspecified in source
Bolivia	3.7	2.3	
Kenya	77.0	50.6	
Brazil			2.0
Egypt			2.3
Philippines	3.0		

Source: Bolivia and Kenya from Orazem et al. (2008), Table 4.
Egypt from Janssens et al. (2001).
Other countries from Patrinos (2007), Tables 2 and 4.

is shown to be regressive: private returns are higher than social returns where the latter is defined on the basis of private benefits but total resource costs

Average returns to schooling are highest in the Latin America and the Caribbean region and for the sub-Saharan Africa region. Returns to schooling for Asia are at about the world average. The returns are lower in the high-income countries of the OECD. Based on the social calculation, primary education exhibits the highest returns, followed by secondary and higher education.

Table 6.3 Social and private returns to investment in education by level and region (%)

Region	Social			Private		
	Primary	Secondary	Higher	Primary	Secondary	Higher
Asia[*]	16.2	11.1	11.0	20.0	15.8	18.2
Europe/Middle East/North Africa[*]	15.6	9.7	9.9	13.8	13.6	18.8
Latin America/Caribbean	17.4	12.9	12.3	26.6	17.0	19.5
OECD	8.5	9.4	8.5	13.4	11.3	11.6
Sub-Saharan Africa	25.4	18.4	11.3	37.6	24.6	27.8
World	18.9	13.1	10.8	26.6	17.0	19.0

Source: Psacharopoulos and Patrinos (2002).
* Non-OECD.

World Bank 2012 Compilation

The estimates in Table 6.4 were based on the Mincerian method, hence only private returns are given. Returns to tertiary education are highest among the three levels. It should be noted, however, that returns to education estimates on the basis of the Mincerian method grossly underestimate the true returns because of the tacit inclusion of foregone earnings to the cost of keeping children in school.

The OECD 2013 Compilation

Given that primary education is universal in OECD countries, the OECD produces estimates of the returns to education only for upper secondary and tertiary education (Table 6.5).

A common finding in other studies is that educating girls has a higher rate of return relative to educating boys. Summers (1992) reports that in Pakistan the wide social rate of return on girls' education exceeds 20 percent.

Education Quality

In contrast to these studies on the amount of education delivered, many econometric studies have found that increased resources have not led to statistically significant improvements in test scores – a standard measure of education quality (Hanushek, 2007). In a survey of 376 education production functions relating school resources to

Table 6.4 Private returns to investment in education by region (%)

Region	Primary	Secondary	Tertiary
Middle East and North Africa	9.4	3.5	8.9
South Asia	9.6	6.3	18.4
Eastern and Central Europe	8.3	4.0	10.1
High-Income Economies	4.8	5.3	11.0
East Asia and Pacific	11.0	6.3	15.4
Latin America and Caribbean	9.3	6.6	17.6
Sub-Saharan Africa	13.4	10.8	21.9
World	10.3	6.9	16.8

Source: Psacharopoulos and Patrinos (2002).

Table 6.5 Average returns to education in 29 OECD countries (%)

	Educational level	
Return type	Upper secondary	Tertiary
Social	8.4	11.2
Private	14.5	13.0

Source: Data extracted from OECD (2013a), men.

student achievement, most studies report negative or insignificant effects of expenditure per student, teacher salaries, or class size (Hanushek, 2003).

Similarly, there is little evidence of the real improvements from alleged school quality enhancing interventions such as textbooks, improved buildings, or smaller class sizes (Kremer et al., 2013).

Institutional changes such as the introduction of monitoring and evaluation systems, central examinations, teacher incentives, and accountability are more likely to improve school quality, although they are difficult to cost (Hanushek and Woessmann, 2011).

The evidence on the cost side of school quality improvements is problematic. Glewwe (1996) reports a social rate of return of improving middle school quality in Ghana of about 25 percent. Following our conversion methodology this corresponds to 5 and 8.3 benefit-cost ratios for discount rates 5 percent and 3 percent, respectively.

From another study in Chile, we know that an improvement of 1 standard deviation of test scores is associated with about a 700 increase in annual earnings (Patrinos and Sakellariou, 2011 and correspondence with the authors). So, and given the many caveats associated with this statistic, one may be tempted to conclude that the benefit-cost ratio of quality improvements is roughly 7. The same study in Chile reports a 17 percent average private rate of return to test score improvements that must correspond to about 13 percent social returns.

A study on Pakistan found that attending a higher quality rather than a poor quality primary school has a 13 percent social rate of return (Behrman et al., 2008, Table 3). Adopting a 15 percent average social return to investments in school quality improvements from the preceding studies gives 5 and 3 benefit-cost ratios for school quality at 3 percent and 5 percent discount rates, respectively. However, it should be emphasized that the benefit-cost ratios for school quality are not based on an equally rich research base as those for school quantity reported earlier.

Vocational Education

According to an OECD study, "[T]he question 'Is it worthwhile to invest in VET?' remains open at

Table 6.6 Social returns to investment in upper secondary school streams, Tanzania

Curriculum type	Rate of return (%)
Academic	6.3
Technical	1.7

Source: Psacharopoulos (1995).

this stage" (OECD, 2008). In many countries, the wage returns to academic qualifications are significantly higher than the returns to vocational qualifications, government training programs, and adult basic skills training (Blundell, Dearden, Mdghir, and Sianesi, 1999; Carneiro and Heckman, 2003; Dearden et al., 2002; Dickerson 2005).

Within levels of education, and counterintuitively, general secondary education is more profitable than vocational education (Table 6.6) because the vocational track of secondary schools costs about twice that of the general track without creating any differential in earnings (Psacharopoulos and Loxley, 1985).

Education Financing

One of the broad goals of the post-2015 MDG proposals is "sufficient financing" of education systems, measured by the expenditure per student or the share of GDP devoted to education. It should be noted, however, that education financing is a means of achieving goals, not a goal in itself. Hence it cannot be subjected to cost-benefit analysis.

Lessons from the literature

It seems clear that investments in expanding any level and type of education passes in general a cost-benefit test evaluated at a 3 percent or 5 percent discount rate, but some education investments are more profitable than others.

Economics Nobel Laureate James Heckman, in a series of papers, has succinctly summarized priorities in educational investments as in Figure 6.3, concluding that skill formation is most efficient in the early ages and levels of education (Cunha et al., 2006; Heckman, 2008).

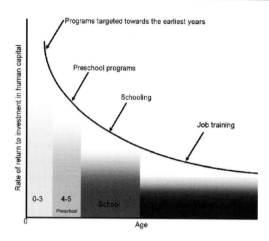

Figure 6.3 *A grand summary of education investment returns*

Source: Heckman (2008).

Table 6.7 Primary school enrollment ratio, latest data (%)

Region	Preschool (Gross)	Primary (Net)	Secondary (Net)
East Asia & Pacific	50	96.9	73.0
European Union/ OECD	81	98.5	92.2
Latin America & Caribbean	69	95.3	76.1
Middle East & North Africa	22	94.3	70.3
South Asia	47	92.7	50.1
Sub-Saharan Africa	18	77.3	24.7
World	46	91.2	62.7

Source: Preschool from UNICEF (2014), no net available. Primary and secondary from World Bank (2014).

Present Conditions

Before assessing specific targets among the Post-2015 MDG goals, let us review where the world stands in terms of educational development.

On the eve of the MDG-2015 target for having achieved universal primary education, there are about 60 million children out of school, more than half of them in sub-Saharan Africa. Table 6.7 shows the latest data on school coverage in three levels of schooling. The gross enrollment ration refers to the number of school-level children enrolled in a particular school level, regardless of age, expressed as a percentage of the total number of children of official school age in the population. The net enrollment ratio refers to the number of children of the official age group expressed as a percentage of that age group in the population.

Twenty-three percent of primary school-age children in sub-Saharan Africa are out of school. Even advanced industrial countries fall short of the 100 percent net enrollment ratio – the main MDG indicator for monitoring progress toward the 100 percent zero-target date.

In fact, there seems to be an asymptote below the 100 percent mark regarding school coverage

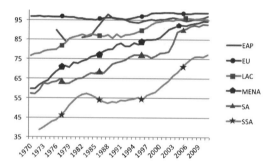

Figure 6.4 *Net primary enrollment ratio trend by region*

Source: Plotted from World Bank (2014) data.

for many reasons other than failed education policy or lack of finance, as noted earlier.

Figure 6.4 illustrates the long way toward universal primary education and the impossibility (sharp deviation from the trend) of achieving the 2015 zero-target of 100 percent enrollment in Africa.

Clemens (2004) demonstrates the impossibility of achieving universal education in Burkina Faso by 2015. Following past trends, a more likely target date is 2100.

Table 6.8 Preprimary gross enrollment ratio (%)

Region	Enrollment ratio 2010 or latest year
Sub-Saharan Africa	18
Middle East & N. Africa	22
South Asia	47
East Asia & Pacific	50
Latin America and Caribbean	69
Industrialized countries	81
World	46

Source: UNICEF (2014).

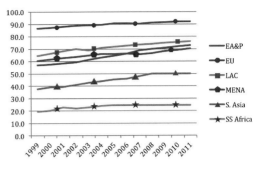

Figure 6.5 *Net secondary enrollment ratio (%)*

Source: World Bank (2014).

Table 6.9 Secondary enrollment indicators, 2011 or latest year

Region	Out of lower secondary (millions)	Net secondary enrollment ratio (%)
East Asia	9.0	73.0
European Union	0.7	92.2
Latin America & Caribbean	1.5	76.1
Middle East & N. Africa	2.8	70.3
South Asia	31.2	50.1
Sub-Saharan Africa	22.8	24.7
World	69.5	62.7

Source: World Bank (2014).

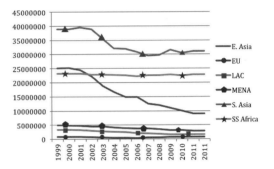

Figure 6.6 *Out-of-school children of lower secondary age*

Source: World Bank (2014).

Preschool

Table 6.8 shows that preschool coverage varies widely between regions – from an enrollment ratio of 18 percent in sub-Saharan Africa to 81 percent in industrialized countries.

Regarding secondary education, there are about 70 million children without access to it, most of whom are in South Asia and sub-Saharan Africa (See Table 6.9, also Figures 6.5 and 6.6).

Universities

The number of students enrolled in tertiary education per 100,000 inhabitants is listed among the post-2015 goals, although no specific targets are given. Figure 6.7 shows the vast disparities between regions in tertiary education coverage.

Education Quality

Regarding the quality of schooling, 123 million youth ages 15 to 24 lack basic reading and writing skills Over 60 percent of them are young women (United Nations, 2013). In Ethiopia the best-off children are almost 20 times more likely to be literate than the poorest children (Save the Children, 2013). In Pakistan less than half of grade 5 children in Balochistan could solve a two-digit subtraction, compared to 73 percent in the wealthier province of Punjab (UNESCO, 2014). Table 6.10 shows the vast disparities between

Table 6.10 Countries at the top and bottom of the 2012 PISA score

Country	Mathematics	Reading	Science
Shanghai-China	613	570	580
Singapore	573	542	551
Hong Kong–China	561	545	555
Chinese Taipei	560	523	523
Korea	554	536	538
Brazil	391	410	405
Argentina	388	396	406
Tunisia	388	404	398
Jordan	386	399	409
Colombia	376	403	399
Qatar	376	388	384
Indonesia	375	396	382
Peru	368	384	373

Source: Extract from OECD (2013b).

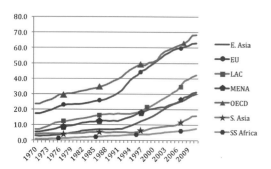

Figure 6.7 *Tertiary education gross enrollment ratio by region*

Source: World Bank (2014).

countries in terms of educational achievement measured by OECD's standardized PISA score.

Assessing the Post-2015 MDG Targets

Out of the three rate-of-return compilations presented earlier, the one reported in Table 6.3 is the most suitable to use as a base for a benefit-cost assessment of the post-2015 targets. (The OECD one refers mainly to advanced industrial countries,

and the World Bank 2012 compilation refers only to private returns.) Table 6.11 presents benefit-cost ratios of expanding at the margin education coverage under current conditions. All benefit-cost ratios exceed 1 and are highest for primary education. In sub-Saharan Africa the benefit-cost ratio is about 9 at 3 percent discount rate. It should be noted that the benefit-cost ratios reported in Table 6.11 are lower estimates of the wide-social profitability of investment in education, as they are based only on labor market rewards omitting externalities.

From the Base Scenario to the Zero Target. Universal primary education is the most prominent target in the post-2015 MDG goals. Given in most regions primary school enrollment is converging toward the below 100 percent asymptote described earlier, let us focus on sub-Saharan Africa that presents the greatest challenge of meeting the zero-target by 2030 (dotted line in Figure 6.8).

To increase the net primary enrollment ratio 23 percentage points to 100 percent by 2030 raises issues of cost and feasibility. Most studies attempting to cost Education for All multiply the additional number of students by the average cost per student in the base year (Devarajan, 2002; Bruns et al., 2003).

Although the average cost of schooling might be valid for a marginal expansion of the school system, it cannot hold for expanding school capacity by one-quarter of its present value. Building more schools in rural areas, hiring qualified teachers, and operating more schools puts a strain on resources hence raising the marginal cost of schooling.

From economics 101 we know that the marginal cost of schooling increases after the minimum average cost point (Figure 6.9). Because the benefit cost ratios in Table 6.11 have been estimated on the basis of the average cost of schooling, they have to be adjusted downward as we move to the zero-target.

Assuming that education systems operate somewhere in the region of the lowest average cost, we assume that a 5 percentage points increment of the enrollment ratio is associated with a 5 percent increase in cost over the previous cost value. In other words, given there are no cost observations beyond the base scenario, we assume that the

Table 6.11 Benefit-cost ratios by level of schooling and region – base scenario

Region/Educational level	3% discount rate			5% discount rate		
	Primary	Secondary	Higher	Primary	Secondary	Higher
Asia	5.4	3.7	3.7	3.2	2.2	2.2
Europe/M. East/N. Africa	5.2	3.2	3.3	3.1	1.9	2.0
Latin America/Caribbean	5.8	4.3	4.1	3.5	2.6	2.5
OECD	2.8	3.1	2.8	1.7	1.9	1.7
Sub-Saharan Africa	8.5	6.1	3.8	5.1	3.7	2.3
World	6.3	4.4	3.6	3.8	2.6	2.2

Source: Based on the social returns in Table 6.3, and the returns to B-C ratio conversion process described in Appendix 2.

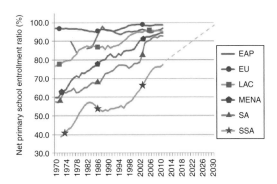

Figure 6.8 *Moving toward the zero-target of primary school coverage*

Source: Adapted from World Bank (2014).

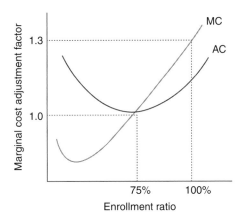

Figure 6.9 *The marginal cost of schooling increases with enrollment*

Source: Author.

elasticity of the marginal cost curve in Figure 6.9 is equal to 1. Given this scenario, the direct cost per primary school student would increase over the years as shown in Table 6.11, col. (3).

It should be noted that the cost increase applies only to the direct cost of schooling, which is about 20 percent of the total cost of schooling at the primary level according to evidence from developing countries, the rest being foregone earnings (Psacharopoulos, 1995, Table 1). Hence the benefit-cost ratios should be adjusted downward by 20 percent of the incremental values in Table 6.11, col. (3). The last two columns in Table 6.12 show the adjusted benefit-cost ratios for achieving the zero target of full primary school coverage in sub-Saharan Africa by 2030. Depending on the discount rate, the benefit-cost ratios range from about 5 to 9.

Table 6.13 reports the results of the same exercise for the world, the benefit-cost ratios ranging from 2.6 to 6.3.

Needless to say that the 15-year projection raises issues of general equilibrium, such as the increased share of the labor force with primary education reducing the rate of return on the investment. Yet it has been observed that rates of return over time do not fluctuate much because of what Tinbergen (1975) described as the race between education and technology. As the supply of educated labor increases, so does the demand for higher skills, hence not depressing the returns to education.

Preschool

One of the post-2015 MDG targets is to reduce by 50 percent the proportion of children who are not

Table 6.12 Benefit-cost ratios of meeting the 100 percent net primary enrollment target in sub-Saharan Africa by 2030

Year	Primary enrollment ratio (%)	MC index	Direct cost adjustment factor	MC-adjusted B/C ratio	
				3% discount	5% discount
(1)	(2)	(3)	(4)	(5)	(6)
2015	75	1.00	1.00	8.5	5.1
2018	80	1.05	1.01	8.4	5.0
2021	85	1.10	1.02	8.3	5.0
2024	90	1.16	1.03	8.3	5.0
2027	95	1.22	1.04	8.2	4.9
2030	100	1.28	1.06	8.0	4.8

Notes: Col. (2), hypothetical net primary enrollment ratio.
Col. (3), marginal cost index assuming a unitary elasticity of direct schooling costs to enrollment.
Col. (4), marginal cost index applicable to the direct cost of schooling in the benefit-cost estimation.
Cols. (5) and (6), sub-Saharan benefit-cost ratios from Table 6.11 for base year divided by Col. (4) for successive years.

Table 6.13 Benefit-cost ratios of meeting the 100 percent net primary enrollment target in world by 2030

Year	Primary enrollment ratio (%)	MC index	Direct cost adjustment factor	MC-adjusted B/C ratio	
				3% discount	5% discount
(1)	(2)	(3)	(4)	(5)	(6)
2015	90	1.0	1.0	6.3	3.8
2018	92	1.1	1.0	6.2	3.8
2021	94	1.1	1.0	6.2	3.7
2024	96	1.2	1.0	6.1	3.7
2027	98	1.2	1.0	6.1	3.7
2030	100	1.3	1.1	5.9	3.6

Notes: Col. (2), hypothetical net primary enrollment ratio.
Col. (3), marginal cost index assuming a unitary elasticity of direct schooling costs to enrollment.
Col. (4), marginal cost index applicable to the direct cost of schooling in the benefit-cost estimation.
Cols. (5) and (6), world benefit-cost ratios from Table 6.12 for base year divided by Col. (4) for successive years.

attending early childhood care and education programs. Table 6.14 presents the preschool enrollment ratios in the base and target years under this scenario.

Focusing again on sub-Saharan Africa that presents the greatest challenge in meeting the target, one could use Kenya's known benefit-cost ratio for preschool programs of 77. Because the intervention on which this benefit-cost ratio is based includes a nutrition element, we adopted half of its value. Table 6.15 shows that the benefit-cost ratios exceed 28 to 39 depending on the discount rate.

Externalities

One important qualification regarding the cost-benefit figures presented in this chapter is that they are based on observed market returns to education excluding externalities. Educating one member of society is associated with a series of benefits that accrue not only to the educated person but also to others (UNESCO, 2013). Including such externalities would raise the benefit-cost ratios reported in this chapter. And because different levels of education may be associated with differential externalities, priorities for investment in education could be reversed.

Table 6.14 Preschool enrollment ratio 2010 and target year (%)

Region	Enrollment ratio 2010 or latest year	2030 target enrollment ratio
(1)	(2)	(3)
Sub-Saharan Africa	18	59
Middle East and N. Africa	22	61
South Asia	47	74
East Asia & Pacific	50	75
Latin America & Caribbean	69	85
Industrialized countries	81	91
World	46	73

Note: Col. (3) =100 − [(100 − col. (2) * 0.5]
Source: UNICEF (2014).

Table 6.15 Benefit-cost ratios of meeting the 50 percent reduction of children who are not attending preschool in sub-Saharan Africa by 2030

Year	Primary enrollment ratio (%)	MC-adjusted B/C ratio 3% discount	MC-adjusted B/C ratio 5% discount
(1)	(2)	(5)	(6)
2010	18	39	30
2015	24	38	29
2018	31	38	29
2021	37	38	29
2024	44	37	29
2027	51	37	28
2030	59	37	28

Notes: Col. (2), hypothetical preschool enrollment progression to target year.
2010 benefit-cost ratios from Table 6.2, Kenya row, adjusted to 5 percent discount rate and reduced by one-half to exclude the nutrition component of the intervention. Other years based on a 1 percent increase of cost of preschooling for every seven percentage points of increase in the enrollment ratio.

Quantifying education externalities has been the holy grail of empirical work in the economics of education (Foster and Rosenzweig, 1994). Barring the difficulties, we have solid evidence that parents' education has a positive effect on health and child survival. Children of better-educated parents have a higher chance of survival and are more likely to go to school and receive regular health checks. More educated women have lower maternal and infant mortality rates and improved reproductive health. From the Netherlands (Groot and Maassen van den Brink, 2007) and Pakistan (Asghar et al., 2009) to Morocco (Glewwe, 1999) and Mozambique (Lindelow, 2008), it has been found that education has positive externalities though its effect on health and child survival. The case is especially strong for mother's education (Schultz, 2002).

In Pakistan, for example, more than one-third of men with less than primary education are in poor health, versus 5 percent for those with higher education (Asghar et al., 2009). One well-documented nonmarket effect is that educating women reduces fertility and child mortality. Also in Pakistan, it has been found that giving 1000 girls one extra year of schooling reduces fertility and child mortality rates by about 8 percent (Summers, 1992). In Taiwan mothers with 9 versus 6 years of education resulted in saving one child life per 1000 births (Chou et al., 2010). A child born to a mother who can read stands a 50 percent greater chance of surviving past age five (United Nations, 2014).

Beyond health, it has been found that each additional year of education on average reduces a country's chances of falling into civil war by 3.6 percent (Winthrop and Graff, 2010).

What Will It Cost?

After the Jom Tien conference in 1990 there have been many estimates of what it would cost to achieve education for all, over and above what governments are already spending for primary education. Due to the lack of data in many countries, differing demographic projections of the school-age population and the effect of HIV, the estimates vary wildly.

Lassibille and Navarro Gomez (1990) put the cost at $7.2 billion per year in 1985 dollars). Colclough and Lewin (1993) estimated that achieving a gross primary enrolment ratio of 100 would require an additional annual public expenditure of $5–6 billion during the 1990s (in 1986 dollars).

After setting the 2015 MDG goals in 2000, UNICEF put the annual additional cost of achieving education for all in developing countries at $9.1 billion per year in 1998 dollars (Delamonica et al., 2001). The World Bank estimated the same cost between $10 and $30 billion annually depending on assumptions (Devarajan et al., 2002).

In 2010 UNESCO estimated that it would take another $16 billion per year in external financing to achieve basic education for in low-income countries by 2015. The latest UNESCO estimate is that it would take an additional $29 billion per year to achieve basic education by 2015 (UNESCO, 2014).

Post-2015 global education goals are expected to be more ambitious than the EFA goals extending to lower secondary education. UNESCO (2014) estimates that the shortfall in the financing necessary to achieve universal basic and lower secondary education by 2015 is estimated at US$38 billion annually. Thus, a conservative assumption is that extra financing of this order would be required to meet the 2030 targets. Adding extended preschool coverage would bring the cost above not only what governments can afford, but also foreign aid.

According to the latest data, there are 57 million children out of school, most of them in sub-Saharan Africa. A rough estimate of the cost per primary school student in sub-Saharan Africa is $300 (based on UNESCO, 2011). Thus an additional $17 billion per year would be needed to reach the zero target by 2030. To put the preceding figures in context, total international aid for basic education in low-income countries in 2011 was $5.8 billion. Looking at the other side of the coin, UNESCO (2014) reports that the cost of 250 million children not learning the basics is equivalent to $129 billion.

Bringing in the cost perspective and the declining trend of international aid for education in recent years enhances the case on how unrealistic are the post-2015 education targets.

Concluding Comments

The estimates presented earlier must be considered approximate given data limitations and the many assumptions involved. In addition, for education to translate to earnings and productivity a host of necessary conditions must hold, such as a country to be in nonconflict and have established protection of property rights. Such conditions may not hold in many sub-Saharan countries that rank high in the Fund for Peace (2013) failed States Index.

On the other hand, and subject to the preceding qualifications, the benefit-cost ratios presented earlier are based on the market benefits of education. Given a long list of nonmarket benefits of education, they should be considered as lower estimates of the true wide-social benefit-cost ratios for expanding a particular level of education.

The generality, ambiguousness, and optimism of the post-2015 MDG targets in the present discourse do not augur well for their implementation by 2030, if not well beyond. Would a more modest and pragmatic approach be warranted, such as giving priority and focusing action where the social returns on the investment are highest?

Instead of setting well-meaning global targets, should these be country-specific depending on initial conditions in each country? Would progress toward a given target, rather than achieving a zero target, be more appropriate for monitoring progress?

Perhaps, should "Education for All" be replaced by "Education for Some," i.e., the most needy? But such a mundane term would never fly in international parlance.

Appendix 1

Education Targets in the Post-2015 MDG Proposals

Target			Indicator	Definition
Establish Sufficient Education System Accessible to All at All Levels (Inputs)	Capacity and Accessibility	Continued Pursuit of Lifelong Learning	Adjusted net intake rate (percentage of population in the same age group)	Total enrollment in primary education of pupils of official primary school entrance age, expressed as a percentage of the population of the same age in a given school year.
			Age-specific enrollment rate (percentage of cohort)	Enrollment of a specific single age enrolled, irrespective of the level of education, as a percentage of the same age.
			ECCE	Programs that, in addition to providing children with care, offer a structured and purposeful set of learning activities, either in a formal institution or as part of a nonformal child development program. ECCE programs are typically designed for children age three years and over, occurring before primary education.
	Sufficient Financing	Public Expenditure	Government expenditure on education to poorer families	No agreed/universal/ international definition.
			Public expenditure on education, total (percentage of GDP)	Total public expenditure (current and capital) on education, expressed as a percentage of the GDP in a given year.
			Public expenditure on education, total (percentage of government expenditure)	Current and capital expenditures on education by local, regional and national governments, expressed as a percentage of total government expenditure on all sectors.
			Expenditure per student, per level (percentage of GDP per capita)	No agreed/universal/ international definition.
		Private	Total private expenditure on educational institutions and educational administration, as percentage of GDP	Private expenditure on educational institutions and administration at a given level of education, expressed as percentage of GDP.
	Equal Right to Education	Equal Right to Education	Ratio of female to male by level of education (percentage)	No agreed/universal/ international definition.
			Ratio of female to male net intake rate (percentage)	No agreed/universal/ international definition.
			Percentage of female teachers	Number of female teachers at a given level of education, expressed as a percentage of total number of teachers at the same level in a given school year.

(cont.)

(cont.)

Target		Indicator	Definition
	Socioeconomic Equality	Duration of compulsory school years	No agreed/universal/ international definition.
		Children out of primary school, female and male (percentage of cohort)	Number of children of official primary school age who are not enrolled in primary or secondary school, expressed as a percentage of the population (by gender) of official primary school age.
		Economically active children, ages 7–14, female and male (percentage of cohort)	Economically active children refer to children involved in economic activity (non-school attendance) for at least one hour in the reference week of the survey.
		Ratio of school attendance of orphans to school attendance of nonorphans	No agreed/universal/ international definition.
		Population from 5–24 years of age by school attendance, urban and rural residence	No agreed/universal/ international definition.
Ensure Active Participation in EFA (Throughputs)	Continued Pursuit of Lifelong Learning	Survival Ratio	Percentage of repeaters	Total number of pupils who are enrolled in the same grade as the previous year, expressed as a percentage of total enrollment in the given grade of education.
		Dropout rate by grade (percentage)	Proportion of pupils from a cohort enrolled in a given grade in a given school year who are no longer enrolled in the following school year.
		Attendance rate (percentage)	Total number of pupils actually attending schools as a percentage of the total registered enrollment.
		Survival rate by grade	Percentage of cohort of pupils enrolled in the first grade of a given level or cycle of education in a given school year who are expected to reach successive grades.
		Persistence to last grade of primary, female and male (percentage of cohort)	Participants in all components of an educational program involved in primary education, irrespective of the result of any potential assessment of the achievement of learning objectives as a percentage of total enrollment registered at the entrance.
		Primary completion rate, female and male (percentage of cohort)	No agreed/universal/ international definition.
	Lifelong Learning	Firms offering formal training	Number of firms with formal training programs.
		Adult education	Education specifically targeting individuals who are regarded as adults to improve their technical or professional qualifications, further develop their abilities,

(cont.)

(cont.)

Target	Indicator	Definition
		enrich their knowledge with the purpose to complete a level of formal education or to acquire knowledge, skills and competencies in a new field, or to refresh or update their knowledge in a particular field.
	Number of students in tertiary education	Number of students enrolled in tertiary education in a given academic year per 100,000 inhabitants.
	Year input per graduate	Estimated average number of pupil-years spent by pupils from a given cohort who graduate from a given cycle or level of education, considering the years of dropout and repetition.
Advancement	Promotion rate by grade	Proportion of pupils from a cohort enrolled in a given grade at a given school year that study in the next grade in the following school year.
	Effective transition rate	The likelihood of a student moving to a higher level of education represented by the number of new entrants to the first grade of the higher level of education in the following year, expressed as a percentage of the students enrolled in the last grade of the given level of education in the given year who do not repeat that grade the following year.
	New entrants to primary education with ECCE	Pupils entering primary education for the first time and who attended some organized ECCE programs
	Students enrolled by type of institution	For example, students enrolled in adult education programs are categorized separately from the total number of students.

Source: Adapted from CIGI (2012), Table 4.

Appendix 2

From Rates of Return to Benefit-Cost Ratios

Because of the detailed nature of data entering a rate of return estimation, papers reporting returns to education do not contain the full age–earnings profiles on which the estimates are based. So it is not possible to use the original benefit and cost streams to estimate benefit-cost ratios for comparison with other sectors. For this purpose we would have to convert the available rates of return to benefit-cost ratios.

From cost-benefit analysis 101 we know that the rate of return (r) and the discount rate (i) relate to each other in the way depicted in Figure 6.10, where NPV denotes the net present value of the investment.

Therefore, we know from theory that the benefit-cost ratio is an inverse function of the discount rate – the lower the discount rate used to estimate the net present value, the higher the benefit-cost ratio.

Given that we have no information on the net present value, we could make an approximation of the size of the benefit-cost ratio by using the short-cut formula described earlier to estimate the benefit-cost ratio of an investment for a given discount rate knowing only its rate of return.

Let B denote the annual benefit of the investment, say how much university graduates are earning on average above secondary school graduates $\left(\overline{W}_u - \overline{W}_s\right)$, and the annual cost equal foregone earnings $\left(\overline{W}_s\right)$ plus direct costs $\left(\overline{C}_u\right)$. According to the shortcut formula the rate of return of the investment can expressed as

$$(1)\ r = \frac{\overline{W}_u - \overline{W}_s}{4\left(\overline{W}_s + \overline{C}_u\right)} = \frac{B}{PVC}$$

where PVC is the lump sum cost of the investment with no discounting involved given the relatively short period within which the costs are incurred.

The present value of the benefits of the investment (PVB) for a given discount rate (i) can be expressed as

$$(2)\ PVB = B/i.$$

Combining equations (1) and (2), B cancels out giving the required conversion:

$$\frac{PVB}{PVC} = \frac{r}{i} = \text{Benefit-cost ratio}$$

Of course, the conversion described earlier is an approximation, given we do not have information on the elasticity of the NPV–i curve in Figure 6.10. An experiment was conducted to find out how much a true benefit-cost ratio would be off relative

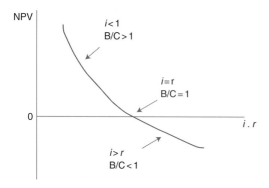

Figure 6.10 *Benefit-cost ratio, discount rate, and rate-of-return relationship*

Source: Author.

Table 6.16 Testing the sensitivity of the internal rate of return to B/C ratio conversion

Discount rate i	Present value of benefits PVB	Present value of costs PVC	True B/C ratio PVB/PVC	Estimated B/C ratio r/i
3%	405,296	297,368	1.4	1.6
4.9%	284,901	284,336	1.0	1.0
6%	236,821	277,208	0.85	0.8

Note: Internal rate of return, r = 4.9%

to the approximation described earlier. "True" in this case means a cost-benefit ratio estimated on the basis of discounted age-earnings profiles by level of education.

Assuming annual flat annual earnings of $\overline{W}_s$ = $80,000 and $\overline{W}_u$ = $100,000 associated with a four-year university degree and a working life of 42 years, the rate of return of the investment is 4.9 percent. In Table 6.16 a comparison is made between the true benefit-cost ratio of the investment to the estimated one for three alternative discount rates. As expected, the conversion does not match exactly the true benefit-cost ratio, but it is very close.

References

Asghar, Zahid, Nazia Attique, Amena Urooj, and Naushin Mahmood (2010). "Measuring impact of education and socio-economic factors on health for Pakistan," *The Pakistan Development Review* 48(4): 653–74.

Banerjee, Abhijit V., Shawn Cole, Esther Duflo, and Leigh Linden (2007). "Remedying education: evidence from two randomized experiments in India." *The Quarterly Journal of Economics* 122(3): 1235–64.

Behrman, J. R., Y. Cheng, and P. Todd. (2004) "Evaluating pre-school programs when length of exposure to the program varies: a nonparametric approach." *Review of Economics and Statistics* 86(1): 108–32.

Behrman, Jere R., David Ross, and Richard Sabot (2008). "Improving quality versus increasing the quantity of schooling: estimates of rates of return from rural Pakistan." *Journal of Development Economics* 85(1–2): 94–104.

Blundell, R., Dearden, L., Meghir, C., and Sianesi, B. (1999) "Human capital investment: the returns from education and training to the individual, the firm and the economy." *Fiscal Studies* 20(1): 1–23.

Bruns, Barbara, Alain Mingat, and Ramahatra Rakotomalala (2003). *Achieving Universal Primary Education by 2015: A Chance for Every Child*. Washington, DC: The World Bank.

Carl Bialik (2013). "No easy lessons in assessing preschool payoff," *Wall Street Journal*, p. A2.

Carneiro, P., Lorraine Dearden, and Anna Vignoles (2010). "The economics of vocational education and training." In P. Peterson, E.

Baker and B. McGaw (eds.), *International Encyclopedia of Education*, Vol 8. Amsterdam: Elsevier: 255–61.

Carneiro, P. and J. Heckman (2003). "Human capital policy." In James Heckman and Alan Krueger (eds.), *Inequality in America: What Role for Human Capital Policies*. Cambridge, MA: MIT Press.

Center for International Governance Innovation (CIGI) (2012). *Post-2015 Development Agenda: Goals, Targets and Indicators Special Report*. New York: United Nations.

Chetty, R., J. N. Friedman, N. Hilger, E. Saez, D. W. Schanzenbach, and D. Yagan. (2011). "How does your kindergarten classroom affect your earnings? Evidence from Project STAR." *Quarterly Journal of Economics* 126(4): 1593–1660.

Chou, Shin-Yi, Jin-Tan Liu, Michael Grossman, and Ted Joyce (2010), "Parental education and child health: evidence from a natural experiment in Taiwan." *Applied Economics* 2(1): 33–61.

Clemens, M. (2004). *The Long Walk to School: International education goals in historical perspective*. Washington, DC: Center for Global Development, Working Paper 37.

Clemens, M, C. Kenny, and J. Moss (2007). "The trouble with the MDGs: confronting expectations of aid and development success." *World Development* 35(5): 735–51.

Colclough, Christopher, and Keith Lewin (1993). *Educating All the Children: Strategies for Primary Schooling in the South*. New York: Oxford University Press.

Cunha, F., J. J. Heckman, L. J. Lochner, and D. V. Masterov (2006). "Interpreting the evidence on life cycle skill formation." In E. A. Hanushek and F. Welch (eds.), *Handbook of the Economics of Education*. Amsterdam: Elsevier: 697–812.

Dearden L., S. McIntosh, M. Myck, and A. Vignoles (2002), "The returns to academic and vocational qualifications in Britain," *Bulletin of Economic Research*, 54: 249–74.

Delamonica, Enrique, Santosh Mehrotra, and Jan Vandemoortele (2001). "Is EFA affordable? Estimating the global minimum cost of 'education for all'." Innocenti Working Paper No. 87. Florence: UNICEF Innocenti Research Centre.

Devarajan, Shantayana, Margaret Miller, and Eric Swanson (2002). "Goals for development: history, prospects and costs." Policy Research

Working Paper No. 2819. Washington, DC: The World Bank.

Dickerson A. P. (2005), "A study on rates of return to investment in level 3 and higher Qualifications." Department of Trade and Industry, December 2005.

European Commission (2000). "Lisbon European Council 23–24 March 2000." European Commission.

(2009). "Progress towards the Lisbon objectives: Benchmarks and indicators." European Commission.

Eurostat (2013). "Early school leavers." http://epp.eurostat.ec.europa.eu/statistics_explained/index.php/School_enrolment_and_early_leavers_from_education_and_training#Youth_education_attainment_level_and_early_leavers_from_education_and_training.

Foster, A. and M. Rosenzweig (1994). "Human resources, technical adoption, and externalities." Department of Economics, University of Pennsylvania.

Fund for Peace (2013). "Failed states index." Fund for Peace. http://ffp.statesindex.org/rankings-2013-sortable.

Gertler, Paul, James Heckman, Rodrigo Pinto, et al. (2013). "Labor market returns to early childhood stimulation: a 20-year followup to an experimental intervention in Jamaica." NBER Working Paper No. 19185.

Glewwe, Paul (1996). "The relevance of standard estimates of rates of return to schooling for education policy: a critical assessment." *Journal of Development Economics* 51(2): 267–90.

(1999). "Why does mother's schooling raise child health in developing countries? Evidence from Morocco." *Journal of Human Resources* 34(1): 124–59.

Glewwe, Paul, Meng Zhao, and Melissa Binder (2006). "Achieving universal basic and secondary education: How much will it cost?" American Academy of Arts and Sciences. www.amacad.org/multimedia/pdfs/publications/researchpapersmonographs/Glwwe.pdf.

Global Campaign for Education (2003). *Must Try Harder: A School Report on 22 Rich Countries' Aid to Basic Education in Developing Countries.* Brussels: Global Campaign for Education.

Gould, J. R. (1972). "On investment criteria for mutually exclusive projects." *Economica* 39 (153): 70–7.

Groot, W. and H. Maassen van den Brink (2007). "The health effects of education." *Economics of Education Review* 26(2), 186–200.

Hanushek, Eric A. (1999). "Some findings from an independent investigation of the Tennessee STAR experiment and from other investigations of class size." *Educational Evaluation and Policy Analysis* 21(2): 143–163.

(2003). The Failure of Input-Based Schooling Policies. *Economic Journal.* 113(485), 64–98.

(2007). "The alchemy of 'costing out' an adequate education." In M. R. West and P. E. Peterson (eds.), *School Money Trials: The Legal Pursuit of Educational Adequacy.* Washington, DC: Brookings Institution.

Hanushek Eric A. and Ludger Woessmann (2011). "Educational outcomes." *Economic Policy.* July.

Heckman, J. J. (2000). "Policies to foster human capital." *Research in Economics* 54: 3–56.

(2008). "Schools, Skills, and Synapses." Forschungsinstitut zur Zukunft der Arbeit Institute for the Study of Labor. IZA DP No. 3515.

(2011), "Effective child development strategies." In Edward Zigler, Walter S. Gilliam, and W. Steven Barnett (eds.), *The pre-K debates - Current Controversies and Issues.* Baltimore, MD: Paul H. Brookes Pub. Co.

Heckman, J. J., and Kautz, T. (2012). "Hard Evidence on Soft Skills." IZA DP No. 6580.

Hirshleifer J. (1958). "On the Theory of Optimal Investment Decision." *Journal of Political Economy* 66(4): 329–52.

Janssens, Wendy, Jacques Van Der Gaag, and Shinichiro Tanaka (2001). *Arab Republic of Egypt: An Economic Analysis of Early Childhood Education Development.* Washington, DC: World Bank.

Jung, Haeil and Amer Hasan (2014). "The Impact of Early Childhood Education on Early Achievement Gaps: Evidence from the Indonesia Early Childhood Education and Development (ECED) Project." World Bank Policy Research Working Paper 6794.

Krafft, Caroline (2013). "Is School the Best Route to Skills? Returns to Vocational School and Vocational Skills in Egypt." Minnesota Population Center Working Paper Series No. 2013–09. Minnesota Population Center Working Paper Series.

Kremer, M., Conner Brannen, and Rachel Glennerster (2013). "The challenge of education and learning in the developing world." *Science* 340: 297–300.

Lassibille, G. and M. L. Navarro Gomez (1990). "Forecast of primary-education expenditure in developing countries in the year 2000." *Prospects* 20(4): 513–24.

Levin, H., Clive Belfiel, Peter Muennig, and Cecilia Rouse (2007). "The public returns to public educational investments in African-American males." *Economics of Education Review* 26(6): 699–708.

Lindelow, Magnus (2008). "Health as a family matter: do intra-household education externalities matter for maternal and child health?" *Journal of Development Studies* 44(4): 562–85.

McEwan, Patrick J. (2013). "Improving learning in primary schools of developing countries: a meta-analysis of randomized experiments." Mimeo. Wellesley, MA: Wellesley College.

Mincer, J. (1974). *Schooling, Experience, and Earnings*. Cambridge, MA: National Bureau of Economic Research.

Moenjak, Thammarak and Christopher Worswick (2003). "Vocational education in Thailand: a study of choice and returns." *Economics of Education Review* 22(1): 99–107.

Newhouse, D. and D. Suryadarma (2011). "The value of vocational education: high school type and labor market outcomes in Indonesia." *The World Bank Economic Review* 25(2): 296–322.

North-South Institute (2013). "Post-2015 Tracking Tool." http://cidpnsi.ca/blog/portfolio/tracking-post-2015/cidpnsi.ca/wp-content/uploads/2013/07/NSI-Post-2015-Tracking-Tool-Database-September-2013.xlsx.

Organization for Economic Co-operation and Development (OECD) (2008). *Costs and Benefits in Vocational Education and Training*. Paris: OECD.

(2013a). *Education at a Glance, 2013*. Paris: OECD.

(2013b). *PISA 2012 Results*. Paris: OECD.

Orazem, P., P. Glewwe, and H. Patrinos (2008). "The Challenge of Education." Copenhagen Consensus Center.

Oxfam (2002). "Broken promises? Why donors must deliver on the EFA action plan." Global Campaign for Education Briefing Paper, September 23.

Patrinos, H. (2007), "Living conditions of children." In Bjorn Lomborg (ed.), *Solutions for the World's Biggest Problems: Costs and Benefits*, Cambridge, UK: Cambridge University Press: 358–75. (Also: World Bank Policy Research Working Paper 4251, The World Bank.)

Patrinos, H. and C. Sakellariou (2011). "Quality of schooling, returns to schooling and the 1981 vouchers reform in Chile." *World Development* 39(12): 2245–56.

Psacharopoulos, George (1989). "Why educational reforms fail: a comparative analysis." *International Review of Education* 35(2): 179–95.

Psacharopoulos, G. (1995). "The Profitability of Investment in Education: Concepts and Methods." The World Bank, Human Capital Development and Operations Policy, Working Papers, no. 63.

Psacharopoulos, G. and R. Layard (1979). "Human capital and earnings: British evidence and a critique." *Review of Economic Studies* 46(3): 485–503.

Psacharopoulos, G. and W. Loxley (1985). *Diversified Secondary Education and Development: Evidence from Colombia and Tanzania*, Baltimore, MD: Johns Hopkins University Press.

Psacharopoulos, G. and R. Mattson (1998). 'Estimating the returns to education: a sensitivity analysis of methods and sample size.' *Journal of Educational Development and Administration* 12(3): 271–287.

Psacharopoulos, G. and H. Patrinos (2002). "Returns to investment in education: A further update." World Bank Policy Research Working Paper 2881.

Pugatch, Todd (2012). "Safety valve or sinkhole? Vocational schooling in South Africa." IZA Discussion Paper Series No. 7015. IZA Discussion Paper Series. Bonn, Germany.

Said, Mona and Fatma El-Hamidi (2008). "Taking technical education seriously in MENA: determinants, labor market implications and policy lessons." Economic Research Forum Working Paper Series No. 450.

Salehi-Isfahani, Djavad, Insan Tunali, and Ragui Assaad (2009). "A comparative study of returns to education of urban men in Egypt, Iran, and Turkey." *Middle East Development Journal* 12/01(02): 145–187.

Save the Children (2013). *Ending the Hidden Exclusion*. London: Save the Children.

Schultz, T. Paul (2002). "Why governments should invest more to educate girls." *World Development* 30(2): 207–25.

Summers, Lawrence H. (1992). "Investing in all the people." *The Pakistan Development Review* 31(4): pp. 367–404.

Temple, J. A and A. J. Reynolds (2007). "Benefits and costs of investments in preschool education: evidence from the Child-Parent Centers and related programs." *Economics of Education Review* 26(1): 126–44.

Tinbergen, J. (1975). *Income Distribution*. Amsterdam: Elsevier.

UNESCO (1961a). "Conference of Africa States on the development of education in Africa: Final report." Paris: UNESCO. http://unesdoc.unesco.org/images/0007/000774/077416e.

(1961b). "Outline of a plan for African educational development." http://unesdoc.unesco.org/images/0007/000774/077414e.pdf, http://unesdoc.unesco.org/images/0007/000774/077416e.

(1993). *Global monitoring report 1993*. Paris: UNESCO.

(2002). *Global monitoring report 2002*. Paris: UNESCO.

(2010). *Education and the Millennium Development Goals*. Paris: UNESCO, www.unesco.org/fileadmin/MULTIMEDIA/HQ/ED/GMR/pdf/gmr2010/MDG2010_Facts_and_Figures_EN.pdf.

(2011). *Financing education in sub-Saharan Africa*. Montreal, Quebec, Canada: Institute of Statistics.

(2013). *Education transforms lives, Global Monitoring Report, 2013*. Paris: UNESCO.

(2014). *Education for All Global Monitoring Report. Teaching and Learning: Achieving quality for all 2013/4*. Paris: UNESCO.

UNICEF (2014). "ChildInfo." www.childinfo.org/education_preprimary.php.

United Nations (2013). "A new global partnership: eradicate poverty and transform economies through sustainable development – Report of the High-level panel of eminent persons on the Post-2015 development agenda." New York: United Nations.

(2014). "Open working group brief: sustainable development goal on equitable learning." New York: National Assembly, United Nations.

United Nations Development Program (UNDP) (2013). "The Millennium Development Goals Report, 2013." www.undp.org/content/dam/undp/library/MDG/english/mdg-report-2013-english.pdf.

Winthrop, R. and C. Graff (2010). *Beyond Madrasas: Assessing the Links between Education and Militancy in Pakistan*. Washington, DC: Brookings Institution.

Woessmann, L. (2007). "International evidence on expenditure and class size: a review." In Tom Loveless and Frederick M. Hess (eds.), *Brookings Papers on Education Policy 2006/2007*. Washington, DC: Brookings Institution: 245–272.

Word, E., Johnston, J., Bain, H. P., et al. (1990). "Student/Teacher Achievement Ratio (STAR), Tennessee's K–3 class size study: Final summary report, 1985–1990." Nashville: Tennessee State Department of Education.

World Bank (2002). "Arab Republic of Egypt Strategic Options for Early Childhood Education." Washington, DC: World Bank.

(2011). *Education Strategy 2020*. The World Bank.

(2014). World Bank Indicators. http://databank.worldbank.org/data/views/variableselection/selectvariables.aspx?source=education-statistics-~-all-indicators#.

World Conference on Education for All (WCEFA) (1990). *Meeting Basic Learning Needs: A New Vision for the 1990's*. New York: The World Bank, UNESCO, UNICEF.

Alternative Perspective

CAROLINE KRAFFT AND PAUL GLEWWE

Summary

Overall, we generally agree with Psacharopoulos on the value of improving school quality, and we share his skepticism of vocational and technical education. Yet we would also argue that the evidence for expanding preprimary and primary education in sub-Saharan Africa is not as strong as he claims.

The task set is a very difficult one, and we question the very idea of this undertaking, largely because the field of education suffers particularly from output-driven goals rather than outcomes. Setting goals that focus on outputs or proxies, such as enrollment rates, creates an incentive to attain that specific goal, which will not necessarily lead to the essential goals or benefits of education, such as human capital, knowledge, and skills.

It is this "how to proceed" that is crucially absent from Psacharopoulos's chapter. For instance, improving school quality by increasing student test scores is stated to have a benefit-cost ratio between 3.0 and 5.0, but how to improve test scores and school quality is effectively not discussed. Even if ways to achieve more years of schooling can be found and costed, calculating the benefit-cost ratio can be misleading given the lack of data on externalities, measurement errors (particularly in developing countries), the absence of the self-employed from the estimate, and the inclusion of government workers, whose salary reflects government policy rather than productivity.

We are therefore concerned about the likely inaccuracy of the quoted figures. This is compounded by the low quality of the evidence presented (and perhaps the quality of evidence available). A further factor is the uncertainty around estimates and potential outliers. In particular, the benefit-cost ratio of preschool programs in sub-Saharan Africa is based on a study in Kenya, with a ratio an order of magnitude higher than others, with no adequate justification.

A weakness of the chapter is that it provides no economic justification for public subsidy of education because social rates of return quoted are lower than private rates of return. Although Psacharopoulos alludes to wider social benefits, he is not able to provide sufficient hard evidence to support his case.

Research from developed countries shows that the best investment a country can make is likely to be in preprimary education, particularly for disadvantaged children. This is the most cost-effective stage to invest in, and the opportunity cost of children's time is low at this age. Good-quality preprimary education consistently improves child development and enhances later attainment. On the other hand, investing in universal primary education in sub-Saharan Africa is problematic, given that half of the 57 million children out of school are in conflict zones. For those outside conflict zones, primary education is likely to be a worthwhile investment, but schools must be of sufficiently high quality to allow significant learning. In the case of secondary education, there are unfortunately too few jobs requiring formal education to make this a good investment in some less-developed countries.

The issue of education quality is important but priorities for cost-effective interventions are difficult to set. However, in all cases studied it is important to ensure that teachers are both present and knowledgeable. This in itself may also help to reduce dropout rates.

Although we have pointed a number of difficulties with the underlying challenge and with Psacharopoulos's approach, ultimately we come to similar priority targets. Preprimary education, primary education, and school quality investments are the best education goals. However, there is also a real need for high-quality longitudinal studies to assess the benefits of interventions that may only pay off much later in life.

Alternative Perspective

PETER F. ORAZEM

Summary

Fifty-two percent of all primary-age children who are not attending school are in sub-Saharan Africa. Moreover, 61 percent of the children expected to receive no primary schooling during their lifetimes reside in that region. If we are to meet the Millennium Development Goal of Universal Primary Education for all, the countries of sub-Saharan Africa represent the greatest challenge. It is inconceivable that UNESCO's estimate of the need for an extra $26 billion annually to achieve universal global primary education will be met via increased foreign aid. This allows international agencies to blame failures to achieve Universal Primary Education (UPE) on lack of funds, but we should note that the estimated funding gap has steadily increased while the number of children out of school has decreased.

There are, in fact, other reasons for the failure. First, it is clear that not all governments are using their resources for the intended purpose; corrupt countries show poor returns to human capital. Some of the worst countries as measured by the Fund for Peace's Fragile States index are in sub-Saharan Africa, and it is unsurprising that their schooling record is also poor. Out-of-school children in countries such as the Democratic Republic of the Congo, Somalia, or Zimbabwe are unlikely to attend school even if aid is increased.

A second major problem in the region is the large proportion of children who have lost one or both parents. Sub-Saharan Africa has 36 percent of the children worldwide who have lost at least one parent, and 47 percent of those who have lost both. The effects of parental loss on schooling are insignificant in some countries where there are strong extended family linkages to provide support. However, in most countries the problem is getting worse rather than better, with concerns that extended families can no longer provide enough financial and emotional support.

There is widespread acceptance that policies aimed at enhancing human capital investments should focus on the very young, but it is less clear how best to target resources. Experiments such as the famous Perry preschool program for disadvantaged children showed higher cognitive scores on entering school for children who had followed a two-year preschool program. Although these differences soon disappeared, these children were found to have advantages in later life, being more likely to finish high school, go to college, have steady employment, and avoid criminal activity.

The difficulty is that the Perry program included other interventions with the family in addition to preschooling, so the effect of preschool alone is not easy to define. Similarly, in developing countries there are numerous preschool programs that appear to have generated positive long-term results, but these might in part be due to the provision of nutritional supplements or health services. Devoting substantial resources to preschool programs without first deconstructing past successes into the value added from each subcomponent is premature. And any effort to expand preschool must also establish why these programs have not been universally successful.

In conclusion, we must assess whether insufficient preschool access is the root cause of failure to achieve UPE. It seems unlikely that a country will ever attain UPE without first addressing the problems of orphans and dysfunctional government institutions.

Benefits and Costs of the Energy Targets for the Post-2015 Development Agenda

ISABEL GALIANA

Introduction

The global energy system is undergoing a rapid and significant transformation both from demand and supply perspectives. The former is due in large part to the growth and rapid urbanization of emerging economies, both of which are extremely energy intensive. The latter is due primarily to the "shale gas revolution," the disaster at Fukushima, and the push for renewables. Governments are defining policies regulating all aspects of energy systems, including extraction, transportation, distribution, accessibility, fuel mix, transmission, and so on.

The World Energy Council's definition of energy sustainability is based on three core dimensions – energy security[1], social/economic equity, and environmental sustainability. Policy objectives should strive to address these three partially conflicting dimensions.

Further confounding the complexity of establishing appropriate targets are the following facts: there are currently about 1.3 billion people without electricity and 2.6 billion people who rely on traditional biomass for cooking and heating; energy demand is expected to double by 2050; and there is a strong international desire to halve greenhouse gas (GHG) emissions to mitigate global warming. Energy planning must also be linked to goals and priorities in other sectors of the economy.

Regional differences abound, with regions least able to finance an energy shift most in need of one. Energy poverty[2] in Africa in particular is a priority as less than 30 percent of the population has access to electricity in sub-Saharan Africa. In Asia 700 million people still have no access to electricity, and almost 2 billion people still burn wood, dung, and crop waste to cook and to heat their homes (Asian Development Bank, 2014). Lack of access to modern forms of energy results in the use of more-polluting and-less sustainable fuels, including biomass.

In this chapter we examine six potential targets for a post-2015 development agenda.

1. The zero target of increasing access to modern forms of energy to 100 percent of the population
   a. Universal provision of electrification
   b. Universal provision of modern cooking facilities
2. Doubling the rate of energy efficiency improvement globally
3. Doubling the share of renewable energy in the global energy mix
4. Phasing out fossil fuel energy subsidies
5. Providing access to modern cooking fuels to 30 percent of the population
6. Increasing investment in R&D in energy technologies

Part 1

Existing Global Energy Programs

In 2011 the Sustainable Energy for All initiative (SE4ALL) was launched based on the recommendations of the Secretary-General's Advisory Group on Energy and Climate Change (AGECC). This

---

[1] Energy security in this context relates to reducing volatility in energy supply and prices.
[2] Definitions abound for energy poverty; here we define energy poverty as a lack of access, financial or physical, to sufficient modern energy to meet basic needs of cooking, lighting, and heating.

focuses on drawing attention and financing to three objectives:

1. Ensuring universal access to modern energy services by 2030
2. Doubling the rate of improvements in energy efficiency by 2030
3. Doubling the share of renewable energy to 30 percent of the global energy mix by 2030

Numerous reports highlight the importance of energy services in achieving the MDGs (Modi, McDade, et al., 2005; United Nations [UN], 2005). The designation of 2012 as the International Year of Sustainable Energy for All was in part an appeal to governments to support the MDGs through energy policy.

In June of 2014 Secretary-General Ban Ki-moon declared the decade from 2014–2024 as the United Nations Decade of Sustainable Energy for All (DSEA). The DSEA was launched within the SE4ALL program and highlights the importance of energy in developing the post-2015 development agenda.

Energy – The Basics

Modern forms of energy increase the productivity of agriculture and labor, improve the health of the population, lower transaction and transport costs, and provide important services such as lighting to consumers. Energy policy targets tend to focus on consumption through efficiency or production through energy portfolio preferences. Efficiency measures are driven by both environmental concerns though reduced damages associated with lower total energy consumption[3] and economic growth ambitions, as reduced energy use per unit produced lowers costs. Production targets focus on the energy mix or the quality of energy services within an economy, often though renewable targets and/or increased distribution. The quality of energy services is often described with the "energy ladder" hypothesis, which states that as incomes rise, a household's energy choice moves from traditional fuels, such as wood, first to transitional fuels, like kerosene, and then to modern fuels, such as electricity from the grid. Higher-quality energy is portrayed as more productive, environmentally less damaging, and more flexible.

The energy ladder hypothesis was studied by Burke (2013) based on data from 134 countries for the period 1960–2010. He shows that economic development results in an overall substitution from the use of biomass to energy sourced from fossil fuels, and then increasingly toward primary electricity from nuclear power and certain low-carbon modern renewables such as wind power. An important consideration will be the possibility of skipping rungs on the ladder, for example, jumping from biomass to clean electricity, skipping the fossil fuel rung. Unfortunately, there is no clear answer regarding the welfare-enhancing potential and cost effectiveness of this option.

Lastly, with respect to production objectives, energy life cycle impacts must be examined; extraction, transformation, transportation distribution, and consumption of energy are governed by unyielding laws of physics that constrain possibilities.

Current Trends in Energy Production and Use

According to the International Energy Outlook 2013 (Energy Information Administration [EIA], 2013a) world energy consumption is projected to grow 56 percent between 2010 and 2040. Figure 7.1 illustrates the growth over the last two decades and projections to 2040. The main driver is strong economic growth in non-OECD (Organization for Economic Co-operation and Development) countries. In fact, projected energy use in non-OECD countries increases by 90 percent, whereas in OECD countries, the increase is only 17 percent.

Action is needed to tackle the lack of significant growth in sub-Saharan Africa, where less than 30 percent of the population had access to electricity in 2012.

Figure 7.2 looks at the fuel mix of energy demand from 1990 to 2010 with projections out to 2040. Renewable energy and nuclear power are the world's fastest-growing energy sources to

---

[3] An exception may be particular cases of total rebound (discussed in more detail in Target 2).

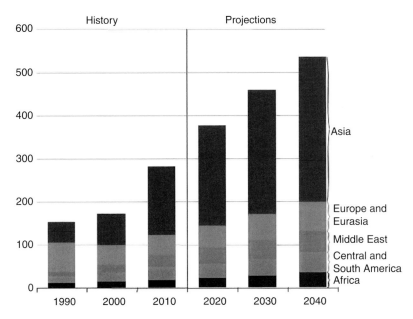

Figure 7.1 *Non-OECD energy consumption (quadrillion Btu) by country grouping*

Source: EIA 2013a.

2035, both increasing by 2.7 percent per year, but fossil fuels continue to dominate supply, largely due to their wide availability, low costs, and integration in existing infrastructure (lock-in).

Csereklyei, Rubio Varas, and Stern (2014) find evidence for the following five stylized facts on energy and economic growth[4] that have implications for the development of suitable energy policy objectives.

- First, elasticity of energy with respect to income is stable and less than unity. CVS1 has a number of important implications. Energy use per capita increases over time as an income grows. The elasticity of global energy intensity with respect to income is around –0.3. The growth rate of energy intensity is negatively correlated with the growth rate of income, thus rapid growth implies rapid improvements in energy efficiency.
- The second CVS stylized fact is that both global energy intensity and the energy to capital ratio are converging across countries.
- Third, elasticity of the energy-to-capital ratio with respect to income is around –0.4, implying that the decline in energy intensity is driven

mainly by energy efficiency improvements rather than structural change. However, it is not unusual for the opposite trend to be found in the early stages of development.
- Fourth, based on data from the U.S., the UK, and Sweden, the cost share of energy declines over time.
- Fifth, energy quality increases with income.

The World Energy Outlook provides a series of scenarios to assess various potential futures. The New Policies Scenario takes into account policy commitments and plans that have been announced by countries. These policies include climate targets and plans to phase out fossil-energy subsidies that have not been implemented but rather only announced and consequently are extremely optimistic. This scenario serves as the International Energy Agency (IEA) baseline scenario. The New Policies Scenario shows a gradual decline in the number of people without electricity, bringing

---

[4] The stylized facts will be referred to as CVS1–CVS5.

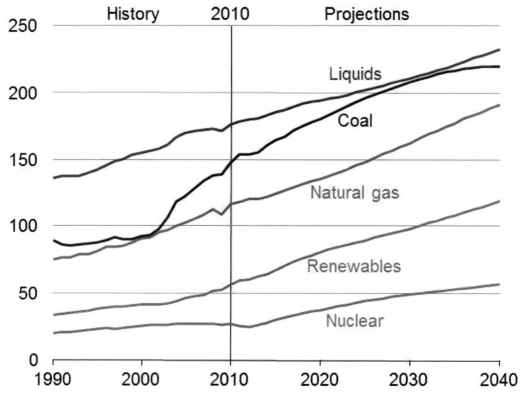

Figure 7.2 *World energy consumption* (quadrillion Btu)

Source: EIA, 2013a.

this below 1 billion in 2030, but a much smaller net fall in those without clean cooking facilities.

Investments in energy supply have doubled since 2000 to over $1.6 trillion. Moreover, $130 billion went to improve energy efficiency and $250 billion to renewables. However, fossil fuel extraction and infrastructure accounts for more than $1 trillion per year (World Energy Investment Outlook, 2014). It will become increasingly difficult for developing and emerging economies to supply the massive investments in infrastructure needed to support booming electricity demand.

IEA (2014a) projections under the New Policies Scenario show annual investment in energy supply rising to $2 trillion in 2035, with expenditures on energy efficiency expanding to $550 billion. Low-carbon technologies account for almost three-quarters of energy supply investment with renewables at a

cumulative $6 trillion and nuclear at $1 trillion over the 2012–2035 period. Given the strong expected growth, nearly two-thirds of energy-supply investment takes place in emerging economies, with investment spreading beyond the BRICS. Achieving the widely discussed climate target of 2°C would require double the investments in the New Policies Scenario by 2035.

Shale Gas and the Growth of Liquefied Natural Gas

The availability of primary energy sources has never been greater; for the most part, the increased supply is due to the "shale gas revolution." Shale gas is now part of the energy lexicon as technological innovation has increased proven gas reserves to unprecedented levels. However, both government policy and export constraints interfere with the ability of resource-rich regions to move their product to high-valued external markets.

Together, multi-stage hydraulic fracturing and horizontal drilling along with 3-D seismic technologies, have dramatically increased proven reserves; in 2013, the EIA estimated global technical recoverable shale gas resources of 7,299 trillion cubic feet (EIA, 2013a).

However, the process of fracking is controversial. Much of Europe and pockets of North America have banned the practice. Antifracking campaigns focus on seismicity resulting from deep fractures, chemical contamination of freshwater aquifers from surface seepage, and subsurface migration. Shale gas exploitation also has climate change implications via methane leakages and carbon emissions from combustion.

With a massive increase in supply, the price of gas is depressed in well-developed basins. However, the price remains high in areas without natural gas or without the necessary pipeline capacity, giving rise to a nascent global liquefied natural gas (LNG) industry. Thus natural gas can replace higher-cost input fuels such as coal, oil, or other petroleum products, even in areas without natural gas reserves. The shale gas revolution has also reduced electricity prices across those regions with access to the natural gas.

The EIA expects world LNG production to double from about 10 trillion cubic feet in 2010 to around 20 trillion cubic feet in 2040. The liquefaction facilities are currently, or are expected to be, located Australia, Qatar, and North America (EIA, 2014). The total capacity of the 19 facilities currently planned in North America would be 219 metric tonnes per annum (MTPA). More than 28 other countries have announced plans to build LNG facilities.

As technology evolves and disperses, significant opportunities will present themselves to regions that currently have poor access to energy supply, are without the necessary infrastructure and investment capital, but have technically recoverable shale gas. For example, the EIA (2014) estimates that China and Africa have some of the world's largest technically recoverable shale gas resources. By 2020, the number of countries with import capacity could double, with India, China, and Japan all having significant demand.

Implications of Fukushima

With its energy-intensive industrial base, Japan's decision to invest heavily in nuclear energy was a pragmatic one. Prior to the earthquake in 2011, 30 percent of Japan's electricity came from its 40 GW of nuclear generating capacity. However, following the incidents at Fukushima, Japan systematically shut down the country's nuclear fleet, and at present its energy needs are being met by coal, oil, and liquefied natural gas.

As Japan's carbon-free nuclear energy was replaced with higher carbon sources, the country's carbon emissions have increased. Although policy makers globally are reluctant to expand the role of nuclear energy, the climate implications of switching to carbon-intensive sources is clear. Germany's Energiewende has seen their emissions increase as base load coal facilities are required to offset the nuclear closures.

The Rise of Coal in China and India

In 2012, 41 percent of the world's electricity generation was coal fired, and the top three importers of coal for electricity production were China, Japan, and India.

Between 1990 and 2010, the Chinese and Indian economies grew by an average of 10.4 and 6.4 percent per year, respectively (EIA, 2013b, 2013c). Since 2010, the growth rates in both those countries dipped slightly; however, coal consumption continues to rise. EIA (2013b) estimates Chinese coal consumption tripled between 2000 and 2010, and in 2011 China became the largest coal importer in the world. China alone consumed 47 percent of global coal in 2012 and accounted for 82 percent of the global incremental coal demand in that year.

The strong growth of India's economy is driving the consumption of coal as the country's primary energy source. In 2012, India ranked third in the world in both the production and the consumption of coal; 639.6 and 721.4 million short tons, respectively. The EIA forecasts that coal will remain the second-largest energy source globally due to the significant increases in use in China and India and other non-OECD countries (EIA, 2013c).

Energy and Development

Economic development represents a restructuring of a country's economy in terms of technological and social progress. Economic growth is closely linked to economic development, as it represents an expansion in a country's gross domestic product (GDP). Csereklyei and Humer (2012) describe four theories that relate economic growth and energy consumption. Of the hypotheses outlined (Neutrality, Feedback, Conservation, and Growth), only the Growth Hypothesis postulates a unidirectional relationship between energy consumption and GDP growth.

The importance of energy forms the core of the Growth theory; economic growth is driven by the use of more resources, which increases per capita GDP (Soubbotina, 2005). Smil (2000) hypothesizes that "civilization's advances during the twentieth century are closely bound with an unprecedented rise of energy consumption" (p. 21). In the twentieth century, fossil fuel consumption rose by over 1300 percent while population tripled; annual per capita energy consumption more than quadrupled.

In contrast, the Neutrality Hypothesis asserts that there is no relationship between energy consumption and GDP. It assumes a unidirectional relationship wherein GDP growth increases energy consumption and suggests that policies aimed at conserving energy will not impact GDP.

The Feedback Hypothesis assumes bidirectional causality between energy access and economic development. When this feedback mechanism is known to occur, a means of decoupling the two would allow for a reduction in energy consumption without a deleterious impact on economic growth.

Empirically, evidence can be found to support each of these hypotheses. The only conclusion that is clear is that the relationship between energy or electricity, and GDP growth is uncertain and can support any one of the four hypotheses. Each suggests different energy development paradigms, but hypothesis testing is very difficult at very low income levels.

Energy and the Environment

Environmental and energy policies are fundamentally linked because all forms of energy have some degree of environmental damage associated with them. There is a strong push to reduce negative impacts associated with energy systems at all levels of government.

At the global level, energy and climate change are strongly related, with an urgent need to reduce GHG emissions from energy systems. It is also urgent to decrease indoor and outdoor air pollution from fuel combustion and its impacts on human health and ecosystems, as well as to reduce other adverse effects and ancillary risks associated with some energy systems. Fossil fuel extraction causes significant damage at both the local and regional levels.

Nuclear energy's main environmental impact is the disposal of spent fuel and the risk of a nuclear catastrophe. Despite a NIMBY (not in my backyard) attitude toward nuclear, it is one of the most environmentally sound sources of base load energy[5].

Hydropower's environmental impacts are linked to the flooding of large areas and the alteration of natural river flows, disturbing wildlife. Other renewable energy sources, such as wind and solar, have minimal environmental impacts. However both require rare earth metals (REMs), the extraction and refining of which can cause contamination.

All major forms of electricity generation save for wind require large amounts of water either for cooling in the case of nuclear, coal, NG, and solar thermal, or cleaning of solar panels. There is evidence that the needs of generating systems will conflict with irrigation and consumption needs as populations increase, particularly in drought-prone areas.

With respect to biofuels, decentralized traditional biomass such as wood or cow dung can lead to biodiversity loss and deforestation, not to mention the adverse health effects of traditional three-stone cooking. Environmental concerns

---

[5] Base load energy – reliable, consistent source of power, i.e., not intermittent such as wind or solar.

associated with modern biofuels, principally etha-
nol and biodiesel, include carbon emissions, deforestation and biodiversity loss, and the food versus
fuel dilemma, whereby croplands are diverted from
food to fuel, potentially causing food prices to
spike.

Part 2

Target 1: Increase Access to Modern Forms of Energy to 100 Percent of the Population (The "Zero Target")

Modern energy access is defined as "household
access to electricity and clean cooking facilities
(e.g., fuels and stoves that do not cause air pollution
in houses)" (IEA, 2014b). There are currently 1.3
billion people without access to electricity, and 2.6
billion are without access to modern forms of
energy, most of who live in rural areas of Africa
and South-east Asia. In sub-Saharan Africa only
31 percent of the population has access to electricity, the lowest level in the world (Centurelli, 2011).

The target of providing universal modern energy
access has four subrequirements: access to

electricity for rural populations, 100 percent access
to the grid for rural populations, providing modern
cooking facilities to the rural poor, and providing
LPG stoves to urban populations.

Electrification and modern cooking facilities provide lighting, mechanization, and improved cooking
efficiency, which reduces time spent on household
chores while increased productivity allows fewer
adult labor hours to replace child labor, thereby
freeing up time for children to attend school (Department for Internal Development [DFID], 2014).

Modern energy access improves health in a
number of ways, for example by reducing indoor
air pollution, increasing agricultural productivity,
and providing refrigeration. Women are freed from
their traditional role of gathering cooking fuel and
can use the considerable amount of time saved for
income generation.

Universal Electrification

Bazilian et al. (2010) undertook a comprehensive
study and summarized the costs and assumptions
associated with universal electrification from
12 different studies. The results are shown in
Figure 7.3.

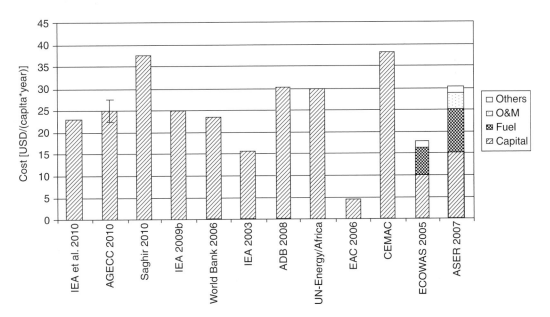

Figure 7.3 *Estimates of universal electrification costs*

Source: Bazilian et al., 2010.

In each case the total costs are disassembled into fuel, O&M, capital, and others. From the chart it is clear that only two of the studies include expenses other than capital, which would suggest a gross underestimation of the costs of universal electrification. They rectified the issues by creating an algorithm that utilizes levelized costs to incorporate capital, fuel, and O&M costs associated with various generating technologies. Transmission and distribution are included, based on the IEA assumption that these costs are roughly equivalent to the capital costs associated with providing the universal electrification.

Bazilian et al. (2010) estimate a range of $14 to $134 billion per year and explain that $100 billion per year would be the best approximation of cost. They estimate that 950 TWh of incremental energy would be required by 2030, generated from an additional 250 GW of capacity. The welfare gain associated with household lighting alone could be $0.15 to $0.65 per kWh (IEG World Bank, 2013) in rural areas. Applying this range to the total electricity requirement of 950 TWh results in benefits ranging from $142.5 to $617.5 billion. A more recent study found that the willingness to pay for electricity in Ghana was in the $0.2734/kWh (Twerefou, 2014). Using this more modest value, the benefits attributable to universal electrification are $259.7 billion per year once the target has been met.

Access to Modern Cooking Fuels

Table 7.1 shows the estimated costs of providing modern cooking fuels. These vary considerably depending on the assumptions made.

More recently, Pachauri et al. (2013) estimated the cost of achieving global access to modern cooking facilities to be $1,210.92 billion in 2010 dollars or $60.6 billion per year, including fuel price support with grants for low-cost financing for stove purchases.

Each year, 4.3 million people die from indoor air pollution (IAP). We assume each death corresponds to about 32 DALYS. Using a low estimate of $1,000 and a high estimate of $5,000 for DALYS,[6] the added health benefit of modern cooking access ranges from $137.6–$688 billion per year. In terms of avoided morbidity benefits,

Table 7.1 Cost estimates for global modern cooking facilities

Capital ($US billion)	Fuel ($US billion)	Source
.0		IEA et al., 2010
0.9		AGECC, 2010
0.6		EAC, 2006
1.3	8.3	ECOWAS, 2005
5.0	18.1	IIASA, 2011

Source: From Bazilian et al., 2010.

World Health Organization (WHO, 2009) estimates that 41 million DALYS are attributable to negative health impacts of indoor air pollution. The avoided health costs are $41–$205 billion per year.

Universal Energy Access

Providing global electrification and access to modern cooking fuels encompasses the benefits of achieving to the two goals individually. The morbidity and mortality associated with indoor air pollution from solid fuel use would be eliminated. The welfare benefits that result from electrification would also be achieved (Table 7.2).

Target 2: Double the Rate of Energy Efficiency Improvement Globally

Improving energy efficiency (EE, the ratio of GDP to energy) is a popular policy tool presented as cost saving, job creating, and environmentally friendly. Benefits of improvements in energy efficiency are numerous and span the three core dimensions of energy sustainability – energy security, social/economic equity, and environmental sustainability.

---

[6] DALYS are disability adjusted life years. "One DALY can be thought of as one lost year of 'healthy' life. The sum of these DALYs across the population, or the burden of disease, can be thought of as a measurement of the gap between current health status and an ideal health situation where the entire population lives to an advanced age, free of disease and disability"; www.who.int/healthinfo/global_burden_disease/metrics_daly/en/.

Table 7.2 Benefits and costs of energy targets

Goal	Cost	Benefits	Benefit-cost ratio (BCR)
Universal electrification	$14–$134 billion (Bazilian et al., 2010)	Welfare: $142.5–$617.5 billion (Bazilian et al., 2010)	4.6–10.2
Modern cooking fuels	$60.6 billion (Pachauri et al., 2013)	Avoided morbidity: $41–$205 billion Avoided mortality: $137.6–$688 billion Total health benefits: $178.6–$893	2.9–14.7
Universal energy Access	$74.6–$194.6 billion	Welfare and health benefits: $321.1–$1,510.5 billion	4.3–7.8

EE can improve the security of energy systems by increasing fuel availability, accessibility, and affordability and can reduce a country's dependence on fossil fuels (Asia Pacific Energy Research Center [APERC], 2007; Kruyt et al., 2009). Economically, EE reduced energy prices, through lesser demand, eases infrastructure needs and frequency of temporary power shortfalls as well as improving industrial competitiveness through reduced operating costs. The "negawatt" argument, whereby conservation (the "negawatt") is much cheaper than expanding energy production capacity, cannot be overstated. Resources are conserved, emissions are reduced, and policies can be implemented rapidly.

Energy efficiency is especially important for developing countries as it can accelerate productivity growth and lead to further economic development. Developing countries with abundant energy resources are relatively inefficient in their energy generation and use.

In least-developed countries, energy access naturally takes priority over energy efficiency measures. However, according to Koskimäki (2012), African countries also have very strong reasons to focus on energy efficiency. First, EE can expand access to a greater number of people as per capita demand levels are lower. Domestic energy bills are reduced, alleviating poverty and freeing up resources for other uses. More efficient cooking devices also reduce health impacts of traditional stoves and provide social benefit, not to mention saving forests. Last, the rapid rate of urbanization is associated with greater energy use, and in particular electricity consumption, giving an opportunity to build efficient supply networks.

The average rate of energy efficiency (EE) improvement has been ~1.2 percent for the period from 2000–2012 (EIA, 2013a). Figure 7.4 illustrates the IEA reference case[7] energy intensity forecasts for certain key regions as well as the world. Energy efficiency is expected to improve at a rate of 2.04 percent per annum to 2040. A doubling of the rate of energy efficiency improvements thus means achieving a 2.4 percent decline in energy intensity by 2040, an increase of ~0.4 percent over the IEA reference scenario.

Csereklyei, Rubio, and Stern (2014) analyzes a global data set from 1971–2010 and finds the geometric mean energy intensity decrease is 0.40 percent per annum and the arithmetic average is 1.07 percent per annum. The accelerated rate of energy intensity decline associated with China over the last decade may increase the feasibility of doubling the rate of longer-term energy efficiency improvement. However, given the evidence of convergence in EE discussed earlier, it is important to understand the physical limits to energy intensity.

Figure 7.4 is consistent with Csereklyei, Rubio, and Stern (2014) second stylized fact that global energy intensity is converging across countries.

Linares and Labandeira (2010) present a review of the literature associated with two "paradoxes" that influence energy efficiency policies, the rebound effect and the energy-efficiency gap. The rebound effect describes a situation in which an improvement in energy efficiency does not bring about a proportional reduction in energy demand.

[7] IEA reference case: Recall this is the optimistic future in which all currently announced policies are successfully implemented.

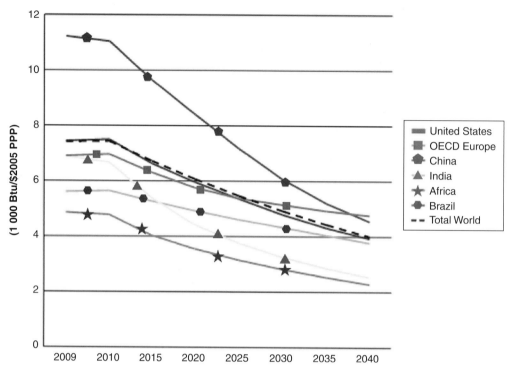

Figure 7.4 *Energy efficiency outlook*

Source: IEA, 2013d, Reference Case.

Rebound is measured using the elasticity of energy demand with respect to energy efficiency. For example, if elasticity is between –1 and 0 there will be a less than the proportional decrease in energy demand. For positive elasticities, energy demand would increase. Although this effect is negative in the context of climate change, from a developmental perspective rebound is something that can be capitalized on to spur growth objectives by increasing consumption. From a social welfare perspective, it will be optimal for governments in developing countries to give greater attention to economic growth, job creation, or industrial productivity than energy conservation.

The energy efficiency gap is the unexploited economic potential for energy efficiency, the low-hanging fruit that doesn't get picked. A difficulty in assessing the energy efficiency gap as well as potential costs and benefits from EE policies is that the opportunities for efficiency improvements are fragmented and found at all scales (light bulb to

generating plant). Another market failure that distorts energy use is underpricing of energy by regulators, exacerbated by energy subsidies. Tackling the gap between potential and actual investment will be a key element of realizing EE targets post-2015.

The International Energy Agency (IEA) first Energy Efficiency Market Report estimates total global investment in energy efficiency measures in 2011 was between $147 and $300 billion (IEA, 2013a). The World Energy Investment Outlook (IEA, 2014a) finds the current energy efficiency investment for 2012 to be $130 billion, equivalent to 13 percent of fossil fuel investment and compares to $240 billion investment in renewable energy sources.

In the New Policies Scenario, EE investment quadruples to $550 billion toward 2035 with 62 percent being spent in the transport sector, 29 percent in buildings, and 9 percent in industry. Figure 7.5 shows forecasts for annual spending

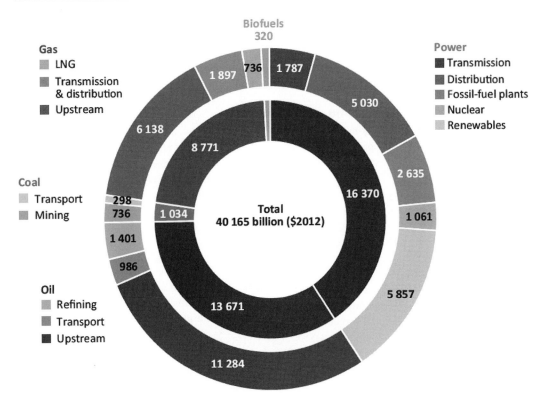

Figure 7.5 *Cumulative global energy efficiency investment by end-use sector in the new policies scenario 2014–2035*

Source: IEA, 2014a.

on energy efficiency for EE investments by sector, the vast majority being in the fossil fuel energy supply chain.

In the IEA 450 scenario with rapid decarbonization of the energy sectors, energy efficiency investment increase to $1.1 trillion in 2035, eight times current levels. This cumulative investment of $14 trillion in efficiency reduces energy consumption by almost 15 percent in 2035 relative to the reference scenario. It is unlikely this type of investment will materialize given current economic trends and objectives.

There are two main linkages between energy efficiency and GDP: increased investment and increased consumption. A study by Vivid Economics (2013) finds evidence from OECD countries for a 0.1 GDP growth elasticity of energy efficiency. That is to say a 1 percent increase in the level of energy efficiency causes a 0.1 percentage point

increase in the growth rate of GDP per capita per annum. This was confirmed in a separate study in the UK. This evidence of rebound suggests energy efficiency should be considered as part of mainstream economic policy rather than an energy or environmental issue only (Ryan and Campbell, 2012).

Given the estimate for GDP rebound, if energy efficiency levels are increasing each year by 1 additional percentage point, combined GDP for the OECD countries considered would be $612 billion larger in 2030 than currently projected, representing a 1.78 percent increase. If energy efficiency improves at an additional percentage point from 2012 through to 2030 (almost double its current rate), it would reach 20 percent above the projected baseline by 2030. (Vivid Economics, 2013).

In Serbia and Montenegro, where energy intensity is three times higher than the rest of Europe, a UN study (UNDP, 2004) identified that energy efficiency measures could boost the GDP growth rate to 5 percent to 7 percent a year. Other high energy-intensity regions have similar potential.

It has been shown that Germany's Energy-efficient Construction and Refurbishment program yielded €5 in tax revenue for every €1 of public funds spent on the program in 2010, created 340,000 jobs, and saved €1.8 billion in unemployment benefits. Ultimately the program achieved returns of 12.5 percent on investments,[8] excluding environmental benefits.

The IEA's World Energy Outlook 2006 estimates that an investment of US$3.2 trillion will be required worldwide to double the rate of energy efficiency improvement, US$2.3 trillion of which will be invested by the G8 countries, while avoiding new supply investments of US$3 trillion worldwide. This $200 billion net efficiency investment generates significant additional benefits in improved business productivity and reduced consumer energy bills worth approximately US$500 billion annually by 2030. This implies a BCR of greater than 1 within three to five years, rising thereafter.

If G8 countries pledge to double their historical rate of energy efficiency improvement to ~2.5 percent and maintain it to 2030, it would reduce their energy demand by about 20 percent in 2030 and avoid the consumption of 55 exajoules (EJ) of primary energy in the G8 Making a 2.5 percent efficiency improvement worldwide would save 97 EJ and return energy consumption to 2004 levels by 2030.[9]

At the industrial level, investments of ~US$360 billion in energy efficient technology will be needed, and lifetime savings in energy costs are estimated to be more than US$900 billion (IEA, 2006). In order to meet growing energy demand to 2030, China and India are forecast to spend an additional US$4 trillion on capacity. Ensuring this is done with the most energy-efficient plants is estimated to add about US$30 per kW to capital costs, but fewer plants would be needed (Massachusetts Institute of Technology [MIT], 2007). This is expected to generate capital expenditure savings of more than US$24 billion in Europe and US$270 billion worldwide along with fuel savings of almost US$0.001 per kWh that would

offset the capital cost in only four years (MIT, 2007). The imposition of efficiency standards for coal-fired plants could save OECD countries US$5 billion per year and reduce CO_2 emissions by almost 1.8 billion tonnes per year in 2030. Moreover, a 60 percent efficiency standard in natural gas generation would reduce total OECD power generation costs by almost US$60 billion in 2030 and would cut carbon emissions by 400 million tonnes per annum. If replicated globally, this policy would reduce projected CO_2 emissions in 2030 by 5 billion tonnes per year (Moss, Chandler, et al., 2007).

Summary

Cost of double the rate of energy efficiency Improvement globally: US$3.2 trillion.

Benefits double the rate of energy efficiency improvement globally:

1. US$3 trillion in avoided new supply investments
2. Improved business productivity and reduced consumer energy bills worth approximately US$500 billion annually by 2030
3. CO_2 reductions – increasing linearly to 25 US$ billion (5$/ton CO_2) – 250 US$ billion ($50/ton CO_2) annually in 2030

BCR: 2.4–3.0.

Target 3: Double the Share of Renewable Energy in the Global Energy Mix

The growth in the use of renewable energy technologies is aimed at decreasing global carbon emissions from electricity production. At the same time, these technologies, such as wind and solar

---

[8] KfW Bankengruppe (2011) KfW Programmes: Energy-efficient Construction and Refurbishment. Public budgets benefit up to fivefold from "promotional euros." Press Release No. 092. See www.kfw.de/kfw/en/KfW_Group/ Press/Latest_News/ PressArchiv/PDF/2011/092_E_Juelich-Studie.pdf.

[9] The calculation assumes the Reference Case of the IEA World Energy Outlook 2006 (IEA, 2006) as the baseline scenario.

photovoltaic (PV), have the potential to be deployed at a small scale in remote areas.

Renewable energy technologies, other than large-scale storage hydro, are dependent on variable fuel sources such as the sun and wind, and the inevitable intermittency requires backup from other sources, thus increasing costs. Wind- and solar-generating capacity tends to be remote from the demand centers and requires more transmission infrastructure, which also increases costs. The net carbon benefit associated with renewable energy technologies is ambiguous when backup is by coal- and gas-fired power stations.

In theory, doubling renewable energy in the global energy mix has the potential to mitigate carbon emissions and provide economic and health benefits.

Subsidies, and other inducements such as feed-in-tariffs (FITs) and renewable portfolio standards (RPSs) have been shown to be extremely cost ineffective and have not impacted emissions as hoped. The UK-based Renewable Energy Foundation finds the cost of abatement under FITs to be between £174 and £800 per tonne of CO_2 (Constable, 2011). In Spain, FITs have led to a record deficit of US$8.3 billion for a total five-year deficit of about US$20 billion.[10] But there are many justifications beyond current carbon abatement for increasing the share of renewables including energy security and reduced imports, issues of technological change, and path dependence. For example, van Benthem, Gillingham, and Sweeney (2008) find that California's solar subsidies are economically justified by learning spillovers, although the environmental benefits alone fall short of the costs.

The European Union has set a goal of 27 percent share of renewables in energy consumption by 2030; currently it is approximately 14 percent. Globally, renewables excluding large hydro accounted for 8.5 percent of electricity generation in 2013. Krozer (2013) looks at the case of Europe's renewables policies between 2002 and 2011 and considers benefits in terms of reductions of CO_2 emissions and fossil-fuel imports. He finds that benefits have only been higher than the FIT costs for on-shore wind and small hydro, and then only during periods of high oil prices (Krozer, 2013). Del Rio and Gual (2007) find that the total

support costs outweigh the external costs avoided by renewable energy deployment for all technologies.

Fundamentally, goals that target the share of renewables have potential in some cases. CBAs could be quite high for select regions, but globally poor without significant technological breakthroughs to deal with the intermittency and non-dispatchability of renewables.[11]

The International Renewable Energy Agency (IRENA), in a recent study, found that doubling renewable energy from its current share of 18 percent to 36 percent in 2030 was feasible. The reference case estimates renewable energy production under a business-as-usual scenario, with current and planned renewable energy policies and estimates that 93EJ of renewable energy would be produced worldwide.

However, this study has significant limitations. A number of assumptions are questionable, including the benefits (too high) and the costs (too low). In the basic scenario, final renewable energy use increases to 132 EJ but relies heavily on biomass that represents 61 percent of renewable energy.[12] The net increase is 39 EJ of renewable energy. To a large extent, developing countries are not accounted for in the study, but additional benefits would accrue if much of Africa and many of the Asia Pacific nations were the beneficiaries via improved energy access.[13]

To achieve the goal of doubling the renewable energy share, worldwide incremental energy system costs are estimated to be $93 billion annually until 2030, while average incremental

---

[10] www.economist.com/node/21524449.

[11] This, of course, does not apply to storage hydro but rather solar and wind.

[12] Biomass is somewhat controversial as a low-carbon renewable energy source. Over shorter time horizons, biomass combustion produces almost as much carbon as coal.

[13] REmap analysis covers 75 percent of projected global total final energy consumption (TFEC) in 2030, with analysis of the following 26 countries: 2 Australia, Brazil, Canada, China, Denmark, Ecuador, France, Germany, India, Indonesia, Italy, Japan, Malaysia, Mexico, Morocco, Nigeria, Russia, Saudi Arabia, South Africa, South Korea, Tonga, Turkey, Ukraine, the United Arab Emirates (UAE), the United Kingdom (UK), and the United States (p. 3).

investment needs are $200 billion annually to 2030 (IRENA, 2014b). The study reveals that the annual net incremental investment required to achieve the goal is US$265 billion until 2030, falling to US$133 billion when fuel cost savings are taken into account. To incentivize the substitution toward renewable energy, an estimated US$315 billion per year in subsidies is required. Thus the total annual cost of doubling the share of renewable energy is in the range of $448 billion to US$580 billion (IRENA, 2014b).

Relative to the reference case, the REmap option shows that additional deployment of renewable energy can reduce CO_2 emissions by 8.6 Gt by 2030, valued at $165–$640 billion per year (IRENA, 2014b). The benefits associated with removing both outdoor and indoor air pollution include improved health outcomes and fewer deaths. The benefits associated with displacing some coal and biomass combustion through a savings of $200 billion per year.

Fossil fuel subsidies would be reduced through the displacement of high-carbon energy with renewable energy. Thus the current fossil fuel subsidy of $544 billion (IRENA, 2014a) would presumably decline as more renewable energy displaces fossil fuel-fired generation.[14] However, the ability for renewables to displace fossil fuel–fired generation in the countries that are part of the study is suspect.

Expecting renewable energy to fully displace fossil fuels, as is assumed in the IRENA study, overstates the capacity of variable energy resources and understates the importance placed on grid reliability. For these reasons, our assessment of the benefits associated with doubling renewable energy will not include the substantial reduction in fossil fuel subsidies. In addition, CO_2 mitigation is valued at approximately $75/tCO_2$, which is 50 percent higher than the typical estimate for carbon emissions reductions. At $50/tCO_2$ and expecting only half the carbon emissions reductions, the environmental benefit of doubling renewable energy would be a maximum of $215 billion.

Summary

Total costs of doubling renewable energy: $448–$580 billion per year.

Total benefits of doubling renewable energy: $415 billion per year.
  BCR: 0.72–0.92.

Target 4: Phasing Out Fossil Fuel Subsidies

Since 2009, the G20 has been committed to phasing out fossil fuel subsidies, which undermine efforts to deal with issues such as climate change and wasteful energy consumption. Nevertheless, the 2013 IEA World Energy Report estimates that worldwide fossil fuel subsidies rose to $US544 billion in 2012, up from $400 billlion in 2010. Most of the increase has been tied to energy price increases as well as the global economic crisis during which governments have increased support to industry. Against this background, efforts to reduce subsidies continue in the G20 and other international groupings.

It has been well documented that some EU countries subsidize fossil fuel energy production and distribution, although some efforts are being made across the EU to phase them out.

The benefits of eliminating fossil fuel subsidies are numerous: simplification of tax system, efficiency gains, reducing trade distortions, and meeting environmental goals. Depending on the number of countries that participate and the speed at which they remove their subsidies, subsidy reform could lead to a predictable source of governmental funding, from a few billion to many billion dollars a year. As higher-income households capture most subsidy benefits, energy subsidies have important distributive consequences that are often not fully understood.

Globally, subsidies have been shown to encourage wasteful consumption, exacerbate energy-price volatility by blurring market signals, incentivize black market fuel, and undermine the competitiveness of renewables and more efficient energy

---

[14] Increasing renewable energy through variable energy sources such as wind and solar technologies does not decrease firm energy (likely produced with fossil fuels as a primary energy input) one-for-one, as additional energy is required to backstop any intermittency and deliver other necessary ancillary services that variable sources cannot provide.

technologies. By acting as an indirect barrier to private investment in energy efficiency and clean energy, fossil fuel subsidies are a significant obstacle to the mobilization of finance to cleaner sectors.

The International Energy Agency (IEA) identifies phasing out fossil fuel subsidies as one of four policies to keep the world on course for the 2° global warming target. Similarly, the World Energy Outlook Special Report: Redrawing the Energy-Climate Map, published in June 2013, identified reforming fossil-fuel subsidies as one of the measures that could halt the increase in emissions by 2020 without harming economic growth. Redirecting subsidies away from fossil fuels, collecting adequate royalties on their extraction, and taxing activities that emit GHGs could fight climate change and finance green alternatives all at the same time.

The International Monetary Fund has documented that eliminating fossil fuel subsidies together with imposing carbon taxes would immediately reduce worldwide carbon dioxide (CO_2) emissions by 13 percent. If the fossil fuel subsidies were eliminated only in certain developing countries, GHG emissions would be reduced by more than 10 percent by 2050, compared to the baseline (IEA, 2013a).

European Union

In 2009 the EU's influence on energy issues increased with the adoption of the Treaty of Lisbon within which energy is identified as shared competence between the EU and member states. In March 2009 the European Commission enacted binding legislation within its climate and energy package in order to achieve the "20–20-20" targets. These targets include a 20 percent reduction in EU GHG emissions from 1990 levels, raising the share of EU energy consumption produced from renewable resources to 20 percent, and a 20 percent improvement in the EU's energy efficiency.

Subsequently, in 2010, the EU Council Decision 2010/787/EU stipulated the phase-out of subsidies for the production of coal from uncompetitive mines by end of 2018. Europe's growth strategy for the decade from 2010–2020, Europe 2020, includes a call to member states "to phase out environmentally harmful subsidies (EHS), limiting exceptions to people with social needs."

Germany

The production of hard coal in Germany has traditionally attracted government support for geological, historical, and political reasons. The total, nominal value of estimated financial assistance for hard coal amounted was reduced from €5 billion in 1999 to €2.27 billion in 2011. In accordance with the EU Council decision, Germany plans to discontinue subsidized coal mining in a socially acceptable manner by the end of 2018, in part because hard coal mining in Germany remains fundamentally uneconomic.[15]

According to a Cambridge Econometrics (2013) report to the European Commission Germany, removal of three subsidies[16] to producers would result in a very small increase in GDP (up to 0.03 percent for all three subsides combined) compared to the baseline and a 0.1 percent fall in energy consumption and CO_2 emissions.

United Kingdom

The UK has significant producer and consumer subsidies that are in the process of reforms. The main type of producer subsidy remaining in the UK is in the oil and gas sector and relates to tax allowances to partially offset the petroleum revenue tax (PRT). In 2011 The United Kingdom gave £280 million in tax credits to the oil and gas sector. Domestic support, the largest subsidy for fossil fuels in the UK, is the lower VAT rate of 5 percent for domestic energy supplies (compared to 20 percent for the economy as a whole). The UK also imposes a climate change levy (CCL), an end-use carbon tax; however, discounts are offered for eligible energy-intensive users. Exemptions from the CCL are considered a subsidy within the

---

[15] German production costs are on average four times the price of imported coal
[16] Energy-tax breaks for agriculture and manufacturing, peak equalization scheme, and the tax relief for energy-intensive processes.

OECD and International Monetary Fund (IMF) methods of identifying subsidies.

Cambridge Econometrics (2013) finds that phasing out the UK VAT exemption on heating fuels would have small net impacts at the macro-economic and sectoral level. GDP is almost unchanged by 2020, with a very slight increase.

Sweden

Sweden's fossil fuel subsidies are limited to exemptions and reductions from energy and CO_2-taxes that benefit particular users and uses of fossil fuels.

Until the end of 2010, greenhouses and the agricultural sector were granted a full energy-tax rebate for fossil fuels used for heating. In 2011, the energy-tax exemption was replaced by a 30 percent reduction in the standard tax rate on heating fuels. Since its introduction in 1991 the exemptions from the carbon tax have evolved and been reformed twice in recent years. The Swedish government has outlined objectives to phase out all energy and CO_2 tax exemptions. The Swedish experience shows that worries about competitiveness and carbon leakage can be mitigated through gradually declining tax exemptions for affected sectors.

Cambridge Econometrics (2013) finds that phasing out Swedish fossil fuel subsidies would lead to modest reductions in energy consumption and emissions, at no economic cost (i.e., no reduction in GDP). If the consequent revenues are used in an efficient manner, then a small economic benefit might be possible, largely due to reduced imports of fossil fuels.

Norway

Subsidies in the Norwegian oil and gas industry are limited to a faster rate of capital depreciation in the oil and gas sector for tax purposes compared to other industries, the funding of petroleum research and funding of seismic exploration. Norway uses the taxing of fossil fuels to pay for the R&D and exploration subsidies. There are nine subsidies that are offered to the oil and gas sector, totalling around $4 billion per year in 2009, although these are forecast to be declining over time (Econ Pöyry, 2012).

Rest of the World

Many African countries need to subsidize energy so that their citizens can afford the energy services, often provided by imported energy. Subsidies are targeted at the poor but may miss their original target and are a heavy burden on the public purse. The progressive elimination of subsidies and redirection of public support toward energy efficiency and other mitigation measures means that government resources may be more efficiently allocated (Koskimäki, 2012).

The IEA's latest estimates indicate that fossil-fuel consumption subsidies worldwide amounted to $544 billion in 2012, slightly up from 2011 as moderately higher international prices,[17] and increased consumption offset some notable progress that is being made to rein in subsidies. Subsidies to oil products represented over half of the total (IEA, 2013d).

In 2011, fossil fuel consumer subsidies in developing and emerging economies were estimated at US$523 billion (IEA, 2012), up to six times that of OECD countries. Unfortunately, although there are likely to be many benefits, the case for reform in developing countries is less clear, particularly because of the potentially regressive welfare effects. Despite the fact that the wealthiest 20 percent generally benefit the most from energy subsidies, the poorest 20 percent would be hardest hit by reforms (IMF, 2013). Yemtsov (2010) summarizes the effects of various energy subsidy reforms on the poorest 20 percent in nine developing countries and finds a negative effect on real income ranging from 1.8 to 16 percent. However, the very poor without access to modern energy derive no benefit from subsidies and so reform would certainly benefit them with appropriately recycled revenues.

Some regional studies of the impacts of fossil fuel reform in developing countries find negative outcomes for GDP in the short to medium run. For example, Lin and Jiang (2011) examined the impacts of energy subsidy reform in China and found lowered energy demand and emissions but also reduced welfare, GDP, and employment (− 2.03 percent, − 1.56 percent, and − 1.41 percent,

---

[17] Higher international prices amplify local macroeconomic volatility by increasing subsidies (expenditures) for fossil fuel producing countries.

respectively). If one considers the nonpriced benefits such as the social cost of carbon, the impacts on welfare may be improved. In the 2014 IMF report "Getting Energy Prices Right," the potential revenue from correcting energy prices (subsidy removal and appropriate taxation for externalities) is equivalent to 2.6 percent of GDP globally. In addition, they find a reduction of carbon dioxide emissions of up to 23 percent and a reduction of mortality due to outdoor air pollution of 63 percent. The benefit of these reforms will depend heavily on the manner in which the revenue is recycled but if done with the intention of minimizing the impacts to the poor, they will be extremely large and equitably distributed. The OECD 2011 working paper, "The Trade Effects of Phasing Out Fossil-Fuel Consumption Subsidies," finds that multilateral subsidy removal results in a slight increase in global real income but with only non-OECD subsidy reform they find regional welfare improvements ranging from 0.4–4 percent by 2050. This suggests that developing countries would benefit from taking the lead on this target.

Notwithstanding the potential distributional and welfare risks associated with reform, there have been significant developments recently in non-OECD countries, for example in Ghana, Indonesia, Pakistan, and India. It is imperative that fossil fuel subsidy reform in developing countries be accompanied by offsetting measures to the hardest hit.

Summary

The difficulties in defining and identifying fossil fuel subsidies make accurate estimates about costs and benefits of their removal at an aggregate level impractical. However, all evidence suggests that the benefits in terms of government savings, reduced energy demand, improved health and reduced emissions would largely exceed the transitional costs. In particular if reform were undertaken simultaneously across the world to minimize competitiveness and trade effects, the potential damages would be limited.

Total benefits: ~$600–$750 billion/year + health benefits + emission reductions.

Total costs: Administrative costs and distributional impacts to the poorest but these can be mitigated through appropriate revenue recycling.

BCR: Likely >>15 with proper revenue recycling.

Target 5: Provide Access to Modern Cooking Fuels to 30 Percent of the Population Currently Using Traditional Fuels

A less-ambitious but potentially more fruitful avenue than tackling the enormous task of universal energy provision is to concentrate on first providing modern cooking fuels to the 30 percent of the population who currently rely on traditional solid fuels.

It is estimated that by 2030, 2.6 billion people will rely on solid fuels (e.g., wood, coal, and other solid fuels such as animal waste), and this fuel use pattern is the cause of 4.3 million deaths due to exposure to IAP during cooking, which disproportionately affects women and small children. Time savings from collecting and/or preparing the solid fuels for cooking detracts from the time that could be spent engaging in more productive economic activities.

There is evidence that a targeted approach would yield higher benefit-cost ratios when compared to the goal of universal access. Jeuland and Pattanayak (2012) find that the best options for a household are fuel switching from traditional wood-burning stoves to kerosene or LPG, or from traditional to improved charcoal-burning stoves.

Pachauri et al. (2013) developed cost curves for providing modern cooking energy carriers and stoves under different levels of fuel price support and microfinance loans (Figure 7.6).

Providing access to 30 percent of the population without access to modern fuels in 2030 would reduce the total number of people without access by about 780,000. This improvement could be achieved at a cumulative cost of less than $200 billion in US2005 dollars, or about 2010US $223.3. In annual terms this amounts to $11.2 billion over the 20-year period.

Using the same assumptions from Target 1 (death from IAP = 32 DALYS lost, $1,000 to $5,000 per DALY), access to modern cooking facilities provide $41.3–$206.4 billion in benefits (from avoided deaths) when 30 percent of the population is served. 30 percent of the 41 million DALYS currently attributed to IAP is 12.3 million

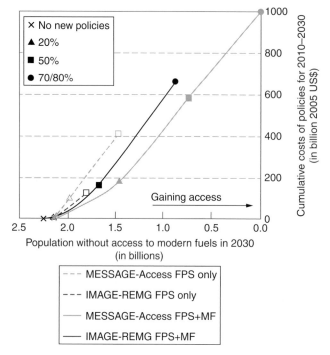

Figure 7.6 *Cost curves of improving access to modern cooking fuels under differing levels of fuel price support and microfinance loans*

Source: Pathways to achieve universal household access to modern energy by 2030 Shonali Pachauri et al 2013 Environ. Res. Lett. 8 024015 https://doi.org/10.1088/1748-9326/8/2/024015).

DALYS avoided. Using low and high estimates gives an additional health benefit in the range $12.3–$61.5 billion.

Costs of achieving 30 percent access to modern cooking fuels: <$11.2 billion per year.

Benefits of achieving 30 percent access to modern cooking fuels: $53.6–$267.9 billion per year.

BCR: >4.8–23.9.

Target 6: Doubling Investment in R&D in Energy Technologies

Research, development, and demonstration (RD&D) of advanced technologies will be crucial to meeting future energy challenges. Margolis and Kammen (1999) wrote a seminal paper on the low levels of energy R&D in the United States and globally, and this has been supported by a number of other studies. Total investments in R&D for all sectors as a share of GDP are around 2.5 percent

for the Americas, 1.9 percent for Asia and Europe, and 0.9 percent for the rest of the world. Energy R&D is forecast to increase 4.8 percent to $22 billion globally for 2014, equivalent to approximately 1.4 percent of total global R&D and just 0.02 percent of gross world product.

From a developing country perspective RD&D at the regional and local levels will be key to developing appropriate technologies to meet the needs of each region. Focus areas include smart grids, storage, clean coal, solar, wind, advanced nuclear, hydrogen, and fuel cell technologies, among others. Increased R&D expenditure may lead to better energy efficiency and renewable technologies that may also benefit environmental sustainability, but estimates of these benefits are extremely imprecise.

Systems approaches to R&D are coming of age as an awareness of their benefits becomes clear. Holmes (2013) discusses the benefits of energy system R&D and shows that the benefit-to-cost ratio of R&D systems research can be substantially higher than for individual technology development. Because systems approaches are still in the early phases, there is potential for significant results in the short term, another example of cost-effective low-hanging fruit.

Leng Wong, Chia, and Chang (2013) look at the impacts of economic growth and renewable energy R&D on fossil fuel consumption. With respect to energy R&D, they find that higher economic growth promotes renewable energy R&D, and renewable energy R&D in turn reduces fossil fuel consumption. They provide a novel view of the short-term benefits of energy R&D showing that output is dependent not only on energy consumption but also on energy R&D. They show that in countries that remain highly dependent on fossil fuels, fossil fuel R&D is found to be more important for economic growth than fossil fuel consumption by improving efficiency and reducing manufacturing costs. Renewable energy R&D is shown to cause significant positive effects (1–1.4 percent) on economic growth in countries without oil reserves. If output is in fact more responsive to changes in fossil fuel R&D than fossil fuel consumption, this may suggest increasing energy R&D could be a powerful policy instrument in developing countries.

Energy R&D has numerous potential cobenefits, including spillovers into other sectors, employment, and environmental benefits in the short run (2030), as well as the expectation of technological breakthroughs to address the long-term issues (2050–2100; Galiana and Green 2010).

Galiana and Green (2009, 2010, 2012) have shown BCAs of increasing clean energy RD&D can be expected to be anywhere from 2–30 depending on chances of success and discount rates. The results from Leng Wong et al. (2013) alone virtually guarantee a BCA of greater than 1; add to that the cobenefits, breakthroughs and environmental and welfare gains, and it is easy to see the benefit of such a policy. Moreover, the transfer of current subsidies to fossil fuels toward energy R&D could cover the costs of the policy.

Part 3

Target Recommendations for Post-2015

What is clear from an energy perspective is that all considered targets have positive BCAs. Our analyses suggest that Target 5 (Provide access to modern cooking fuels to ~30 percent of the population currently using traditional fuels) and Target 6 (Doubling investment in R&D in energy technologies) should be the top priorities for a post-2015 development agenda.

Universal electrification, energy access, and access to modern cooking facilities are all valuable targets but the universality implies increasing costs at the limit and thus suggests a more restrained target would result in greater benefit-cost ratios (Table 7.3). As ambitions and hopes for the future, they are all valid, but they are primarily limited by the lack of technological readiness to achieve them. Technological innovations will be required to improve benefit-cost ratios of energy targets, and subsidizing RD&D,

Table 7.3 Benefit-cost summary – universal energy access goals

	BCR (range)	Comments
Target 1: Universal Energy Access	4.3–7.8	Aspirational goal but BCR can be improved by redefining as a
Target 1a: Universal electrification	4.6–10.2	subset (global electrification, universal modern cooking) of the
Target 1b: Universal modern cooking facilities	2.9–14.7	original target
Target 2: Double the rate of energy efficiency improvement globally	2.4–3.0	Much higher for specific regional programs particularly in inefficient rapidly growing regions. BCAs up to ~15–20
Target 3: Double the share of renewable energy globally	0.72–0.92	Difficult due to intermittency and storage issues.

although not the only route, appears to be the most likely to accelerate the appearance of these innovations. Energy is essential to development, and as such any target that stimulates greater energy access will yield positive benefit-cost ratios. Moreover, if inequality is considered, energy access becomes the most important target. It is unfortunate that current technologies require a trade-off between sustainability and full energy access. Until low-carbon energy sources solve the issues of intermittency and storage, energy access will be shaped primarily by fossil fuels. The benefits of appropriately pricing energy, in particular fossil energy, through subsidy and taxation reform will be all the more important until alternative low-carbon energies can be reliably delivered.

References

Adair-Rohani H. et al. (2013). "Limited electricity access in health facilities of sub-Saharan Africa: a systematic review of data on electricity access, sources, and reliability." *Global Health: Science and Practice.* 9:249–261. doi: 10.9745/GHSP-D-13–00037.

Advisory Group on Energy and Climate Change (AGECC) (2010). The Secretary-General's Advisory Group on Energy and Climate Change (AGECC) Summary Report and Recommendations. Available from www.unido .org/fileadmin/user_media/Publications/download/AGECCsummaryreport.pdf.

Asian Development Bank (2014). Access to Energy. Retrieved August 2014, from www.adb.org/sectors/energy/issues/access-energy.

Asia Pacific Energy Research Center (APERC) (2007). *Understanding International Energy Initiatives in the APEC Region.* Tokyo: Asia Pacific Energy Research Center.

Barker, T. B., P. Ekins, and T. Foxon (2008). "The macro-economic rebound effect and the UK economy." *Energy Policy* 35(10): 4935–46.

Bazilian, M. (2013). Towards Universal Energy Access by 2030: Areas requiring further research. Available from sciencepolicy.colorado.edu.

Bazilian, M. et al. (2010). *Understanding the Scale of Investment for Universal Energy Access.* Geopolitics of Energy (October–November): 21–42.

Bazilian, M., Sagar, A., Detchon, R., and Yumkella, K. (2010). "More heat and light." *Energy Policy* 38: 5409–12.

Birol, F. (2007). "Energy economics: a place for energy poverty in the agenda?" *The Energy Journal* 28(3). Available at: www.iea.org/papers/2007/Birol_Energy_Journal.pdf.

Bloom, D and Zaidi, A. K. M. (2002). *The Demographic Impact of Biomass Fuel Use, Department of Population and International Health.* Boston, MA: Harvard School of Public Health.

Bonjour, S., Adair-Rohani, H., Wolf, J., et al. (2013). "Solid fuel use for household cooking: country and regional estimates for 1980–2010." *Environmental Health Perspectives* 121: 784–90.

Brew-Hammond, A. (2010). "Energy access in Africa: challenges ahead." *Energy Policy* 38: 2291–2301.

Bruce, N., W. Rehfuess, and K. Smith. (2011). Household energy solutions in developing countries, in J. Nriagu (ed.), *Encyclopedia of Environmental Health.* Burlington, MA: Elsevier, Available from: http://ehs.sph .berkeley.edu/krsmith/publications/2011/Household%20energy%20Enc%20EH.pdf

Burke, P. J. (2013). "The national-level energy ladder and its carbon implications." *Environment and Development Economics* 18(04): 484–503.

Burniaux, J., J. Chateau, and J. Sauvage (2011). *"The Trade Effects of Phasing Out Fossil-Fuel Consumption Subsidies," OECD Trade and Environment Working Papers,* 2011/05. Paris: OECD Publishing.

Cambridge Econometrics (September 2013), Modelling of Milestones for achieving resource efficiency: phasing out environmentally harmful subsidies, Final report to the European Commission.

Centurelli, R. 2011. Energy Poverty: Can We Make Modern Energy Access Universal – Focus on Financing Appropriate Sustainable Energy Technologies,

Canadian Energy Research Institute (CERI). (2013). Global LNG: Now, Never or Later? Available from www.ceri.ca/images/stories/2013-02-04_CERI_Study_131_-_Global_LNG.pdf.

Chen, S. T., Kuo, H. I., Chen, C. C. (2007). "The relationship between GDP and electricity consumption in 10 Asian Countries." *Energy Policy* 35: 2611–21.

Constable, J. (2011). *The Green Mirage: Why a Low-Carbon Economy May Be Further Off Than We Think*. London: Civitas.

Council of Canadian Academies. (2014). *Environmental Impacts of Shale Gas Extraction in Canada*. Ottawa, Ontario, Canada: The Expert Panel on Harnessing Science and Technology to Understand the Environmental Impacts of Shale Gas Extraction, Council of Canadian Academies.

Csereklyei, Z. and Humer, S. (2012). Modelling Primary Energy Consumption under Model Uncertainty. Department of Economics, Vienna University of Economics and Business (WU), available from http://epub.wu.ac.at/3706/1/wp147.pdf

Csereklyei, Z., Rubio Varas, M.d.M. and Stern, D. I. (2014). *Energy and Economic Growth: The Stylized Facts*. CCEP Working Paper 1417, November 2014. Crawford School of Public Policy, The Australian National University.

Del Río, P. and M. A. Gaul (2007). "An integrated assessment of the feed-in tariff system in Spain." *Energy Policy* 35(2): 994–1012.

Department for Internal Development (DFID). (2014). Correlation and Causation between Energy Development and Economic Growth. Available from http://dx.doi.org/10.12774/eod_hd.january2014.eca.

Dincer, I. and M. A. Rosen (2012). *EXERGY: Energy, Environment and Sustainable Development*. Amsterdam: Elsevier.

Dobbs, R. et al. (2011). *Resource Revolution: Meeting the World's Energy, Materials, Food, and Water Needs*. New York: McKinsey Global Institute.

East African Community (EAC). (2006). Strategy on Scaling up Access to Modern Energy Services in Order to Achieve the Millennium Development Goals. East African Community. Available at: www.eac.int/energy/index.php?option=com_docman&task=doc_download&gid=15&Itemid=70.

Economic Community of West African States (ECOWAS) (2005). White Paper for a Regional Policy – Geared Towards Increasing Access to Energy Services for Rural and Periurban Populations in Order to Achieve the Millennium Development Goals. Economic Community of West African States. Available at: www.gm.undp.org/Reports/ECOWAS energy white paper.pdf.

Econ Pöyry (2012). *Fossil Fuels – At What Cost? Government Support for Upstream Oil and Gas Activities in Norway*. Geneva: Global Subsidies Initiative of the IISD.

Energy Information Administration (EIA). (2013a). International Energy Outlook 2013. Available from www.eia.gov/forecasts/ieo/nat_gas.cfm.

(2013b). Today in Energy: China Consumes Nearly as Much Coal as the Rest of the World Combined. Available from www.eia.gov/todayinenergy/detail.cfm?id=9751.

(2013c). Today in Energy: India's Economic Growth Is Driving Its Energy Consumption. Available from www.eia.gov/todayinenergy/detail.cfm?id=10611d.

(2014). Technically Recoverable Shale Gas. Available from www.eia.gov/analysis/studies/worldshalegas/.

Energy Sector Management Assistance Program (ESMAP). (2007). *Technical and Economic Assessment of Off-grid, Mini-grid and Grid Electrification Technologies*. Washington, DC: Energy Sector Management Assistance Program, The World Bank Group. Available at: http://siteresources.worldbank.org/EXTENERGY/Resources/336805–1157034157861/ElectrificationAssessmentRptAnnexesFINAL17May07.pdf.

Ernst & Young. (2012). Global LNG: Will new demand and new supply mean new pricing? Available from www.ey.com/Publication/vwLUAssets/Global_LNG_New_pricing_ahead/$FILE/Global_LNG_New_pricing_ahead_DW0240.pdf.

Erol, U. and E. S. H. Yu (1987a). "On the causal relationship between energy and income for industrialized countries." *Journal of Energy and Development* 13: 113–22.

Eskom (2009). Annual Report. Available at: www.eskom.co.za/annreport09/ar_2009/index_annual_report.html.

Esso, L. J. (2010). "Threshold cointegration and causality relationship between energy use and growth in seven African countries." *Energy Economics* 30: 2391–2400.

Fields, S. (2011). An assessment of solid fuel use reveals that continued widespread global dependence on such fuels for household needs will impede success in meeting the UN Millennium Development Goals. http://dx.doi.org/10.6084/m9.figshare.38743

Fullerton, D. G., Bruce, N., and Gordon, S. B. (2008). "Indoor air pollution from biomass fuel smoke is a major health concern in the developing world." *Transactions of the Royal Society of Tropical Medicine and Hygiene* 102(9): 843–51.

Galiana, I. and C. Green (2009). "Let the global technology race begin." *Nature* 462(7273): 570–71.

(2010). Technology-led climate policy, in B. Lomborg (ed.), *Smart Solutions to Climate Change: Comparing Costs and Benefits.* Cambridge, UK: Cambridge University Press.

(2012). A technology-led climate policy in a changing landscape, in B. Lomborg (ed.), *Global Problems, Smart Solutions: Costs and Benefits.* Cambridge, UK: Cambridge University Press.

Grieshop, A., J. Marshall, and M. Kandlikar (2011). "Health and climate benefits of cook stove replacement options." *Energy Policy* 29: 7530–42.

Guan, D., X. Su, Q, Zhang, G. P. Peters, Z. Liu, Y. Lei, and , K. He (2014). "The socioeconomic drivers of China's primary $PM_{2.5}$ emissions." *Environmental Research Letters*, 9: 024010.

Habermhel, H. (2007). *Economic Evaluation of the Improved Household Cooking Stove Dissemination Programme in Uganda.* Eschborn, Germany: German Technical Cooperation (GTZ).

(2008). *Costs and Benefits of Efficient Institutional Cook Stoves in Malawi.* Eschborn, Germany: German Technical Cooperation (GTZ). Available from www.giz.de/Themen/en/ dokumente/en-costs-benefits-institutional-stoves-malawi-2008.pdf.

Hirst, E. and M. Brown. (1990). "Closing the efficiency gap: barriers to the efficient use of energy." *Resources, Conservation and Recycling* 3(4): 267–281.

Hoffert, M. (2011). "Governments must pay for clean-energy innovation." *Nature* 472(7342): 137.

Holmes, J. (2013). "A more perfect union: energy systems integration studies from Europe." *Power and Energy Magazine, IEEE* 11 (5): 36–45.

Hutton, G., H. Rehfuess, and F. Tediosi (2007). Evaluation of the costs and benefits of interventions to reduce indoor air pollution, *Energy for Sustainable Development* 11: 34–43.

Independent Evaluation Group (IEG) – World Bank. (2013). Approach Paper: Evaluation of the World Bank Group's Support for Electricity Access, available from lnweb90.worldbank.org.

International Energy Agency (IEA). (2003). *World Energy Investment Outlook 2003.* Paris: International Energy Agency.

(2004). *World Energy Outlook 2004.* Paris: International Energy Agency.

(2005). *World Energy Outlook 2005.* Paris: International Energy Agency.

(2006). *World Energy Outlook 2006.* Paris: I. E. A. Publications.

(2008). *Energy Statistics of non-OECD countries.* Paris: International Energy Agency.

(2009a). *Comparative Study on Rural Electrification Policies in Emerging Countries.* Paris: International Energy Agency. Available at: www.iea.org/papers/2010/rural_elect.pdf.

(2009b). *World Energy Outlook 2009.* Paris: International Energy Agency.

(2010). *Projected Costs of Generating Electricity.* Paris: International Energy Agency, Nuclear Energy Agency, Organisation for Economic Co-operation and Development.

(2011). WEO – 2011. Energy for All: Financing Access for the Poor. Available from www.iea.org.

(2012). Universal Access to Energy Would Herald Enormous Economic and Social Benefits. Available from www.iea.org.

(2013a). *Energy Efficiency Market Report 2013: Market Trends and Medium-Term Prospects.* Paris: IEA.

(2013b). FAQs: Coal. Available from www.iea.org/aboutus/faqs/coal/.

(2013c). Global Tracking Framework. Available from www.iea.org/publications/ freepublications/publication/name,38535, en.html.

(2013d). *World Energy Outlook 2013.* Paris: International Energy Agency.

(2014a). *World Energy Investment Outlook 2014.* Paris: International Energy Agency.

(2014b). Energy Poverty. Available from www.iea.org/topics/energypoverty/.

International Energy Agency (IEA), United Nations Development Programme (UNDP), and United Nations Industrial Development Organization (UNIDO). (2010). *Energy Poverty – How to Make Modern Energy Access Universal?* Paris: International Energy Agency. Available at:

www.worldenergyoutlook.org/docs/weo2010/
weo2010_poverty.pdf.

International Institute for Applied Systems Analysis
(IIASA). (2011). Global Energy Assessment.
Available from www.globalenergyassessment.org.

International Monetary Fund (IMF) (2013a). *Case
Studies on Energy Subsidy Reform: Lessons and
Implications*. Washington, DC: IMF.

(2013b). *Energy Subsidy Reform: Lessons and
Implications*. Washington, DC: IMF.

International Renewable Energy Agency (IRENA).
(2014a). Remap 2030 Report: A Renewable
Energy Road Map. Available from http://
irena.org/remap/REmap_Report_June_2014.pdf

(2014b). Remap 2030: A Renewable Energy
Roadmap Questions and Answers.
Available from www.irena.org/remap/
REmap_QandA.pdf.

Jeuland M. A. and S. K. Pattanayak (2012). "Benefits
and costs of improved cookstoves: assessing the
implications of variability in health, forest and
climate impacts." *PLoS ONE* 7(2): e30338.
doi:10.1371/journal.pone.0030338.

Kahsaia M. S., C. Nondob P. V. Schaeffer, and G. G.
Tesfa (2011). "Income level and the energy
consumption–GDP nexus: Evidence from Sub-
Saharan Africa. *Energy Economics*,"
doi:10.1016/j.eneco.2011.06.006.

Koskimäki, P.-L. (2012). "Africa could take a leap to
energy efficiency: what lessons could
Sub-Saharan countries learn from European
energy efficiency policy implementation?"
Energy for Sustainable Development 16(2):
189–96.

Krozer, Y. (2013). "Cost and benefit of renewable
energy in the European Union." *Renewable
Energy* 50: 68–73.

Kruyt, B., D. P. van Vuuren, H. De Vries,
and H. Groenenberg (2009). "Indicators
for energy security." *Energy Policy* 37(6):
2166–81.

Lee, C. C. 2005. "Energy consumption and GDP in
developing countries: A co-integrated panel
analysis." *Energy Economics* 27: 415–427.

Leng Wong, S., W.-M. Chia, and Y. Chang (2013).
"Energy consumption and energy R&D in
OECD: perspectives from oil prices
and economic growth." *Energy Policy* 62:
1581–90.

Lin, B. and Z. Jiang (2011). "Estimates of energy
subsidies in China and impact of energy subsidy
reform." *Energy Economics* 33(2): 273–83.

Linares, P. and X. Labandeira. (2010). Energy
efficiency: Economics and policy. *Journal of
Economic Surveys* 24: 573–92.

Liu, Z., D. Guan, D. Crawford-Brown, Q. Zhang, K.
He, and J. Liu (2013). "Energy policy:
A low-carbon roadmap for China." *Nature*
500: 143–5.

Mestl, H. E. S., K. Aunan, and H. M. Seip (2007).
"Health benefits from reducing indoor air
pollution from household solid fuel use in China
—three abatement scenarios." *Environment
International* 33: 831–40.

Marcantonini, C. and A. D. Ellerman (2013). The cost
of abating CO2 emissions by renewable energy
incentives in Germany. *2013 10th International
Conference on the European Energy Market
(EEM)*. Stockholm, Sweden: IEEE.

Margolis, R. M. and D. M. Kammen. (1999).
"Underinvestment: the energy technology and
R&D policy challenge." *Science* 285(5428):
690–2.

Massachusetts Institute of Technology (MIT). (2007).
*The Future of Coal: Options for a Carbon-
Constrained World*, Cambridge, MA:
Massachusetts Institute of Technology. http://
web.mit.edu/coal/The_Future_of_Coal.pdf.

Menegaki, A. (2011). "Growth and renewable energy
in Europe: a random effect model with evidence
for neutrality hypothesis." *Energy Economics*
33: 257–63.

Menyah, K. and Y. Wolde-Rufael. (2010). "Energy
consumption, pollutant emissions and economic
growth in South Africa." *Energy Economics*
32(6): 1374–82.

Modi, V. et al. (2005). *Energy Services for the
Millennium Development Goals*. Washington,
DC: United Nations Development Programme.

Moss, R. et al. (2007). *Realizing the Potential of
Energy Efficiency: Targets, Policies, and
Measures for G8 Countries*. Washington, DC:
United Nations Foundation.

Nemet, G. F. (2009). "Demand-pull, technology-
push, and government-led incentives for non-
incremental technical change." *Research Policy*
38(5): 700–9.

Nemet, G. F. and D. M. Kammen. (2007). "US
energy research and development: declining
investment, increasing need, and the
feasibility of expansion." *Energy Policy*
35(1): 746–55.

Pachauri, S. et al. (2013). "Pathways to achieve
universal household access to modern energy by

2030." *Environmental Research Letters* 8(2), doi: 10.1088/1748–9326/2/02042015.

Parshall, L., D. Pillai, S. Mohan, A. Sanoh, and V. Modi (2009). "National electricity planning in settings with low pre-existing grid coverage: development of a spatial model and case study of Kenya." *Energy Policy* 37: 2395–2410.

Pope, D. P. et al. (2010). "Risk of low birth weight and stillbirth associated with indoor air pollution from solid fuel use in developing countries." *Epidemiologic Reviews* 32(1): 70–81. doi:10.1093/epirev/mxq005.

Popp, D. and R. Newell. (2012). "Where does energy R&D come from? Examining crowding out from energy R&D." *Energy Economics* 34(4): 980–991.

Prins, G. et al. (2010). *The Hartwell Paper: A New Direction for Climate Policy after the Crash of 2009*. London: London School of Economics Mackinder Programme.

(2013). *The Vital Spark: Innovating Clean and Affordable Energy*. London: London School of Economics Mackinder Programme.

Ryan, L. and N. Campbell. (2012). *Spreading the Net: The Multiple Benefits of Energy Efficiency Improvements*. Paris: OECD/IEA.

Sagar, A. D. and B. Van der Zwaan. (2006). "Technological innovation in the energy sector: R&D, deployment, and learning-by-doing." *Energy Policy* 34(17): 2601–08.

Saito, M. (2014). In post-Fukushima policy test, Japan town rallies for nuclear re-start. Reuters. Available from www.reuters.com/article/us-japan-nuclear-restarts/in-post-fukushima-policy-test-japan-town-rallies-for-nuclear-re-start-idUSBREA3C0NG20140413.

Siemens. (2013). Connecting Possibilities – Scenarios for Optimizing Energy Systems. Available from www.energy.siemens.com/hq/en/energy-topics/publications/connecting-possibilities-study.htm.

Smil, Vaclav. (2000). "Energy in the twentieth century: resources, conversions, costs, uses and consequences." *Annual Review of Energy and the Environment* 25: 21–51.

(2005). *Energy at the Crossroads: Global Perspectives and Uncertainties*. Cambridge, MA: MIT Press.

Sopinka, A. and Pitt, L. (2013). "Variable energy resources: a very interesting impacts for the western interconnect." *The Electricity Journal* 26: 20–5.

Soubbotina, T. P. (2005). *Beyond Economic Growth. An Introduction to Sustainable Development* (2nd ed.). Washington, DC: World Bank. Available from www.worldbank.org/depweb/english/beyond/global/index.html.

Sovacool, B. (2012). "The political economy of energy poverty: A review of key challenges." *Energy for Sustainable Development* 16(3): 272–282. doi:10.1016/j.esd.2012.05.006.

Soytas, U., and R. Sari (2003). "Energy consumption and GDP: causality relationship in G-7 countries and emerging markets." *Energy Economics* 25: 33–7.

Sterlacchini, A. (2012). "Energy R&D in private and state-owned utilities: an analysis of the major world electric companies." *Energy Policy* 41: 494–506.

Stern, D. I. (1993). "Energy and economic growth in the USA, a multivariate approach." *Energy Economics* 15: 137–150.

Stern, D. (2000). "A multivariate cointegration analysis of the role of energy in the US macroeconomy." *Energy Economics* 22: 267–83.

(2004). Economic growth and energy, in C. J. Cleveland (ed.), *Encyclopedia of Energy*. Amsterdam: Elsevier, 35–51.

Sudhakara Reddy, B. (2013). "Barriers and drivers to energy efficiency – A new taxonomical approach." *Energy Conversion and Management* 74: 403–16.

Sussan, T. E., V. Ingole, J. H. Kim, S. McCormick, J. Negherbon, J. Fallica, and S. Biswal (2013). "Source of biomass cooking fuel determines pulmonary response to household air pollution." *American Journal of Respiratory Cell and Molecular Biology* 50(3): 538–48.

Twerefou, D. K. (2014). "Willingness to pay for improved electricity supply in Ghana." *Modern Economy* 5(5): 489–98.

United Nations (UN). (2005). *The Energy Challenge for Achieving the Millennium Development Goals*. New York: United Nations.

United Nations Development Programme (UNDP) (2004). *Stuck in the Past, Energy, Environment and Poverty in Serbia and Montenegro*. Belgrade: UNDP.

UN-Energy/Africa. (2009). *Energy for Sustainable Development: Policy Options for Africa*. New York: United Nations.

van Benthem, A., J. L. Sweeney, and K. Gillingham (2008). "Learning-by-doing and the optimal solar policy in California." *The Energy Journal* 29 (3): 131–151.

Vivid Economics. (2013). *Energy Efficiency and Economic Growth*. London: The Climate Institute.

World Health Organization (WHO). (2004). Indoor Smoke from Solid Fuels: Assessing the Environmental Burden of Disease at National and Local Levels. Available from www.who.int/quantifying_ehimpacts/publications/9241591358/en/.

⸻ (2008). Evaluating Household Energy and Health Interventions: A Catalogue of Methods. Available from who/int/indoor air/publications/methods/full_catalogue_method.pdf.

⸻ (2012). Health indicators of sustainable energy in the Context of the Rio +20 UN Conference on Sustainable Development. Available from www.who.int/hia/green_economy/indicators_energy 2.pdf.

World Health Organization/United Nations Development Programme (WHO/UNDP). (2008). The Global Burden of Disease: 2004 Update, WHO, Geneva. Available from, www.who.int/healthinfo/global_burden_disease/2004_report_update/en/.

⸻ (2009). *The Energy Access Situation in Developing Countries: A Review Focusing on the Least Developed Countries and Sub-Saharan Africa*. New York: UNDP.

Wong, S. L. et al. (2013). "Energy consumption, energy R&D and real GDP in OECD countries with and without oil reserves." *Energy Economics* 40: 51–60.

World Bank Group. (2008). *The Welfare Impact of Rural Electrification: A Reassessment of the Costs and Benefits*. Washington, DC: World Bank. Available at: http://lnweb90.worldbank.org/oed/oeddoclib.nsf/DocUNIDViewForJavaSearch/EDCCC33082FF8BEE852574EF006E5539/$file/rural_elec_full_eval.pdf.

World Bank. (2011). One Goal, Two Paths: Achieving Universal Access to Modern Energy in East Asia and the Pacific. Available from http://documents.worldbank.org/curated/en/2011/01/15156077/one-goal-two-paths-achieving-universal-access-modern-energy-east-asia-pacific.

⸻ (2014). Data. Regional UN Classification, Least Developing Countries. Accessed on June 30, 2014, from http://data.worldbank.org/region/LDC.

World Energy Council. (1999). The Challenge of Rural Energy Poverty in Developing Countries. Available from http://my.ewb-usa.org/theme/library/myewb-usa/project-resources/technical/ruralelectrification.pdf.

Yemtsov, R. (2010). "Development effective reform strategies: safety nets to protect poor and vulnerable groups from the negative impacts of reform." Increasing the Momentum of Fossil Fuel Subsidy Reform Conference, Geneva, 14–15 October.

7.1 Alternative Perspective

ADELE MORRIS

Summary

This perspective reviews the targets and their priorities and proposes a seventh, policy-based target. Morris believes that the chapter convincingly explains how access to modern energy resources is critical for economic development and improving the welfare of poor households. Few doubt the merits of expanding modern energy access in principle, but there remain questions about where the benefits are highest and what policies may best be used.

The targets proposed pose several challenges to cost-benefit analysis. In particular, they are mainly target levels of desirable outcomes, without specific policies to bring them about. There is also an issue of rising marginal costs as the easier sectors are served first, and finally, aggregate welfare increases may mask important underlying distributional outcomes, which calls for careful design of policies.

Although the benefits of access to electricity are great, the challenges of delivering this to all make it difficult to deliver. The more modest target of expanding access to modern cooking is likely to provide strong net benefits, particularly now that newer, better-built stoves are coming to market.

The objective of doubling the rate of decline in energy use per unit of GDP (SDG 2) does not make much sense in itself, as the energy intensity of an economy tends to shrink with economic growth as the service sector expands. That means that a more energy-efficient economy can be both a cause and an effect of development. Targeting a particular sector would make more sense, but only if there is also a specific cost-

effective policy proposal. As for the "energy-efficiency gap," it is difficult to substantiate claims of a significant and pervasive gap. What are apparent benefits to society many actually negatively impact consumers, who have to pay the full cost.

Target 3 is to double the share of renewable energy. If the primary purpose is to reduce emissions of carbon dioxide and pollutants, this should be compared with other strategies. Peer-reviewed literature provides strong evidence that policies to promote renewables are less cost effective than policies to price carbon.

The benefits of reducing "pretax consumption-distorting" subsidies on fossil fuels depend on how they were implemented and what would happen to the resources that would have been spent on the subsidies. The net result of the spending shift could be more progressivity, particularly if fossil fuel subsidies are replaced with income support and other programs targeted to the poor.

Although it is clear that energy research should be devoted to developing technologies that are cheap, reliable, and scalable, to ease the transition from fossil fuels, much R&D takes place in the private sector, so companies need incentives to expand this activity. However, there may be other research areas that are even more underfunded, so Morris suggests a modest increase in public funding plus appropriate carbon price signals to the private sector.

Her suggestion for a more policy-oriented target is to phase out implicit fossil fuel subsidies by imposing energy taxes that reflect external costs. One study that benchmarks the potential benefit-cost ratio of climate policy appears in the technical documentation of the recent proposed rule from the US Environmental Protection Agency (EPA) to reduce CO_2 emissions from existing power plants. EPA figures suggest a benefit-cost ratio of up to 8.4 for global climate and health impacts. Because the EPA proposal is likely to be less cost effective than a well-designed carbon tax, such a policy could actually achieve BCRs in excess of most if not all of the other sustainable development goals.

Alternative Perspective

7.2

MADELEINE GLEAVE AND TODD MOSS

Summary

The invigorated focus on energy on the development agenda is a positive step reflecting what governments, business leaders, and citizens across the developing world agree: increasing access to energy is a top priority and central to solving other challenges in health, education, and job creation. The first set of MDGs acknowledged energy's role, but left access as an implicit step required to meet other targets. The draft list of new Sustainable Development Goals now includes a proposal to "ensure access to affordable, reliable, sustainable and modern energy for all."

However, although there is general agreement on the need for universal access to electricity, determining what specifically constitutes "modern access" is a more difficult task, with no clear-cut definition. Modern energy access entails less a physical connection than the availability of reliable and affordable power necessary to sustain a dignified lifestyle, one that is consistently free from depravation and intimately connected with the global community. At present, nearly all definitions provide a gross underestimate of what a growing class of the world's poor expect and demand in the way of energy services.

According to the IEA definition, a household is considered to have "modern electricity access" at a consumption minimum of 250 kWh per year (or roughly 50 kWh/person/year) in rural areas and 500 kWh per year (100 kWh/person/year) in urban areas. But these are indefensibly low thresholds. An average of 100 kWh/year equates to powering a single 60-watt light bulb for five hours each day; a typical American would use the same amount of energy in just three days.

We propose three possible alternative ways to set thresholds that would capture a more realistic level of consumption at modern levels and provide a better target:

1. A simple peer-level threshold, based on average consumption levels in middle-income countries such as Tunisia (1,300 kWh/year) or South Africa (4,600 kWh/year). This would provide targets that are closer to what is needed for a modern standard of living.
2. The World Bank's Global Tracking Framework has developed a classification of energy access over a system of five tiers. One approach could set the global goal for all citizens to have reliable, affordable, and safe energy for household use and cooking by 2030 – which is at minimum Tier 4. Countries already at Tier 4 could aim to reach Tier 5.
3. In the same way as we can estimate daily nutritional needs, an energy access goal could be based on the energy required for a basket of fundamental services needed to sustain modern life. This could, for example, be the power needed to run basic energy-intensive assets, initially a mobile phone, radio, television, and fridge plus standard cooking and lighting appliances.

Our purpose is to affirm that access to affordable, safe, and clean energy is a worthwhile goal and potentially a post-2015 global development goal.

Although the nature of energy access, services, and consumption makes estimating specific targets complex, we are failing the world's poor if we underestimate true demand and collectively do not aim for a brighter, fully powered future.

Benefits and Costs of the IFF Targets for the Post-2015 Development Agenda

ALEX COBHAM

Introduction: Illicit Financial Flows*

This chapter covers the important issue of illicit financial flows (IFFs) and ways in which they may be addressed. The Sustainable Development Goals (SDGs) target to curtail IFFs (16.4) currently has no defined indicators. Discussions are ongoing, but there is a risk that policy focus is lost. The proposal made here is for a set of three indicators that offer clear policy prioritization and are likely to exhibit very high benefit-cost ratios.

The limitations of cost-benefit analysis should be kept in mind throughout. The power of the SDGs' predecessor, the Millennium Development Goals (MDG) framework, lay in its contribution to setting norms rather than in the specifics of individual targets. Most important, perhaps, MDG 3 fixed the still-emerging norm on the need for gender equality – with a reach that has gone far beyond the handful of areas in which targets were actually specified.

The value of economic cost-benefit analysis is of second order in comparison to that norm-setting role, and the UN Open Working Group rightly weighed political and social issues highly. Imagine that cost-benefit analysis showed that including the most marginalized 1 percent of populations politically or, in service basic provision, was prohibitively expensive. It is unthinkable that the principle (and norm) of universality would be sacrificed to a more "realistic" 99 percent target – which would effectively formalize a commitment to exclude the most excluded.

Where cost-benefit analysis can play a role, however, is in relation to the other major contribution of the MDGs: the creation of a framework for shared policy prioritization among national and other actors. Two caveats apply: the extent of uncertainties in any assessment should be fully reflected when this analysis is weighed alongside other evidence, and the second-order nature of economic costs and benefits in the political decisions being taken should not be forgotten.

In the current study, a narrowly economic approach provides conservative estimates because although the costs of the proposed targets are measured relatively well, only limited economic benefits are captured (ignoring the potential for political, social, and environmental benefits). In the case of illicit flows, therefore, there is unlikely to be a conflict between cost-benefit analysis and rights-based arguments.

Illicit financial flows comprise tax evasion, the theft of state assets, the laundering of the proceeds of crime, and a range of market and regulatory abuses under cover of anonymity – including, importantly, multinational tax avoidance.[1] The leading estimates suggest that developing countries in total may currently be losing close to a trillion dollars a year and more than half a

* This chapter draws on material prepared for the Tana High Level Forum on Peace and Security in Africa (Cobham, 2014) and for the UNECA High Level Panel on Illicit Financial Flows out of Africa. I am grateful for comments from participants and technical committee members of each and for the research assistance of Alice Lépissier.

[1] Multinational tax avoidance is a dominant issue in the report of the UNECA High Level Panel on Illicit Financial Flows out of Africa, which is the key UN document underpinning the global adoption of SDG 16.4. A concerted corporate pushback is currently underway, seeking retrospectively to exclude multinationals from the specific target, but we assume here that this attempt will be unsuccessful, and that the scope of SDG 16.4 will remain as intended.

trillion dollars a year on average over the last decade (Global Financial Integrity [GFI], 2013). Although such estimates of deliberately hidden phenomena are fraught with uncertainty, at the very least, it seems likely that illicit outflows are substantially larger than official aid receipts, and that tax abuse, typically through trade mispricing, is the major element of illicit outflows. Damage is likely to be substantial – in the form of tax losses, foregone economic growth, greater inequality, and the undermining of institutions, political represen-tation, and trust.

There is no single, agreed-on definition of illicit financial flows (IFFs), due to both the vagueness of the term and the hidden nature of its content. The Oxford dictionary definition of "illicit" is: "forbid-den by law, rules or custom." The first three words alone would define "illegal," and this highlights an important feature of any definition: illicit financial flows are not necessarily illegal. Flows forbidden by "rules or custom" may encompass those that are socially and/or morally unacceptable and not necessarily legally so.

A legal definition would not necessarily be pre-cise either. Behavior of uncertain legality is more likely to go unchallenged by a tax system with little to no capacity to uncover corporate tax eva-sion, or a political system with little to no will to address the theft of state funds – the absence of legal findings of criminality is not, therefore, an unbiased indicator of the legality of financial flows. A strictly legal definition of IFFs is therefore likely to result in systematically – and wrongly – under-stating the scale of the problem in lower-income, lower-capacity states. For this reason, such a defin-ition should be rejected.[2]

Consistent with the definition of illicit as for-bidden is the idea of IFFs as hidden – whether technically illegal in each context or not, they would be frowned on at the very least as a form of abuse, and so are deliberately obscured from public view. Following from this, IFFs can be thought of in the four categories shown in Figure 8.1. Generally, it is possible to be rather clearer about the legality of the underlying capital than of the transaction – for example, legal profits may be subject to illicit transactions with the aim of tax abuse.

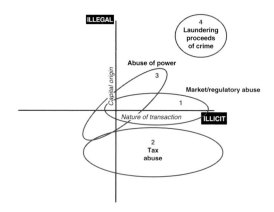

Figure 8.1 *Stylized representation of major IFF types*

Source: Cobham (2014).

The categories are

1. Market and/or regulatory abuse (including the use of anonymity to hide political conflicts of interest or to break regulations)
2. Tax abuse (both by individuals and companies related to hidden assets and income streams, and by multinational groups related to profit shifting)
3. Abuse of power, including the theft of state funds and assets, and the bribery of public officials
4. The laundering of the proceeds of crime (pri-marily the trafficking of drugs and of humans)

The historic emphasis in policy has been on IFFs relating to illegal capital – i.e., abuse of power and corruption – and laundering of criminal proceeds. More recently, and since the financial crisis in particular, greater prominence has been given to

---

[2] Blankenburg and Khan (2012) provide an interesting, related argument: that in cases of state illegitimacy there may be legal flows that are illicit and indeed illegal flows that are licit. Where a state is unrepresentative and predatory, its adjudications over legality may be considered illegitimate. A tax-evading flow, under such circumstances, could be con-sidered justified – and even, depending on the interpretation of "rules or custom," as licit. Relatedly, some illegal flows (and possibly some illicit ones) may not be detrimental if the set of rules or laws that they breach are themselves flawed.

measures against tax and market abuse. These include the manipulation of trade prices and hidden transfers of ownership, for example.

Because most of the identified channels can be used for multiple types of illicit flow, any attempt to clamp down on one or more IFF types while leaving others open is likely to fail. In addition, because there are consistently damaging effects on revenues and on regulatory effectiveness, it may make sense to seek broader progress.

Illicit Financial Flows in the Sustainable Development Goals

The issue of illicit financial flows is among a number that have come to much greater prominence in the period since the MDGs were set. It was of little surprise then that the High-Level Panel (HLP) report on the post-2015 development agenda proposal for the successor framework to the MDGs included not only a lengthy discussion of the issue, but also importantly a specific illicit flows target:

> 12e. Reduce illicit flows and tax evasion and increase stolen-asset recovery by $x

This was an important and early milestone in the debate, and reflects the extent of consensus that had developed in the preceding five years in particular. The final SDG framework settled on the following formulation:

> 16.4 By 2030, significantly reduce illicit financial and arms flows, strengthen the recovery and return of stolen assets and combat all forms of organized crime

The question now facing the UN's Inter-Agency Task Force is how to track the required significant reduction in IFFs. There are a number of obstacles to address.

First, there may not be globally accepted estimates of the components mentioned that could credibly be targeted in such a precise way. Leading multilateral institutions including the World Bank and IMF have neither offered support for the most widely used estimates (those of Global Financial Integrity, e.g., GFI, 2013), nor proposed their own

alternatives. Given recent academic criticism of the approaches (e.g., Hong and Pak, 2016; Johannesen and Pirttilä, 2016; Nitsch, 2016), it is unclear whether there is sufficient political confidence in any one set of estimates.

A broader concern is that, in the absence of specific policy measures and national responsibilities, the target does not provide the kind of clarity or lines of accountability necessary to drive progress. If estimated IFFs out of country X are large, it is not immediately clear who should take what action under the SDG framework. If it is the policy makers of country X, it is not necessarily clear which issues they should prioritize: high IFFs may reflect anything from multinational profit-shifting to citizens' creation of undeclared offshore assets.

It is also clear that policy makers in country X do not hold sole responsibility. IFFs are an international problem, where the secrecy provided in other jurisdictions is likely to be at least as important as the action taken domestically (see, e.g., World Bank, 2013). Also important are international rules and processes such as those relating to corporate tax and to the multilateral exchange of tax information.

A limited number of subtargets or indicators will not, of course, capture the entirety of IFF causality. But careful design can ensure that SDG 16.4 provides a great deal of support to the specific policy progress that will deliver a meaningful reduction in illicit flows. The following section summarizes the damaging impacts of IFFs, explaining the importance of such an aim. Three subtargets to sit under 16.4 are then proposed, with a cost-benefit analysis for each.

Development Impacts of IFFs

Illicit financial flows may have impacts in four important areas: on economic growth, on social development outcomes, on income distribution and inequality, and on governance and institutional strength. In each area the evidence is indicative rather than comprehensive, although the literature is developing apace. Here we highlight some major findings.

Economic Growth Impact

Illicit outflows can be considered as lost GDP. The GFI and African Development Bank assessed the scale of losses in Kar et al. (2013), finding that all but 2 of the 20 most heavily affected African countries, have lost more than 10 percent of their recorded GDP on average.[3]

A number of studies have looked at the revenue impact of IFFs, or more specifically of trade mispricing. Christian Aid (2008) used Baker's (2005) survey-based estimates to estimate a tax loss for all developing countries of $160 billion, and a subsequent study (Christian Aid, 2009) based on detailed trade data was broadly consistent in scale, as was GFI's analysis (Hollingshead, 2010). The overall sub-Saharan African loss is estimated at 3.4 percent of total government revenues, although given the broad rise in African IFFs since the early 2000s we might expect this to have worsened since. Individual countries show marked differences, however, with four of the top ten revenue losers from the region: Zimbabwe loses most (31.5 percent of revenues), Mali comes in fifth (25.1 percent of revenues lost), Republic of Congo sixth (24.9 percent), and Zambia eighth (21.7 percent).

In terms of economic growth, these losses show the scale of lost opportunities to develop infrastructure and human capital. To give just one example: Andersen and Dalgaard (2013) find that a 1 percent increase in power outages across the region reduces GDP per capita, in the long run, by 2.6 percent; or alternatively, "if all African countries had experienced South Africa's power quality, the continent's average annual rate of real GDP per capita growth would have been increased by 2 percentage points" (p. 22).

Social Development Impact

Only one academic study has looked directly at social development impacts of IFFs. Following Christian Aid (2008), O'Hare et al. (2014) model the potential impacts of IFFs on child (under five) and infant mortality, identifying potential pathways from IFFs to mortality: lost revenue and lost national resources (GDP), combined with losses in state capacity, result in worse household access to basic necessities, and this – mediated through the resource allocation within the household – gives rise to worse child health outcomes, including higher mortality rates.

The authors draw on a previous meta-analysis of studies of the relationship between GDP and mortality rates, to establish a baseline for the impact of GDP losses in sub-Saharan Africa. These are then applied to GFI estimates of IFFs, to establish how much quicker progress toward MDG 4 (reductions in child mortality) would have been if IFFs were eliminated.

Some reductions are striking – e.g., in Swaziland, the projected reduction is from 155 years at current progress, to just 27, or in Mauritania from 198 to 19 years. Others are more modest, e.g., Mozambique, which falls from 16 to 11 years. The regional picture lies in between, of course, with the projected date to reach MDG 4 coming forward from 2029 to 2016.

Income Distribution Impact

IFFs are likely, by and large, to be an elite phenomenon: because this is where the incidence of direct taxation will overwhelmingly lie and because political and corporate power in many cases will facilitate IFFs. If tax systems are in theory progressive, then incentives for abuse are likely to be strongest at the top of the income distribution – and opportunities will also be concentrated here, for those with access to foreign bank accounts, or for businesses operating internationally. Lost taxation on high (individual and corporate) income makes the system less progressive and increases inequality. Analysis of IFFs estimates suggests that income hidden through illicit financial flows may result in as big a shift in national income inequality as has been seen by allowing for new data on the taxed incomes of the richest households (Cobham, Davis, Ibrahim, and Sumner, 2016).

There is an additional effect on the tax system itself. Because revenues cannot be raised through direct taxation when the system is porous to IFFs,

---

[3] Although see, e.g., Jerven (2013) on the well-known problems with GDP statistics themselves; and note the criticism that the GFI approach – unlike, say, that of Boyce and Ndikumana (2001) – deals with gross rather than net outflows and so is likely to overstate simple GDP effects if used in this way.

this results in pressure for less progressive – or, all too often, downright regressive – modes of taxation such as value-added tax (VAT). Such moves make higher inequality inevitable.

A third, and the most indirect potential channel, is the political one. If IFFs are associated with greater rent-seeking rather than productive economic activity, then more of the economy – and politics – is tied up in a battle for control of limited resources. This type of power struggle will almost inevitably reduce opportunities for those outside the elite, reducing social mobility and crystallizing inequality. Inequality is associated with a range of negative outcomes, in areas ranging from the intellectual and psychosocial development of children to the probability of conflict (UNICEF/UN Women, 2013), and the costs are likely to be substantial also in terms of foregone economic growth.

Nigeria provides a striking illustration of elite gains in a country widely recognized as suffering large illicit flow. In 2014, central bank governor Lamido Sanusi was removed after he had highlighted the multi-billion-dollar deviation between Nigeria's recorded (oil) exports and the apparent worldwide level of imports from Nigeria.

Without making an explicit causal link, we can use Edward and Sumner (2014) data to consider the pattern of consumption growth by centile of Nigeria's population between 1990 and 2010 and compare that to the pattern across the continent. Despite Nigeria's massive growth during the period, only above the 95th percentile did Nigerian citizens see consumption growth greater than that elsewhere on average; and the vast majority saw their consumption fall while elsewhere it rose. When Nigeria rebased its GDP series in 2014, it not only revealed the country to have the largest economy in Africa, but also showed a level of revenue typically associated with state "fragility," just 10.6 percent of GDP (of which tax revenues were less than 3.9 percent).[4]

Governance Impacts

The final major impact of IFFs is likely to be on governance, and IFFs of all types are associated with either ineffective state functioning or illegitimate use of state power. As a result, there are multiple channels through which IFFs present a threat to governance, undermining both political institutions and the confidence in them. Figure 8.2 shows the linkages of different IFF types to security, where negative security is defined as the ability of states to prevent insecurity at the personal, community, and political levels, and positive security is defined as the ability of states to provide secure conditions in which rapid human development can take place.

The relationship between taxation and governance is complex and strong (Brautigam et al., 2008). Most simply, states with a ratio of tax to GDP below 15 percent or 20 percent of GDP are often thought of as "fragile" (Stewart et al., 2009), simply due to the resulting weakness in state capacity to deliver services, including its own administration. The more governments can fund themselves without directly taking money from citizens (say, from natural resource wealth or high, long-term levels of aid), the less likely is effective accountability. The role of direct taxation appears to be especially important (Mahon, 2005), supporting the view that it is precisely the salience of tax that strengthens the accountability mechanism and so, over time, the governance outcome.

The potential economic growth effects will again be substantial through this channel. Fayissa and Nsiah (2013) used a panel of 39 African countries, from 1995–2004, and found that governance is consistently important for growth, and especially for those countries at the lowest and highest per capita income levels. On average, a 10 percent improvement in a broad governance measure would imply an increase in per capita GDP of 1.5 percent, or (allowing for dynamic effects) as much as a 6.1 percent increase.

The likely impacts of IFFs are both large and wide ranging, although there are substantial uncertainties. In addition, the counterfactuals are unclear and vary according to the type of IFF. For example, restricting corporate profit-shifting and generating additional revenue should produce a fairly direct benefit in the country in question. However, this

---

[4] See: http://www.cgdev.org/blog/nigerias-upward-revision-gdp-should-sound-alarm-tax-gdp-ratio.

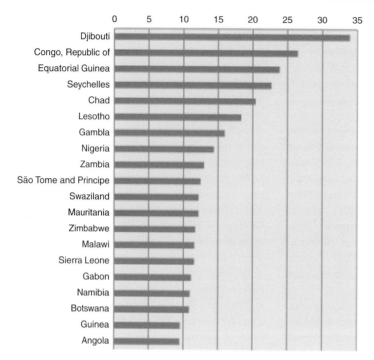

Figure 8.2 *Ratio of average IFF to GDP, 1980–2009*

may effectively result in a redistribution away from shareholders, giving rise to economic losses elsewhere, and possibly dynamic effects on investment if one government is seen as particularly aggressive in targeting tax abuse. Limiting the returns to crime by preventing money-laundering may potentially reduce economic activity, at least in the short term. Even preventing the theft of state assets will reduce the business of foreign banks involved in the transaction and may also lead to lower investment or consumption in that jurisdiction. As a result, it would be impossible to provide a full and precise estimate of either the gross benefits of a 1 percent reduction in IFFs, or of the benefits net of any offsetting losses.

Proposed Targets[5]

Because of the hidden nature of IFFs, policy responses have focused on financial transparency. Major policy change is underway in three key areas, namely the ABC of measures that formed the original Tax Justice Network policy platform in 2003–05:

- Automatic exchange of tax information: to prevent the hiding of offshore assets and income streams, as a deliberate shift away from the dysfunctional "on-request" system of tax information exchange that was the Organization for Economic Co-operation and Development (OECD) standard
- Beneficial ownership information, collation in fully public registers to eliminate the potential for anonymous ownership of companies, trusts, and foundations
- Country-by-country reporting from multinational enterprises, again fully public to expose the major misalignments between the distribution of profit and the location of real economic activity, which result in major revenue losses to tax avoidance

Although initially the proposals were seen as utopian, radical, or simply impractical, by 2013 they

---

[5] This section draws on material prepared for the Open Government Guide (Cobham, 2013) and the Tana High Level Forum on Peace and Security in Africa (Cobham, 2014).

had come to form the main policy agenda of the G8, G20, and OECD groups of countries. Each of the three areas gives rise to a potential subtarget of SDG 16.4, which would provide clear lines of accountability.

For the issue of beneficial ownership, the legal title to companies is not always the same as the name of the people who actually control it (the "beneficial owners"). For example, companies can be listed under the name of "Nominee" shareholders or be held in the name of another company (or trust or foundation), or anonymous "bearer shares" may be used, making it impossible to trace relationships. As the World Bank study *The Puppet Masters* showed (van der Does de Willebois et al., 2011), anonymous ownership of companies, trusts, and foundations is often the central element of financial secrecy in illicit financial flows.

Often, anonymous vehicles are formed in foreign jurisdictions, adding to the problems because this compels authorities to engage in the complicated and often difficult process of a cross-border investigation. Commonly used jurisdictions have a particular responsibility to others in respect of providing transparency.

The Financial Action Task Force (FATF) recommends that countries ensure that information on the real, beneficial owners of companies, trusts, and foundations are available to the authorities in an adequate, accurate, and timely manner (Recommendations 24 and 25). A range of countries, including the UK, have introduced a public registry of beneficial ownership of companies, with more than 50 planning to follow suit under the Extractive Industries Transparency Initiative and all EU member states about to act under the fourth Anti Money Laundering Directive.

Making such registries public not only gives easier access to law enforcement authorities, but also allows citizens, journalists, and civil society to hold companies (and their owners) to account for their actions (Open Societies Foundation, 2013).

The specific target would take the form of a zero target for companies and other legal arrangements without publicly available beneficial ownership information. It might be argued that achieving the last few percent of coverage could be high cost and of relatively low benefit; however, we rely on the argument that partial responses to financial secrecy are somewhat like squeezing a sausage: the total volume (of IFFs) does not change, only the distribution as agents seek alternative secrecy jurisdictions if one becomes transparent. In that light, a zero target is necessary:

i. *Reduce to zero the legal persons and arrangements for which beneficial ownership information is not publicly available.*

Data collated on such a target would highlight the extent to which each jurisdiction had met their responsibilities, so accountability for financial secrecy affecting others would be clear.

The second target relates to multilateral, automatic exchange of tax information. The rationale is to provide a powerful deterrent to undeclared foreign income and hidden assets and a powerful tool to tackle continuing abuse. Automatic exchange was the subject of declarations at the G20 and G8, and with the latter's explicit mandate the OECD (2014) has published the new international standard: the Common Reporting Standard, or CRS:

To prevent circumventing the CRS, it is designed with a broad scope across three dimensions:

- The financial information to be reported with respect to reportable accounts includes all types of investment income (including interest, dividends, income from certain insurance contracts, and other similar types of income) but also account balances and sales proceeds from financial assets.
- The financial institutions that are required to report under the CRS do not only include banks and custodians but also other financial institutions such as brokers, certain collective investment vehicles, and certain insurance companies.
- Reportable accounts include accounts held by individuals and entities (which includes trusts and foundations), and the standard includes a requirement to look through passive entities to report on the individuals that ultimately control these entities.

An "early adopters" group has now begun the process to pilot the standard. Encouragingly, this involves a number of traditional "tax haven" jurisdictions, such as Jersey, Cayman, and the British Virgin Islands, which have typically resisted such information exchange – but few lower-income countries, not even all the G20 members. In total, jurisdictions responsible for more than 90 percent of financial services exports, and around two-thirds of world population, are now included. But it looks increasingly clear that most lower-income countries will have to seek bilateral agreements where a requirement for immediate, full reciprocity may be an obstacle.[6] Most worryingly, some of the most important financial secrecy jurisdictions, such as Switzerland and the United States (ranked first and third, respectively, on the Financial Secrecy Index [Tax Justice Network, 2015]), have indicated they will only provide information to a handful of (high-income) countries.

The proposed target is to ensure that all jurisdictions that share bilateral trade or investment flows also exchange the relevant information to prevent abuse within those transactions. Again, this takes the form of a zero target:

ii. *Reduce to zero the cross-border trade and investment relationships between jurisdictions for which there is no bilateral automatic exchange of tax information*

Reporting on progress would show the progress of individual countries and jurisdictions, allowing identification of blockages. In addition, at the national level, reporting would identify major partners with whom information exchange should be prioritized.

The potential scale of corporate tax abuse in IFFs is large. Leading estimates suggest that annual revenue losses globally may reach $600 billion, ranging from 2–3 percent of total tax revenues in OECD countries to 6–13 percent in non-OECD countries (Cobham & Janský, 2018; Cobham, Janský & Loretz, 2016; Crivelli, de Mooij, and Keen, 2016). The third target therefore relates to corporate reporting.

The OECD was mandated in 2013 to produce a global standard for country-by-country reporting to tax authorities, and this standard – which closely resembles the original Tax Justice Network proposal – is now increasingly in effect around the world. This type of reporting is designed to allow a simple system of red-flagging potentially tax-abusive misalignments of profit and economic activity (Murphy, 2012). A red flag might be raised if, for example, local subsidiaries account for half of the economic activity but only 5 percent of the declared profit; while a subsidiary in Luxembourg, for example, is in the opposite position.

Making this information public allows analysis and comparison between countries, which is likely to discipline behavior and to support effective policy responses. Importantly, it would also contribute to public confidence in fair tax being applied (Cobham, Gray, and Murphy, 2017). Regrettably, the OECD standard at present refers only to the provision of information privately to tax authorities in headquarters countries. Information exchange arrangements are in place to allow access to other tax authorities, but as with financial information these arrangements so far have largely excluded lower-income countries. There are active political debates underway at the national level and across the EU on making the information public. In September 2016, the UK parliament voted to give Treasury the power to require publication; as of May 2017, this power has not yet been exercised. The European Parliament is increasingly supportive of full public reporting, but a final agreement with the European Commission awaits.

The proposed target is therefore to:

iii. *Reduce to zero the number of multinational businesses that do not report publicly on a country-by-country basis*

Either companies or tax authorities could choose to publish the information, with resulting indications of the transparency commitment or otherwise.

These three measures, between them, point the way toward a set of subtargets for SDG 16.4 that have the potential to generate the type of illicit flow reductions sought.

A further potential target area may be considered. The estimates of Global Financial Integrity tend to suggest that for most countries, in most periods, trade misinvoicing is responsible for half

---

[6] See: http://www.taxjustice.net/2014/02/13/press-release-tjn-responds-new-oecd-report-automatic-information-exchange/ and Cobham (2014).

or more of all illicit financial flows. This leads to proposals to address the trade channel directly.

As discussed in section 1, misinvoicing can be used for a broad range of IFF types – from laundering the proceeds of crime and individual tax evasion, to abusive corporate profit-shifting. Tackling it directly may be effective in reducing any or all of these. Proposals for government to use customs data more closely and in international collaboration (see, e.g., Cobham, 2013) are certainly worth pursuing. GFI (2014) also propose measures to increase individual accountability in customs declarations and related company accounts.

There are, however, serious question marks over the use of national-level trade data, as in the GFI methodology. Both Hong and Pak (2016) and Nitsch (2016) find that such an approach is likely to generate results of a scale that is unrelated to the underlying IFF reality – and possibly of the opposing direction. It would be incautious, therefore, to take these estimates as the basis for prioritizing one IFF channel over others.

Setting aside the question of evidence, it may not be sensible to assume that making one IFF channel more difficult or expensive to use will not simply push IFFs into other channels. It seems reasonable to think that misinvoicing is a sufficiently large channel that there would not be 1:1 substitution into other channels, but it also seems unlikely that no substitution would take place.

The alternative is to seek to reduce the benefits to having successfully undertaken any given illicit flow via the three targets listed earlier. The combination of beneficial ownership transparency and automatic information exchange greatly reduces the chances of tax evasion, successful bribery or theft of state assets, and effective money laundering. This is unlikely to provide perfect discipline, but will certainly reduce the incentives. The three targets each seek to raise the transparency of the IFF process and/or the final position achieved, and thereby to raise the risks of challenge and to reduce the expected returns.

On balance, although there is certainly value in exploring the potential for closing the trade channel of IFFs, the potential for substitution to other channels if the underlying incentives are not

changed leads us to exclude these from further consideration here.

Finally, the proposed targets are much more likely to provide accountability than previous formulations. Measuring compliance as proposed would make it possible to state that a given country or jurisdiction (i) has x percent of companies, trusts, and foundations for which no beneficial ownership information is publicly available; (ii) has no bilateral automatic exchange of tax information for y percent of its cross-border investment and trade flows; and (iii) has z percent of the multinationals operating and/or headquartered there reporting publicly on a country-by-country basis.

The core idea is that these targets, measured in this way, give developing countries leverage. For example,[7] Zambia can fail to meet its IFF target of zero trade without automatic information exchange, or Zambia can ask a major trade partner like Switzerland to sign up to provide it with tax information automatically, or Zambia can trade less with Switzerland.[8] Conversely, any given set of possible trading or investment partners can be compared according to their performance on these targets to see which is likely to embody the highest IFF risk (an approach we piloted for the HLP on IFFs out of Africa).

Discussion of Costs and Benefits[9]

Proposed target (i) relates to the publication of registers of beneficial ownership of companies,

---

[7] I'm grateful to Claire Kumar for capturing this point so clearly in an interview.

[8] Bjorn Lomborg has raised an interesting counterargument: might such a mechanism create the potential to reduce progress toward, or even to roll back, free trade – perhaps being exploited by special-interest groups to erect barriers? Although this is plausible, it is not currently the situation that the technical means to limit free trade are lacking; the extent to which they are used is primarily a question of local and international politics. To the extent that this proposal might empower some countries that have historically found it harder, for example, to use WTO mechanisms to pursue a more managed trade agenda, it could potentially open up new obstacles, but it seems unlikely to be a major outcome.

[9] This section benefits from the careful research assistance of Emily Alpert.

trusts, and foundations. No substantive assessments of compliance costs for trusts and foundations exist, unfortunately. This absence of good data on the numbers of such arrangements or the costs of beneficial ownership registration is a concern not only for this exercise but also for the broader questions of financial transparency and illicit flows. In what follows, the analysis is necessarily limited to companies.

There are three relevant studies for company ownership, two relating to the UK and one to the European Union. The latter, the study of Savona et al. (2007), although wider in scope, is also the least recent and the least transparent in its calculations. It considers two models of beneficial ownership disclosure based on the Third EU Anti Money Laundering Directive (Directive 2005/60/EC): Model 0 assumes an intermediary-based disclosure system whereby accountants and banks generally would be responsible for obtaining and disclosing information with an ownership threshold of 25 percent, while Model 1 assumes the duty to disclose beneficial ownership of public and private unlisted companies is placed on the same beneficial owner, who should notify the company of his ownership details. It is then expected that the company should collect this information and file it in a Central National Registry available online to law enforcement agencies and to the wider public. The ownership threshold is raised to 10 percent.

The EU study relies on a combination of quantitative and qualitative data, primarily obtained through questionnaires submitted to experts and authorities in each of the EU-27 member states. Estimates were used to fill gaps in the data, but fundamental assumptions are not explicit. Direct costs of implementation are considered, along with indirect costs through the effects on economic activity.

Overall, this study found costs at the aggregate EU-27 level as follows: the net direct cost for implementing Model 0 is estimated at approximately €6,774 million and the net indirect cost at €10,143 million; while for Model 1, the net direct cost is estimated at €125 million and the net indirect cost at €11,171 million. The bulk of the costs for Model 0 are associated with the activities of "intermediaries," whereas they are greatest for "government" under Model 1.

For the UK, the total cost estimates are €11,425 million for Model 0 and €11,005 million for Model 1. Under both models, the greatest costs to the UK are attributed to (1) a loss in tax revenue and (2) the loss of bank clientele, whereas the offsets (benefits) to either governments or intermediaries were negligible in comparison. The results show the UK as incurring the highest direct and indirect costs of any of the member states under both models, and ultimately accounting for the majority of costs to the EU as a whole: 61.1 percent under Model 0, but 97.6 percent under Model 1. The costs are offset by aggregate benefits that are projected to accrue to more than half of the EU member states.

The first UK study we consider was commissioned by the NGO Global Witness from lawyers John Howell & Co. (2013), to update the analysis contained in the UK government's own 2002 assessment. The study considers transition costs and ongoing costs to companies and Companies House under four different scenarios: (1) companies collect and maintain an internal registry of their own beneficial ownership; (2) companies declare to Companies House; (3) information is made public; and (4) companies provide ID verification of each beneficial owner. In line with the Third Anti-Money Laundering Directive (AMLD), the proposed Fourth AMLD and the recommendations of the Financial Action Task Force (FATF), the GW Study determines the threshold for beneficial ownership at 25 percent. The study does not assess any potential benefits.

Based on estimates of 5.5 million individual shareholdings in private companies and the likelihood of 410,000 unregistered beneficial owners in the UK, implementing a disclosure system for beneficial ownership would cost at minimum £14.08 million for companies to collect and maintain an internal registry (scenario 1) plus an additional £10.02 million to declare this information to companies house on an annual basis (scenario 2). To require declaration more frequently (on event), would cost £14.59 million (Scenario 3) or approximately £4.57 million more than annual disclosure. No extra cost is foreseen for the information to be made public; however it would cost an estimated £49.65 million extra for companies to provide ID verification of each beneficial owner. Ongoing

Table 8.1 Cost estimates for public register of UK company beneficial ownership, US$

	EU study (2007)		GW study (2013)	
Initial costs		38.04		38.23
Of which:	Data filing for unregistered beneficial owners	1.89	Companies collect and maintain an internal registry of their own beneficial ownership	22.02
	Record keeping and filing with a central registry	36.14	Companies declare to Companies House (central registry)	15.67
			Transition costs for Companies House (central registry)	0.55
Ongoing costs		4.57		3.60
Of which:	Updating for unregistered owners	0.77	Maintaining registry annually	0.42
	Data updating with registry	3.80	Declaring annually to Companies House (central registry)	3.17
Total costs		42.61		41.83

Note: Table shows, in 2013 US$, a comparison of "Model 1" in Savona et al. (2007), the EU study; and "Scenario 2" in Howell & Co. (2013), the GW study. For the EU study we use average USD/EUR exchange rate for 2007: 1EUR = $1.37, and a conversion rate of 0.89 to account for inflation of 2007 dollars in 2013. For GW study we use average GBP/USD exchange rate for 2013: 1GBP = $0.635.

costs are calculated at £0.27 million (Scenario 1), £2.03 million (Scenario 2), £3.84 million (Scenario 3), and £6.45m (Scenario 4). Excluding the requirement for ID verification, the estimated transition cost for annual disclosure is £24.10 million plus £2.3 million in ongoing costs (Scenario 2), and the estimated transition cost for disclosure on event is £29.67 million plus £4.11 million in ongoing costs.

The transition costs estimates from Scenario 2 from Howell & Co. (2013) with the direct costs in Model 1 for "Businesses" and "Individuals" in the UK from the EU study are the most reasonable to compare of all the scenarios and models because both assume the costs are borne by the companies; the EU study breaks out individuals from businesses, but identifies the costs for "individuals" as personnel time, much as Howell & Co. do, and both studies consider upfront and ongoing costs. The costs of both analyses are nearly equivalent when converted into 2013 dollars: see Table 8.1.

The most recent study, however, is the UK government's own impact assessment (Department of Business Innovation and Skills, 2013). This takes a more granular approach, assessing the 3.19 million companies according to the relative complexity of their ownership structures and

estimating costs accordingly and using existing costs of government initiatives to estimate the IT, staff, and bureaucratic elements. Costs to government are estimated to be £51,000–110,000 for the IT development of the registry and communication to industry, and £220,000 annually for maintenance. Costs to businesses are estimated to be £226 million initially, and £78 million annually thereafter. In total, costs over ten years are estimated at £899 million (using a discount factor of 3.5 percent), which is equivalent, using the 2013 exchange rate, to $1.405 billion.[10]

It is striking how far above the existing studies these new estimates are. The reliance on self-reported costs from businesses, even after excluding the least plausible values at the top end and zeros at the bottom, is noted as a concern in Department of Business Innovation and Skills (2013) and seems likely to be responsible for the discrepancy. We therefore use the "High" estimates from Department of Business Innovation and Skills (2013) for our high-costs scenario; the "Low" estimates for the medium-cost scenario, and the GW study for the low-cost scenario.

[10] Average of bid and ask prices from oanda.com for 2013 of 0.63963 pence to a dollar.

Table 8.2 Range of benefit-cost ratios for proposed target (i), UK–global extrapolation

Benefit estimates:	Low	Medium	High
Cost estimates:	10% reduction of 2002–2011 average IFF estimate	25% reduction of 2002–2011 average IFF estimate	50% reduction of 2011 IFF estimate
High UK 2013, "High"	13.3 (12.9)	33.4 (32.1)	114.8 (110.6)
Medium UK 2013, "Low"	20.0 (19.3)	50.1 (48.2)	172.3 (165.9)
Low GW 2013	363.3 (338.2)	908.3 (845.6)	3125.1 (2909.5)

Note: Values given are benefit-cost ratios for 3% discount rate (for 5% discount rate in brackets). Extrapolation assumes that UK costs/GDP ratio is globally applicable.

Finally, we show the results for two different extrapolations. In the first, we simply scale up from the UK results to the global level on the basis of the UK's share of world GDP (3.4 percent on the World Bank's most recent [2012] data). This assumes, in effect, that the cost/GDP ratio faced by the UK is applicable globally. In the second extrapolation, we scale up from UK costs to EU costs on the basis of the EU study, which finds a great range of costs (both positive and negative). We then scale from EU to global level by assuming the cost/GDP ratio faced by the EU is applicable globally. Extrapolation I, therefore, provides a substantially higher estimate of global costs than does extrapolation II.

The Department of Business Innovation and Skills (2013) study does not put a value to the benefits, but discusses a broad range of areas in which these are likely to arise – from the statements of multiple law enforcement agencies of the value of such a register, to estimates of the cost of fraud (£523 million annually), to academic studies of the value in GDP terms of recovering trust.

Because beneficial ownership transparency has a role to play in combating each IFF type, we use GFI estimates of total IFFs as the basis to examine potential benefits of meeting this target. As noted, the methodology of the trade component has been criticized, suggesting it may result in overstatement of the true scale of IFFs. On the other hand, as discussed in section 2, there are many costs associated with IFFs. Using reductions in dollar scale as a measure of benefit ignores a great many wider benefits, although also some offsetting costs. The GFI estimates also do not account for net illicit outflows from high-income countries, so will understate global gross outflows. On balance, we expect the approach to understate the benefits, but recognize these are inevitably highly uncertain.

We consider three possible benefit scenarios. For the high-benefit scenario, we take the GFI (2013) estimate for illicit flows in 2011 as the baseline and assume a 50 percent reduction due to global commitment to public registries of company ownership. For the medium-benefit scenario, we take the GFI estimate for average illicit flows during 2002–2011 as the baseline and assume a 25 percent reduction. For the low-benefit scenario, we take the same baseline and assume only a 10 percent reduction. In all cases we assume a consistent growth rate to 2030, based on IMF projections for average world economic growth in 2016 – and assume that IFFs will simply grow in line with global GDP. Table 8.2 shows the range of benefit-cost ratios from the combination of different scenarios, for extrapolation I; while Table 8.3 shows the same for extrapolation II.

We next consider target (ii), of automatic tax information exchange. Although there are no published benefit-cost studies, as of October 2016 the OECD is tracking 84 countries and jurisdictions with arrangements in place for automatic exchange of tax information under the Common Reporting

Table 8.3 Range of benefit-cost ratios for proposed target (i), UK–EU–global extrapolation

Benefit estimates:	Low	Medium	High
Cost estimates:	10% reduction of 2002–2011 average IFF estimate	25% reduction of 2002–2011 average IFF estimate	50% reduction of 2011 IFF estimate
High UK 2013, "High"	87.7 (84.5)	219.3 (211.1)	754.5 (726.4)
Medium UK 2013, "Low"	131.6 (126.7)	329.0 316.8)	1132.1 (1090)
Low GW 2013	2387.3 (2222.5)	5968.1 (5556.4)	20534.4 (19117.6)

Note: Values given are benefit-cost ratios for 3% discount rate (for 5% discount rate in brackets). Extrapolation assumes that UK/EU costs ratio is as per Model 1 in Savona et al. (2007); and that EU costs/GDP ratio is globally applicable.

Standard (CRS).[11] From the range of countries and jurisdictions committing, it seems unlikely that none have considered the costs; so although any such estimates remain private, it would appear that they are lower than the expected benefits.

Out of the 83 possible exchange relationships for each jurisdiction, however, the maximum number of bilateral relationships to exchange in practice is just 46. This level was achieved only by a handful of OECD countries, including the UK and Spain. Switzerland, which will start exchanges in 2018, so far has just 29 relationships – and all are with EU countries. A group of 54 "early adopters" will begin exchange in 2017, but this will be far from the comprehensive multilateral exchange that was originally envisaged. Whether it develops in that direction, or remains patchy and systematically excluding lower-income countries, remains to be seen.

As such, a subtarget in the SDG 16.4 to drive progress toward comprehensive multilateral exchange can be a powerful tool for the inclusion of lower-income countries, and for the reduction of IFFs that they face.

The specific benefit for those countries that are able to receive data will be hard to assess, in part because the deterrent effect is expected to be significantly larger than any criminal convictions that emerge. The more substantive issues are that the initiative has sufficiently long lead times before any information exchange; and more than 2 billion people living primarily in lower-income countries

are currently not included in any form. A target of zero bilateral trade and investment flows without automatic information exchange is therefore needed to ensure that the poorest people are not excluded as rich countries act to protect their own tax bases.

In addition, the process of introducing FATCA (the USA's unilateral requirement affecting all other countries) has forced financial institutions around the world to adopt appropriate systems. Many consulting firms now offer technology platforms that cover the entire set of related requirements. A detailed study of the leading offers, combined with data on the distribution of financial institutions globally, would offer an alternative means of reaching a well-founded estimate on the cost side.

On the benefit side, we can carry out a back-of-the-envelope calculation to envisage the potential scale. To consider the potential effect of automatic information exchange, the best available data appears to be that published periodically by the Internal Revenue Service in the US on the recorded compliance rates of different taxes, where these are disaggregated according to the extent of "matching" information – that is, of

[11] www.oecd.org/tax/automatic-exchange/international-frame work-for-the-crs/exchange-relationships/ (accessed 20 October 2016). See also updated analysis at www.taxjustice.net/ 2017/05/05/developing-countries-access-to-cbcr-guess-whos-not-coming-oecd-dinner/ (accessed 16 May 2017).

information publicly known to be provided to the tax authority by someone other than the taxpayer, e.g., an employer.

Over time, these data show a consistent pattern: as the most recent IRS study, Black et al. (2012) states, "the net misreporting percentage, or NMP (defined as the net misreported amount expressed as a ratio of the true amount), for amounts subject to substantial information reporting and withholding is 1 percent; for amounts subject to substantial information reporting but no withholding, it is 8 percent; and for amounts subject to little or no information reporting, such as business income, it is 56 percent" (p. 3). Comparing the second and third categories implies that the availability of matching information alone cuts the extent of misreporting to just a seventh of the level otherwise.

The most recently published study of undeclared overseas assets is that of Zucman (2013), who finds that "individuals held unrecorded portfolios worth \$4.5tr in tax havens ... My estimate [of all offshore wealth], \$5.9tr in 2008, is at the low-end of the scale [compared to estimates from the Tax Justice Network, Boston Consulting Group, Cap Gemini and Merrill Lynch]" (p. 19). We take the \$4.5 trillion, which is the minimum unreported, from this most conservative of the available estimates.

The benefit of transparency is potentially of the order of six-sevenths of the income stream derived from this \$4.5 trillion. If we conservatively assume the entirety was invested in U.S. Treasury bills at around 3.5 percent, then the total annual income would be \$157.5 billion, and if six-sevenths of that were to be reported due to information exchange, it would bring \$135 billion of taxable income a year – even before any benefits of reduced criminality of other types were taken into effect.

A low-end estimate might assume that tax authorities in general are much less effective than the IRS, and therefore that the availability of information would have much a weaker deterrent effect. A one-seventh, rather than six-sevenths reduction, implies additional taxable income of \$22.5 billion a year. (Alternatively, of course, a less-effective tax authority might well discover a higher initial share of unreported income, so this may be unduly conservative.)

Over the SDG period from 2016–2030, these simple low- and high-end scenarios generate a range of additional taxable income globally of \$277 billion to \$1660 billion (with a 3 percent discount rate), or \$245 billion to \$1471 billion (5 percent discount rate). Although cost estimates remain lacking, it seems reasonable to expect that in most scenarios the likely net benefit would remain high and positive. In particular, the marginal costs for countries with financial centers of including additional lower-income countries in exchange arrangements is likely to be small, while the marginal benefits for these countries that face larger IFFs may be large.

Finally, we consider target (iii), relating to the publication of multinationals' country-by-country reporting. Here, even without substantial evidence of either costs or benefits, the case seems clearly positive. This is because the ongoing OECD process is intended to result in a template used by all tax authorities to require consistent reporting from all multinationals of their country-by-country economic activity, including taxes paid.

As noted earlier, the publication of this information provides a tool to support the accountability of companies, tax authorities, and governments to their citizens and provides tax authorities with a global rather than purely national dataset with which to make comparisons of the behavior of multinational companies in their jurisdiction.

Following the example of such initiatives as International Aid Transparency Initiative (IATI), the mechanism would be straightforward. Rather than send data in the template (in the XML format) privately to one or more tax authorities, companies would simply publish the XML file and record the location of the information in the online, machine-readable register. A public database for CBCR information, which nests various reporting formats including those for EU banks and extractive industries, is now being piloted by the Open Data for Tax Justice Coalition.

This would almost certainly reduce costs for each multinational in terms of employee time. In addition, it would do the same for tax authorities who would have no role in passing on data between themselves and would simply query the data they wanted more or less instantly via the

Table 8.4 Range of benefit-cost ratios for proposed targets

Proposed target	Benefits	Costs	BCR
(i) Reduce to zero the legal persons and arrangements for which beneficial ownership info is not publicly available	$768 billion–$7.5 trillion	$0.35 billion–$66 billion	13–20,000
(ii) Reduce to zero the cross-border trade and investment relationships between jurisdictions for which there is no bilateral automatic exchange of tax information	Possible additional taxable income of $277 billion to $1660 billion (or $245 billion to $1471 billion)	Unknown: but certainly not prohibitive for the 64 jurisdictions now committed to the OECD standard	Likely to be high (high confidence)
(iii) Reduce to zero the number of multinational businesses that do not report publicly on a country-by-country basis	Unknown; but highly likely to be in billions of dollars a year	Unknown, but close to zero and possibly negative	Likely to be high (high confidence)

register. The remaining question on the cost side is whether publication imposes nontrivial costs on the multinationals. A poll of business leaders conducted by a PwC (2014) poll found 59 percent in favor of publication, suggesting that there is only limited concern here.

Now if we envisage that the greater accountability discussed would deliver tangible benefits in the form, for example, of greater alignment between profits and economic activity (the goal of the OECD's Base Erosion and Profit Shifting initiative, and an important issue for lower-income countries in particular), then the resulting benefit-cost ratio is likely to be substantial.

Zucman (2014) estimates that U.S.-headquartered multinationals' tax avoidance via "tax havens" results in revenue losses of 20–30 percent or more; around $200 billion in 2013. Cobham, Janský, and Loretz (2016) found that the relevant part of the corporate tax base would increase significantly in most countries at all income levels, if profit declaration were to be completely aligned with economic activity (measured by sales, assets, and employment). As those authors survey, global revenue losses in the region of $600 billion annually appear to be broadly supported by the work of both IMF and other researchers, using different approaches and different data.

Because country-by-country reporting would make public the specific multinational groups responsible, a disciplining effect on the most egregious misalignment seems likely. Based on Zucman's (2014) results only, a 2 percent reduction could add $4 billion a year to U.S. revenues, or $56 billion–$64 billion by 2030; a 10 percent reduction $279 billion–$320 billion. The global scale, including the dynamic behavioral effects of more effective corporate taxation, remains in need of further research – but is, of course, likely to be very substantially higher.

A final caveat: given the relatively untested nature of the three targets, it may just be possible that their introduction would have precisely zero impact on illicit financial flows – so that even low-end estimates are overstated. As discussed earlier, however, this seems unlikely as each target is central to the way in which different types of illicit flow are hidden, and it is in their hidden nature that the damage is done.

Conclusion

Two main findings emerge from the analysis here. First, there are potentially powerful subtargets for SDG 16.4, which could ensure the framework delivers major progress in reducing illicit financial flows. Each of targets (i)–(iii) seem likely to have high benefit-cost ratios in any reasonable scenario; Table 8.4 provides a summary of the findings.

Second, there is scope to improve significantly the evidence base over the next two years as initiatives in each area go forward – and those involved, not least the OECD, should ensure that the collation of performance data is prioritized so that these gains do indeed crystallize.

Our Recommendation

We propose three subtargets that are more precise than the SDG target 16.4 and provide a much better degree of accuracy, measurability, and accountability. For each of the three proposed subtargets, there is currently insufficient evidence to provide precise cost-benefit analyses. However, available data indicate that in even the most conservative scenarios, they are likely to exhibit high ratios of benefit to cost. The targets are

i. Reduce to zero the legal persons and arrangements for which beneficial ownership info is not publicly available.
ii. Reduce to zero the cross-border trade and investment relationships between jurisdictions for which there is no bilateral automatic exchange of tax information.
iii. Reduce to zero the number of multinational businesses that do not report publicly on a country-by-country basis.

There are ongoing international processes in respect of each of these targets, and those involved should be encouraged to prioritize the collection of data that would enable a more complete impact assessment.

Given the likely minimum ranges of benefit-cost ratios, however, there is a strong case to include these specifics in the post-2015 framework. Since the analysis in this chapter was first undertaken, the UNODC and UNCTAD have been tasked with developing indicators for SDG 16.4. While the initial request is for dollar-value scale estimates, indicators of the type evaluated here are also under discussion (see Cobham & Janský, 2017).

References

Andersen, T. and C.-J. Dalgaard, 2013, "Power outages and economic growth in Africa," *Energy Economics* 38, 19–23.

Baker, R., 2005, *Capitalism's Achilles Heel: Dirty Money and How to Renew the Free-Market System*. Hoboken, NJ: John Wiley.

Berg, A. and J. Ostry, 2011, "Inequality and Unsustainable Growth: Two Sides of the Same Coin?" IMF Staff Discussion Note SDN/11/08.

Black, T., K. Bloomquist, E. Emblom, A. Johns, A. Plumley, and E. Stuk, 2012, "Federal Tax Compliance Research: Tax Year 2006 Tax Gap Estimation," IRS Research, Analysis & Statistics Working Paper.

Blankenburg, S. and M. Khan, 2012, "Governance and illicit flows," in P. Reuter (ed.), *Draining Development? Controlling Flows of Illicit Funds from Developing Countries*. Washington DC: World Bank.

Boyce, J. and L. Ndikumana, 2001, "Is Africa a net creditor? New estimates of capital flight from severely indebted sub-Saharan African countries, 1970–96," *Journal of Development Studies* 38(2), 27–56.

Brautigam, D., O.-H. Fjeldstad, and M. Moore, 2008, *Taxation and State-Building in Developing Countries: Capacity and consent*. Cambridge: Cambridge University Press.

Christian Aid, 2008, *Death and Taxes: The True Toll of Tax Dodging*. London: Christian Aid.

2009, *False Profits*. London: Christian Aid.

Cobham, A., 2013, "Topic Guide: Tax and Illicit Flows," in Open Government Guide. www.opengovguide.com/topics/illicit-flows/.

2014, "The Impacts of Illicit Financial Flows on Peace and Security in Africa," Study for Tana High-Level Forum on Peace and Security in Africa. www.tanaforum.org/index.php?option=com_docman&task=doc_download&gid=44&Itemid=272.

Cobham, A., W. Davis, G. Ibrahim, and A. Sumner, 2016, "Hidden inequality: how much difference would adjustment for illicit financial flows make to national income distributions?" *Journal of Globalization and Development* 7(2), 1–18.

Cobham, A., J. Gray, and R. Murphy, 2017, "What Do They Pay? Towards a Public Database to Account for the Economic Activities and Tax Contributions of Multinational Corporations," CityPERC Working Paper 2017/01. London: City, University of London.

Cobham, A. and P. Janský, 2017, "Measurement of Illicit Financial Flows," UNODC-UNCTAD Expert consultation on the SDG Indicator on Illicit financial flows: Background paper prepared for UNCTAD: https://www.unodc.org/documents/data-and-analysis/statistics/IFF/Background_paper_B_Measurement_of_Illicit_Financial_Flows_UNCTAD_web.pdf.

2018, "Global distribution of revenue loss from corporate tax avoidance: re-estimation and country results," *Journal of International Development*, 30(2), 206–32.

Cobham, A., P. Janský, and S. Loretz, 2016, "Key findings from global analyses of multinational profit misalignment," in S. Picciotto (ed.), *Taxing Multinational Enterprises as Unitary Firms*. Brighton: International Centre for Tax and Development at the Institute of Development Studies.

Cobham, A. and S. Loretz, 2014, "International Distribution of the Corporate Tax Base: Implications of Different Apportionment Factors under Unitary Taxation," International Centre for Tax and Development Working Paper Series.

Coster van Voorhout, J., T. Alleblas, and T. Zhang, 2014. *Curbing Illicit Financial Flows: The Post-2015 Agenda and International Human Rights Law*. The Hague: The Hague Institute for Global Justice.

Crivelli, E., R. De Mooij, and M. Keen 2016. "Base erosion, profit shifting and developing countries." *FinanzArchiv: Public Finance Analysis* 72(3).

Department of Business Innovation and Skills, 2013, *Transparency and Trust: Enhancing the Transparency of UK Company Ownership and Increasing Trust in UK Business*, Discussion Paper. London: Department for Business Innovation and Skills.

Edward, P. and A. Sumner, 2014, "The poor, the prosperous and the 'inbetweeners': a fresh perspective on global society, inequality and growth." *International Policy Center for Inclusive Growth Working Paper* 122. www.ipc-undp.org/pub/IPCWorkingPaper122.pdf.

Fayissa, B. and C. Nsiah, 2013, "The impact of governance on economic growth in Africa." *Journal of Developing Areas* 47(1), 91–108.

Global Financial Integrity (GFI), 2013, *Illicit Financial Flows from Developing Countries: 2002–2011*. Washington, DC: Global Financial Integrity.

2014, *Hiding in Plain Sight: Trade Misinvoicing and the Impact of Revenue Loss in Ghana, Kenya, Mozambique, Tanzania, and Uganda: 2002–2011*. Washington, DC: Global Financial Integrity.

Government Accountability Office (GAO), 2006, "*Company Formations: Minimal Ownership Information Is Collected and Available*," Report to the Permanent Subcommittee on Investigations, Committee on Homeland Security and Governmental Affairs, Washington, DC: U.S. Senate, Government Accountability Office.

Harrison, E., 2013, "The Foreign Account Tax Compliance Act," *STEP Journal* (March). www.step.org/foreign-account-tax-compliance-act.

Hollingshead, A., 2010, *The Implied Tax Revenue Loss from Trade Mispricing*. Washington, DC: Global Financial Integrity.

Hong, K. and S. Pak, 2016, "Estimating trade misinvoicing from bilateral trade statistics: The devil is in the details." *The International Trade Journal*, DOI: 10.1080/08853908.2016.1202160.

Howell & Co., 2013, "Costs of Beneficial Ownership Declarations," report prepared for Global Witness.

Jerven, M., 2013, *Poor Numbers: How We Are Misled by African Development Statistics and What to Do about It*. Ithaca, NY: Cornell University Press.

Johannesen, N. and J. Pirttilä, 2016, "Capital flight and development: An overview of concepts, methods, and data sources," *UNU-WIDER Working Paper* 95.

Kar, D., S. Freitas, J. M. Moyo, and G. S. Ndiaye, 2013, Illicit Financial Flows and the Problem of Net Resource Transfers from Africa: 1980–2009, African Development Bank/Global Financial Integrity. http://bit.ly/ADBgfi.

Lusiani, N., 2014, "A Post-2015 Fiscal Revolution: Human Rights Policy Brief, Center for Economic and Social Rights/Christian Aid. www.cesr.org/downloads/fiscal.revolution.pdf (accessed 16 June 2014).

Mahon, J., 2005, "Liberal states and fiscal contracts: Aspects of the political economy of public finance", Paper presented at American Political Science Association conference (Washington, DC, September).

Murphy, R., 2012, "Country-by-country reporting: Accounting for globalisation locally," report prepared for Tax Justice Network. www.taxresearch.org.uk/Documents/CBC2012.pdf (accessed 16 June 2014).

Nitsch, V., 2016, "Trillion dollar estimate: illicit financial flows from developing countries." *Darmstadt Discussion Papers in Economics* 227.

O'Hare, B., I. Makuta, N. Bar-Zeev, L. Chiwaula, and A. Cobham, 2014, "The effect of illicit financial flows on time to reach the fourth Millennium Development Goal in sub-Saharan Africa: a quantitative analysis," *Journal of the Royal Society of Medicine* 107(4), 148–56.

Open Society Foundations, 2013, "Terrorism Inc: How shell companies aid terrorism, crime and corruption." www.opensocietyfoundations.org/sites/default/files/Terrorism%20INC%20Final%2010-24-13%20FINAL.pdf (accessed 16 June 2014).

Open Working Group, 2014. "Introduction and Proposed Goals and Targets on Sustainable Development for the Post2015 Development Agenda." http://sustainabledevelopment.un.org/content/documents/4044140602working document.pdf (accessed 16 June 2014).

Organisation for Economic Cooperation and Development (OECD), 2014, *Standard for Automatic Exchange of Financial Account Information: Common Reporting Standard.* Paris: Organisation for Economic Cooperation and Development.

PwC, 2014, *CEO Survey 2014*. London: PwC. www.pwc.com/gx/en/ceo-survey/2014/explore-the-data.jhtml (accessed 16 June 2014).

Ross, M., 2004, "Does taxation lead to representation?" *British Journal of Political Science* 34, 229–49.

Savona, E., M. Maggioni, B. Vettori, J. Ponticelli, M. Riccardi, F. Andrian, and C. Ciuretti, 2007, "Cost Benefit Analysis of Transparency Requirements in the Company/Corporate Field and Banking Sector Relevant for the Fight against Money Laundering and Other Financial Crime," Final report to the European Commission.

Stewart, F., G. Brown, and A. Cobham, 2009, "The implications of horizontal and vertical inequalities for tax and expenditure policies," CRISE (Oxford) Working Paper 65.

Tax Justice Network, 2015, *Financial Secrecy Index 2015*. London: Tax Justice Network, http://financialsecrecyindex.com/ (accessed June 16, 2014).

UNICEF/UN Women (eds.), 2013, Synthesis Report on the Global Thematic Consultation on Addressing Inequalities. Available at www.worldwewant2015.org/file/299198/download/324584.

van der Does de Willebois, E., E. Halter, R. Harrison, J. Won Park, and J. Sharman, 2011, *The Puppet Masters: How the Corrupt Use Legal Structures to Hide Stolen Assets and What to Do about It.* Washington, DC: World Bank/UNODC Stolen Asset Recovery Initiative. http://star.worldbank.org/star/sites/star/files/puppetmastersv1.pdf.

World Bank, 2013, *Financing for Development Post-2015*. Washington, DC: World Bank.

2014, *World Bank national accounts data (2012)*, Washington, DC: World Bank, http://data.worldbank.org (accessed June 16, 2014).

Zucman, G., 2013, "The missing wealth of nations: are Europe and the US net debtors or net creditors?" *Quarterly Journal of Economics* 128(3), 1321–64.

2014, "Tax evasion on offshore profits and wealth," draft prepared for *Journal of Economic Perspectives*, available at http://gabriel-zucman.eu/files/Zucman2014JEP.pdf.

8.1 Alternative Perspective

PETER REUTER

Summary

The issue of illicit financial flows came to prominence as a public policy issue with the publication of Raymond Baker's *Capitalism's Achilles Heel* in 2005, but it is striking that today we know little more about the issue. Moreover, all the current estimates of such flows are based on those of Global Financial Integrity, set up by Baker after his book was published, and use a single methodology. The state of the art on IFFs is essentially prescience, with no empirical basis for assessing the effectiveness of proposed policies. Nevertheless, Cobham does much to improve on the High-Level Panel's proposed objective. His goals are precise and, although ambitious, are not wholly unfeasible.

One way to look at the possible consequences for IFFs is to examine the international money laundering control regime, aimed at many IFF-related phenomena. This is a relatively well-resourced and high-profile effort, with all but a handful of countries claiming to have implemented the recommendations of the OECD-affiliated Financial Action Task Force (FATF). However, in practice it is striking how few countries, even among those that were progenitors of the system, such as the United States, France, and the UK, have close to a perfect scorecard. Nevertheless, the FATF can and does put countries on a "blacklist" for noncompliance and there is evidence that countries care about this.

The FATF regime has led to important changes in the routines of the financial sector. Nonetheless, there is little evidence that opportunities for money laundering have been restricted. Indeed, one astonishing feature is that many major international banks flagrantly flout the regime. The Anti-Money Laundering (AML) system is a carefully designed and universally accepted framework to control an important method of protecting the fruits of crimes, but no one can show any evidence that it has had its intended effect of reducing the level of such crimes.

What Cobham proposes is in effect a vast extension of the AML system, covering much more than criminally generated revenues, because it would also strike at that which is illicit, such as transfer pricing abuses, as well as the purely illegal. Although AML measures are inherently complex and varied, Cobham's three proposed rules seem much easier to design, implement, and monitor. Still, the AML experience is instructive in considering how the transparency requirements might be met. Asking a kleptocratic state to create an effective AML system is to ask the fox to create a better henhouse; it is the governing political elite that benefits most substantially from the weakness of the existing system of controls. Experience to date is that nations will meet the letter of the law without placing any substantial barriers to the flow of laundered money.

Cobham adopts an apparently very conservative approach to estimate the benefit-cost ratio. Yet these calculations involve a very bold and unarticulated assumption, namely that the implementation of the beneficial ownership disclosure requirement will reduce IFFs. The experience with AML regulations surely provides cautions here. There are still opportunities to move substantial sums simply by carrying cash across borders, and trade misinvoicing is not prevented via the proposed transparency measures. On the one hand, it should be noted that crime displacement turns out to be far less complete and ubiquitous that expected. Studies in the Netherlands show that drug dealers are highly conventional in the ways they conceal their assets.

None of this is to suggest that IFFs are a poor target, but we need to know more about the phenomenon itself and the effects of various interventions before it can be placed high on the list of recommendations for the post-2015 development challenges.

8.2 Alternative Perspective

DEV KAR AND TOM CARDAMONE

Summary

Global Financial Integrity (GFI) agrees with Cobham that the original targets proposed by the High-Level Panel (HLP) were undermined by framing them in dollars rather than percentage terms, that illicit flows are substantially larger than Overseas Development Aid, and that they adversely affect economic growth, development outcomes, inequality, and governance. However, in contrast to the challenge chapter, we believe that the Open Working Group's reframing of the original proposals both muddies the focus and detracts from the primary objective.

We also feel that Cobham's proposals do not adequately advance the current state of play and therefore miss an opportunity to make significant progress. Although the proposed steps toward financial transparency are extremely important, they are already being addressed in numerous global for a, and great progress has been made toward their implementation. Their inclusion in the post-2015 SDG targets could therefore be seen as redundant.

Financial transparency is only one side of the coin, and only limited progress can be made toward curtailing IFFs without also making efforts in source countries to detect and interdict misinvoiced trade. An appropriate SDG target would lead to developing country governments taking responsibility for addressing their part of the problem.

We agree with Cobham that "... the [current] specific proposal is flawed – but this does not imply that it should be dropped ..." Rather, it should be changed in two important ways. First it

should stand alone rather than being linked to reductions in corruption and related issues; our data suggest that a very low percentage of illicit flows is due to corruption and is likely under 20 percent of the total. Second, more precise language is needed than that used in the current draft. Specifically, it should read: "reduce illicit financial flows related to trade misinvoicing by 50 percent."

This concentrates on the largest part of the IFF problem (about 80 percent according to our data), depoliticizes the issue by eliminating any linkage to government corruption, and provides a specific role for donor countries and agencies to build capacity in customs departments in developing countries. It would have numerous benefits, particularly as a development enabler. Including an SDG target on IFFs will generate revenue needed to help achieve the other likely SDG targets such as ending malnutrition and achieving universal health coverage.

Given that about 80 percent of IFFs are due to trade misinvoicing, we see a focused effort to modernize customs departments as the primary way to address this problem. Based on estimates by the World Bank, we assess the costs at $2 million per country, or a little more than $300 million for all developing nations. However, government tax revenue on the profits earned from international trade could equal about $8 billion, which is more than 26 times the cost. It should also be understood that the cost is a one-off, while the benefits would continue to accumulate over time. The international community has taken action to address the demand side of the equation, and a target on misinvoicing is a critical next step to address the supply side.

Benefits and Costs of the Trade Targets for the Post-2015 Development Agenda

KYM ANDERSON

Opportunities to Lower Trade Barriers

Lowering trade barriers would contribute to all four of the likely main goals of the United Nations' post-2015 development agenda: poverty alleviation, ending hunger, reducing income inequalities, and strengthening global partnerships for sustainable development (United Nations, 2014).

Stronger global partnerships for sustainable development would result from promoting a more open, rules-based, nondiscriminatory and equitable multilateral trading system by successfully completing the Doha Development Agenda (DDA) negotiations at the World Trade Organization (WTO). Remaining barriers to trade harm most the economies imposing them, but the worst of the merchandise barriers (in agriculture and textiles) are particularly harmful to the world's poorest producers. Reforming those policies would thus alleviate poverty, reduce income inequality within and between nations, reduce malnutrition and hunger globally, and boost employment and economic growth sustainably, particularly in rural areas of developing countries, where three-quarters of the world's poor reside (World Bank, 2007).

It is within the power of national governments to lower their own barriers to trade unilaterally, of course, but often that is difficult to achieve politically. Lowering them is politically easier when other countries do so at the same time, as with a multilateral or regional trade and integration agreement. For developing countries that is especially so if that agreement includes an aid-for-trade package.[1]

Among the possible strategies to reduce remaining price- and trade-distorting measures, five current opportunities stand out. The most

beneficial involves multilaterally completing the stalled Doha Development Agenda (DDA) of the World Trade Organization (WTO). If that continues to prove to be too difficult politically to bring to a conclusion in the near future, three other opportunities considered here are the proposed Trans-Pacific Partnership (TPP), extending the free-trade area among the ten-member Association of South East Asian Nations to include China, Japan, and South Korea (ASEAN+3), and freeing up trade among all APEC countries (a free trade area of the Asia-Pacific, FTAAP).[2] One more potential opportunity involves bringing disciplines to export restrictions to match those for import restrictions, especially for farm products.

In the absence of any proposals directly involving the world's poorest regions (South Asia and sub-Saharan Africa) people here could benefit indirectly and substantially from new opportunities

---

[1] A secondary goal that has been proposed for the post-2015 agenda is to implement the principle of special and differential treatment for developing countries, and in particular least-developed countries. This is commonly interpreted to mean developing countries need not commit in WTO agreements to as much policy reform as high-income countries. Yet developing and especially least-developed countries would gain far more from their own policy reforms than from those of high-income countries, so allowing them to continue to deny themselves prospective gains from trade liberalization is not going to contribute to their economic growth.

[2] The 11 current countries in TPP negotiations are Australia, Brunei, Canada, Chile, Japan, Malaysia, Mexico, New Zealand, Peru, Singapore, and Vietnam. The 21 members of APEC include the TPP participants plus the other main ASEAN+3 economies plus Hong Kong, Papua New Guinea, Russia, and Taiwan.

to trade with East Asia's booming economies that would result from greater integration of Asia-Pacific economies. Their indirect benefit would be greater, the more they unilaterally lower their own trade barriers. They could do so by liberalizing their border measures (import tariffs, export taxes, nontariff barriers) but also by removing regulations or investing more in infrastructures that lower the costs of doing business across borders.

Why Do Trade Barriers Persist?

Despite the net economic and social benefits of reducing most government subsidies[3] and barriers to international trade and investment, almost every national government intervenes in markets for goods, services, and capital in ways that distort international commerce.[4] The policy instruments considered here will focus mainly on those trade-related ones over which a government's international trade negotiators have some influence both at home and abroad.[5] It should be kept in mind, though, that policies affecting the services sector can also add to the cost of doing business across borders (Borchert, Gootiiz, and Mattoo, 2014; Francois and Hoekman, 2010).

The General Agreement on Tariffs and Trade's (GATT's) Uruguay Round of multilateral trade negotiations led to agreements signed in 1994 that contributed to trade liberalization over the subsequent ten years. But many subsidies and trade restrictions remained, including not just trade taxes-cum-subsidies but also contingent protection measures such as antidumping, regulatory standards that can be technical barriers to trade, and domestic producer subsidies. At the same time, the ongoing proliferation of preferential trading and bilateral or regional integration arrangements adds complexity to international economic relations, which may be welfare reducing for some excluded economies.

Although reducing trade distortions could often benefit treasuries, they remain in place largely because further liberalization would redistribute jobs, income, and wealth in ways that those in government fear would reduce their chances of remaining in power (and, in countries where corruption is rife, possibly reduce their own wealth). The challenge involves finding politically attractive ways to phase out remaining distortions to world markets for goods and services.

Arguments for Lowering Trade Barriers

Even before examining the empirical estimates of the benefits and costs of grasping various trade-liberalizing opportunities, the case can be made that such reform in principle is beneficial economically.[6]

Static Economic Gains from Own-Country Trade Reform

The standard comparative static analysis of national gains from international trade emphasizes the economic benefits from production specialization and exchange to exploit comparative advantage. This is part of the more general theory of the welfare effects of distortions in a trading economy, as summarized by Bhagwati (1971) and Corden (1997).

The gains from opening an economy are larger, the greater the variance of rates of protection among industries – especially within a sector (Lloyd, 1974). Likewise, the more-productive

---

[3] Not all subsidies are welfare-reducing, and in some cases a subsidy-cum-tax will be the optimal government intervention to overcome a gap between private and social costs that cannot be bridged à la Coase (1960). Throughout this chapter all references to "cutting subsidies" refer to bringing them back to their optimal level (which will be zero in all but those relatively few exceptional cases).

[4] Labor market interventions also are rife, including barriers to international migration. For estimates of the potential global economic benefits from reducing the latter, see Anderson and Winters (2009).

[5] That thereby excludes measures such as generic taxes on income, consumption and value added, government spending on mainstream public services, infrastructure and generic social safety nets in strong demand by the community, and subsidies (taxes) and related measures set optimally from the national viewpoint to overcome positive (negative) environmental or other externalities. Also excluded from consideration here are policies affecting markets for foreign exchange.

[6] This survey does not pretend to provide comprehensive coverage of the gains-from-trade theory. For more, readers are referred to the handbooks by Grossman and Rogoff (1995) and Harrigan and Choi (2003) and the textbook by Feenstra (2003).

domestic firms within industries expand by drawing resources from less-productive firms. Indeed theory and empirical studies suggest the shifting of resources within an industry may be more welfare-improving than shifts between industries.[7] Furthermore, if trade barriers are managed by inefficient institutions (such as distributors of import or export quota licences), gains from removal of such barriers will be larger than removal of standard trade taxes (Khandelwal, Schott, and Wei, 2013).

The static gains from trade tend to be greater as a share of national output the smaller the economy, particularly where economies of scale in production have not been fully exploited and where consumers (including firms importing intermediate inputs) value variety. Less-than-full exploitation of scale economies is more common in smaller and poorer economies where industries have commensurately smaller numbers of firms. This is especially the case in the service sector, for example for utilities, where governments have been inclined to sanction monopoly provision.[8]

Those gains from opening up will be even greater if accompanied by a freeing up of domestic markets and the market for currency exchange. The more stable and market friendly is domestic economic policy, the more attractive will an economy be to capital inflows and the greater the likelihood that adjustments by firms and consumers to trade liberalization will lead to a more-efficient utilization of national resources and greater economic welfare (Corden, 1997). If domestic policy reforms included improving the government's capacity to redistribute income and wealth more efficiently and in ways that better matched society's wishes, concerns about the distributional consequences of trade liberalization also would be lessened.

The ICT revolution has enabled firms to take advantage of factor cost differences across countries for specific tasks without having to sacrifice gains from product specialization or move the whole of their production operation offshore (Hanson, Mataloni, and Slaughter, 2005). Trade in many tasks (e.g., emailing data files) is not even recorded in official trade statistics and so is not directly subject to trade policies. That suggests the variance of import protection across all traded items is even greater than across just recorded trade

in goods, so the welfare gains from reducing the latter could well be greater than that captured by conventional trade models.

Dynamic Economic Gains from Own-Country Trade Reform

The standard comparative static analysis needs to be supplemented with links between trade and economic growth. The mechanisms by which openness contributes to growth are gradually being better understood by economists, following the pioneering work of such theorists as Grossman and Helpman (1991) and Rivera-Batiz and Romer (1991). Factors affecting an economy's growth rate include the scale of the market when knowledge is embodied in the products traded, the degree of redundant knowledge creation that is avoided through openness, and the effect of knowledge spillovers (Acharya and Keller, 2007; Romer, 1994; Taylor, 1999). The latest surge of globalization has been spurred also by the technology "lending" that is involved in offshoring an ever-rising proportion of production processes. As Baldwin (2011) points out, this joining of a supply chain has made industrialization potentially far less complex and far faster – especially for countries with reliable workers, a hospitable business environment, and a location near large industrial countries such as China.

The dynamic gains from openness can be greater when accompanied by reductions in domestic distortions. When trade reform includes financial markets, more is gained than just a lower cost of credit. The resulting financial deepening can stimulate growth too (Townsend and Ueda, 2010). Kose et al. (2009) add two other indirect growth-enhancing benefits of financial reform: they discipline firms to look after the interests of

---

[7] Melitz (2003) provides the theory behind this point, and many econometricians have since provided strong empirical support for that theory.

[8] The argument for allowing such monopolies is that they could provide greater technical efficiency via their larger scale. The contrary argument is that, being sheltered from competition, they fall so short of that potential as to be less productive than two or more smaller-scale competing suppliers.

shareholders better, and they discipline governments to provide greater macroeconomic stability.

The available empirical evidence strongly supports the view that open economies grow faster (see the surveys by Billmeier and Nannicini, 2009; Francois and Martin, 2010; U.S. International Trade Commission [USITC], 1997; and Winters, 2004,). Notable early macroeconometric studies of the linkage between trade reform and the rate of economic growth include those by Sachs and Warner (1995) and Frankel and Romer (1999). More-recent studies also provide some indirect supportive econometric evidence. For example, freeing up the importation of intermediate and capital goods promotes investments that increase growth (Wacziarg, 2001). Indeed, the higher the ratio of imported to domestically produced capital goods for a developing country, the faster it grows (Lee, 1995; Mazumdar, 2001). Greater openness to international financial markets also boosts growth via the stimulation to investment that more risk-sharing generates.

In a study that revisits the Sachs and Warner data and then provides new time-series evidence, Wacziarg and Welch (2008) show that dates of trade liberalization do characterize breaks in investment and GDP growth rates. Specifically, for the 1950–1998 period, countries that have liberalized their trade (defined as those raising their trade-to-GDP ratio by an average of 5 percentage points) have enjoyed on average 1.5 percentage points higher GDP growth compared with their prereform rate.

There have also been myriad case studies of liberalization episodes. In a survey of 36 of them, Greenaway (1993) reminds us that many things in addition to trade policies were changing during the studied cases, so ascribing causality is not easy, suggesting to some authors that the link between economic growth and trade reform has been overstated. But the same has been said about the contributions to growth of such things as investments in education, health, agricultural research, and so on, but it is clear that people respond to incentives (Easterly, 2001). Removing unwarranted subsidies and trade barriers is an important part of creating the right incentives. Additional evidence from 13 new case studies reported in Wacziarg and Welch (2008) supports that view, as does the fact that there are no examples of autarkic economies that have enjoyed sustained economic growth, in contrast to the many examples since the 1960s of reformed economies that boomed after opening up.

Specifically, economies that commit to less market intervention tend to attract more investment funds. Faini (2004) found that trade liberalization in the 1990s fostered inward foreign investment, while backtracking on trade reform had a negative impact. More-open economies also tend to be more innovative because of greater trade in intellectual capital and because greater competition spurs innovation (Aghion and Griffith, 2005; Aghion and Howitt, 2006), leading to higher rates of capital accumulation and productivity growth (Lumenga-Neso, Olarreaga, and Schiff, 2005).[9]

Industry studies provide additional support for the theory that trade reform boosts the rate of productivity growth.[10] It appears more-productive firms are innately better at exporting, so opening an economy leads to their growth and the demise of the least-productive firms (Bernard et al., 2007). That leads to better exploitation of comparative advantage by both industries and also individual firms. If those more-productive firms are also foreign owned, as is clearly the case in China (Whalley, 2010), then being open to FDI multiplies the gains from product trade openness. And if those foreign firms are involved in retailing, they can put pressure on below-par domestic suppliers to raise their productivity. Walmart's influence in Mexico provides one example of this force at work (Javorcik, Keller, and Tybout, 2008). Furthermore, if the foreign firms are supplying lower-cost services inputs into manufacturing, that can boost the productivity growth of local manufacturers using those service inputs, according to a recent study of the Czech Republic (Arnold, Javorcik, and Mattoo, 2011).[11]

---

[9] More open economies also tend to be less vulnerable to foreign shocks such as sudden stops in capital inflows, currency crashes, and severe recessions (Frankel and Cavallo, 2008).

[10] For an overview of this new theory, see Helpman, Marin, and Verdier (2008).

[11] For a survey of the growth effects of opening to trade in services, see Francois and Hoekman (2010).

It need not be just the most-productive firms that engage in exporting. For lower-productivity firms, incurring the fixed costs of investing in newly opened foreign markets may be justifiable if accompanied by the larger sales volumes. Lower foreign tariffs will induce these firms to simultaneously export and invest in productivity (while inducing higher-productivity firms to export without more investing, as in Melitz, 2003; Melitz and Ottaviano, 2008; and Melitz and Redding, 2014). Lileeva and Trefler (2010) model this econometrically using a heterogeneous response model. Unique "plant-specific" tariff cuts serve as their instrument for the decision of Canadian plants to start exporting to the United States. They find that those lower-productivity Canadian plants that were induced by the tariff cuts to start exporting increased their labor productivity, engaged in more product innovation, and had high adoption rates of advanced manufacturing technologies. These new exporters also increased their domestic (Canadian) market share at the expense of nonexporters, which suggests that the labor productivity gains reflect underlying gains in total factor productivity.

Liberalizing international financial flows also has been shown to have boosted economic growth (Bordo and Rousseau, 2012; Schularick and Steger, 2010). A study by Hoxha, Kalemli-Ozcan, and Vollrath (2013) examines potential gains from financial integration and finds that a move from autarky to full integration of financial markets globally could boost real consumption permanently by 9 percent in the median developing country, and up to 14 percent in the most capital-scarce countries.[12]

In short, international trade and investment liberalization can lead not just to a larger capital stock and a one-off increase in productivity but also to higher rates of capital accumulation and productivity growth in the reforming economy because of the way reform energizes entrepreneurs. For growth to be maximized and sustained, though, there is widespread agreement that governments also need to (a) have in place effective institutions to efficiently allocate and protect property rights, (b) allow domestic factor and product markets to function freely, and (c) maintain macroeconomic and political stability (Baldwin, 2004; Chang,

Kaltani and Loayza, 2005; Rodrik, 2007; Wacziarg and Welch, 2008).

Rutherford and Tarr (2002) bring these factors together in a paper using a dynamic, stochastic numerical open economy growth model. They simulate a halving of the only policy intervention (a 20 percent tariff on imports) and, in doing so, fully replace the government's lost tariff revenue with a lump-sum tax. That modest trade reform produces a welfare increase (in terms of Hicksian equivalent variation) of 10.6 percent of the present value of consumption in their central model. Systematic sensitivity analysis showed that there is virtually no chance of a welfare gain of less than 3 percent, and a 7 percent chance of a welfare gain larger than 18 percent of consumption. Further work found that the welfare estimates for the same tariff cut ranged up to 37 percent when international capital flows are allowed and down to 4.7 percent when using the most inefficient replacement tax (a tax of capital). Even this very inefficient tax on capital is superior to the tariff as a revenue raiser.

Increasing the size of the tariff cuts results in roughly proportional increases in the estimated welfare gains. Large welfare gains in the model arise because the economy benefits from increased varieties of foreign goods. In the case that the additional varieties result in no increase in total factor productivity, there is a small welfare gain of about 0.5 percent, similar to the gains emerging from static general equilibrium studies. Their results also illustrate the importance of complementary reforms to fully realize the potential gains from trade reform. In particular, with the ability to access international capital markets, the gains are roughly tripled, and the use of inefficient replacement taxes significantly reduces the gains. These combined results underscore the point that complementary macroeconomic, regulatory, and financial market reforms to allow capital flows and efficient alternate tax collection are crucial to realizing the potentially large gains from trade liberalization.

[12] In a case study of Thailand, Townsend and Ueda (2010) estimate welfare gains from financial liberalization as high as 28 percent.

Key Opportunities for Trade Barrier Reductions

The most obvious feasible opportunity currently open is a nonpreferential, legally binding, partial liberalization of goods and services trade following the WTO's current round of multilateral trade negotiations, the Doha Development Agenda (DDA). That continues to prove to be difficult politically to bring to a conclusion, however, notwithstanding the progress made at the Bali Trade Ministerial in December 2013 (including on trade facilitation – see Neufeld, 2014).[13]

Three other opportunities considered here involve prospective subglobal regional integration agreements. One is the proposed Trans-Pacific Partnership (TPP) among a subset of 12 member countries of the Asia Pacific Economic Cooperation (APEC) grouping; another involves extending the free-trade area among the ten-member Association of South East Asian Nations to include China, Japan and Korea (ASEAN+3); and the third opportunity is a free-trade area among all APEC countries.[14] Also considered later is a potential opportunity to include on the WTO's agenda, namely, bringing discipline to export restrictions to match those for import restrictions on farm products.

The TPP began in 2006 when just four small APEC members (Brunei, Chile, New Zealand, and Singapore) got together to begin negotiations for greater economic integration. Being already open liberal economies, their leaders saw this not as an end in itself but rather as a pathway for a more-expansive club. In September 2008 the United States announced its interest in joining the TPP. By 2010 Australia, Malaysia, Peru, and Vietnam also joined in, and since then Canada, Japan, and Mexico have joined the negotiations, to make a total of 12 of APEC's 21 members as of April 2014. Following President Trump's election in late 2016, however, the United States has withdrawn from the TPP negotiations.

Meanwhile, discussions have been under way between the ten members of ASEAN, who already have their own free-trade agreement (AFTA), and their three big northern neighbors (China, Japan, and Korea), with a view to forming a broader East Asian FTA that is generally referred to as ASEAN+3.

APEC leaders have endorsed both of those regional integration tracks and see them as potential pathways to an FTA involving all APEC members (Asia Pacific Economic Cooperation [APEC], 2010). We therefore consider this more-encompassing prospect as the third regional opportunity.

These Asia-Pacific regional initiatives are also important to other parts of the world because the region represents a growing share of the world economy: almost 60 percent in 2011 (http://icp.worldbank.org).

The final opportunity, bringing greater discipline to export restrictions, has become important as a result of policy responses to the three spikes in international food prices between 2008 and 2012. Some grain-exporting countries responded by restricting their exports, while some grain-importing countries lowered or suspended their import tariffs, effectively neutralizing each other's actions by pushing up prices. This exposed the asymmetry in WTO disciplines, which are much tougher on import measures than on those affecting exports. It also underlined the potential value in having food exporting members convert their export restrictions to trade taxes, bind them, and agree to phase them out.

Estimates of Benefits from Reducing Trade Barriers

Empirical comparative static model simulation studies of the potential economic welfare gains from prospective multilateral or large regional trade liberalization agreements typically generate positive gains for the world and for most participating countries.

---

[13] If WTO member countries can agree to sign up to the proposed Trade Facilitation Agreement negotiated in Bali, the gains could be very considerable. See Moïsé and Sorescu (2013) and Zaki (2014).

[14] Whether such reciprocal preferential trade agreements are stepping-stones or stumbling blocks to freer global trade is a much-debated point among economists. For a survey of the impact of regionalism on the multilateral trading system, see Baldwin (2009).

All the estimates considered later of the costs of current policies and the potential economic welfare gains from these reform opportunities are generated using computable general equilibrium (CGE) models of the global economy. The CGE welfare gains refer to the equivalent variation in income (EV) as a result of each of the shocks described.[15] Although not without their shortcomings (see Anderson, 2003; Francois and Martin, 2010 and the caveats described later), CGE models are far superior for current purposes to both partial equilibrium models and macroeconometric models.

In the case of subglobal preferential trade reform studies, the estimated gains to the countries involved are almost always smaller, and some excluded countries – and even some participating ones – may lose. When increasing returns to scale and monopolistic competition (IRS/MC) are assumed instead of constant returns to scale and perfect competition (CRS/PC), and firms are assumed to be heterogeneous rather than homogeneous, and when trade is liberalized not just in goods but also in services and investment flows, the estimates of potential gains can increase several-fold. However, the projected GDP gains are rather small because this approach fails to capture the growth-enhancing dynamic effects of reform. Experience in, for example, Korea, Chile, and India suggests growth can actually be boosted considerably (Irwin, 2002).

We need to consider this background when estimating the economic gains from the identified options.

Economic Consequences of Doha Multilateral Reform

Following the stalling of the Doha round in 2008, there have been some more recent studies of the benefits of a successful outcome. Laborde, Martin, and van der Mensbrugghe (2011) estimate that if the basic formula approach to reducing trade barriers and subsidies, as currently proposed, were to be adopted by all WTO member countries, then global GDP would be 0.36 percent higher. Making allowance for the various flexibilities in the proposals, the gains drop to 0.22 percent of global GDP: 0.25 percent for high-income (including Europe's transition) economies and 0.17 percent for developing countries. This is considered here as the lower-bound estimate of the gains from this opportunity.

Not all developing countries are estimated to gain, though: GDP would drop 0.19 percent in Bangladesh and 0.10 percent in sub-Saharan Africa. That loss is partly because of the erosion of tariff preferences and partly because developing and especially least-developed countries are not required to open their own markets. However, they could avoid being worse off simply by opening their own markets more, if they so choose.

When economies of scale and monopolistic competition are assumed instead of constant returns to scale and perfect competition, and firms are assumed to be heterogeneous rather than homogeneous, and when trade is liberalized not just in goods but also in services and investment flows, the estimates of potential gains tend to be raised several-fold. In their previous contribution to this project, Anderson and Winters (2009) reviewed past literature of modeling efforts that added such features and concluded that an upper-bound estimate of those gains could be five times the lower-bound estimate. That would bring the gains as a share of GDP to 1.1 percent globally: 1.25 percent for high-income countries and 0.85 percent for developing countries. As for timing, again following Anderson and Winters (2009), it is assumed those gains would accrue fully after 2020, following a six-year phase-in period.

There are dynamic gains from trade to consider in addition to the preceding comparative static ones. An estimate might be that reform boosts GDP growth rates – projected from 2010 to 2025 by the Asian Development Bank (2011, p. 57) and Fouré, Bénassy-Quéré, and Fontagné (2010) to be around 2.0 percent for high-income countries and 5.0 percent for developing countries and so

---

[15] EV is defined as the income that consumers would be willing to forego and still have the same level of well-being after as before the reform. For a discussion of the merits of EV versus other measures of change in economic welfare, see, for example, Just, Hueth, and Schmitz (2004).

3.0 percent globally[16] – by 0.4 of a percentage point for high-income countries and 0.6 of a percentage point for developing countries, that is, to 2.4 and 5.6 percent, respectively, and hence from 3.0 to 3.47 percent globally through to 2025.[17] As for the period after 2025, a review of the literature by Winters (2004) suggests that the growth increments due to trade liberalization could last several decades. Thus we assume the incremental boost to GDP declines linearly from its 2025 value to the long run average growth rate by 2050, so there is just the continuing comparative static gain of 0.22 percent globally, 0.25 percent for high-income countries and 0.17 percent for developing countries from 2050 to 2100.

Economic Consequences of Preferential Reforms in the Asia-Pacific Region

Each of the current trade liberalization initiatives in the region – the TTP, ASEAN+3, and an APEC free-trade area – is assumed to be preferential, in the sense that trade is freed within the group but not between group members and the rest of the world.

Estimates of prospective gains from these three opportunities are provided by Petri, Plummer, and Zhai (2012). They use the latest GTAP database (version 8.1, with a 2007 baseline, see Narayanan et al., 2012) but their CGE model of the global economy is, in several respects, more sophisticated than the one used in the earlier Doha analysis (see Zhai, 2008). In particular, it is distinguished from the standard Linkage model in two important ways. First, it assumes economies of scale and monopolistic competition in the manufacturing and private services sectors instead of constant returns to scale and perfect competition. Second, following Melitz (2003), firms are assumed to be heterogeneous rather than homogeneous: each industry with monopolistic competition consists of a continuum of firms that are differentiated by the varieties of products they produce and their productivity. Furthermore, trade is liberalized by these authors not just by reducing applied bilateral tariffs on goods but also by raising utilization rates of tariff preferences, lowering nontariff barriers to both goods and services, and reducing costs

associated with meeting rules of origin (for details see the Appendixes in Petri, Plummer, and Zhai, 2012). Even so, the results summarized later can be considered conservative for reasons mentioned in the following caveat section.

With these model refinements, the estimated gains from preferential liberalization of trade within this region are nontrivial, in part because of the growing economic importance of the region. Specifically, the TPP12 countries are projected by Petri, Plummer, and Zhai to account for one-quarter of the global economy, the ASEAN+3 economies for just over one-quarter, and the whole of APEC's 21 members for more than half of global GDP in 2025 (see Table 9.1).

Prior to the US withdrawal from the negotiations, it was estimated that the 12 members of the Trans-Pacific Partnership would get a 0.42 percent boost to their GDP if they removed their bilateral barriers to trade in goods and services; global GDP would be boosted by 0.22 percent (see Table 9.1). If instead the three large northeast Asian countries formed an FTA with the ASEAN members, global GDP growth would rise by a similar amount (0.21 percent). But if all 21 APEC members were to form a free-trade area (FTAAP), the global gains would be four times greater (0.85 percent). The corresponding gains for all developing countries would be 0.06 percent of GDP from TPP, 0.33 percent from ASEAN+3, and 1.17 percent from FTAAP, and for all high-income and transition countries the gains would be 0.36, 0.10, and 0.56 percent of GDP (Table 9.2).

---

[16] The growth rate of developing countries typically converges on that of high-income countries over time. Hence it is assumed in the baseline that the GDP of developing countries grows at a rate of 4.0 percent during 2025–2050 and at 3.0 percent during 2050–2100.

[17] Econometric support for the claim that this assumed increase in GDP growth rates is conservative is provided by Romalis (2007), who estimates that the elimination of just import tariffs, and only by high-income countries, would boost annual GDP growth in developing countries by up to 1.6 percentage points. In the model by Rutherford and Tarr (2002), their ten percentage point cut in tariffs led to a rise in the steady-state growth rate of 2 percent p.a. to 2.6 percent over the first decade and 2.2 percent over the first five decades (and even after 50 years their annual growth rate is 2.1 percent).

Table 9.1 Comparative static effects on economic welfare of trade reform under three different prospective Asia–Pacific preferential free-trade agreements, 2025

	Baseline share of world GDP (%), 2025	US$ billion			Percent of GDP		
		TPP12	ASEAN+3	FTAAP	TPP12	ASEAN +3	FTAAP
TPP12 countries	26	112	26	172	0.42	0.11	0.73
ASEAN+3 countries	28	129	219	596	0.45	0.78	2.12
All 21 APEC countries	57	239	216	912	0.41	0.37	1.57
All non-APEC countries	43	−16	−1	−50	−0.00	−0.00	−0.11
World	100	223	215	862	0.22	0.21	0.85

(Annual difference from baseline, 2007 US dollars and percent)
Source: Petri, Plummer, and Zhai (2012, Table 7).

This progression in gains is due to several factors: greater trade complementarity as the mix of economies broadens, greater trade barriers (especially in agriculture) between the full set of APEC economies and the two smaller subsets prior to their removal, and greater scope for exploiting gains within the manufacturing sectors among the ASEAN+3 countries than among the TPP12 countries.

Two other points are worth noting. One is that non-APEC countries lose very little in aggregate, reflecting the fact that trade creation dominates trade diversion in these three cases. China would lose from being excluded from the TPP, however. The other point is that the estimated gain from full liberalization of trade among all APEC countries is higher than that estimated for the partial Doha multilateral reform summarized earlier. That would provide the wherewithal for those participating countries to share some of their gain with those poorer countries elsewhere that may lose from such regional trading arrangements.

To make the present value of estimated gains from these prospective preferential reforms comparable with the earlier estimates of gains from partial multilateral reform under the WTO's Doha agenda, it is assumed the gains would accrue fully after 2020, following a six-year phase-in period during which the gains begin in 2015 at one-sixth of the full amount as of 2025 and rise by a further one-sixth each year until 2020.

Consistent with the Doha analysis, we assume that reform boosts the GDP growth rates of the participating APEC countries and their key trading partners by one-fifth between 2010 and 2025. For the period after 2025, we assume, again very conservatively, that the dynamic boost to GDP growth diminishes linearly after 2025 and disappears by 2050, so the benefits from reform return to just the comparative static gains for the latter half of the century.

Economic Consequences of Not Insulating Domestic Markets from Price Volatility

As both food-exporting and food-importing countries alter their trade restrictions when prices spike, each has less impact domestically because of the other group's action. Both sets of actions also turn the terms of trade even more in favor of the exporter group. Global gains or losses depend on whether total world trade expands or contracts. The effect on numbers in poverty will depend on the impacts of these policies both domestically and in other countries.

A recent study by Anderson and Nelgen (2012) found that both exporting and importing countries contributed substantially to the international food price spike of 2006–8. In that period international prices rose 113 percent for rice, 70 percent for wheat, and 83 percent for maize. Using a simple model they estimated that the insulating actions of national governments were responsible for 0.4 of

Table 9.2 Assumptions used in the benefit-to-cost calculus

	Baseline GDP levels and assumed growth rates to 2100:				
	Real GDP (US$ billion)		Real GDP growth rate, %/year		
	2010	2025	2010–2025	2025–2050	2050–2100
Developing countries	19,400	40,331	5.0	4.0	3.0
High-income countries	38,800	50,342	2.0	2.0	2.0
World	58,200	90,674	3.0	3.0	2.6

Higher growth rates in alternative policy reform scenarios, 2010–25:					
	Doha "Low"	Doha "High"	TPP12	ASEAN+3	FTAAP
Developing countries	5.6	5.6	5.1	5.5	5.6
High-income countries	2.4	2.4	2.2	2.2	2.2
World	3.47	3.47	3.1	3.3	3.4

Additional comparative static gross benefit from reform (expressed as % of GDP for each year after 2020 and phased in linearly from one-sixth of that rate in 2015 and one-sixth more each year to 2020):					
	Doha "Low"	Doha "High"	TPP12	ASEAN+3	FTAAP
Developing countries	0.17	0.85	0.06	0.33	1.17
High-income countries	0.25	1.25	0.36	0.10	0.56
World	0.22	1.10	0.22	0.21	0.85

Cost of reforms (US$ billion per year), for each year from 2015 to 2020 inclusive:					
	Doha "Low"	Doha "High"	TPP12	ASEAN+3	FTAAP
Developing countries	7	17	4	13	24
High-income countries	13	33	10	10	15
World	20	50	14	23	39

A high-income includes Eastern European and former Soviet Union transition economies.
Source: See text.

the price rise for rice, 0.2 for wheat, and 0.1 for maize. A more-sophisticated study using the global economy wide GTAP model by Jensen and Anderson (2017) came up with a smaller number for wheat (0.05) but very similar estimates for rice (0.36) and maize (0.09). Global welfare fell slightly, there was a large transfer of economic welfare from importing to exporting countries, and domestic grain price rises in developing countries rose almost independent of attempts to insulate the markets.

Anderson, Ivanic, and Martin (2014) took the analysis one step further and found that the insulating behavior of national governments helped poverty reduction more than hindered nationally, but when the international price consequences of those governments' combined actions are taken into account, the number of poor in the world is estimated to have risen slightly.

Together these results suggest that using trade policy to deal with a domestic social concern exacerbates price spikes and runs the risk of reducing global welfare and raising global poverty. Anderson and Nelgen (2012) also show that an equal and opposite outcome is possible when national governments respond in the opposite way to a slump in world prices – as they did in the mid-1980s, for example. A clear implication of this result is that what the G-33 group of developing countries are calling for as part of the WTO Doha Development Agenda's agricultural negotiations, namely a Special Safeguard Mechanism, is exactly the opposite of what the world needs (Hertel, Martin, and Leister, 2010; Thennakoon and Anderson, 2015).

We cannot undertake the same type of benefit-cost analysis for this issue because of the impossibility of predicting the pattern of price spikes.[18] Nonetheless, stronger disciplines on export as well as import measures at the WTO (e.g., tariffying and binding export measures) would reduce the tendency to insulate and would thus add to the gains from general trade reform.

Estimated Costs Associated with Trade Reform

The benefits from reform are not costless. There is expenditure on negotiating, and policy development, but more significant are the private costs of adjustment for firms and workers (Francois, 2003; Matusz and Tarr, 2000). Those costs are ignored in the CGE models discussed earlier, where the aggregate level of employment is held constant. There are also social costs to consider, including unemployment payments plus training grants to build up new skills.

Those one-off costs, which need to be weighed against the nonstop flow of economic benefits from reform, tend to be smaller, the longer the phase-in period or smaller the tariff cut per year (Furusawa and Lai, 1999), and also smaller than the changes associated with normal economic growth (Porto and Hoekman, 2010). In recent debates about trade and labor, analysts have not found a significant link between import expansion and increased unemployment. One example is a study of the four largest EU economies' imports from East Asia (Bentivogli and Pagano, 1999). Another is a study of the UK footwear industry, which found liberalizing that market would incur unemployment costs only in the first year because of the high job turnover in that industry, and they were less than 1.5

percent of the estimated benefits from cutting that protection (Winters and Takacs, 1991). A similar-sized estimate is provided by de Melo and Tarr (1990) for U.S. textile, steel, and auto protection cuts (later reported by Jacobson, LaLonde, and Sullivan, 1993). For developing countries also the evidence seems to suggest low costs of adjustment, not least because trade reform typically causes a growth spurt (Krueger, 1983). In a study of 13 liberalization efforts for nine developing countries, Michaely, Papageorgiou, and Choksi (1991) found only one example where employment was not higher within a year.[19]

---

[18] Even so, see Bouët and Laborde-Debucquet (2012) on the potential costs of export restrictions.

[19] A further impact of trade policy reform about which concern is often expressed is the loss of tariff revenue for the government. This is of trivial importance to developed and upper-middle-income countries where trade taxes account for only 1 and 3 percent of government revenue, respectively. For lower-middle-income countries that share is 9 percent, and it is more than 20 percent for more than a dozen low-income countries for which data are available, so how concerned should those poorer countries be? The answer depends on whether/how much that revenue would fall and, if it does fall, on whether/how much more costly would be the next best alternative means of raising government revenue. On the first of those two points, government revenue from import taxes will rise rather than fall with reform if the reform involves replacing, with less-prohibitive tariffs, any of import quotas or bans, or tariffs that are prohibitive (or nearly so) or that encourage smuggling or underinvoicing or corruption by customs officials. It is possible even in a tariff-only regime that lower tariffs lead to a sufficiently higher volume and value of trade that the aggregate tariff collection rises. Examples of trade policy reforms that led to increased tariff revenue are Chile and Mexico (Bacchetta and Jansen, 2003, p. 15) and Kenya (Glenday, 2002). See also Greenaway and Milner (1993) and Nash and Takacs (1998). Because the economy is enlarged by opening up, income and consumption tax collections will automatically rise too. On the second point, about the cost of raising government revenue by other means if tax revenue does fall, Corden (1997, Chapter 4) makes it clear that in all but the poorest of countries it will be more rather than less efficient to collect tax revenue in other ways. Even countries as poor as Cambodia have managed to introduce a value-added tax. Hence from a global viewpoint there is no significant cost that needs to be included in response to this concern. Income and consumption tax revenue also will rise as the economy expands following reform. In any case CGE modelers typically alter those other tax rates when trade tax revenues change so as to keep the overall government budget unchanged.

If the adjustment costs are so small and may lead to more rather than less jobs even during the adjustment period, why are governments so reluctant to open their economies? The reason is because the anticipated losses in jobs and asset values are very obvious and concentrated, whereas the gains in terms of new job and investment opportunities are thinly spread, are less-easily attributed to the trade reform, and are taken up often by people other than those losing from the reform. Moreover, there is considerable uncertainty about who in fact will end up bearing the costs or reaping net benefits, leading all groups to be less enthusiastic about reform (Fernadez and Rodrik, 1991).

Thus reform has political, and possibly employment, costs for politicians, and one should not underestimate the difficulties of political action. We do not factor these into the economic cost-benefit analysis for society as a whole, however, because they are not of a comparable form. Nor do we count the transfers among people within each country as part of the gross benefits and costs of reform. Rather, we implicitly assume society costlessly compensates the losers using the extra tax revenue from those whose incomes rise.

The existing estimates of the adjustment costs to trade reform are very small, but they are concentrated on particular individuals and so perhaps deserve a large weight socially. It is certainly possible that those estimates omit some elements too, such as the disutility of one-off uncertainty and disruption experienced by everyone in adjusting to policy changes. Hence, so as not to exaggerate the estimated net gains from trade reform, it is assumed here that there would be an adjustment period of six years following the beginning of liberalization (assumed to start in 2015), and that in each of those years the adjustment costs would be 10 percent of the estimated annual comparative static benefits as of 2025 (and zero thereafter) in the case of Doha "low" and also in the cases of subregional FTA formation in the TPP12 and ASEAN+3 cases.[20] For the more-comprehensive Doha "high" and the FTAAP cases, where benefits are far higher because reform is far more widespread, costs of adjustment are assumed to be 2.5 times greater than in the other cases (that is, 5 percent of the 2025 comparative static benefit).

Net Benefits and Benefit-Cost Ratios

The assumptions used to calculate the present (i.e., 2015) value of the net benefits and the benefit-cost ratios associated with the policy reform opportunities are summarized in Table 9.2. Those indicators are calculated using two alternative discount rates: 3 and 5 percent per year. In the Doha trade reform scenarios, the "low" case refers to global comparative static gains of just 0.22 percent of GDP, while the "high" case refers to global gains five times higher, to take into account the unmeasured gains due to such things as economies and scale, imperfect competition, and services and foreign investment reforms.

In present value terms the net benefit of a Doha agreement are shown in Table 9.3 to range from $291 trillion to $772 trillion. The costs are less than $300 billion in present value terms: they are mostly private rather than government costs and are dwarfed by the gross benefits. Today's developing countries would reap around half of those net gains, as their share of the global economy is assumed to grow throughout this century (although at a progressively slower rate after 2025). The benefit-cost ratios from the trade reform opportunity offered by the Doha round are between ~2,100 and 4,700 for developing countries, which means it is an extremely high payoff activity, if only the political will can be found to bring about a successful conclusion to negotiations. The global benefit-cost ratios from Doha are lower but still impressive, at between 1,300 and 2,800.

If for political reasons the Doha round cannot be brought to a successful conclusion, governments still have the opportunity to form preferential trade agreements. Of the three possibilities being discussed among countries in the Asia-Pacific region, Table 9.4 shows that the greatest estimated gain would come if all APEC member countries agreed to form a region-wide free-trade area (FTAAP). That is assumed to involve completely freeing all trade, albeit preferentially within the Asia-Pacific

---

[20] Except for developing countries in the case of the TPP12, where the aggregate adjustment cost is assumed to be one-fifth that in high-income countries.

Table 9.3 Net present value of benefits and costs to 2100, and benefit-to-cost ratios, from reducing trade barriers and farm subsidies globally under the WTO's Doha Development Agenda

	Benefit-cost ratio			
	3% discount rate		5% discount rate	
	Low	High	Low	High
World	6,011	2,769	2,730	1,252
Developing countries	10,093	4,721	4,606	2,130

Net present value in 2015 of benefits and costs (in 2007 US trillion dollars).

	3% discount rate						5% discount rate					
	Low			High			Low			High		
	Gross Benefit	Cost	Net Benefit	Gross Benefit	Cost	Net Benefit	Gross Benefit	Cost	Net Benefit	Gross Benefit	Cost	Net Benefit
World	671	0.1	671	772	0.3	772	291	0.1	291	334	0.3	333
Developing countries	394	0.04	394	448	0.1	448	172	0.04	172	193	0.1	193

Source: Author's calculations based on Table 9.2 and assumptions in text.

region (including Russia and China), in contrast to a Doha agreement, which would only partially open up trade, albeit nonpreferentially, so that all engaged trading partners are involved. Because the APEC members are projected to comprise nearly three-fifths of global GDP by 2025 (see Table 9.1), it is not surprising that an FTA among them could yield a benefit to the world that is three-quarters of what Doha is projected to deliver. Furthermore, the FTAAP is projected to deliver a slightly greater benefit to developing countries as a group than is Doha. This is partly because under Doha developing countries are assumed to reform less than high-income countries and partly because by 2025 the APEC grouping will account for around two-thirds of the GDP of all developing countries. The two other opportunities analyzed involve subregional FTAs in the Asia-Pacific region and so necessarily yield smaller benefits: fewer countries are liberalizing, and only for their trade with a subset of APEC members. Of those two, the ASEAN+3 proposal would yield slightly more global and developing country benefits than the TPP, even though the latter's global benefit-cost ratios are slightly higher (Table 9.4).

Social and Environmental Benefits and Costs of Trade Reforms

Because trade reform generates large and ongoing economic gains while incurring comparatively minor one-off adjustment costs, it would allow individuals and governments the freedom to spend more on other pressing problems, thereby indirectly contributing to society's other post-2015 agenda targets.[21] But in addition, trade reform would also directly apply to some of those goals, specifically poverty alleviation, the environment, and malnutrition and hunger.[22]

---

[21] On the intrinsic benefits of freedom of opportunity and action that freer markets provide people, apart from their positive impact in boosting income and wealth, see Sen (1999). A recent examination of the evidence from globalization suggests that indeed the benefits of greater openness do spread well beyond just narrow economic ones (Potrafke, 2014).

[22] The economic and social impacts of freeing up international migration are not discussed here, but they were explicitly included in the predecessor to the present project, where they are shown to be potentially enormous in aggregate (Anderson and Winters, 2009). Not every small developing country will have less poverty if migration is freed up because it will depend on the skill mix of the migrants and the extent of remittances

Table 9.4 Net present value of benefits and costs to 2100, and benefit-to-cost ratios, from reducing trade barriers and subsidies under three alternative Asia–Pacific regional trade agreements

	Benefit-cost ratio					
	3% discount rate			5% discount rate		
	TPP12	ASEAN+3	FTAAP	TPP12	ASEAN+3	FTAAP
World	1693	2631	2380	765	1196	1076
Developing countries	3308	4712	3532	431	2163	1586

Net present value in 2015 of benefits and costs, 3% discount rate (in 2007 US trillion dollars).

	TPP12			ASEAN+3			FTAAP			
	Gross Benefit	Cost	Net Benefit	Gross Benefit	Cost	Net Benefit	Gross Benefit	Cost		Net Benefit
World	126	0.07	126	338	0.1	338	518	0.2	2262	546
Developing countries	74	0.02	74	342	0.1	342	473	0.1	2318	401

Net present value in 2015 of benefits and costs, 5% discount rate (in 2007 US trillion dollars).

	TPP12			ASEAN+3			FTAAP		
	Gross Benefit	Cost	Net Benefit	Gross Benefit	Cost	Net Benefit	Gross Benefit	Cost	Net Benefit
World	55	0.1	55	147	0.1	146	224	0.2	223
Developing countries	39	0.1	39	150	0.1	150	203	0.1	203

Source: Author's calculations based on Table 9.2 and assumptions in text.

Poverty Alleviation

Evidence presented by Dollar and Kraay (2002), Sala-i-Martin (2006), Dollar, Kleineberg, and Kraay (2014) and others carefully surveyed in Ravallion (2006), suggests aggregate economic growth differences have been largely responsible for the differences in poverty alleviation across regions. Initiatives that boost economic growth are therefore likely to be helpful in the fight against poverty. But cuts to trade barriers also alter relative product prices domestically and in international markets, which in turn affect factor prices. Hence the net effect on poverty depends also on the way those price changes affect poor households' expenditures and their earnings net of remittances. If the consumer and producer price changes are pro-poor, then they will tend to reinforce any positive growth effects of trade reform on the poor.

The effects of trade reform on global poverty can be thought of at two levels: on the income gap between developed and developing countries, and on poor households within developing countries. On the first, CGE estimates such as by Anderson, Martin, and van der Mensbrugghe (2006) and Valenzuela, van der Mensbrugghe, and Anderson (2009) suggest that current developing countries would enjoy nearly half of the global static plus dynamic gains from reducing trade barriers, substantially lowering the income gap with developed countries.

How poor households within developing countries are affected is more difficult to say (Winters, 2002; Winters and Martuscelli, 2014). Developed countries' agricultural policies of and lower barriers to textiles and clothing trade would boost the demand for unskilled labor and for farm products produced in poor countries. Because two-thirds of the world's poor live in rural areas and, in

they send back, among other things; but in most cases the evidence on international migration's impact on poverty is overwhelmingly positive (World Bank, 2006, Chapter 3).

least-developed countries, the proportion is as high as 90 percent (Organisation for Economic Co-operation and Development [OECD], 2003a, p. 3), and because many poor rural households are net sellers of farm labor and/or food, one would expect such reforms to reduce the number in absolute poverty. A set of analyses reported in Anderson, Cockburn, and Martin (2011) for nearly a dozen developing countries finds strong support for this hypothesis in most of the country case studies considered.[23] If full global trade reform were to be undertaken, that study concludes that it would reduce by at least 26 million the number of people in extreme poverty, and 87 million would be alleviated from $2/day poverty (Anderson, Cockburn, and Martin, 2011, Table 9.4).

Those estimates are only from comparative static models and so are underestimates because they do not include the poverty-reducing dynamic growth effects of such reforms. We also made a crude estimate of how many people might be pulled out of poverty under the Doha High scenario when both the comparative static and dynamic growth effects are included. That calculation suggests that by 2030 the number of poor could be reduced by two-fifths, or around 300 million people, if an ambitious outcome were to emerge from the WTO's Doha Development Agenda. The reduction would be about one-eighth less under the Doha Low scenario. If liberalization was confined just to the Asia-Pacific region, which now has only a minority of the world's poor, the impact on global poverty may be considerably smaller.

The Environment

Until recently environmentalists have tended to focus mainly on the direct environmental costs they perceive from trade reform, just as they have with other areas of economic change.[24] That approach does not acknowledge areas where the environment might have been improved or weigh the costs of any net worsening of the environment against the economic benefits of policy reform.

The reality is that although there are both negative and positive impacts, there are many examples

where cuts to subsidies and trade barriers would reduce environmental damage (Anderson, 1992; Irwin, 2002, pp. 48–54). For some time the OECD has been encouraging analysis of these opportunities (OECD 1996, 1997, 1998, 2003b). Environmental and many development NGOs seem to be coming to the view that the net social and environmental benefits from reducing subsidies and at least some trade barriers may indeed be positive, and that the best hope of reducing environmentally harmful subsidies and trade barriers is via the WTO negotiations (see, e.g., Cameron, 2007; de Melo and Mathys, 2012).

If there remains a concern that the net effect of trade reform on the environment may be negative, the aim should be to ensure first-best environmental policy measures are in place rather than failing to correct trade distortions. We would then know that the direct economic gains from trade reform would exceed society's evaluation of any extra environmental damage, other things being equal (Corden, 1997, Chapter 13).

Much environmental damage in developing countries is a direct consequence of poverty so, as trade reform reduces poverty, it will reduce such damage. Because richer people have a greater demand for a clean environment, income rises (above certain levels) tend to be associated with better environmental outcomes.[25] Abatement practices have been more than enough to compensate for increases in consumption of polluting products. Openness to trade also accelerates that spread of abatement ideas and technologies.

Estimating the net global cost to society of all environmental damage that might accompany a reduction in trade barriers is extraordinarily

---

[23] For more on this methodology, see Hertel et al. (2011).
[24] See the critique by Lomborg (2001).
[25] This is the theme of the book by Hollander (2003). For statistical evidence of the extent to which different environmental indicators first worsen and then improve as incomes rise (sometimes called the environmental Kuznets curve), see the special issue of the journal *Environment and Development Economics*, Volume 2, Issue 4 in 1997 and the more-recent papers by and cited in Harbaugh, Levinson, and Wilson (2002), Cole (2003), Johansson and Kristrom (2007), and Vollebergh, Melenberg, and Dijkgraaf (2009).

difficult both conceptually and empirically.[26] It is safest to assume that the net effect of reform on the environment would be zero.

When the environmental impact is global rather than local, as with greenhouse gases and their apparent impact on climate change, international environmental agreements may be required (see Cline, 2004; de Melo and Mathys, 2012; Yohe et al., 2009). When developing countries are not party to such agreements, however, it is difficult to prevent "leakage" through relocation of carbon-intensive activities. An alternative approach that should reduce emission reductions while generating national and global economic benefits is to lower coal subsidies and trade barriers. Phasing out distortionary policies that encourage excessive extraction and consumption of coal and oil has both improved the economy and lowered greenhouse gas emissions globally, which is a win–win Pareto improvement for the economy and the environment (Anderson and McKibbin, 2000).

Malnutrition and Hunger

Although poor countries have feared that reducing agricultural subsidies and protectionism globally would raise the price of food imports, enhancing food security is mainly about alleviating poverty. That suggests this issue needs to be considered from a household rather than national perspective. And the discussion earlier argues that poverty is more likely than not to be alleviated by cuts to trade barriers.

Hunger and undernutrition can be eased by trade not only in goods but also in agricultural technologies, in particular newly bred varieties of staple crops. The introduction of high-yielding dwarf wheat and rice varieties during the Green Revolution that began in Asia in the 1960s is a previous case in point, whereby producers and consumers shared the benefits.

A prospective case in point is the possibility of breeding crop varieties that are not only less-costly to grow but also contain vitamin and mineral supplements. The most promising is so-called golden rice, genetically engineered to contain a higher level of beta-carotene in the endosperm of the grain and thereby provide a vitamin A supplement (so

alleviating childhood blindness and mortality rates). By being cheaper and/or more nutritionally beneficial, it would improve the health of poor people and also boost their labor productivity. Anderson, Jackson, and Nielsen (2005) estimate that the latter economic benefit from this new technology could be as much as ten times greater than just the traditional benefits of lower production costs – not to mention that poor people would live longer and healthier lives. This new technology has yet to be adopted, however, because the European Union and some other countries will not import food from countries that may contain genetically modified organisms (GMOs) – even though there is no evidence that GM foods are a danger to human health (see, e.g., King, 2003; European Academies Science Advisory Council [EASAE], 2013). The cost of that trade barrier to developing countries – which is not included in the earlier estimates – has been very considerable (Anderson, 2010).

Caveats

Measuring both the benefits and the costs of liberalizing trade is still an inexact science, so we have provided a range of estimates and erred on the conservative side.[27] Nonetheless, it is worth reviewing the key areas where analytical improvements are still needed. On the cost side, more empirical research on the real costs of adjustments would be helpful. Those costs could be much lower than assumed. On the benefit side, economists have made more progress but plenty of scope remains for further improvements, particularly on

---

[26] A beginning nonetheless has been made, with several governments funding ex ante evaluations of the WTO Doha round's potential impact on the environment. The EU's efforts include a workshop on methodological issues that are laid out in Centre d'Études Prospectives et d'Informations Internationales (CEPII, 2003), and further work has been contracted to the University of Manchester, whose progress can be traced at http://idpm.man.ac.uk/sia-trade/Consultation.htm. Ex post analyses are also being undertaken by NGOs. See, for example, Bermudez (2004) for WWF's sustainability impact assessment of trade policies during 2001–3.

[27] Parts of this section draw on the survey by Francois and Martin (2010).

the size and longevity of dynamic gains from trade reform. Key areas are discussed later.

The standard approach used in evaluating the consequences of international trade agreements is to compare the agreed tariff binding with the previously applied tariff rate and to treat the postagreement tariff rate as the lesser of the two rates. This essentially involves treating the current applied rate as a deterministic forecast of future protection rates in the absence of the agreement. In fact, the trend rate of protection responds systematically to underlying determinants that evolve over time, and annual protection rates fluctuate substantially around that trend. This can significantly affect estimated benefits.

Anderson and Hayami (1986) and Lindert (1991) provide insights into the likely evolution of agricultural trade policies in the absence of international agreements. There is a tendency for agricultural protection to be low or negative in very poor countries because the number of farmers is large, it is difficult for them to organize to apply pressure on governments, and they have little surplus to sell. By contrast, the urban population in a poor country is far smaller and easier to organize, and food is an important part of consumer budgets. As economies develop, however, farmers become fewer in number and more commercial in orientation, so that their real incomes are more strongly influenced by agricultural output prices. At the same time, the urban population increases, and the importance of food in consumer budgets and hence in real wage determinations declines. The end result can be a very rapid increase in agricultural protection rates in high-growth economies – as is already showing up in Asia's three largest economies (see Anderson, 2014).

Also striking is the large variation in national rates of agricultural protection over time. This is because trade and subsidy policies are frequently used also to stabilize domestic agricultural prices in the face of variations in world prices (Anderson and Nelgen, 2012; Tyers and Anderson, 1992). The value of legal bindings on those policies via trade agreements, even when the bindings are well above applied rates at the time of the agreement, is nontrivial and yet is not captured in most models because those models are not stochastic.

As Francois and Martin (2004) show, even bindings that are set well above average rates of protection may greatly diminish the costs of protection when international prices peak. This is another reason why current CGE models are understating the gains from reducing tariff and subsidy bindings, particularly for farm products.

As for services, new estimates of the extent to which policies inhibit their efficient provision (see Borchert et al., 2014; Francois and Hoekman, 2010) suggest reforms to those policies, particularly in developing countries, could generate far greater benefits than previous estimates have suggested. Moreover, those potential benefits are multiplying as the importance of global value chains grows with the fragmentation of production into ever-more footloose processes. This is yet another reason to expect the earlier estimates of net benefits and associated benefit-cost ratios from reform of trade-related policies to be very much on the low side.

Conclusion

The theory and available evidence show that trade-restricting policies are very wasteful. Preannounced, gradual reductions in trade barriers, especially if agreed multilaterally under the WTO's DDA, would yield huge economic benefits and relatively little economic cost, with extremely high benefit-cost ratios (up to 2,800 globally and between ~2,100 and 4,700 for the developing country group). Such reform would also assist in the achievement of several of the other targets in the UN's post-2015 agenda, including alleviating poverty, promoting equality among nations, reducing malnutrition and hunger, and boosting employment and economic growth sustainably, particularly in rural areas. A successful DDA outcome would also make it less pressing to lower immigration barriers insofar as trade in products is a substitute for international labor movements. Cuts in trade barriers also would provide a means for citizens to spend more on other pressing problems.

In the absence of a comprehensive DDA agreement, freeing up trade in the Asia-Pacific region provides the next-best targets. The Trans-Pacific

Partnership (TPP) would yield a B/C ratio of ~800–1,700 for the world economy and 1,800–3,300 for developing countries, but if that were to be expanded into a free trade area of the Asia-Pacific (FTAAP), those ratios would rise to ~1,100–2,400 for the world economy and ~1,600–3,500 for developing countries.

The total value of benefits is higher with the DDA (up to $772 trillion in 2007 U.S. dollars globally) than with a full FTAAP (up to $448 trillion globally). The FTAAP may be able to deliver a little more to the developing country group, but mostly to the relatively affluent developing countries of East Asia and possibly at the expense of some poorer developing countries in South Asia and sub-Saharan Africa. This could be avoided if the more affluent countries were prepared to share some of the benefits with poorer countries, via aid-for-trade initiatives, for example.

The ICT revolution is reducing the costs of conditional cash transfers, making it increasingly feasible for governments to provide social protection to any losers from any policy reforms (World Bank, 2014). Such social protection can even contribute to economic growth, thereby potentially also pulling more people out of poverty (Alderman and Yemtsov, 2014). To the extent that the more-widespread scope for providing social protection lowers the political resistance to trade policy reforms, there may be room for more optimism in the future than there has been in the past about prospects for both unilateral and plurilateral trade liberalization.

References

Acharya, R. C. and W. Keller (2007), "Technology Transfers Through Imports," NBER Working Paper 13086, Cambridge, MA: National Bureau of Economic Research.

Aghion, P. and R. Griffith (2005), *Competition and Growth: Reconciling Theory and Evidence*, Cambridge MA: MIT Press.

Aghion, P. and P. Howitt (2006), "Appropriate Growth Policy: A Unified Framework," *Journal of the European Economic Association* 4: 269–314.

Alderman, H. and R. Yemtsov (2014), "How Can Safety Nets Contribute to Economic Growth?" *World Bank Economic Review* 28(1): 1–20.

Anderson, K. (1992), "Effects on the Environment and Welfare of Liberalising World Trade: The Cases of Coal and Food," in *The Greening of World Trade Issues*, edited by K. Anderson and R. Blackhurst, Ann Arbor: University of Michigan.

(2003), "Measuring Effects of Trade Policy Distortions: How Far Have We Come?" *The World Economy* 26(4): 413–40.

(2010), "Economic Impacts of Policies Affecting Biotechnology and Trade," *New Biotechnology* 27(5): 558–64.

(2014), "Food Price and Trade Policy Evolution since the 1950s: A Global Perspective," *World Food Policy* 1(1): 12–33.

Anderson, K., J. Cockburn, and W. Martin (2011), "Would Freeing Up World Trade Reduce Poverty and Inequality? The Vexed Role of Agricultural Distortions," *The World Economy* 34(4): 487–515.

Anderson, K. and Y. Hayami (1986), *The Political Economy of Agricultural Protection East Asia in International Perspective*, London: Allen and Unwin.

Anderson, K., M. Ivanic, and W. Martin (2014), "Food Price Spikes, Price Insulation, and Poverty," in *The Economics of Food Price Volatility*, edited by J.-P. Chavas, D. Hummels, and B. Wright, Chicago: University of Chicago Press for NBER.

Anderson, K., L. A. Jackson, and C. P. Nielsen (2005), "GM Rice Adoption: Implications for Welfare and Poverty Alleviation," *Journal of Economic Integration* 20(4): 771–88.

Anderson, K., W. Martin, and D. van der Mensbrugghe (2006), "Market and Welfare Implications of the Doha Reform Scenarios," in *Agricultural Trade Reform and the Doha Development Agenda*, edited by K. Anderson and W. Martin, London: Palgrave Macmillan (co-published with the World Bank).

Anderson, K. and W. McKibbin (2000), "Reducing Coal Subsidies and Trade Barriers: Their Contribution to Greenhouse Gas Abatement," *Environment and Development Economics* 5(4): 457–81.

Anderson, K. and S. Nelgen (2011), "What's the Appropriate Agricultural Protection Counterfactual for Trade Analysis?" in *Unfinished Business? The WTO's Doha Agenda*, edited by W. Martin and A. Mattoo, London:

Centre for Economic Policy Research and the World Bank.

(2012), "Agricultural Trade Distortions during the Global Financial Crisis," *Oxford Review of Economic Policy* 28(2): 235–60.

Anderson, K. and L. A. Winters (2009), "The Challenge of Reducing International Trade and Migration Barriers," in *Global Crises, Global Solutions* (2nd ed.), edited by B. Lomborg, Cambridge: Cambridge University Press.

Asia Pacific Economic Cooperation (APEC) (2010), Leaders' Declaration, www.apec.org/Meeting-Papers/Leaders-Declarations/2010/2010_aelm .aspx.

Arnold, J. M., B. S. Javorcik, and A. Mattoo (2011), "Does Services Liberalization Benefit Manufacturing Firms? Evidence from the Czech Republic." *Journal of International Economics* 85(1): 136–46.

Asian Development Bank (2011), *Asian Development Outlook 2011*, Manila: ADB.

Bacchetta, M. and M. Jansen (2003), "Adjusting to Trade Liberalization: The Role of Policy, Institutions and WTO Disciplines," Special Studies 7, Geneva: World Trade Organization.

Baldwin, R. E. (2004), "Openness and Growth: What's the Empirical Relationship?" in *Challenges to Globalization: Analysing the Economics*, edited by R. E. Baldwin and L. A. Winters, Chicago: University of Chicago Press for NBER and CEPR.

(2009), "Big-Think Regionalism: A Critical Survey," in *Regional Rules in the Global Trading System*, edited by A. Estevadeordal, K. Suominen, and R. Teh, Cambridge: Cambridge University Press.

(2011), Trade and Industrialization after Globalization's 2nd Unbundling: How Building and Joining a Supply Chain Are Different and Why It Matters, NBER Working Paper 17716, Cambridge MA: National Bureau of Economic Research

Beghin, J., D. van der Mensbrugghe, and D. Roland-Holst (2002), *Trade and the Environment in General Equilibrium: Evidence from Developing Economies*, Norwell, MA: Kluwer Academic Publishers.

Bendivogli, C. and P. Pagano (1999), "Trade, Job Destruction and Job Creation in European Manufacturing," *Open Economies Review* 10: 156–84.

Bermudez, E. (2004), *Sustainability Assessments of Trade Policies and Programmes*, Gland: WWF International.

Bernard, A. B., J. B. Jensen, S. J. Redding, and P. K. Schott (2007), "Firms in International Trade," *Journal of Economic Perspectives* 21(3): 105–30.

Bhagwati, J. N. (1971), "The Generalized Theory of Distortions and Welfare," in *Trade, Balance of Payments and Growth*, edited by J. N. Bhagwati et al., Amsterdam: North-Holland.

Billmeier, A. and T. Nannicini (2009), "Trade Openness and Growth: Pursuing Empirical Glasnost," *IMF Staff Papers* 56: 447–75.

Bordo, M. and P. Rousseau (2012), "Historical Evidence on the Finance-Trade-Growth Nexus," *Journal of Banking and Finance* 36(4): 1236–43.

Bouët, A. and D. Laborde-Debucquet (2012), "Food Crisis and Export Taxation: The Cost of Non-Cooperative Trade Policies," *Review of World Economics* 148(1): 209–33.

Borchert, I., B. Gootiiz, and A. Mattoo (2014), "Policy Barriers to International Trade in Services: Evidence from a New Database," *World Bank Economic Review* 28(1): 162–88.

Cameron, H. (2007), "The Evolution of the Trade and Environment Debate at the WTO," in *Trade and Environment: A Resource Book*, edited by A. Najam, M. Halle, and R. Melendez-Ortiz, Geneva: International Centre for Trade and Sustainable Development (ICTSD), see www.trade-environment.org.

Centre d'Études Prospectives et d'Informations Internationales (CEPII) (2003), Methodological Tools for SIA: Report of the CEPII workshop held on 7–8 November 2002 in Brussels, Paris: CEPII Working Paper No. 2003–19. Download at www.cepii.fr/anglaisgraph/workpap/pdf/ 2003/wp03-19.pdf.

Chandy, L., N. Ledlie, and V. Penciakova (2013), *The Final Countdown: Prospects for Ending Extreme Poverty by 2030*, Washington, DC: Brookings Institution.

Chang, R., L. Kaltani, and N. Loayza (2005), "Openness Can be Good for Growth: The Role of Policy Complementarity," Policy Research Working Paper 3763, Washington, DC: World Bank, and NBER Working Paper 11787.

Cline, W. R. (2004), "Climate Change," in *Global Crises, Global Solutions*, edited by B. Lomborg, Cambridge: Cambridge University Press.

Cline, W. R., T. O. Kawanabe, M. Kronsjo, and T. Williams (1978), *Trade Negotiations in the Tokyo Round: A Quantitative Assessment*, Washington, DC: Brookings Institution.

Coase, R. (1960), "The Problem of Social Cost," *Journal of Law and Economics* 3: 1–44.

Cole, M. A. (2003), "Development, Trade, and the Environment: How Robust Is the Environmental Kuznets Curve?" *Environment and Development Economics* 8(4): 557–80.

Copland, B. and M. S. Taylor (2003), *Trade and the Environment: Theory and Evidence*, Princeton, NJ: Princeton University Press.

Corden, W. M. (1997), *Trade Policy and Economic Welfare* (2nd ed.), Oxford: Clarendon Press.

Deardorff, A. V. and R. M. Stern (1979), *An Economic Analysis of the Effects of the Tokyo Round of Multilateral Trade Negotiations on the United States and Other Major Industrial Countries, MTN Studies 5*, Washington, DC: U.S. Government Printing Office.

   (1986), *The Michigan Model of World Production and Trade: Theory and Applications*, Cambridge, MA: MIT Press.

de Melo, J. and N. A. Mathys (2012), "Reconciling Trade and Climate Policies," CEPR Discussion Paper No. 8760, London.

de Melo, J. and D. Tarr (1990), "Welfare Costs of US Quotas on Textiles, Steel and Autos," *Review of Economics and Statistics* 72: 489–97.

Diebold, W., Jr. (1952), *The End of the ITO, International Finance Section, Essays in International Finance No. 16*, Princeton, NJ: Princeton University Press.

Dollar, D., T. Kleineberg, and A. Kraay (2014), "Growth, Inequality, and Social Welfare: Cross-country Evidence," Policy Research Working Paper 6842, World Bank, Washington, DC, April.

Dollar, D. and A. Kraay (2002), "Growth Is Good for the Poor," *Journal of Economic Growth* 7(3): 195–225.

EASAC (European Academies Science Advisory Council) (2013), *Planting the Future: Opportunities and Challenges for Using Crop Genetic Improvement Technologies for Sustainable Agriculture, EASAC Policy Report 21*, Halle: EASAC Secretariat.

Easterly, W. (2001), *The Elusive Quest for Growth*, Cambridge, MA: MIT Press.

Faini, R. (2004), "Trade Liberalization in a Globalizing World," CEPR Discussion Paper No. 4665, London, October.

Feenstra, R. C. (2003), *Advanced International Trade: Theory and Evidence*, Princeton, NJ: Princeton University Press.

Fernandez, R. and D. Rodrik (1991), "Resistance to Reform: Status Quo Bias and the Presence of Individual Specific Uncertainty," *American Economic Review* 81: 1146–55.

Fouré, J., A. Bénassy-Quéré, and L. Fontagné (2010), "The World Economy in 2050: A Tentative Picture," CEPII Working Paper 2010–27, Paris: CEPII, December.

Francois, J. F. (2003), "Assessing the Impact of Trade Policy on Labour Markets and Production," pp. 61–88 in *Methodological Tools for SIA*, CEPII Working Paper No. 2003–19, Paris: CEPII.

Francois, J. F. and B. Hoekman (2010), "Services Trade and Policy," *Journal of Economic Literature* 48(3): 642–92.

Francois, J. F. and K. A. Reinert (eds.) (1997), *Applied Methods for Trade Policy Analysis: A Handbook*, Cambridge: Cambridge University Press.

Francois, J. F. and W. Martin (2004), "Commercial Policy, Bindings and Market Access," *European Economic Review* 48: 665–79.

   (2010), "Ex Ante Assessments of the Welfare Impacts of Trade Reforms with Numerical Models," in *New Developments in Computable General Equilibrium Analysis for Trade Policy*, edited by H. Beladi and E. K. Choi, London: Emerald Group Publishing.

Frankel, J. A. and E. A. Cavallo (2008), "Does Openness to Trade Make Countries More Vulnerable to Sudden Stops, Or Less? Using Gravity to Establish Causality", *Journal of International Money and Finance* 27(8): 1430–52.

Frankel, J. A. and D. Romer (1999), "Does Trade Cause Growth?" *American Economic Review* 89(3): 379–99.

Freeman, R. B. (2004), "Trade Wars: The Exaggerated Impact of Trade in Economic Debate," *The World Economy* 27(1): 1–23.

Furusawa, T. and E. L. C. Lai (1999), "Adjustment Costs and Gradual Trade Liberalization" *Journal of International Economics* 49: 333–61.

Glenday, G. (2002), "Trade Liberalization and Customs Revenue: Does Trade Liberalization

Lead to Lower Customs Revenue? The Case of Kenya," *Journal of African Finance and Economic Development* 5(2): 89–125.

Greenaway, D. (1993), "Liberalizing Foreign Trade through Rose-Tinted Glasses," *Economic Journal* 103: 208–22.

Greenaway, D. and C. Milner (1993), "The Fiscal Implication of Trade Policy Reform: Theory and Evidence," UNDP/World Bank Trade Expansion Program Occasional Paper 9, Washington, DC: World Bank.

Grossman, G. M. and E. Helpman (1991), *Innovation and Growth in the Global Economy*, Cambridge, MA: MIT Press.

Grossman, G. M. and K. Rogoff (eds.) (1995), *Handbook of International Economics Volume III*, Amsterdam: North-Holland.

Hanson, G. H., R. J. Mataloni and M. J. Slaughter (2005), "Vertical Production Networks in Multinational Firms," *Review of Economics and Statistics* 87(4): 664–78.

Harbaugh, W. T., A. Levinson, and D. M. Wilson (2002), "Re-examining the Empirical Evidence for an Environmental Kuznets Curve," *Review of Economics and Statistics* 84(3): 541–51.

Harrigan, J. and E. K. Choi (eds.) (2003), *Handbook of International Trade*, Oxford: Blackwell.

Helpman, E. and O. Itskhoki (2010), "Labor Market Rigidities, Trade and Unemployment," *Review of Economic Studies* 77(3): 1100–37.

Helpman, E., D. Marin, and T. Verdier (eds.) (2008), *The Organization of Firms in a Global Economy*, Cambridge, MA: Harvard University Press.

Hertel, T. W., W. Martin, and A. M. Leister (2010), "Potential Implications of a Special Safeguard Mechanism (SSM) in the WTO: The Case of Wheat," *World Bank Economic Review* 24: 330–59.

Hertel, T. W., M. Verma, M. Ivanic, and A. R. Rios (2011), "GTAP-POV: A Framework for Assessing the National Poverty Impacts of Global Economic and Environmental Policies," GTAP Technical Paper 31, West Lafayette, IN: Purdue University.

HLP (2013), *A New Global Partnership: Eradicate Poverty and Transform Economies through Sustainable Development, Report of the High-level Panel of Eminent Persons on the Post-2015 Agenda*, New York: United Nations.

Hollander, J. (2003), *The Real Environmental Crisis: Why Poverty, Not Affluence, Is the Environment's Number One Enemy*, Berkeley: University of California Press.

Hoxha, I., S. Kalemli-Ozcan, and D. Vollrath (2013), "How Big Are the Gains from International Financial Integration?" *Journal of Development Economics* 103: 90–98.

Irwin, D. A. (2002), *Free Trade Under Fire*, Princeton, NJ: Princeton University Press.

Jacobson, L. S., R. J. LaLonde, and D. G. Sullivan (1993), "Earnings Losses of Displaced Workers," *American Economic Review* 83(4): 685–709.

Javorcik, B., W. Keller, and J. Tybout (2008), "Openness and Industrial Responses in a Walmart World: A Case Study of Mexican Soaps, Detergents and Surfactant Producers," *The World Economy* 31(12): 1558–80.

Jensen, H. G. and K. Anderson (2017), "Grain Price Spikes and Beggar-Thy-Neighbor Policy Responses: A Global CGE Analysis," *World Bank Economic Review* 31(1): 158–75.

Johansson, P. and B. Kristrom (2007), "On a Clear Day You Might See an Environmental Kuznets Curve," *Environmental and Resource Economics* 37: 77–90.

Just, R. E., D. L. Hueth, and A. Schmitz (2004), *The Welfare Economics of Public Policy*, London: Edward Elgar.

Khandelwal, A. K., P. K. Schott, and S.-J. Wei (2013), "Trade Liberalization and Embedded Institutional Reform: Evidence from Chinese Exporters", *American Economic Review* 103(6): 2169–95.

Kindleberger, C. P. (1989), "Commercial Policy between the Wars," in *The Cambridge Economic History of Europe*, Vol. 8, edited by P. Mathias and S. Pollard, Cambridge: Cambridge University Press.

King, D. K. (2003), GM Science Review: First Report, Prepared by the GM Science Review Panel under the chairmanship of Sir David King for the UK Government, July.

Kose, M. A., E. Prasad, K. Rogoff, and S. Wei (2009), "Financial Globalization: A Reappraisal," *IMF Staff Papers* 56(1): 8–62.

Krueger, A. O. (1983), *Trade and Employment in Developing Countries, Volume 3: Synthesis and Conclusions*, Chicago: University of Chicago Press for NBER.

Laborde, D., W. Martin, and D. van der Mensbrugghe (2011), "Potential Real Income Effects of Doha Reforms," in *Unfinished Business? The WTO's*

Doha Agenda, edited by W. Martin and A. Mattoo, London: Centre for Economic Policy Research and Washington, DC: World Bank.

Laborde, D., W. Martin, and D. van der Mensbrugghe (2012), "Implications of the Doha Market Access Proposals for Developing Countries," *World Trade Review* 11(1): 1–25.

Lakner, C. and B. Milanovic (2013), "Global Income Distribution: From the Fall of the Berlin Wall to the Great Recession," Policy Research Working Paper 6719, Washington, DC: World Bank.

Lee, J.-W. (1995), "Capital Goods Imports and Long-Run Growth," *Journal of Development Economics* 48: 91–110.

Lileeva, A. and D. Trefler (2010), "Improved Access to Foreign Markets Raises Plant-Level Productivity . . . For Some Plants," *Quarterly Journal of Economics* 125(3): 1051–99.

Lindert, P. (1991), "Historical Patterns of Agricultural Protection," in *Agriculture and the State*, edited by P. Timmer, Ithaca, NY: Cornell University Press.

Lloyd, P. J. (1974), "A More General Theory of Price Distortions in an Open Economy," *Journal of International Economics* 4(4): 365–86.

Lomborg, B. (2001), *The Skeptical Environmentalist: Measuring the Real State of the World*, Cambridge: Cambridge University Press.

Lomborg, B. (ed.) (2004), *Global Crises, Global Solutions*, Cambridge: Cambridge University Press.

(ed.) (2009), *Global Crises, Global Solutions* (2nd ed.), Cambridge: Cambridge University Press.

(ed.) (2013), *Global Problems, Smart Solutions: Costs and Benefits*, Cambridge: Cambridge University Press.

Lumenga-Neso, O., M. Olarreaga, and M. Schiff (2005), "On 'Indirect' Trade-Related R&D Spillovers," *European Economic Review* 49(7): 1785–98.

Matusz, S. and D. Tarr (2000), "Adjusting to Trade Policy Reform," in *Economic Policy Reform: The Second Stage*, edited by A. O. Krueger, Chicago: University of Chicago Press.

Mazumdar, J. (2001), "Imported Machinery and Growth in LDCs," *Journal of Development Economics* 65: 209–24.

Melitz, M. J. (2003), "The Impact of Trade on Intra-industry Reallocations and Aggregate Industry Productivity," *Econometrica* 71(6): 1692–1725.

Melitz, M. J. and G. I. P. Ottaviano (2008), "Market Size, Trade and Productivity," *Review of Economic Studies* 75(1): 295–316.

Melitz, M. J. and S. J. Redding (2014), "Missing Gains from Trade," *American Economic Review* 104(5): 317–21.

Michaely, M., D. Papageorgiou, and A. Choksi (eds.) (1991), *Liberalizing Foreign Trade, 7: Lessons of Experience in the Developing World*, Cambridge, MA: Basil Blackwell.

Moïsé, E. and S. Sorescu (2013), "Trade Facilitation Indicators: The Potential Impact of Trade Facilitation on Developing Countries," Trade Policy Paper 144, OECD, Paris.

Narayanan, G., A. A. Badri, and R. McDougall, eds. (2012), *Global Trade, Assistance, and Production: The GTAP 8 Data Base*, West Lafayette, IN: Center for Global Trade Analysis, Purdue University.

Nash, J. and W. Takacs (1998), "Lessons from the Trade Expansion Program," in *Trade Policy Reform: Lessons and Implications*, edited by J. Nash and W. Takacs, Washington, DC: World Bank.

Neufeld, N. (2014), "The Long and Winding Road: How WTO Members Finally Reached a Trade Facilitation Agreement," Staff Working Paper ERSD-2014–06, World Trade Organization, April.

Organisation for Economic Co-operation and Development (OECD) (1996), *Subsidies and the Environment: Exploring the Linkages*, Paris: OECD.

(1997), *Reforming Energy and Transport Subsidies: Environmental and Economic Implications*, Paris: OECD.

(1998), *Improving the Environment through Reducing Subsidies*, Paris: OECD.

(2003a), *Agricultural Trade and Poverty: Making Policy Analysis Count*, Paris: OECD.

(2003b), *Environmentally Harmful Subsidies: Policy Issues and Challenges*, Paris: OECD.

Olsen, M. (1965), *The Logic of Collective Action*, Cambridge, MA: Harvard University Press.

Petri, P. A., M. G. Plummer, and F. Zhai (2012), The Trans-Pacific Partnership and Asia-Pacific Integration: A Quantitative Assessment, Policy Analyses in International Economics 98, Washington DC: Peterson Institute for international Economics, November (with updated results that include Japan in the TPP,

uploaded March 2013 at http://asiapacifictrade
.org/?page_id=106).

Porto, G. and Hoekman, B. (eds.) (2010), *Trade
Adjustment Costs in Developing Countries:
Impacts, Determinants and Policy Responses*,
London: CEPR and Washington, DC: World
Bank.

Potrafke, N. (2014), "The Evidence on
Globalization," CESIFO Working Paper
No. 4708, IFO Institute, University of Munich.

Ravallion, M. (2006), "Looking Beyond Averages in
the Trade and Policy Debate," *World
Development* 34(8): 1374–92.

Rivera-Batiz, L. and P. Romer (1991), "International
Integration and Endogenous Growth," *Quarterly
Journal of Economics* 106: 531–56.

Rodriguez, F. and D. Rodrik (2001), "Trade Policy and
Economic Growth: A Skeptic's Guide to Cross-
National Evidence," in *NBER Macroeconomics
Annual 2000*, edited by B. S. Bernanke and K.
Rogoff, Cambridge, MA: MIT Press.

Rodrik, D. (2007), *One Economics, Many Recipes:
Globalization, Institutions and Economic
Growth*, Princeton, NJ: Princeton University
Press.

Romalis, J. (2007), "Market Access, Openness and
Growth," NBER Working Paper 13048,
Cambridge, MA.

Romer, P. (1994), "New Goods, Old Theory, and the
Welfare Costs of Trade Restrictions," *Journal of
Development Economics* 43(1): 5–38,

Rutherford, T. F. and D. G. Tarr (2002), "Trade
Liberalization, Product Variety and Growth in a
Small Open Economy: A Quantitative
Assessment," *Journal of International
Economics* 56(2): 247–72.

Sachs, J. D. and A. Warner (1995), "Economic
Reform and the Process of Global Integration,"
Brookings Papers on Economic Activity 1: 1–95.

Sala-i-Martin, X. (2006), "The World Distribution of
Income: Falling Poverty and . . . Convergence,
Period," *Quarterly Journal of Economics*
121(2): 351–97.

Schularick, M. and T. M. Steger (2010), "Financial
Integration, Investment, and Economic Growth:
Evidence from Two Eras of Financial
Globalization," *Review of Economics and
Statistics* 92(4): 756–68.

Sen, A. (1999), *Development as Freedom*, New York:
Anchor Books.

Taylor, M. S. (1999), "Trade and Trade Policy in
Endogenous Growth Models," in *International

Trade Policy and the Pacific Rim*, edited by
J. Piggott and A. Woodland, London: Macmillan
for the IAE.

Thennakoon, J. and K. Anderson (2015), "Could the
Proposed WTO Special Safeguard Mechanism
Protect Farmers from Low International Prices?"
Food Policy 50(1): 106–113.

Townsend, R. M. and K. Ueda (2010), "Welfare
Gains from Financial Globalization,"
International Economic Review 51(3): 553–97.

Tyers, R. and Anderson, K. (1992), *Disarray in World
Food Markets: A Quantitative Assessment*.
Cambridge: Cambridge University Press.

United Nations (2014), "Final Compilation of
Amendments to Goals and Targets by Major
Groups and Other Stakeholders," to inform the
Thirteenth and last Session of the Open Working
Group on Sustainable Development Goals,
New York, 14–18 July.

UNDESA (2013), *World Population Prospects,
The 2012 Revision, Volume II: Demographic
Profiles*, http://esa.un.org/wpp/Documentation/
pdf/WPP2012_Volume-II-Demographic-
Profiles.pdf.

U.S. International Trade Commission (USITC)
(1997), *The Dynamic Effects of Trade
Liberalization: An Empirical Analysis,
Publication 3069*, Washington, DC: US
International Trade Commission.

Valenzuela, E., D. van der Mensbrugghe, and K.
Anderson (2009), "General Equilibrium Effects
of Price Distortions on Global markets, Farm
Incomes and Welfare," in *Distortions to
Agricultural Incentives: A Global Perspective,
1955–2007*, edited by K. Anderson, London:
Palgrave Macmillan.

van Beers, C. and A. de Moor (2001), *Public
Subsidies and Policy Failures: How Subsidies
Distort the Natural Environment, Equity and
Trade and How to Reform Them*, Cheltenham:
Edward Elgar.

van der Mensbrugghe, D. (2011), "Linkage Technical
Reference Document: Version 7.1", mimeo,
World Bank, Washington DC, March. Freely
available at http://go.worldbank.org/
12JVZ7A910 or http://siteresources.worldbank
.org/INTPROSPECTS/Resources/
334934–1314986341738/TechRef7.1_
01Mar2011.pdf.

Vollebergh, H., B. Melenberg, and E. Dijkgraaf
(2009), "Identifying Reduced-Form Relations
with Panel Data: The Case of Pollution and

Income," *Journal of Environmental Economics and Management* 58: 27–42.

Wacziarg, R. (2001), "Measuring the Dynamic Gains from Trade," *World Bank Economic Review* 15(3): 393–429.

Wacziarg, R. and K. H. Welch (2008), "Trade Liberalization and Growth: New Evidence," *World Bank Economic Review* 15(3): 393–429.

Whalley, J. (1985), *Trade Liberalization among Major World Trading Areas*, Cambridge, MA: MIT Press.

(2010), "China's FDI and Non-FDI Economies and the Sustainability of Future High Chinese Growth," *China Economic Review* 21(1): 123–35.

Winters, L. A. (2002), "Trade Liberalisation and Poverty: What Are the Links?" *The World Economy* 25(9): 1339–68.

(2004), "Trade Liberalization and Economic Performance: An Overview," *Economic Journal* 114: F4–F21.

Winters, L. A. and A. Martuscelli (2014), "Trade Liberalization and Poverty: What Have We Learned in a Decade?" *Annual Review of Resource Economics* 6: 493–512.

Winters, L. A. and W. E. Takacs (1991), "Labour Adjustment Costs and British Footwear Protection," *Oxford Economic Papers* 43: 479–501.

World Bank (2006), *Global Economic Prospects 2006: Economic Implications of Remittances and Migration*, Washington, DC: The World Bank.

(2007), *World Development Report 2008: Agriculture for Development*, Washington, DC: The World Bank.

World Bank (2012), "An Update to the World Bank's Estimates of Consumption Poverty in the Developing World," http://siteresources .worldbank.org/INTPOVCALNET/ Resources/Global_Poverty_Update_2012_ 02–29-12.pdf.

(2014), *The State of Social Safety Nets 2014*, Washington, DC: World Bank.

Yohe, G. W., R. S. J. Tol, R. G. Richels and G. J. Blanford (2009) "Climate Change," in *Global Crises, Global Solutions* (2nd ed.), edited by B. Lomborg, Cambridge: Cambridge University Press.

Zaki, C. (2014), "An Empirical Assessment of the Trade Facilitation Impact: New Econometric Evidence and Global Economic Effects," *World Trade Review* 13(1): 103–30.

Zhai, F. (2008), "Armington Meets Melitz: Introducing Firm Heterogeneity in a Global CGE Model of Trade," *Journal of Economic Integration* 23(3): 575–604.

9.1 Alternative Perspective

BERNARD HOEKMAN

Summary

Anderson points out that global trade has grown strongly since 1990 and has been accompanied by rising real incomes. However, although average incomes in the East Asia and Pacific region have risen more than 1500 percent since 1960, the rise has been just 30 percent in sub-Saharan Africa. Economic policies that increased the costs of trade have been an important factor in this disappointing performance. Anderson, in his chapter, makes a compelling case for the large welfare benefits that could come from liberalizing trade in the Asia-Pacific region in the absence of a global agreement on the Doha Development Agenda, but it would seem important to include consideration of reforms that encompass developing countries in the rest of the world.

Analysis shows that many developing countries impose import restrictions, which are generally much higher for agricultural produce and that non-tariff measures (NTMs) represent a substantial share of merchandise trade barriers. Barriers to trade in services are also on average substantially higher in emerging economies than OECD countries. This makes it important to consider reductions in NTMs and service trade restrictions as well as tariffs and trade-distorting agricultural support policies in the assessments of gains from trade reform. The DDA therefore only partially captures the potential net benefits of global trade reforms.

Although there is scope for widening and improving the DDA, it has delivered one positive outcome that will generate large net benefits: the Bali Trade Facilitation Agreement (TFA). Full implementation has been estimated to reduce average trade costs in developing nations by about 10 percent, which will generate large welfare gains.

Overall gains from raising trade facilitation performance to even half that of global best practice could increase global GDP by 5 percent, six times more than removing all remaining import tariffs. Higher implementation costs would mean BCRs are lower than for tariff reform and subsidy reduction, but the overall benefits would be far greater.

Trade is not and should not be a goal in itself. Instead the focus should be on enhancing opportunities for firms to use trade and enhancing the real incomes of consumers in developing countries. Current goals proposed for the post-2015 agenda have a mercantilist focus on exports as opposed to trade overall. Imports can benefit local firms by providing inputs needed for exports, reducing prices, and improving the quality of goods on the domestic market.

A possible goal that would provide a focal point for actions to be undertaken by governments according to local circumstances, and for which they could be held accountable, would be a certain level of trade cost reduction, such as a 10 percent reduction for firms operating in low-income countries by 2020. This would be economically superior to the export-focused approach in the current proposals. Reducing trade costs is neutral in the sense of benefiting exporters and importers: lower trade costs will benefit households in developing countries by reducing prices of goods.

Using a trade cost reduction target as the focal point for trade reforms post-2015 is not a panacea. Lack of guidance to governments could result in inefficient use of resources, and a country-by-country approach may lead governments to miss opportunities for cooperation. Nevertheless, there is a strong case for the SDGs to revisit business as usual and for governments to adopt a specific target to reduce the costs of trade.

9.2 Alternative Perspective

PATRICK LOW

Summary

Overall, Anderson's chapter provides an excellent and comprehensive analytical review of contemporary trade policy issues in manufacturing and agriculture, and of the case for policy reform. However, it pays limited attention to services, when it is becoming increasingly apparent that their contribution to the economy has been underestimated for a long time.

Services make up a dominant share of income in most economies and account for about 70 percent of global GDP. On average, the lower a country's income as measured by GDP, the less will services represent national economic activity. Unsurprisingly, the prominence of services as a source of income translates into jobs. Despite this importance to the economy, services have received relatively little attention from economists and policy makers. One reason for this is the long shadow cast by classical economic thought, starting with Adam Smith, who regarded services as having zero value because they did not result in something physical and storable. More recently, Baumol's Cost Disease hypothesized a continual rise in the unit costs in service industries because productivity could not be improved.

In fact, changes to technology, particularly advances in ICT, allow storability and the delivery of many services at a distance. Moreover, services are frequently packaged with goods in production and consumption. The only distinguishing feature of services is their intangibility. Meanwhile, services are becoming increasingly dominant in the world economy and integrated into global value chains. Notwithstanding methodological challenges, the use of total factor productivity rather than output for a given unit of labor shows that services can themselves contribute to productivity growth.

Because up to two-thirds of trade is in intermediate goods, which may be imported and then reexported after further processing, there is a strong argument for measuring trade in value-added terms and banishing the double-counting implicit in gross trade flow data. Several important consequences flow from this. First, bilateral trade balances can look quite different. Second, the technology content of particular trade flows may also vary significantly from what the gross trade values might suggest. Third, the value-added numbers provide a much more accurate picture of the nature of trade dependency among countries. For example, studies on Apple products show that a high-tech export from China, such as an iPhone, contains a small fraction of China-generated value, with the rest coming from other countries.

Using this approach shows services' share of trade to go from around 23 percent measured by balance-of-payments statistics to nearly 50 percent. This all means that services are traded and tradable to a far greater degree than is generally realized, not least by policy makers. Services are more regulation-intensive than goods, yet we know much less about how policies affect the wide range of service activities in an economy. Inefficient supply or restricted access can seriously hobble economies.

Given the predominance of services in economic activity and the nature and range of service activities, they offer valuable opportunities for diversification and development in emerging economies. However, it is not easy to see how to incorporate trade in services into the post-2015 agenda in a comparatively data-starved environment. One option might be to produce a composite of the World Bank's and the OECD's service policy databases to derive key indicators that might help to enhance opportunities for participation by developing and emerging economies. Another approach might be to develop a metric for tracking developing country participation on global value chains.

Benefits and Costs of the Health Targets for the Post-2015 Development Agenda

PRABHAT JHA, RYAN HUM, CINDY L. GAUVREAU, AND KEELY JORDAN

Introduction

A variety of development priorities have been proposed for 2030 as Sustainable Development Goals (SDGs) to follow the highly-influential 2015 Millennium Development Goals (MDGs). These proposed goals cover a wide range of development objectives, including SDG3, "Ensure healthy lives and promote well-being for all at all ages." Within the overarching health goal, many subgoals have been proposed, some of which are realistic and others that are not (Norheim et al., 2014). Common frameworks to evaluate these disparate goals are required by national governments and global agencies.

One proposed method to evaluate goals is benefit-cost analyses (BCAs), expressed as some monetary value of the benefits divided by the costs (benefit-cost ratios, or BCR) of achieving these benefits. A BCR greater than one for an assessed intervention indicates that it is socially beneficial compared to the next best use of the same resources. A ranking of interventions by the size of their BCRs is one step in allowing the prioritization according to the relative benefits they provide to society. (Note that a goal with a high societal benefit, such as universal education of girls, might not necessarily have a higher BCR than other interventions). In the case of health, high coverage of individual interventions are seldom achieved without an extensive delivery system comprising community outreach of services, first referral, and specialty hospitals, as well as supportive services for quality, patient safety, monitoring and evaluation, and other services (Jha and Laxminarayan, 2009). Moreover, some interventions (such as immunization) reduce deaths beyond the specific diseases they cover, by,

for example, increasing the nutritional standing of children. The impact of increased access through universal healthcare is also not easily quantified through BCA. Therefore, traditional BCA, applied to individual interventions, fails to fully capture the cumulative and synergistic benefits or costs of implementation within a health system and in tandem with other health-promoting activities.

Thus, overall goals of reducing child and adult mortality are required as an overarching framework target. However, it should also be emphasized that within this framework, careful consideration be given to the specific subpopulation needs for each major age group (0–4, 5–49, and 50–69 years), as they differ in disease patterns.

In this chapter, we attempt to provide a BCR for an overall outcome of reducing premature mortality in low- and lower-middle-income countries by 40 percent by 2030 (40 × 30). This method quantifies the value of a broad-based expansion of healthcare resources for services and interventions rather than an incremental intervention-by-intervention approach. We propose this outcome as a new subgoal of SDG3 (Norheim et al., 2014). Additionally, important especially for low- and lower-middle-income countries, we try to indicate the affordability of achieving this goal by estimating its cost per capita. A secondary objective is to identify interventions that contribute positively to a reduction in premature mortality within the framework of the SDG3 subgoals and frame these within the context of the overall goal to reduce premature mortality.

By focusing on mortality we do not mean to deny the importance of the subgoals to reduce disability and suffering, such as that aimed at improving mental health or palliative care.

219

However, the burden of disability and suffering, as captured in the disability-adjusted life year (DALY) in low- and middle-income countries (LMICs), is relatively smaller than mortality (Jha, 2014), especially in lower-income countries (Murray et al., 2012). Because most causes of premature mortality are highly correlated with those of disability, a reduction in the former will result in a reduction of the latter. However, the benefits of healthy years gained takes into account (albeit crudely) the ratio of disability to mortality.

Death in old age is not avoidable, but prior to old age it is (Doll, 1994). Our focus on deaths before age 70 is not at the exclusion of strategies to reduce deaths at older ages. Rather, the main interventions relevant to reducing adult mortality can also be made available at older ages, and reducing premature deaths and disability prior to old age (such as from diabetes or smoking-related disease) can make the time period between onset of disease and death in older age shorter and less painful (the so-called compression of morbidity in old age, by reducing key risk factors and deaths in middle age [Mathers et al., 2014]).

Methodology

Section One

In developing an appropriate approach to estimating benefits and costs, we draw on the methodology of previous work of the Copenhagen Consensus process and base the potential avoidance of premature mortality on that estimated recently (Norheim et al., 2014).

Premature mortality is defined as dying before the age of 70, the current global average lifespan. We focus on a 40 percent reduction in premature mortality as proposed recently (Norheim et al., 2014). The focus of this analysis is on 0.9 billion people living in 34 low-income countries (GNI per capita <$1045 in 2013 as defined by the World Bank) and 2.6 billion people living in 50 lower-middle-income countries (GNI per capita $1046 to $4125 in 2013). The United Nations Population Division (UNPD) estimates that populations will rise to 1.2 billion and 3.1 billion,

respectively, in these two regions by 2030 (UNPD, 2012). Where relevant, we also discuss all low- and middle-income countries.

To determine an overarching, achievable, and quantitative goal that is more inclusive across ages and diseases, we conducted an analysis of the trends in mortality from 1970 to the present as well as the current projections to 2030. We used the UN Population Division historical life tables (UNPD, 2012); these cover each five-year time period from 1950 to 2010, with medium-fertility projections for 2010–15. For every fifth year from 1970 to 2010, we estimated the death rates in it by averaging the age-specific risks in the five-year periods before and after it (so our 1970 rates describe risks in 1965–75); this method reduces year-to-year changes in mortality changes. From the historical life tables, we extracted for particular calendar years the risks in the age ranges 0–4, 5–49, or 50–69 years. The risk is the probability that someone who had survived to the start of an age range would die in it.

Cause-specific mortality rates for 2000 and 2010 for the world as a whole and for each World Bank income grouping were from the World Health Organization (WHO) Global Health Observatory (WHO, 2014). Application of these 2000 and 2010 rates to the UNPD medium-fertility projection of the 2030 population yielded two numbers of deaths, the comparison of which gave the change (% per decade); this is also the change in the death rate from 2000 to 2010, if standardized to the projected 2030 population being analyzed. Such age-standardized comparisons avoid issues of competing risks. A full explanation of the methods can be found in the article by Norheim and colleagues (2014).

To determine the BCR for the proposed goal (for low-income and lower-middle-income regions only), we converted deaths averted to averted DALYs using the WHO's Global Health Estimates (for all cause death, by income level, and for three broad age groups 0–4, 5–49, and 60–69). Conversion factors of 95 and 97 DALYs per child death at ages 0–4 years were used for low-income countries and lower-middle-income countries, respectively. For deaths between ages 5 and 49, we used a conversion factor of 91 and 97; and for deaths between ages 50 and 69, we used a factor of 43 and 42, respectively. Rough estimates of the conversion factors were determined by taking the 2012 estimates for total "All-cause death" values for that age group divided by the total all cause DALYs from the WHO (2014; Appendix A). We calculated the DALYs for each region over a 20-year period (2010–2030) assuming they achieved the mortality projections estimated by the UNPD in 2030 (for a standardized 2030 population) as well as the DALYs assuming the regions achieved a higher premature mortality reduction articulated in the proposed goal (in the year 2030). For this analysis, the benefits were the difference between the DALYs averted by achieving a higher premature mortality reduction and the UNPD 2030 status quo medium projections. To convert the DALYs into a monetary value, we assumed each DALY was valued at (1) $1000, (2) $5000, or (3) by multiplying the DALYs by twice the GDP per capita income in that region for that year (Jamison, Jha, et al., 2013). We applied a 3 percent and 5 percent discounting function to the stream of benefits achieved over the 20-year gradual increase in deaths/DALYs averted.

To determine the costs of achieving the goal, we estimated the incremental government health expenditures required to reduce premature mortality to the proposed level. WHO estimates (WHO, 2014) that current public spending on health is about 2 percent of GDP in low-income countries, and slightly lower for lower-middle-income countries, but that a higher share of GDP to health (crudely at ~5 percent) would allow countries to achieve a "grand convergence" in health (Jamison, Summers, et al., 2013). We used this method as the majority of the funds required to achieve this goal would be derived from national health spending, and it would be difficult to identify the full suite of interventions for each individual country or region and further estimate the cost to achieve a specific level of intervention coverage. In this chapter, we assume that increases to government health expenditures will lead to higher access to basic health services such as promotion, prevention, and treatment services. However, Section Two also highlights highly cost-effective interventions that could be explored given a country's

particular context and epidemiological profile. A review of the benefits of expanded health coverage (via government health expenditure increases and universal healthcare) to population health outcomes can be found in the article by Moreno-Serra and Smith (2012).

We used the following cutoffs for all BCRs in this chapter. A BCR of 15 or above was considered "excellent," a BCR between 5 and 15 was considered "good," a BCR between 1 and 5 was considered "fair," a BCR or less than 1 (or the target was internally inconsistent, poorly specified, or unrealistic) was considered "poor," To conduct a crude sensitivity analysis on the costs, we use an alternative study to estimate the expenditures required to reduce child and adult mortality to the proposed levels. In a country-level panel data study, using instrumental variable specifications, Moreno-Serra and Smith (2015) show an estimated reduction of about 7.9 deaths of children under 5 years old per 1000 for a 10 percent increase in government health expenditures per capita; this reduction increases to about 12 deaths per 1000 when considering only low- and middle-income countries. For adults in low- and middle-income countries, they find a less-dramatic impact at about 2.2 deaths averted per 1000 for the same 10 percent increase in government health expenditures. We linearly extrapolated the benefits of government funded health spending on child and adult mortality (by averaging the benefits across both sexes) according to their income level and calculated the required increase in health expenditures necessary to achieve higher target mortality goal from the UN 2030 mortality projected levels in the low- and lower-middle-income regions.

Section Two

Our second objective was to comment on the health-related proposed SDG3 and its subgoals, particularly where they are likely to be poor in terms of BCR. We conducted a literature review to identify, where available, existing BCRs for the subgoals of SDG3. Priority was given to benefit-cost ratios from previous Copenhagen Consensus exercises (Jamison, Jha, and Bloom, 2008; Jamison et al., 2012; Jha et al., 2012), the Commission on Investing in Health (Jamison, Summers, et al., 2013), Global Burden of Disease (Lozano et al., 2012), and other large global health reviews. All of these papers build on the results of the second edition of "Disease Control Priorities" (DCP2), which engaged over 350 authors and estimated the cost-effectiveness of 315 interventions (Jamison et al., 2006; Jamison, 2015). These papers examine nine key interventions in terms of their cost-effectiveness and the size of the disease burden they address (summarized in Table 10.4).

The benefit-cost methodology used for most of the health interventions builds on the analysis framework in the Copenhagen Consensus 2008 Challenge Paper on disease control (Jamison, Jha, and Bloom, 2008). The basic approach to cost-benefit analysis was to start with the cost-effectiveness (CE) results from the extensive comparative analyses reported in DCP2 (Jamison et al., 2006; Laxminarayan, Chow, and Shahid-Salles, 2006). These results are expressed as the cost of buying a DALY.

The DCP2 experience shows that there is a broad range of reasonable estimates of the cost-effectiveness of most interventions. This results partly from (often highly) incomplete information and uncertainty. It results also, and even more important, from the responsiveness of the cost-effectiveness function to variations in prices, in the scale of the intervention (and of its substitutes and complements), and in the epidemiological environment specific to the country in which the study is set. Most CE studies have limited generalizability, and caution is advised in extrapolating results to other jurisdictions and countries.

Given these often broad ranges in CE ratios, and hence in BC ratios, it makes little sense to conclude with precise estimates or with attempts to quantify statistical uncertainty around the point estimates. Rather, we have identified major opportunities for investment in interventions that address a large disease burden highly cost effectively (Table 10.4). Even valuing DALYs at a conservative $1,000 the benefit to cost ratios associated with investing in these opportunities is enormously high. Overall this suggests that the conclusions in our Table 10.4 are conservative.

Results

Table 10.1 presents the overall reduction of 40 percent in premature death by 2030 over 2010 death rates by age ranges 0–4, 5–49, and 50–69, by major disease globally and stratified by low-income and lower-middle-income countries, as well as the 2030 deaths at ages 0–69 years compared to 2030 UNPD baseline projections. The broad target translates to reductions of: two-thirds in child and maternal deaths; two-thirds tuberculosis (TB), HIV, and malaria deaths; one-third in premature deaths from noncommunicable diseases; and one-third among remaining causes.

These goals are broadly consistent with goals proposed by the Commission on Investing in Health (Jamison, Summers, et al., 2013), the World Health Organization's call for a 25 percent reduction in selected NCDs by 2025 (WHO, 2011). Importantly, many of the specific interventions calculated for earlier rounds of the Copenhagen Consensus are subsumed within these age and disease-specific goals. Note that although death rates fell about 24 percent and 16 percent from 2000 to 2010 in low- and lower-middle-income countries, there is no certainty that these rates of progress will continue. In early childhood, the proportion of neonatal deaths (in the first month of life) is rising as deaths at ages 1–59 months fall faster, and such neonatal deaths are more difficult to reduce (Jamison, Summers, et al., 2013). Similarly, the effects of smoking are increasing among adults, so that deaths attributable to smoking are falling less than deaths from other causes (Jha and Peto, 2014). However, to be conservative, we make our calculations against the 2030 UN forward projections.

Table 10.2 summarizes the figures used to determine the BCR for achieving a 40 percent reduction in premature death. In low-income countries, a 40 percent reduction in premature death (achieved through a 66 percent reduction in child mortality, and 33 percent reduction for the ages 5–49 and 50–69 years) would avert an additional 2.2 million deaths in the year 2030 or 195 million DALYs compared to UN projections for 2030. For lower-middle-income countries, the comparable total averted is 4.5 million deaths and 360 million

Table 10.1 Premature deaths in 2030 (millions): Unaltered and targeted reductions, by age, specific disease, and World Bank income groupings

	Low-income				Lower-middle-income				World					
	ages 0–49		ages 50–69		ages 0–49		ages 50–69		ages 0–4		ages 5–49		ages 50–69	
	unaltered	targeted reduction	unaltered	targeted reduction	unaltered	targeted reduction	unaltered	targeted reduction	unaltered	targeted reduction	unaltered	targeted reduction	unaltered	targeted reduction
Neonatal or maternal*	1.01	0.68	–	–	1.63	1.09	–	–	2.5	–	0.3	0.2	–	–
HIV*	0.83	0.55	0.09	0.06	0.64	0.43	0.12	0.08	0.1	–	1.5	1.0	0.3	0.2
TB and malaria*	0.52	0.34	0.17	0.12	0.56	0.37	0.41	0.28	0.5	–	0.5	0.3	0.7	0.4
Other communicable**	1.87	0.62	0.38	0.13	2.31	0.77	0.88	0.29	2.8	–	1.9	0.6	1.6	0.5
Noncommunicable**	1.04	0.34	1.55	0.52	2.61	0.87	6.69	2.23	0.9	–	4.9	1.6	17.5	5.8
Fatal injuries**	0.95	0.32	0.20	0.07	1.62	0.54	0.63	0.21	0.4	–	3.3	1.1	1.6	0.5
All deaths	6.21	2.86	2.40	0.89	9.37	4.07	8.74	3.08	7.2	4.8	12.4	4.9	21.7	7.5
All deaths at 0–69 years compared to 2010 rates			8.62	3.74			18.11	7.15			19.5	9.7	41.3	17.3
All deaths at 0–69 years compared to 2030 UNPD projections			7.58	2.18			16.29	4.52			NA		NA	

Notes: Unaltered = deaths at unaltered 2010 rates. Targeted reduction = deaths avoided through targeted reduction. Targeted reductions not estimated for world population ages 0–4 by disease grouping.
* Conditions for which there is a targeted reduction of two-thirds.
** Conditions for which there is a targeted reduction of one-third.

Table 10.2 Benefit-to-cost ratio for overarching goal: Avoiding 40 percent reduction in premature death

	Low-income countries (Population of 1.2 billion in 2030)	Lower-middle-income countries (Population of 3.1 billion in 2030)
Costs*		
GDP per capita (in 2010)	$572	$1599
GDP growth per capita	3.7%	5.3%
Increase in government health expenditures (by 2030)	$42 million	$402 million
Total costs over 20 years	$434 million	$4.3 billion
Benefits**		
Additional deaths and DALYs averted from 0–4 (in 2030)	0.9 million deaths 86 million DALYs	0.9 million deaths 89 million DALYs
Additional deaths and DALYs averted from 5–49 (in 2030)	1.1 million deaths 102 million DALYS	2.2 million deaths 201 million DALYs
Additional deaths and DALYS averted from 50–69 (in 2030)	0.16 million deaths 7 million DALYS	1.5 million deaths 62 million DALYs
Total Monetary Value of DALYs in 2030 (where 1 DALY = $1000)	$195 billion	$3.6 trillion
Total Monetary Value of DALYs in 20 years (where 1 DALY = $5000)	$973 billion	$18 trillion
Cumulative deaths averted from 2001–2030	21.76 million	45.25 million
Benefit-to-Cost Ratio		
BCR @ $1000/DALY with 3% discounting	4.5	0.8
BCR @ $5000/DALY with 3% discounting	22.3	4.2
Population weighted average BCR @$1000/DALY = 1.9 to 1		
Population weighted average BCR @$5000/DALY = 9.3 to 1		

* Calculated to be an increase from 2 to 5 percent of GDP per capita over 20-year period.
** Calculated by taking the difference between UN death projections to 2030 and a 40 percent reduction in 2010 death rates (standardized to the 2030 population distribution).

DALYs. Over the two decades leading up to 2030, the cumulative averted deaths would be 21.8 million and 45.3 million in low-income and lower-middle-income countries, respectively.

For these income groups, it is estimated that an additional $34 and $128 in government health expenditures per capita would be required to achieve these mortality reductions, respectively. At a value of $5000 per DALY, this suggests a benefit-to-cost ratio of approximately 22 to 1 for low-income countries and 4 to 1 for lower-middle-income countries or a population-weighted overall BCR of 9 to 1. (An aggregate total BCR would be slightly lower at 6 to 1.)

Table 10.3 outlines the results of other methods to determine the BCR of achieving this goal, varying the monetary value of each DALY, and various health expenditures increments. In particular, we used Moreno-Serra and Smith's study to determine the percentage increase in baseline government health expenditures to achieve our proposed goal; for low-income countries, this was determined to be a 235 percent increase from a 2 percent baseline (or 4.7 percent GDP) and for lower-middle-income countries, it was 325 percent (or 6.5 percent of GDP); these values very much approximate the 5 percent GDP devoted to health expenditures advocated by other global health researchers. For

Table 10.3 Benefit-to-cost ratio sensitivity analysis using a variety of methods

Country income group	Option 1: Base scenario from 2 to 5% GDP, $5000/DALY	Option 2: $1000/DALY	Option 3: monetary value of 2xGDP/DALY	Option 4: increasing health expenditures according to Moreno-Serra & Smith, $5000/DALY
Benefit-to-Cost Ratio				
Low-income	22 to 1	4.5	8 to 1	25 to 1
Lower-middle-income	4 to 1	1 to 1	5 to 1	3 to 1
Combined	6 to 1	1 to 1	6 to 1	6 to 1

low-income countries, the BCR ranged from 4.5 to 1 to 25 to 1. Although the range is large, even the lowest BCR ratio suggests a good return on investment. For lower-middle-income countries, the BCR ranged from 1 to 1 to 5 to 1, which is fair to good rating, as we defined earlier. The results for both income regions were highly influenced by the monetary value of the DALY and less so by the different cost calculations. Notwithstanding the heterogeneity in the BCR across the two regions, taking a combined median BCR yielded a 5 to 1 ratio (across both income regions and averaged across all sensitivity analyses).

Table 10.4 summarizes the BCRs associated with the SDG3 targets. In addition to the preceding classification of BCRs, we add an "uncertain" rating when the economic evidence was unclear or the policy response to reach the goal was uncertain. Table 10.4 also presents alternative targets based on the Commission on Investing in Health (CIH; Jamison, Summers, et al., 2013) or avoiding 40 percent of premature deaths in each country 2010–30 (Norheim et al., 2014) where applicable. The first two SDG3 subgoal targets were categorized by maternal and child health. Target 1, to reduce the global maternal mortality rate (MMR) to less than 70 per 100,000 live births by 2030, was rated "unrealistic." Alternative targets proposed consist of a global MMR of 94 per 100,000 live births by the CIH or to avoid two-thirds of maternal deaths by 2030 as proposed by Norheim and colleagues (2014). Essential surgical interventions to address difficult childbirth, trauma, and other complications have a BCR of 10 and are therefore "good" interventions to focus on (Jamison et al., 2012). Target 2, to end preventable deaths of newborns and under-five children by 2030, was also

assessed "unrealistic." The CIH proposes an under-five mortality rate of 20 per 1,000 live births and a newborn mortality rate of 11 per 1,000 live births, while the Norheim paper proposes to avoid two-thirds of child deaths by 2030. Interventions aimed at childhood diseases and expanded immunization coverage have an "excellent" BCR of 20 (Jamison et al., 2012).

The second category within the SDG3 subgoal health targets were disease specific. Target 3, to end the epidemics of AIDS, tuberculosis, malaria, and neglected tropical diseases and combat hepatitis, water-borne diseases, and other communicable diseases by 2030, was rated "unrealistic." Alternative, more realistic targets are CIH's proposal to reverse the spread of HIV/AIDS and reduce annual AIDS deaths to 3 per 100,000 persons in 2030; reverse the spread of TB and reduce TB deaths to 4 per 100,000 persons; and to reverse the spread of malaria and reduce annual malaria deaths by 95 percent from 2010 to 2030. Norheim and colleagues suggest avoiding two-thirds of TB, HIV, and malaria deaths by 2030 (Norheim et al., 2014). HIV "combination prevention" was found to have a "good" BCR of 12 (Jamison, Jha, and Bloom 2008), whereas appropriate case finding and treatment of TB (including dealing with MDR TB) has a "excellent" BCR rating of 15, and subsidy for appropriate malaria treatment via a novel subsidy to reputable private providers has an "excellent" BCR rating of 35 (Jamison et al., 2012).

Category three consists of noncommunicable diseases and injury. The fourth target, to reduce by one-third premature mortality from noncommunicable diseases (NCDs) through prevention and treatment and promote mental health and well-being

Table 10.4 Benefit-to-cost ratio for proposed targets

Proposed Target	BCR	Rating
3.1 By 2030 reduce the global MMR to less than 70 per 100,000 live births		Unrealistic
Essential surgery to address difficult childbirth, trauma, and other conditions	10	Good
3.2 By 2030 end preventable deaths of newborns and under-five children		Unrealistic
Childhood diseases: expanded immunization coverage	20	Excellent
3.3 By 2030 end the epidemics of AIDS, tuberculosis, malaria, and neglected tropical diseases and combat hepatitis, water-borne diseases, and other communicable diseases		Unrealistic
HIV: "combination prevention"	12	Good
TB: appropriate case finding and treatment, including dealing with MDR TB	15	Excellent
Malaria: subsidy for appropriate treatment via Affordable Medicines Facility-malaria	35	Excellent
3.4 By 2030 reduce by one-third pre-mature mortality from NCDs through prevention and treatment and promote mental health and well-being		Uncertain
Cancer, heart disease, other: tobacco taxation	40	Excellent
Heart attacks: acute management with low-cost drugs	25	Excellent
Heart disease, strokes: salt reduction	20	Excellent
Hepatitis B immunization	10	Good
Heart attacks and strokes: secondary prevention with 3–4 drugs in a "generic risk pill"	4	Fair
3.5 Strengthen prevention and treatment of substance abuse, including narcotic drug abuse and harmful use of alcohol	NI	Uncertain
3.6 By 2020 halve global deaths and injuries from road traffic accidents*	NI	Unrealistic
Combined intervention strategy that simultaneously enforces speed limits, drunk-driving laws, and motorcycle helmet use	NI	
3.7 By 2030 ensure universal access to sexual and reproductive healthcare services, including for family planning, information and education, and the integration of reproductive health into national strategies and programmes	NI	Excellent
Providing adequate services for all 867 million women in developing countries who want to avoid a pregnancy in 2012	NI	Excellent
3.8 Achieve universal health coverage (UHC), including financial risk protection, access to quality essential healthcare services, and access to safe, effective, quality, and affordable essential medicines and vaccines for all	NI	Uncertain
3.9 By 2030 substantially reduce the number of deaths and illnesses from hazardous chemicals and air, water, and soil pollution and contamination	NI	Uncertain
3.a Strengthen the implementation of the World Health Organization Framework Convention on Tobacco Control in all countries, as appropriate	NI	Uncertain, but likely to be Good to Excellent if tobacco taxation is central
3.b Support the research and development of vaccines and medicines	NI	Uncertain
3.c Substantially increase health financing and the recruitment, development, training, and retention of the health workforce	NI	Uncertain
3.d Strengthen the capacity of all countries, in particular developing countries, for early warning, risk reduction, and management of national and global health risks	NI	Uncertain

Note: NI = No information on CE or BCR is available.
* By error, the year 2020 and not 2030 was printed in the official UN SDG3 goals for road traffic accidents, and the prospects for achieving this goal by 2020 are of course poor. By 2030, the prospects are uncertain.

by 2030, was rated "uncertain" due to the lack of economic evidence. The paper by Norheim and colleagues proposes to reduce by one-third premature deaths from NCDs and one-third of those from the remaining causes between ages 5 and 69 years (other communicable diseases and injuries). The Copenhagen Consensus paper in 2012 on chronic diseases (Jha et al., 2012) found tobacco taxation to prevent cancer, heart disease, and other diseases, acute management with low-cost drugs to reduce heart attacks, and salt reduction to address heart disease and strokes all have excellent BCRs of 40, 25, and 20, respectively.

The same paper found Hepatitis B immunization to have a "good" BCR of 10 and secondary prevention with 3–4 drugs in a "generic risk pill" to reduce heart attacks and strokes has a "fair" BCR rating of 4. The fifth target, to strengthen prevention and treatment of substance abuse including narcotic drug abuse and harmful use of alcohol, was also rated "uncertain" with low priority. The sixth and final target within this category, to halve global deaths and injuries from road traffic accidents, was rated as "uncertain." A mathematical modeling study in the *BMJ* on the cost effectiveness of strategies to combat road traffic injuries in sub-Saharan Africa and South East Asia (Chisholm et al., 2012) found that combining intervention strategies that simultaneously enforces speed limits, drunk-driving laws, and motorcycle helmet use saves one DALY for a cost of $Int1380.

The fourth category covers healthcare access. Target seven; to ensure universal access to sexual and reproductive healthcare services, including family planning information and education, and the integration of reproductive health into national strategies and programs by 2030 was rated "excellent." The CIH proposes in their report 50 percent coverage with modern family planning methods to reduce the global total fertility rate (TFR) to 2.2 by 2030. The Guttmacher Institute and UNFPA estimate that it costs $30 to prevent each unintended pregnancy, making this target highly cost-effective (Singh et al., 2009). Target eight, to achieve universal health coverage, including financial risk protection, access to quality essential healthcare services, and access to safe, effective, quality and affordable essential medicines and vaccinations for

all, though an excellent goal, is rated "uncertain" due to the lack of cost-effective data. The CIH proposes a set of pro-poor pathways to universal health coverage (progressive universalism) in their report, with similar proposals made earlier for India (Jha and Laxminarayan, 2009).

Target nine, which we categorized as environmental hazards, aims to substantially reduce the number of deaths and illnesses from hazardous chemicals and air, water, and soil pollution and contamination by 2030. This target was rated "uncertain" due to the lack of cost-effectiveness data we were able to find. Finally, targets 3.a, 3.b, 3.c, and 3.d are concerned with improving health systems and policies and are therefore outside the scope of this review. We ranked them "uncertain" due to the lack of available cost-effective data.

Discussion

Our analyses suggest that an overarching goal of 40 percent reduction in premature mortality is cost-beneficial under a range of assumptions about the economic value of an extra DALY and a range of costs required to achieve such gains (Table 10.5). Broader goals of mortality reduction of 40 percent are comparable in terms of BCR to some of the specific subconstitutions, such as maternal delivery services. However, the reality is that most political and administrative decisions are seldom about a single intervention, but rather about adopting and supporting broad health system goals. The 40 percent reduction is also relatively easy to monitor, as global systems from the UNPD provide reasonable estimates of age-specific mortality for every country. However, expanded efforts to evaluate cause-specific mortality changes are required, as most countries do not have adequate registration and medical certification of deaths (Jha, 2014).

Our analysis has the advantage of introducing quantification to the target-setting process, based on rigorous analysis of mortality trends by age as well as by disease category. The proposed targets focus on premature mortality before age 70 and avoid more complex metrics that are much harder to measure and track over time, such as changes in DALYs' similar composite measures.

For this study, we were unable to identify each specific intervention to achieve the 40 percent reduction, but instead gave a general estimation of the level of incremental increase in government health expenditures required to achieve the proposed goal. Our estimated values draw largely from research by Moreno-Serra and Smith (2015), but others have also studied publicly funded health expenditures and concluded similar impacts on under-5 and maternal mortality (Bidani and Ravallion, 1997; Bokhari, Gai, and Gottret, 2007; Wagstaff and Claeson, 2004). We did not attempt to do a full meta-analysis/systematic review on the subject, but rather prioritized the general costing of 5 percent of GDP devoted to health expenditures as advocated by the Lancet Commission on Investing in Health (Jamison, Summers, et al., 2013). To conduct a sensitivity analysis regarding the 5 percent GDP costing, we used Moreno-Serra and Smith's analysis given its statistical rigor via the use of the most recent cross-country data from 1995 to 2008, an instrumental variable analysis, an allowance for differential impacts on low- versus higher-income countries, and the inclusion of both adult and child mortality as outcome variables. We note that the values we derived from the Moreno-Serra and Smith analysis yielded suggested increases of 4.7 percent and 6.5 percent of GDP devoted to health expenditures for low-income and lower-middle-income regions, approximating the 5 percent suggested by others.

The level of increase in health expenditures remains a topic of research. Jamison and colleagues (2013), using WHO data (2014), estimate that current public spending on health is about 2 percent of GDP in low-income countries and slightly lower for lower-middle-income countries,

but the opportunity (as income grows) to devote a higher share of GDP to health exists – with some countries able to achieve a 4 percent allocation completely from domestic resources and others supplemented via development assistance for health. Alternatively, Evans and colleagues (2001) estimated that health system performance increased greatly with expenditure up to about $100 per capita a year (in 2010 adjusted dollars). We were, nonetheless, unable to cost out the full suite of specific interventions required to achieve this goal for each country. We do provide a list of existing BCR and CERs that have been developed for well-researched interventions. This can be used to assist governments in determining highly cost-effective interventions that would be achievable within their government budgets and appropriate for their population health context.

Technological progress, of course, can reduce the costs of these interventions and thereby also reduce the necessary public spending on health (Hum et al., 2012). Our previous research shows that the cost to save a child's life has fallen by half from 1970 to 2010, with the greatest decline achieved after 1990, coinciding with actions following the UN's World Summit for Children (Hum et al., 2012). Unfortunately, the spread of HIV/AIDS, an increase in smoking in LMICs, and less political attention devoted to adult mortality (Jha and Peto, 2014) have allowed the costs to rise for older populations. Indeed, a goal of reducing premature mortality would not necessarily give preferential treatment by age or disease and could stimulate research that can reduce the adult mortality cost curve already achieved in children.

In sum, ambitious but feasible goals of reducing premature mortality before age 70 by 40 percent by 2030 worldwide are likely to be cost-beneficial.

Table 10.5 Estimating the ratio of "disability adjusted life years" (DALYs) to total "all-cause deaths," by age group, below age 70 years in the year 2012

Income Group	Indicator	0 to 4 years	5 to 49 years	50 to 69 years
Low-income countries	Deaths	2,170,484	2,345,348	1,324,540
	DALYs	207,114,297	213,531,697	56,866,398
	Ratio	**95**	**91**	**43**
Lower-middle-income countries	Deaths	3,535,967	4,668,495	5,265,371
	DALYs	341,469,034	454,202,863	223,579,101
	Ratio	**97**	**97**	**42**

* Data is extracted from the WHO's Global Health Observatory Data (2014).

References

Bidani, Banu, and Martin Ravallion. 1997. "Decomposing social indicators using distributional data." *Journal of Econometrics* 77 (1):125–39.

Bokhari, F. A., Y. Gai, and P. Gottret. 2007. "Government health expenditures and health outcomes." *Health Economics* 16 (3):257–73. doi: 10.1002/hec.1157.

Chisholm, D., H. Naci, A. A. Hyder, N. T. Tran, and M. Peden. 2012. "Cost effectiveness of strategies to combat road traffic injuries in sub-Saharan Africa and South East Asia: mathematical modelling study." *BMJ* 344:e612. doi: 10.1136/bmj.e612.

Doll, Richard. 1994. Foreword. In *Mortality from Smoking in Developed Countries 1950–2000*, edited by R. Peto, A. D. Lopez, J. Boreham, and M. Thun. Oxford: Oxford University Press.

Evans, D. B., A. Tandon, C. J. Murray, and J. A. Lauer. 2001. "Comparative efficiency of national health systems: cross national econometric analysis." *BMJ* 323 (7308):307–10.

Hum, R. J., P. Jha, A. M. McGahan, and Y. L. Cheng. 2012. "Global divergence in critical income for adult and childhood survival: analyses of mortality using Michaelis-Menten." *Elife* 1: e00051. doi: 10.7554/eLife.00051.

Jamison, D. T. 2015. "Disease Control Priorities, 3rd edition: improving health and reducing poverty." *Lancet*, Feb. 5, doi: 10.1016/S0140–6736(15)60097–6.

Jamison, D. T., Joel G. Breman, Anthony R. Measham, et al. 2006. *Disease Control Priorities in Developing Countries*. 2nd ed. Washington, DC: World Bank Publications.

Jamison, D. T., P. Jha, and D. Bloom. 2008. "Disease control." *Copenhagen Consensus 2008 Challenge Paper.*

Jamison, D. T., P. Jha, R. Laxminarayan, and T. Ord. 2012. "Infectious disease, injury and reproductive health." *Copenhagen Consensus 2012 Challenge Paper.*

Jamison, D. T., P. Jha, V. Malhotra, and S. Verguet. 2013. "Human health: the twentieth-century transformation of human health – its magnitude and value." In *How Much Have Global Problems Cost the World? - A Scorecard from 1900 to 2050* edited by B. Lomberg. Cambridge: Cambridge University Press.

Jamison, D. T., L. H. Summers, G. Alleyne, et al. 2013. "Global health 2035: a world converging within a generation." *Lancet* 382 (9908):1898–955. doi: 10.1016/s0140–6736(13)62105–4.

Jha, P. 2014. "Reliable direct measurement of causes of death in low- and middle-income countries." *BMC Med* 12:19. doi: 10.1186/1741–7015–12–19.

Jha, P., and Ramanan Laxminarayan. 2009. *Choosing Health: An Entitlement for All Indians*. Toronto, Ontario, Canada: Centre for Global Health Research.

Jha, P., Rachel Nugent, Stephane Verguet, David Bloom, and Ryan Hum. 2012. "Chronic disease prevention and control." In *Third Copenhagen Consensus: Chronic Disease*. Copenhagen: Copenhagen Consensus Center.

Jha P., and R. Peto 2014. "Global effects of smoking, of quitting, and of taxing tobacco." *New England Journal of Medicine* 370: 60–8.

Laxminarayan, R., J. Chow, and S. A. Shahid-Salles. 2006. "Intervention cost-effectiveness: overview of main messages." In *Disease Control Priorities in Developing Countries*, edited by

D. T. Jamison, J. G. Breman, A. R. Measham, et al. Washington, DC: World Bank.

Lozano, R., M. Naghavi, K. Foreman, et al. 2012. "Global and regional mortality from 235 causes of death for 20 age groups in 1990 and 2010: a systematic analysis for the Global Burden of Disease Study 2010." *Lancet* 380 (9859): 2095–128. doi: 10.1016/s0140–6736(12)61728–0.

Mathers, C. D., G. A. Stevens, T. Boerma, R. A. White, and M. I. Tobias. 2014. "Causes of international increases in older age life expectancy." *Lancet.* doi: 10.1016/s0140–6736 (14)60569–9.

Moreno-Serra, Rodrigo, and Peter C. Smith. 2012. "Does progress towards universal health coverage improve population health?" *Lancet* 380:917–23.

—— 2015. "Broader health coverage is good for the nation's health: evidence from country level panel data." *Journal of the Royal Statistical Society: Series A (Statistics in Society)* 178 (1):101–124. doi: 10.1111/rssa.12048.

Murray, C. J., M. Ezzati, A. D. Flaxman, et al. 2012. "GBD 2010: design, definitions, and metrics." *Lancet* 380 (9859):2063–6. doi: 10.1016/ s0140–6736(12)61899–6.

Norheim, O. F., P. Jha, K. Admasu, et al. 2014. "Avoiding 40% of the premature deaths in each country, 2010–30: review of national mortality trends to help quantify the UN Sustainable Development Goal for health." *Lancet.* doi: 10.1016/s0140–6736(14)61591–9.

Singh, Susheela, Jacqueline E. Darroch, Lori S. Ashford, and Michael Vlassoff. 2009. *Adding It Up: The Costs and Benefits of Investing in Family Planning and Maternal and Newborn Health.* New York: Guttmacher Institute and United Nations Population Fund.

United Nations Population Division (UNPD). 2012. *World Population Prospects: the 2012 Revision.* New York: UN Population Division.

Wagstaff, Adam, and Mariam Claeson. 2004. *The Millennium Development Goals for Health: Rising to the Challenges.* Washington, DC: The World Bank.

World Health Organization (WHO). 2011. *Global Status Report on Non-Communicable Diseases 2010.* Geneva: World Health Organization.

—— 2014. *WHO Global Health Observatory* [cited Oct. 28 2014]. Available from www.who.int/ healthinfo/global_burden_disease/estimates/en/ index1.html.

Benefits and Costs of the Noncommunicable Disease Targets for the Post-2015 Development Agenda

RACHEL NUGENT AND ELIZABETH BROUWER

Introduction

We discuss the role of noncommunicable diseases (NCDs) in the development goal discourse, especially how NCDs fit into the overall health goal and why it is essential to have an NCD target to meet Goal 3 of the proposed SDGs: *Ensure healthy lives and promote well-being for all at all ages.* The interventions presented and analyzed here will reduce mortality by 28.5 percent in 2030, primarily from cardiovascular and respiratory diseases, as well as some cancers.

Rationale for Addressing NCDs in Development

NCDs are the largest cause of mortality both globally and in the majority of low- and middle-income countries (LMICs). NCD mortality exceeds that of communicable, maternal, perinatal, and nutritional conditions combined (Commission, 2013). NCDs account for 65 percent of global deaths (Murray and Lopez, 2013), accounting for a majority of deaths in all regions except Africa. Eighty percent of NCD deaths (28 million people) occur in LMICs, making NCDs a major cause of poverty and an urgent development issue. Bloom et al. (2011) estimated that $47 trillion in economic output would be lost due to NCDs by 2030, concluding that "inaction would likely be far more costly [than interventions for NCDs]."

NCDs are wrongly perceived as diseases only of the rich. There has been a dramatic transition from infectious disease to NCD burden – in Mexico, for example, NCD was the cause of death in 45.4 percent of cases in 1980, but this increased to 74.4 percent by 2009. The reach of NCD risk factors is striking: a study in Argentina, Chile, and Uruguay found that 43.4 percent of the population has high blood pressure, 11.9 percent has diabetes and 35.5 percent are obese. Nineteen percent of Kenyan HIV patients are obese and 8.2 percent have high blood pressure. Ninety percent of NCD deaths before age 60 are in LMICs, resulting in loss of household heads, wasted education investments, and huge out-of-pocket costs to families. Most of these deaths are from preventable causes, and lack of access to affordable medicines and health care services are also major contributors.

Adding urgency to the NCD debate is the likelihood that the number of people affected will rise substantially in the coming decades. Globally, the NCD burden will increase by 17 percent in the next ten years, and in the African region by 27 percent. The highest absolute number of deaths will be in the Western Pacific and South-East Asia regions. From a demographic perspective, both rising and aging populations are behind the projected increase in NCDs. From an epidemiological perspective, rising exposure to the main risk factors will also contribute to the urgency, particularly as globalization and urbanization take greater hold in the developing world.

NCD Targets and Indicators

Following the Political Declaration on NCDs adopted by the United Nations (UN) General

Assembly in 2011, the World Health Organization (WHO) developed a global monitoring framework (GMF) to enable tracking of progress in preventing and controlling major NCDs – cardiovascular disease (CVD), cancer, chronic lung diseases, and diabetes – and their key risk factors (NCD, 2012). As part of the GMF, the World Health Assembly in 2013 adopted nine voluntary global NCD targets to be reached by 2025. Those targets were accompanied by 25 indicators, covering NCD mortality and morbidity, risk factors, and national health system response. That process paved the way for NCDs to become a central component in the post-2015 development goals. It provided ready-made outcomes from a completed consensus process within the NCD communities and significant buy-in within the UN system.

The proposed post-2015 NCD target (3.4) for the SDGs is drawn directly from that agreed outcome – adjusted to fit the 2030 end date. The eventually chosen indicators are expected to closely track the

GMF global targets. Table 11.1 presents the proposed post-2015 NCD target and the WHO-agreed NCD targets in the GMF for which sufficient evidence is available to estimate benefits and costs. The table presents the definition or indicator for each target from the WHO Framework, along with the rationale for including the indicators analyzed in this chapter (World Health Organization, 2013a).

To analyze the actions needed to address the preceding global agenda, we have chosen to focus on the primary GMF-agreed NCD target and the subsidiary GMF targets that reflect high-priority diseases and with well-proven, cost-effective interventions available. We examine prevention and treatment interventions that will reduce mortality from cardiovascular disease, stroke, chronic obstructive pulmonary disease (COPD), and some cancers.

The proposed NCD target (3.4) to reduce premature NCD mortality by one-third refers to the

Table 11.1 Health and NCD goals, targets, and indicators

Goal, Target, Indicator	Definition or Indicator	Rationale
Goal 3: Ensure healthy lives and promote well-being for all at all ages		
Proposed NCD Target 3.4 and GMF Target #1: By 2030, reduce by one-third premature mortality from noncommunicable diseases through prevention and treatment and promote mental health and well-being.	Refers to the unconditional probability of dying between ages 30 and 70 years from cardiovascular diseases, cancer, diabetes, or chronic respiratory diseases.	There is political agreement on the numerical part of the target from the WHO World Health Assembly. The target is felt to be sufficiently ambitious, realistic, and feasible.
GMF Target: A 30% relative reduction in mean population intake of salt/sodium.	Age-standardized mean population intake of salt (sodium chloride) per day in grams in persons aged 18+ years.	Moderate reduction in salt intake can lower systolic blood pressure by small but meaningful amounts. Salt reduction is a WHO "Best Buy."
GMF Target: A 30% relative reduction in prevalence of current tobacco use in persons ages 15+ years.	Prevalence of current tobacco use among adolescents. Age-standardized prevalence of current tobacco use among persons age 18+ years.	Each 10% increase in tobacco tax leads to at least a 4% reduction in demand, about half of which is from current consumption.
GMF Target: A 25% relative reduction in the prevalence of raised blood pressure or contain the prevalence of raised blood pressure according to national circumstances.	Age-standardized prevalence of raised blood pressure among persons age 18+ years (defined as systolic blood pressure ≥ 140 mmHg and/or diastolic blood pressure ≥ 90 mmHg).	High blood pressure is responsible for at least 50% of cardiovascular disease, particularly stroke and ischemic heart disease.
GMF Target: Achieve 50% coverage in drug therapy and counseling (including glycemic control) to prevent heart attacks and strokes.	Proportion of eligible persons (defined as age 40 years and over with a 10-year cardiovascular risk $\geq 30\%$, including those with existing cardiovascular disease) receiving drug therapy and counseling (including glycemic control) to prevent heart attacks and strokes.	Multidrug therapy for adults with heart disease lowers the 10-year risk of rehospitalization or death from 50% to 16%.

unconditional probability of dying between ages 30 and 70 years from cardiovascular diseases, cancer, diabetes, or chronic respiratory diseases. Most NCD deaths in high-income countries occur after age 70. Further, NCD mortality has been in a long decline in high-income countries thanks to existing high coverage of effective prevention and treatment interventions. Thus, the target will only be achieved through dramatic reductions of NCD mortality in low- and middle-income countries. For this reason, we focus the analysis on the benefits to be obtained by substantially increasing the coverage and effectiveness of NCD interventions in LMICs.

Cardiovascular Disease

About 35 million people have an acute coronary or cerebrovascular event every year. An estimated 100 million people in the world are known to have cardiovascular disease, which gives them a five times greater risk of an event compared to people not diagnosed with cardiovascular disease (Kerr et al., 2009; Yusuf, 2002). Treating those with known disease or at high risk of disease with drug therapy – what is referred to as "secondary prevention" – will avert many deaths through a targeted approach. Earlier analysis suggests the multidrug package could effectively reduce chronic disease death rates by 1.5 percent per year, at an average yearly cost of $1.08 per person in 23 high-burden LMICs (Lim et al., 2007). High-risk patients are relatively easy to identify because they have already accessed health services due to their heart disease history, or through noninvasive assessment of combined risk factors (tobacco use, weight, blood pressure, age, and sex). For resource-limited environments, official guidelines generally include the use of four medications: aspirin, ACE-inhibitors, beta blockers, and statins. All of these are available in cheap, generic formulations, although not all are affordable to low-income patients. Further, the simplicity of this regimen suggests it can be brought to scale in low-resource settings through primary health or outpatient facilities (Lim et al., 2007).

Treatment of acute heart attacks with inexpensive drugs is less demanding of system resources and also cost-effective (Gaziano et al., 2006). It is a high priority to make drugs available to reduce mortality.

High Blood Pressure

High blood pressure is implicated in about half of all deaths from heart disease and stroke (World Health Organization, 2013b), but is amenable to a very similar drug regimen as that for secondary prevention. Those at high risk of stroke would be advised to replace the beta blocker with an antihypertensive. The global population with high blood pressure is estimated at about 1 billion (World Health Organization, 2011), with a prevalence of 46 percent among adults in African which is even higher than in HICs (prevalence of 35 percent) (World Health Organization, 2013c). The recommended interventions include opportunistic screening and treatment for those with raised blood pressure and population education to encourage awareness and reduction of dietary salt. Studies have shown population level salt reduction to be cost-saving (Wang and Labarthe, 2011) and drug treatment for those with raised blood pressure to be highly cost-effective (Barton et al., 2011).

Depending on the diet composition in a population, greater effect may occur through interventions to reduce salt in food processing or at the cooking or eating stages. Processors in parts of Latin America have agreed to reduce salt levels in formulations, but in much of India and Asia salt is mostly added at the table, and changing consumer behavior can be more difficult.

Increasing numbers of countries are implementing national policies to reduce salt consumption, and experience in the United States and other developed countries suggest that substantial reduction from current levels is feasible with little or no consumer resistance. Selecting the appropriate level of intervention to achieve the greatest possible reduction in salt intake requires understanding local consumption habits and food systems. For instance, Argentina and South Africa are focusing on salt reduction in bread (Bertram et al., 2012; Rubinstein et al., 2010). Reducing salt in bread has been found to be very cost effective in Argentina with an ICER of (2007) I$1407 or a cost of US$703 per disability-adjusted life year (DALY) gained. The cost-effectiveness of 15–30 percent reduction in salt intake in Mexico through the two channels of voluntary and legislated manufacturing changes and labeling was modeled. The average cost-effectiveness across the population is US$286 (in 2005 US$) per DALY gained (Salomon et al., 2012).

Tobacco Control

The number of tobacco-attributable deaths that will occur in 2030 given business as usual (BAU) has been estimated by the WHO as more than eight million, with others claiming as many as 10 million total deaths, mostly in LMICs (Alwan, 2011; Jha and Peto, 2014). Although the health effects of tobacco (stroke, heart disease, COPD, TB, and cancer) can take years to become apparent, as many as half of tobacco attributable deaths occur in people under the age of 70.

Reducing smoking levels has been demonstrated to be well within the control of public policy. The WHO Framework Convention on Tobacco Control provides a comprehensive package of evidence-based policies, and the WHO MPOWER package assists countries to implement the interventions. These include warning labels, mass media campaigns, advertising bans, and taxation. Of these, tobacco taxation is particularly effective – with a 10 percent price increase leading to a 4–8 percent drop in consumption (Alwan, 2011).

These policy measures have already reduced consumption in high-income countries, but smoking in developing countries is rising. Tobacco taxation is widely considered to be the most effective intervention to decrease use (Blecher and Van Walbeek, 2004; Jha and Peto, 2014; Jha et al., 2012). Taxes are underutilized, accounting for about 54 percent of the final price of cigarettes in low- and middle-income countries, but 71 percent (as of 2006) in high-income countries (Jha and Chaloupka, 2000).

Methods

Number of Deaths to Be Averted

Given what we know about potential life expectancy in some high-income countries, a reasonable estimate is 70 years of age, so deaths occurring before that may be considered premature. This is also the cutoff used by the UN to measure progress toward reduction in premature deaths.

This analysis relies on the WHO's Global Health Estimates (GHE) from 2013 (WHO Global Health Estimates, 2013). GHE 2013 estimates that of the projected 70 million deaths that will occur in 2030, 23.7 million will be of people between the ages of 30 and 69, and approximately 17.6 million of those deaths will be from an NCD (WHO Global Health Estimates, 2013). According to this projection, 5.9 million deaths in 30- to 69-year-olds would need to be averted to reach the target of a one-third reduction.

Norheim et al. (2014) projected the effect of avoiding 40 percent of premature deaths by 2030 using UN mortality trends from 1970–2010 and applying those country-standardized trends to projected 2030 population rates. They estimate that between 17.5 and 23 million people between the ages of 50–69 and 0–69, respectively, will die from NCDs in the year 2030, about 90 percent of which would occur in LMICs. Based on these estimates, 5.8 to 7.7 million NCD deaths would need to be averted to reach the one-third goal. The midpoint of this range is 6.8 million.

Combining these two data sources, we estimate that interventions would need to avert between 5.9 and 6.8 million NCD deaths in people between the ages of 30 and 69 to reduce premature NCD mortality by one-third in 2030 (Table 11.2).

Interventions to Avert NCD Deaths

We considered five interventions that would need to be in place to come close to reaching the NCD target.

- **Tobacco tax** – Tax tobacco at sufficiently high rates to achieve a 50 percent relative reduction in user prevalence. In this target, we concentrate on low- and middle-income countries (LMICs) because many high-income countries (HIC) have already implemented significant tax increases.
- **Aspirin therapy for AMI** – Provide aspirin to 75 percent of patients at the onset of an acute myocardial infarction (AMI).
- **Salt reduction** – 30 percent reduction in the mean dietary intake of salt through voluntary reformulation of processed foods.

Table 11.2 Projected deaths from noncommunicable diseases in 2030

	Age range	Total projected deaths in 2030 (in millions)	Deaths to be averted to reach reduction goal (in millions)
WHO Global Health Estimates (2013)	30–69	17.60	5.87
Norheim et al. (2014)	0–69	23.02	7.67
Norheim et al. (2014)	50–69	17.57	5.86
Calculated Target	**30–69**		**5.87 – 6.77***

* 6.77 is the midpoint between 5.86 and 7.67.

Table 11.3 Tobacco taxation, calculation inputs

Metric	Values	Source
Tobacco attributable deaths in 2030 (business as usual)	10 million	Jha and Peto (2014)
Percent of tobacco attributable deaths that will occur in people <70 years old	50%	Jha and Chaloupka (2000)

Target percent decrease in tobacco product consumption (based on the following)
  Price elasticity of demand for tobacco products
  Prevalence elasticity of demand as a percentage of price elasticity of demand
  Increase in price of tobacco products to achieve relative reduction target
	50%
	−0.4 to −1.2
	(Midpoint −0.8)
	50%
	125%
		Kontis et al. (2014)
		Jha and Chaloupka (2000)
		Jha and Chaloupka (2000)
		Calculation

Tobacco deaths averted in 2030 among 30- to 69-year-olds	2.5 million	Calculation
Average annual cost per capita to implement revised tobacco tax system	$0.50 USD	Asaria et al. (2007); estimate $0.1 for 10% tax, adjusted to $0.5 for 125% cumulative tax
Projected population of LMICs in 2030	7.1 billion	WHO Global Health Estimates (2013)
Total Cost	$3.55 billion	Calculation

Source: Jha P., Peto R. Global effects of smoking, of quitting, and of taxing tobacco. *New England Journal of Medicine* 2014; 370(1): 60–8. Jha P., Chaloupka F. J. The economics of global tobacco control. *BMJ: British Medical Journal* 2000; 321(7257): 358. Kontis V., Mathers C.D., Rehm J., et al. Contribution of six risk factors to achieving the 25× 25 non-communicable disease mortality reduction target: a modelling study. *The Lancet* 2014. World Health Organization, *WHO Report on the Global Tobacco Epidemic, 2013: Enforcing bans on tobacco advertising, promotion and sponsorship*. Geneva, Switzerland: World Health Organization, 2013.

- **Hypertension management** – Use of antihypertension medicines by 50 percent of those at medium to high risk.
- **Secondary prevention of cardiovascular disease** – 70 percent coverage and 60 percent adherence to a multipill regimen for those at a high risk of a cardiovascular event.

Tobacco Taxation

We consider the effect of raising the price of tobacco in LMICs only, where tobacco use is rising. The agreed GMF target is a 30 percent relative reduction in the prevalence of tobacco use (World Health Organization, 2013a). Jha and Peto (2014) find that a reduction of about one-third could be achieved by doubling the inflation-adjusted price of cigarettes. However, we calculate the benefits and costs of a more ambitious target that would achieve a 50 percent relative reduction in user prevalence. This goal is deemed to be achievable based on recent evidence (Kontis et al., 2014).

All other assumptions are shown in Table 11.3.

Table 11.4 Aspirin therapy, calculation inputs

Metric	Values	Source
Projected global deaths from ischemic heart disease in 2030 among 30- to 60-year-olds	2.8 million	WHO Global Health Estimates (2013)
CVD burden averted with aspirin therapy for acute myocardial infarctions (AMIs)	2%	WHO Best Buys (2011)
Projected IHD deaths averted in 30- to 69-year-olds in 2030	56,212	Calculation
Aspirin therapy for AMI, cost per treated case	$13	WHO Best Buys (2011)
Aspirin therapy coverage	75%	Author assumption
Total cost of providing aspirin therapy	$27.4 million	Calculation

Source: World Health Organization, *WHO Report on the Global Tobacco Epidemic, 2013: Enforcing bans on tobacco advertising, promotion and sponsorship.* Geneva, Switzerland: World Health Organization, 2013. *From burden to "best buys": Reducing the economic impact of non-communicable diseases in low- and middle-income countries, 2015 Global Status Report on NCDs.* Geneva, Switzerland: World Health Organization, World Economic Forum, 2011.

Although not included in our benefit-cost calculations, we also calculated the revenue incurred from the tax increase, as this often makes tobacco taxes attractive to governments. Using the 2030 LMIC population numbers, we assumed 20 percent of men and 5 percent of women would be smokers based on current rates (World Health Organization, 2013d). We assumed that average consumption in the smoking population is 12 packs of cigarettes per year at $1/pack, and then adjusted revenue downward to reflect an estimated 5 percent loss to smuggling and assumed 50 percent decrease in usage (Hum et al., 2015; Lim et al., 2013). If we assume that the tax increase is at least 75 percent of the price, tax revenues in LMICs would exceed $2.5 billion.

Aspirin Therapy

Taking an aspirin at the onset of an acute myocardial infarction is a WHO Best Buy for preventing premature mortality. Aspirin therapy prevents as much as 2 percent of all CVD mortality (World Health Organization, 2011). We considered the projected 2030 deaths due to ischemic heart disease in the relevant age range and applied the 2 percent burden reduction assuming that 75 percent of the population would have access to the low-cost drug (WHO Global Health Estimates, 2013; World Health Organization, 2011). The WHO estimates that the cost per treated case of an AMI

patient who takes aspirin, including clinical visits and diagnostic tests, is $13–$15 USD (Table 11.4) (Alwan 2011).

Population Salt Reduction

A 30 percent salt reduction (the GMF target) over ten years is estimated to avert 16 million deaths, of which about 6.7 million would occur under the age of 70 (Asaria et al., 2007). We used this number, adjusted to reflect one year and the projected 2030 LMIC population, to estimate the premature deaths averted from reduced salt intake. The same study estimated the average annual cost per person to implement voluntary salt reduction in the 23 high-burden LMICs considered to be $0.09 USD (Asaria et al., 2007). We estimate the annual population cost of the intervention (Table 11.5) (WHO Global Health Estimates, 2013).

Hypertension Management

The WHO estimates that between 12 and 15 percent of the current population has elevated blood pressure, and the Global Burden of Disease study estimated that over 9 million deaths worldwide were attributable to high blood pressure in 2010 (Lim et al., 2013; World Health Organization, 2013b). Almost 40 percent of all hypertension deaths occurred in the 30- to 69-year-old age range, with 18 percent of all deaths in that age

Table 11.5 Population salt reduction, calculation inputs

Metric	Values	Source
Total deaths averted by reducing population salt intake by 30 percent over 10 years in 30- to 69-year-old age range*	6.7 million	Asaria et al. (2007)
Population increase from 2015–2030	22%	WHO Global Health Estimates (2013)
Projected deaths averted in 30- to 69-year-old age range in year 2030	.815 million	Calculation
Average annual cost per person to implement voluntary salt reduction in processed foods	$0.09 USD	Asaria et al. (2007)
Projected population of LMICs in 2030	7.1 billion	WHO Global Health Estimates (2013)
Total cost of implementing the intervention in LMICs in 2030	$639 million	Calculation

* Numbers from study represent only 23 low- and middle-income countries that represent 80 percent of the global salt burden.
Source: Asaria P., Chisholm D., Mathers C., Ezzati M., Beaglehole R. Chronic disease prevention: health effects and financial costs of strategies to reduce salt intake and control tobacco use. *The Lancet* 2007; 370(9604): 2044–53. World Health Organization, *WHO Report on the Global Tobacco Epidemic, 2013: Enforcing bans on tobacco advertising, promotion and sponsorship.* Geneva, Switzerland: World Health Organization, 2013.

range attributable to high blood pressure (HBP) (Lim et al., 2013; WHO Global Health Estimates, 2013). We calculated the number of deaths due to high blood pressure in 2030, assuming 50 percent intervention coverage and 50 percent successful adherence to the regimen. To avoid double counting the averted deaths from the salt reduction and hypertension management interventions, we subtracted our projected deaths averted from salt reduction from the estimated deaths averted from treatment of high-risk hypertension patients.

We only considered the LMIC population, as most people in HICs already have good access to healthcare services. Assuming only 40 percent of hypertensive patients needed to be on medication, and applying our assumption of 50 percent coverage, we used the Lancet Commission on Hypertension (Olsen et al., 2016) estimate of $19.50 USD per person per year to diagnose and treat hypertension to calculate the cost of expanded hypertension management (Table 11.6).

Secondary Prevention of CVD

Secondary prevention of CVD generally means putting those at high risk of CVD, or those who have had a nonfatal coronary heart disease or cerebrovascular event, on a multidrug regimen, which can prevent approximately 20 percent of deaths, assuming a 60 percent adherence to the daily regimen (Lim et al., 2007). We calculated the number of premature deaths that could be averted if at least 70 percent of high-risk people had access to secondary prevention care (WHO Global Health Estimates, 2013).

The same study estimated that the average annual cost to provide secondary prevention treatment to an individual would be about $55 USD (Lim et al., 2007). We used that figure to estimate the cost of reaching 70 percent of the high-risk population with the polydrug regimen (Table 11.7). We assumed a high-risk population of 100 million.

Value of a Statistical Life

We assumed each DALY was valued at $1,000 LMICs based on World Bank Data (Jha et al., 2012), as well as $5,000 for sensitivity as used in the CC2015 consensus paper on health (Hum et al., 2016). We considered the average age of premature death and the assumed life expectancy to move from deaths averted to DALYs. We then applied a 3 percent and 5 percent discounting function to the projected future DALYs averted before multiplying them by the aforementioned monetary value.

Table 11.6 Hypertension management, calculation inputs

Metric	Values	Source
Percent of 30- to 69-year-old deaths attributable to high blood pressure (HBP) in 2010	18%	Lim et al. (2013)
Total deaths in LMICs in 30–69 age range in 2030	21.6 million	WHO Global Health Estimates (2013)
Number of deaths in 30–69 age range attributable to HBP	3.9 million	Calculation
Hypertension management coverage	50%	Author assumption
Adherence to hypertension management	50%	Author assumption
Number of deaths averted from hypertension in 2030 in LMICs in the 30–69 age range	.77 million	Calculation
Number of people living with hypertension 30–69	573 million	WHO Global Brief on Hypertension (2013)
Percent of hypertension patients at medium to high risk	40%	Author assumption
Annual cost of hypertension diagnostics and medications per head	$19.50	Lancet Commission on Hypertension 2016 (Olsen et al., 2016)
Total cost of implementing hypertension management for medium- to high-risk patients at 50% coverage	$2.236 million	Calculation

Source: Lim S. S., Vos T., Flaxman A. D., et al. A comparative risk assessment of burden of disease and injury attributable to 67 risk factors and risk factor clusters in 21 regions, 1990–2010: a systematic analysis for the Global Burden of Disease Study 2010. *The Lancet* 2013; 380(9859): 2224–60. World Health Organization, *WHO Report on the Global Tobacco Epidemic, 2013: Enforcing bans on tobacco advertising, promotion and sponsorship.* Geneva, Switzerland: World Health Organization, 2013. WHO. *A global brief on hypertension: Silent killer, global public health crisis.* WHO/DCO/WHD/2013.2. Geneva, Switzerland: World Health Organization, 2013.

Table 11.7 Secondary prevention of CVD with polydrug, calculation inputs

Metric	Values	Source
Projected number of deaths due to cardiovascular disease in 2030 ages 30–69	6.3 million	WHO Global Health Estimates (2013)
Secondary prevention coverage	70%	Author assumption
Percent of deaths averted with polydrug over 10-year period, assuming a 60% adherence rate	20%	Lim et al. (2007)
Projected CVD deaths averted in 2030 in 30- to 69-year-olds due to secondary prevention	.88 million	Calculation
Number of individuals who would benefit from a polydrug treatment, ages 30–69	100 million	Author Assumption
Average cost per treated individual	$55	Lim et al. (2007)
Intervention cost of providing polydrug treatment at 70% coverage	$3,850 million	Calculation

Source: World Health Organization, *WHO Report on the Global Tobacco Epidemic, 2013: Enforcing bans on tobacco advertising, promotion and sponsorship.* Geneva, Switzerland: World Health Organization, 2013. Lim S. S., Vos T., Flaxman A. D., et al. A comparative risk assessment of burden of disease and injury attributable to 67 risk factors and risk factor clusters in 21 regions, 1990–2010: a systematic analysis for the Global Burden of Disease Study 2010. *The Lancet* 2013; 380(9859): 2224–60.

Results

This section provides an overview of the most cost-beneficial interventions to achieve the post-2015 NCD target. There is a broad range of reasonable estimates of the cost-effectiveness of most interventions (Gaziano et al., 2017; Jha et al., 2012), due to a combination of uncertainties in the data and sensitivity to prices and other factors.

Given the broad range of BCRs, we have simply identified major opportunities for investment in interventions that address a large disease burden highly cost effectively. Even valuing DALYs at a conservative $1,000 the benefit-to-cost ratios associated with investing in these opportunities are enormously high. This suggests that our results are conservative.

Earlier in the chapter the five interventions that we selected are listed. Costs of each intervention were taken from published estimates cited in Tables 11.2–11.7 to depict as closely as possible the full social costs of intervening but, absent social values in most instances, the costs reflect financial estimates. An indicative benefit-cost ratio is calculated.

Table 11.8 ranks interventions by benefit cost-ratio – from 31:1 aspirin therapy at the onset of an AMI to 3:1 for the multidrug therapy for cardiovascular disease prevention. Every intervention in the table has not only a high estimated benefit-cost ratio but also addresses major NCD disease burden. For example, despite considerable cost of $3.85 billion per year, secondary prevention with the multidrug regimen would avoid annually about 881,600 fatal heart attacks and strokes a year.

Taking aspirin at the onset of an acute myocardial infarction offers the highest benefit-cost ratio among the interventions in our list. It garners $31 in benefits for each $1 invested. Although the magnitude of lives saved is not as large as other interventions, the drug's low price and ease of administration makes it a feasible and affordable intervention.

Secondary prevention of CVD was the least cost-effective of the considered interventions, but still was effective at saving $3 for every $1 invested and averted the second highest absolute number of deaths.

These analyses are consistent with a recent World Health Organization (2011) report that examined both population-wide and individual-focused measures that low- and middle-income countries can take to reduce the burden of chronic diseases, and with the 2015 Global Status Report on NCDs (World Health Organization, 2011).

Table 11.8 Selected interventions to achieve post-2015 NCD target: benefits and costs, BCR (3% discounting)

| Target | Annual costs ($m) | Annual benefits ($m)* | | BCR | | Rating |
		DALY = 1000	DALY = 5000	DALY = 1000	DALY = 5000	(DALY = 1000)
Aspirin therapy at the onset of AMI (75% coverage)	$27.40	$836	$4,181	31	153	Excellent
Reduce mean population salt consumption by 30%	$638	$12,121	$60,607	19	95	Excellent
Increase the price of tobacco by 125%	$3,548	$37,194	$185,968	10	52	Good
Chronic hypertension management for medium- to high-risk patients (50% coverage)	$1,663	$11,446	$57,228	7	34	Good
Secondary prevention of CVD with polydrug (70% coverage)	$3,850	$13,116	$65,580	3	17	Fair
Total	**$9,727**	**$74,713**	**$373,564**	**8**	**38**	

Adding interventions that focus on individuals would result in a total cost of US$ 11.4 billion, implying an annual per capita investment of less than US$ 1 in low-income countries and approximately US$ 3 in upper-middle-income countries. Our estimates are in the mid-range of WHO's estimates for fully implementing high-priority population and individual level Best Buys.

Discussion

The opportunities identified earlier don't explicitly address the challenge of strengthening of health system capacity, nor the investment needed for the public sector to impose change on the private sector. This means we may be underestimating the full costs of health system improvements that are needed to scale up NCD interventions. The costs used in our BCRs are "fully loaded," in that they account for administrative and delivery costs, but most LMICs currently provide virtually no NCD services and will need to put in place systems to do so. In this respect, our results are intended as a complement to the Copenhagen Consensus recommendations for health system strengthening.

One might consider there to be two broad approaches to strengthening health systems. One involves relatively nonspecific investments in capacity and reforms of process. The second involves creating specific capacity to deliver priority services in volume and with high quality, with capacity strengthening spreading out from high-performing nodes. The approach that this chapter implicitly advocates is very much in the spirit of the latter.

NCDs are different from most infectious and child diseases in fundamental ways that suggest changes in traditional global health programming models are needed. The following characteristics of NCDs are useful to keep in mind.

NCDs require complex care usually involving different kinds of caregivers, across different levels of care. A substantial care gap exists in the implementation of proven NCD interventions, including the WHO "Best Buys" and the MPOWER guidelines for tobacco control and prevention. One study found that the economic status of a country accounted for about two-thirds of the variation in use of recommended prevention therapy, while the other one-third related to individual patient factors (Yusuf et al., 2011). Even in high-income countries, a significant segment of patients with established heart disease are not adequately treated (Kotseva et al., 2009). Most hypertensive people are asymptomatic for years prior to having a cardiovascular event that could kill them. This creates challenges to finding and treating high-risk people, and the absence of obvious symptoms also impedes long-term adherence to medication.

The quality of care is also particularly important for NCD prevention and control because patients are often unmotivated to seek care and uninformed about risks and potential outcomes. Because NCDs progress in a more variable manner than acute conditions, and patients in LMICs often present late in disease progression, healthcare providers must be prepared to handle a broad range of conditions.

Behavior can place an individual at greater risk for developing NCDs. Individuals might engage in risk-taking behavior such as smoking or insufficient physical activity, for a variety of reasons.

NCD prevention and control require action outside the health sector and often through population-based measures. Yet coordination with actors outside the health sector can be difficult. Coordination in itself is costly and may involve significant political capital and upfront cost.

A broad set of changes will be needed for countries to meet the proposed NCD Target for Sustainable Development Goal #3: *Ensure healthy lives and promote well-being for all at all ages.* These must include more and better trained healthcare providers; simplifying treatment guidelines, formulations, and delivery; improving affordability; and more education and training for patients to take responsibility for their own disease management.

Conclusion

NCDs are the dominant health issue in almost all countries and regions. Even in poor countries, they are a current problem. They involve significant costs to society, to governments, and to individuals and households, especially where governments and donors are not providing many services (Bloom et al., 2011; Kankeu et al., 2013). One might reasonably ask, then, why are NCDs not among the stated priorities of more developing country health strategies and, by extension, the major global health funders?

Many factors interact to establish issues as global and donor priorities (Shiffman, 2009, 2010). Prominent among those that impede the advancement of investments and action for NCDs is the view that LMIC health systems are not "strong" enough or sufficiently geared toward complex, chronic needs to effectively implement NCD prevention and control (Ali et al., 2013). If this is true – and even if it is, it is true by degree – then one solution (the one taken by major external funders so far) is to wait until LMICs become wealthy enough to gradually add NCD services to their public health provision and let the private market provide whatever services can be paid for privately. This approach is socially and morally vacuous and raises the specter of undermining years of investments in LMIC health systems and economic development.

Fortunately, a diverse array of new programs and projects are underway to test the defeatist view that NCDs are too complicated for LMIC health systems to deal with. These include transferring knowledge and practice from existing areas of global health strength (such as HIV/AIDS) (Lamptey et al., 2011; Mattke, 2013); reconceptualizing primary healthcare to better align with population health needs (in SE Asia [Narain, 2011] and in Africa [Bukhman and Kidder, 2013]); developing new partnerships and methods that challenge current healthcare models (Alleyne and Nishtar, 2013); and filling in specific gaps in knowledge to strengthen existing systems (Smith and Yadav, 2013). All of these and other nascent efforts are establishing a new development paradigm that includes a broader definition of health and health systems (Wood and Babbington, 2011). This chapter demonstrates opportunities for improving health and well-being by reducing mortality from NCDs globally, achieving the SDG health goal, and strengthening health system capacities.

References

Ali MK, Rabadán-Diehl C, Flanigan J, et al. 2013. Systems and capacity to address noncommunicable diseases in low-and middle-income countries. *Science Translational Medicine* **5**(181): 181cm4–cm4.

Alleyne G, Nishtar S. 2013. Sectoral cooperation for the prevention and control of non-communicable diseases. In: Galambos L, Sturchio JL, eds. *Addressing the Gaps in Global Policy and Research for Non-Communicable Diseases.* Baltimore, MD: Johns Hopkins University.

Alwan A. 2011. *Global Status Report on Noncommunicable Diseases 2010.* Geneva: World Health Organization.

Asaria P, Chisholm D, Mathers C, Ezzati M, Beaglehole R. 2007. Chronic disease prevention: health effects and financial costs of strategies to reduce salt intake and control tobacco use. *The Lancet* **370**(9604): 2044–53.

Barton P, Andronis L, Briggs A, McPherson K, Capewell S. 2011. Effectiveness and cost effectiveness of cardiovascular disease prevention in whole populations: modelling study. *BMJ* **343**.

Bertram Y, Steyn K, Wentze-Viljoen E, Tollman S, Hofman J. 2012. Reducing the sodium content of high-salt foods: effect on cardiovascular disease in South Africa. *SAMJ: South African Medical Journal* **102**(9): 743–5.

Blecher E, Van Walbeek C. 2004. An international analysis of cigarette affordability. *Tobacco Control* **13**(4): 339–46.

Bloom D, Cafiero E, Jané-Llopis E, et al. 2011. *The Global Economic Burden of Non-Communicable Diseases.* Geneva: World Economic Forum.

Bukhman G, Kidder A (eds.). 2013. *The PIH Guide to Chronic Care Integration for Endemic Non-Communicable Diseases.* Boston, MA: Partners in Health.

Commission OM. 2013. *Now for the Long Term, the Report of the Oxford Martin Commission for Future Generations.* University of Oxford.

CVD. Prevention Roadmap Summit. www.world-heart-federation.org/publications/heart-beat-e-newsletter/heart-beat-july-2014/advocacy-news/cvd-roadmap/ (accessed January 5, 2015).

Galambos L, Sturchio JL, Whitehead RC. 2013. *Noncommunicable Diseases in the Developing World: Addressing Gaps in Global Policy and Research.* Baltimore, MD: Johns Hopkins University Press.

Gaziano TA, Opie LH, Weinstein MC. 2006. Cardiovascular disease prevention with a multidrug regimen in the developing world: a cost-effectiveness analysis. *The Lancet* **368**(9536): 679–86.

Gaziano, T., Suhrcke M, Elizabeth Brouwer, Carol Levin, Irinia Nikolic, Rachel Nugent. 2017. Costs and cost-effectiveness of interventions and policies to prevent and treat cardiovascular and respiratory diseases, Chapter 19 in Cardiovascular, Respiratory, and Related Diseases, Volume 5 in Disease Control Priorities, 3rd Edition, World Bank.

Hum R, Jordan K, Gauvreau CL, Jha P. 2015. Health: reducing premature mortality by 40% in the post-2015 consensus. Copenhagen Consensus.

Jha P, Chaloupka FJ. 2000. The economics of global tobacco control. *BMJ: British Medical Journal* **321**(7257): 358.

Jha P, Jacob B, Gajalakshmi V, et al. 2008. A nationally representative case–control study of smoking and death in India. *New England Journal of Medicine* **358**(11): 1137–47.

Jha P, Nugent R, Verguet S, Bloom D, Hum R. Chronic Disease Prevention and Control. Copenhagen Consensus 2012 Challenge Paper. 2012.

Jha P, Peto R. 2014. Global effects of smoking, of quitting, and of taxing tobacco. *New England Journal of Medicine* **370**(1): 60–8.

Kankeu HT, Saksena P, Xu K, Evans DB. 2013. The financial burden from non-communicable diseases in low- and middle-income countries: a literature review. *Health Research Policy and Systems* **11**: 31.

Kerr AJ, Broad J, Wells S, Riddell T, Jackson R. 2009. Should the first priority in cardiovascular risk management be those with prior cardiovascular disease? *Heart* **95**(2): 125–9.

Kontis V, Mathers CD, Rehm J, et al. 2014. Contribution of six risk factors to achieving the 25×25 non-communicable disease mortality reduction target: a modelling study. *The Lancet*.

Kotseva K, Wood D, De Backer G, et al. 2009. Cardiovascular prevention guidelines in daily practice: a comparison of EUROASPIRE I, II, and III surveys in eight European countries. *The Lancet* **373**(9667): 929–40.

Lamptey P, Merson M, Piot P, Reddy KS, Dirks R. 2011. Informing the 2011 UN Session on Noncommunicable Diseases: applying lessons from the AIDS response. *PLoS Medicine* **8**(9): e1001086.

Lim SS, Gaziano TA, Gakidou E, et al. 2007. Prevention of cardiovascular disease in high-risk individuals in low-income and middle-income countries: health effects and costs. *The Lancet* **370**(9604): 2054–62.

Lim SS, Vos T, Flaxman AD, et al. 2013. A comparative risk assessment of burden of disease and injury attributable to 67 risk factors and risk factor clusters in 21 regions, 1990–2010: a systematic analysis for the Global Burden of Disease Study 2010. *The Lancet* **380**(9859): 2224–60.

Liu B-Q, Peto R, Chen Z-M, et al. 1998. Emerging tobacco hazards in China: 1. Retrospective proportional mortality study of one million deaths. *BMJ* **317**(7170): 1411–22.

Mattke S. 2013. Learning from the HIV/AIDS experience to improve NCD interventions. In: Galambos L, Sturchio JL, eds. *Addressing the Gaps in Global Policy and Research for Non-Communicable Diseases*. Baltimore, MD: Johns Hopkins University.

Murray CJ, Lopez AD. 2013. Measuring the global burden of disease. *New England Journal of Medicine* **369**(5): 448–57.

Narain JP. 2011. Integrating services for noncommunicable diseases prevention and control: Use of primary health care approach. *Indian Journal of Community Medicine: Official Publication of Indian Association of Preventive & Social Medicine* **36**(Suppl1): S67.

NCD. 2012. *Global Monitoring Framework*. Geneva: World Health Organization.

Norheim OF, Jha P, Admasu K, et al. 2014. Avoiding 40% of the premature deaths in each country, 2010–30: review of national mortality trends to help quantify the UN Sustainable Development Goal for health. *The Lancet* **385**(9964): 239–52.

Nugent RA, Jamison DT. 2011. What can a UN health summit do? *Science Translational Medicine* **3**(100): 100cm25–cm25.

Olsen, M, et al. 2016. A call to action and a lifecourse strategy to address the global burden of raised blood pressure on current and future generations: the Lancet Commission on hypertension. *The Lancet* **388**(10060): 2665–2712.

Rubinstein A, Colantonio L, Bardach A, et al. 2010. Estimation of the burden of cardiovascular disease attributable to modifiable risk factors and cost-effectiveness analysis of preventative interventions to reduce this burden in Argentina. *BMC Public Health* **10**(1): 627.

Salomon JA, Carvalho N, Gutiérrez-Delgado C, et al. 2012. Intervention strategies to reduce the burden of non-communicable diseases in Mexico: cost effectiveness analysis. *BMJ* **344**.

Shiffman J. 2009. A social explanation for the rise and fall of global health issues. *Bulletin of the World Health Organization* **87**: 608–13.

2010. A framework on generating political priority for global health issues. *Injury Prevention* **16**(Suppl 1): A280–A.

Smith L, Yadav P. 2013. Improving access to medicines for non-communicable diseases through better supply chains. In: Galambos L, Sturchio JL, eds. *Addressing the Gaps in Global Policy and Research for Non-Communicable Diseases*. Baltimore, MD: Johns Hopkins University.

Sridhar D, Brolan CE, Durrani S, et al. 2013. Recent shifts in global governance: implications for the response to non-communicable diseases. *PLoS Medicine* **10**(7): e1001487.

Sweeney S, Obure CD, Maier CB, Greener R, Dehne K, Vassall A. 2011. Costs and efficiency of integrating HIV/AIDS services with other health services: a systematic review of evidence and experience. *Sexually Transmitted Infections* 88(2): 85–99.

United Nations General Assembly. 2011. Political declaration of the high level meeting of the general assembly on the prevention and control of non-communicable diseases. United Nations General Assembly. New York, NY.

Vassall A. 2014. Benefits and costs of the tuberculosis targets for the post-2015 development agenda. Copenhagen Consensus.

Wang G, Labarthe D. 2011. The cost-effectiveness of interventions designed to reduce sodium intake. *Journal of Hypertension* **29**(9): 1693–9.

WHO Global Health Estimates. 2013. Summary Tables: Projection of Deaths by Cause, Age, and Sex. July 2013 ed. Geneva: World Health Organization.

Wood J, Babbington G. 2011. *Healthcare in Asia: The Innovation Imperative*. London: The Economist.

World Health Organization. 2011. From burden to "best buys": Reducing the economic impact of non-communicable diseases in low- and middle-income countries, 2015 Global Status Report on NCDs. Geneva, Switzerland: World Health Organization, World Economic Forum.

2013a. Draft comprehensive global monitoring framework and targets for the prevention and control of noncommunicable diseases. Geneva: World Health Organization.

2013b. *A Global Brief on Hypertension: Silent Killer, Global Public Health Crisis*. Geneva: World Health Organization.

2013c. Global action plan for the prevention and control of noncommunicable diseases 2013–2020. World Health Organization.

2013d. *WHO Report on the Global Tobacco Epidemic, 2013: Enforcing Bans on Tobacco Advertising, Promotion and Sponsorship*. Geneva: World Health Organization.

Yusuf S, Islam S, Chow CK, et al. 2011. Use of secondary prevention drugs for cardiovascular disease in the community in high-income, middle-income, and low-income countries (the PURE Study): a prospective epidemiological survey. *The Lancet* **378**(9798): 1231–43.

Yusuf S. 2002. Two decades of progress in preventing vascular disease. *The Lancet* **360**(9326): 2–3.

CHAPTER 12

Benefits and Costs of the Women's Health Targets for the Post-2015 Development Agenda

DARA LEE LUCA, JOHANNE HELENE IVERSEN, ALYSSA SHIRAISHI LUBET, ELIZABETH MITGANG, KRISTINE HUSØY ONARHEIM, KLAUS PRETTNER, AND DAVID E. BLOOM

Introduction

Economists have long recognized the positive association between population health and income per capita. Traditionally, this association was viewed as reflective of a causal link from income to health. In recent years, robust evidence has been offered in support of the view that the association also reflects a reverse causal link from population health to income. However, this growing body of research has yet to identify the specific and essential role of women's health as a driver of economic growth. We believe that there are strong reasons to believe that female-specific health interventions are a sound investment for promoting economic well-being at both individual and population levels. In particular, we focus on vaccination against human papilloma virus (HPV), largely motivated by the substantial cervical cancer burden borne by women in resource-poor countries during what is often the most productive years of their lives.

Background

Cervical Cancer in a Global Context

Globally, cervical cancer is the fourth most common cancer among women, with more than a half-million cases diagnosed and more than 200,000 deaths reported every year. The burden of cervical cancer is disproportionately high in the developing world: about 85 percent of cases occur in less-developed countries, where the disease

represents the second-deadliest cancer among women (following breast cancer) (Ferlay et al., 2013). The impact of the disease is further accentuated by the young average age at death, often when women are most likely to be bearing children, raising and supporting families, and participating in the workforce (Arbyn et al., 2011). For these reasons, cervical cancer conveys potentially large negative familial and societal externalities, particularly detrimental to children of affected women.

In developed countries, adequate health system infrastructure, resources, and personnel have reduced the cervical cancer burden substantially, but fundamental challenges remain in developing countries (Gakidou, Nordhagen and Obermeyer, 2008). Virtually all cervical cancer cases are related to HPV infection, a sexually transmitted virus that can cause different types of cancer in both women and men (World Health Organization, 2007). It should be emphasized that the majority of women with HPV do not develop cervical cancer; rather, women become susceptible to developing cervical cancer following HPV infection, and other environmental factors are required for the cancer to develop.

Cervical Cancer Prevention: HPV Vaccination

In 2006, two vaccines[1] that protect against HPV came to market. Studies show that both vaccines

[1] Gardasil©, manufactured by Merck & Co., is a quadrivalent vaccine licensed to protect against HPV 16/18-related cervical, anal, vaginal, and vulvar precancers and cancers,

are safe and highly effective in preventing HPV 16 and HPV 18 – responsible for around 70 percent of cervical cancer – among girls who have not been previously infected (Lu et al., 2011; Markowitz et al., 2007; Pomfret, Gagnon, and Gilchrist, 2011). Immunizing girls before they begin to initiate sexual activity is a key strategy for preventing cervical cancer. The two vaccines have been licensed in over 100 countries as of 2014, and the list continues to grow (GAVI Alliance, 2014).

The HPV vaccination series requires three doses over six months; thereafter, the vaccine has been shown to remain effective for at least five years (dependent on full compliance with the vaccine schedule). Recent and ongoing research suggests that the vaccine remains efficacious even when fewer than three doses are administered (Kreimer et al., 2011). The American Cancer Society (ACS) recommends routine HPV vaccination for females ages 11 to 12 years, as well as for females ages 13 to 18 years to complete missed vaccination opportunities and finish the series (Saslow et al., 2007). The ACS also recommends screening according to the age-specific recommendations for the general population, including for women at any age with a history of HPV vaccination.

The market price of the HPV vaccine is considerably higher than prices for the traditional vaccines included in World Health Organization's (WHO's) Expanded Program on Immunization (EPI), and this can be partly attributed to the complex, patent-protected technologies involved (Light, 2006; Masia, 2008). Vaccine prices differ also by market. However, the Global Alliance of Vaccines and Immunization (GAVI) has recently successfully negotiated a price reduction for quadrivalent vaccine to US $4.50 per dose for GAVI-eligible countries (GAVI Alliance, 2014) (compared to upwards of $300 for the series in high-income countries such as the US (Jit et al., 2014). This dramatic price reduction will likely play a major role in facilitating the expansion of HPV vaccine coverage.

Cervical Cancer Prevention: Screening

The low-cost Papanicolaou test, commonly referred to as the "Pap test" or "Pap smear," is one of the most reliable and widely used cervical cancer screening tests available (Chen et al., 2011). Cells collected from the cervix during a pelvic examination are analyzed under a microscope for evidence of precancers. Through such screening programs, cell changes on the cervix can be detected and treated appropriately before potentially developing into cervical cancer. Screening guidelines vary by country, but in general, screening is recommended to start at about the age of 20 or 25, continue until about the age of 50 or 60, and occur every three to five years (Strander, 2009).

Widespread screening and subsequent diagnosis has led to a dramatic drop in cervical cancer rates and deaths in developed countries (Arbyn et al., 2010; Schiffman et al., 2007), but not in developing countries (Miller et al., 2000). Screening programs have been implemented in developing countries since the early 1980s, yet have failed to reduce cervical cancer mortality rates, in part due to lack of information, access, and infrastructure (Denny, Quinn, and Sankaranarayanan, 2006). Conventional cytology screening is resource- and time-intensive, and in 2002 the WHO estimated that only 5 percent of women in developing countries were screened appropriately (Saleh, 2013).

There has hence been considerable interest in alternative methods for cervical cancer screening, such as visual inspection with acetic acid (VIA) and DNA testing for HPV. VIA is as effective as Pap tests in detecting precancerous cells (Qureshi, Das, and Zahra, 2010), but is easier to use and lower cost. VIA also has the advantage of a "screen-and-treat" feature, whereby acetic acid elicits acetowhitening in the presence of cervical intraepithelial neoplasia (CIN), or premalignant growth, which can be detected and treated in the same visit (Denny, Quinn, and Sankaranarayanan, 2006).

Although both Pap and VIA tests are effective and relatively low-cost cervical cancer screening methods, it is still a challenge to expand screening

and HPV 6/11-related genital warts; it provides protection against 70 percent of cervical cancer cases. Cervarix©, produced by GlaxoSmithKline, is a bivalent vaccine that protects against HPV types 16/18.

coverage sufficiently to developing countries. It is not clear that pushing VIA would necessarily reduce cervical cancer incidence substantially, as critical barriers remain both within and outside the healthcare system. In the absence of a vaccine, all HPV-related treatment and care depends on patients having the time and resources needed to travel to appointments, receive treatments, and recover. This may not be the optimal strategy for tackling cervical cancer given the high costs of treatment in developing countries (Denny, Quinn, and Sankaranarayanan, 2006).

We therefore argue that wide-scale implementation of HPV vaccination programs, specifically through programs at schools, may be more effective in reducing cervical cancer incidence in developing countries. Ideally, screening using VIA should also be continued in conjunction with vaccination, as recommended in most developed countries. However, screening women within 5–10 years of first sexual intercourse, as currently recommended by guidelines in many developed countries, may not be efficient. Combined with increased coverage of vaccination, we recommend that screening begin closer to peak ages of cervical cancer risk, starting from around age 35 and peaking near age 65 (Gustafsson et al., 1997), after which incidence rates decline dramatically.

Conceptual Framework and Supporting Evidence

In this section, we consider the full economic benefits of increasing HPV vaccination.

Direct Health Gains

This category of benefit refers to a reduction in disease or mortality resulting from vaccination. Increasing HPV vaccination may directly reduce morbidity and mortality from HPV types 16/18, 6/11 (and others) through cross-protection. Furthermore, because HPV infection may increase the risk of acquiring HIV (Averbach et al., 2010; Smith et al., 2010), it is plausible to consider further the role HPV vaccination could serve in providing cross-protection against other sexually transmitted infections (STI) (also see Figure 12.1). Anal cancer, 90 percent of which is caused by HPV, could be averted either via the direct vaccination of men or through cross-protection from vaccinating women. HPV vaccination could also lead to fewer vaginal and vulvar cancers, roughly 40 percent of which are caused by HPV. Finally, the mental health strain that accompanies disease and treatment should also be considered. Studies have shown that cervical cancer survivors may suffer from the

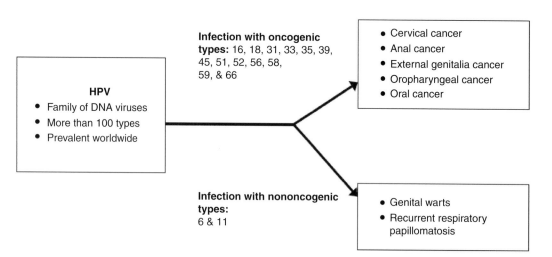

Figure 12.1 *The HPV virus family, comprised of more than 100 related viruses, and the health complications specific to oncogenic and nononcogenic types, respectively*

Source: Bärnighausen et al., 2012

lingering effects of depression for many years after treatment (Greimel et al., 2009).

Healthcare Cost Savings

For HPV vaccination, healthcare cost savings can result from avoiding direct medical costs (e.g., medications, doctor visits, lab costs, hospitalizations) and direct, nonmedical costs (e.g., transport) because the burden of illness is reduced. There may also be health cost savings in other dimensions realized from averted treatment of mental health strains, other cancers, and other STIs via increasing HPV vaccination. This category of benefit is almost universally accounted for in economic evaluations of vaccination.

Care-Related Productivity Gains

There is an opportunity cost to seeking treatment, receiving care, or recovering from HPV-related health outcomes: time away from wage-earning work for both the individual receiving care and the caregiver. Family, friends, and others may participate in caregiving. With higher HPV vaccination coverage, there could be productivity gains from averted missed work for vaccinated individuals, as well as averted missed work for potential caregivers.

Outcome-Related Productivity Gains

It is not uncommon for patients with HPV-related cancers to disengage from the workforce temporarily or permanently, leading to lost productivity and income, with disease tending to strike during economically active years. In particular, age-specific incidence and mortality owing to cervical cancer often overlap with the age range when the majority of women are economically active in many countries. Although patterns differ by country, the data suggest that withdrawal from the workforce could hurt productivity at both the household and national levels, and these losses in future earnings and productivity would be mitigated if effective vaccination programs were in operation. Other potential gains could result from the prevention of HPV-related disease, such as anal cancer in men. In summary, productivity gains may lead to less need for care, fewer career interruptions and impacts, and higher lifetime hours worked (length of the productive period), as well as higher productivity and earnings per hour worked. These substantive gains in productivity are typically not taken into account in cost-effective analyses of HPV vaccination.

Behavior-Related Productivity Gains

Behavior-related productivity gains can result when vaccination improves health and survival and thereby changes individual behavior. With regard to HPV vaccination, there are two main ways this can happen. First, reduced risk of HPV may impact educational choices and investment for the children of the vaccinated person. Second, reduced risk of HPV could also impact protective behavior. There is already well-established evidence that household-level behavior changes as a result of cervical cancer, for example, decreased daily food consumption among patients in Argentina (Arrossi et al., 2007). Among these households, a host of education-related impacts were also incurred, including absenteeism and difficulty paying for education. With a successful vaccination program, and a subsequent reduction in cervical cancer, we anticipate these negative behavior effects to be mitigated. Human capital investments in women could also be positively impacted as a result of women's improved longevity and health (Jayachandran and Lleras-Muney, 2009).

Community Health and Economic Externalities

Positive externalities include improved health outcomes among unvaccinated community members, including vaccination-related herd immunity effects (John and Samuel, 2000; Roberts, Mensah, and Weinstein, 2010). With regard to HPV vaccination, the specific community health externalities could include reduced incidence of HPV and HPV-related disease in unvaccinated community members. On a macrolevel, higher vaccination rates and reduced rates of cancer could potentially make an economy more desirable for foreign direct investment.

Given the sexually transmitted nature of HPV, herd effects could theoretically be realized in two ways: (Ferlay et al., 2013) by vaccinating both males and females, who would confer protection directly to their unvaccinated sexual partners; or (Arbyn et al., 2011) by vaccinating just females, which would reduce transmission to their unvaccinated male partners and, in turn, reduce transmission to their subsequent, unvaccinated female partners (Kim, Andres-Beck and Goldie, 2007), and so on. That said, most existing studies indicate that vaccinating girls along with screening would be more effective than vaccinating both boys and girls (Kim, Andres-Beck and Goldie, 2007; Kim and Goldie, 2009; Newall et al., 2007; Taira, Neukermans, and Sanders, 2004).

Mathematical models can predict the impact of herd effects from HPV vaccination, but recent empirical data have also made it possible to quantify and confirm them. A 2012 study from the United States reports a decrease in vaccine-type-specific HPV prevalence in both vaccinated and unvaccinated girls in the vaccinated cohort four years after introduction of the vaccine, suggesting evidence of herd effects in the community (Kim, Andres-Beck and Goldie, 2007). Data from Australia suggest a 44 percent decline in the incidence of male genital warts as a result of female HPV vaccination (Read et al., 2011).

Finally, health benefits may also accrue to children of the vaccinated person via reduction in the incidence of recurrent respiratory papillomatosis (RRP), though it should be noted that although serious, RRP is a rare condition (Venkatesan, Pine, and Underbrink, 2012). By reducing HPV-related genital warts in the mothers, the children would no longer be at risk for juvenile-onset RRP that occurs as a result of exposure to HPV in the perinatal period (Chesson et al., 2008). Consideration of these intergenerational health benefits is not currently standard practice in economic evaluations of HPV vaccination.

Costs of Increasing Coverage of HPV Vaccination

Substantial benefits could accrue from increased HPV vaccination coverage. We now move on to briefly discuss the related costs and infrastructure

that would be needed to substantially scale up HPV vaccination in less-developed countries.

The first thing to consider is the market price of the HPV vaccine. The vaccine is available (as of 2013) at the substantially reduced cost of under $5 in GAVI-eligible countries. However, there are also substantial system costs for an immunization program, including for introducing a new vaccine (e.g., investments in cold chain infrastructure and personnel training), as well as maintaining the vaccine in the national immunization program (e.g., costs of transportation, cold chain maintenance, and wastage). Research suggests that almost half of all systems costs spending are directed toward human resources items (Lydon et al., 2008), followed by investments in cold chain and maintenance, and then vehicles and transportation. In conducting a comprehensive benefit-cost analysis, it is critical to properly assess the systems costs required.

Given that the HPV vaccine does not align with other routine vaccinations, and that the vaccine is to be given in three doses over 12 months, there could be significant time costs incurred for seeking vaccination against HPV. However, when introduced through a school-based immunization program, these costs would be relatively low for school-age girls who regularly attend school. There is growing evidence from Africa, Asia, and Latin America that school-based HPV vaccination programs can be successful (Fregnani et al., 2013). In areas where the rate of school enrollment among girls is low, the time costs would be greater, and more involved community-based efforts will be needed to reach young girls.

Although adverse effects of vaccination are always a concern, there are reassuringly few adverse events following HPV immunization (CDC, 2013; Lu et al., 2011; Markowitz et al., 2007; Pomfret, Gagnon, and Gilchrist, 2011). Further, there is little evidence of risk compensation, i.e., individuals engaging in riskier sexual behavior after receiving the vaccine (Brewer et al., 2007; Marlow et al., 2009).

Comparison of Benefit-Cost Analyses

We present in Table 12.1 the benefit-cost ratios (BCRs) of four major female-specific interventions that have been examined in the literature.

Table 12.1 Comparison of benefit-cost ratios

Type of Intervention	Benefit-Cost Ratio (BCR) DALY = $1,000	Benefit-Cost Ratio (BCR) DALY = $5,000	Description of Strategy	Source Study	First Author	Year
Vaccination						
World*	3.39	16.97	Vaccination of 70% a single birth cohort of 9-year-old girls in 2007 with a 100% effective vaccine. Cost per vaccinated girl is I$25.	Health and economic outcomes of HPV 16,18 vaccination in 72 GAVI-eligible countries	Goldie	2008
Afr	3.37	16.85				
Emr	2.74	13.70				
Eur	2.68	13.42				
Amr	4.88	24.41				
Wpr	3.65	18.24				
Sear	3.37	16.86				
VIA (5, 35, 45 years of age) + Treatment						
World*	1.73	8.67	Visual inspection after application of 3–5% acetic acid (VIA) once every five years between the ages of 35 and 45; plus treatment.	Screening, prevention and treatment of cervical cancer – A global and regional generalized cost-effectiveness analysis	Ginsberg	2009
Afr	2.03	10.17				
Emr	1.60	7.99				
Eur	1.39	6.96				
Amr	1.57	7.83				
Wpr	0.99	4.96				
Sear	2.53	12.65				
Pap Smear (3, 20, 65) + Treatment						
World*	0.83	4.16	Administration of Pap smear once every three years between the ages of 20 and 65; plus treatment.			

(cont.)

Table 12.1 (*cont.*)

Type of Intervention	Benefit-Cost Ratio (BCR) DALY = $1,000	Benefit-Cost Ratio (BCR) DALY = $5,000	Description of Strategy	Source Study	First Author	Year
Afr	0.94	4.70				
Emr	0.56	2.78				
Eur	0.64	3.19				
Amr	0.83	4.13				
Wpr	0.37	1.87				
Sear	1.46	7.28				
Family Planning						
World*	30.00	50.00	Family planning programs broadly refer to programs that provide information about contraception, as well as contraceptives themselves and related reproductive health services	Copenhagen Consensus 2012: Challenge Paper on "Population Growth"	Kohler	2012

Notes: All data are discounted at a rate of 3 percent.

*The world averages for "VIA+Treatment" and "Pap Smear+Treatment" are weighted figures based on the number of countries included in each author's analysis.

**These figures reflect Kohler's lower-bound benefit-cost ratios, which account only for reduced infant and maternal mortality (not income growth realized through life cycle, distributional, and intergenerational benefits). When these additional income growth benefits are considered, Kohler's BCRs increase dramatically to 90 and 150, respectively. We hypothesize that capturing similar benefits in the HPV vaccination BCRs would also result in compelling increases across all world regions.

Source: Kohler, HP. Copenhagen Consensus 2012: Challenge Paper on Population Growth. PSC Working Paper Series. 2012: 1–79. Goldie SJ et al., Health and economic outcomes of HPV 16,18 vaccination in 72 GAVI-eligible countries. *Vaccine.* 2008: 26(32):4080–93. Ginsberg GM et al., C. Screening, prevention and treatment of cervical cancer – a global and regional generalized cost-effectiveness analysis. *Vaccine.* 2009: 27(43): 6060–79.

We first present data from HPV vaccination, followed by those from Pap smears administered according to current US recommendations (tri-annual between ages of 20 and 65), and penta-annual VIA screening from ages 35–45 (proposed as a more feasible and efficient strategy in low-resource settings). Finally, we present the BCR of family-planning programs, which has been previously studied as a Copenhagen Consensus Center (CCC) intervention and found to be highly cost-effective (Kohler, 2012).

As shown in Table 12.1, the BCRs from vaccination range from 2.7 to 4.9 depending on the region (assuming a disability-adjusted life year (DALY) is valued at $1,000),[2] but the BCRs are consistently higher than for the traditional screen-and-treat strategy. The average BCRs of Pap tests and VIA screening are lower at 0.83 and 1.73, respectively. When we assume that the cost per DALY is $5,000, the BCRs are even higher. The main assumption here is that the cost per vaccinated girl is I$25 (I),[3] which includes the three-dose vaccine (at I$5 per dose), wastage, freight and supplies, administration, immunization support, and programmatic costs (Goldie et al., 2008). Most existing studies suggest that HPV vaccination would be a cost-effective strategy if the cost per vaccinated girl were less than I$25. More complex models that take into account interaction effects from both vaccination and screening indicate that vaccination combined with screening at later ages would be even more cost-effective (Diaz et al., 2008; Goldie et al., 2007; Kim et al., 2007; Kim et al., 2008). An additional potential benefit that has not been taken into account is the savings that result from reduced frequency of screening.

While analyzing the BCR is appealing because of its simplicity, we caution that these ratios are aggregated from different sources. Although we attempt to standardize our inputs (e.g., adjusting all costs to 2005 international dollars when possible) there remain significant differences in the details of the assumptions. More important, as we emphasized earlier, an economic valuation of HPV vaccination should take into account the broader benefits of vaccination, and hence the estimates in Table 12.1 should be considered as conservative, lower-bound estimates.

Conclusion

Although cervical cancer is one of the most common and deadliest cancers, it is also one of the most preventable (Markowitz et al., 2012). Introducing wide-scale HPV vaccination to the developing world will reap substantial rewards. This strategy is consistent with the WHO Global Action Plan 2013–2020, for which one global target is to achieve a 25 percent relative reduction in risk of premature mortality from cardiovascular diseases, cancer, diabetes, or chronic respiratory diseases (WHO, 2013). Although the benefit-cost ratio of HPV vaccination is lower than previously studied CCC interventions such as family planning programs, it is also potentially more scalable and replicable, especially if school-based vaccination programs can be implemented and sustained.

A key prior barrier to wider adoption of the HPV vaccination in developing countries was the cost of the vaccine. However, at the greatly reduced cost of $5 per dose for GAVI-eligible countries, existing studies would suggest that HPV vaccination combined with screening could be very cost-effective. Nonetheless, any country considering adoption of an HPV immunization program will need to carefully evaluate the disease burden and existing healthcare infrastructure and determine whether it has the necessary resources to implement such a program. Other considerations include whether there exist competing and more cost-effective programs, and whether such a program would garner political and public support (Agosti and Goldie, 2007). For eligible countries, GAVI does provide different forms of support, from developing smaller-scale demonstration projects to national introduction.

[2] The regions featured in this analysis are aggregate figures adopted from the existing studies of Goldie et al., 2008 and Ginsberg et al., 2009, respectively, and reflect data representative of six WHO geographic areas: Africa (Afr), Eastern Mediterranean (Emr), Europe (Eur), Americas (Amr), Western Pacific (Wpr), and South East Asia (Sear).

[3] According to the World Bank, in any given country, an international dollar would buy an equivalent amount of goods and services as that of a U.S. dollar in the United States and is often used along with purchasing power parity. This hypothetical currency is commonly abbreviated as "I."

To conclude, we believe that scaling up HPV vaccination to 70 percent coverage – in conjunction with judicious screening guidelines – could be the key to reducing the burden of cervical cancer in developing countries. According to several studies (Ginsberg et al., 2009; Goldie et al., 2008; Jit et al., 2014; Van Kriekinge et al., 2014) a ten-year vaccination intervention has the potential to reduce the number of cervical cancer deaths by nearly 3 million. There could be substantial broader economic benefits that are not captured in existing analyses of cervical cancer vaccination. Our comparison demonstrates that the average benefit-cost ratio of HPV vaccination across GAVI-eligible regions is around 3.4, but we emphasize that this should be considered a lower-bound estimate, as it only captures health cost savings. If we take into account the broader economic and health externality benefits of HPV vaccination, the benefit-cost ratio should increase substantially.

References

Agosti JM, Goldie SJ. 2007. Introducing HPV vaccine in developing countries – key challenges and issues. *New England Journal of Medicine* 356(19):1908–10.

Arbyn M, Anttila A, Jordan J, et al. 2010. European Guidelines for Quality Assurance in Cervical Cancer Screening. Second edition – summary document. *Annals of Oncology* 21(3):448–58.

Arbyn M, Castellsagué X, de Sanjosé S, et al. 2011. Worldwide burden of cervical cancer in 2008. *Annals of Oncology* 22(12):2675–86.

Arrossi S, Matos E, Zengarini N, et al. 2007. The socio-economic impact of cervical cancer on patients and their families in Argentina, and its influence on radiotherapy compliance. Results from a cross-sectional study. *Gynecologic Oncology* 105(2):335–40.

Averbach SH, Gravitt PE, Nowak RG, et al. 2010. The association between cervical human papillomavirus infection and HIV acquisition among women in Zimbabwe. *AIDS* 24(7):1035–42.

Brewer NT, Cuite CL, Herrington JE, Weinstein ND. 2007. Risk compensation and vaccination: can getting vaccinated cause people to engage in risky behaviors? *Annals of Behavioral Medicine* 34(1):95–9.

Centers for Disease Control (CDC). 2013. Human papillomavirus (HPV) vaccine. www.cdc.gov/vaccinesafety/vaccines/HPV/index.html. Accessed November 13, 2014.

Chen MK, Hung HF, Duffy S, Yen AM, Chen HH. 2011. Cost-effectiveness analysis for Pap smear screening and human papillomavirus DNA testing and vaccination. *Journal of Evaluation in Clinical Practice* 17(6):1050–8.

Chesson HW, Forhan SE, Gottlieb SL, Markowitz LE. 2008. The potential health and economic benefits of preventing recurrent respiratory papillomatosis through quadrivalent human papillomavirus vaccination. *Vaccine* 26(35):4513–8.

Denny L, Quinn M, Sankaranarayanan R. 2006. Chapter 8: Screening for cervical cancer in developing countries. *Vaccine* 24 Suppl 3: S3/71–7.

Diaz M, Kim JJ, Albero G, et al. 2008. Health and economic impact of HPV 16 and 18 vaccination and cervical cancer screening. *India British Journal of Cancer* 99: 230–238.

Ferlay J, Soerjomataram I, Ervik M, et al. 2013. GLOBOCAN 2012 v1.0, Cancer Incidence and Mortality Worldwide. IARC CancerBase. http://globocan.iarc.fr. Accessed November 13, 2014.

Fregnani JH, Carvalho AL, Eluf-neto J, et al. 2013. A school-based human papillomavirus vaccination program in Barretos, Brazil: final results of a demonstrative study. *PLoS ONE* 8(4):e62647.

GAVI Alliance. 2014. 206,000 more girls to benefit from HPV vaccine with GAVI Alliance support. 10 countries approved in latest round of HPV vaccine demonstration programmes. www.gavi.org/library/news/press-releases/2014/206-000-more-girls-to-benefit-from-hpv-vaccine-with-gavi-alliance-support/. Accessed January 11, 2018.

Gakidou E, Nordhagen S, Obermeyer Z. 2008. Coverage of cervical cancer screening in 57 countries: low average levels and large inequalities. *PLOS Medicine* 5(6):e132.

Ginsberg GM, Tan-Torres Edejer T, Lauer JA, Sepulveda, C. 2009. Screening, prevention and treatment of cervical cancer – a global and regional generalized cost-effectiveness analysis. *Vaccine* 27(43): 6060–79.

Goldie SJ, Kim JJ, Kobus K, et al. 2007. Cost-effectiveness of HPV 16, 18 vaccination in Brazil. *Vaccine* 25(33):6257–70.

Goldie SJ, O'Shea M, Campos NG, et al. 2008. Health and economic outcomes of HPV 16,18 vaccination in 72 GAVI-eligible countries. *Vaccine* 26(32):4080–93.

Greimel ER, Winter R, Kapp KS, Haas J. 2009. Quality of life and sexual functioning after cervical cancer treatment: a long-term follow-up study. *Psychooncology* 18(5):476–82.

Gustafsson L, Pontén J, Zack M, Adami HO. 1997. International incidence rates of invasive cervical cancer after introduction of cytological screening. *Cancer Causes and Control* 8(5):755–63.

Jayachandran, S and Lleras-Muney A. 2009. Life expectancy and human capital investments: Evidence from maternal mortality declines. *National Bureau of Economic Research* 124 (1): 349–97.

Jit M, Brisson M, Portnoy A, Hutubessy R. 2014. Cost-effectiveness of female human papillomavirus vaccination in 179 countries: a PRIME modelling study. *Lancet Global Health* 2(7):e406–14.

John TJ, Samuel R. 2000. Herd immunity and herd effect: new insights and definitions. *European Journal of Epidemiology* 16(7):601–6.

Kim JJ, Andres-Beck B, Goldie SJ. 2007. The value of including boys in an HPV vaccination programme: a cost-effectiveness analysis in a low-resource setting. *British Journal of Cancer* 97(9):1322–8.

Kim JJ, Goldie SJ. 2009. Cost effectiveness analysis of including boys in a human papillomavirus vaccination programme in the United States. *BMJ* 339:b3884.

Kim JJ, Kobus KE, Diaz M, et al. 2008. Exploring the cost-effectiveness of HPV vaccination in Vietnam: insights for evidence-based cervical cancer prevention policy. *Vaccine* 26(32): 4015–24.

Kim JJ, Kobus KE, O'Shea M, et al. 2007. Impact of HPV vaccine duration and efficacy on cost-effectiveness of vaccination in Vietnam [Abstract: PS19–35]. *In: Proceedings of the 24th International Papillomavirus Conference and Clinical Workshop*. Beijing, China: CNKI.

Kreimer AR, Rodriguez AC, Hildesheim A, et al. 2011. Proof-of-principle evaluation of the efficacy of fewer than three doses of a bivalent HPV16/18 vaccine. *Journal of the National Cancer Institute* 103(19):1444–51.

Light DW. 2006. Pricing pharmaceuticals in USA. In: Temple NJ and Thompson A, eds. *Excessive medical spending: facing the challenge*. London: Radcliffe Publishing, 63–99.

Lu B, Kumar A, Castellsagué X, Giuliano AR. 2011. Efficacy and safety of prophylactic vaccines against cervical HPV infection and diseases among women: a systematic review & meta-analysis. *BMC Infectious Diseases* 11:13.

Lydon P, Levine R, Makinen M, et al. 2008. Introducing new vaccines in the poorest countries: what did we learn from the GAVI experience with financial sustainability? *Vaccine* 26(51):6706–16.

Markowitz, LE, Dunne, EF, Saraiya, M, Lawson, H, Chesson, H, Unger, ER. 2007. Quadrivalent Human Papillomavirus Vaccine Recommendations of the Advisory Committee on Immunization Practices (ACIP). MMWR. http://origin.glb.cdc.gov/MMWR/preview/mmwrhtml/rr5602a1.html. Accessed November 13, 2014.

Markowitz LE, Tsu V, Deeks SL, et al. 2012. Human papillomavirus vaccine introduction – the first five years. *Vaccine* 30 Suppl 5:F139–48.

Marlow LA, Forster AS, Wardle J, Waller J. 2009. Mothers' and adolescents' beliefs about risk compensation following HPV vaccination. *Journal of Adolescent Health* 44(5):446–51.

Masia N. 2008. The cost of developing a new drug. IIP Digital. http://iipdigital.usembassy.gov/st/english/publication/2008/04/20080429230904myleen0.5233981.html#axzz3Iy3tAKMB. Accessed November 13, 2014.

Miller AB, Nazeer S, Fonn S, et al. 2000. Report on consensus conference on cervical cancer screening and management. *International Journal of Cancer* 86(3):440–7.

Newall AT, Beutels P, Wood JG, Edmunds WJ, Macintyre CR. 2007. Cost-effectiveness analyses of human papillomavirus vaccination. *Lancet Infectious Diseases* 7(4):289–96

Pomfret TC, Gagnon JM, Gilchrist AT. 2011. Quadrivalent human papillomavirus (HPV) vaccine: a review of safety, efficacy, and pharmacoeconomics. *Journal of Clinical Pharmacy and Therapeutics* 36(1):1–9.

Qureshi S, Das V, Zahra F. 2010. Evaluation of visual inspection with acetic acid and Lugol's iodine as cervical cancer screening tools in a low-resource setting. *Tropical Doctor* 40(1):9–12.

Read TR, Hocking JS, Chen MY, et al. 2011. The near disappearance of genital warts in young women 4 years after commencing a national human papillomavirus (HPV) vaccination programme. *Sexually Transmitted Infections* 87(7):544–7.

Roberts RR, Mensah EK, Weinstein RA. 2010. A guide to interpreting economic studies in infectious diseases. *Clinical Microbiology and Infection* 16(12):1713–20.

Saleh, HS. 2013. Can visual inspection with acetic acid be used as an alternative to Pap smear in screening cervical cancer? *Middle East Fertility Society Journal* 19(3): 187–91.

Saslow D, Castle PE, Cox JT, et al. 2007. American Cancer Society Guideline for human papillomavirus (HPV) vaccine use to prevent cervical cancer and its precursors. *CA: A Cancer Journal for Clinicians* 57(1):7–28.

Schiffman M, Castle PE, Jeronimo J, Rodriguez AC, Wacholder S. 2007. Human papillomavirus and cervical cancer. *Lancet* 370(9590):890–907.

Smith JS, Moses S, Hudgens MG, et al. 2010. Increased risk of HIV acquisition among Kenyan men with human papillomavirus infection. *Journal of Infectious Diseases* 201(11): 1677–85.

Strander B. 2009. At what age should cervical screening stop? *BMJ* 338:b809.

Taira AV, Neukermans CP, Sanders GD. 2004. Evaluating human papillomavirus vaccination programs. *Emerging Infectious Diseases* 10(11):1915–23.

Van Kriekinge G, Castellsagué X, Cibula D, Demarteau N. 2014. Estimation of the potential overall impact of human papillomavirus vaccination on cervical cancer cases and deaths. *Vaccine* 32(6): 733–739.

Venkatesan NN, Pine HS, Underbrink MP. 2012. Recurrent respiratory papillomatosis. *Otolaryngologic Clinics of North America* 45(3):671–94, viii–ix.

World Health Organization (WHO). 2007. *Human papillomavirus and HPV vaccines: technical information for policy-makers and health professionals.* Geneva: WHO.

——— 2013. *Global action plan for the prevention and control of noncommunicable diseases 2013–2020.* Geneva: WHO.

Benefits and Costs of TB Control for the Post-2015 Development Agenda

ANNA VASSALL

Introduction

The economic case for investment in tuberculosis (TB) control is compelling. TB control has been part of an essential package of health services for most low- and middle-income countries (LMICs) for decades, based on TB control's relatively high returns. The economic case, put simply, is that TB treatment is low cost and highly effective and on average may give an individual in the middle of their productive life around 20 additional years of life, resulting in substantial economic and health return. Yet, to date, globally TB control is underfunded, both in relative and absolute terms (Floyd et al., 2013). The most recent global estimates suggest a resource gap of around US$2 billion per year (World Health Organization, 2014), with TB receiving less than 4 percent of total development assistance for health (compared to HIV receiving 25 percent, and maternal and child health around 20 percent) in 2011 (Viz Hub).

Background

In 2010, TB was ranked 13th in terms of its contribution to the global burden of disease, primarily impacting LMICs and the world's poor (Lozano et al., 2012). Over 9 million individuals fell ill with TB in 2013, and the annual number of deaths from TB was estimated at 1·4 million persons in 2013, which is on par with other major killers such as HIV and malaria (Murray et al., 2014). Around 13 percent of the annual cases of TB and around 30 percent of all TB deaths are among persons living with HIV (Zumla et al., 2013). HIV increases the risk of mortality, and the presentation of TB in those living with HIV is atypical, meaning

that TB, in those living with HIV, can be difficult to diagnose (Zumla et al., 2013).

TB has two stages: latent infection and active TB. Over two billion people worldwide are latently infected, and 5 percent of those develop active TB within 18 months, with a further 5 percent risk of developing active TB over a lifetime. The risk of developing the active form increases substantially after HIV infection. Most TB responds well to standard drug treatment, but there were almost half a million cases of multi-drug-resistant TB (MDR-TB) in 2013, with over 10 percent of these cases being extensively drug-resistant (XDR-TB) in some countries.

Between 1990 and 2010 there was a 38 percent reduction in the disease burden from TB (per 100,000 population) (Murray et al., 2012), and the mortality rate had fallen by 45 percent by 2013. Since 1995 it is estimated that 37 million lives have been saved (World Health Organization, 2016). However, absolute numbers continue to rise, with 7.1 million cases among HIV-negative individuals. The post-2015 strategy aims to end the global TB epidemic, with targets to reduce TB deaths by 95 percent and new TB cases by 90 percent between 2015 and 2035, while ensuring no family is burdened with catastrophic expenses due to the disease. Although progress in the last two decades suggests that TB control is beginning to work, an effective response has been hampered by weak health systems, poverty, and suboptimal medical technologies.

TB Control Interventions Required to Reach Post-2015 Goals

TB can be difficult to diagnose, and most programs rely on passive case finding. However, about 30 percent of all active TB cases go unrecognized, and latent TB is asymptomatic. The symptoms of (active) pulmonary TB include cough, fever, night sweats, and weight loss, many of which are similar to symptoms of common diseases. Pulmonary TB in those with HIV may be asymptomatic or may present with a lesser range and intensity of symptoms. Extrapulmonary TB can affect any organ of the body with varied symptoms and manifestations, and these symptoms may also present differently in those with HIV (Zumla et al., 2013). Some countries have adopted more active policies to find cases of TB among high-risk populations.

Providing preventative TB treatment in those populations with a high risk of developing active TB is recommended by the World Health Organization (WHO). The treatment of drug-susceptible TB involves delivering a standard low-cost (around $21 per person for drugs only) regimen of TB treatment, usually for six months. With good treatment adherence, treatment is very successful, with over a 90 percent cure rate in most settings. The treatment of MDR-TB is far more complex, can take 24 months or longer, and is also much less effective.

Strengthening TB control to achieve the post-2015 targets requires investment both in technology and the health systems that support the delivery of services (Stop TB, 2008). In order to identify TB cases, the health system has to be strengthened to recognize symptomatic patients quickly, even if patients are visiting clinics for other diseases or symptoms.

Despite the availability of screening, diagnostic, and treatment technologies for TB, there remains substantial scope for improvement. Investment in new diagnostic and treatment technologies may both substantially improve the efficacy of TB control and help address some of the numerous health system and patient side barriers to deliver service.

The Cost Effectiveness of TB Control

Using evidence from recent studies, a very broad cost per disability-adjusted life year (DALY) averted (across all studies) can be calculated for three main areas of intervention required to achieve the post-2015 goals: the identification and treatment of latent TB, the diagnosis and treatment of drug-susceptible TB, and the diagnosis and treatment of MDR-TB. However, working out one BCR that summarizes the overall cost-benefit of reaching the post-2015 is complex.

The cost-effectiveness of screening and treatment of latent TB in those with HIV is long established with over a dozen studies (Baltussen et al., 2005; Currie et al., 2005; Foster et al., 1997; Hausler et al., 2006; Maheswaran and Barton, 2012; Masobe et al., 1995; Pho et al., 2012; Rose, 1998; Shrestha et al., 2007; Sutton et al., 2009; Terris-Prestholt et al., 2008; Uhler et al., 2010) finding this intervention cost-effective: a selection of the more recent studies is provided in Table 13.1. Studies have typically arrived at estimates between US $100 and US$ 200 per quality-adjusted life year (QALY) or DALY averted for intensified case finding among those with HIV (or testing for HIV) in a range of LMICs settings, depending on the population group screened and the method used. There is much less known about the cost-effectiveness of more active forms of case detection.

The cost-effectiveness and affordability of first-line regimens for treatment of active TB is long established. The World Development Report in 1993 identified TB treatment as one of the most cost-effective components of a basic package of healthcare. Currently the cost-effectiveness of TB treatment (including costs of passive case detection and diagnosis) is estimated at between US$20 and US$270 per DALY, depending on the income level of the settings and the cost of the health system. One of the few cost-benefit studies for an LMIC setting conducted for TB (examining 10 years investing in TB control in India) finds a BCR of 115:1. The results are summarized in Table 13.2.

Diagnosing and treating MDR-TB may be more costly than treating drug-susceptible TB, but it has still been found to be cost effective. A systematic review by Fitzpatrick and Floyd, summarizes the evidence on the cost-effectiveness of treatment MDR-TB (Fitzpatrick and Floyd, 2012). It finds that the best estimates of the cost per DALY averted were US$598, $US163, $US143, and US$ 745, from studies in Estonia, Peru, the Philippines, and Russia, respectively. When these results are extrapolated to

Table 13.1 Summary of recent studies on intensified and active case finding, screening, and the treatment of latent TB

Setting	Population Group	Primary Result*	Approach Used	Source
Uganda	HIV-infected adults	Compared to no program, the incremental cost-utility of the targeted testing program was US$102/QALY gained	Empirical cohort study	Shrestha et al. (2007)
South Africa	All those being tested for HIV	Costs of US$ 81–166 for detecting a TB case compared to "do-nothing"	Empirical cohort study	Hausler et al. (2006)
Sub-Saharan Africa	All those testing positive with HIV	Screening all those testing positive with HIV with sputum microscopy, compared to a "do nothing" base case is US$149 per QALY. At prevalence higher than 10%, other strategies become cost-effective	Hypothetical modeled cohort of sub-Saharan Africa population parameterized from literature	Maheswaran and Barton (2012)
South Africa	All those starting HIV treatment	The incremental cost of intensive screening including culture was $360 per additional tuberculosis case identified.	Empirical cohort study	Bassett et al. (2010)
South Africa	All those visiting mobile services in community with high HIV prevalence	The cost of the intervention was US$1,117 per tuberculosis case detected and US$2,458 per tuberculosis case cured.	Empirical cohort study	Kranzer et al. (2012)
Mexico	Individuals at high risk for HIV infection over 20 years	The incremental cost per case of LTBI detected was US$730, cost per active TB averted was US$529 and cost per QALY gained was US$108.	Markov model for parameterized for Mexico	Burgos et al. (2009)
Population in a high burden country	Young household contacts	The discounted societal cost of care per life year saved ranged from US$237 (no-testing) to US$538 (IGRA only testing).	A decision analysis model was developed to estimate health and economic outcomes of five TB infection screening strategies in young household contacts	Mandalakas et al. (2013)
Population of India, China, and South Africa	General population using a combination of discrete (2-year) campaigns and as continuous activities integrated into ongoing TB control program	Discrete campaigns costing up to $1,200 per case actively detected and started on treatment in India, $3,800 in China, and $9,400 in South Africa were all highly cost-effective (using WHO thresholds)	Transmission model	Azman and Dowdy (2014)

* Results reported in the dollar years reported by each study.
Source: Shrestha et al.: Cost-utility of tuberculosis prevention among HIV-infected adults in Kampala, Uganda. *International Journal of Tuberculosis and Lung Disease* 2007, 11:747–54. Hausler et al.: Costs of measures to control tuberculosis/HIV in public primary care facilities in Cape Town, South Africa. *Bulletin of the World Health Organization* 2006, 84:528–36. Maheswaran H, Barton P: Intensive case finding and isoniazid preventative therapy in HIV infected individuals in Africa: economic model and value of information analysis. *PLoS ONE* 2012, 7:e30457. Bassett et al.: Intensive tuberculosis screening for HIV-infected patients starting antiretroviral therapy in Durban, South Africa. Clinical Infectious Diseases 2010, 51:823–9. Kranzer et al.: Feasibility, Yield, and Cost of Active Tuberculosis Case Finding Linked to a Mobile HIV Service in Cape Town, South Africa: A Cross-sectional Study. *PLoS Medicine* 2012, 9:e1001281. Burgos et al.: Targeted screening and treatment for latent tuberculosis infection using QuantiFERON-TB Gold is cost-effective in Mexico. The international journal of tuberculosis and lung disease: the official journal of the International Union against *Tuberculosis and Lung Disease* 2009, 13:962–68. Mandalakas et al.: Modelling the cost-effectiveness of strategies to prevent tuberculosis in child contacts in a high-burden setting. *Thorax* 2013, 68:247–55. Azman AS, Dowdy DW: Bold thinking for bold results: modeling the elimination of tuberculosis. *International Journal of Tuberculosis and Lung Disease* 2014, 18:883.

Table 13.2 Summary of key recent studies in the diagnosis and treatment of drug-susceptible TB

Setting	Population group	Primary result*	Approach used	Source
India	TB control in the general population	The cost of TB control averaged just US$26 per DALY gained over 1997–2006 and generated a return of US$115 per dollar spent.	Economic modeling based on country-level programme and epidemiological data from 1997 to 2006	Goodchild et al. (2011)
Ethiopia	TB patients	The cost per successfully treated patient was US$161.9 and US$60.7, depending on whether health facility or community DOT was used	Community randomized trial	Datiko and Lindtjorn (2010)
Ukraine	TB patients	The cost per DALY was US$ 55 using an ambulatory model of care	Empirical cross-sectional study	Vassall et al. (2009)
India	TB patients in public–private mix project	Average societal cost per patient successfully treated fell from US $154 to US$132 in the 4 years following the initiation of PPM	Empirical cross-sectional study	Pantoja et al. (2009)
South Africa	TB patients in public–private mix project	Cost per case cured ranges from (US $354–979) in private providers and public sites (US $700–1000)	Empirical cross-sectional study	Sinanovic and Kumaranayake (2006)
Five southern African settings	Presumptive TB cases	Xpert has an estimated cost-effectiveness of US$959 (633–1,485) DALY averted over 10 y. Across countries, cost-effectiveness ratios ranged from US $792 (482–1,785) in Swaziland to US$1,257 (767–2,276) in Botswana.	Transmission model	Menzies et al. (2012)
India, South Africa, Uganda	Presumptive TB cases	Average cost per DALY of TB diagnosis and treatment ranges from US$25 per DALY to US$ 85 per DALY (for a range of algorithms (including culture) and with and without Xpert)	Decision analytic cohort model	Vassall et al. (2011)

* Results reported in the dollar years reported by each study.

other settings, systematic review finds cost per DALY averted was lower than GDP per capita in all 14 WHO subregions considered.

Summary of Benefit-Cost Findings

Using the studies on cost-effectiveness outlined earlier (selected studies referenced in Table 13.3, and adjusted to 2013 US$) and then simply valuing health benefits using the Copenhagen Consensus methods, we find BCRs for TB diagnosis and treatment ranging from 11–192:1, depending on the cost and valuation of benefit used.

The **BCR for the diagnosis and treatment of TB** based on current screening practices is likely to be somewhere in the range of **11–192:1, depending on how the DALY is valued.**

For countries adopting **intensified case detection and treatment of latent TB for those living with HIV** to reach the post-2015 goals (most likely countries with high levels of HIV coinfection) this additional investment has a BCR of **6–47:1.**

Finally, for countries, also needing to **diagnosis and treat MDR-TB,** this additional investment has a **BCR of 0–5:1.**

Using the weighted average, based on 2013 global TB incidence and HIV coinfection, the

Table 13.3 Summary of benefit-cost ratios for key TB strategies

Intervention	Cost per DALY Range (2013 US$)		Benefit-Cost Ratio (low-range DALY) (2013 US$)		Benefit-Cost Ratio (high-range DALY) (2013 US$)	
Intensified case finding and treatment of latent TB (Maheswaran and Barton, 2012; Shrestha et al., 2007)	107	156	9	6	47	32
TB diagnosis and treatment (drug sensitive TB) (Goodchild et al., 2011; Vassall et al., 2011)	26	89	38	11	192	56
TB diagnosis and treatment (MDR-TB) (Fitzpatrick and Floyd, 2012; Oxlade et al., 2012)	217	2192	5	0	23	2

Source: Goodchild et al.: A cost-benefit analysis of scaling up tuberculosis control in India. *International Journal of Tuberculosis and Lung Disease* 2011, 15:358–62. Datiko DG, Lindtjorn B: Cost and cost-effectiveness of smear-positive tuberculosis treatment by Health Extension Workers in Southern Ethiopia: a community randomized trial. *PLoS ONE* 2010, 5:e9158. Vassall et al.: Reforming tuberculosis control in Ukraine: results of pilot projects and implications for the national scale-up of DOTS. *Health Policy Planning* 2009, 24:55–62. Pantoja et al.: Economic evaluation of public-private mix for tuberculosis care and control, India. Part II. Cost and cost-effectiveness. *International Journal of Tuberculosis and Lung Disease* 2009, 13:705–12. Sinanovic E, Kumaranayake L: Financing and cost-effectiveness analysis of public-private partnerships: provision of tuberculosis treatment in South Africa. *Cost Effectiveness and Resource Allocation* 2006, 4:11. Menzies NA, Cohen T, Lin HH, Murray M, Salomon JA: Population health impact and cost-effectiveness of tuberculosis diagnosis with Xpert MTB/RIF: a dynamic simulation and economic evaluation. *PLoS Medicine* 2012, 9:e1001347. Vassall A, van Kampen S, Sohn H, Michael JS, John KR, den Boon S, Davis JL, Whitelaw A, Nicol MP, Gler MT, et al.: Rapid Diagnosis of Tuberculosis with the Xpert MTB/RIF Assay in High Burden Countries: A Cost-Effectiveness Analysis. *PLoS Medicine* 2011, 8:e1001120.

Table 13.4 Benefit for every dollar spent on reducing incidence of tuberculosis

Target	Annual Cost for First Year (US$ millions)	Benefits ($millions)				Benefit for Every Dollar Spent			
		Discount Rate = 3%		Discount Rate = 5%		Discount Rate = 3%		Discount Rate = 5%	
		DALY = $1000	DALY = $5000	DALY = $1000	DALY = $5000	DALY = $1000	DALY = $5000	DALY = $1000	DALY = $5000
Reduce TB deaths by 95% and TB incidence by 90% between 2015 and 2035	$8,092	$132,856	$664,279	$111,288	$556,438	**$16**	**$82**	**$14**	**$69**

following overall BCR is estimated for reaching the post -2015 TB control goals. It should be noted that costs and benefits here represent total, not incremental, benefits of TB control from the current baseline. It should also be noted that annual total costs and DALYs averted are top end and assume full coverage from year 1 at incidence levels in 2015. Both cost and DALYs are likely to change over the next 20 years. The overall level of intervention and therefore total costs are likely to be lower at many points, either due to the time it takes to reach full coverage, or later on in the period due to the transmission impact of the interventions. The level of total DALYs averted may also vary, with earlier efforts having a greater transmission impact, but in the absence of country level data this cannot be determined in the analysis.

Conclusion

The WHO estimates that between 2002 and 2011, 43 million people were successfully treated for TB at a unit cost of between US$100–500 per person (Floyd et al., 2013). Continuing this effort may result in a return of up to US$56 per dollar spent.

This benefit will primarily accrue to the very poorest globally (Table 13.4). TB control continues to be chronically underfunded, yet the costs of addressing TB are not substantial compared to other development and health investments. The economic case for strengthening the health systems and services to support TB control presented here is therefore one of the most convincing in the area of public health today – and must be a core part of the post-2015 development effort.

References

Albert H. 2004. Economic analysis of the diagnosis of smear-negative pulmonary tuberculosis in South Africa: incorporation of a new rapid test, FASTPlaqueTB, into the diagnostic algorithm. *International Journal of Tuberculosis and Lung Disease* 8:240–247.

Anderson C, Inhaber N, Menzies D. 1995. Comparison of sputum induction with fiber-optic bronchoscopy in the diagnosis of tuberculosis. *American Journal of Respiratory and Critical Care Medicine* 152:1570–1574.

Andrews JR, Lawn SD, Rusu C, et al. 2012. The cost-effectiveness of routine tuberculosis screening with Xpert MTB/RIF prior to initiation of antiretroviral therapy: a model-based analysis. *AIDS* 26:987–995. 910.1097/QAD.1090b1013e3283522d3283547.

Atun R, Lazarus JV, Van Damme W, Coker R. 2010a. Interactions between critical health system functions and HIV/AIDS, tuberculosis and malaria programmes. *Health Policy Planning* 25 Suppl 1:i1–3.

Atun R, Weil DE, Eang MT, Mwakyusa D. 2010b. Health-system strengthening and tuberculosis control. *Lancet* 375:2169–78.

Azman AS, Dowdy DW. 2014. Bold thinking for bold results: modeling the elimination of tuberculosis. *International Journal of Tuberculosis and Lung Disease* 18:883.

Azman AS, Golub JE, Dowdy DW. 2014. How much is tuberculosis screening worth? Estimating the value of active case finding for tuberculosis in South Africa, China, and India. *BMC Medicine* 12:216.

Baltussen R, Floyd K, Dye C. 2005. Cost effectiveness analysis of strategies for tuberculosis control in developing countries. *BMJ* 331:1364.

Barter DM, Agboola SO, Murray MB, Barnighausen T. 2012. Tuberculosis and poverty: the contribution of patient costs in sub-Saharan Africa – a systematic review. *BMC Public Health* 12:980.

Bassett IV, Wang B, Chetty S, et al. 2010. Intensive tuberculosis screening for HIV-infected patients starting antiretroviral therapy in Durban, South Africa. *Clinical Infectious Diseases* 51:823–9.

Boccia D, Hargreaves J, Lonnroth K, et al. 2011. Cash transfer and microfinance interventions for tuberculosis control: review of the impact evidence and policy implications. *International Journal of Tuberculosis and Lung Disease* 15 Suppl 2:S37–49.

Burgos JL, Kahn JG, Strathdee SA, et al. 2009. Targeted screening and treatment for latent tuberculosis infection using QuantiFERON-TB Gold is cost-effective in Mexico. *The International Journal of Tuberculosis and Lung Disease: The Official Journal of the International Union against Tuberculosis and Lung Disease* 13:962–8.

Chihota VN, Grant AD, Fielding K, et al. 2010. Liquid vs. solid culture for tuberculosis: performance and cost in a resource-constrained setting. *International Journal of Tuberculosis and Lung Disease* 14:1024–31.

Currie CS, Floyd K, Williams BG, Dye C. 2005. Cost, affordability and cost-effectiveness of strategies to control tuberculosis in countries with high HIV prevalence. *BMC Public Health* 5:130.

Datiko DG, Lindtjorn B. 2010. Cost and cost-effectiveness of smear-positive tuberculosis treatment by Health Extension Workers in Southern Ethiopia: a community randomized trial. *PLoS ONE* 5:e9158.

Davis JL, Cattamanchi A, Cuevas LE, Hopewell PC, Steingart KR. 2013. Diagnostic accuracy of same-day microscopy versus standard microscopy for pulmonary tuberculosis: a systematic review and meta-analysis. *Lancet Infectious Diseases* 13:147–54.

Dawson R, Diacon A. 2013. PA-824, moxifloxacin and pyrazinamide combination therapy for tuberculosis. *Expert Opinion on Investigational Drugs* 22:927–32.

Denkinger CM, Kampmann B, Ahmed S, Dowdy DW. 2014a. Modeling the impact of novel diagnostic tests on pediatric and extrapulmonary tuberculosis. *BMC Infectious Diseases* 14:477.

Denkinger CM, Pai M, Dowdy DW. 2014b. Do we need to detect isoniazid resistance in addition to rifampicin resistance in diagnostic tests for tuberculosis? *PLoS ONE* **9:**e84197.

Denkinger CM, Schumacher SG, Boehme CC, et al. 2014c. Xpert MTB/RIF assay for the diagnosis of extrapulmonary tuberculosis: a systematic review and meta-analysis. *European Respiratory Journal* **44:**435–46.

Diacon AH, Dawson R, Von Groote-Bidlingmaier F, et al. 2013. Randomized dose-ranging study of the 14-day early bactericidal activity of bedaquiline (TMC207) in patients with sputum microscopy smear-positive pulmonary tuberculosis. *Antimicrobial Agents and Chemotherapy* **57:**2199–203.

Diacon AH, Pym A, Grobusch MP, et al. 2014. Multidrug-resistant tuberculosis and culture conversion with bedaquiline. *New England Journal of Medicine* **371:**723–32.

Dooley KE, Nuermberger EL, Diacon AH. 2013. Pipeline of drugs for related diseases: tuberculosis. *Current Opinion in HIV and AIDS* **8:**579–85.

Dowdy DW, Lourenco MC, Cavalcante SC, et al. 2008. Impact and cost-effectiveness of culture for diagnosis of tuberculosis in HIV-infected Brazilian adults. *PLoS ONE* **3:**e4057.

Dowdy DW, Maters A, Parrish N, Beyrer C, Dorman SE. 2003. Cost-effectiveness analysis of the gen-probe amplified mycobacterium tuberculosis direct test as used routinely on smear-positive respiratory specimens. *Journal of Clinical Microbiology* **41:**948–53.

Dowdy DW, O'Brien MA, Bishai D. 2008. Cost-effectiveness of novel diagnostic tools for the diagnosis of tuberculosis. *International Journal of Tuberculosis and Lung Disease* **12:**1021–29.

Dowdy DW, van't Hoog A, Shah M, Cobelens F. 2014. Cost-effectiveness of rapid susceptibility testing against second-line drugs for tuberculosis. *International Journal of Tuberculosis and Lung Disease* **18:**647–654.

Dye C, Williams B. 2000. Criteria for the control of drug-resistant tuberculosis. *Proceedings of the National Academy of Sciences* **97(14):**8180–85.

Ferroussier O, Kumar MKA, Dewan PK et al. 2007. Cost and cost-effectiveness of a public-private mix project in Kannur District Kerala, India, 2001–2002. *International Journal of Tuberculosis and Lung Disease* **11:**755–61.

Fitzpatrick C, Floyd K. 2012. A systematic review of the cost and cost effectiveness of treatment for multidrug-resistant tuberculosis. *Pharmacoeconomics* **30:**63–80.

Floyd K, Arora VK, Murthy KJ, et al. 2006. Cost and cost-effectiveness of PPM-DOTS for tuberculosis control: evidence from India. *Bulletin of the World Health Organization* **84:**437–45.

Floyd K, Fitzpatrick C, Pantoja A, Raviglione M. 2013. Domestic and donor financing for tuberculosis care and control in low-income and middle-income countries: an analysis of trends, 2002–11, and requirements to meet 2015 targets. *Lancet Global Health* **1:**e105–15.

Floyd K, Skeva J, Nyirenda T, Gausi F, Salaniponi F. 2003. Cost and cost-effectiveness of increased community and primary care facility involvement in tuberculosis care in Lilongwe District, Malawi. *International Journal of Tuberculosis and Lung Disease* **7:**S29–37.

Floyd K, Wilkinson D, Gilks C. 1997. Comparison of cost effectiveness of directly observed treatment (DOT) and conventionally delivered treatment for tuberculosis: experience from rural South Africa. *BMJ* **315:**1407–11.

Fofana MO, Knight GM, Gomez GB, White RG, Dowdy DW. 2014. Population-level impact of shorter-course regimens for tuberculosis: a model-based analysis. *PLoS ONE* **9:**e96389.

Foster S, Godfrey-Faussett P, Porter J. 1997. Modelling the economic benefits of tuberculosis preventive therapy for people with HIV: the example of Zambia. *AIDS* **11:**919–25.

Gler MT, Skripconoka V, Sanchez-Garavito E, et al. 2012. Delamanid for multidrug-resistant pulmonary tuberculosis. *New England Journal of Medicine* **366:**2151–60.

Goodchild M, Sahu S, Wares F, et al. 2011. A cost-benefit analysis of scaling up tuberculosis control in India. *International Journal of Tuberculosis and Lung Disease* **15:**358–62.

Hausler HP, Sinanovic E, Kumaranayake L, et al. 2006. Costs of measures to control tuberculosis/HIV in public primary care facilities in Cape Town, South Africa. *Bulletin of the World Health Organization* **84:**528–36.

Hughes R, Wonderling D, Li B, Higgins B. 2012. The cost effectiveness of nucleic acid amplification techniques for the diagnosis of tuberculosis. *Respiratory Medicine* **106:**300–7.

Islam MA, Wakai S, Ishikawa N, Chowdhury AM, Vaughan JP. 2002. Cost-effectiveness of community health workers in tuberculosis control in Bangladesh. *Bulletin of the World Health Organization* **80**:445–50.

Jack W. 2001. The public economics of tuberculosis control. *Health Policy* **57**:79–96.

Johnston JC, Shahidi NC, Sadatsafavi M, Fitzgerald JM. 2009 Treatment outcomes of multidrug-resistant tuberculosis: a systematic review and meta-analysis. *PLoS ONE*, **4**:e6914.

Kerkhoff AD, Kranzer K, Samandari T, et al. 2012. Systematic review of TST responses in people living with HIV in under-resourced settings: implications for isoniazid preventive therapy. *PLoS ONE* **7**:e49928.

Khan MS, Coker RJ. 2014a. How to hinder tuberculosis control: five easy steps. *Lancet* **384**:646–48.

2014b. Tuberculosis control: hard questions – Authors' reply. *Lancet* **384**:1744–45.

Knight GM, Griffiths UK, Sumner T, et al. 2014. Impact and cost-effectiveness of new tuberculosis vaccines in low- and middle-income countries. *Proceedings of the National Academy of Sciences* **111**:15520–25.

Kranzer K, Afnan-Holmes H, Tomlin K, et al. 2013. The benefits to communities and individuals of screening for active tuberculosis disease: a systematic review. *International Journal of Tuberculosis and Lung Disease* **17**:432–46.

Kranzer K, Houben RM, Glynn JR, et al. 2010. Yield of HIV-associated tuberculosis during intensified case finding in resource-limited settings: a systematic review and meta-analysis. *Lancet Infectious Diseases* **10**:93–102.

Kranzer K, Lawn SD, Meyer-Rath G, et al. 2012. Feasibility, yield, and cost of active tuberculosis case finding linked to a mobile HIV service in Cape Town, South Africa: a cross-sectional study. *PLoS Medicine* **9**:e1001281.

Lozano R, Naghavi M, Foreman K, et al. 2012. Global and regional mortality from 235 causes of death for 20 age groups in 1990 and 2010: a systematic analysis for the Global Burden of Disease Study 2010. *Lancet* **380**:2095–128.

Lu C, Liu Q, Sarma A, et al. 2013. A systematic review of reported cost for smear and culture tests during multidrug-resistant tuberculosis treatment. *PLoS ONE* **8**:e56074.

Maheswaran H, Barton P. 2012. Intensive case finding and isoniazid preventative therapy in HIV infected individuals in Africa: economic

model and value of information analysis. *PLoS ONE* **7**:e30457.

Mandalakas AM, Hesseling AC, Gie RP, et al. 2013. Modelling the cost-effectiveness of strategies to prevent tuberculosis in child contacts in a high-burden setting. *Thorax* **68**:247–55.

Marra F, Marra CA, Sadatsafavi M et al. 2008. Cost-effectiveness of a new interferon-based blood assay, QuantiFERON-TB Gold, in screening tuberculosis contacts. *International Journal of Tuberculosis and Lung Disease* **12**:1414–24.

Martinson NA, Barnes GL, Moulton LH, et al. 2011. New regimens to prevent tuberculosis in adults with HIV infection. *New England Journal of Medicine* **365**:11–20.

Masobe P, Lee T, Price M. 1995. Isoniazid prophylactic therapy for tuberculosis in HIV-seropositive patients – a least-cost analysis. *South African Medical Journal* **85**:75–81.

Menzies NA, Cohen T, Lin HH, Murray M, Salomon JA. 2012. Population health impact and cost-effectiveness of tuberculosis diagnosis with Xpert MTB/RIF: a dynamic simulation and economic evaluation. *PLoS Medicine* **9**: e1001347.

Moalosi G, Floyd K, Phatshwane J, et al. 2003. Cost-effectiveness of home-based care versus hospital care for chronically ill tuberculosis patients, Francistown, Botswana. *International Journal of Tuberculosis and Lung Disease* **7**:S80–85.

Mueller DH, Mwenge L, Muyoyeta M, et al. 2008. Costs and cost-effectiveness of tuberculosis cultures using solid and liquid media in a developing country. *International Journal of Tuberculosis and Lung Disease* **12**:1196–202.

Murray CJ, DeJonghe E, Chum HJ, et al. 1991. Cost effectiveness of chemotherapy for pulmonary tuberculosis in three sub-Saharan African countries. *Lancet* **338**:1305–08.

Murray CJ, Ortblad KF, Guinovart C, et al. 2014. Global, regional, and national incidence and mortality for HIV, tuberculosis, and malaria during 1990–2013: a systematic analysis for the Global Burden of Disease Study 2013. *Lancet* **384**:1005–1070.

Murray CJ, Vos T, Lozano R, et al. 2012. Disability-adjusted life years (DALYs) for 291 diseases and injuries in 21 regions, 1990–2010: a systematic analysis for the Global Burden of Disease Study 2010. *Lancet* **380**:2197–223.

Nganda B, Wang'ombe J, Floyd K, Kangangi J. 2003. Cost and cost-effectiveness of increased community and primary care facility involvement in tuberculosis care in Machakos District, Kenya. *International Journal of Tuberculosis and Lung Disease* **7**:S14–20.

Nunn AJ, Rusen ID, Van Deun A, et al. 2014. Evaluation of a standardized treatment regimen of anti-tuberculosis drugs for patients with multi-drug-resistant tuberculosis (STREAM): study protocol for a randomized controlled trial. *Trials* **15**:353.

Nunn P, Williams B, Floyd K, et al. 2005. Tuberculosis control in the era of HIV. *Nature Reviews Immunology* **5**:819–826.

Okello D, Floyd K, Adatu F, Odeke R, Gargioni G. 2003. Cost and cost-effectiveness of community-based care for tuberculosis patients in rural Uganda. *International Journal of Tuberculosis and Lung Disease* **7**:S72–79.

Orenstein EW, Basu S, Shah NS, et al. 2009. Treatment outcomes among patients with multidrug-resistant tuberculosis: systematic review and meta-analysis. *Lancet Infectious Diseases* **9**:153–61.

Owens JP, Fofana MO, Dowdy DW. 2013. Cost-effectiveness of novel first-line treatment regimens for tuberculosis. *International Journal of Tuberculosis and Lung Disease* **17**:590–96.

Oxlade O, Falzon D, Menzies D. 2012. The impact and cost-effectiveness of strategies to detect drug-resistant tuberculosis. *European Respiratory Journal* **39**:626–34.

Pantoja A, Fitzpatrick C, Vassall A, Weyer K, Floyd K. 2013. Xpert MTB/RIF for diagnosis of tuberculosis and drug-resistant tuberculosis: a cost and affordability analysis. *European Respiratory Journal* **42**:708–20.

Pantoja A, Floyd K, Unnikrishnan KP, et al. 2009. Economic evaluation of public-private mix for tuberculosis care and control, India. Part I. Socio-economic profile and costs among tuberculosis patients. *International Journal of Tuberculosis and Lung Disease* **13**:698–704.

Pantoja A, Lonnroth K, Lal SS, et al. 2009. Economic evaluation of public-private mix for tuberculosis care and control, India. Part II. Cost and cost-effectiveness. *International Journal of Tuberculosis and Lung Disease* **13**:705–12.

Pho MT, Swaminathan S, Kumarasamy N, et al. 2012. The cost-effectiveness of tuberculosis preventive therapy for HIV-infected individuals in southern India: a trial-based analysis. *PLoS ONE* **7**:e36001.

Pooran A, Booth H, Miller RF, et al. 2010. Different screening strategies (single or dual) for the diagnosis of suspected latent tuberculosis: a cost effectiveness analysis. *BMC Pulmonary Medicine* **10**:7.

Pooran A, Pieterson E, Davids M, Theron G, Dheda K. 2013. What is the cost of diagnosis and management of drug resistant tuberculosis in South Africa? *PLoS ONE* **8**:e54587.

Rao NA, Anwer T, Saleem M. 2009. Magnitude of initial default in pulmonary tuberculosis. *Journal of the Pakistan Medical Association* **59**:223–25.

Roos BR, van Cleeff MR, Githui WA, et al. 1998. Cost-effectiveness of the polymerase chain reaction versus smear examination for the diagnosis of tuberculosis in Kenya: a theoretical model. *International Journal of Tuberculosis and Lung Disease* **2**:235–41.

Rose DN. 1998. Short-course prophylaxis against tuberculosis in HIV-infected persons. A decision and cost-effectiveness analysis. *Annals of Internal Medicine* **129**:779–86.

Salomon JA Lloyd-Smith J, Getz WM, et al. 2006. Prospects for advancing tuberculosis control efforts through novel therapies. *PLoS Medicine* **3**(8).

Samandari T, Agizew TB, Nyirenda S, et al. 2011. 6-month versus 36-month isoniazid preventive treatment for tuberculosis in adults with HIV infection in Botswana: a randomised, double-blind, placebo-controlled trial. *Lancet* **377**:1588–98.

Scherer LC, Sperhacke RD, Ruffino-Netto A, et al. 2009. Cost-effectiveness analysis of PCR for the rapid diagnosis of pulmonary tuberculosis. *BMC Infectious Diseases* **9**:216.

Shah M, Dowdy D, Joloba M, et al. 2013. Cost-effectiveness of novel algorithms for rapid diagnosis of tuberculosis in HIV-infected individuals in Uganda. *AIDS* **27**:2883–92.

Shrestha RK, Mugisha B, Bunnell R, et al. 2006. Cost-effectiveness of including tuberculin skin testing in an IPT program for HIV-infected persons in Uganda. *International Journal of Tuberculosis and Lung Disease* **10**:656–62.

2007. Cost-utility of tuberculosis prevention among HIV-infected adults in Kampala, Uganda. *International Journal of Tuberculosis and Lung Disease* **11**:747–54.

Sinanovic E, Kumaranayake L. 2006a. Financing and cost-effectiveness analysis of public-private partnerships: provision of tuberculosis treatment in South Africa. *Cost Effectiveness and Resource Allocation* **4**:11.

2006b. Quality of tuberculosis care provided in different models of public-private partnerships in South Africa. *International Journal of Tuberculosis and Lung Disease* **10**:795–801.

2006c. Sharing the burden of TB/HIV? Costs and financing of public-private partnerships for tuberculosis treatment in South Africa. *Tropical Medicine and International Health* **11**:1466–74.

2010. The motivations for participation in public-private partnerships for the provision of tuberculosis treatment in South Africa. *Global Public Health* **5**:479–92.

Sinanovic E, Ramma L, Vassall A, et al. 2015. Impact of reduced hospitalisation on the cost of treatment for drug-resistant tuberculosis in South Africa. *International Journal of Tuberculosis and Lung Disease* 19(2):172–78.

Skripconoka V, Danilovits M, Pehme L, et al. 2013. Delamanid improves outcomes and reduces mortality in multidrug-resistant tuberculosis. *European Respiratory Journal* **41**:1393–400.

Steingart KR, Henry M, Ng V, et al. 2006. Fluorescence versus conventional sputum smear microscopy for tuberculosis: a systematic review. *Lancet Infectious Diseases* **6**:570–81.

Sterling TR, Villarino ME, Borisov AS, et al. 2011. Three months of rifapentine and isoniazid for latent tuberculosis infection. *New England Journal of Medicine* **365**:2155–66.

Stop TB Partnership. 2006. *Global plan to stop TB 2006–2015*. Geneva: Stop TB Partnership.

Stop TB. 2008. *Contributing to health systems strengthening: guidance to National Tuberculosis Programmes*. Geneva: World Health Organization.

Sutton BS, Arias MS, Chheng P, Eang MT, Kimerling ME. 2009. The cost of intensified case finding and isoniazid preventive therapy for HIV-infected patients in Battambang, Cambodia. *International Journal of Tuberculosis and Lung Disease* **13**:713–18.

Tanimura T, Jaramillo E, Weil, D. Raviglione, M, Lonroth K. 2014. Financial burden for tuberculosis patients in low- and middle-income countries: a systematic review. *European Respiratory Journal* 1763–75.

Terris-Prestholt F, Kumaranayake L, Ginwalla R, et al. 2008. Integrating tuberculosis and HIV services for people living with HIV: Costs of the Zambian ProTEST Initiative. *Cost Effectiveness and Resource Allocation* **6**:2.

Theron G, Peter J, Dowdy D, et al. 2014a. Do high rates of empirical treatment undermine the potential effect of new diagnostic tests for tuberculosis in high-burden settings? *Lancet Infectious Diseases* **14**:527–32.

Theron G, Zijenah L, Chanda D, et al. 2014b. Feasibility, accuracy, and clinical effect of point-of-care Xpert MTB/RIF testing for tuberculosis in primary-care settings in Africa: a multicentre, randomised, controlled trial. *Lancet* **383**:424–35.

Uhler LM, Kumarasamy N, Mayer KH, et al. 2010. Cost-effectiveness of HIV testing referral strategies among tuberculosis patients in India. *PLoS ONE* **5**.

van Cleeff M, Kivihya-Ndugga L, Githui W, et al. 2005. Cost-effectiveness of polymerase chain reaction versus Ziehl-Neelsen smear microscopy for diagnosis of tuberculosis in Kenya. *International Journal of Tuberculosis and Lung Disease* **9**:877–83.

Vassall A. 2013. Cost-effectiveness of introducing bedaquiline in MDR-TB regiments – an exploratory analysis. London: London School of Hygiene and Tropical Medicine.

Vassall A, Bagdadi S, Bashour H, Zaher H, Maaren PV. 2002. Cost-effectiveness of different treatment strategies for tuberculosis in Egypt and Syria. *International Journal of Tuberculosis and Lung Disease* **6**:1083–90.

Vassall A, Chechulin Y, Raykhert I, et al. 2009. Reforming tuberculosis control in Ukraine: results of pilot projects and implications for the national scale-up of DOTS. *Health Policy Planning* **24**:55–62.

Vassall A, van Kampen S, Sohn H, et al. 2011. Rapid diagnosis of tuberculosis with the Xpert MTB/RIF assay in high burden countries: a cost-effectiveness analysis. *PLoS Medicine* **8**: e1001120.

Viz Hub. Financing Global Health [http://vizhub.healthdata.org/fgh/]

Wells CD, Nelson LJ, Laserson KF, et al. 2007. HIV infection and multidrug-resistant tuberculosis: the perfect storm. *Journal of Infectious Diseases* **196 Suppl 1**:S86–107.

World Health Organization. 2011. *Guidelines for intensified tuberculosis case-finding and isoniazid preventive therapy for people living with HIV in resource-constrained settings.* World Health Organization.

2014. *Global tuberculosis report 2014.* Geneva: World Health Organization.

2016. Factsheet: Post 2015 Global Tuberculosis Strategy. http://who.int/tb/post2015_ TBstrategy.pdf?ua=1.

Zignol M, van Gemert W, Falzon D, et al. 2012. Surveillance of anti-tuberculosis drug resistance in the world: an updated analysis, 2007–2010.

Bulletin of the World Health Organization **90:**111–19D.

Zumla A, Raviglione M, Hafner R, von Reyn CF. 2013. Tuberculosis. *New England Journal of Medicine* **368:**745–55.

Zwerling A, White RG, Vassall A, et al. 2014. Modeling of novel diagnostic strategies for active tuberculosis – a systematic review: current practices and recommendations. *PLoS ONE* **9:**e110558.

Benefits and Costs of the Infant Mortality Targets for the Post-2015 Development Agenda

GÜNTHER FINK

Introduction and Background

The High-Level Panel of Eminent Persons (HLPEP) notes in its work on developing post-2015 goals that "... [i]nvesting more in health, especially in health promotion and disease prevention, like vaccinations, is a smart strategy to empower people and build stronger societies and economies" (United Nations, 2014, p. 38). It argues that solutions for child mortality are simple and affordable, and that therefore all preventable deaths should be averted by 2030, with a specific aim "... for an upper threshold of 20 deaths per 1000 live births in all income quintiles of the population" (United Nations, 2014, p. 38).

While estimating the feasibility of reducing infant deaths overall, we zoom in on neonatal mortality (deaths in the first 28 days of children's life), which accounts for over 40 percent of total under-five mortality today and will become the main area to tackle for most countries if major progress in under-five mortality is to be made over the next 15 years.

Under-five Mortality Today and Global Progress Made over the Period 1990–2013

Major progress has been made in the realm of child mortality over the past 40 years. While close to 18 million children died before reaching their fifth birthday globally in 1970, this had been reduced to less than 7 million in 2013 (UN Inter-agency Group for Child Mortality Estimation [IGME], 2014), at the same time as the number or births has increased.

Table 14.1 shows that there has also been a shift in the distribution of deaths within the first five years: while early neonatal mortality (deaths in the first seven days of children's lives) accounted only for about 22 percent in 1970, it accounts for 32 percent of total mortality today; less than 29 percent of total under-five deaths today occur among children after the first 12 months of their life.

Figure 14.1 shows the current child mortality burden by cause of death, highlighting the relatively large share of current under-five mortality occurring in the neonatal period (first 28 days) and that the most common cause is simple prematurity.[1] This analysis also shows the rather remarkable progress in reducing mortality from infectious diseases. However, this means that the global burden of under-five mortality would still exceed 4 million deaths per year, even if the world was to eradicate all of these infectious diseases and the number of births per year was to remain constant.

Trends and Projections: What Improvements Are Feasible?

The remarkable reduction in the number of infant deaths has been accompanied by a change in geographic distribution. While only one-third of under-five deaths occurred in Africa in 1990, the continent accounts for more than 50 percent of under-five deaths today (see Table 14.2). Going forward, Africa is likely to account for an even larger fraction of child deaths due to both continued high fertility rates and the generally slower rates of progress made for child mortality.

[1] Prematurity is defined as delivery prior to 37 weeks of gestation.

Table 14.1 Global trends in neonatal, infant, and under-five mortality

	1970	1990	2013	% change 1970–1990	% change 1990–2013
Early neonatal deaths (0–6 days)	3,886.0	3,256.8	2,001.4	−16.2%	−38.5%
Late neonatal deaths (7–28 days)	1,999.8	1,207.9	610.7	−39.6%	−49.4%
Post neonatal deaths (29–364 days)	5,636.5	3,853.7	1,847.8	−31.6%	−52.1%
Childhood deaths (1–4 years)	6,088.4	3,826.8	1,816.0	−37.1%	−52.5%
Total under-5 deaths	17,610.7	12,145.2	6,275.9	−31.0%	−48.3%

Source: Wang et al. (2014), own calculations. Numbers in columns 1–3 are in thousands.

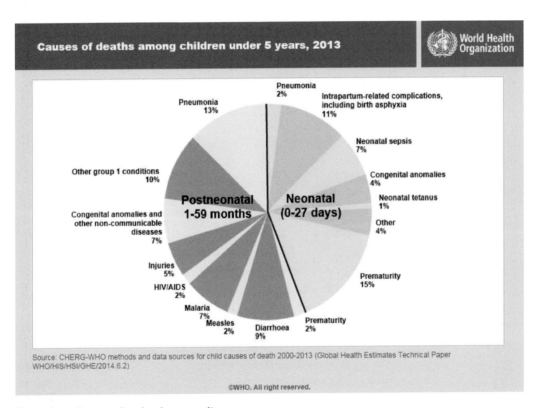

Figure 14.1 *Causes of under-five mortality*

In general, the last decades have seen a remarkable amount of convergence in health outcomes, with countries with initially high mortality achieving the largest improvements in health, even in settings with poor or negative economic growth. As a result of these trends, countries with the same levels of incomes experience substantially lower child mortality outcomes today compared to 40 years ago, a pattern that was highlighted in the seminal work by Preston (1975) and subsequent work by Soares (2005) and Bloom et al. (Bloom, Canning, et al., 2009). This pattern of convergence in mortality is illustrated in Figure 14.2, which shows the improvements in infant mortality over the period 1990–2013 as a function of infant mortality levels in 1990.

Table 14.2 Regional distribution of child death by age group

	Under-5 deaths ('000)		Infant Deaths ('000)		Neonatal Deaths ('000)	
	1990	2013	1990	2013	1990	2013
Africa	4,076	3,208	2,508	2,166	1,086	1,120
Asia	7,735	2,784	5,682	2,228	3,211	1,490
Europe	167	50	140	42	89	28
Latin America	628	196	497	167	255	101
North America	47	31	39	27	24	18
Oceania	17	16	13	12	6	7
World	12,670	6,285	8,879	4,642	4,671	2,764

Source: UN Inter-agency Group for Child Mortality Estimation (2014).

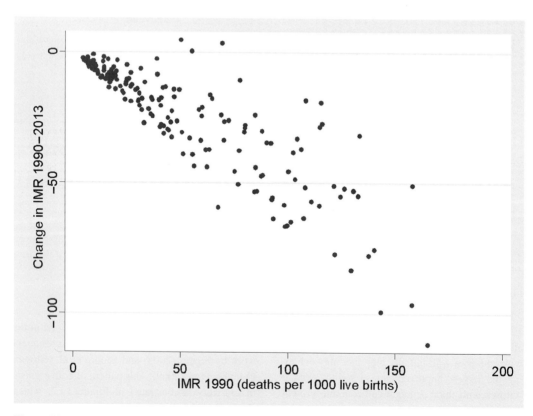

Figure 14.2 *Changes in infant mortality, 1990–2013*

Source: Mortality data from IGME (2014); own calculations.

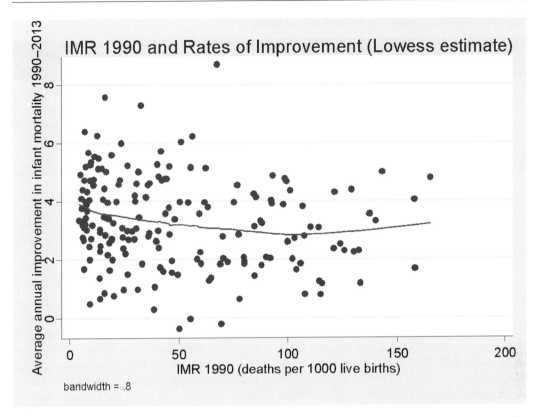

Figure 14.3 *Annual rates of improvements in infant mortality, 1990–2013, versus infant mortality in 1990*

The much lower rates of infant mortality today naturally raise the question of how much of an improvement could or will be possible over the coming few years. On average, IMR improved by 3 percent annually over the 1990–2013 period. If the same annual improvements can be achieved over the period 2013–2030, average IMR would be 20.5 globally in 2030. This is close to the overall target of 20 deaths per 1000 outlined by the HLPEP (2014), but our calculations do not take mortality after age one into account (which would mean an additional 5–10 deaths per 1000); they also just reflect a global average, which is very different from setting this common objective for all countries.

At a country level, current differences in mortality outcomes are large, and these differences are likely to persist in future years. Assuming constant rates of annual improvements between 2015 and 2030, more than 30 countries will have infant mortality rates in excess of 30 per 1000 in 2030 (and many more will have under-five mortality rates above this level). Figure 14.3 shows the annual rates of improvement in IMR between 1990 and 2013 as a function of 1990 infant mortality rates – there is very little evidence that countries with higher initial rates have been able to improve faster.

An alternative approach to assess what is feasible for countries is to look at the likely distribution of income per capita in 2030. Given the relatively large amounts of private and public health resources needed to achieve positive health outcomes, the cross-sectional relationship between infant mortality rates and income per capita is rather strong (−0.53 direct correlation, −0.79 when taking the natural logarithm of income).

One of the primary concerns with a uniform target is that countries with low incomes might not be able to achieve low rates of infant mortality.

Table 14.3 Income per capita and distribution of infant mortality rates

| | Income per capita 2011 | | Infant mortality rate 2013 (deaths per 1000) | | |
Quintile	From	To	Mean	Min	Max
1	291	2,217	55	14	107
2	2,339	5,146	36	8	102
3	5,219	12,155	17	6	69
4	12,403	25,081	10	2	47
5	25,556	124,720	4	2	13

Table 14.3 quite nicely illustrates the strong associations between income per capita and health: average infant mortality rates are 55 in the lowest quintile, and only 4 deaths per 1000 in the top bracket.

What is more remarkable, though, is the large heterogeneity in mortality outcomes in the bottom two brackets. In the lowest income quintile (< US$ 2220 per capita in 2013), the country with the best performance by far in 2013 was El Salvador, with an estimated IMR of 13.5; the only other country with an IMR of < 30 is Kyrgyzstan; both countries do, however, constitute outliers, with few other countries achieving levels below 40.

In the second bracket (US$ 2300–5150), outcomes look on average much more positive, with four countries having achieved IMR < 15 (Jamaica, Moldova, Sri Lanka, and Syria), and several more having achieved rates below 30.

Overall, these results suggest that infant mortality rates decline by about five deaths for every 1000 US$ of income per capita; the overwhelming majority of children today die in the bottom two quintiles, where average income per capita is about US$ 2500. Even if these countries should develop well economically in the period 2015–2030, large improvements in the average resources locally available do not seem likely, and meeting the uniform target is infeasible.

Infant Mortality Interventions, Targets, and Cost Effectiveness

We now concentrate on neonatal mortality. Several recent studies have highlighted that the majority of

neonatal deaths (as well as under-five deaths) occur in relatively few countries. In the case of neonatal mortality, eight countries – with a combined population of 3.5 billion, or 50 percent of the world population today, account for about two-thirds of all neonatal deaths. Table 14.4 shows the relative importance of the three main causes of neonatal deaths in these countries. Although the overall patterns appear fairly consistent, a few differences are worth highlighting: first, the relative contribution of prematurity in India is substantially higher than in other countries, likely related to frequently small maternal stature and the high prevalence of maternal undernutrition. Ethiopia fares worst with respect to interpartum complications, which is likely related to very low rates of births attended by skilled providers in the country.

Major progress is only possible via improved health services. Several recent studies have attempted to estimate the global cost of scaling up health services as summarized in Bhutta et al. (2014):

1. **Antenatal care services**: folic acid supplementation to prevent congenital anomalies; multi-micronutrient and energy supplementation as well as malaria prevention in pregnancy to reduce the likelihood of low birth weight and prematurity.
2. **Care during childbirth**: clean birth at facilities (reducing sepsis and tetanus) and antibiotics to treat infections.
3. **Care after birth**: Kangaroo mother care for preterm children; warmth, feeding/intravenous fluids, oxygen, antibiotics at secondary health centers for small neonates or neonates with health issues. Oral rehydration supplements for diarrhea, and antibiotics to treat pneumonia.

Table 14.4 Country-specific estimates of main causes of neonatal mortality

| | Neonatal deaths per year | | Estimated Percentage of Neonatal Deaths due to | |
	(1000 deaths per year)	Prematurity (%)	Interpartum-related complications including asphyxia (%)	Neonatal sepsis (%)
India	706.6	43.7	19.2	14.8
Nigeria	247.3	32.8	29.4	15.8
Pakistan	163.3	35.6	23.2	19.9
China	115.7	23.3	24.8	3.8
Ethiopia	89.7	24.5	33.7	18.0
DR Congo	87.2	34.1	28.7	16.2
Bangladesh	76.7	31.2	22.2	16.2
Indonesia	69.5	36.4	19.2	13.1

Source: WHO Global Health Observatory.

In terms of current coverage, access to antenatal care services has improved substantially in virtually all countries over the past two decades, which makes delivering supplements as well as malaria prevention relatively straightforward; in terms of the actual material cost, the entire antenatal care package is unlikely to cost more than US$10 per child, even when staff time is taken into account. In terms of total cost, this is a relatively small amount: with an estimated 120 Million births per year in developing countries, the total annual cost would be less than US$1.5 billion per year globally. However, things are more complicated and costly for safe deliveries and postnatal care.

Given these health system challenges, generating cost estimates is complicated (Table 14.5). On one hand, one may want to only account for the direct and additional marginal cost generated by the outlined set of essential interventions (facility use time, medical staff time, input cost, etc.); this "marginal cost" approach was taken in the most recent *Lancet* neonatal series (Bhutta, Das, et al., 2014) and resulted in an estimate of US$5.65 billion per year for the 75 countries with the highest burden of child mortality. Estimates get substantially higher when the cost of building additional capacity is taken into account; two recent papers using different costing tools find total annual cost estimates of US$ 9.2 and US$10.9 billion, respectively (Bhutta, Yakoob et al., 2011; Guttmacher Institute, 2009).

In practice, both approaches are unlikely to fully capture the investment required to achieve high coverage of essential services. For example, most high-income countries have a physician density of three physicians per 1000 population or higher; in low- and middle-income countries, the average current physician density is about 0.5 physicians per 1000 population. Figure 14.4 shows the cross-sectional relationship between physician density and infant mortality: no country with a physician density of one or more physicians per 1000 population has an infant mortality rate > 50.

Taking these figures, and assuming that each country needs an average of one physician per 1000 population, the total need for new physicians is about 1.3 million doctors today (not counting other staff). Assuming that doctors earn on average twice the national income per capita, the global annual salary cost would be US$7.7 billion, not counting the cost of training. Clearly this cost would generate benefits much greater than the reductions in neonatal mortality, and the same would be true for other staff as well as improved infrastructure overall.

The critical question for costing is thus what proportion of the total additional investment and cost should be attributed to the neonatal health improvements. Under the ideal scenario of one doctor per 1000 population, each doctor would have to assist only about 30 births per year, which would clearly only take up a small amount of a

Table 14.5 Estimated cost of scaling up essential maternal and neonatal child health services

Author	Cost Estimate	Costing Assumptions
(a) Bhutta et al. (2014)	US$ 5.65 billion	Running cost only, including staff time, but no additional staffing or infrastructure (Lives Saved Tool-LiST).
Guttmacher Institute (2009)	US$ 9.2 billion	Running cost, capital cost plus overhead for management.
Bhutta et al. (2011)	US$ 10.9 billion	Running cost plus amortized facility cost (LiST, WHO CHOICE).
Stenberg et al. (2014)	US$ 17.3–30 billion	Running cost plus health system improvements including construction of health centers and hospitals. High cost scenario also includes interventions to increase demand for and utilization of essential health services.

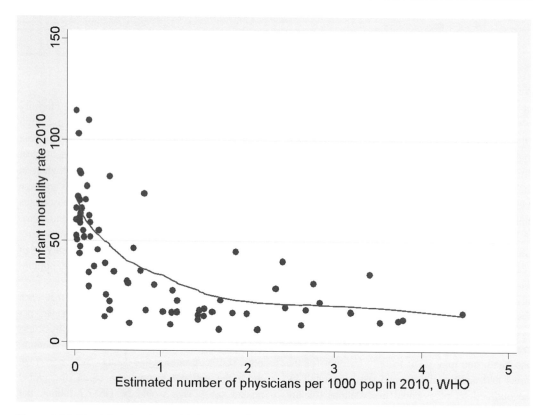

Figure 14.4 *Physician density and infant mortality rates in low and middle income*

physician's overall time allocation. Other health service system improvements would similarly have benefits well beyond reducing neonatal mortality.

In the most comprehensive analysis to date, the Study Group for the Global Investment Framework for Women's and Children's Health made a major attempt to assess the total investment needed to comprehensively improve health systems for child and maternal health (Stenberg et al., 2014). Under the most ambitious scenario – including new infrastructure, health worker training, improved supply chains, improved information systems as well as financial incentives to increase demand for health services – the total estimated cost was US$678 billion, which translates to an annual cost of approximately US$30 billion over the 2013–2035 period.

Table 14.6 Benefit-cost ratios for a comprehensive intervention package to reduce neonatal mortality by 70 percent

Assumptions		3% Discounting			5% Discounting		
		Benefit	Cost	B-C	Benefit	Cost	B-C
Cost	Benefit	(US$ billions)		Ratio	(US$ billions)		Ratio
Low	Low	63.1	10.9	5.8	40.3	10.9	3.7
Low	High	315.4	10.9	28.9	201.7	10.9	18.5
High	Low	63.1	17.3	3.6	40.3	17.3	2.3
High	High	315.4	17.3	18.2	201.7	17.3	11.7

Notes: All numbers reflect total benefits and costs per year. Total benefits are based on all surviving neonates experiencing typical high-income country life expectancies. Total cost includes all costs directly attributable to pre-, peri-, and postnatal health services required to achieve the improvements in neonatal survival. For further details on costing, see Stenberg et al. (2014).

Benefit-Cost Estimation

We assume that a comprehensive investment package could prevent 70 percent of neonatal deaths, which corresponds to 1.93 million infant deaths prevented per year. Following WHO guidelines (WHO, 2003), we assume that all surviving children will experience Japanese life expectancy.[2] At a discounting rate of 3 percent per year, this means 32.6 DALYs per life saved; at a discounting rate of 5 percent, each life saved yields an additional 20.8 DALYs.

For costing, we take the most recent comprehensive supply side cost estimate of US$17.3 billion as our main estimate and show alternative (more optimistic) estimates using a cost number of US$ 10.9 billion (running cost and infrastructure only).

Table 14.6 summarizes the main results. With the more commonly used discounting rate of 3 percent and an average benefit of US$5000 per life year saved (which seems the more reasonable assumption, given that the average GDP per capita in low- and middle-income countries today is US$ 4500), our calculations yield an estimated benefit-cost ratio of 18.2 with the more conservative cost estimate of US$17.3 billion. With a more conservative discounting rate of 5 percent per year, the benefit-cost ratio declines to 11.7; with a more optimistic cost estimate of US$10.9 billion per year and 3 percent discounting, the benefit-cost ratio increases to 28.9. Under all scenarios, benefit-cost ratios are positive and returns to investment high.

Discussion

The results presented in this chapter suggest that large improvements in neonatal mortality are possible, and that the required health interventions are likely to be highly cost effective. Achieving these improvements will, however, be challenging because neonatal risk factors and neonatal mortality are harder to prevent than most other causes of under-five mortality, and major progress for neonatal mortality will likely only be possible if health services (and the health system more generally) are substantially improved, requiring major financial investment. The most recent cost estimates suggest that an additional US$17–30 billion per year will be needed to reduce neonatal mortality by 70 percent. Major shifts in global health financing will likely be needed if ambitious targets are to be reached for neonatal mortality within the next 15 years.

In terms of the overall mortality targets to be defined as part of the new development goals, a

[2] Assuming lower life expectancies changes the overall numbers only marginally due to the relatively high discounting rates applied to future years. At 3 percent discounting, the net present value of a life year at age 60 (which infants would experience in 60 years from today) is only 17 percent of the value of a life year today; at 5 percent discounting, the net present value of a life year at age 60 is only 5.3 percent. Accordingly, the total DALYs gained from one infant life saved change by less than 10 percent if Japanese survival rates are replaced with survival rates from a typical developing country today.

global target of 20 per 1000 seems reasonable for infant as well as for under-five mortality. However, a uniform and absolute mortality target of 20 as proposed by the HLPEP seems neither very attractive nor practical; any fixed target would be very difficult (if not impossible) to achieve for many of the poorest countries and essentially not pose any challenge for the more advanced middle-income nations. Aiming at smaller differences in health outcomes across income quintiles is clearly also a worthy target.

In summary, all the evidence presented in this chapter suggests that large further reductions in neonatal as well as child mortality are possible and should be targeted by the new development goals. All available evidence suggests that the returns to investing in these resources would be large; major changes in global health financing may, however, be necessary if these benefits are to be reaped within the coming 15 years (Table 14.7).

Appendix

Table 14.7 Neonatal mortality by country

Rank	Country	Deaths	Rank	Country	Deaths	Rank	country	Deaths
1	India	706.6	41	South Sudan	12.2	81	Turkmenistan	2.4
2	Nigeria	247.3	42	Algeria	12.1	82	Lesotho	2.1
3	Pakistan	163.3	43	Senegal	12.1	83	UK	2.1
4	China	115.7	44	Burundi	11.4	84	Gambia	2.0
5	Ethiopia	89.7	45	Morocco	10.7	85	Paraguay	1.9
6	DR Congo	87.2	46	Uzbekistan	10.7	86	Sri Lanka	1.7
7	Bangladesh	76.7	47	Zimbabwe	10.4	87	Jordan	1.7
8	Indonesia	69.5	48	Rwanda	9.2	88	Malaysia	1.7
9	Tanzania	44.0	49	Russia	8.0	89	Nicaragua	1.6
10	Uganda	39.9	50	Sierra Leone	7.9	90	France	1.5
11	Kenya	32.9	51	Benin	7.9	91	Germany	1.4
12	Afghanistan	32.1	52	Cambodia	7.7	92	Japan	1.4
13	Brazil	30.2	53	Togo	7.4	93	Palestine	1.4
14	Philippines	29.5	54	Colombia	6.7	94	Tunisia	1.4
15	Mali	28.5	55	Haiti	6.5	95	Italy	1.4
16	Mozambique	26.7	56	Peru	6.4	96	Poland	1.3
17	Cameroon	25.7	57	CAR	6.1	97	Gabon	1.2
18	Côte d'Ivoire	25.7	58	Argentina	5.3	98	Canada	1.2
19	Sudan	25.1	59	Thailand	4.6	99	Mongolia	1.2
20	Chad	22.8	60	Tajikistan	4.6	100	Romania	1.1
21	Angola	22.6	61	Papua NGa	4.6	101	Spain	1.0
22	Ghana	21.5	62	Bolivia	4.6	102	Namibia	1.0
23	Niger	21.2	63	Laos	4.5	103	Libya	0.9
24	Egypt	20.3	64	Eritrea	4.5	104	South Korea	0.9
25	Burkina Faso	18.9	65	Guatemala	4.4	105	Chile	0.9
26	Mexico	18.5	66	Mauritania	4.3	106	Eq. Guinea	0.8
27	Burma	16.5	67	Syria	4.3	107	El Salvador	0.8
28	Malawi	16.1	68	Kazakhstan	4.0	108	Swaziland	0.8
29	South Africa	15.8	69	Venezuela	3.9	109	Botswana	0.7
30	Yemen	15.6	70	North Korea	3.8	110	Australia	0.7
31	USA	15.3	71	Liberia	3.8	111	Timor	0.7
32	Madagascar	15.2	72	Congo	3.6	112	Georgia	0.6
33	Iraq	15.0	73	Dom. Rep	3.6	113	Comoros	0.6
34	Iran	15.0	74	Saudi Arabia	3.4	114	Panama	0.6
35	Somalia	14.6	75	Azerbaijan	3.0	115	Djibouti	0.5
36	Guinea	14.2	76	Ecuador	3.0	116	Jamaica	0.5

(*cont.*)

Table 14.7 (*cont.*)

Rank	Country	Deaths	Rank	Country	Deaths	Rank	country	Deaths
37	Vietnam	13.6	77	Ukraine	2.8	117	United Arab	0.4
38	Zambia	13.0	78	Guinea- Bis.	2.5	118	Taiwan	0.4
39	Nepal	12.8	79	Kyrgyzstan	2.5	119	Lebanon	0.4
40	Turkey	12.3	80	Honduras	2.4	120	Netherlands	0.4
Column % of total	88%			9%			2%	

Source: Bhutta et al., 2011, 2014 for mortality estimates; own calculations.

References

Bhutta, Z. A., J. K. Das, R. Bahl, et al. (2014). "Can available interventions end preventable deaths in mothers, newborn babies, and stillbirths, and at what cost?" *The Lancet* 384 (9940): 347–70.

Bhutta, Z. A., M. Y. Yakoob, J. E. Lawn, et al. (2011). "Stillbirths: what difference can we make and at what cost?" *Lancet* 377(9776): 1523–38.

Bloom, D. E., D. Canning, and G. Fink (2009). "Disease and Development Revisited." NBER Working Paper 15137.

Feenstra, R. C., R. Inklaar, and M. P. Timmer (2013). "The Next Generation of the Penn World Table."

Guttmacher Institute (2009). Facts on investing in family planning and maternal and newborn health. Guttmacher Institute. http://www .guttmacher.org/pubs/AddingItUp2009.pdf.

Open Working Group (2014). Open Working Group proposal for Sustainable Development Goals. http://sustainabledevelopment.un.org/ focussdgs.html. Accessed November 2, 2014, United Nations Division for Sustainable Development, Department of Economic and Social Affairs.

Preston, S. H. (1975). "The changing relation between mortality and level of economic development." *Population Studies* 29(2): 231–48.

Soares, R. R. (2005). "Mortality reductions, education attainment, and fertility choice." *American Economic Review* 95(3): 580–601.

Stenberg, K., H. Axelson, P. Sheehan, et al. (2014). "Advancing social and economic development by investing in women's and children's health: a new Global Investment Framework." *Lancet* 383(9925): 1333–54.

UN Inter-agency Group for Child Mortality Estimation (2014). "Levels and Trends in Child Mortality Report 2014. Estimates Developed by the UN Inter-agency Group for Child Mortality Estimation.

UN Inter-agency Group for Child Mortality Estimation (IGME) (2014). "Child Mortality Estimates." www.childmortality.org/, UN.

United Nations (2014). "A New Global Partnership: Eradicate Poverty and Transform Economies through Sustainable Development." New York. www.post2015hlp.org/wp-content/ uploads/2013/05/UN-Report.pdf, United Nations.

(2014). "Global, regional, and national levels of neonatal, infant, and under-5 mortality during 1990–2013: a systematic analysis for the Global Burden of Disease Study 2013." *Lancet* 384(9947), 957–79.

Wang, H., C. A. Liddell, M. M Coates, et al. (2014). "Global, regional, and national levels of neonatal, infant, and under-5 mortality during 1990–2013: a systematic analysis for the Global Burden of Disease Study 2013." *Lancet* 384(9947), 957–79.

WHO (2003). *Making Choices in Health: WHO Guide to Cost-Effectiveness Analysis*. Geneva: World Health Organization.

CHAPTER 15

Benefits and Costs of the HIV/AIDS Targets for the Post-2015 Development Agenda

PASCAL GELDSETZER, DAVID E. BLOOM,
SALAL HUMAIR,[1] AND TILL BÄRNIGHAUSEN

Introduction

Thirty years after the human immunodeficiency virus (HIV) was first identified, the HIV epidemic continues to cause large-scale human suffering and economic losses. Since featuring prominently in the MDGs, HIV has received unprecedented global political and financial commitment, being allocated 25 percent of all international assistance for health in 2011. But, despite significant successes, the goal will not be achieved, and the HIV epidemic in sub-Saharan Africa is still one of the most important causes of loss of life and health. The global HIV response will thus have to be a major continued focus of national and international development strategies after 2015.

Two Goals to Address the HIV Epidemic in the Most Affected Countries

Sub-Saharan Africa is home to 70 percent of those living with HIV globally (UNAIDS, 2013b). Within Africa, the Southern region has been hit hardest by the epidemic, with Botswana, Lesotho, South Africa, Swaziland, and Zimbabwe being termed hyperendemic (having an HIV prevalence greater than 15 percent among the adult population). We recommend two goals to address this:

Goal 1: Achieve ART (antiretroviral therapy) coverage of at least 90 percent among HIV-infected adults with a CD4 count <350 cells/μL before expanding the HIV treatment scale-up to people with higher CD4 counts.
Goal 2: Attain circumcision coverage of at least 90 percent among HIV-uninfected adult men.

Why Focus ART First on Those Most in Need?

Since the advent of ART, the WHO has gradually increased its recommended threshold for starting patients on ART to include increasingly healthy patients. WHO treatment thresholds are based on the CD4 count, a cell count that decreases in concentration with deteriorating immune system function. In 2011, a clinical trial, hailed as a game changer in the HIV field, provided evidence for even earlier initiation of ART. It showed that providing ART early in the course of the disease reduces the chance of an infected person passing HIV to an uninfected partner by 96 percent (Cohen et al., 2011). Currently, several large ongoing trials aim to establish the causal effect of providing ART to all HIV patients regardless of CD4 count, i.e., Treatment as Prevention (TasP), when implemented at the population level in sub-Saharan Africa (Essex, DeGruttola, Lebelonyane, and Habibi, 2013; Havlir and Kamya, 2013; Hayes et al., 2014; Iwuji et al., 2013; Stop AIDS Now! 2014).

However, in the real world, where financial and human resources are limited, countries in sub-Saharan Africa, including the hyperendemic countries in Southern Africa, are still far from

[1] Salal Humair's contribution is based on work done when he was at the Harvard School of Public Health. Amazon.com, Inc. provided no support for SH's contributions to this study, either in salaries, time off, or other resources. Amazon.com, Inc. did not play any additional role in the study design, data collection and analysis, decision to publish, or revisions of the manuscript.

reaching universal ART coverage among those with lower CD4 counts. As of 2012, only an estimated 61 percent of all HIV-infected individuals with a CD4 count <350 cells/μL and 34 percent of those with a CD4 count <500 cells/μL (the current WHO threshold) were receiving ART in sub-Saharan Africa (UNAIDS, 2013b), in part because only about half (48 percent) of those infected with HIV know their status (UNAIDS, 2014a). Compared with providing ART only to those with a CD4 count <350 cells/μL, TasP would roughly double the number of ART-eligible patients in hyperendemic countries (UNAIDS, 2013b, 2014a), which would require very large additional financial investments. Using a discount rate of 3 percent, an estimate indicated that implementing TasP in South Africa in 2009 would have cost an additional US $11.8 billion over the following 12 years as compared with maintaining the current coverage level of ART (Bärnighausen, Bloom, and Humair, 2012a). In this situation, we recommend first reaching those at highest risk, for two main reasons.

The first reason is that providing ART to an individual with a CD4 count <350 cells/μL is, on average, more cost effective than offering ART to a patient with a higher CD4 count because the weaker a patient's immune system is, the more dramatic is their health status improvement with ART. Additionally, the preventive effect of ART is higher among those with lower CD4 counts because, with the exception of a very early acute infection stage lasting one to four months, patients with CD4 <200 cells/μL are significantly more infectious than those with higher CD4 counts (Hollingsworth, Anderson, and Fraser, 2008).

The second reason for a gradual rollout of ART from sickest to healthiest patients is that implementing TasP immediately may lead to a "crowding-out" effect, whereby healthier patients may prevent sicker ones from receiving ART (Bärnighausen, Bloom, and Humair, 2014; Bärnighausen, Humair, and Bloom, 2012b).

Why Circumcision?

If effectively implemented, male medical circumcision (MMC) is plausibly a highly cost-beneficial intervention to address the HIV epidemic for several reasons. First, MMC has been shown to be efficacious in preventing new HIV infections. Second, although MMC targets men, after some delay, rates of infection in women also reduce substantially as fewer of their sexual partners are infected. Third, MMC is a one-off intervention that lasts for life. Fourth, the implementation costs of MMC will be comparatively. Fifth, great potential exists for scaling up MMC in hyperendemic countries and sub-Saharan Africa as a whole; the level of acceptability of MMC is encouraging with a review finding that a median of 65 percent of uncircumcised men in sub-Saharan Africa are willing to be circumcised (Westercamp and Bailey, 2007).

A Model to Project the Cost-Benefits of ART and Circumcision

We have developed a mathematical model to determine the cost effectiveness of increasing ART coverage under different CD4 count thresholds and of MMC in HIV-hyperendemic countries. A detailed description of the model and its assumptions can be found elsewhere (Bärnighausen et al., 2012a; Eaton et al., 2012). Here, we build on this model to determine the costs and benefits of scaling up ART among HIV-infected individuals with a CD4 count <350 cells/μL (henceforth referred to simply as ART) and MMC among HIV-uninfected adult men in all five hyperendemic countries globally, using data from South Africa, but we are scaling to apply to all hyperendemic countries.

The model computes the number of new HIV infections and HIV-related deaths for different coverage combinations of ART and MMC using both behavioral and biological variables. Compared with other models that typically furnish cost-effectiveness estimates of single HIV interventions, this model allows us to project the combined effects of multiple HIV interventions that may affect different biological or behavioral variables, as discussed in Bärnighausen et al. (2012a). Figure 15.1 provides an overview of the model's basic structure.

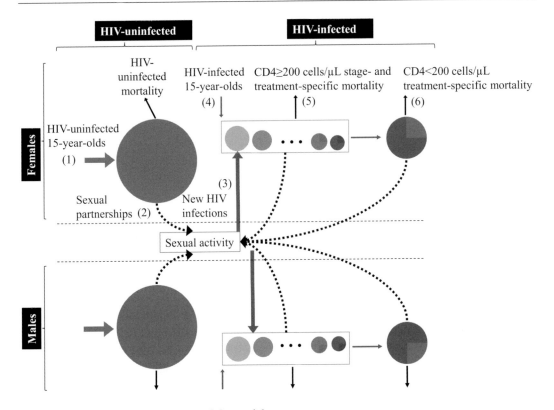

Figure 15.1 *Diagrammatic summary of the model*
(1) HIV-uninfected individuals enter the pool of uninfected sexually active people. (2) Sex acts occur between HIV-uninfected individuals and other HIV-uninfected and HIV-infected individuals. (3) Sex acts between HIV-uninfected and HIV-infected individuals lead to new HIV infections. (4) These newly infected individuals together with HIV-infected 15-year-olds add to the pool of HIV-infected individuals. (5) HIV-infected individuals progress through different stages of the disease. (6) When the disease has progressed to the point that the CD4 count drops below 200 cells/μL, the individual dies and drops out of the pool of HIV-infected individuals. The striped parts represent those individuals who receive ART.

Source: Adapted from Bärnighausen et al. (2012a).

The following two assumptions need to be kept in mind. First, the model assumes that an HIV-infected individual will not progress to the next stage of the disease as long as the person is on ART. Second, it assumes that MMC provides protection from HIV over and above that offered by ART because MMC and ART operate through different biological mechanisms.

For each calendar year between 2015 and 2030, the model computes the cost of the interventions and number of HIV-related deaths if ART or MMC had been scaled up. The scenario that serves as a comparison, i.e., the counterfactual, is the cost and

number of HIV-related deaths when maintaining the approximate current coverage levels of ART (50 percent among those with a CD4 count <350 cells/μL; WHO, 2014b) and MMC (45 percent among adult men; Williams et al., 2006). The two scenarios compared with this benchmark scale up MMC among adult men (90 percent MMC and 50 percent ART coverage) or scale up ART (45 percent MMC and 90 percent ART coverage). By subtracting the number of deaths in each intervention scenario from the number of deaths in the counterfactual scenario, we calculated the number of deaths averted in each calendar year for each

Table 15.1 Life years gained and cost of each goal

Goal	3% Discount			5% Discount		
	Life years gained (1,000s)	Cost (US $1,000s)	Additional cost (US$1,000s)[1]	Life years gained (1,000s)	Cost (US $1,000s)	Additional cost (US$1,000s)[1]
Goal 1: 90% ART coverage	64,106	37,190,000	19,311,250	48,843	32,193,300	16,452,647
Goal 2: 90% MMC coverage	5,101	18,328,150	451,873	3,886	16,265,760	524,737

[1] This is the cost of reaching the goal minus the cost of maintaining the current coverage levels of MMC and ART.

Table 15.2 Benefit, cost, and benefit-to-cost ratio at US$1,000 per life year gained

Goal	3% Discount			5% Discount		
	Benefit (US$1,000s)	Cost (US$1,000s)	B:C ratio	Benefit (US$1,000s)	Cost (US$1,000s)	B:C ratio
Goal 1: 90% ART coverage	64,105,816	19,311,250	3.3	48,842,526	16,452,647	3.0
Goal 2: 90% MMC coverage	5,100,549	451,873	11.3	3,886,133	524,737	7.4

Table 15.3 Benefit, cost, and benefit-to-cost ratio at US$5,000 per life year gained

Goal	3% Discount			5% Discount		
	Benefit (US $1,000s)	Cost (US $1,000s)	B:C ratio	Benefit (US $1,000s)	Cost (US $1,000s)	B:C ratio
Goal 1: 90% ART coverage	320,529,080	19,311,250	16.6	244,212,632	16,452,647	14.8
Goal 2: 90% MMC coverage	25,502,746	451,873	56.4	19,430,663	524,737	37.0

ART and MMC scale-up scenario. We calculated from data collected in KwaZulu-Natal in the largest population cohort in Southern Africa (Tanser et al., 2013) that without ART, a person would die 10 years after the point of infection (Bacchetti and Moss, 1989; Bailey, 1997) and that the individual has a life expectancy of 70 years (Bor et al., 2013). Using this approach, we calculated that, on average, an undiscounted 33.5 years of life are gained for each death averted.

Findings

Table 15.1 shows the projected life years gained and the implementation costs for each of the two goals. The life years gained are more than ten times higher for ART as compared with MMC, but the additional cost of scaling up MMC is only about US$500 million, compared to $16.5–19.3 billion for ART. In fact, as the projected cost of maintaining the current coverage levels of ART and MMC is $15.8–17.9 billion, the cost of scaling up ART would require an additional 92–122 percent investment while rollout of MMC would only need roughly 3 percent in additional investment.

Tables 15.2 and 15.3 show the benefit-to-cost ratios for each goal. The benefit-to-cost ratio for MMC is considerably higher, but scaling up ART is also a highly cost-beneficial intervention and, in our view, an important goal for HIV and AIDS for the period 2015 to 2030.

Limitations

We decided to calculate the cost-benefit using life years gained rather than DALYs gained. This is a reasonable simplification as MMC averts deaths through preventing new infections, meaning that the survivors are likely to be in full health; similarly, patients on ART are likely to be healthy. Also, for simplicity, we considered costs and benefits as if both ART and MMC were scaled up immediately in 2015 to 90 percent coverage. In addition, the model does not account for the effect of MMC and ART on the beneficiaries' social and economic outcomes. HIV is strongly associated with poor socioeconomic outcomes, such as loss of employment (International Monetary Fund, 2004).

Comparing the Results with the "Rethink HIV" Exercise

In 2011, the Copenhagen Consensus Center, with funding from the Rush Foundation, commissioned a group of academics to analyze the costs and benefits of different approaches to tackling the HIV epidemic. The resulting book, entitled *Rethink HIV,* contains an assessment paper on approaches to preventing sexual transmission of HIV by Jere Behrman and Hans-Peter Kohler (Behrman and Kohler, 2011) and a paper on treatment of HIV/AIDS by Mead Over and Geoffrey Garnett (Over and Garnett, 2011). Although based on different models and assumptions, the findings in both these assessment papers are comparable to our results here.

Implementation Challenges for Increasing ART Coverage

The main implementation challenges for our first proposed goal are to (1) identify HIV-infected people who are unaware of their status and (2) improve uptake of and retention in national ART programs.

As an estimated 48 percent of HIV-infected individuals globally do not know their status

(UNAIDS, 2014a), this strategy has clearly fallen short of achieving universal testing coverage. Because an estimated 48 percent of those with HIV infection do not know their status, new intensified testing efforts are needed, which may have the added benefit of reducing HIV-related risk behavior (Fonner et al., 2012) and possibly even HIV incidence (Coates et al., 2014). Facility-based testing alone, however, is unlikely to achieve universal testing coverage, and countries may therefore also need to implement extensive community-based testing programs, which have the potential to reach a large proportion of the population (Suthar et al., 2013).

The second main challenge to increasing ART coverage is to link those identified as HIV-infected to national ART programs and to ensure high levels of ART retention and adherence. A systematic review found that in sub-Saharan Africa only an average of 57 percent of patients who knew their positive HIV status completed assessment for ART eligibility. Of those eligible for ART, only 66 percent started ART, and of those who started ART, only 65 percent were still on ART after three years (Kranzer et al., 2012). Evidence shows that mobile phone text message reminders and other types of reminders (e.g., diary cards), directly observed therapy, treatment supporters, food supplements, and education and counseling can significantly increase ART adherence (Bärnighausen et al., 2011; Finitsis, Pellowski, and Johnson, 2014).

Implementation Challenges for Increasing MMC Coverage

The implementation challenges for increasing MMC coverage can be divided into supply- and demand-side obstacles. On the supply side, the main challenges are human resource constraints and monetary costs. HIV-hyperendemic countries face serious shortages of trained staff. Thus, MMC campaigns that require a large chunk of clinicians' time will inevitably incur an opportunity cost of decreased availability and/or quality of care for other healthcare services. To minimize this opportunity cost, MMC programs should not only emphasize efficiency through simple measures, such as providing prebundled MMC kits to reduce preparation time and increasing the number of surgical bays in operating rooms, but also focus on task shifting from higher to lower healthcare cadres without compromising quality of care. New technologies, such as the PrePex device or the Shang Ring, would obviate the need for a surgical procedure and could therefore further facilitate task shifting in MMC programs.

The costs of scaling up MMC to achieve 90 percent coverage in hyperendemic countries will only be an additional $500 million. However, as international resources for HIV prevention decline, MMC scale-up can only be successful if international donors and developing country governments prioritize funding for MMC.

Although ethnic, cultural, and religious identities strongly influence the rates and timing of circumcision, the acceptability of MMC is high across sub-Saharan Africa, including in hyperendemic countries. A review of acceptability studies found that a median of 65 percent of uncircumcised men in sub-Saharan Africa were willing to become circumcised, 69 percent of women were in favor of circumcision for their partner, and 71 percent of men and 81 percent of women were willing to circumcise their son (Westercamp and Bailey, 2007). Despite this high level of acceptability, low demand for MMC, especially among older men, is seen as a key reason for the low rates of circumcision (Chinkhumba, Godlonton, and Thornton, 2014; Sgaier et al., 2014).

Thus far, the main demand creation strategies for MMC programs have consisted of mass media campaigns, community mobilization activities, mobile MMC clinics that bring the service closer to the customer, and MMC campaigns at strategic times of the year, such as during school holidays (Lissouba et al., 2010; Mahler et al., 2011). In addition, although they would add to the cost of MMC programs, financial incentives are a particularly promising strategy for increasing demand for MMC.

Vague versus Specific Goals

In our view, the current proposed HIV targets are too vague to be useful to developing country governments and international organizations as they do not provide guidance on how progress should be measured or what interventions should be implemented. We have thus proposed goals that specify *how* the HIV epidemic should be targeted. Although more instructive to both implementers and policy makers, this approach has the disadvantage that more cost-beneficial measures to address HIV may arise in the future through new technologies (e.g., an HIV vaccine) or new scientific evidence on existing technologies. If politically feasible, an ideal solution, therefore, would be the use of specific targets and indicators with an opportunity for regular (e.g., five-yearly) revision in light of new scientific evidence.

Conclusion

In summary, scaling up MMC is a highly cost-beneficial intervention to address the HIV epidemic in hyperendemic countries for the period 2015–2030. In addition, our economic evaluation has demonstrated that increasing coverage of ART among the patients who need it most (i.e., those with a CD4 count <350 cells/μL) is also cost beneficial, albeit significantly less cost beneficial than MMC. Further, focusing ART first on those with a CD4 count <350 cells/μL before gradually increasing the pool of ART-eligible patients to higher CD4 count thresholds is more cost effective than immediate expansion of ART eligibility to healthier HIV-infected patients.

References

Aghokeng, A. F., Monleau, M., Eymard-Duvernay, S., et al. (2014). Extraordinary heterogeneity of virological outcomes in patients receiving highly antiretroviral therapy and monitored with the World Health Organization public health approach in sub-Saharan Africa and southeast Asia. *Clinical Infectious Diseases: An Official Publication of the Infectious Diseases Society of America, 58*(1), 99–109. doi:10.1093/cid/cit627.

Auvert, B., Taljaard, D., Lagarde, E., et al. (2005). Randomized, controlled intervention trial of male circumcision for reduction of HIV infection risk: the ANRS 1265 Trial. *PLoS Medicine*, *2*(11), e298. doi:10.1371/journal.pmed.0020298.

Bacchetti, P., & Moss, A. R. (1989). Incubation period of AIDS in San Francisco. *Nature*, *338*(6212), 251–3. doi:10.1038/338251a0.

Bailey, N. T. (1997). A revised assessment of the HIV/AIDS incubation period, assuming a very short early period of high infectivity and using only San Francisco public health data on prevalence and incidence. *Statistics in Medicine*, *16*(21), 2447–58. Retrieved from http://www.ncbi.nlm.nih.gov/pubmed/9364653.

Bailey, R. C., Moses, S., Parker, C. B., et al. (2007). Male circumcision for HIV prevention in young men in Kisumu, Kenya: a randomised controlled trial. *Lancet*, *369*(9562), 643–56. doi:10.1016/S0140-6736(07)60312-2.

Bärnighausen, T., Bloom, D. E., & Humair, S. (2012a). Economics of antiretroviral treatment vs. circumcision for HIV prevention. *Proceedings of the National Academy of Sciences of the United States of America*, *109*(52), 21271–6. doi:10.1073/pnas.1209017110.

(2014). Human resources for treating HIV/AIDS: are the preventive effects of antiretroviral treatment a game changer? *PLoS One, 11*(10), e0163960.

Bärnighausen, T., Chaiyachati, K., Chimbindi, N., et al. (2011). Interventions to increase antiretroviral adherence in sub-Saharan Africa: a systematic review of evaluation studies. *The Lancet. Infectious Diseases*, *11*(12), 942–51. doi:10.1016/S1473-3099(11)70181-5.

Bärnighausen, T., Humair, S., & Bloom, D. (2012b). Is HIV treatment-as-prevention a "game-changer"? An economic evaluation of HIV combination prevention. In *International HIV Treatment as Prevention (TasP) Workshop*. Vancouver.

Behrman, J. R., & Kohler, H.-P. (2011). Assessment Paper: Sexual Transmission of HIV. In B. Lomborg (Ed.), *Rethink HIV*. New York: Cambridge University Press. Retrieved from http://www.copenhagenconsensus.com/sites/default/files/behrman_kohler.pdf.

Bollinger, L., Adesina, A., Forsythe, S., et al. (2014). Cost drivers for voluntary medical male circumcision using primary source data from sub-Saharan Africa. *PLoS One*, *9*(5), e84701. doi:10.1371/journal.pone.0084701.

Bor, J., Herbst, A. J., Newell, M.-L., & Bärnighausen, T. (2013). Increases in adult life expectancy in rural South Africa: valuing the scale-up of HIV treatment. *Science (New York, N.Y.)*, *339*(6122), 961–5. doi:10.1126/science.1230413.

Bor, J., Tanser, F., Newell, M.-L., & Bärnighausen, T. (2012). In a study of a population cohort in South Africa, HIV patients on antiretrovirals had nearly full recovery of employment. *Health Affairs (Project Hope)*, *31*(7), 1459–69. doi:10.1377/hlthaff.2012.0407.

Chinkhumba, J., Godlonton, S., & Thornton, R. (2014). The Demand for Medical Male Circumcision. *American Economic Journal: Applied Economics*, *6*(2), 152–177. doi:10.1257/app.6.2.152.

Coates, T. J., Kulich, M., Celentano, D. D., et al. (2014). Effect of community-based voluntary counselling and testing on HIV incidence and social and behavioural outcomes (NIMH Project Accept; HPTN 043): a cluster-randomised trial. *The Lancet. Global Health*, *2*(5), e267–77. doi:10.1016/S2214-109X(14)70032-4.

Cohen, M. S., Chen, Y. Q., McCauley, M et al. (2011). Prevention of HIV-1 infection with early antiretroviral therapy. *The New England Journal of Medicine*, *365*(6), 493–505. doi:10.1056/NEJMoa1105243.

Curran, K., Njeuhmeli, E., Mirelman, A., et al. (2011). Voluntary medical male circumcision: strategies for meeting the human resource needs of scale-up in southern and eastern Africa. *PLoS Medicine*, *8*(11), e1001129. doi:10.1371/journal.pmed.1001129.

Dieleman, J. L., Graves, C. M., Templin, T., et al. (2014). Global health development assistance remained steady in 2013 but did not align with recipients' disease burden. *Health Affairs (Project Hope)*, *33*(5), 878–86. doi:10.1377/hlthaff.2013.1432.

Eaton, J. W., Johnson, L. F., Salomon, J. A., et al. (2012). HIV treatment as prevention: systematic comparison of mathematical models of the potential impact of antiretroviral therapy on HIV incidence in South Africa. *PLoS Medicine*, *9*(7), e1001245. doi:10.1371/journal.pmed.1001245.

Essex, M., DeGruttola, V., Lebelonyane, R., & Habibi, S. El. (2013). Botswana Combination Prevention Project. Retrieved February 20, 2015, from https://clinicaltrials.gov/ct2/show/NCT01965470.

Finitsis, D. J., Pellowski, J. A., & Johnson, B. T. (2014). Text message intervention designs to promote adherence to antiretroviral therapy (ART): a meta-analysis of randomized controlled trials. *PloS One*, *9*(2), e88166. doi:10.1371/journal.pone.0088166.

Fonner, V. A., Denison, J., Kennedy, C. E., O'Reilly, K., & Sweat, M. (2012). Voluntary counseling and testing (VCT) for changing HIV-related risk behavior in developing countries. *The Cochrane Database of Systematic Reviews*, *9*, CD001224. doi:10.1002/14651858.CD001224.pub4.

Ford, N., Chu, K., & Mills, E. J. (2012). Safety of task-shifting for male medical circumcision: a systematic review and meta-analysis. *AIDS (London, England)*, *26*(5), 559–66. doi:10.1097/QAD.0b013e32834f3264.

Gray, R. H., Kigozi, G., Serwadda, D., et al. (2007). Male circumcision for HIV prevention in men in Rakai, Uganda: a randomised trial. *Lancet*, *369*(9562), 657–66. doi:10.1016/S0140-6736 (07)60313-4.

Hankins, C., Forsythe, S., & Njeuhmeli, E. (2011). Voluntary medical male circumcision: an introduction to the cost, impact, and challenges of accelerated scaling up. *PLoS Medicine*, *8*(11), e1001127. doi:10.1371/journal.pmed.1001127.

Havlir, D., & Kamya, M. (2013). Sustainable East Africa Research in Community Health. Retrieved February 20, 2015, from https://clinicaltrials.gov/show/NCT01864603.

Hayes, R., Ayles, H., Beyers, N., et al. (2014). HPTN 071 (PopART): rationale and design of a cluster-randomised trial of the population impact of an HIV combination prevention intervention including universal testing and treatment – a study protocol for a cluster randomised trial. *Trials*, *15*, 57. doi:10.1186/1745-6215-15-57.

High-Level Panel of Eminent Persons on the Post-2015 Development Agenda. (2014). *A new global partnership: eradicate poverty and transform economies through sustainable development.* New York City. Retrieved from http://www.post2015hlp.org/wp-content/uploads/2013/05/UN-Report.pdf.

Hollingsworth, T. D., Anderson, R. M., & Fraser, C. (2008). HIV-1 transmission, by stage of infection. *The Journal of Infectious Diseases*, *198*(5), 687–93. doi:10.1086/590501.

International Monetary Fund. (2004). *The Macroeconomics of HIV/AIDS*. (M. Haacker, Ed.) (Vol. 19, p. 344). Washington DC: International Monetary Fund.

Iwuji, C. C., Orne-Gliemann, J., Tanser, F et al. (2013). Evaluation of the impact of immediate versus WHO recommendations-guided antiretroviral therapy initiation on HIV incidence: the ANRS 12249 TasP (Treatment as Prevention) trial in Hlabisa sub-district, KwaZulu-Natal, South Africa: study protocol for a cluster randomised controlled trial. *Trials*, *14*, 230. doi:10.1186/1745-6215-14-230.

Kennedy, C. E., Fonner, V. A., Sweat, M. D., et al. (2013). Provider-initiated HIV testing and counseling in low- and middle-income countries: a systematic review. *AIDS and Behavior*, *17*(5), 1571–90. doi:10.1007/s10461-012-0241-y.

Kranzer, K., Govindasamy, D., Ford, N., Johnston, V., & Lawn, S. D. (2012). Quantifying and addressing losses along the continuum of care for people living with HIV infection in sub-Saharan Africa: a systematic review. *Journal of the International AIDS Society*, *15*(2), 17383. doi:10.7448/ias.15.2.17383.

Lissouba, P., Taljaard, D., Rech, D., et al. (2010). A model for the roll-out of comprehensive adult male circumcision services in African low-income settings of high HIV incidence: the ANRS 12126 Bophelo Pele Project. *PLoS Medicine*, *7*(7), e1000309. doi:10.1371/journal.pmed.1000309.

Lomazzi, M., Borisch, B., & Laaser, U. (2014). The Millennium Development Goals: experiences, achievements and what's next. *Global Health Action*, *7*, 23695. Retrieved from http://www.pubmedcentral.nih.gov/articlerender.fcgi?artid=3926985&tool=pmcentrez&rendertype=abstract.

Mahler, H. R., Kileo, B., Curran, K., et al. (2011). Voluntary medical male circumcision: matching demand and supply with quality and efficiency in a high-volume campaign in Iringa Region, Tanzania. *PLoS Medicine*, *8*(11), e1001131. doi:10.1371/journal.pmed.1001131.

Mills, E. J., Nachega, J. B., Bangsberg, D. R., et al. (2006). Adherence to HAART: a systematic review of developed and developing nation patient-reported barriers and facilitators. *PLoS Medicine*, *3*(11), e438. doi:10.1371/journal.pmed.0030438.

Mwandi, Z., Murphy, A., Reed, J., et al. (2011). Voluntary medical male circumcision: translating research into the rapid expansion of services in Kenya, 2008–2011. *PLoS Medicine*, *8*(11), e1001130. doi:10.1371/journal. pmed.1001130.

Njeuhmeli, E., Forsythe, S., Reed, J., et al. (2011). Voluntary medical male circumcision: modeling the impact and cost of expanding male circumcision for HIV prevention in eastern and southern Africa. *PLoS Medicine*, *8*(11), e1001132. doi:10.1371/journal.pmed.1001132.

Open Working Group of the General Assembly on Sustainable Development Goals. (2014). *Open Working Group proposal for Sustainable Development Goals*. New York City. Retrieved from http://sustainabledevelopment.un.org/ content/documents/1579SDGs Proposal.pdf.

Ortblad, K. F., Lozano, R., & Murray, C. J. L. (2013). The burden of HIV: insights from the Global Burden of Disease Study 2010. *AIDS (London, England)*, *27*(13), 2003–17. doi:10.1097/ QAD.0b013e328362ba67.

Over, M., & Garnett, G. (2011). Assessment Paper: Treatment. In B. Lomborg (Ed.), *Rethink HIV*. New York: Cambridge University Press. Retrieved from www.copenhagenconsensus .com/sites/default/files/over_garnett.pdf.

Rosen, S., Larson, B., Rohr, J., et al. (2014). Effect of antiretroviral therapy on patients' economic well being: five-year follow-up. *AIDS (London, England)*, *28*(3), 417–24. doi:10.1097/ QAD.0000000000000053.

Sgaier, S. K., Reed, J. B., Thomas, A., & Njeuhmeli, E. (2014). Achieving the HIV prevention impact of voluntary medical male circumcision: lessons and challenges for managing programs. *PLoS Medicine*, *11*(5)., e1001641. doi:10.1371/ journal.pmed.1001641.

Stop AIDS Now! (2014). MaxART – Implementation Study on Treatment as Prevention. Retrieved October 23, 2014, from www.stopaidsnow .org/maxart-implementation-study-treatment- prevention.

Sustainable Development Solutions Network. (2014). *Proposed Sustainable Development Goals (SDGs) and Targets*. New York City. Retrieved from http://unsdsn.org/wp-content/uploads/ 2014/04/140417-Goals-and-Targets1.pdf.

Suthar, A. B., Ford, N., Bachanas, P. J., et al. (2013). Towards universal voluntary HIV testing and counselling: a systematic review and meta- analysis of community-based approaches. *PLoS Medicine*, *10*(8), e1001496. doi:10.1371/journal. pmed.1001496.

Tanser, F., Bärnighausen, T., Grapsa, E., Zaidi, J., & Newell, M.-L. (2013). High coverage of ART associated with decline in risk of HIV acquisition in rural KwaZulu-Natal, South Africa. *Science (New York, N.Y.)*, *339*(6122), 966–71. doi:10.1126/science.1228160.

Thirumurthy, H., Masters, S. H., Rao, S., et al. (2014). Effect of providing conditional economic compensation on uptake of voluntary medical male circumcision in Kenya: a randomized clinical trial. *JAMA*, *312*(7), 703–11. doi:10.1001/jama.2014.9087.

Tobian, A. A. R., Kacker, S., & Quinn, T. C. (2014). Male circumcision: a globally relevant but under-utilized method for the prevention of HIV and other sexually transmitted infections. *Annual Review of Medicine*, *65*, 293–306. doi:10.1146/ annurev-med-092412-090539.

UNAIDS. (2005). AIDS in Africa: Three scenarios to 2025. Geneva. Retrieved from http://data.unaids .org/publications/IRC-pub07/jc1058- aidsinafrica_en.pdf.

    (2013a). Access to antiretroviral therapy in Africa: Status report on progress towards the 2015 targets. Geneva. Retrieved from www.unaids.org/sites/default/files/media_asset/ 20131219_AccessARTAfricaStatusReport Progresstowards2015Targets_en_0.pdf.

    (2013b). Global Report – UNAIDS report on the global AIDS epidemic 2013. Geneva. Retrieved from www.unaids.org/en/media/unaids/ contentassets/documents/epidemiology/2013/ gr2013/UNAIDS_Global_Report_2013_en.pdf.

    (2014a). The Gap Report. Geneva. Retrieved from http://www.unaids.org/en/media/unaids/ contentassets/documents/unaidspublication/ 2014/UNAIDS_Gap_report_en.pdf.

    (2014b). What are the different epidemiological scenarios? Geneva. Retrieved from http:// hivpreventiontoolkit.unaids.org/support_pages/ faq_diff_epi_scenarios.aspx.

UNICEF. (2014). Protection, care and support for children affected by HIV and AIDS. Retrieved October 01, 2014, from http://data.unicef.org/ hiv-aids/care-support.

United Nations. (2001). *Declaration of Commitment on HIV/AIDS. New York City*. Retrieved from www.unaids.org/en/media/unaids/ contentassets/dataimport/publications/irc-pub03/ aidsdeclaration_en.pdf.

    (2006). *Political Declaration on HIV/AIDS. New York City*. Retrieved from www.unaids.org/

en/media/unaids/contentassets/dataimport/pub/report/2006/20060615_hlm_politicaldeclaration_ares60262_en.pdf.

(2011). *Political Declaration on HIV and AIDS: Intensifying Our Efforts to Eliminate HIV and AIDS. New York City.* Retrieved from www.unaids.org/en/media/unaids/contentassets/documents/document/2011/06/20110610_UN_A-RES-65-277_en.pdf.

(2014). *United Nations Millennium Development Goals.* United Nations. Retrieved September 30, 2014, from www.un.org/millenniumgoals/aids.shtml.

Vasilakis, C. (2012). The social economic impact of AIDS: Accounting for intergenerational transmission, productivity and fertility. *Economic Modelling, 29*(2), 369–81. doi:10.1016/j.econmod.2011.11.006

Westercamp, N., & Bailey, R. C. (2007). Acceptability of male circumcision for prevention of HIV/AIDS in sub-Saharan Africa: a review. *AIDS and Behavior, 11*(3), 341–55. doi:10.1007/s10461-006-9169-4.

WHO. (2006). Antiretroviral therapy for HIV infection in adults and adolescents: recommendations for a public health approach. Geneva. Retrieved from www.who.int/hiv/pub/guidelines/artadultguidelines.pdf?ua=1.

(2008). Task shifting: global recommendations and guidelines. Geneva: World Health Organization. Retrieved from www.who.int/workforcealliance/knowledge/resources/taskshifting_guidelines/en/.

(2010a). Antiretroviral therapy for HIV infection in adults and adolescents: recommendations for a public health approach. Geneva. Retrieved from http://whqlibdoc.who.int/publications/2010/9789241599764_eng.pdf?ua=1.

(2010b). Considerations for implementing models for optimizing the volume and efficiency of male circumcision services. Geneva. Retrieved from www.malecircumcision.org/programs/documents/mc_MOVE_2010_web.pdf.

(2013). Consolidated guidelines on the use of antiretroviral drugs for treating and preventing HIV infection. Geneva. Retrieved from http://apps.who.int/iris/bitstream/10665/85321/1/9789241505727_eng.pdf.

(2014a). WHO Progress Brief – Voluntary medical male circumcision for HIV prevention in priority countries of East and Southern Africa. Geneva: World Health Organization. Retrieved from http://www.who.int/hiv/topics/malecircumcision/male-circumcision-info-2014/en/.

(2014b). World Health Statistics 2014. Geneva. Retrieved from http://apps.who.int/iris/bitstream/10665/112738/1/9789240692671_eng.pdf?ua=1.

Williams, B. G., Lloyd-Smith, J. O., Gouws, E., et al. (2006). The potential impact of male circumcision on HIV in Sub-Saharan Africa. *PLoS Medicine, 3*(7), e262. doi:10.1371/journal.pmed.0030262.

World Bank and USAID. (2011). *The Ethics of Material Incentives for HIV Prevention.* Washington DC: Author Retrieved from http://siteresources.worldbank.org/INTHIVAIDS/Resources/375798–1297872065987/WorldBankUSAIDDebate5Report.pdf.

Benefits and Costs of the Malaria Targets for the Post-2015 Consensus Project

NEHA RAYKAR

Introduction

Despite a 42 percent decrease in global malaria mortality since 2000, the disease was estimated to cause 627,000 estimated deaths worldwide in 2012. Ninety percent of all estimated deaths occurred in sub-Saharan Africa, and 77 percent were in children under age five. Malaria-endemic countries also bear considerable indirect long-term costs associated with physical and cognitive retardation, malnutrition, anemia, and increased disease susceptibility.

Macroeconomic nonhealth costs to the economy result from reduced labor market productivity and loss of tourism and business investment, in addition to lost capital and purchasing power (Mills and Shillcutt, 2004). Annual per-capita GNP growth also suffers; this is particularly costly for malaria-endemic countries, which are among the world's poorest.

In addition to malaria being the focus of MDG 6, in 2007, the World Health Assembly passed a resolution calling for a 75 percent reduction in the global malaria burden by 2015. Between 2000 and 2010, the substantial expansion of malaria interventions has led to a 26 percent decline in malaria-specific mortality rates globally while the estimated global incidence of malaria declined by 17 percent. In the decade since 2000, 1.1 million deaths from malaria were averted and reported malaria cases reduced by more than 50 percent in 43 of the 99 countries with ongoing transmission (WHO, 2012).

The past decade of malaria control has seen significant changes in antimalarial drug policies, mass distribution of insecticide-treated bed nets, and corresponding declines in the incidence of malaria (Fegan et al., 2007). A big push is being contemplated to eliminate malaria in areas of unstable transmission, with the eventual goal of global elimination (Smith et al., 2013). However, despite impressive gains, potential resistance to the first-line drug, artemisinin, looms large; besides declining financial support for malaria control, artemisinin resistance is likely one of the greatest threats to the gains made globally in rolling back malaria, while long-lasting insecticide-treated bed nets (LLITNs) have yet to be fully deployed in some parts of the world where they could be useful.

Here, we consider two targets that could be useful in the context of an overall malaria eradication strategy:

A. Delay artemisinin resistance greater than 1 percent until 2025 through a combination of quality artemisinin combination therapies (ACTs), multiple first-line therapies (MFTs), and resistance containment efforts.

B. Reduce malaria incidence by 50 percent between 2015 and 2025 through mass distribution of long-lasting insecticide treated bed nets (LLITNs).

Target A

Delay emergence of artemisinin resistance greater than 1 percent until 2025 through the use of quality ACTs and MFTs

Artemisinin resistance is one of the greatest threats to global malaria control efforts today.

Artemisinins have been responsible for averting millions of deaths from falciparum malaria, and there are no other drugs available today or in the late stages of development that are nearly as effective. Artemisinins entered into routine use in the Greater Mekong Sub-region (GMS) much earlier than in other regions, mainly as monotherapy. This may also to explain why resistance also arose there first, but other factors may also be at play. Resistance to the last mainstay of treatment, chloroquine, also arose in the region (and was not first used there), as did resistance to pyrimethamine.

Several factors, including indiscriminate use of drugs at high intensity, increase the chances of selection of resistant parasite populations. Combination therapies delay the emergence of resistance to antimalarial drugs and also halt the spread and further increase of established resistance. Increase in disease burden from rising drug resistance to conventional antimalarials in endemic countries prompted the WHO in 2001 to recommend the use of ACTs as first-line therapy for uncomplicated cases of *P. falciparum* malaria (Bosman and Mendis, 2007). In the last decade, an increasing number of endemic countries have deployed highly effective ACTs to delay the evolution of drug resistance.

MFTs simulate the idea of combinations, but at the population scale. As of 2014, no country had implemented a national MFT strategy, although a de facto MFT strategy is operational in many countries. Using a diversity of combinations introduces significant operational challenges, but the underlying ecological argument is strong, and MFTs could be an important complement to the use of combinations in delaying resistance.

The World Wide Antimalarial Resistance Network (WWARN) was established to accurately assess the spread of artemisinin resistance through a worldwide system for collating information on antimalarial resistance and standardizing key parameters of in vitro tests to overcome inter- and intralaboratory variability. Our proposed target of delaying the emergence of artemisinin resistance above 1 percent is based on their measurement standards.

Target B

Reduce malaria incidence by 50 percent between 2015 and 2025 through mass distribution of long-lasting insecticide-treated bed nets (LLITNs)

LLITNs have been proven to prevent malaria transmission. LLITNs, mostly impregnated with a pyrethroid insecticide, physically reduce human vector contact and reduce the vector population by killing the mosquitoes that come into contact with the nets. Use of LLITNs by a majority of a target community provides protection even to those who do not sleep under LLITNs (Hawley et al., 2003). A review of LLITN randomized trials estimates that they reduce the incidence of uncomplicated malaria by 50 percent compared to no use of nets at all and by 39 percent compared to the use of untreated nets (Lengeler, 2004). Scaling up of LLITN distribution by providing them free of charge or at highly subsidized rates has led to a substantial increase in coverage in several endemic areas (Cohen and Dupas, 2010).[1]

Although a powerful and accessible intervention, LLITNs requires coverage of a large proportion of the at-risk population to produce larger community-wide effects (Hawley et al., 2003). LLITNs typically last for less than five years and maintaining a high level of coverage can be challenging. Millions of vulnerable people continue to use untreated bed nets or nets treated with less-effective insecticides, and the development of resistance to the preferred pyrethroids can be an additional problem.

Cost-Benefit Estimates

Morel et al. (2005) evaluated the cost effectiveness of combinations of selected malaria-control

---

[1] Cohen and Dupas (2010) find that although subsidies through cost-sharing arrangements may increase usage intensity relative to free distribution, it may also reduce program uptake by dampening demand. They argue that free distribution of ITNs could save many more lives and at a lower cost per life saved (due to large externality effects) compared to cost-sharing programs.

Table 16.1 Western Africa: at-risk population

| Interventions | Western Africa: 98% of the population at risk | | |
	Average yearly DALYs averted	Average yearly costs (2000 Int$)	Average cost effectiveness (Int$/DALY averted)
Case management with ACTs (80% coverage)	7,771,018	72,386,626	9
ITNs + case management with ACTs+ intermittent presumptive treatment with SP during pregnancy (95% coverage)	12,972,791	315,546,119	24

Table 16.2 Southern and Eastern Africa: at-risk population

| Interventions | Southern and Eastern Africa: 69% of the population at risk | | |
	Average yearly DALYs averted	Average yearly costs (2000 Int$)	Average cost effectiveness (Int$/DALY averted)
Case management with ACTs (95% coverage)	5,886,159	73,000,256	12
ITNs + case management with ACTs (95% coverage)	9,138,452	254,755,715	28

interventions[2] separately for two subregions of sub-Saharan Africa (SSA), both of which have high transmission rates but differ in disease burden.[3] The interventions were evaluated at differing target coverage rates (50 percent, 80 percent, and 95 percent) to allow unit costs and effectiveness to vary with coverage. Costs include the value of resources needed to implement the interventions over a ten-year horizon and human resource training costs. Effects were measured as disability-adjusted life years (DALYs) averted by an intervention program of ten years. In Western Africa, the region with a greater at-risk population, case management including treatment with ACTs at 80 percent target coverage is the most cost effective intervention (Int$9 per DALY averted). In Southern and Eastern Africa, for this intervention to be the most cost effective, the target coverage needed is 95 percent. In both regions, use of ITNs plus case management with ACTs is the next most cost-effective intervention. In Western Africa (with a larger at-risk population), adding presumptive treatment with sulfadoxine-pyrimethamine (SP) during pregnancy is also cost-effective. The cost effectiveness ratios for these two sets of interventions are presented in Tables 16.1 and 16.2.

We rely on these cost-effectiveness ratios to evaluate the benefit-cost ratio of MFTs for the most cost-effective interventions in SSA, assuming

DALY values of $1000 and $5000. We assume a life expectancy at birth of 68 years and average ages of death from malaria in high transmission areas of SSA to be 2 years among under-five children and 20 years among the rest of the population (Goodman et al., 1999). Further, there is evidence that 77 percent of all malaria deaths are among under-five children (WHO Global Health Observatory). Using these parameters, we compute the weighted average years gained from surviving malaria which are then discounted at 3 percent and 5 percent to arrive at the discounted annual benefits of the two recommended interventions for DALY values of $1000 and $5000. The results are presented in Tables 16.3 and 16.4.

Delaying artemisinin resistance through case management with ACTs results in a higher benefit-cost ratio compared to a combination of

[2] Interventions evaluated were combinations of: ITNs, indoor residual spraying, case management with ACTs, case management with chloroquine, case management with SP, case management with nonartemisinin-based combination treatment and intermittent presumptive treatment with SP in pregnancy.
[3] For a systematic review of studies on cost-effectiveness analysis of malaria interventions, see White et al., 2011. Also see Mills and Shillcutt (2004) for a summary of benefit-cost ratios of three interventions and of scaling up ACTs coverage in sub-Saharan Africa.

Table 16.3 Benefit, cost, and benefit-to-cost ratio at US$1,000 per life year gained

Value of a Life: 1000 USD/DALY	3% discount rate			5% discount rate		
	Annual Benefits ($m)	Annual Costs ($m)	BCR	Annual Benefits ($m)	Annual Costs ($m)	BCR
Delay artemisinin resistance greater than 1% until 2025 in SSA	5,844	145	40	3,878	145	27
Delay artemisinin resistance and reduce malaria incidence by 50% between 2015 and 2025 in SSA	9,461	570	17	6,279	570	11

Table 16.4 Benefit, cost, and benefit-to-cost ratio at US$5,000 per life year gained

Value of a Life: 5000 USD/DALY	3% discount rate			5% discount rate		
	Annual Benefits ($m)	Annual Costs ($m)	BCR	Annual Benefits ($m)	Annual Costs ($m)	BCR
Delay artemisinin resistance greater than 1% until 2025 in SSA	29,220	145	201	19,391	145	133
Delay artemisinin resistance and reduce malaria incidence by 50% between 2015 and 2025 in SSA	47,307	570	83	31,394	570	55

ITNs and case management with ACTs, although this excludes the benefits and costs of providing MFTs due to lack of information on these. In comparison, Mills and Shillcutt (2004) present benefit-cost ratios (in Int$2003) in annual terms for various malaria-control measures for SSA and find that switching from SP to ACT has the highest benefit-cost ratio (38.6), followed by scaling up ACTs (19.1). The benefit-cost ratio of using ITNs alone is 10.4.

Although these interventions focus on Africa, these are a good approximation of the more generalized non-region-specific targets because Africa accounts for a large majority of global malaria morbidity and mortality.

Although the study by Morel and colleagues evaluates multiple combinations of antimalarial interventions, it is nondynamic in nature and does not account for local malaria transmission patterns and their evolution over time. The model assumes a fixed number of cases or deaths averted per unit of service provided. However, dynamic models have only been developed for preventive interventions and are not directly applicable to ACTs treatment.

Morel and colleagues' model also does not include the costs of comorbidities such as anemia and low birth weight among young children, which are indirectly linked to malarial infections and further increase the susceptibility to and severity of other infectious diseases. Thus, malaria contributes to child mortality beyond the direct fatal consequences of malaria infection, which means that the analysis underestimates the DALYs averted by effective malaria prevention and treatment.

Challenges

Diagnosis of Malarial Cases

Diagnostic medical services in malaria-endemic countries are limited, poor in quality, or expensive, resulting in malaria treatment being administered on the basis of either clinical or self-diagnosis, or microscopy, which is generally limited to larger clinics and does not reach remote endemic areas because it is resource-intensive. This means that a significant number of patients with fever are treated for malarial parasites they do not have.

Drugs are wasted, and other infections remain undiagnosed.

There is rising evidence that rapid diagnostic tests (RDTs) for malaria have the potential to be highly cost effective across most of Africa if they are accurate and are used to guide treatment decisions (Goodman, 1999; Jonkman et al., 1995; Rolland et al., 2006; Shillcutt et al., 2008). They have achieved greater than 95 percent sensitivity for *P. falciparum* malaria, although they are less sensitive for non-falciparum parasites (Wongsrichanalai et al., 2007). Shillcutt and colleagues' model evaluates the cost effectiveness of RDTs and microscopy relative to presumptive treatment in rural health facilities in Africa and finds that RDTs could save many costly and unnecessary ACT treatments and improve treatment of nonmalarial febrile infections, thus making RDTs highly cost effective (Shillcutt et al., 2008).

Affordability of ACTs

Most patients in the malaria-endemic areas of Africa (50–75 percent) seek treatment through the private sector, which is often unregulated. Quality-assured treatment with an ACTs has emerged as the most cost-effective malaria intervention, but this is more expensive than other antimalarial drugs.

In 2004, an Institute of Medicine (IOM) committee recommended establishing an international fund to purchase artemisinin combinations at producer cost and resell them to distributors (government or private wholesalers) at a subsidized cost. If ACTs drugs enter the supply chain at a low price and the supply chain is adequate, the price to consumers is expected to be similar to the price of chloroquine. This centralized procurement of ACTs drugs at the international level would ensure quality standards, remove artemisinin shortage by encouraging drug manufacturers to enter the market in lieu of guaranteed purchase of drugs on behalf of countries, and ease the delivery of foreign aid by reducing administrative bottlenecks within country governments (Arrow et al., 2005).

An independent evaluation of an 18-month Affordable Medicines Facility-malaria (AMFm) pilot starting in 2009 revealed that AMFm met or exceeded the benchmarks for availability, price,

and market share of quality-ensured ACTs (Arrow et al., 2012). In November 2012, the Global Fund Board decided to modify the existing AMFm by integrating it into the regular Global Fund model called the Private Sector Co-payment Mechanism (PSCM), whereby countries would choose how much of their country budgets would be reallocated to AMFm and mobilize resources for the copayment. Arrow et al. (2012) argue that such an approach will destabilize artemisinin demand, increase ACTs prices, discourage ACTs manufacturers, and deprive access to ACTs drugs. Since the transition, of the seven participating countries, Cambodia, Niger, and Zanzibar stopped AMFm implementation after the first phase, and Ghana, Madagascar, and Tanzania have integrated the PSCM into existing Global Fund grants. Providing subsidized access to effective antimalarial drugs, especially in the private sector, poses a considerable challenge.

Policy Considerations

In general, reducing malaria incidence requires substantial scale-up of treatment coverage. However, incremental costs of scaling up coverage can be expected to be much higher than, say, switching treatment because scale-up involves additional infrastructural costs, staff salaries, training and supervision costs, and costs incurred by patients. The estimated incremental cost of scaling up treatment coverage with ACTs is approximately Int$20 per patient for averting 0.22 DALYs (Mills and Shillcutt, 2004). A combination of nationwide distribution of ACTs and LLITNs to all under-five children has been associated with reductions in inpatient morbidity and deaths in Rwanda and Ethiopia (Otten et al., 2009). Substantially high coverage of ACTs (and correspondingly, low coverage of component drugs' monotherapy) is required if additional cost of ACTs is to be matched by the benefits of reduction in drug resistance. Besides improvements in public-sector services, this also requires addressing private-sector dispensing and home-based case management practices such as drug packaging, retailer training, and consumer education (Mills and Shillcutt, 2004).

References

Alonso, P. L., S. W. Lindsay, J. R. M. Armstrong Schellenberg, et al. "A malaria control trial using insecticide-treated bed nets and targeted chemoprophylaxis in a rural area of The Gambia, West Africa 6. The impact of the interventions on mortality and morbidity from malaria." *Transactions of the Royal Society of Tropical Medicine and Hygiene* 87, no. Supplement 2 (1993): 37–44.

Arrow, Kenneth J., Claire Panosian, and Hellen Gelband, eds. *Saving Lives, Buying Time: Economics of Malaria Drugs in an Age of Resistance*. Washington, DC: National Academies Press, 2004.

Arrow, Kenneth J., Hellen Gelband, and Dean T. Jamison. "Making antimalarial agents available in Africa." *New England Journal of Medicine* 353, no. 4 (2005): 333–5.

Arrow, Kenneth J., Patricia M. Danzon, Hellen Gelband, et al. "The Affordable Medicines Facility—malaria: killing it slowly." *The Lancet* 380, no. 9857 (2012): 1889–90.

Bacon, David J., Ronan Jambou, Thierry Fandeur, et al. "World Antimalarial Resistance Network (WARN) II: in vitro antimalarial drug susceptibility." *Malaria Journal* 6, no. 1 (2007): 120.

Barat, Lawrence M. "Four malaria success stories: how malaria burden was successfully reduced in Brazil, Eritrea, India, and Vietnam." *The American Journal of Tropical Medicine and Hygiene* 74, no. 1 (2006): 12–16.

Barnes, Karen I., David N. Durrheim, Francesca Little, et al. "Effect of artemether-lumefantrine policy and improved vector control on malaria burden in KwaZulu–Natal, South Africa." *PLoS Medicine* 2, no. 11 (2005): e330.

Bhattarai, Achuyt, Abdullah S. Ali, S. Patrick Kachur, et al. "Impact of artemisinin-based combination therapy and insecticide-treated nets on malaria burden in Zanzibar." *PLoS Medicine* 4, no. 11 (2007): e309.

Boni, Maciej F., David L. Smith, and Ramanan Laxminarayan. "Benefits of using multiple first-line therapies against malaria." *Proceedings of the National Academy of Sciences* 105, no. 37 (2008): 14216–21.

Bosman, Andrea, and Kamini N. Mendis. "A major transition in malaria treatment: the adoption and deployment of artemisinin-based combination therapies." *The American Journal of Tropical Medicine and Hygiene* 77, no. 6 Suppl (2007): 193–7.

Breman, Joel G., Anne Mills, Robert W. Snow, et al. "Conquering malaria" in D. R. Jamison, J. G. Breman, A. R. Measham, et al. (eds.), *Disease Control Priorities in Developing Countries*, 2nd ed. (New York: Oxford University Press, 2006): 413–32. Available: www.dcp-3.org/sites/default/files/dcp2/DCP21.pdf. Accessed November 1, 2014.

Chizema-Kawesha, Elizabeth, John M. Miller, Richard W. Steketee, et al. "Scaling up malaria control in Zambia: progress and impact 2005–2008." *The American Journal of Tropical Medicine and Hygiene* 83, no. 3 (2010): 480–8.

Cohen, Jessica, and Pascaline Dupas. "Free distribution or cost-sharing? Evidence from a randomized malaria prevention experiment." *Quarterly Journal of Economics* 125, no. 1 (2010): 1.

Dapeng, Luo, Yao Renguo, Song Jinduo, Huo Hongru, and Wang Ze. "The effect of DDT spraying and bed nets impregnated with pyrethroid insecticide on the incidence of Japanese encephalitis virus infection." *Transactions of the Royal Society of Tropical Medicine and Hygiene* 88, no. 6 (1994): 629–31.

Dondorp, Arjen M., Rick M. Fairhurst, Laurence Slutsker, et al. "The threat of artemisinin-resistant malaria." *New England Journal of Medicine* 365, no. 12 (2011): 1073–5.

Fegan, Greg W., Abdisalan M. Noor, Willis S. Akhwale, Simon Cousens, and Robert W. Snow. "Effect of expanded insecticide-treated bednet coverage on child survival in rural Kenya: a longitudinal study." *The Lancet* 370, no. 9592 (2007): 1035–9.

Fumiya, Shiga, Virasakdi Chongsvivatwong, Uchiyama Saburo, and Suwich Thammapalo. "The feasibility of a bed net impregnation program to enhance control of Malayan filariasis along a swamp forest in southern Thailand." *Southeast Asian Journal of Tropical Medicine and Public Health* 32, no. 2 (2001), 235–239.

Goodman, C. A. "The economic evaluation of malaria diagnosis." *Draft Position Paper prepared for informal consultation on "Malaria diagnostics at the turn of the century."* organized by WHO and USAID, Geneva (1999): 25–7.

Guerin, Philippe J., Piero Olliaro, Francois Nosten, et al. "Malaria: current status of control, diagnosis, treatment, and a proposed agenda for research and development." *The Lancet Infectious Diseases* 2, no. 9 (2002): 564–73.

Guerin, Philippe J., Piero Olliaro, Francois Nosten, et al. "Malaria: current status of control, diagnosis, treatment, and a proposed agenda for research and development." *The Lancet Infectious Diseases* 2, no. 9 (2002): 564–73.

Guillet, Pierre, R. N'guessan, Frédéric Darriet, et al. "Combined pyrethroid and carbamate 'two-in-one' treated mosquito nets: field efficacy against pyrethroid-resistant Anopheles gambiae and Culex quinquefasciatus." *Medical and Veterinary Entomology* 15, no. 1 (2001): 105–12.

Hawley, William A., Penelope A. Phillips-Howard, Feiko O. ter Kuile, et al. "Community-wide effects of permethrin-treated bed nets on child mortality and malaria morbidity in western Kenya." *The American Journal of Tropical Medicine and Hygiene* 68, no. 4 suppl (2003): 121–7.

Jonkman, A., R. A. Chibwe, C. O. Khoromana, et al. "Cost-saving through microscopy-based versus presumptive diagnosis of malaria in adult outpatients in Malawi." *Bulletin of the World Health Organization* 73, no. 2 (1995): 223.

Laxminarayan, Ramanan, Ian W. H. Parry, David L. Smith, and Eili Y. Klein. "Should new antimalarial drugs be subsidized?" *Journal of Health Economics* 29, no. 3 (2010): 445–56.

Laxminarayan, Ramanan. "Act now or later? Economics of malaria resistance." *The American Journal of Tropical Medicine and Hygiene* 71, no. 2 suppl (2004): 187–95.

Lengeler, Christian. "Insecticide-treated bed nets and curtains for preventing malaria." *Cochrane Database Syst Rev* 2, no. 2 (2004).

Lourens, Chris, William M. Watkins, Karen I. Barnes, et al. "Implementation of a reference standard and proficiency testing programme by the World Wide Antimalarial Resistance Network (WWARN)." *Malaria Journal* 9 (2010): 375.

Mills, Anne, and Sam Shillcutt. *The Challenge of Communicable Diseases*. (Tewksbury, MA: Copenhagen Consensus, 2004).

Morel, Chantal M., Jeremy A. Lauer, and David B. Evans. "Cost effectiveness analysis of strategies to combat malaria in developing countries." *BMJ* 331, no. 7528 (2005): 1299.

Otten, Mac, Maru Aregawi, Wilson Were, et al. "Initial evidence of reduction of malaria cases and deaths in Rwanda and Ethiopia due to rapid scale-up of malaria prevention and treatment." *Malaria Journal* 8, no. 1 (2009): 14.

Rolland, Estelle, Francesco Checchi, Loretxu Pinoges, et al. "Operational response to malaria epidemics: are rapid diagnostic tests cost-effective?" *Tropical Medicine & International Health* 11, no. 4 (2006): 398–408.

Ross, Amanda, Nicolas Maire, Elisa Sicuri, Thomas Smith, and Lesong Conteh. "Determinants of the cost-effectiveness of intermittent preventive treatment for malaria in infants and children." *PloS One* 6, no. 4 (2011): e18391.

Sabot, Oliver, Justin M. Cohen, Michelle S. Hsiang, et al. "Costs and financial feasibility of malaria elimination." *The Lancet* 376, no. 9752 (2010): 1604–15.

Sachs, Jeffrey, and Pia Malaney. "The economic and social burden of malaria." *Nature* 415, no. 6872 (2002): 680–5.

Shillcutt, Samuel, Chantal Morel, Catherine Goodman, Paul et al. "Cost-effectiveness of malaria diagnostic methods in sub-Saharan Africa in an era of combination therapy." *Bulletin of the World Health Organization* 86, no. 2 (2008): 101–10.

Shillcutt, Samuel, Chantal Morel, Catherine Goodman, et al. "Cost-effectiveness of malaria diagnostic methods in sub-Saharan Africa in an era of combination therapy." *Bulletin of the World Health Organization* 86, no. 2 (2008): 101–10.

Smith, David L., Eili Y. Klein, F. Ellis McKenzie, and Ramanan Laxminarayan. "Prospective strategies to delay the evolution of anti-malarial drug resistance: weighing the uncertainty." *Malaria Journal* 9, no. 1 (2010): 217.

Smith, David L., Justin M. Cohen, Christinah Chiyaka, et al. "A sticky situation: the unexpected stability of malaria elimination." *Philosophical Transactions of the Royal Society B: Biological Sciences* 368, no. 1623 (2013): 20120145.

Watkins, W. M. and Mosobo, M. "Treatment of *Plasmodium falciparum* malaria with pyrimethamine-sulphadoxine: selective pressure for resistance is a function of long elimination half-life." *Transactions of the Royal Society of Tropical Medicine and Hygiene* 87, (1993): 75–8.

White, Michael T., Lesong Conteh, Richard Cibulskis, and Azra C. Ghani. "Costs and cost-effectiveness of malaria control interventions-a systematic review." *Malaria Journal* 10, no. 337 (2011): 1475–2875.

White, N. J. "Assessment of the pharmacodynamic properties of antimalarial drugs in vivo." *Antimicrobial Agents and Chemotherapy* 41, no. 7 (1997): 1413.

White, Nicholas. "Antimalarial drug resistance and combination chemotherapy." *Philosophical Transactions of the Royal Society of London. Series B: Biological Sciences* 354, no. 1384 (1999): 739–49.

Wongsrichanalai, Chansuda, Mazie J. Barcus, Sinuon Muth, Awalludin Sutamihardja, and Walther H. Wernsdorfer. "A review of malaria diagnostic tools: microscopy and rapid diagnostic test (RDT)." *The American Journal of Tropical Medicine and Hygiene* 77, no. 6 Suppl (2007): 119–27.

World Health Organization. "Insecticide-treated mosquito nets: a WHO position statement" (Geneva: WHO, 2007).

"World malaria report 2012" (Geneva: WHO, 2012).

World Malaria Report 2008 Geneva: World Health Organization, 2008).

CHAPTER 17

Benefits and Costs of Digital Technology

Infrastructure Targets for the Post-2015 Development Agenda

EMMANUELLE AURIOL AND ALEXIA LEE
GONZÁLEZ FANFALONE

Introduction: The Importance of Information Communication Technologies (ICTs) for Development

Expanding affordable access to information communication technologies (ICTs) infrastructure has become a priority for policy makers, both in developing and developed countries, as ICTs are important enablers for social inclusion and economic development. ICT infrastructure has an impact on growth through several channels: productivity gains, enhanced innovation and new ways to market goods and services, employment, and firm creation, among others (Pepper et al., 2009). The social inclusion dimension is the potential to offer services (e.g., health, education, and e-government) to all communities, however remote.

Sustainable Development Goals and Targets Regarding ICTs

Millennium Development Goals and Post 2015 Agenda: Where Do the Targets Lie in Terms of ICTs?

The International Telecommunications Union (ITU) has followed up on the Millennium Development Goal (MDG) 8F (*Develop a Global Partnership for Development*), which states: "In cooperation with the private sector, make available the benefits of new technologies, especially information and communication technologies." The ITU uses the following indicators to track this target: telephone lines and cellular subscribers per 100 inhabitants, and computers and Internet subscribers per 100 inhabitants.[1] For example, Figure 17.1 displays mobile subscribers per 100 inhabitants (i.e., mobile voice penetration) in developed and developing regions of the world based on ITU statistics.

There has been extensive debate of what goals should be included in the Post-2015 Agenda with regard to ICTs. Although covered explicitly in Goal 9 of the June 2014 *Outcome Document of the Open Working Group on Sustainable Development Goals* (SDGs), the availability of ICTs also has a bearing on other areas such as lifelong learning and gender equality. Goal 9c states: "Significantly increase access to ICT and strive to provide universal and affordable access to Internet in LDCs [least developed countries] by 2020." The question is, what is a "significant" increase? In addition, this target seems to imply universal access to the Internet in five years' time, which may be unrealistic.

Reducing the Scope of ICT Targets and Focusing on Broadband: Why Broadband?

All these different targets beg the question: which targets to choose in order to undertake a cost benefit analysis of such goals for the post 2015 agenda? In order to conduct such analysis, targets must be measurable and with a specific time frame.

---

[1] www.itu.int/en/ITU-D/Statistics/Pages/intlcoop/mdg/default.aspx, and www.unmillenniumproject.org/goals/gti.htm.

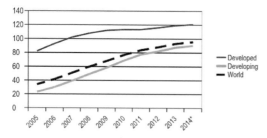

Figure 17.1 *Mobile-cellular subscriptions per 100 inhabitants (mobile voice penetration)*

Note: The developed/developing country classifications are based on the UN M49.[2]
Source: ITU World Telecommunication/ICT Indicators database.

In addition, the scope of the ICT infrastructure goals should be reduced (e.g., broadband, mobile communications) as to improve impact.

The suggestion is to focus on broadband indicators. The justification is twofold. First, it is consistent with what is already written in the latest draft of Sustainable Development Goals (SDGs) in June 2014, which specifically states expanding Internet access in its Goal 9c: "significantly increase access to ICT and strive to provide universal and affordable access to Internet in LDCs by 2020."[3] Second, broadband is a transformative platform that impacts the ICT sector as well as other sectors of the economy. It can contribute to economic growth and enhance productivity, create jobs, and increase consumer surplus as consumers gain access to more services and applications at lower prices.

Figure 17.2 shows a road map for assessing the benefits of broadband infrastructure:

With this in mind, governments in both developing and developed regions of the world since the 2009 economic crisis, have increased investment in broadband as part of their economic stimulus packages. For instance, large investments in broadband infrastructure have been carried on around the world, and numerous National Broadband Plans have been implemented. There are several prominent examples of investment in networks since 2009. For instance, the United States invested USD 97.7 billion in network deployment, China has invested USD 7.44 billion in broadband since 2009, Malaysia USD 1.6 billion since 2009, and Australia has invested AUS 43 billion for the

deployment of a fiber network in eight years' time (LIRNEasia, 2014b).[4]

However, what is called the "digital divide" (within and among countries) remains a key impediment to development (ITU, 2014b). In particular, developing countries are still lagging in broadband deployment, whether it is mobile or fixed infrastructure. For example, in 2014 the developing world displayed less than 6.1 percent fixed broadband penetration versus 27.5 percent in the developed world, and mobile broadband penetration in developing countries was 21.1 percent in 2014 compared to 83.7 percent in the developed world.

All the preceding reasons stress the importance of establishing specific Sustainable Development Goals concerning broadband deployment in the Post-2015 Agenda so that developing countries can reap the benefits that this infrastructure can deliver.

What Is Broadband, and How Can It Be Measured?

Broadband has been defined as an Internet service of at least 256 kbps by the "Partnership for Measuring ICT for Development" (ITU, 2011a, 2011b). At present, OECD countries are revising this definition. The World Bank defines Broadband as an ecosystem, which includes users and applications in an interconnected high-capacity communications network (World Bank, 2011).[5]

---

[2] See the following link for the UN M49 classification: www.itu.int/en/ITU-D/Statistics/Pages/definitions/regions .aspx.

[3] Refer to the June 2014 draft of the SDGs here: http:// sustainabledevelopment.un.org/focussdgs.html.

[4] http://broadbandasia.info/wp-content/uploads/2014/03/ Ford-Lecture-Session-March-7.pdf.

[5] Definitions may vary. For instance, in the World Bank's Broadband Policy Toolkit it says the following: "Despite its worldwide growth and promotion by policymakers, network operators, content providers and other stakeholders, broadband does not have a single, standardized definition. The term 'broadband' may refer to multiple aspects of the network and services, including: 1) the infrastructure or 'pipes' used to deliver services to users; 2) high-speed access to the Internet; and/or 3) the services and applications available via broadband networks, such as Internet protocol television (IPTV) and voice services that may be bundled in a 'triple play' package with broadband Internet access. Further, many countries have established definitions of broadband based on

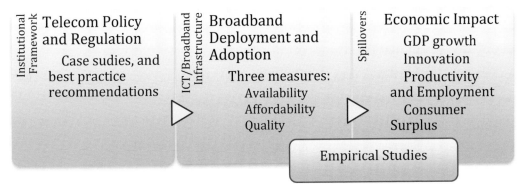

Figure 17.2 *Analytical framework to assess the impact of broadband on the economy*

Broadband services can be measured through three main dimensions: (1) availability, (2) quality, and (3) affordability. Hence, in principle, specific targets surrounding broadband access could take into account these three dimensions if reasonable indicators exist.

Targets regarding **availability** or access to broadband can be formulated around the number of broadband subscriptions per 100 inhabitants (i.e., broadband penetration rates), or by geographical coverage.

Quality of broadband is typically measured by the download speed of the Internet connection. Broadband penetration targets could have the dimension of speed embedded in them. For instance, the Digital Agenda Europe set the goal of that 100 percent of European Union (EU) citizens should have access to basic broadband by the year 2013, 100 percent of broadband coverage by the year 2020 at 30 Mbps (megabytes per second), and 50 percent of households in the year 2020 should have subscriptions with speeds above 100 Mbps (European Commission [EC], 2010).[6] Placing targets in terms of speed will, of course, have an influence on the network deployment cost. It should be noted that there are inherent difficulties surrounding the indicators that measure actual broadband speed (opposed to advertised speeds). Nevertheless, there are three main sources that measure broadband speeds: Ookla, Akamai, and Google.[7]

An example and very useful way of picturing broadband services offered by country is to combine broadband penetration figures with actual

speeds observed in the connections as shown in Chapter 4 of the OECD Communications Outlook 2013 for OECD countries (see OECD, 2013b and Figure 17.3 below).

Affordability of broadband is measured by prices of service packages. It should be noted that prices of telecommunication services depend greatly in the regulatory framework and competitive conditions of the market in each country. The complexity of broadband service plans (e.g., bundles, usage patterns, promotional discounts) makes it difficult to construct indicators to track "pricing" targets at a global scale. The OECD has provided a pricing methodology that incorporates usage baskets (for fixed and mobile broadband) in

speed, typically in Mbps or kilobits per second (Kbps), or based on the types of services and applications that can be used over a broadband network (i.e., functionality). Due to each country's unique needs and history, including economic, geographic and regulatory factors, definitions of broadband vary widely."

[6] See http://eur-lex.europa.eu/legal-content/EN/ALL/;ELX_SESSIONID=sNLXJNSWfJh3TTG5xkL4hrpFLjhwX1HLdWTvCnsvxL1T8zl2SJyb!1619291392?uri=CELEX:52010DC0245R(01).

[7] A caveat should be noted regarding the indicators that may be used to monitor speed targets. There are inherent difficulties surrounding the indicators that measure actual broadband speed (opposed to advertised speeds) as it depends on where servers are located when they measure the connection speed, depends on the user's terminal device, and also varies according to the type of broadband connection (i.e., mobile of fixed broadband). Nevertheless, there are three main sources that measure broadband speed: Ookla, Akamai and Google. See http://explorer.netindex.com/maps for Broadband speed tests from Ookla.

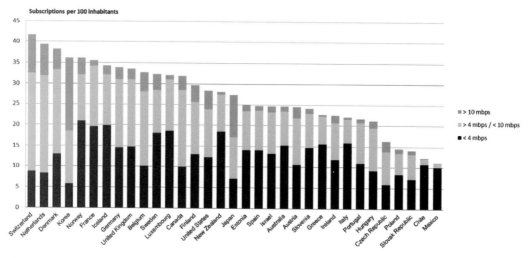

Figure 17.3 *Broadband penetration rates by speed tiers, 2012*

Source: OECD, 2013b. Note: Based on OECD subscription data (June 2012) merged with Akamai's actual speed data.

order to compare prices of broadband services across OECD member countries (see Chapter 7 of OECD, 2013b).[8] However, this methodology requires exhaustive data collection of service plans, at a significant cost. The picture is further complicated by the improvement in the quality of services available over time.[9]

Existing Broadband Targets Proposed by the ITU Broadband Commission in 2010 and Where We Stand in Terms of Achieving Them by 2015

In 2010, the Broadband Commission was set up by the ITU in order to achieve the MDG 8F: "In cooperation with the private sector, make available the benefits of new technologies, especially information and communications technologies."[10] The Broadband Commission established the following targets:

- Target 1: Making broadband policy universal. By 2015, all countries should have a national broadband plan or strategy or include broadband in their Universal Access/Service Definitions.
- Target 2: Making broadband affordable. By 2015, entry-level broadband services should

be made affordable in developing countries through adequate regulation and market forces (amounting to less than 5 percent of average monthly income).

[8] The OECD methodology requires exhaustive data collection of service plans, so even if it would be desirable that a similar benchmark be made available for developing countries, the data collection exercise would require funds in order to be undertaken. The link to the OECD basket methodology is: www.oecd.org/sti/broadband/price-baskets .htm. Nevertheless, some telecommunications research tanks in developing regions have attempted to replicate the OECD pricing methodology of telecom services (see Calandro et al. (2012) for African countries, and Galperin (2012) for Latin American countries).

[9] What adds complexity to the price comparison of ICTs is the adjustment of quality of these services over time. For instance, the quality features of a broadband service plan in the year 2000 differ greatly from those offered in 2014 (e.g., in terms of speed of the connection, or data allowances). For instance, a 100 Mbps Internet offer perhaps was nonexistent some years ago, so comparing offers from, for example, 2007 to 2014, in terms of price per megabyte, would imply comparing different baskets of products. Research using hedonic regression techniques has recently attempted to tackle this problem.

[10] www.broadbandcommission.org/Documents/Broadband _Targets.pdf.

- Target 3: Connecting homes to broadband. By 2015, 40 percent of households in developing countries should have Internet access.
- Target 4: Getting people online. By 2015, Internet user penetration should reach 60 percent worldwide, 50 percent in developing countries, and 15 percent in LDCs.

By mid-2014, none of these seemed likely to be achieved in 2015. The ITU claims that Target 2 was reached by stating the following in the MDG 2014 report: "*The price of broadband services has continued to drop. Globally, between 2008 and 2012, fixed-broadband prices fell by 82 per cent, with the biggest drop occurring in developing countries.*"[11] However, the possible achievement of the affordability criterion is hard to ascertain given that telecommunication prices depend on third-degree price discrimination and bundling techniques (as discussed earlier), making it difficult to compare price figures over time and across countries.

Figures 17.4 and 17.5 show some of the trends in terms of household access to Internet and mobile broadband penetration.

Proposed Broadband Targets for the Post-2015 Agenda

This study focuses on one dimension of broadband, its availability, measured in terms of penetration. This would allow for targets to be concise and measurable.

The specific targets that are suggested and examined for the time frame 2015–2030 are the following:

- Increase world fixed broadband penetration by threefold.
- Increase fixed broadband penetration around threefold in developing regions.
- Increase world mobile broadband penetration around threefold.
- Increase mobile broadband around threefold in the developing regions.
- Achieve 100 percent fixed + mobile broadband penetration (world and developing regions).
- Achieve universal fixed broadband penetration (world and developing regions).

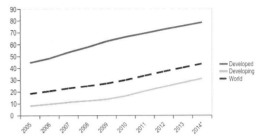

Figure 17.4 *Percentage of households with Internet access at home*

Note: The developed/developing country classifications are based on the UN M49.[12]
Source: ITU World Telecommunication/ICT Indicators database.

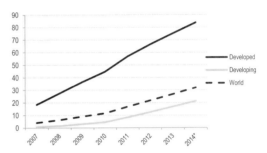

Figure 17.5 *Mobile broadband subscriptions per 100 inhabitants*

Note: The developed/developing country classifications are based on the UN M49.[13]
Source: ITU World Telecommunication/ICT Indicators database.

- Achieve universal mobile broadband penetration (world and developing regions).

A cost-benefit analysis (CBA) is conducted for these targets that will allow us to compare global

[11] See www.un.org/millenniumgoals/2014%20MDG%20report/MDG%202014%20English%20web.pdf, page 53.
[12] See the following link for the UN M49 classification: www.itu.int/en/ITU-D/Statistics/Pages/definitions/regions.aspx.
[13] Idem.

targets (world penetration) versus regional goals (developing regions), as well as universal access by 2030 compared to increasing 2014 broadband penetration levels by threefold. We take into account the 2014 broadband penetration levels as the status quo and then calculate the expected deployment as a function of the stipulated targets.

Cost Benefit Analysis of Deploying Broadband Infrastructure

The challenges with the CBA in the case of broadband infrastructure are twofold. First, it is extremely difficult to calculate the cost of deploying infrastructure at a global level given differences in technologies, geographical situation, market conditions, and connection speed targets. Furthermore, the cost of the deployment will depend on whether governments wish to deploy basic, fast, or ultrafast broadband. Second, there is much debate on how to calculate the benefits of ICT infrastructure given the spillovers it has on GDP. Broadband has become a general purpose technology (GPT), with significant effects on growth, but to quantify the externality has been the subject of an entire research agenda over the past few years.

In addition to these challenges, given the evolving cost structures and demand patterns, there is an inherent degree of uncertainty in such a dynamic sector. With these caveats in mind, we estimate illustrative CBAs of each suggested target against the status quo of current broadband penetration levels.

Measuring the Benefits of Broadband Deployment

In economic literature, the following empirical approaches have been taken into account to quantify the impact of broadband on the economy:

- Input-output tables: What is the impact of broadband infrastructure deployment on output and employment generation within a country?
- Multivariate regression techniques: What is the contribution to GDP growth, productivity, and employment?
- Consumer surplus perspective: What are the benefits that broadband represents to the end user?

European Commission (2013) shows the cumulative benefits of meeting the targets in the Digital Agenda for Europe (DAE) by deploying high-speed broadband in Europe from 2012 to 2020. With modest state aid, the European Union can expect to receive cumulative benefits of between EUR 200 billion and EUR 600 billion in the period 2012 to 2020, representing a benefit cost ratio of 2.7 and 2.9.

The present study establishes the benefits of broadband deployment focusing in the impact that this infrastructure has on GDP growth. Katz (ITU, 2012) summarizes three main channels for this. First, the deployment of broadband technology across firms improves their productivity given the adoption of more efficient business processes. Second, extensive broadband deployment increases innovation through new applications and services. Third, broadband leads to a more efficient functioning of firms by maximizing their reach to labor pools or access to raw materials or consumers.

A study conducted by the World Bank (Qiang and Rossotto, 2009) showed that broadband has the largest impact on growth compared to other telecommunication investments For instance, in low- and medium-income economies, this World Bank study estimated that a 10 percent increase in broadband penetration would represent an increase in economic growth of almost 1.4 percent.

There exists consensus in the literature that there is a positive relationship between broadband and growth. Whether this relationship is causal has been tackled by some studies. That is, countries with high GDP growth may also have the means to invest in broadband deployment and hence will exhibit higher broadband penetration levels. On the other hand, it could be that broadband investment leads to GDP growth. The latter issue is known in the literature as reverse causality or endogeneity concerns

Reverse causality – i.e., the hypothesis that broadband investment boosts growth rather than itself

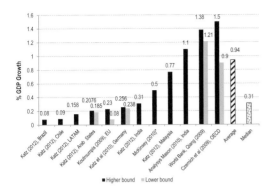

Figure 17.6 *Percentage increase of GDP for each 10 percent increase in broadband penetration*

Source: Authors' elaboration using the World Bank Broadband Policy Toolkit and ITU (2012); McKinsey & Company analysis Report 2010 for the WEF.[14]

being a consequence of growth – has been particularly addressed in the study by Koutroumpis (2009). With this study in mind, we derive the potential benefits of broadband in the present study by calculating the percentage impact on GDP growth using as reference the elasticities presented in the study by Koutroumpis (2009). These range from 0.008 to 0.023 percent increase on GDP growth for each 1 percent increase in broadband penetration.

A summary of empirical studies that have assessed the impact of broadband on economic growth can be seen in Figure 17.6. As shown in this figure, the economic impact of every 10 percent increase of broadband penetration on GDP growth varies from 0.08 to 1.5 percent due to differences in model specifications and datasets used. It should be noted that some of these studies are only done for one country in particular, while other studies include data from a cross section of countries.

Measuring the Costs of Broadband Deployment

Understanding the Costs: How Does a Broadband Network Work?

There are two elements of a broadband network: the access network connects the end user with the nearest network node, and the backhaul and core network are connectivity links over large distances within a country.

The access network connects the core and backhaul network to the final user, which can be a local wireless or wireline access to the end user. In the case of a wireline (or fixed network) the access network is comprised of a copper, fiber, or a cable that connects the end user to a backhaul node. In the case of a wireless network, it is the connection of a cellular tower to the end user using spectrum for this last mile. The core network is comprised of the national backbone network, usually made out of fiber. The backhaul network is comprised of metropolitan lines that connect the local access network to the national backbone through fiber or microwave links.

Figure 17.7 illustrates the different elements of a broadband network and the types of technology used for each of these network elements.

The cost of deployment depends on the speed targets embedded in the broadband coverage targets. For instance, Katz et al. (2010) in their study of the German digital agenda found that the cost of deployment per line in order to reach 50 percent of German households with ultrafast broadband (i.e., fiber-to-the-home [FTTH] with speeds up to 100 Mbps) would translate into a cost per line of EUR 1150–1425. On the other hand, in Brazil, a basic broadband line at 1 Mbps speeds would cost around USD 300 in case of an upgrade and USD 450 in case of new line deployment (ITU, 2012).

It is important to note that deployment cost per line will also depend on technology used and population density, as shown in the study of the deployment costs of ultrafast broadband in Spain by Feijóo and Barroso (2010). For instance, these authors found that wireless technology such as long-term evolution (LTE) was more expensive than fixed solutions where population density exceeded 3000 inhabitants per square kilometer, whereas fiber deployments (i.e., fiber-to-the home or FTTH) became more expensive in less-dense areas (WIK, 2012).

---

[14] See the McKinsey & Company analysis Report 2010 for the WEF here: www.weforum.org/pdf/GITR10/Part1/Chap%205_Fostering%20the%20Economic%20and%20Social%20Benefits%20of%20ICT.pdf.

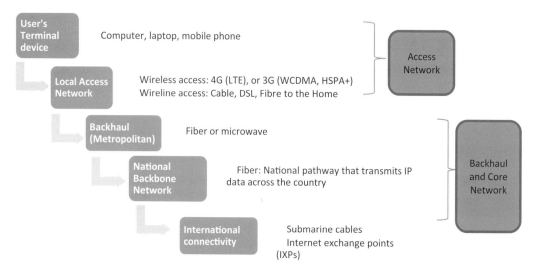

Figure 17.7 *Elements of a broadband network, access, and core/backhaul network*

Source: Authors' elaboration based on European Union Guide to Broadband Investment (EU, 2011; TRAI, 2014).

The Telecom Regulatory Authority of India (TRAI) calculated that the cost per line to reach an Indian household through cable technology was around USD140 (8450 Rp.), whereas, TRAI calculated that the cost per line using FTTH technology was USD510 in capital expenditures (CAPEX), plus USD116 in operational expenditures (OPEX) per year (31200 Rp. of CAPEX plus 7089 Rp. annually in OPEX). The latter translates to a total cost per line of around USD1700.

The Challenges of Assessing Costs in an Aggregated Form

There are many challenges to establishing cost per line deployment at a global level, given that it is highly unlikely to have "one size fits all" infrastructure within and across countries. In addition, the cost of deployment will ultimately depend on the bandwidth requirements envisaged for the network.

Despite these difficulties, this section will use as a benchmark the cost per line calculated in studies related to network deployment investments within the context of national broadband plans and digital agendas, bearing in mind the caveats noted earlier.[15]

A Simplified Methodology to Assess the Benefit-Cost Ratio

The explicit targets to be analyzed are found in Table 17.1.

To calculate the stream of costs and benefits and to bring them to present value, the first step is to calculate the expected change in terms of subscriptions that are embedded in each target. For this calculation, a United Nations estimate of the projected population in 2030 was used to derive the number of expected lines to be covered in the world and in developing regions in 2030.

[15] A useful reference to several countries undertaking broadband investments and National Broadband plans to increase quality, price and availability of Broadband can be found in the study undertaken by Harvard's Berkman Center for Internet and Society, commissioned by the FCC as a background paper for their broadband stimulus package in 2009. See http://transition.fcc.gov/stage/pdf/Berkman_Center_Broadband_Study_13Oct09.pdf. Another useful reference is the ITU, 2012 publication "Impact of Broadband in the Economy," which provides an extensive review of the studies measuring the impact to date, with several tables about investment carried on in different countries. See www.itu.int/ITU-D/treg/broadband/ITU-BB-Reports_Impact-of-Broadband-on-the-Economy.pdf.

Table 17.1 Targets to be analyzed in the CBA

	Broadband penetration targets for 2030
Target 1	Increase world fixed broadband penetration by threefold from 2014 levels (from 10% to 30% in 2030).
Target 2	Increase Developing countries' fixed broadband penetration by approximately threefold from 2014 levels (from 6% to 20% in 2030).
Target 3	Increase world mobile broadband penetration by approximately threefold from 2014 levels (from 32% to 90% in 2030).
Target 4	Increase developing countries' mobile broadband penetration by approximately threefold (from 21% in 2014 to 60% in 2030).
Target 5*	Increase world penetration of fixed+ mobile broadband from 42% in 2014 to 100% 2030 (assuming to reach the target with one-third of fixed lines and two-thirds of mobile connections).
Target 6*	Increase developing countries' penetration of fixed+ mobile broadband from 27% in 2014 to 80% in 2030 (reaching the target with one-third of fixed lines and two-thirds of mobile connections).
Target 7	Universal fixed broadband penetration by the year 2030.
Target 8	Universal mobile broadband penetration by the year 2030.

Note: (*) For targets 5 and 6 (i.e., targets that refer to mobile plus fixed broadband penetration), it is assumed that one-third of the target would be fulfilled with fixed networks and two-thirds with wireless networks.
Source: Analysys Mason and Tech4i2: www.analysysmason.com/About-Us/News/Press- releases1/broadband-benefit- for-EU-Mar2013/.

The global population is projected as 8,218 million, with 6,952 million people living in developing regions.[16]

Table 17.2 shows how many lines (subscriptions) would be covered with the eight proposed targets.

Calculating the Benefits

The benefits of this increase of broadband lines are mapped to the potential GDP growth impact using the elasticities from the empirical studies mentioned in Figure 17.6, using this as a proxy of social welfare.

In all three scenarios (i.e., conservative, medium, and optimistic) displayed in Table 17.4, the benefits are calculated taking into account the elasticity of impact on GDP growth by Koutroumpis (2009), recognizing that it is a conservative estimate.

In order to derive the Compound Annual Growth Rate (CAGR) of GDP due to broadband penetration, the formula described in Annex 1 is used, which is based on the formula used in Koutroumpis (2009) and originally presented by Roeller and Waverman (2001).

A growth rate of the economy is assumed for the time period and is applied to the status quo of world GDP, and GDP in developing regions in 2013 (World Bank data), which corresponds to USD 74.9 trillion and USD 24.5 trillion, respectively.[17] Then, the CAGR of GDP due to broadband is applied to these initial levels of GDP. Only the incremental GDP resulting from the attributed growth rate derived from broadband penetration during the period 2015–2030 is counted as a benefit. Finally, the flow of incremental GDP from broadband is brought to net present value.

The Cost per Line Assumptions

For the analysis to be feasible, to determine the cost per line by type of network (i.e., mobile or fixed broadband), some very simplistic assumptions must be used. These cost assumptions vary in the three scenarios of the CBA due to possible cost variations inherent to heterogeneous geographic conditions, technology used, and other country specific conditions.

---

[16] See developing and developed world classification used by the United Nations in http://unstats.un.org/unsd/methods/m49/m49regin.htm#developed and www.itu.int/en/ITU-D/Statistics/Pages/definitions/regions.aspx. As mentioned in the note, the population estimates in order to derive the number of lines aimed to be covered for 2030 embedded in these penetration rates targets were retrieved from the United Nations population estimates http://esa.un.org/unpd/wpp/Excel-Data/population.htm.

[17] The growth rates assumed are based on World Bank projections of the growth of the economy for the year 2016.

Table 17.2 Mapping penetration targets to change in lines needed for each target

	Penetration 2014	Subscribers 2014 in millions	Penetration target 2030	Change in penetration 2014–2030	Subs. in 2030** (millions)	Change in subs. 2014–2030 (millions)
Target 1 Fixed broadband (BB) World	10%	711.13	30%	20%	2465.49	1754.36
Target 2 Fixed BB Developing Regions	6%	366.31	20%	14%	1390.36	1024.05
Target 3 Mobile BB World	32%	2315.26	90%	58%	7396.47	5081.21
Target 4 Mobile BB Developing Regions	21%	1265.11	60%	39%	4171.08	2905.97
Target 5* Fixed+ Mobile BB World	42%	3026.40	99%	57%	8136.12	5109.72
Target 6* Fixed+ Mobile BB Dev. regions	27%	1631.42	80%	53%	5561.44	3930.02
Target 7 Universal fixed BB World	10%	711.13	99%	89%	8136.12	7424.98
Target 8 Universal mobile BB World	32%	2315.26	99%	67%	8136.12	5820.86

Note: (*) For targets 5 and 6 (i.e., targets that refer to mobile plus fixed broadband penetration), it is assumed that one-third of the target would be fulfilled with fixed networks and two-thirds with wireless networks. (**) To estimate world and developing region targets in terms of subscribers, the estimated population figures of the UN with constant mortality rate were used.
Source: Katz, Raul and Javier G. Avila (2010), The Impact of Broadband Policy on the Economy, *Proceedings of the 4thd ACORN-REDECOM Conference*, Brasilia, May 14–15, 2010 (2010).

The different costs of deployment assumed for the different scenarios (i.e., high/medium/low cost of deployment) are based on the cost per line by type of technology shown in Table 17.3.

In the **conservative scenario** (i.e., high cost of deployment), the cost per fixed line considered is EUR 1500 (USD 1910) per line, based on WIK (2012).[18] The assumed cost per fixed line in the **medium scenario** is EUR 1150 (USD 1460), based on Katz et al. (2010) analysis of Germany's digital agenda targets.[19] For wireless deployment costs, the **medium and conservative scenario** takes the cost estimates presented in WIK (2012) report (i.e., EUR 500 per line, or USD 640). Based on WIK (2012), the **optimistic scenario**

considers a cost of EUR 400 (USD 510) and EUR 600 (USD 770) per wireless and fixed line, respectively.

These cost assumptions seem in line with the cost per line from other sources, such as the OECD

[18] This figure used by the WIK, 2012 report uses data from Feijóo and Gomez-Barroso (2010), which are similar to Katz et al. (2010) cost per line of deploying fiber in less dense areas.

[19] However, we only base the cost of a fixed line connection from this study given that other sources indicate that wireless lines are less expensive to deploy. See www.polynomics.ch/dokumente/Polynomics_Broadband_Brochure_E.pdf.

Table 17.3 Cost per line assumptions used for the cost-benefit analysis

	Cost per line	Currency	USD (2010)	Source
LTE (Wireless)	400	EUR	509.55	WIK 2012 (based on Feijóo and Gómez Barroso, 2010)
	500	EUR	636.94	WIK 2012 (based on Feijóo and Gómez Barroso, 2010)
VDSL* (Fixed)	300	EUR	382.17	Katz et al. (2010) report for Germany; WIK 2012
	400	EUR	509.55	Katz et al. (2010) report for Germany
FTTH (Fixed)	600	EUR	764.33	WIK 2012 (based on Feijóo and Gómez Barroso, 2010)
	1150	EUR	1464.97	Katz et al. (2010) report for Germany
	1425	EUR	1815.29	Katz et al. (2010) report for Germany
	1500	EUR	1910.83	WIK 2012 (based on Feijóo and Gómez Barroso, 2010)

* Very-high bit-rate digital subscriber line.

Note: Source of annual exchange rate USD/EUR of 0.785 in 2010 is from the US Internal Revenue Service.
Source: Authors' elaboration based on WIK (2012) and Katz et al. (2010)

report, "Network developments in support of innovation and user needs" (OECD, 2009b).[20]

Results of the Cost-Benefit Analysis

The results of the cost-benefit ratios are shown in Table 17.4.

The rapid rate of technological change makes it particularly difficult to assess costs and benefits for ICT investments. Because the standard 3 percent and 5 percent discount rates are low compared to those used by telecom companies when they make investment decisions, Table 17.4 also shows results using a discount factor of 8.8 percent based on a study by WIK (2013).[21]

We now focus our attention on the conservative scenario given that it underestimates the impact of broadband on GDP and overestimates the costs of deployment. In all cases, the cost-benefit ratios are quite high. For the purpose of comparing these targets with other development targets, Table 17.5 shows only the 3 percent and 5 percent discount factor results.

In all three scenarios (i.e., conservative, medium, or optimistic scenario), the targets for the expansion of broadband penetration (either mobile or fixed) by threefold in developing regions

of the world exhibit the highest B/C ratios (Targets 2 and Target 4). The next most attractive target is expanding world mobile broadband by threefold (Target 3). Increasing world fixed broadband penetration threefold (from 10–30 percent, Target 1) also exhibits a large B/C ratio. Universal penetration goals have the lowest B/C ratios, with the exception of achieving this goal through mobile broadband.

A valuable takeaway is that it is more cost effective to meet universal penetration goals via wireless deployment. In fact, the B/C ratio of achieving universal coverage through mobile broadband is quite high (i.e., 11.43). However,

---

[20] This was one of the first studies attempting to analyze the cost and benefits of broadband deployment at an international level and assumes costs of EUR 500 per VDSL line and EUR 1500 per fiber-to the-home line (OECD, 2009b). The OECD 2009 report also mentions that the Dutch regulator OPTA arrived at the estimate of EUR 1000 per fast-broadband line, while the in the United Kingdom costs per line were estimated around GBP 980. In addition, the report highlights that the telecommunications operator, Verizon, in the United States estimated a cost per ultrafast broadband line of USD 1400 (OECD, 2009b).

[21] http://stakeholders.ofcom.org.uk/binaries/consultations/fixed-access-markets/responses/TalkTalk_Group_second_addit1.pdf.

Table 17.4 Cost-benefit ratios depending on three scenarios

B/C	Conservative Scenario			Medium Scenario			Optimistic Scenario		
Disc. Factor	3%	5%	8.8%	3%	5%	8.8%	3%	5%	8.8%
Target 1	12.25	12.05	11.70	21.16	20.71	19.92	52.79	51.38	48.89
Target 2	13.64	13.34	12.82	21.58	21.01	20.02	50.19	48.62	45.88
Target 3	13.00	12.76	12.35	17.51	17.10	16.38	29.47	28.59	27.06
Target 4	14.41	14.08	13.52	17.60	17.13	16.30	27.29	26.41	24.88
Target 5*	7.86	7.72	7.46	12.33	12.04	11.52	25.42	24.65	23.31
Target 6*	6.49	6.35	6.09	9.26	9.00	8.56	17.64	17.06	16.03
Target 7	3.02	2.97	2.87	5.32	5.19	4.97	13.58	13.17	12.45
Target 8	11.43	11.22	10.85	15.46	15.09	14.44	26.13	25.34	23.95

Notes: All three scenarios consider the elasticity of impact on GDP growth from Koutroumpis (2009). The conservative scenario assumes an elasticity equal to 0.008, a high cost of deployment, and low expected annual growth rate of GDP. The medium scenario assumes an elasticity of 0.014, medium costs of deployment, and medium expected growth rate of the economy. The optimistic scenario assumes an elasticity of 0.023, a low cost of deployment, and a high growth rate of the economy. For the explicit assumptions, please refer to Annex 2.

Table 17.5 Net present value (NPV) of benefits and costs of conservative scenario, USD millions

Conservative Scenario		3%			5%		
TARGETS		NVP Benefits	NPV Costs	B/C	NVP Benefits	NPV Costs	B/C
Target 1	Increase world fixed broadband penetration by threefold	32,068,336	2,616,850	**12.25**	27,213,741	2,257,829	**12.05**
Target 2	Increase developing countries' fixed broadband penetration by threefold	20,841,084	1,527,503	**13.64**	17,587,457	1,317,936	**13.34**
Target 3	Increase world mobile broadband penetration by approximately threefold	33,176,665	2,553,024	**13.00**	28,109,846	2,202,759	**12.76**
Target 4	Increase developing countries' mobile broadband penetration by threefold	21,034,511	1,460,090	**14.41**	17,742,743	1,259,771	**14.08**
Target 5*	100% world penetration of (fixed+ mobile broadband) by 2030	33,426,217	4,252,173	**7.86**	28,311,555	3,668,792	**7.72**
Target 6*	80% (fixed+ mobile broadband penetration) in developing regions	21,236,609	3,270,460	**6.49**	17,904,963	2,821,766	**6.35**
Target 7	Universal fixed broadband penetration by the year 2030	33,460,381	11,075,333	**3.02**	28,339,167	9,555,842	**2.97**
Target 8	Universal mobile broadband penetration by the year 2030	33,440,094	2,924,655	**11.43**	28,322,771	2,523,404	**11.22**

Notes: All currency figures in USD millions. For targets 5 and 6, it is assumed that one-third of the target would be fulfilled with fixed networks and two-thirds with wireless networks.
Source: WIK (2012), Re-thinking the Digital Agenda for Europe (DAE): A richer choice of technologies, Independent analysis conducted by WIK-Consult GmbH on behalf of Liberty Global, September 2012. Katz, Raul and Javier G. Avila (2010), The Impact of Broadband Policy on the Economy, Proceedings of the 4thd ACORN-REDECOM Conference Brasilia May 14–15, 2010 (2010).

these results depend on the cost assumptions and the available indicators chosen to measure these targets. Nevertheless, it should be noted that network deployment targets should be met with the principle of technology neutrality.

The Importance of Wireless for the Developing World

The costs savings of deploying mobile network are quite significant. Some studies suggest that the cost per user of a wired network may be three times higher than a wireless network (Rahunathan, 2005). The main reason for this cost difference is that in a wireless network, the "last mile" (i.e., the access to the end user in the local network) is shared through a cellular site using radio-electric spectrum rather than requiring substantial investment in cabling.[22]

Moreover, LTE wireless technology already achieves mobile broadband connections with speeds of 10–30 Mbps in some parts of the world. It is expected that new innovations in wireless, such as cognitive radio and making available more spectrum, should ensure that higher broadband speeds in the future (LIRNEasia, 2014a).

For the case of a country like India, with high population density and prevalent TV networks, cable seems a cost-effective option for broadband deployment (Marcus and Jain, 2010). Also, with mobile voice networks having grown strongly, in contrast to fixed networks, there is a strong case for mobile broadband as a cost-effective solution in India and other developing countries.[23]

In addition to cost savings of wireless technology, a report by McKinsey and Co., "Fostering the Economic and Social Benefits of ICT," for the World Economic Forum (WEF, 2010), estimated that bringing mobile broadband penetration in emerging markets to the levels of penetration of mature markets could add $300–400 billion to global GDP and translate into 10–14 million direct jobs in emerging regions (WEF, 2010).

Finally, most Internet connections in the developing regions of the world are bound to be from wireless devices. An ICT research think tank in Southeast Asia, LIRNEasia, pointed out

that most people from developing countries get connected to the Internet through mobile phones (LIRNEasia, 2014a).[24]

There are interesting examples in Africa and Asia of how mobile Internet access is becoming more and more important for developing countries based on survey data. For instance, in 2012 in Ethiopia and Uganda, 81 percent of users accessed the Internet through a mobile device in the previous 12 months, and around 70 percent of users in these countries accessed the Internet for the first time using a mobile device. Access through mobile Internet makes sense given that in 2012 only 0.9 percent and 0.5 percent of households had a working fixed Internet connection at home in Ethiopia and Uganda, respectively (Calandro et al., 2012).

Other examples include Tanzania, Namibia, and Nigeria, where about 50 percent of users accessed the Internet for the first time on a mobile phone (Calandro et al., 2012). In China, by the end of 2012, there were 422 million mobile Internet users (64.4 million more than in 2011), and among the total of Chinese Internet users, 75.4 percent accessed the Internet using their mobile phones (China Internet Network Information Center, 2013).

Sensitivity Analysis of the Conservative Scenario

A sensitivity analysis can be conducted by varying the parameters of the CBA, such as the growth rate of the economy, the elasticity of broadband impact

---

[22] Civil engineering costs in a wired or fixed network, including trenches, ducts, posts, cable, and rights of way, may represent 30 percent to 80 percent of the total network's capital expenditures. See European Regulatory Group (2007), p. 17; Ofcom (2008), p. 14; and OECD (2008), p. 20.

[23] In fact, fixed voice networks are very insipient in India (almost nonexistent with only 3 percent penetration), whereas mobile voice penetration has exploded in the past decade (from 3 percent in 2003 to 72 percent in 2011 according to ITU data).

[24] LIRNEasia highlighted in September 2014, within the context of a consultation document of India's National Broadband Plans, the importance of wireless networks to boost access in developing countries.

Table 17.6 Main parameter assumptions by scenario

SCENARIOS	
Optimistic	• High elasticity of the impact of broadband penetration on growth (0.023) • Low deployment costs (USD 510 per wireless line and USD 770 per fixed line) • High growth rate of the economy (3.5% for world, and 5.5% for developing regions)
Medium	• High elasticity of the impact of broadband penetration on growth (0.014) • Medium deployment costs (USD 640 per wireless line and USD 1460 USD per fixed line) • Medium growth rate of economy (3% for world and 5% for developing regions)
Conservative	• Low elasticity of the impact of broadband penetration on growth (0.008), • High deployment costs (USD 640 for wireless technology and USD 1900 for fixed line), • Low growth rate of economy (2.5% for the world and 4.5% for developing regions)

on GDP growth, or the deployment cost assumptions. Table 17.6 shows the main parameters used for each of the scenarios. The sensitivity analysis is based on the conservative scenario results shown in Table 17.5 earlier.

The results of the benefit-to-cost ratios in Table 17.5 change slightly when different elasticities of broadband impact on economic growth are assumed. For instance, when assuming a medium elasticity (0.014 percent), the ratios increase around 8 percent, whereas the elasticity of the optimistic scenario (0.023 percent) improve around 21 percent. If one takes into account the elasticity presented in Qiang and Rossotto (2009), the ratios greatly improve (almost 2.5 times higher).

If one assumes a medium growth rate of the economy, as a whole ratios improve around 14 percent (depending on the target). A high growth rate of the economy would lead to an increase of these ratios by 23–30 percent.

When varying the assumed costs, the ratios can greatly improve. If we change to the optimistic scenario costs (keeping constant the conservative scenario growth rates and assumed elasticities), the ratios improve around 25–147 percent. If we

assume the costs per line of the medium scenario, the ratios improve 16–30 percent.

Robustness Check: A Different Methodology to Assess the Benefits

The CBA analysis in Table 17.5 uses Roeller and Waverman's (2001) formula for the CAGR of the economy attributed to broadband; this method tends to underestimate changes in the levels of broadband penetration for the same time period.

Another way of calculating the benefits is to take the elasticity estimated by Koutroumpis (2009) and multiply it by the percent change in broadband penetration given the established penetration targets. This "percent impact" on the economic growth is assumed to be linear across the period (i.e., divided by the number of years, which in our case is 16). This "yearly percent impact" on the GDP growth is additional to the baseline assumed GDP growth rate.

The advantage of this method is that it allows accounting for greater changes in the penetration levels embedded in the targets. The caveat is that the benefits may be overestimated given that the elasticity of the impact of broadband penetration on economic growth (which is a local concept) is applied linearly over the whole period. In contrast, the benefit calculation used for Table 17.5 implicitly assumes by the nonlinearity of the benefits.

The B/C ratios calculated by this methodology are shown in Table 17.7. In this case, the highest ratios are those of Targets 3, 4, and 8, which all relate to increases in mobile broadband penetration (which is much cheaper to deploy than fixed networks). The target that is robust to both methodologies is to increase mobile broadband penetration by threefold in the developing world (Target 4). In addition, if universal targets are desired, this is best achieved with mobile broadband (Target 8).

Institutional Framework as the Foundation to Reap the Benefits of ICT

Given the importance of ICTs for development, what should governments do to foster ICT networks? The World Bank points out that

Table 17.7 CBA using different methodology to assess the benefits

Conservative Scenario		3%			5%		
TARGETS		NVP Benefits	NPV Costs	B/C	NVP Benefits	NPV Costs	B/C
Target 1	Increase world fixed broadband penetration by threefold	42,390,809	2,616,850	**16.20**	36,066,886	2,257,829	**15.97**
Target 2	Increase developing countries' fixed broadband penetration by threefold	23,256,962	1,527,503	**15.23**	19,657,414	1,317,936	**14.92**
Target 3	Increase world mobile broadband penetration by approximately threefold	75,098,009	2,553,024	**29.42**	63,424,511	2,202,759	**28.79**
Target 4	Increase developing countries' mobile broadband penetration by threefold	31,739,474	1,460,090	**21.74**	26,698,437	1,259,771	**21.19**
Target 5*	100% world penetration of (fixed+ mobile broadband) by 2030	74,316,157	4,252,173	**17.48**	62,773,903	3,668,792	**17.11**
Target 6*	80% (fixed+ mobile broadband penetration) in developing regions	37,104,968	3,270,460	**11.35**	31,129,633	2,821,766	**11.03**
Target 7	Universal fixed broadband penetration by the year 2030	109,094,260	11,075,333	**9.85**	91,588,082	9,555,842	**9.58**
Target 8	Universal mobile broadband penetration by the year 2030	84,188,760	2,924,655	**28.79**	70,978,911	2,523,404	**28.13**

Note: (*) For targets 5 and 6 (i.e., targets that refer to Mobile plus fixed broadband penetration), it is assumed that one-third of the target would be fulfilled with fixed networks and two-thirds with wireless networks.

governments should ensure that markets work more efficiently and should ensure equitable ICT access for all (World Bank, 2011). Some key enablers for ICT infrastructure development as a way to promote efficiency and extend ICT coverage can be summarized as follows:

- Competition in the telecommunications service provider market
- Policies that foster the access and adoption of ICTs
- Development of applications and local content
- Government aid to extend ICT network coverage and provide services in underserved areas (i.e., investment in strategic parts of the network)

Pepper et al. (2009) mention two key elements to foster ICT access and use: (1) the ecosystem, such as ICT market competition and ICT policies and regulation, and (2) infrastructure, which includes

physical infrastructure (international connectivity, domestic networks), as well as ICT skilled human capital in the country. In order to foster ICT infrastructure, policy makers should strive to tackle both institutional and regulatory framework conditions as well as to provide incentives for network deployment.

Specific Policy and Regulatory Interventions to Foster Network Deployment

Deployment of broadband infrastructure is an expensive undertaking, given the large fixed costs that it entails, so any measures that reduce the cost of deployment should help public funding make a greater impact as well as rendering investment by private operators more attractive. In general, any policy or regulation that reduces deployment costs should maximize the social impact of the investment.

To reduce entry barriers and provide incentives to invest in networks, governments can take the following set of actions:

- Institutional framework to tackle anticompetitive behavior
- Regulatory telecommunications framework focused on wholesale remedies
- Efficient interconnection policies (i.e., wholesale access obligations, as well as access fees regulated at costs)
- Efficient spectrum management
- Re-use of existing infrastructure (e.g., ducts and trenches from other utilities as well as infrastructure-sharing policies among established operators)
- Streamlining the provision of rights of way when deploying infrastructure (this may depend of municipal authorities)
- State aids in broadband infrastructure should be analyzed as to not crowd out private investment, the tendering process should be transparent and technology neutral, and state aids should be accompanied by open access regulations to the subsidized networks

Regulations That May Help Reduce the Cost of Network Deployment

Bottlenecks in telecommunications networks exist where network facilities would be uneconomically duplicated and where new entrants must purchase services from incumbents (e.g., wholesale broadband access; OECD, 2012a). The aim of ex ante regulation is "to prevent a dominant operator from engaging in anticompetitive practices such as 'deny, delay and degrade' tactics in the provision of essential wholesale access products to new entrant competitors" (OECD, 2012a). Thus, regulators set ex ante conditions of access to network elements of the incumbent or dominant player's network.[25]

In the case of fixed network deployment, it has been estimated that the largest costs are associated to the access network. For instance, construction costs for fiber-to-the-home networks are estimated at around 60–80 percent of total roll out costs (OECD, 2011).

As incumbents may have a significant advantage over entrants because of their historical monopoly position and existing rights of way, European and OECD countries have recognized that ex ante regulations need to be put in place to reduce bottlenecks. For instance, Korea and Hong Kong, both leaders in fiber deployment in the world, have promoted open access to the inside wiring of apartment buildings, which in turn has facilitated infrastructure competition (OECD, 2013a).

With regard to wireless networks, the access network, or "last mile," consists basically of antennas, towers, and spectrum. Because, as discussed earlier, wireless networks may become very important to reach broadband penetration targets in developing regions of the world, it is worthwhile to focus on two important elements that may drive the cost of deploying wireless networks down: effective spectrum management and infrastructure sharing.

Spectrum Management

Wireless technologies require spectrum as an essential input, thus spectrum management is crucial in promoting market entry. Efficient spectrum management not only means making spectrum available, but also ensuring its efficient allocation so that players in the market have incentives to deploy networks and effectively compete in the market. Allowing the purchase of spectrum holdings by new entrants has been a useful tool to increase competition in telecommunications markets.

Infrastructure Sharing

Infrastructure sharing is becoming more and more common in European and OECD countries, especially in rural areas (OECD, 2012a). For instance, Vodafone and Telefonica have reached an

---

[25] These conditions include the fees, and a typical example of ex ante regulation in Europe and OECD countries is wholesale interconnection of networks. For example, in Europe mobile termination (i.e., interconnection) fees are regulated ex ante by the NRAs following a Long Run Incremental Cost (LRIC) methodology, given that all mobile operators have a monopoly in the termination of their calls.

agreement of sharing infrastructure in European markets wherever both firms are present (OECD, 2014b).

There are two main infrastructure-sharing agreements: passive, which involves the sharing of masts, towers or sites, and cabinets, and active infrastructure sharing (involving antennas, nodes, and even spectrum). Analysis Mason (2010b) estimated that wireless infrastructure sharing might reduce operators' capital expenditures in 30 percent and 15 percent of operational expenditures.

One of the most important elements in the development of a mobile network is the location of towers and antennas. To promote the entry of new competitors into the market, regulatory authorities in various countries have implemented policies aimed at fostering site and tower sharing among mobile operators.

The Importance of an Independent Regulator and Competition Authority

There should be an institutional and regulatory framework to tackle anticompetitive behavior and to enforce ex ante regulation in a sector where the nature of the cost structure naturally results in an oligopoly market. Independent national regulatory agencies and competition authorities are very important, as they play an essential role in facilitating sector development and growth by providing regulatory certainty and a level playing field in the market.

A well-designed independent regulator should enable clear separation between industrial policy and sector regulation aiming to boost competition. This would reduce exposure to political drivers when the regulator takes actions to foster competition. It becomes even more relevant in a setting where there is public ownership of telecommunications operators given that an independent regulator may avoid conflicts of interest (OECD, 2014b).

Competition Authorities should be independent from government to avoid political interference. Also, both the national regulatory agency and the competition authority should have enforcement powers over their decisions, meaning reasonable sanctioning powers to foster compliance of regulation and competition measures.

State Aid When Funding Broadband Investment Projects and Open Access Obligations

Despite the advantages of an active role of government in promoting broadband network deployment, there always exists a risk of crowding out private investments. The 2009 European Commission's State Aid Guidelines for Broadband Investments (henceforth referred to as the EC Broadband Guidelines) provide the safeguards that should be put in place to promote competition while fostering rapid roll-out of broadband networks (EC, 2009). Several broadband state aid projects within the European Union have been granted over the past few years, and all of them comply with the EC Broadband Guidelines (see Table 17.10 in Annex 3 for examples of broadband state aids granted in the EU).[26]

The EC Broadband Guidelines establish that broadband stimulus should be granted where market failure has been established, for instance where no service is available or where coverage is insufficient. In addition, the Guidelines state that publicly funded broadband infrastructure projects should commit to open access to all operators with public documentation of the terms and conditions of access as well as transparent pricing to ensure nondiscrimination (LIRNEasia, 2014a).

What Type of Broadband Infrastructure Should Governments Fund to Reduce Network Deployment Costs?

An important role of the government is to ensure that high-speed robust core backbone networks are available across the country. In many cases, a clear and predictable regulatory environment will attract private investment to build core broadband networks; in others, public investment may be required to generate the externalities that core networks offer (Pepper et al., 2009).

Many governments have opted to provide funds for international connectivity (i.e., submarine cables or satellite links), the core and backhaul

---

[26] See all state aids granted for Broadband Networks in the European Union in the following link: http://ec.europa.eu/com petition/sectors/telecommunications/broadband_decisions.pdf.

network, Internet exchange points, as well as investing in the access network in remote areas. For example, a large number of public broadband investment projects in Europe are centered on elements of the backhaul and core network (EU, 2011). The reasoning behind this is that the backhaul/core network connects large areas within a country, and it is a cost-effective way to ensure coverage of a large number of users. However, the effectiveness of these investments relies on the access infrastructure, as the last mile to the user may be the bottleneck. Thus, authorities should strive to ensure that there is sufficient competition in the access network (EU, 2011).

What Is the Role of International Organizations in Helping Developing Countries Expand ICT Services?

International organizations have a useful role to play. First, they can be platforms for information sharing and for benchmarking best practices regarding regulation and policies that provide incentives for network deployment (OECD, 2009a). Second, the donor community can help with aid for the investments in ICT infrastructure. For instance, the World Bank has financed strategic investments for key parts of broadband infrastructure in developing countries (i.e., submarine cables, backbone networks). Currently, the Inter-American Development Bank is financing critical infrastructure for broadband deployment in Latin America.

Conclusions

Our aim has been to suggest possible ICT infrastructure targets to be included in the Sustainable Development Goals agenda. The suggested targets focused on broadband availability measured in terms of penetration. Existing literature has already generated a considerable amount of evidence of the positive spillovers that broadband has on the economy (ITU, 2012). In fact, policy makers in both the developed and developing regions of the world are taking into account broadband deployment as core aspect of their development strategies as well as economic stimulus packages.

Our cost-benefit analysis should be interpreted with caution as it is based in a series of oversimplifying assumptions regarding the cost per line per according to different types of technology to achieve network coverage. The intention was to provide some sort of reference when comparing ICT infrastructure targets with other development targets in the post-2015 agenda. In addition, the broadband deployment targets are formulated according to the existing indicators in this domain.

With these caveats in mind, generally speaking, the targets related to the expansion of mobile broadband penetration by threefold at a global level or in developing regions exhibit the largest benefit-cost ratios (Targets 3–4). In particular, the highest B/C ratios robust to different methodologies of assessing the benefits are those related to expanding mobile broadband in developing regions (i.e., Target 4, with B/C ratios of 14.41 and 21.74, depending on the way the benefits are assessed). Second, tripling world mobile broadband penetration (from 32 percent to 90 percent as expressed in Target 3) also has large B/C ratios (13 and 29.42 using the different calculation methods).

Additionally, if policy makers insist on universal broadband penetration goals, some important details on how to measure these targets need to be considered (i.e., if the targets should be measured with indicators according fixed or mobile broadband, and if indicators should be measured at a household or individual level). Our work shows that targets for the universal availability of broadband can be more cost effectively achieved via wireless technology (at least in the developing regions of the world). In fact, the B/C ratio of achieving universal mobile broadband penetration by the year 2030, Target 8, is quite high (i.e., 11.43 and 28.79, depending on the methodology used to assess the benefits).

Finally, there are some actions governments can take to drive the cost of deployment down and provide incentives for network deployment. Governments should implement policies and regulations to improve market competition, while fostering incentives to invest in network deployment by the private sector. In this sense, institutional and regulatory framework conditions are key in providing a fertile ground for ICT infrastructure deployment.

Annex 1

Compound Average Growth Rate (CAGR) of GDP Due to Broadband Penetration Growth (Formula) (Table 17.8)

To calculate the effect of broadband penetration on total GDP growth (world and developing regions), the following formula is used:

$$CAGB = \left[\frac{\left(PEN_{2030}/_{1-PEN_{2030}} \right) - \left(PEN_{2014}/_{1-PEN_{2014}} \right)}{PEN_{2030}/_{1-PEN_{2030}}} \right.^* \\ \left. \propto +1 \right]^{1/16}$$

This formula was used originally used by Roeller and Waverman (2001) as a measure of the annual percent change of fixed telephone penetration multiplied by the estimated penetration coefficient. This formula was adapted from Koutroumpis (2009) for broadband penetration, and it equals to a measure of the compound annual growth effect of broadband on economic growth. The parameter $\propto$ is the elasticity of the impact of broadband penetration on economic growth derived from the simultaneous regression equation approach of Koutroumpis (2009).[27]

Table 17.8 Compound annual growth rate due to increase in broadband penetration, by broadband penetration target

		Percentage of growth rate	
Target 1	0.001065	0.030415	Fixed world
Target 2	0.001056	0.019192	Fixed developing
Target 3	0.001349	0.038532	Mobile BB world
Target 4	0.001171	0.021289	Mobile BB developing
Target 5*	0.001412	0.040343	Fixed+ mobile world
Target 6*	0.001291	0.023467	Fixed+ mobile developing
Target 7	0.001421	0.040591	Universal fixed
Target 8	0.001416	0.040444	Universal mobile

Note: For targets 5 and 6, it is assumed that one-third of the target would be fulfilled with fixed networks and two-thirds with wireless networks.

[27] http://ac.els-cdn.com/S0308596109000767/1-s2.0-S0308596109000767-main.pdf?_tid=04dd9e9c-4332–11e4–843e-00000aacb360&acdnat=1411484464_291de3a2327fe69f40587e6b4adad44d.

Annex 2

Assumptions for the Three Different Scenarios (Table 17.9)

The **conservative scenario** assumes a high cost of deployment for both fixed and wireless technologies (i.e., USD1900 and USD640, respectively) based on estimates of several studies and on industry report estimates. In addition, total capital expenditures (CAPEX) are assumed uniformly distributed among the years 2015–2030. This means that total CAPEX is divided evenly among the years. To calculate the benefits, a low growth rate of the economy is assumed based on World Bank estimates for the year 2016 (i.e., 2.5 percent for world growth rate and 4.5 percent for the developing regions), and the lowest elasticity of the impact of broadband penetration on GDP from Koutroumpis (2009) is taken into account (i.e., 0.008).

The **medium scenario** takes into account slightly lower costs per line for fixed networks and the same cost as the conservative scenario for a wireless line (i.e. USD1460 per fixed line, and same cost per wireless line as the conservative scenario). A medium growth rate of the economy is assumed (i.e., 3 percent for the world and 5 percent for developing regions), and the assumed elasticity is that 1 percent increase on broadband penetration will impact GDP growth in 0.014 percent (a medium elasticity based on Koutroumpis 2009).

The **optimistic scenario** assumes high economy growth rates (i.e., 3.5 percent for the world and 5.5 percent for developing regions), low costs of

Table 17.9 Main parameters of CBA

Inputs	
Discount factor (percent)	0.03
	0.05
	0.088
Elasticity of broadband impact in GDP growth (percent)	0.023
	0.014
	0.008
	0.025
	0.018
	0.09
	0.15
World GDP 2013 in millions (Source: World Bank)	USD 74,899,882
Developing regions GDP in 2013 in millions (Source: World Bank)	USD 24,487,857
Population 2030 world millions (Source: UN)	8 218
Population 2030 developing world millions (Source: UN)	6 952
Average GDP growth world (Source: World Bank, estimates for 2016)	2.5
	3
	3.5
Average GDP growth developing world (Source: World Bank, estimates for 2016)	4.5
	5
	5.5

infrastructure deployment (i.e., USD510 for a wireless line and USD770 for a fixed line), and a high impact of broadband on GDP (i.e., elasticity of 0.023 from Koutroumpis 2009).

Annex 3

Broadband State Aids in the EU

Several broadband state aid projects within the European Union have funded over the past few years complying with the EC Broadband Guidelines.[28] In particular they comply with paragraph 79 of the Broadband Guidelines, which refers to open access obligations of the subsidized network.[29] Table 17.10 shows some examples of funded EU broadband projects.

Table 17.10 Examples of broadband state aids in the European Union, 2013–2014

Country	Name of broadband investment project	State aid (EUR millions)	Duration
Greece	Prolongation of broadband network development in white rural areas of Greece[30]	161.077	2014–2015
Portugal	High-speed broadband in Portugal[31]	106.2	2014–2015
Finland	Modifications in the aid scheme concerning high-speed broadband construction in sparsely populated areas in Finland[32]	160	2014–2015
Germany	NGA Sachsen-Anhalt[33]	125	2014–2017
Rumania	Ro-NET project[34]	84	2013–2015
Ireland	Next generation (backhaul) network (NGN) alongside a gas pipeline in Galway and Mayo[35]	10.06	2013–2028
Poland	Regional broadband network of Łódź-2nd stage[36]	6	2013–2015
Germany	Entwicklungskonzept Brandenburg Glasfaser 2020 II[37]	54	2013–2015

[28] See all state aids granted for Broadband Networks in the European Union in the following link: http://ec.europa.eu/com petition/sectors/telecommunications/broadband_decisions.pdf.

[29] For instance, the United Kingdom in February 2012 launched a EUR 1.8 billion state aid for broadband delivery to comply with the Digital Agenda Europe and the National Broadband Strategy of the UK. The aid followed an open and transparent tender process, and one of the stipulated conditions was that the direct beneficiaries of the scheme would provide third parties with effective wholesale access for seven years. This open access clause ensures that existing access seekers can migrate customers to an NGA network as soon as the subsidized network is in place (EC, 2012).

[30] See EC decision in: http://eur-lex.europa.eu/legal-con tent/EN/TXT/PDF/?uri=OJ:C:2014:050:FULL&from=EN.

[31] See EC decision in: http://eur-lex.europa.eu/legal-content/ EN/TXT/PDF/?uri=OJ:C:2014:117:FULL&from=EN.

[32] See EC decision in: http://eur-lex.europa.eu/legal-con tent/EN/TXT/PDF/?uri=OJ:C:2014:117:FULL&from=EN.

[33] See EC decision in: http://ec.europa.eu/competition/ state_aid/cases/248494/248494_1501760_125_3.pdf.

[34] See EC decision in: http://ec.europa.eu/competition/ state_aid/cases/250354/250354_1501667_115_2.pdf.

[35] See EC decision in: http://ec.europa.eu/competition/ state_aid/cases/243213/243213_1504550_221_2.pdf.

[36] See EC decision in: http://ec.europa.eu/competition/ state_aid/cases/247159/247159_1484945_88_2.pdf.

[37] See EC decision in: http://ec.europa.eu/competition/ state_aid/cases/248698/248698_1471122_81_2.pdf.

References

Analysys Mason (2010a), Assessment of Economic Impact of Wireless Broadband in South Africa, Report for GSMA (Nov. 2010).

(2010b), Wireless Infrastructure Sharing Saves Operators 30% in CAPEX and 15% in OPEX, article of May 6 2010, www.analysysmaso.com/About-Us/News/Insight/Wireless-infrastructure-sharing-saves-operators-capex-and-opex/#.Ujh0xpKG0y5.

Australian Department of Communication (2014), Independent Cost-Benefit Analysis of Broadband and Review of Regulation, Australian Government, August 2014, www.communications.gov.au/__data/assets/pdf_file/0003/243039/Cost-Benefit_Analysis_-_FINAL_-_For_Publication.pdf.

Berkman Center (2009), Next Generation Connectivity: A Review of Broadband Internet Transitions and Policy around the World, Harvard University, Berkman Center for Industry and Society, http://transition.fcc.gov/stage/pdf/Berkman_Center_Broadband_Study_13Oct09.pdf.

Body of European Regulators for Electronic Communication (BEREC) (2011), BEREC-RSPG Report on Infrastructure and Spectrum Sharing in Mobile/wireless Networks, BEREC, BoR (11) 26, June 2011, http://berec.europa.eu/eng/document_register/subject_matter/berec/reports/?doc=224.

Broadband Commission for Digital Development (2010), Broadband Targets for 2015, www.broadbandcommission.org/Documents/Broadband_Targets.pdf.

Broadband Commission for Sustainable Development (2013), The State of Broadband, Paris: International Telecommunication Union (ITU).

Buttkereit, S., Enriquez, L., Grijpink, F., Moraje, S., Torfs, W., and Vaheri-Delmulle, T. (2009), Mobile Broadband for the Masses: Regulatory Levers to Make It Happen, Louvain-la-Neuve, Belgium: McKinsey & Company.

Calandro, E., Stork, C., and Gillwald, A. (2012), Internet Going Mobile: Internet Access and Usage in 11 African Countries, info, 15 (5), 34–51, www.researchictafrica.net/presentations/Presentations/2012%20Calandro%20Stork%20Gillwald%20-%20Internet%20Going%20Mobile-%20Internet%20access%20and%20usage%20in%20eleven%20African%20countries%20.pdf.

China Internet Network Information Center (2013), Statistical Report on Internet Development in China, www1.cnnic.cn/IDR/ReportDownloads/201302/P020130221391269963814.pdf.

CIGI and KDI (2012), Post-2015 Development Agenda: Goals, Targets and Indicators, Special Report www.cigionline.org/sites/default/files/mdg_post_2015v3.pdf.

Clarke, G. (2008), Has the Internet Increased Exports for Firms from Low and Middle-Income Countries? Information Economics and Policy 20 (1), 16–37.

Crandall, R., Jackson, C., and Singer, H. (2003), The Effect of Ubiquitous Broadband Adoption on Investment, Jobs, and the U.S. Economy, Washington, DC: Criterion Economics.

Crandall, R., Lehr, W., and Litan, R. (2007), The Effects of Broadband Deployment on Output and Employment: A Cross-sectional Analysis of U.S. Data, Issues in Economic Policy, 6.

Czernich, N., Falck, O., Kretschmer T., and Woessman, L. (2009), Broadband Infrastructure and Economic Growth (CESifo Working Paper No. 2861). Retrieved from www.ifo.de/DocCIDL/cesifo1_wp2861.pdf.

Dixon, A. N., Sallstrom, L., Leung Wasmer, A., and Damuth, R. J. (2007), The Economic and Societal Benefits of ICT Use: An Assessment and Policy Roadmap for Latin America and the Caribbean, Arlington, VA: CompTIA.

European Commission (EC) (2009), Community Guidelines for the Application of State aid Rules in Relation to Rapid Deployment of Broadband Networks, http://ec.europa.eu/competition/consultations/2009_broadband_guidelines/index.html.

(2010), Digital Agenda Europe, 26 August 2010, http://eur-lex.europa.eu/legal-content/EN/TXT/HTML/?uri=CELEX:52010DC0245R(01)&from=EN.

(2012), State Aid SA.33671 (2012-N-United Kingdom, National Broadband scheme for the UK-Broadband Delivery UK, Brussels, November 20, 2012.

(2013), The Socio-Economic Impact of Bandwidth, Study Conducted by Analysys Mason and Techi4 Limited for the European Commission DG-Communication Networks Content and Technology, Final report 2013.

European Regulatory Group (2007), ERG Opinion on Regulatory Principles of NGA, April 2007, ERG (07) 16rev2.

European Union (EU) (2011), Guide to Broadband Investment, September 2011, http://ec.europa.eu/regional_policy/sources/docgener/presenta/broadband2011/broadband2011_en.pdf

Feijóo, C. and Gómez-Barroso, J.-L. (2010), A Prospective Analysis of the Deployment of Next Generation Access Networks: Looking for the Limits of Market Action: The Case of Spain, Report for NEREC.

Galperin, H. (2012), Prices and Quality of Broadband in Latin America: Benchmarking and Trends. *Economics of Networks eJournal*, 4 (64), 12. http://dx.doi.org/10.2139/ssrn.2171788.

ITU (2011a), Measuring the WSIS Targets, A Statistical Framework, www.itu.int/en/ITU-D/Statistics/Pages/publications/wsistargets2011.aspx.

(2011b), Handbook for the Collection of Administrative Data on Telecommunications/ICT, p. 44, www.itu.int/en/ITU-D/Statistics/Pages/publications/handbook.aspx.

(2012), Impact of Broadband on the Economy, Broadband Series, Raul Katz, www.itu.int/ITU-D/treg/broadband/ITU-BB-Reports_Impact-of-Broadband-on-the-Economy.pdf.

(2014a), ITU World Telecommunication/ICT Indicators database, www.itu.int/en/ITU-D/Statistics/Pages/publications/wtid.aspx.

(2014b), The World Summit on the Information Society (WSIS) Review report 2014, Introduction, www.itu.int/en/ITU-D/Statistics/Documents/publications/wsisreview2014/WSIS2014_review_introduction.pdf.

Katz, R. L. (2009a), Estimating Broadband Demand and Its Economic Impact in Latin America, paper submitted to the ACORN REDECOM Conference 2009, Mexico City, September 5, 2009. www.acorn-redecom.org/program.html.

(2009b), *La Contribución de las tecnologías de la información y las comunicaciones al desarrollo económico: propuestas de América Latina a los retos económicos actuals*, Madrid, España: Ariel.

(2009c), The Economic and Social Impact of Telecommunications Output: A Theoretical Framework and Empirical Evidence for Spain, *Intereconomics*, 44 (1), 41–8.

Katz, R. and Avila, J. G. (2010), The Impact of Broadband Policy on the Economy. In *Proceedings of the 4thd ACORN-REDECOM Conference*, Brasilia, May 14–15, 2010.

Katz, R., L. and Suter, S. (2009), Estimating the Economic Impact of the Broadband Stimulus Plan (Columbia Institute for Tele-Information Working Paper). Retrieved from www.elinoam.com/raulkatz/Dr_Raul_Katz_-_BB_Stimulus_Working_Paper.pdf.

Katz, R. L., Vaterlaus, S., Zenhäusern, P., and Suter, S. (2010), The impact of broadband on jobs and the German economy, Intereconomics, January-February, Volume 45, Number 1, 26–34.

Katz, R. L., Zenhäusern, P., and Suter, S. (2008), An Evaluation of Socio-economic Impact of a Fiber Network in Switzerland, Polynomics and Telecom Advisory Services, LLC.

Kim, Y., Kelly, T., and Raja, S. (2010), *Building Broadband: Strategies and Policies for the Developing World, Global Information and Communication Technologies Department*, Washington, DC: World Bank.

Koutroumpis, P. (2009), The Economic Impact of Broadband on Growth: A Simultaneous Approach, *Telecommunications Policy*, 33, 471–85.

Kretschmer, T. (2012), Information and Communication Technologies and Productivity Growth: A Survey of the Literature, OECD Digital Economy Papers, No. 195, OECD Publishing. DOI: 10.1787/5k9bh3jllgs7-en

LIRNEasia (2014a), Consultation Paper on India's National Broadband Plan, Comments by LIRNEASIA on the Consultation Paper on Delivering Broadband Quickly: What Has to Be Done? October 13, 2014, http://lirneasia.net/wp-content/uploads/2014/10/TRAI-Consultation-Response_Final.pdf.

(2014b), Research on the Significance of Broadband, Ford Foundation Lecture on Broadband Policy, March 2014, New Delhi, http://broadbandasia.info/wp-content/uploads/2014/03/Ford-Lecture-Session-March-7.pdf.

Marcus, J. S. and Jain, R. (2010), Fast Broadband Deployment in India: What Role for Cable Television? Unpublished Working Paper, Ahmedabad, December 2010.

OECD (2008), Developments in Fibre Technologies and Investment, www.oecd.org/sti/broadband/40390735.pdf.

(2009a), *ICTs for Development, Improving Policy Coherence, OECD and infoDEV*, Paris: OECD Publishing.

(2009b), *Network Developments in Support of Innovation and User Needs*, Paris: OECD Publications.

(2011), Next Generation Access Networks and Market Structure, *OECD Digital Economy Papers*, No. 183, OECD Publishing. http://dx .doi.org/10.1787/5kg9qgnr866g-en.

(2012a), Fixed and Mobile Networks: Substitution, Complementarity and Convergence, *OECD Digital Economy Papers*, No. 206, Paris: OECD Publishing. DOI: 10.1787/5k91d4jwzg7b-en.

(2012b), *OECD Review of Telecommunication Policy and Regulation in Mexico*, Paris: OECD Publishing. DOI: 10.1787/9789264060111-en.

(2013a), Broadband Networks and Open Access, *OECD Digital Economy Papers*, No. 218, Paris: OECD Publishing. DOI: 10.1787/ 5k49qgz7crmr-en.

(2013b), *OECD Communications Outlook 2013*, Paris: OECD Publishing. DOI: 10.1787/comms_ outlook-2013-en.

(2014a), *OECD Review of Telecommunication Policy and Regulation in Colombia*, Paris: OECD Publishing. DOI: 10.1787/ 9789264208131-en.

(2014b), Broadband Portal, www.oecd.org/sti/ broadband/oecdbroadbandportal.htm.

(2014c), The Development of Fixed Broadband Networks, *OECD Digital Economy Papers*, No. 239, Paris: OECD Publishing. DOI: 10.1787/5jz2m5mlb1q2-en.

(2014d), International Traffic Termination, *OECD Digital Economy Papers*, No. 238, Paris: OECD Publishing. DOI: 10.1787/5jz2m5mnlvkc-en.

Ofcom (2008), Next Generation New Build: Delivering Super-Fast Broadband in New Build Housing Developments, p. 14, www.ofcom.org .uk/__data/assets/pdf_file/0029/53759/new_ build_statement.pdf.

Pepper, R., Rueda-Sabater, E. J., Boeggeman, B. C., and Garrity, J. (2009), From Mobility to Ubiquity: Ensuring the Power and Promise of Internet Connectivity... for Anyone, Anywhere, Anytime. In *The Global Information Technology Report 2008–2009*, Cologny, Switzerland: World Economic Forum.

Qiang, C. Z.-W. (2010), Broadband Infrastructure Investment in Stimulus Packages: Relevance for Developing Countries, *info*, 12 (2), 41–56, http://siteresources.worldbank.org/ EXTINFORMATIONANDCOMMUNICA TIONANDTECHNOLOGIES/Resources/ 282822–1208273252769/ Broadband_ Investment_in_Sti.

Qiang, C. Z.-W., and Rossotto, C. M. (2009), Economic Impacts of Broadband. In *Information and Communications for Development 2009: Extending Reach and Increasing Impact*, 35–50. Washington, DC: World Bank.

Rahunathan, A. (2005), *The Economic Advantage of Wireless Infrastructure for Development*, Washington, DC: Inter-American Development Bank, Sustainable Development Department Technical Papers Series.

Roeller, L. H., and Waverman, L. (2001), Telecommunications infrastructure and economic development: A simultaneous approach. *The American Economic Review*, 91(4), 909–23.

Telecommunications Regulatory Authority India (TRAI) (2014), Consultation Paper on Delivering Broadband Quickly: What Do We Need to Do? September 24, 2014, http://trai.gov .in/WriteReadData/WhatsNew/Documents/ Consultation%20Paper%20on%20Broadband% 2024Sep2014.pdf.

Simes, R., Hutley, N., Havyatt, S., and McKibbin, R. (2010), *Australian Business Expectations for the National Broadband Network*, Sydney: Access Economics www.accesseconomics.com.au/ publicationsreports/getreport.php?report=253& id=322.

United Nations (UN) (2000), UN Millennium Declaration (A/Res/55/2). 18 September 2000.

(2006), Millennium Project: Goals, Targets and Indicators, www.unmillenniumproject.org/goals/ gti.htm.

(2013a), The Report of the High-Level Panel of Eminent Persons on the Post-2015 Development Agenda, www.post2015hlp.org/wp-content/ uploads/2013/05/UN-Report.pdf.

(2013b), United Nations System Task Team on the Post-2015 UN Development Agenda, March 2013, www.beyond2015.org/sites/default/files/ global%20partnership%20report.pdf.

(2014a), Outcome Document – Open Working Group on Sustainable Development Goals, June 2014 http://sustainabledevelopment.un.org/ content/documents/4518SDGs_FINAL_ Proposal%20of%20OWG_19%20July%20at% 201320hrsver3.pdf.

(2014b), The Millennium Development Goals Report 2014, www.un.org/millenniumgoals/ 2014%20MDG%20report/MDG%202014% 20English%20web.pdf.

World Economic Forum (2010), McKinsey &
     Company Report 2010 for the WEF, Chapter 1.5
     Fostering the Economic and Social Benefits of I
     www.weforum.org/pdf/GITR10/Part1/Chap
     %205_Fostering%20the%20Economic%20and
     %20Social%20Benefits%20of%20ICT.pdf.

WIK (2012), Re-thinking the Digital Agenda for
     Europe (DAE): A Richer Choice of
     Technologies, Independent Analysis Conducted
     by WIK-Consult GmbH on Behalf of Liberty
     Global, September 2012.
   (2013), Estimating the Cost of GEA, WIK
     Consulting Report for British Telecom in the

United Kingdom, www.ofcom.org.uk/__data/
     assets/pdf_file/0025/78190/talktalk_group_
     second_addit1.pdf.

World Bank (2011), Broadband Strategies
     Toolkit, http://broadbandtoolkit.org/
     1.3#note36.

Zhao, J. and Ruan, L. (2010), Broadband in China:
     Accelerate Development to Serve the Public,
     Value Partners, p. 2 (Mar. 2010), www
     .valuepartners.com/VP_pubbl_pdf/PDF_
     Comunicati/Media%20e%20Eventi/ 2010/
     value-partners-PR_100301_Broadband
     InChin.

17.1 Alternative Perspective

PANTELIS KOUTROUMPIS

Summary

Studies have shown that adoption of broadband is associated with faster economic growth via three broad categories of impact: "direct" effects on employment and GDP during investment, "indirect" effects associated with the telecom sector supply chain, and "induced" effects in the wider economy. But, in fact, there are a number of factors specific to each economy that determine overall impact, with institutions and regulations in particular being key enablers to unlock the economic benefits.

Auriol and Fanfalone make a credible effort to analyze an inherently complex undertaking. The focus on broadband indicators – availability, quality, and affordability – is a valid step forward. However, broadband penetration alone is used to assess costs and benefits, as a proxy of network adoption. Speed is excluded from the list, despite the fact that policy makers around the world are prepared to make considerable investments in faster networks, which they often expect to deliver increased benefits. The analysis presents only a fixed impact across technologies, thus making the cheaper ones score higher in terms of the cost-benefit approach. This is not unexpected, but still represents a simplification of the actual situation.

A common – implicit – assumption in these undertakings is that broadband availability is the same as adoption, which is not necessarily true. Connecting the unconnected yields economic benefits orders of magnitude greater than simply upgrading existing subscribers to higher speeds, especially in the least developed countries (LDC) context. Besides, the marginal impact of broadband in developing countries is never contrasted to the generic effect of the broader global targets. Ideally, these targets should also form part of a

wider approach to some key challenges. For example increasing broadband penetration by 10 percent in LDCs can have a range of effects across the post-2015 agenda: reducing poverty (SDG 1), increasing access to education (SDG 4), improving health monitoring, prevent outbreaks of epidemics (SDG 4), and investing in local infrastructure (SDG 9).

The study builds on projections for developing countries based on evidence from rich economies, which can be misleading. At the same time, it takes a relatively naïve approach in devising broadband targets based on the access medium (fixed or mobile) instead of more cost-effective scenarios that take into account regional population densities and foreseen usage. Mobile broadband is likely to be the best candidate because of the current lack of fixed infrastructure, and older (3G) or alternative (satellite) technologies may be more cost effective in practice. A number of initiatives are already being tested.

Out of the 900 million people residing in LDCs only 6.7 percent are Internet users as estimated by the Broadband Commission (2013). Fixed line networks are rudimentary (0.44 percent only have a fixed broadband connection) making a fixed broadband strategy an unlikely solution. Mobiles already have a substantial footprint in these countries where almost 60 percent of the population uses a mobile device. Rolling this out could immediately help with other challenges. A range of health screening tests could be conducted with results sent directly to hospitals, mobile broadband could build on the One Laptop per Child initiative to boost education, and on-demand transport services could be provided for remote areas.

Despite its benefits, providing broadband to LDCs also faces some substantial challenges, including the need to coordinate spectrum rights and provision alternative modes of access for remote areas, to protect equipment, and to encourage content creation via appropriate governance policies. Information on the issues raised in this paper can help to inform policy makers when formulating plans for broadband.

Viewpoint – Alliance for Affordable Internet

While welcoming the Auriol-Fanfalone paper, the A4AI points out that the authors do not share any evidence of the impact of recent broadband investments in developing countries, nor do they cover the impact beyond economic growth. The implementation of policies that focus on driving down the cost to connect are critical to bringing people online. Achieving the UN Broadband Commission target of entry-level broadband services priced at or below 5 percent of monthly GNI per capita will enable the billions who are currently not online to connect to information and public services available via broadband. The Alliance's *2013 Affordability Report* and recently published country case studies provide several examples of developing countries that are making significant strides in making broadband access more affordable and that are having a real impact on people at all levels of society.

A4AI recommends the following:

- Getting the cost of basic broadband below 2 percent of average income in every country by 2020.
- Achieving universal Internet access — at least 90 percent *active* subscribers or users — in every country by 2030.

CHAPTER 18

Returns to Investment in Reducing Postharvest Food Losses and Increasing Agricultural Productivity Growth

MARK W. ROSEGRANT, EDUARDO MAGALHAES, ROWENA A. VALMONTE-SANTOS, AND DANIEL MASON-D'CROZ

The 2008–2011 food price spikes brought the issue of postharvest losses (PHL) back to the forefront of policy debate, and observers are again calling for a reduction in PHL as a tool to feed the expanding global population. Food losses due to improper postharvest handling, lack of appropriate infrastructure, and poor management techniques have once again become a matter of serious concern. Food losses, defined as "any decrease in food mass throughout the edible food supply chain," can occur in any point of the marketing stages–from production (e.g., crop damage, spillage), postharvest and processing stages (e.g., attacks from insect or microorganisms during storage), distribution, and retail sale until home consumption (e.g., spoilage, table waste; Rosegrant et al., 2013). Kummu et al. (2012) suggest an additional 1 billion people could be fed if food crop losses were halved, which could potentially relieve some of the pressure on the significant increase in production that would be required. Achieving lower levels of food losses, however, requires both investments in technologies that help prevent losses as well as in overall infrastructure. Understanding the magnitude of these investments and their impact is key to establishing that a reduction in PHL has, in fact, an impact on food security.

Seeking to better understand the levels of investment required to effectively reduce PHL requires several steps. First, it is necessary to understand how infrastructure impacts losses. The second step is to quantify the levels of investments required. Third, a cost-benefit analysis of the required infrastructural investments is done to assess economic returns to PHL reduction. Results are subsequently compared to investments in agricultural research and development.

Overview of the Postharvest Loss Debate

A large number of papers have been published focusing on four aspects of PHL: (1) estimates of the magnitudes of losses, (2) the economic impacts of losses in general but also on the poor and the hungry in particular (Gómez et al., 2011), (3) alternatives to decrease losses through the use of both new and traditional technologies, and 4) the economic costs of losses as well as their remedies.

The various papers show widely varying estimates. For instance, estimates of rice losses in Southeast Asia in one publication range from 37–60 percent, while extreme cases in Vietnam are estimated to result in 80 percent of production being lost (Institution of Mechanical Engineers, 2013). But a more comprehensive estimate for rice losses in Asia are at 13–15 percent, based on several studies reported in Parfitt, Barthel, and Macnaughton (2010). Using self-reported measures from household surveys, Kaminski and Christiaensen (2014) estimated that on average between 1.4, 2.9–4.4, and 5.9 percent of the national maize harvest is lost in Malawi, Tanzania, and Uganda, respectively. These estimates are lower than the Food and Agriculture Organization (FAO's) estimate of 8 percent in cereals in sub-Saharan Africa (FAO, 2011).

Estimates of economic losses caused by PHL vary dramatically in both developing and developed worlds. For instance, in the United States, Buzby and Hyman (2012) estimate the economic value of food loss at the retail and consumer levels to be $165.5 billion in 2008 and point out that achieving a 1 percent reduction in food loss would save $1.66 billion. Hodges, Buzby, and Bennett (2011) estimate losses in sub-Saharan Africa to be valued at around $4 billion a year out of an estimated cereal production value of $27 billion (although this is based on questionnaire returns from a subset of 16 countries). The African Postharvest Losses Information System (APHLIS) estimates the value of PHL to be $1.6 billion/year in eastern and southern Africa alone. This large variation is in part caused by multiple stages from farm to retail in which PHL can occur and the nature of the loss, whether avoidable or not.

One important factor to take into consideration is how much of a reduction is actually feasible or realistic and at what cost these goals can be achieved. As part of the UN "Zero Hunger Challenge" announced in 2012, one of the five pillars to achieving this goal was to attain zero food waste. De Gorter (2014) points out that not only is this target unrealistic and impossible to achieve in practice, but also in terms of economic efficiency, the resources used to reach this level of PHL might better be used to eradicate hunger in other ways. Kader (2005) argues that a cost-benefit analysis is needed to evaluate the return to investment to find an acceptable level of loss for different commodities and environments rather than assuming that everyone should aim for zero loss.

Technology and Infrastructure

Reduction in PHL is inherently linked to availability and profitability of appropriate technologies to help abate losses in the various stages postharvest. The potential gains need to be measured against the costs in adopting these technologies. Studies that look at the cost effectiveness of specific technologies to reduce PHL are not abundant, but provide insights into the questions that surround technology adoption.

For example, Kitinoja and AlHassan (2012) find that on-farm technologies, adopting curing on roots, tubers, and bulbs lead to a return to a profit that is 2.5 times larger than the returns on non-adoption. Cooling practices used for vegetables can provide gains up to 7.5 higher than the initial costs. Other technologies such as shading have more limited gains, even though the adopter recoups the investment quickly. Gains for technologies at the value chain stage also vary in magnitude and in the time-span to recoup the investment. Two important factors have to be considered, however, in analyzing these gains. First, some of the technologies do require a substantial amount of production (as well as increases in related inputs, such as labor) in order to be applied, thus limiting their availability to small farmers. Technologies like metal silos may not require additional labor but are expensive to adopt, though the returns are high (Gitonga et al., 2013). Second, technologies such as improved packaging require additional costs in labor and in capacity building, which may reduce the overall profitability.

Perhaps, though, the most telling reason for slow adoption or scaling-up of potential PHL is found in Minten et al. (2014) in a paper on cold storage practices in Bihar, India, and echoed in a number of other papers. They find that over recent years, the adoption of storage practices has increased significantly, by 64 percent between 2000 and 2009, or 5.7 percent per year. The reasons for increased adoption, however, are the improvement of the physical and social infrastructure, which paves the way for producers to have access to profitable technologies.

Not only have recent governments in the region put in place better public services and policy reforms, but they have also invested in roads and infrastructure, thereby increasing the access to markets for farmers in remote areas. At the same time, the rule of law has improved in recent years, as have general governance practices. Kaminski and Christiaensen (2014) also point to the importance of education in reducing PHL. They argue that education combined with economic incentives such as easier access to markets via better infrastructure can significantly reduce losses. One study about the use of metal silos in Kenya points to significant improvements in the adoption of silos with improved infrastructure (Tefera et al., 2011).

Methods

This section covers the econometric analysis as well the application of the Insert International Model for Policy Analysis of Agricultural Commodities and Trade (IMPACT) model to generate long-term projections of food supply, demand, trade, and prices that influences global food security between 2010 and 2050.

Grouped Logistic Regression

The relationship between PHL and infrastructural variables can be modeled using an Ordinary Least Squares (OLS) approach as issues of endogeneity are not present at a country level. The absence of endogeneity arises because the data on losses are collected or estimated at the producer level. For small farmers, particularly in developing countries, the infrastructure that surrounds the farm is therefore taken as a given and thus can be seen as exogenous. Even at the value chain level, firms in a given country also have to use the infrastructure that is available.

The problem that arises from a standard OLS approach is that the dependent variable is expressed as a rate (a percentage). This means that the variable is bounded between 0 and 1. As a result, fitted values obtained from the regression need to fall within this range, but the OLS provides no assurance that this will happen. Following an approach based on Papke and Wooldridge (1996), we have applied a weighted grouped logistic approach in which the logit transformation is applied to the dependent variable, as defined in equation (1).

$$\log\left(\frac{y_i}{1 - y_i}\right) = \beta_0 + \beta_1 x_i + \varepsilon_i \qquad (1)$$

Where y corresponds to the percentage of loss in country i, β_0 is a constant, β_1 is a vector of coefficients for infrastructural, geographical, type of loss and crop variables in x in country i, and ε is an error

term. The transformation applied to the dependent variable ensures that fitted values fall between the specified 0 and 1. As specified, the model becomes a logistic one, hence implying that the coefficients on the right-hand side are to be interpreted as odds ratios. The model is estimated using weighted least squares.

A subsequent step after the estimation of equation 1 is to obtain the marginal effects of the significant variables to calculate the investment needed for a reduction in PHL. Predicted marginal effects were estimated by treating sequential points along the distribution of each of the significant variables as fixed while keeping all other variables at their means. This provided a number of points that could be mapped to show the relationship between losses and increases in selected infrastructural activities. By combining these results with unit cost data for each of the relevant infrastructures, we derived the required levels of investments needed to reduce losses by 5, 10, and 25 percentage points.

The IMPACT Model

IMPACT is a partial equilibrium, multicommodity, multicountry model that covers 56 crop and livestock commodities. The model generates long-term projections of food supply, demand, trade, and prices that enable us to estimate the trends in global food security between 2010 and 2050. It also provides measures of important indicators such as the number of malnourished children under the age of five and the number of people at risk of hunger (Hoddinott, Rosegrant, and Torero, 2013; Robinson et al., 2015; Rosegrant and the IMPACT Development Team, 2012).

The food security and economic impacts of investments to reduce PHL – and increased investments in agricultural research – are modeled here in IMPACT Version 3, updated in 2014 (Robinson et al., 2015). PHL reductions are represented in the model by equivalent increases in commodity yields. Four PHL scenarios were run to simulate the effects of potential improvements in harvest technologies and transportation infrastructure that would allow for a larger percentage of what it planted actually reaching the markets. The results were compared to the impact of increased agricultural research investments. All scenarios were run using the Intergovernmental Panel on Climate Change (IPCC) medium projection on socioeconomics (SSP2) and assuming a constant 2005 climate. Table 18.1 summarizes the assumptions on socioeconomics for SSP2.

The following scenarios (Table 18.2) were then implemented to test the effects of potential decreases in PHL. Scenarios 1–2 follow the same specifications as the baseline, except where described below. Note that a 10 percent reduction in PHL is defined as a reduction by 10 percentage points, for example from 20 percent to 10 percent. Additionally, a scenario with an increase of agricultural research and development (R&D) investment from $5 billion/year to $13 billion/year was included to allow for comparability of the benefits of investments decreasing PHL to the benefits of increasing agricultural R&D.

For this third scenario, we follow the assumptions made by Hoddinott, Rosegrant, and Torero (2013), where the effects of agricultural R&D

Table 18.1 Average annual growth rates (%) to 2050 for GDP, population, and per capita GDP by region under SSP2

Region	GDP[a]	Population[b]	Per capita GDP[c]
East Asia and Pacific	2.9	0.1	2.8
Europe and Central Asia	1.9	0.1	1.8
Latin America and Caribbean (LAC)	2.4	0.5	1.9
Middle East and North Africa (MENA)	3.6	1.1	2.4
North America	1.5	0.5	0.9
South Asia	4.1	0.7	3.3
Sub-Saharan Africa (SSA)	5.4	1.8	3.5
World	2.5	0.6	1.9

Source: SSP Database (https://secure.iiasa.ac.at/web-apps/ene/SspDb/dsd?Action=htmlpage&page=about).

Notes: [a] OECD GDP projections; [b] IIASA population projections; [c] Calculated in the IMPACT model.

Table 18.2 Scenario summary

Scenario	Region	Postharvest Loss Assumptions	
		Less perishable commodities[a]	More perishable commodities[b]
Baseline (BSL)	Global	Standard IMPACT 3 yield projections	
Scenario1 (PL1)	Developing countries[c]	By 2020: postharvest losses decline by 3% By 2025: postharvest losses decline by 6% By 2030: postharvest losses decline by 10%	
Scenario2 (PL2)	Global		
Scenario3 (PL3)	Developing countries[c]	By 2020: postharvest losses decline by 1% By 2025: postharvest losses decline by 3% By 2030: postharvest losses decline by 5%	By 2020: postharvest losses decline by 4% By 2025: postharvest losses decline by 9% By 2030: postharvest losses decline by 15%
Scenario4 (PL4)	Global		
		Yield Assumptions from Investments in Agricultural R&D	
Scenario5 (AR1)	Global	Starting in 2015 All crops: exogenous yield growth increases by 0.4% per year All livestock products: exogenous yield growth increases by 0.2% per year	

Source: Authors.

Notes:
[a] Cereals, pulses, roots and tubers, oilseeds, and other crops.
[b] Fruits, vegetables, and livestock products.
[c] Excludes high-income countries: Australia, Canada, EU27, Israel, Japan, New Zealand, South Korea, Singapore, Switzerland, USA, and high-income Persian Gulf states.

would increase the yield growth for crops by 0.4 percent/year and of livestock by 0.2 percent/year. Three scenarios are presented in Table 18.2 namely, scenarios PL1, PL2, and AR1. The first two scenarios provide insights about the impact of a reduction in PHL on a global scale and in the developing world. AR1 offers the alternative investment option, i.e., to invest in agricultural research instead of PHL reduction.

Data and Results

Data on PHL and infrastructural variables used in the econometric analysis are summarized here, followed by the results from the econometric analysis and IMPACT model projections.

Losses

Data on PHL were drawn for a wide range of sources, including APHLIS and a variety of published work on the subject (Table 18.1).[1] In total, data for 40 countries and 4 aggregates were compiled. The data were collected for four types of losses: on-farm, value chain, consumption, and total losses. Losses were also further classified by region and by type of crop. The following regions are covered: Developed countries, Africa, Middle East, and North Africa (MENA); Latin America and the Caribbean (LAC); and Asia. Six commodity groups were identified: cereals, roots, oilseeds, fruits and vegetables, meat and dairy (henceforth referred as animal), and others. The data set contains 253 observations.

Figure 18.1 illustrates the mean losses by type and by region. Consumption and on-farm losses are higher in developed countries, while value chain losses are higher in developing countries. Africa displays the highest average losses for value chain and the lowest for consumption, which is expected given the continent's lower incomes. For consumption and value chain PHL, Asia, LAC, and MENA show fairly similar averages. MENA's on-farm losses are considerably lower than the average of about 10 percent in other developing regions. The developed world displays a lower overall loss average compared to developing regions, but the differences across regions are surprisingly small. The data show also that the various estimates for different parts of the food chain are not consistent with the estimates for total PHL. In each case estimated total losses are lower than would be expected from the individual component losses. None of the studies reviewed did an integrated estimate of food losses at each part of the value chain to derive a consistent total loss figure.

The mean values are illustrative but mask considerable variation in the distribution of losses across regions. Figure 18.2 shows box plots with bars that represent different stages in the distribution chain. The box in the middle is bounded by the 25th and 75th percentiles and has the median displayed as a horizontal line inside of it. The whiskers show the end points of the distribution. The range of estimated consumption losses in developed countries is considerably higher than in developing regions, as would be expected. A large range is also observed for on-farm losses in the developed world. However, regions like Africa, Asia, and LAC are not too distant from the median loss in the rich world. This scenario of higher losses in the developed world is reversed when value chain losses are considered.

Figure 18.3 shows mean PHL by the type of crop. Fruits and vegetables have the highest on-farm losses. Cereals, roots, and oilseeds observed similar percentages. Losses are also large in the value chain for fruits and for roots and tubers. On-farm losses do not show much variation across commodity groups with the exception of losses originated from animal products, which have significantly lower averages (Figure 18.3). Estimated total losses are lower for cereals than for other commodities.

---

[1] The list of sources of information about postharvest data is available in Appendix Table 2. Sources of Postharvest Data, in Mark W. Rosegrant, Eduardo Magalhaes, Rowena A. Valmonte-Santos, and Daniel Mason-D'Croz (2015). Returns to Investment in Reducing Postharvest Food Losses and Increasing Agricultural Productivity Growth. Post-2015 Consensus. Copenhagen Consensus Center Working Paper, www.copenhagenconsensus.com/sites/default/files/food_security_nutrition_assessment_-_rosegrant_0.pdf.

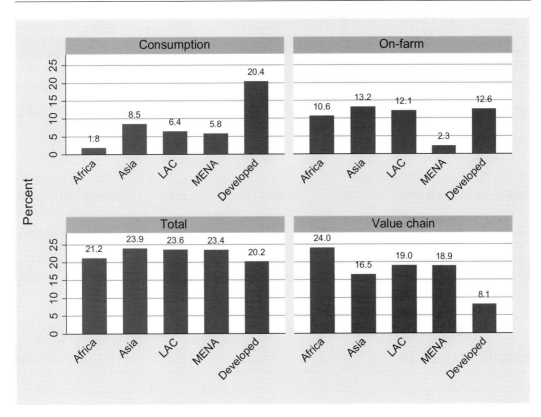

Figure 18.1 *Mean losses by region and type of loss*

Source: Author's calculations using various sources.

Infrastructural Variables

The main principle guiding the selection of choice variables was the importance they play in explaining not only PHL but also economic development in a broader sense. Next we outline the infrastructure and governance variables selected, the reason for selecting them, and the expected direction of the coefficients in the regression analysis. All variables were obtained from the World Bank, via its World Development Indicators (WDI) interface. Table 18.3 presents the selected variables.

Unit cost data to estimate required levels of investments were drawn from a variety of sources. For road infrastructure (both development and maintenance), information was taken from the World Bank's Road Cost Knowledge System.

Costs for electricity were obtained from U.S. Energy Information Administration (www.eia.gov/). We also obtained costs of rail transportation from a Canadian report (DAMF et al., 2007).

Econometric Specification and Results

Two specifications are presented in Table 18.4. Specification number 1 regresses the transformed rate of PHL losses against infrastructural variables and the appropriate dummies. Number 2 adds a governance variable that accounts for the stability of government, a key indicator of governance.

Right-hand-side variables were regressed in their natural log form when appropriate. This was done to reduce issues of nonlinearity, heteroskedasticity, and

Table 18.3 Selected infrastructural variables and rationale

Variable	Rationale	Expected direction
Electric power consumption (kWh per capita)	Access to technology	Reduce PHL directly
Port infrastructure	Access to markets by sea	Reduce PHL indirectly
Air transport, freight (million ton-km)	Access to markets by air	Reduce PHL indirectly
Road density (km of road per 100 sq. km of land area)	Ability to transport goods	Reduce PHL directly
Roads, goods transported (million ton-km)	Intensity of transport capability	Reduce PHL directly
Roads, paved (% of total roads)	Quality of transport capability	Reduce PHL directly
Railways, goods transported (million ton-km)	Access to markets by train	Reduce PHL indirectly
Mobile cellular subscriptions (per 100 people)	Modern access to information	Reduce PHL indirectly
Telephone lines (per 100 people)	Access to information	Ambiguous
Government stability	Provision of an enabling environment	Reduce PHL indirectly
Rural population density	Rural markets	Reduce PHL indirectly

Source: WB WDI, 2013.

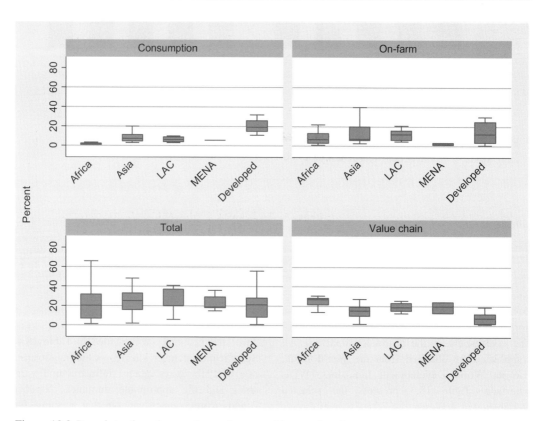

Figure 18.2 *Box plots of postharvest losses by type of loss and region*

Source: Author's calculations using various sources.

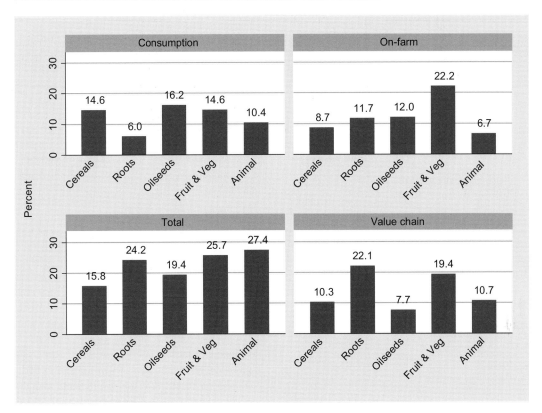

Figure 18.3 *Mean losses by type of loss and commodity*

Source: Author's calculations using various source.

other minor deviations from normality. Because the natural log is a monotonic transformation, the scaling in the data has been preserved.

The coefficients of the results presented in Table 18.4 are expressed in odds ratios, meaning that coefficients measure the impact of changes in the right-hand-side variables on the ratio of PHL over the rate of no PHL (see Methods section). Thus, coefficients greater than one increase the odds of PHL, while coefficients less than one decrease it.

The results provide support for the importance of roads, particularly paved roads, which reduce the odds of PHL by half. Sending more goods by rail also helps decrease PHL. Higher consumption of electricity also helps reduce losses, perhaps signaling the increased use of technologies that require power. Not all infrastructural

coefficients showed the expected signs. Higher capacity of ports seems to increase the odds of PHL, perhaps reflecting significant issues related to the transportation of good to ports, particularly in developing countries. Similarly, increased numbers of landlines per 100 people also seem to increase PHL. We would have expected availability of cell phones to be an important factor in decreasing PHL, as it has been shown to play an important role in speeding up development in general (Aker and Mbiti, 2010). No significant effects were found for the governance variable.

Dummy variables indicating the region, crop, and type of loss all report results that are in line with the descriptive section. For instance, roots and oilseeds increase the odds of PHL relative to cereals. At the same time, regional dummies for

Table 18.4 Econometric results

Variables	-1	-2
Dependent variable: proportion of PHL (between 0 and 1)		
Dummy for port quality (1 = high, 0 = low)	1.481	1.25
	(0.447)	(0.403)
Electric power consumption (kWh per capita)	0.672**	0.688**
	(0.106)	(0.11)
Air transport, freight (million ton-km)	1.048	1.073
	(0.0413)	(0.0516)
Road density (km of road per 100 sq. km of land area)	1.028	1.121
	(0.106)	(0.148)
Roads, goods transported (million ton-km)	0.940	0.876**
	(0.0446)	(0.0485)
Roads, paved (% of total roads)	0.648*	0.573**
	(0.153)	(0.145)
Railways, goods transported (million ton-km)	0.936**	0.921***
	(0.0241)	(0.0262)
Mobile cellular subscriptions (per 100 people)	0.959	0.941
	(0.0897)	(0.0914)
Telephone lines (per 100 people)	2.270***	2.288***
	(0.457)	(0.512)
Port capacity (Container port traffic; TEU: 20 foot equivalent units)	1.092	1.327**
	(0.0790)	(0.151)
Government stability		1.377
		(0.41)
Rural population density	1.222	1.384
	(0.354)	(0.418)
Dummy for roots	1.568*	2.994***
	(0.403)	(0.869)
Dummy for oilseeds	2.200**	2.549**
	(0.839)	(0.979)
Dummy for fruits and vegetables	1.266	1.426
	(0.255)	(0.315)
Dummy for animal	0.596	0.862
	(0.188)	(0.321)
Dummy for other	1.707**	1.904**
	(0.409)	(0.48)
Dummy for on-farm losses	1.204	1.125
	(0.312)	(0.359)
		(cont.)

Dummy for total losses	2.960***	2.088**
	(0.712)	(0.221)
Dummy for value chain losses	0.895	0.546*
	(0.221)	(0.168)
Dummy for Asia	0.485**	0.535
	(0.172)	(0.203)
Dummy for LAC	0.576	0.935
	(0.250)	(0.511)
Dummy for MENA	0.216***	0.292**
	(0.106)	(0.156)
Dummy for developed countries	0.311**	0.142***
	(0.162)	(0.104)
Constant	0.214	0.0216
	(0.456)	(0.0537)
Observations	250	208
R-squared	0.383	0.452

Notes: Standard errors in parenthesis; *** $p < 0.01$, ** $p < 0.05$, * $p < 0.1$.

developed countries and MENA show that these regions are less likely than Africa to incur in PHL.

Based on these estimated coefficients and the unit costs, we estimated the infrastructure investments costs for achieving PHL reductions. The results include simulations for various levels of decreases in PHL. Table 18.5 illustrates the required investments in four types of infrastructure for a 5 percent decrease in PHL.

The estimation of the investments costs for PHL scenarios described in Table 18.2 are based on the results shown in Table 18.5. For Scenario 1, we assumed a 10 percent decrease in PHL, with 2.5 percent from each of the investment categories presented in Table 18.5, resulting in a total investment of $415 billion. The estimated regression coefficients for the investment impacts are conditioned on the underlying values of all of the investments in the data set, so a balanced increase in infrastructure is the most plausible approach. For Scenario 2, we assumed that reducing PHL in developed countries would be less expensive in terms of infrastructure investment given that the physical infrastructure is already in place and therefore most of the effort has to focus on behavioral changes. The recognition of the challenges behind changing behavior has led us to add

Table 18.5 Investment (US$) requirements in infrastructure to reduce PHL by five percentage points

Region	Electricity[a]	Paved Roads[b]	Rail Capacity[c]	Road Capacity[d]
Africa	10,493,751,296	7,027,633,152	57,907,712	6,256,584,192
Asia	80,715,096,064	209,079,418,880	35,974,656,000	403,101,483,008
LAC	32,002,551,808	14,760,436,736	3,956,525,824	22,900,320,256

Notes: [a] Investments for electricity are for a 69 percent increase in per capita consumption. An average of coal and natural gas source was used as a basis. [b] Investments for paved roads are for a 45 percent increase in maintenance and construction (average costs of the two) of paved roads. [c] Rail capacity refers to investments required to increase the millions of tons per kilometer capacity of goods transported by rail by 98 percent. [d] Road capacity refers to investments required to increase the millions of tons per kilometer capacity of goods transported by road by 95 percent

Table 18.6 World prices in 2050 (% change from baseline)

Commodity	PL1	PL2	AR1
Beef	−11.5	−15.1	−11.0
Lamb	−13.9	−16.6	−11.3
Pork	−9.3	−14.9	−10.9
Poultry	−11.8	−17.0	−13.0
Dairy	−6.9	−9.8	−7.0
Eggs	−13.8	−17.2	−12.8
Rice	−19.8	−21.6	−26.3
Wheat	−12.5	−16.6	−20.4
Maize	−0.0	−2.7	−3.0
Groundnuts	−18.5	−21.0	−25.5
Rapeseed	−8.4	−15.4	−19.3
Soybeans	−11.4	−16.9	−21.0
Fruits and vegetables	−14.0	−16.9	−20.7
Pulses	−14.5	−17.4	−21.5
Roots and tubers	−14.3	−16.2	−20.1
Processed oils	−3.4	−4.1	−4.7
Oil meals	0.1	1.7	0.4

Source: Author calculations from IFPRI IMPACT Model version 3 (2014).

25 percent of the developing country investments to achieve the same percentage reductions in developed countries. This results in a global total of $515 billion in investments under Scenario 2.

IFPRI IMPACT Model Results

The decrease in PHL, represented in IMPACT as the equivalent increase in effective crop and animal yields, leads in almost all cases to lower commodity prices by 2050. The price decreases are in the 10–20 percent range with only a few exceptions. World prices decrease more in the scenarios where the PHL assumptions were applied globally (e.g., PL2). The effects of expanding PHL reduction to developed countries contributes an additional 4–5 percentage points to the projected price declines observed under PL1.

Under the scenario of increased investment in agricultural research, price reductions for crops are larger than for PHL reduction scenarios, with prices for most crops declining by more than 20 percent in 2050 relative to the baseline. The livestock price effects are not as great as for crops because of the lower projected yield enhancements for livestock compared to crops (see Table 18.2), but are nevertheless comparable to PHL scenario 1.

As already mentioned above, these changes in prices have significant effects on both consumer and producer behavior. The decreases in agricultural commodity prices seen in Table 18.6 lead to the increased availability of affordable food globally. Tables 18.7 and 18.8 summarize the projected effects that these lower prices would have on food security regionally and globally by 2050.

Increased food availability due to these scenarios is projected to significantly improve food security, as shown in the tables. For developing countries as a group, the population at risk of hunger is projected to decline by 11–15 percent relative to the baseline in 2050. The number of malnourished children would decline by 3.7–5.5 percent. Using both these metrics AR1 followed by the PL2 scenarios show the largest declines in food insecurity: a reduction of over 70 million people at risk of hunger (Table 18.7), and around 5 million children (Table 18.8). Both of these metrics are closely tied

Table 18.7 Population at risk of hunger in 2050

Region	million				% change from baseline		
	BSL	PL1	PL2	AR1	PL1	PL2	AR1
East Asia and Pacific	126	118	116	115	−6.3	−7.5	−8.6
Europe and Central Asia	38	37	37	37	−2.9	−3.7	−4.1
LAC	48	45	44	44	−6.0	−7.7	−8.6
MENA	38	37	36	36	−3.9	−4.9	−5.8
South Asia	162	138	134	131	−15.3	−17.6	−19.2
SS Africa	137	116	112	108	−15.8	−18.6	−21.2
Developing	509	452	442	434	−11.2	−13.1	−14.7
Developed	59	56	55	55	−4.7	−6.1	−6.9
World	568	508	497	489	−10.5	−12.4	−13.9

Source: Author calculations from IFPRI IMPACT Model version 3 (2014).

Table 18.8 Number of malnourished children in 2050

Region					% change from baseline		
	BSL	PL1	PL2	AR1	PL1	PL2	AR1
East Asia and Pacific	8.3	7.9	7.8	8	−4.1	−4.9	−6.0
Europe and Central Asia	1.6	1.5	1.5	1	−4.9	−6.6	−7.6
LAC	2.0	1.8	1.7	2	−10.1	−13.5	−14.8
MENA	2.0	1.8	1.7	2	−8.9	−11.6	−13.8
South Asia	52.6	51.3	50.9	51	−2.5	−3.2	−3.8
SS Africa	36.8	35.1	34.7	34	−4.7	−5.7	−6.9
Developing	103.0	99.2	98.3	97	−3.7	−4.6	−5.5
Developed	0.2	0.2	0.2	0	−2.2	−3.0	−3.4
World	103.2	99.4	98.5	98	−3.7	−4.6	−5.5

Source: Author calculations from IFPRI IMPACT Model version 3 (2014).

to changes in per capita calorie consumption, which explains why PL2 shows the largest effects among the PHL scenarios, as this scenario has the largest reduction in losses of high calorie grains like rice and wheat. The regions where most of the biggest improvements in food security are observed are South Asia and sub-Saharan Africa.

Reductions in commodity prices under these scenarios have a straightforward effect on consumers, where this serves as a relative increase in income, as they are able to purchase more food with the same resources. Most farmers globally are net consumers of food and would benefit from lower prices. Nevertheless, price declines can have a negative effect for producers if they are not compensated by increased productivity. To determine if the price declines are beneficial to society as a whole, we did a welfare analysis and quantified the benefits and losses accrued by different sectors of society. This was done by estimating the producer and consumer surplus and net welfare changes induced by each scenario compared to the baseline. We show here the results of this welfare analysis using a 5 percent discount rate. The results were similar using 3 and 10 percent discount rates.

Table 18.9 Global change in producer surplus, consumer surplus, and welfare by 2050 between baseline and investment scenarios, using a discount rate of 5 percent

	PL1	PL2	AR1	PL1	PL2	AR1
			% change from baseline			
Producer surplus	−2,288	−2,867	−2,043	−3.7	−4.7	−3.3
Consumer surplus	4,508	5,796	4,140	4.9	6.3	4.5
Welfare	2,220	2,929	2,097	3.1	3.9	2.8

Source: Author calculations from IFPRI IMPACT Model version 3 (2014).

The global results of the welfare analysis can be seen in Table 18.9, which shows the percentage changes and economic returns relative to the baseline. The economic value of the percentage changes in consumer surpluses are estimated with respect to projected total world agriculture gross production value through 2050, starting from the 2010 value of $2.3 trillion (FAOSTAT database). The projected lower food prices have a negative effect on producers in all three scenarios because lower prices are only partially offset by increased productivity. The losses for all scenarios are in the range of $2,097–2,867 billion, representing 3.7–4.7 percent declines in producer surpluses, with the largest declines occurring in the global scenarios (PL2), where we see the largest price decreases.

Although producers lose, consumers benefit, and these are larger than the losses observed for producers. This difference is true both in terms of magnitude (gains are $4,140–5,796 billion) and percentage gains. Consequently, society as a whole benefits, as the benefits received by consumers can compensate for the losses observed by producers. Total welfare is projected to increase by 2.8–3.9 percent compared to the baseline. As was observed for price effects, the additional gains from expanding the PHL investments to developed countries has a smaller relative effect (0.8 for PL2) on welfare change than the effects on welfare from improvements in just the developing world (3.1 for PL1). One potentially counterintuitive result is that the agricultural research scenario shows the smallest change despite having the largest price changes by 2050. This result is due to the larger upfront gains

in the PL1–PL2 scenarios, compared to the smaller but growing benefits through 2050 in AR1 (Table 18.9).

Benefit-Cost Analysis

Each of the scenarios is driven by increased investment, with total infrastructure and research investment costs summarized above. In addition to assessing the economic rates of return to PHL reductions for full investment costs, lower cost allocations are considered. The rates of return to investment for infrastructure and technologies that would lead to PHL reductions would likely have large benefits in other sectors of the economy, as expansion of roads, electricity, and railways benefit the economy more broadly beyond the agricultural sector, whereas the scenario focusing on agricultural research investments targets primarily this sector and would have relatively small spillover effects on other sectors of the economy. Therefore infrastructure investment cost allocations to PHL reduction of 50 percent and 25 percent are also assessed for the PHL scenarios. Table 18.10 summarizes the distribution of incremental investment costs over time, and the cost for each of the scenarios as the increased investments are phased in.

Table 18.11 summarizes the benefit-cost analysis for three scenarios with 100 percent attribution of the investment costs to PHL reduction. All of the scenarios generate benefits that are substantially higher than investment costs. The PHL scenarios have benefit-cost ratios (BCR) of 11–12. However, the importance of the growing benefit streams generated by productivity growth and

Table 18.10 Investment scenarios

| Scenario | Years | Annual Investment/Cost Allocation Scenarios (US$ billion per year) | | |
		100%	50%	25%
PL1	From 2014 to 2029	27.67	13.84	6.92
PL2	From 2014 to 2029	34.33	17.17	8.58
AR1	From 2014 to 2025	Starts at 0.67 growing to 8	NA	NA
	From 2026 to 2050	Held constant at 8		

Source: Authors.

Table 18.11 Benefit-cost analysis under 100 percent cost allocation and a 5 percent discount rate

	PL1	PL2	AR1
Benefits derived from investments (US$ billion)	2,220	2,929	2,097
Costs (US$ billion)	203	254	66
BCR	11	12	32

Source: Author calculations from IFPRI IMPACT Model version 3 (2014).

lower costs of investment under the AR1 scenario are clear. The BCR for the AR1 scenario is more than twice to more than three times higher than for the PHL scenarios, depending on the discount rate.

Even when the BCR for the PHL scenarios doubles when only 50 percent of the costs of infrastructure development are allocated to PHL reduction, the BCR for AR1 remains substantially higher than the BCR for the PHL scenarios. The BCR for the PHL scenarios become greater than the AR1 only under the 25 percent cost allocation for PHL.

Conclusions

We have provided a comprehensive review of the state of PHL in various regions of the world as well as across types of losses and commodities. Moreover, we have conducted econometric work to link losses with infrastructural and governance variables. The premise of our work is that

infrastructure is of primary importance in explaining PHL as well as to providing the enabling conditions for adoption of PHL-reducing technologies. Of critical importance, poor infrastructure is a barrier to PHL reduction, and adoption of PHL-reducing technologies is facilitated by the development of improved infrastructure.

Our results show the important roles of electricity, roads (particularly paved ones), and railways in reducing PHL. Dummy variables also revealed significant differences across commodities and regions. For instance, roots and tubers, oilseeds, and fruits all increase the probability of higher of PHL relative to cereals. At the same time, regional dummies indicate that relative to Africa the probability of PHL is lower for all other regions. Infrastructure development is an essential enabling condition for achieving lower PHL.

The scenarios we used show that investment in infrastructure for PHL reduction contributes to lower food prices, higher food availability, and improved food security and has positive economic rates of return. However, comparison with a scenario of increased investments in agricultural research shows that improvements in food security and BCRs and marginal returns to investment are considerably higher for investment in agricultural research than for investment in PHL reduction. Reductions in PHL are not a low-cost alternative to productivity growth for achieving food security. Rather, large-scale reduction in PHL requires large public investments and is complementary to investments in long-term productivity growth to achieve food security.

References

Aker, J. C. and I. M Mbiti. 2010. Mobile Phones and Economic Development in Africa. *Journal of Economic Perspectives* 24: 207–32.

Buzby, J. C. and J. Hyman. 2012. Total and Per Capita Value of Food Loss in the United States. *Food Policy* 37: 561–70.

DAMF, Joseph Schulman Consulting and CANARAIL Consultants Inc. 2007. Estimation of Unit Costs of Rail Transportation in Canada. Final Report www.bv.transports.gouv.qc.ca/mono/0965332.pdf.

de Gorter, H. 2014. Evaluating the Zero Loss or Waste of Food Challenge and Its Practical Implications. Background draft paper prepared for the Food and Agriculture Organization of the United Nations.

FAOSTAT database, accessed on December 18, 2014.

Food and Agriculture Organization of the United Nations (FAO) 2011. *Global Food Losses and Food Waste: Extent, Causes, and Prevention.* Rome: FAO.

Gitonga, Z. M., H. De Groote, M. Kassie, and T. Tefera. 2013. Impact of Metal Silos on Households' Maize Storage, Storage Losses and Food Security: An Application of a Propensity Score Matching. *Food Policy* 43: 44–55.

Gómez, M. I., C. B. Barrett, L. E. Buck, et al. 2011. Research Principles for Developing Country Food Value Chains. *Science* 332: 1154–5.

Hoddinott, J. F., M. W. Rosegrant, and M. Torero. 2013. Hunger and Malnutrition. In *Global Problems, Smart Solutions: Costs and Benefits,* Chapter 6, edited by B. Lomborg. New York: Cambridge University Press.

Hodges, R. J., J. C. Buzby, and B. Bennett. 2011. Postharvest Losses and Waste in Developed and Less Developed Countries: Opportunities to Improve Resource Use. *Journal of Agricultural Science* 149: 37–45.

Institution of Mechanical Engineers. 2013. Global Food: Waste Not, Want Not. Retrieved from www.imeche.org/knowledge/themes/environment/global-food.

Kader, A. A. 2005. Increasing Food Availability by Reducing Postharvest Losses of Fresh Produce. *Proceedings of the 5th International Postharvest Symposium,* edited by F. Mencarelli and P. Tonutti. Leuven, Belgium: International Society for Horticultural Science.

Kaminski, J. and L. Christiaensen. 2014. *Post-Harvest Loss in Sub-Saharan Africa – What Do Farmers Say?* Policy Research Working Paper 6831. The World Bank, http://elibrary.worldbank.org/doi/pdf/10.1596/1813–9450-6831.

Kitinoja, L. and H. AlHassan, 2012. Identification of Appropriate Postharvest Technologies for Improving Market Access and Incomes for Small Horticultural Farmers in Sub-Saharan Africa and South Asia. *Acta Horticulturae* 934: 31–40.

Kummu, M., H. de Moel, M. Porkka, S. Siebert, O. Varis, and P. J. Ward. 2012. Lost Food, Wasted Resources: Global Food Supply Chain Losses and Their Impacts on Freshwater, Cropland, and Fertiliser Use. *Science of the Total Environment* 438: 477–89.

Lundqvist, J., C. de Fraiture and D. Molden. 2008. *Saving Water: From Field to Fork – Curbing Losses and Wastage in the Food Chain.* SIWI Policy Brief. SIWI.

Minten, B., T. Reardon, K. M. Singh, and R. Sutradhar. 2014. The New and Changing Roles of Cold Storages in the Potato Supply Chain in Bihar. *Economic and Political Weekly* 49 (52): 98–108.

Papke, L. E., and J. M. Wooldridge. 1996. Econometric Methods for Fractional Response Variables with an Application to 401(K) Plan Participation Rates. *Journal of Applied Econometrics* 11: 619–32. http://citeseerx.ist.psu.edu/viewdoc/download?doi=10.1.1.473.1598&rep=rep1&type=pdf.

Parfitt, J., M. Barthel, and S. Macnaughton. 2010. Food Waste within Food Supply Chains: Quantification and Potential for Change to 2050. *Philosophical Transactions of the Royal Society, Biological Sciences,* 365.

Robinson, S, D. Mason d'Croz, S. Islam, et al. 2015. *The International Model for Policy Analysis of Agricultural Commodities and Trade (IMPACT): Model description for version 3.* IFPRI Discussion Paper 1483. Washington, DC: International Food Policy Research Institute (IFPRI). http://ebrary.ifpri.org/cdm/ref/collection/p15738coll2/id/129825.

Rosegrant, M. W., S. Tokgoz, P. Bhandary, and S. Msangi. 2013. Looking ahead: Scenarios for the future of food. In *2012 Global Food Policy Report,* Chapter 8, pp. 88–101. Washington, DC: International Food Policy Research Institute.

Rosegrant, M. W. and the IMPACT Development Team. 2012. *International Model for Policy Analysis of Agricultural Commodities and Trade (IMPACT): Model Description.* Washington, DC: International Food Policy Research Institute (IFPRI), www.ifpri.org/book-751/ourwork/program/impact-model.

Swaminathan, M. S. 2006. 2006–07: Year of agricultural renewal. 93 Indian Science Congress in Hyderabad, Public Lecture, January 4.

Tefera, T., F. Kanampiu, H. De Groote, et al. 2011. The Metal Silo: An Effective Grain Storage Technology for Reducing Post-Harvest Insect and Pathogen Losses in Maize While Improving Smallholder Farmers' Food Security in Developing Countries. *Crop Protection* 30: 240–5.

World Bank 2011. *Missing Food: The Case of Postharvest Grain Losses in Sub-Saharan Africa.* Report 60371-AFR, 2011 http://siteresources.worldbank.org/INTARD/Resources/MissingFoods10_web.pdf.

18.1 Alternative Perspective

CHRISTOPHER B. BARRETT

Post-2015 Consensus: Food Security and Nutrition Perspective

Summary

By 2050, there will be far more people to feed, increasingly distant from the rural areas where food is produced, and with the vast majority of the increased demand coming from Africa and Asia. In a world where currently up to 900 million people are chronically malnourished, reducing postharvest losses could play a significant role in meeting the coming challenge.

Rosegrant et al. make the most serious attempt to date to come to a reasonably rigorous answer to the question of the role that lower PHL might play. It is particularly useful that they have compared the effectiveness of reducing losses with the impact of increased spending on agricultural R&D. In the end, they project that both infrastructure investment to reduce PHL and agricultural R&D investment would significantly improve food security, especially in South Asia and sub-Saharan Africa, the regions of greatest global concern. Their conclusion is very sensible: PHL reduction can contribute to improvements in food security globally, but it is relatively less important and less cost-effective an approach than alternative policy instruments available to policymakers.

For a variety of reasons, I suspect that the authors' estimates even err in the direction of exaggerating the role that PHL reduction can play. Their simulations only consider the food security impacts of infrastructure improvements that reduce PHL and ignore the simultaneous impact due to lower prices and uptake of improved production technologies by farmers who have better access to

markets. As an aside, one very noteworthy result of the study is that infrastructure investment in Africa gives a much higher return than in Asia or Latin America. The second reason why the attractiveness of PHL reduction may be exaggerated is that there is no comparison with other potentially high-return interventions.

Another issue is that targeting reductions in food waste is difficult because losses appear for different reasons in different parts of the chain. PHL rates are endogenous to food prices and to incomes and in ways that will naturally make PHL *increase* as food security improves. Lower food prices improve poor people's access to food. But lower food prices also reduce the opportunity cost of food waste; poverty, not PHL, is the principal driver of food insecurity. Better-off consumers discard edible foods that they would eat were they poorer, and a well-off farmer can afford to lose $100 worth of crop willfully that a very poor farmer would work feverishly to capture.

The challenge of ensuring the food security of 9–10 billion people a few decades from now must focus primarily on three pillars. The first is agricultural productivity growth in Africa and Asia. Yet only $3 billion per year is spent annually on research on the seven major crops worldwide, and only 10 percent of that is targeted toward research to help small farmers in Africa and Asia, whose climate and soil conditions and pathogen and pest pressures differ markedly from those faced by farmers in higher-income, temperate zones.

Moreover, because most of the poor in developing countries live in rural areas and derive significant income from agriculture, growth in agriculture has been shown to be two to three times as effective at reducing poverty as growth in nonagricultural sectors, making agricultural investment especially pro-poor and thereby helping with the second pillar: poverty reduction. The third pillar concerns enhancing access to and availability and utilization of micronutrients, the minerals and vitamins that are essential to good health.

Reducing postharvest loss of food is almost certainly a cost-effective intervention. But as Rosegrant et al. convincingly demonstrate, it seems highly unlikely that PHL reduction is among the highest return options in benefit-cost terms.

Benefits and Costs of the Gender Equality Targets for the Post-2015 Development Agenda

CHAPTER 19

IRMA CLOTS-FIGUERAS

Introduction: The Current Situation and the Millennium Development Goals (MDGs), What Has Been Achieved?

Women in the developing world are the ones that suffer the most from poverty, poor health, lack of education, unequal rights, and violence. Remarkable progress has been made in some areas, aided by some of the MDGs, but there is still a long way to go. This chapter reviews the goals and targets relating to gender equality in the UN High Level Panel's (HLP's) "A New Global Partnership" and makes recommendations for the post-2015 development agenda.

Education

The third MDG was specially targeted to achieve gender equality and the empowerment of women. The main target of this goal was to eliminate gender disparity in primary and secondary education. The gender gaps in primary school attendance have been reduced, but access to secondary and university-level education still remains highly unequal.

Figures 19.1, 19.2, and 19.3 plot the female-to-male ratio in enrollments corresponding in primary, secondary, and tertiary education. Differences in enrollment in primary education have decreased in all regions, but sub-Saharan Africa, the Middle East, and North Africa are still lagging behind. The picture for enrollment in secondary education is not that positive, differences have been reduced somewhat but at a lower speed, and sub-Saharan Africa and South Asia are regions that are falling behind. In regard to tertiary education, the reduction in inequality has been very minor everywhere.

Employment

The first MDG includes the target of achieving full and productive employment and decent work for all, including women and young people. According to UN estimates, due to the global financial crisis, both male and female labor force participation rates decreased slightly between 2000 and 2012 (73.8 to 72.7 percent and 48.6 to 47.9 percent, respectively). Figure 19.4 shows the female-to-male labor force participation rates by region between 1989 and 2011. From the graph, it looks like the gender disparity has not decreased much, and disparities are still large in South Asia, the Middle East and North Africa.

To compound the problem, women are paid less for the same work in all regions of the world and have lower access to social benefits.

Maternal Health

The fifth goal is to reduce maternal mortality rates by three-quarters between 1990 and 2015 and provide universal access to reproductive healthcare for all women by 2015. According to the UN, access to prenatal care in developing countries has increased, but not access to contraceptives. Maternal mortality has decreased in South-Asia and sub-Saharan Africa, but is still extremely high (see Figure 19.5). Births in unsafe locations, the practice of unsafe abortions, and poor prenatal and postnatal care are still the reasons behind the estimated 287,000 maternal deaths that occurred worldwide in 2010.

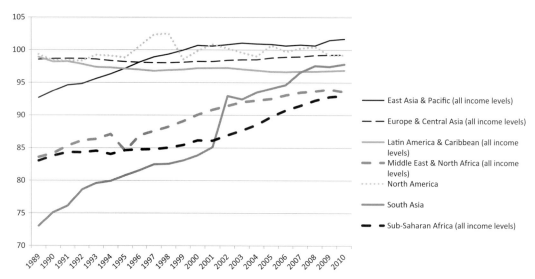

Figure 19.1 *Female-to-male ratio in primary education enrollment*

Source: World Development Indicators 2014, World Bank.

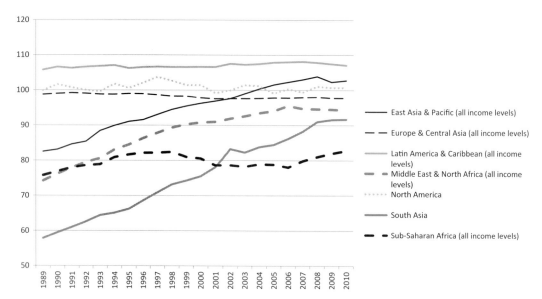

Figure 19.2 *Female-to-male ratio in secondary education enrollment*

Source: World Development Indicators 2014, World Bank.

Water and Sanitation

Finally, the sixth goal had as a target to halve, by 2015, the proportion of people in the world without access to safe water and sanitation. Given that women in the developing world are those who suffer the most from the burden of having to fetch water, increasing access to improved water sources would positively impact the lives of millions of women. Figure 19.6 shows how the proportion of the population with improved access to water has

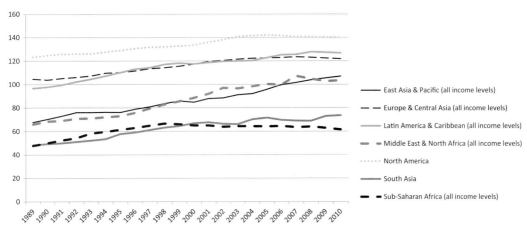

Figure 19.3 *Female-to-male ratio in tertiary education enrollment*

Source: World Development Indicators 2014, World Bank.

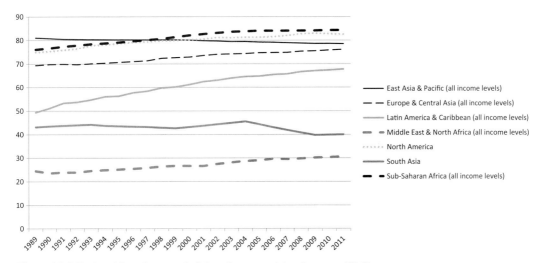

Figure 19.4 *Ratio of female-to-male labor force participation rate (ILO)*

Source: World Development Indicators 2014, World Bank.

increased. But note that in sub-Saharan Africa there is still more than 30 percent of the population who do not have access to safe water.

The Post-2015 Goals

The third MDG was very appropriate, given that education can have effects on health, child care and labor force participation, and it can even prevent early marriage and maybe even reduce violence against women. The targets in the HLP report include preventing and eliminating all forms of violence against girls and women, ending child marriage, ensuring that women have equal access to property, signing contracts, and owning bank accounts, as well as ending all discrimination against women in political, public, and economic life. We consider these four objectives in more depth later. We do this in particular in relation to developing countries, where inequalities remain large.

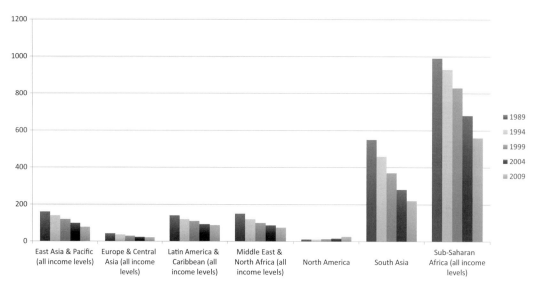

Figure 19.5 *Maternal mortality rates (per 100,000 live births)*

Source: World Development Indicators 2014, World Bank.

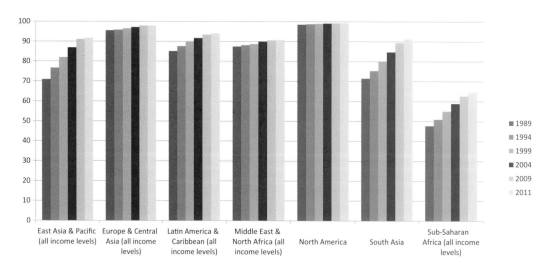

Figure 19.6 *Percentage of the population with access to an improved water source*

Source: World Development Indicators 2014, World Bank.

Proposed Goals: An Evaluation Analyzing the Costs and Benefits of Different Policies to Attain Them

Reduce Violence against Girls and Women

Violence against women of all ages is widespread and persistent. Incidents of rape, domestic violence, violence outside the household, and "honor" killings have been reported in many countries and cultures and seem to happen to women of all ages, irrespective of their socioeconomic status. Further, sex-selective abortions are a form of violence against women that have increased in some countries. Women are also likely to suffer more from violence in conflict and crisis situations.

Obtaining data for violence against women is difficult due to reporting bias and due to the fact that for violent incidents to be reported a minimum degree of female empowerment is needed, which means that we could observe increases in violence that are only due to an increase in the likelihood to report these incidents. There is also very little evidence on how to reduce violence against women, and even if some programs reduce it and the evaluation of the financial costs of these programs is easy to do, it is difficult to estimate their benefits, especially because violence against women not only affects their health and maybe the duration of their lives, but also has severe psychological costs that can affect their education and economic activities. This is something we may not be able to quantify in the context of developing countries.

Table 19.1 shows that domestic violence is very important in all regions in the world but especially high in Africa, the Eastern Mediterranean, and South-East Asia. Sexual violence inflicted by non-partners, which is also very prevalent in times of conflict, is very high in Africa and the Americas. Numbers for the high-income countries seem inflated, but women in these countries may be more likely to report violent incidents than those in low-income countries, where they may not expect institutions to react to them and where violence could even be more "socially acceptable."

There are very few programs whose main goal is to reduce violence against women, although addressing other targets can have a positive effect. For example, Bandiera et al. (2014) show how a life skills and vocational training program in Uganda that took place in after-school clubs decreased the proportion of girls who reported having had sexual relationships without their consent. This program also had other effects, such as an increase in the likelihood that those girls engaged in income-generating activities, raised their monthly consumption expenditures, decreased teen pregnancy and early marriage, and also changed their preferences regarding their preferred age of marriage and childbearing. The program aimed to "empower girls," and the reduction of violence is just one dimension of empowerment.

According to the cost data provided by the authors, the cost of avoiding one violent event is $829.7 – $839.6, computed with a 3 percent or 5 percent discount rate, respectively,[1] see Table 19.2. These estimates should be seen as upper bounds because they include components of the program not directly targeted at reducing sexual violence.

The benefits of reducing sexual violence are many – both physical and psychological – but there are studies that suggest that having sex against one's will also decreases lifetime income (MacMillan, 2000), due to the fact that victims of sexual violence often have to quit education or their jobs. According to the National Alliance to End Sexual Violence, rape is one of the crimes most costly to its victims, and it is estimated that in the United States a rape costs the victim $151,423 (DeLisi et al., 2010).[2] Scaling this number using the Uganda vs. US GDP per capita would mean a cost of $1709.02 (2014 USD). Unfortunately, no similar estimates exist for a developing country, which means that the estimation of a benefit-cost ratio focusing on the prevention of sexual violence

---

[1] Throughout the chapter, 3 percent will be considered the "low" discount rate and 5 percent the "high" discount rate. In order to compute the cost of avoiding one event, I use the coefficient of the effect of the program to compute how many girls need to be treated on average to reduce violence by one incident, and then I multiply this by the cost of treating one girl.

[2] This includes the victim's cost, the justice cost, and the offender productivity cost due to the time spent in jail.

Table 19.1 Violence against women

	Partner physical and sexual violence				Nonpartner sexual violence			
	Mean	CI			Mean	CI		
Africa	36.6	32.7	to	40.5	11.9	8.5	to	15.3
Americas	29.8	25.8	to	33.9	10.7	7	to	14.4
Eastern Mediterranean	37	30.9	to	43.1				
Europe	25.4	20.9	to	30	5.2	0.8	to	9.7
South-East Asia	37.7	32.8	to	42.6	4.9	0.9	to	8.9
Western Pacific	24.6	20.1	to	29	6.8	1.6	to	12
High income	23.2	20.2	to	26.2	12.6	8.9	to	16.2

Source: WHO. Lifetime prevalence of violence with confidence intervals are provided.

Table 19.2 Violence against women, cost-effectiveness estimates

		Low discount rate (3%)	High discount rate (5%)	Low discount rate (3%)	High discount rate (5%)
Paper	**Effect**	**Cost of reducing one violent event during the previous year (2014 US$)**	**Cost of reducing one violent event during the previous year (2014 US$)**	**Cost of treating one girl (2014 US$)**	**Cost of treating one girl (2014 US$)**
Bandiera et al. (2014)	ITT: 6.1 percentage points reduction	829.7	839.6	50.59044	51.1974

part of the program would give a benefit-cost ratio of approximately 2 (1709/840), but this would simply be a guess, given that we are comparing two very different countries.[3]

The authors of the chapter conclude that women's economic and social empowerment can be attained by combining the provision of vocational and life skills even in situations in which social norms are very difficult to change. They report yearly benefits of $32.8 (2008 USD) and yearly costs of $21.8 and $17.9. However, they only use information on household expenditures to compute the benefits. The reduction of sexual violence is not included in the computation, but it would increase the benefits of the program and hence the BCR. In any case, given that these types of programs also have numerous other benefits; their scaling up should definitely be considered.

Intimate partner violence is also a big problem in developing countries and sometimes is related to the contagion of diseases such as HIV. Pronyk et al. (2006) show how a combined microfinance and training intervention could lead to reductions in levels of intimate-partner violence in South Africa. Results of the study show how the incidence of intimate partner violence – sexual or physical – decreased by 55 percent. However, there are no data on costs.

To have reliable data, violence must be reported. Greater empowerment of women can increase reporting and so apparently increase the incidence of violence. Iyer et al. (2012) show how an increase of female political representation in local governments in India caused a large increase in documented crimes against women. Given both the high prevalence of violence and the lack of

---

[3] It is not clear whether scaling up using differences in GDP per capita would be appropriate, due to the differences between these countries.

evidence for programs to reduce it, any such goal cannot have a zero target. And because funds for developing countries are limited, and other policies are effective, programs specifically aimed at reducing crime against women should not be expressly included in the list of post-2015 goals. Therefore, the policy recommended to reduce crimes against women would be to focus more on programs that provide empowerment, education, and economic opportunities for women.

However, note that there are studies, such as Luke and Munshi (2011), which report an increase in female violence following an increase in female income, so improving women's access to income-generating activities may not be the solution in all contexts. Some programs providing informational campaigns have been successful in reducing violence against women or attitudes toward violence, such as the SASA! program in Uganda and the Soul City program in South Africa, see World Bank (2014a) and Fearon and Hoeffler (2014), but BCRs have not been provided for them.

Reduce Child Marriage

Child marriage is defined as marriage before the age of 18 and tends to affect girls disproportionately, who tend to marry older men. This is usually associated with a loss of autonomy, and it is a global issue that affects many cultures, religions, and ethnicities. In addition, it can be considered a form of violence against women if it takes place without the girls' consent. It can have serious consequences for the girls affected because they are more likely to finish their education too early and to end up in poverty. And given that early childbearing can be dangerous for a young mother, they are also at an increased risk of maternal mortality. Early female marriage can also be associated with poorer outcomes for their children.

Field and Ambrus (2008) find that in Bangladesh each additional year that marriage is delayed increases years of schooling by 0.22 and literacy by 5.6 percent. They also find that delayed marriage is associated with an increase in the use of preventive health services.

Very few programs have been designed with the main objective of eliminating child marriage, but

Table 19.3 Percentage of 15- to 19-year-old girls married or in a consensual union by country and year

Country	Year	Percentage of 15- to 19-year-old girls currently married or in consensual union
India	2001	24.50%
	2006	27.10%
Kenya	2003	17.90%
	2008	12.10%
Uganda	2002	28%
	2011	20%
Malawi	2004	32.90%
	2010	23.40%

Source: United Nations, Department of Economic and Social Affairs, Population Division (2013). World Marriage Data 2012 (POP/DB/Marr/Rev2012).

they are not randomized, so causality is difficult to determine. Many other programs include the elimination of early marriages as a subsidiary goal, or it simply appears as the byproduct, mostly of programs that aim to increase the amount of years of education completed by girls.

In this section, four programs will be discussed: one each in India, Uganda, Kenya, and Malawi. The evidence obtained from these programs suggests that the way to reduce child marriage is by extending education, either by providing labor market opportunities that can change perceived returns to education or by providing educational subsidies.

Table 19.3 shows the percentage of adolescent girls ages 15–19 married or in a consensual union in each one of these countries for the last two years for which the United Nations World Marriage data 2012 provided information. The percentage of married adolescents is large in all countries but has decreased in recent years, except for the case of India. One of the consequences of early marriage is early childbearing. Figure 19.7 shows the adolescent fertility rate by region and year. The fertility rate has decreased in all regions, but it is still disproportionately high in sub-Saharan Africa.

In a randomized controlled trial conducted in rural India, Jensen (2012) examined the effect of an exogenous policy change in labor market

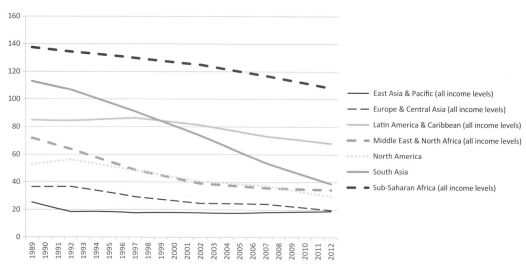

Figure 19.7 *Adolescent fertility rate (births per 1,000 women ages 15–19)*
Source: World Development Indicators 2014. World.

opportunities for women. Some randomly selected villages received recruiters for the business process outsourcing industry (BPO), while the control villages did not receive them. This industry creates very well-paid job opportunities, particularly for women. The intervention provided both awareness and access to these jobs and caused increases in both women's employment and schooling. In addition, women from treatment villages ages 15–21 were 5–6 absolute percentage points less likely to get married or to have given birth over the three-year period of the intervention. Each recruiter were paid $12 per individual treated. This study shows that economic development can not only give employment opportunities to women, but also give them incentives to study, and this will lead to an increase in the age of marriage. To compute the costs of delaying marriage by one year, it will be assumed that the $12 per girl will be divided equally among every year of the three years of the intervention, given that all villages received additional visits in years 1 and 2. It will be also assumed that these are 2006 USD. The effect of the program on the probability of being married in year 2 is a reduction of 5.1 absolute percentage points. Table 19.4 provides the calculation of the cost of delaying marriage by 3 years, which is

$253–$239, depending on the discount factor used.[4]

Duflo et al. (2012) examined the effect of educational subsidies and HIV prevention education on girls' marriage in a randomized experiment in Kenya. The education subsidy provided free school uniforms for the last 3 years of primary school, and the HIV prevention program focused on abstinence until marriage. They found that after three years, girls who received only the education subsidy were 2.6 percent (absolute percentage points, a 20 percent relative risk reduction) less likely to be married. After five years they were 2.9 percent less likely to be married, and after seven years they were 3.9 percent less likely to be married. The effects of the HIV education program or both programs at the same time were not statistically significant.[5] Uniforms in Kenya cost

---

[4] The costs of treating one girl are $4 a year, during three years, discounted with the 3 percent and 5 percent discount factors. With a 5.1 pp reduction in the probability of being married at age 18, 18 girls need to be treated in order to reduce the number of marriages by one unit; this is used in order to compute the cost of delaying the marriage.

[5] The HIV education program is focused on abstinence. These results show that abstinence programs may not be successful.

Table 19.4 Reducing early marriage

Paper	Effect	Cost delaying marriage by X years (2014 US$) Low discount rate (3%)	Cost of delaying marriage by X year (2014 US$) High discount rate (5%)	X	Cost of treating one girl (2014 US$) Low discount rate (3%)	Cost of treating one girl (2014 US$) High discount rate (5%)	Yearly benefits of avoiding pregnancy (forgone annual income)	BCR Low discount rate (3%)	BCR High discount rate (5%)
Jensen (2012)	5.1 percentage points	253.99	259.05	3 years	13.97	14.24	2091.44	22.9	22.9
Duflo et al. (2012)	2.6 percentage points	884.44	902.06	3 years	22.99	23.45	916.24	2.9	2.9
Bandiera et al. (2014)	6.9 percentage points	733.05	741.85	2 years	50.59	51.19	699.92	1.7	1.7
Baird et al. (2011)	7.9 percentage points	2775.13	2802.48	2 years	219.24	221.4	564.72	0.37	0.37

Note that these programs pursue different objectives, such as increasing economic opportunities for women and increasing girls' education, and they did not have as a main objective an increase in the age of marriage. Given that in developing countries the low demand for women's education may be linked to the lack of economic opportunities, results from Jensen (2012) are very encouraging because they show that providing economic opportunities will increase the incentives to stay in education and thus reduce the incentives to get married.

$6 (1.6 percent per capita GDP in 2003), if the students received the subsidy for three years (three new uniforms in total because the children outgrow their old uniforms) that would mean that the cost of avoiding one early marriage during the first three years would be $884–$902.06 in 2014 with low and high discount rates, respectively.[6,7]

The program implemented in Uganda and analyzed by Bandiera et al. (2014), discussed in the previous section, also caused a decrease in early marriage and cohabitation. The program provided both vocational training and sex, reproductive, and marital information and caused a 6.9 percentage points absolute reduction in the probability of being married or cohabiting two years later, which amounts to a 58 percent relative decrease. Given the average costs of the program and the effect of the program, two years for which the marriage is delayed would cost $733–$742 in 2014 USD.

Early marriage can be reduced if girls stay longer in school. In Malawi, Baird et al. (2011) show how unconditional cash transfers were more effective than conditional cash transfers in reducing marriage rates among girls dropping out of school. The program was designed to benefit girls between ages 13 and 22 who had never been married. Treated girls' parents received monthly payments of $4, $6, $8, or $10 each. The girls received $1, $2, $3, $4, or $5 dollars monthly. After one year of the intervention, the effect of the program on the probability of being married was a decrease of 2.6 absolute percentage points. After the two years of intervention, the treatment group that received unconditional transfers was 44 percent less likely to be married than the girls in the control group who did not receive the program, a 7.9 absolute percentage point decrease. Conditional cash transfers did not have a significant impact on the probability of being married. The average cost of the program was $10 per month during 10 months, which amounts to the average yearly transfer that each household was receiving. Given the magnitude of the effects after two years of the program, the cost of increasing the age at marriage by two years is $2775–$2802 in 2014 USD. However, the program was designed as well to increase enrollment and test scores, which

were the main aim of the program. Because married girls do not attend school, those programs that aim to reduce girls' dropouts are going to be successful in increasing the age at marriage.

The three programs described earlier have very different costs, and out of the three, the one providing job opportunities in India seems to be the most cost effective if what we care about is only the increase in age at marriage. The benefits of decreasing the age at marriage include an increase in years of education and literacy, but also a change in the quality of the partner they will eventually marry, their bargaining power within the household, an improvement in health due to delayed childbirth, and a better use of the available health services. All this is very difficult to monetize, and the benefits of each program include achieving objectives other than increasing the age of marriage, so they may not be directly comparable, but it is clear that these programs may well be cost effective, and increasing education or economic opportunities for women is a good way of reducing the age of marriage. The drawback of these programs is that they rarely provide evidence on the long-term effects.

Duflo et al. (2012) find an increase in the age of marriage even seven years after the program was implemented, and they report a decrease in the probability of being married after seven years of four absolute percentage points, which is only significant at the 10 percent level but points to potentially very high benefits of these type of programs (the uniforms were only provided for three years, so a long-term effect does not necessarily imply increased cost).

One of the main problems associated with early marriage is early fertility. Chaaban and

---

[6] Note that a 2.6 percentage point reduction means that around 38 girls should be treated to avoid one early marriage during those three years. The cost of this is the cost of three uniforms for 38 girls, discounted.

[7] The long-term effect of the program is not considered in this study in order to make results more comparable to those from the other programs, in which long-term surveys were not conducted. Note also that if the average girl affected by the program was 13, after seven years she would be 20, and a marriage at that age would not be considered "child marriage."

Cunningham (2011) provide estimates of the costs of early fertility (adolescent pregnancy) by measuring the opportunity costs of lost productivity. Thus the costs are the forgone lifetime earnings due to an early pregnancy. First, they take into account the fact that adolescent mothers will have less years of schooling, and they assume that the wage gap for early mothers is constant over time but assume that there is a "motherhood tax" of 5 percent with one child and 10 percent with two. Given the lack of data on female wages according to the number of children they have, the difference between the average female wage and the average early mother's wage proxies for the cost of early childbearing.[8] These estimates can be used to compute part of the benefits of delaying marriage, even if the costs of early marriage have many more components. It will be assumed that the probability of pregnancy after the first year of marriage will be 90 percent, for simplicity. Table 19.4 shows the yearly benefits of avoiding pregnancy, computed using the data in Chaaban and Cunningham (2011) for each of the four countries, and the BCR for each policy, computed accordingly.[9] As explained before, these estimates overestimate the cost of the programs and underestimate the benefits of delaying marriage. Even if Jensen (2012) has a very large BCR, the policy was not designed to be replicated in other settings, given that it was just a change in the allocation of BPO recruitment services, and this type of firm may not operate in other countries and regions. This means that its BCR should not be considered "generalizable."

Given that we do not know the causal effects of policies directly targeted to reduce child marriage, and given that delaying adolescent and child marriage is almost always associated with staying in school longer, reducing early marriage, which cannot be a zero target, should not be expressly included in the Post-2015 agenda. Instead,

Given the lack of evidence for causal effects of policies aimed specifically at delaying marriage, the more appropriate goals to include are improving economic opportunities for women and increasing the number of years of education attained by girls. Improving women's access to income-generating opportunities will both encourage them to stay longer in school and in the labor force, while educational policies will most probably encourage women to stay longer in school.[10]

Note that a consistent finding of labor economics is that level of education is often the best predictor income. Therefore, the goals of increasing the income of women and the education of women are closely intertwined. In addition, more economic opportunities for women and more education have been shown to be correlated with lower levels of fertility.

Ensure Equal Rights of Women to Own and Inherit Property, Sign a Contract, Register a Business, and Open a Bank Account

Women and men in the developed world have the same legal rights to own property, to sign contracts, to open bank accounts, and so on. However, this is not the case in the developing world, in which women still have fewer rights than men.

Table 19.5 shows data on women's ownership rights, for land, bank loans, and property. A "1" denotes full access, and a "0" denotes complete inability to access. The differences are striking; while in high-income countries or the United States women almost get full access to land, bank loans, and property, in low-income countries the numbers are much lower.

There is a positive correlation between women's rights and development, measured by the Gender Empowerment Measure (GEM) and GDP per capita; see Doepke et al. (2012). The GEM was created by the UNDP and is a mixture of women's rights and women's economic outcomes, but Doepke et al. (2012) also find that women's access to land is correlated with economic development. Other measures of women's rights such as equal custody of children and contraceptive prevalence

---

[8] Selection into being an active participant in the labor market, as opposed to voluntarily choosing not to search for a job, should also be considered because there might be "selection bias," which makes participants different from nonparticipants in the labor market. But this topic is outside the scope of this chapter.

[9] The BCR is the ratio of the discounted forgone income during x years and the costs of avoiding marriage during x years. The value of x varies, depending on the study.

[10] See Jensen (2012) and Duflo et al. (2012).

Table19.5 Women's rights by country's income

	U.S.	High income	Upper- middle income	Lower- middle income	Low income
Women's access to land	1	0.92	0.83	0.79	0.3
Women's access to bank loans	1	0.98	0.92	0.85	0.55
Women's access to property	1	0.98	0.93	0.89	0.52

Source: Doepke et al. (2012). *OECD Gender, Institutions and Development Database.*

are also positively correlated with economic development. In addition, there is evidence that women are more likely than men to direct their income toward children in the family and that women's incomes benefit girls in the household; see Lundberg, Pollak, and Wales (1997), Thomas (1990), and Duflo (2003).

One way to give women property rights and access to some banking services is microfinance. Microfinance programs are often targeted to women and help them set up and run their own finances, which empowers them and gives them more bargaining power in the household. Karlan and Zinman (2011), however, show that in an experiment in the Philippines, microfinance may not have been as beneficial as it was always thought because entrepreneurs decreased their businesses instead of increasing them. In addition, their subjective well-being was reduced, and women did not benefit from the program more than men. If anything, the treatment effect for men and women was the same. More evidence is needed from other countries and other settings, but what is clear is that our knowledge about microfinance is still limited.

Women should also have the right to set up and to run their own enterprises, which would allow them to have their own economic resources. Evidence shows that investing in women's enterprises may not be as lucrative as investing in men's enterprises, which is a problem if funding comes

from profit-maximizing banks or financial companies. But note that women and men work in different sectors and probably work in activities that have different productivities.

One of the roots of the gender-gap in assets is the difference in inheritance rights, which is still prevalent in some countries. Deininger et al. (2013) examine the effect of amendments in inheritance legislation in two states of India on physical and human capital investments and find that the amendment significantly increased daughters' likelihood to inherit land and also increased daughters' educational attainment. Roy (2014) examines the effect on education of giving women inheritance rights. She takes advantage of the fact that different states in India implemented different amendments to the "Hindu Succession Act" at different points in time and finds that women who were in education when the reform was implemented in their state achieve on average 0.5 more years of education. The effect is only present for landowning Hindu families, and the author shows that it could be due to the compensation that the daughters receive due to the fact that they were still disinherited by their fathers after the reform. Actually she finds almost no effect of the reform on the actual inheritance received by women. Field (2003) examines the effect of a land titling reform in Perú on fertility and finds a 22 percent decrease in fertility for households that receive title to property.

In order to improve women's ownership and control of assets, changes in laws, norms, and sometimes even household decisions are needed. In addition, countries introducing changes in laws that give women better access to property rights should make sure that the law is applied properly. For example, in 2014, the Nigeria Supreme Court ruled that a customary law that prevented women from inheriting property was unconstitutional. In Uganda, the Constitution prohibits "laws, cultures, customs or traditions which are against the dignity, welfare or interest of women" (World Bank, 2014). However, BCRs of the policy changes discussed later are not available, so comparisons are impossible.

Having the right to own and inherit property and businesses and having the right to sign contracts and open bank accounts should be regarded as a precondition to achieve women's empowerment, get women out of poverty, and allow women to pursue income-generating activities. Even if we lack evidence on effective policies to achieve this, governments have a big role to play in ensuring that women and men have the same rights, thus this goal should definitely be included in the post-2015 agenda. However, the existence of laws granting the same rights to women and men do not guarantee that women take full advantage of these rights.

Eliminate Discrimination against Women in Political, Economic, and Public Life

This is a very broad goal that includes many issues, such as an improvement in female political representation, which can ensure a better representation of women's needs in not only politics but also in companies and in households and equal access to employment and equal pay and working conditions for women. The goal also includes equal access to education and good access to sexual and reproductive health. Because of this complexity, the goal should be redefined and focus given to smaller subgoals. Next, I describe four of these subgoals: increase women's political representation, improve economic opportunities for women, equal access to education, and sexual and reproductive health.

Increase Women's Political Representation

Women should have equal access to decision-making positions, whether in the political arena, companies, or civil society. According to data from the World Development Indicators, women in 2013 occupied 22 percent of all parliamentary seats in the world, which is low but a considerable increase from the 13 percent political representation they had in 1990. Most of this increase was due to the implementation of quotas for women in many governments. However, when quotas are not present, women are still severely underrepresented. Figure 19.8 shows the percentage of women in national parliaments by region and year. Even if for all regions the percentage of women in national parliaments has increased, the percentage is still lower than 30 percent in all regions.

Evaluating the costs and benefits of increasing female political representation is impossible, and the effect of more female legislators on the welfare and economic development of a country is unknown. However, male politicians may not represent the needs of women because clearly female and male politicians make different policy decisions once in power.

The fact that it is impossible to give a benefit-cost ratio for increasing female political representation in a country does not mean that it should be disregarded as a goal for the post-2015 development agenda, given that it could be a very cheap and effective way to represent the needs of women and improve their lives, especially in developing countries. Countries with low female political representation could implement quotas for women in parliaments or could encourage political parties to field women candidates, which would simply involve a change in the electoral rules, but a change that could have far-reaching consequences.

For developing countries, most of the evidence we have for the effect of quotas and female political representation is from India. The first study to analyze the effect of quotas in a developing country was the one by Chattopadhyay and Duflo (2004), in which they found that reservation of council seats for women increased the public goods more valued by women. In West Bengal, where women complained more about water and roads, reservations lead to more investments in roads and drinking water. In Rajasthan women also complained more than men about drinking water, and reservations for women also resulted in more investments in this infrastructure. In a more recent paper Beaman et al. (2012) find that after two election cycles in which the village headship was reserved for a female politician in India, the gender gap for both parents' and girls' aspirations about education closed. In addition, the gender gap in educational attainment for adolescents disappeared, and girls spent less time doing household work.

Other studies investigate the role of women in state legislatures in India. Given that reservations are not yet in place in that level of government, the fact that some women are elected in close elections, i.e., by very few votes, is used to identify the causal effect of female politicians. One study

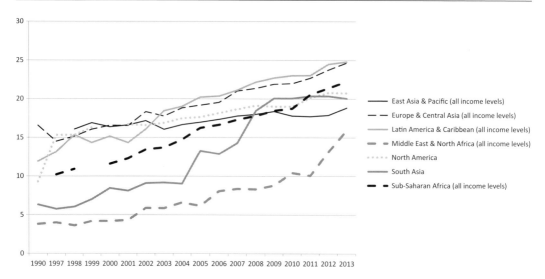

Figure 19.8 *Percentage of women in national parliaments*
Source: World Development Indicators 2014, World Bank.

concludes that raising the share of female politicians results in higher education but only in urban areas (Clots-Figueras, 2012). One additional female politician elected in a district in India increases the probability that an individual completes primary education in an urban area by around 6 percentage points. The other study finds improvements in a wider set of policy variables but shows that these improvements flow from women who hold seats reserved for the lower castes, that is, from "nonelite" women politicians (Clots-Figueras, 2011). Female legislators in seats reserved for lower castes and disadvantaged tribes invest more in health and early education and favor "women-friendly" laws, such as amendments to the Hindu Succession Act, which was designed to give women the same inheritance rights as men.

For Brazil, Brollo and Troiano (2016) use a regression discontinuity design and find that municipalities ruled by female mayors have better health outcomes, receive more federal discretionary transfers, and have lower corruption than those ruled by male mayors. In their study they find that the probability of observing a corruption episode in randomly audited villages is around 30 percent lower when there is a female mayor. Given that corruption

is negatively correlated with GDP and can affect growth negatively, policies that encourage the participation of women in politics should definitely be considered for the post-2015 goals.

Many explanations have been proposed to explain the underrepresentation of women in politics, such as discrimination, lack of female role models, lower ambition, distaste for competition, and family responsibilities. Bhalotra et al. (2014) analyze the effect of a female victory in India on women candidacy and political participation and find that the probability of the female running again increases after a victory; however, there are no effects on women's turnout or political success.

Quotas for women in governments are a controversial measure, but they could be an effective way to increase female political representation. Quotas are designed to compensate for the barriers that women face when entering in politics, but those who are against their implementation argue that they could have a negative effect on meritocracy, they could push more qualified candidates out of the election, and that in general they change the way that political parties and voters behave. However, Besley et al. (2013) analyze the issue using data from Swedish municipalities, in which quotas require parties to alternate male and female names on the ballot. They find that the quota increased the competence of male politicians when it raised the share of female political representation the most. Even if the causal mechanism is unclear, given the difficulties of encouraging female political participation and the huge potential benefits of female political participation, quotas should definitely be considered, and the issue of female political participation should definitely be included as a post-2015 goal.

Improve Women's Access to Economic Opportunities

Even if female labor force participation contributes to household income growth, it is estimated that half of the women in the labor force are in vulnerable employment, and most of them receive less pay than their male counterparts for the same work.[11] Economic opportunities can even affect the value that parents attach to having daughters because it can change the aspirations that parents have for their daughters, and this in turn can change the decisions they make about their daughters' health, nutrition, and education, dramatically changing women's livelihoods.

For example, the experiment conducted by Jensen (2012) in a set of randomly selected rural villages in India, referred to earlier in the context of delaying marriage, shows how employment prospects can be improved by raising awareness of opportunities.

One successful randomized experiment looking at vocational training for girls is the one by Bandiera et al. (2014), also discussed previously. Girls in Uganda were offered both vocational training and information on marriage, sex and reproduction in after-school clubs. Relative to adolescent girls in control communities, those in treatment communities were 72 percent more likely to participate in income-generating activities, mainly via self-employment. Although the authors conducted a cost-benefit analysis of the intervention, the only monetizable benefit was the increase in household expenditure per capita. The result is a BCR of 0.67–0.69, depending on the discount rate used; see the first line in Table 19.6. However, the program had other benefits, apart from the increase in

self-employment activities, but these are difficult to put a monetary value on.

In the following we will try to estimate the net impact of as many of the other benefits as possible. If we consider as well the other benefits attached to the program, such as a the decrease in the probability that girls have sex against their will and the decrease in early marriage and pregnancy rates, the benefits are much larger. Bandiera et al. (2014) find a reduction in early fertility of 2.7 absolute percentage points in treated communities when the survey was conducted in the second year. This means that the benefits per girl would be around $22.76 in 2008 USD. Overall the program would have a BCR of 3.1–3.2, see Table 19.6. If parents change their expectations about the value of investments in girls' human capital after the program is implemented, the benefits would be much larger, but with the current data and the current studies, we do not know whether this would happen.

Figures 19.9 and 19.10 plot the labor force participation rate for young women and the adolescent fertility rate for Bangladesh, Uganda, Tanzania, South Sudan, and Sierra Leone, where similar programs have been run (fertility rate only for South Sudan). Uganda displays consistently higher teenage fertility rates than the other countries, while the labor force participation rate for young women is lower than the one in Tanzania but higher than the ones in Bangladesh and Sierra Leone.

This suggests that the effects of the program could be larger for Uganda than for other regions, which have higher female labor force participation rates and lower teenage fertility rates. The program should be evaluated in other regions, but most probably the BCRs in other countries will still be high enough, and most probably will be larger than 1.

With current data it is impossible to estimate precisely the long-term effects of the program on these girls, but they are likely to be positive, especially if they delay marriage until a much older age, and this protects their health and allows them to accumulate human capital and conduct income-generating activities. If the average age of the girls

---

[11] ILO (2012).

Table 19.6 Economic opportunities for women

| | Low discount rate | | | | | | High discount rate | | | | | |
| | Cost | Benefits | | | Total | BCR | Cost | Benefits | | | Total | BCR |
		HH exp.	Sex. violence	Early fert.				HH exp.	Sex. violence	Early fert.		
Bandiera et al. (2014)	48.8	32.8	96.4	22.8	151.9	3.1	47.4	32.8	96.4	22.8	151.9	3.2
After 4 years (constant benefits)	56.8	95.5	280.8	66.3	442.7	7.8	59.4	93.8	275.6	65.1	369.4	6.2
After 4 years (benefits fade 20% rate)	56.8	78.0	229.4	54.2	361.6	6.4	59.4	76.8	225.8	53.3	355.9	6.0

Note: The costs and benefits refer to the ones of treating one girl and are measured in 2008 U.S. dollars.

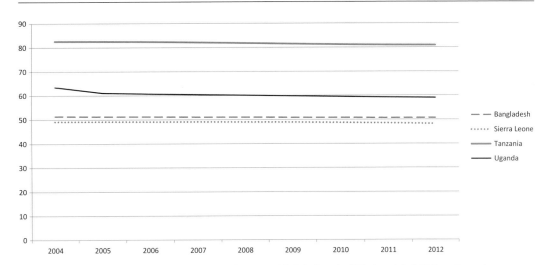

Figure 19.9 *Labor force participation rate for ages 15–24, female (%) (modeled ILO estimate)*

Source: World Development Indicators 2014, World Bank.

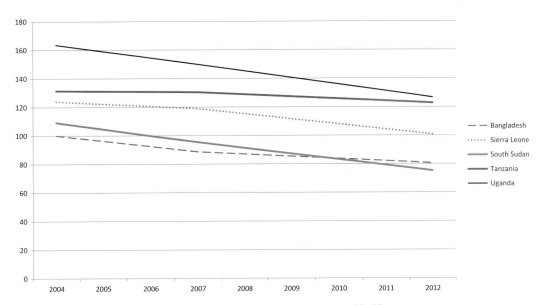

Figure 19.10 *Adolescent fertility rate (births per 1,000 women ages 15–19)*

Source: World Development Indicators 2014, World Bank.

in the program is 16, and girls ages 14–20 are those allowed to attend the after-school clubs in which the vocational and life-skills training are provided, we could expect girls to be in the program for an average of 4 years. If we assume that the fixed costs of the program, which are reported in the paper to be $14.9[12] the first year and $10.7 the

[12] 2008 U.S. dollars.

second year, are only incurred the first two years, and in the third and fourth years the variable costs per affected girl are the same as the variable costs incurred in the second year, which are $7.12, the BCR after four years can be computed if some assumptions are made about the effects of the program. The second and third rows in Table 19.6 provide these estimates under two scenarios, one in which the effects of the program are constant over time and another one in which the effects of the program fade away at a 20 percent rate each year, which is probably more realistic if we consider that a large percentage of girls are likely to be married and maybe have a child by the age of 18. In all cases, both for the optimistic and pessimistic scenarios and with a high and low discount rate, the BCR would be between 5.9 and 7.8.

Another program that was successful in improving income-generating activities for women is the one for disadvantaged youth introduced in Colombia over 2001–2005, analyzed by Attanasio et al. (2011). The program is called "Jóvenes en Acción" and provided three months of classroom training and three months of on-the-job training to young people ages 18–25. The program was not specifically targeted to benefit women, but results from their study show that the program increased earnings and employment for women, while the effects for men were not significantly different from zero. Women who were offered training earned 19.6 percent more and had a 0.068 higher probability of being in paid employment compared with women who were offered no training.

The authors find a gain of $211.16 for women per year, reflecting both the fact that their monthly earnings increased and their salaries also increased due to working in the formal sector. The costs of the program are $750 per person, plus $62 due to the loss of tenure caused by participating in the program. If we assume earnings are constant over time, both with a 3 percent and 5 percent discount rates, the BCR of the program becomes larger than 1 if the women worked 4 years. The authors consider an alternative scenario in which earnings depreciate by 10 percent, in which case women would have to work for 5 years for the program to break even, assuming a high discount rate. Assuming that the women will work for 40 years

more with constant earnings, this amounts to a BCR of 6.19 and 4.68, with 3 percent and 5 percent discount rates, respectively. Assuming earnings depreciate at a 10 percent rate this amounts to a BCR of 2.05–1.8.

Other nonrandomized evaluations of programs in other Latin American countries such as Argentina, Brazil, Chile, Colombia, the Dominican Republic, Panama, Perú, and Uruguay gave similar results. However, without a randomized evaluation, it is very difficult to provide evidence on the causal effect of a program. Card et al. (2011) find that a similar program in the Dominican Republic had effects that were not statistically significant.

The large BCR provided by the program in Bandiera et al. (2014) and the existence of programs such as the one analyzed by Attanasio et al. (2011), which have been proven successful, suggest that the development community should invest in these type of programs, which can be very cost effective and can provide multiple benefits.

Increase the Number of Years of Education Attained by Women

Education is very important for girls and women, not only for the monetary returns and because knowledge empowers women, but also because women who receive more years of schooling are likely to marry later, to have children later in life, to participate in income-generating activities, to make better decisions about their own health and their offspring's health and nutrition, and to have higher bargaining power in the household.

Gender gaps in primary education have narrowed dramatically but there are still disparities in primary education in some regions, and gender differences prevail for secondary and university education.

When considering the decision of whether to target educational investments to girls, or simply to conduct nontargeted educational investments, note that returns to education for girls in low-income countries are higher than returns to education for boys (see Psacharopoulos and Patrinos, 2004, and Schultz, 2002). In addition, girls' education has positive externalities and other non-monetary benefits. For example, an increase in years of schooling also delays marriage and early fertility, which is the most important cause of early dropout for girls.

Out of the articles discussed earlier, Duflo et al. (2012), shows how an educational subsidy that provided primary school girls with free uniforms in grades 6, 7, and 8, when they were more susceptible to dropping out from school, delayed early marriage by 2.6 absolute percentage points after three years. In addition, girls who benefited from the intervention were 3.1 absolute percentage points less likely to have dropped out from school after three years.

This chapter follows Psacharopoulos (2014) and assumes the return to an additional year of education to be 13.8 percent. And together with the average wage in Kenya in 2003 (325.01 2014 U.S. dollars), this allows the computation of the benefits of the additional years of education for each girl. The resulting BCR is between 4.95 and 5.15 (see Table 19.7). This takes into account both the benefits of the additional years of education, together with the benefits due to later marriage. Other benefits could be included, even if they are very difficult to monetize. Educational programs that retain girls in school, especially at the end of primary education, and programs that encourage them to continue with secondary education should definitely be encouraged.

Improve Access to Sexual and Reproductive Health for All Women

It is important to ensure access to healthcare for women, given that according to the UN only half of women in the developing world receive the amount of needed healthcare. The maternal mortality rate has decreased, but it remains unnecessarily high in many areas of the world, which points to a lack of medical care before, during, and after delivery.

Maternal mortality still remains unnecessarily high, but we still know very little about what are the most cost-effective policies that would reduce it. However, an improvement in health facilities and health attention, an increase in the number of antenatal visits attended by women, and ensuring that more women give birth in proper facilities or with the presence of qualified professionals would most probably reduce the maternal mortality rate where it remains high.

Access to contraceptives allows women to decide the moment to have children, which has important implications for their health, the amount of education attained, and for their participation in the labor force. The study by Bandiera et al. (2014) found that the vocational training with life skills intervention in Uganda increased the control that girls have over their bodies. Early childbearing decreased by 26 percent, and self-reported condom use increased by 28 percent relative to baseline levels.

Behrman (2014) provide very high BCRs for achieving universal access to reproductive health services by 2030 and to reduce by 20 percent the maternal mortality rate. They find that the BCRs of implementing family planning programs that would reduce maternal and infant mortality would be of around 90–150, so this should definitely be included in the post-2015 goals.

Reproductive and maternal health is a vitally important issue to be addressed as a precondition for achieving the other targets discussed.

Policy Recommendations and Conclusion

Table 19.8 provides the summary of the recommendations, which will help to improve gender equality.

Two key issues need to be included as preconditions for the rest of the agenda to be achieved.

First is providing education for women, especially at the primary level, in the most deprived areas, in which equality in enrollment and completion rates have not yet been achieved. Second is providing equal access to healthcare, and in particular to reproductive services, both as contraception and as maternal care.

Another precondition is to ensure equal right of women to own and inherit property, sign a contract, register a business, and open a bank account. Although we do not have enough causal evidence, we cannot think about empowering women and

Table 19.7 Education for women

| Paper | Effect (marriage) | Effect (completing primary) | Cost of treating one girl (2014 US$) | | Benefits of more years education (2014 US$) | | Benefits of later marriage (2014 US$) | | BCR | |
			Low discount rate (3%)	High discount rate (5%)	Low discount rate (3%)	High discount rate (5%)	Low discount rate (3%)	High discount rate (5%)	Low discount rate (3%)	High discount rate (5%)
Duflo et al. (2012)	2.6 percentage points after 3 years	3.1 percentage points after 3 years	22.99	23.45	52.43	40.18	66.3	67.6	5.16	4.59

Table 19.8 Summary of recommendations

TARGET	Summary	Summary BCR	Discussion	Recommendation
Increase the number of years of education attained by women	Discourage dropouts from primary education and encourage secondary education enrollment.	4.59–5.16	The BCR also includes benefits from delaying marriage and fertility, but there is evidence of successful educational programs delaying marriage and early fertility.	**Include as a precondition.**
Improve access to sexual and reproductive health for all women	Providing equal access to healthcare, and in particular to reproductive services, both as contraception and as maternal care	90–150 (from Behrman, 2014)	More studies needed.	**Include as a precondition.**
Ensure equal rights of women to own and inherit property, sign a contract, register a business, and open a bank account	Ensure equal right of women to own and inherit property, sign a contract, register a business and open a bank account	Potentially very high with low cost, only change in legislation needed.	More studies needed.	**Include as a precondition.**
Prevent and eliminate all forms of violence against girls and women	Reduce violence against women	Not enough evidence and potentially high costs. Cannot be a zero target.	Programs empowering women, increasing educational attainment, and increasing the availability of income-generating opportunities for women could succeed in reducing violence against women but more evidence is needed.	**Do not include**
End child marriage	Reduce early marriage and teenage fertility rates	Not enough evidence from programs directly targeted to the issue. Cannot be a zero target.	Programs empowering women, increasing educational attainment and increasing the availability of income-generating opportunities for women will most likely succeed in delaying marriage and early fertility.	**Do not include**
Increase women's political representation	Encourage the implementation of quotas at all government levels	Potentially very high. Only changes in electoral laws are needed, so the cost is potentially low.	Evidence suggests that female politicians represent the needs and preferences of women.	**Include**
Improve women's access to economic opportunities	Encourage women to start income-generating activities through vocational training and informational campaigns	6.2–7.8	Evidence of successful programs providing vocational training and information.	**Include**

Table 19.9 Summary of BCRs

TARGET	Program	3% discount rate			5% discount rate		
		Benefit	Cost	BCR	Benefit	Cost	BCR
Increase the number of years of education attained by women	Program in Duflo et al., 2012	118.6	23.0	5.2	107.6	23.5	4.6
Improve access to sexual and reproductive health for all women	Analysis in Behrman, 2014	324–540	3.6	90–150			
Ensure equal right of women to own and inherit property, sign a contract, register a business, and open a bank account	No programs providing BCRs						
Prevent and eliminate all forms of violence against girls and women	No programs directly targeted to the issue providing BCRs						
End child marriage	No programs directly targeted to the issue providing BCRs						
Increase women's political representation	No programs providing BCRs						
Improve women's access to economic opportunities	Program in Bandiera et al., 2014 (after 4 yrs.)	442.7	56.8	7.8	369.4	59.4	6.2

giving them access to income-generating opportunities if they cannot have property rights. The fact that women cannot inherit property means that they will not inherit family land or businesses. If women cannot sign contracts, register businesses, and open bank accounts, this means that there will be a male figure in control of their business, income, and assets, which can weaken not only their incentives to invest in businesses, but also their bargaining power within the household. It is very difficult to calculate BCRs, but this does not mean that this goal should not be included in the post-2015 agenda as one of the most important ones.

We know very little about the effect of programs targeted to reduce violence against women and increase the age at marriage. The programs discussed in these study seem to effectively reduce sexual violence against women and to increase age at marriage, but they are mainly targeted to increase education or women's empowerment in general. We suggest that more should be invested in issues such as education and female economic

and political empowerment, which will probably lead to improvements both as a reduction in violence and as an increase in the age at which girls get married on average.

Women are underrepresented in political positions in all countries in the world, even if some countries have started introducing quotas. Given the increasing evidence that women and men make different policy decisions, the gender goal should definitely mention this as one of the targets. Even if quotas can have drawbacks, the benefits could be larger than the costs for female empowerment and participation in public life.

Finally, development programs that encourage women to start income-generating activities seem to be very successful, not only in getting women into paid employment, but also because they manage to reduce child marriages, change attitudes and expectations, and even to reduce domestic violence. The gender goal in the post-2015 agenda should definitely mention the importance of ensuring that women have access to income-generating activities.

Table 19.9 provides a summary of the benefits, costs, and the benefit-cost-ratio (BCR) of the most successful or representative program for each target analyzed in this chapter. BCRs cannot always be provided due to lack of evidence on programs designed to increase women's political representation or women's rights, but this does not make them less important. The BCRs provided in this study should only be used to indicate that there is scope to find programs and solutions that are successful in tackling a particular problem for which the benefits can be larger than the costs.

References

Attanasio, O., Kugler, A., and Meghir, C. 2011. "Subsidizing Vocational Training for Disadvantaged Youth in Colombia: Evidence from a Randomized Trial." *American Economic Journal: Applied Economics* 3: 188–220.

Bagues, M. and Esteve-Volart, B. 2012. "Are Women Pawns in the Political Game? Evidence from Elections to the Spanish Senate," *Journal of Public Economics* 96: 387–99.

Baird, S., McIntosh, C., and Özler, B. 2011. "Cash or Condition? Evidence from a Cash Transfer Experiment." *The Quarterly Journal of Economics* 126 (4): 1709–53.

Bandiera, O., Buehren, N., Burgess, R., Goldstein, M., Gulesci, S., Rasul, I., and Sulaiman, M. 2014. "Women's Empowerment in Action: Evidence from a Randomized Control Trial in Africa." Mimeo.

Beaman, L., Chattopadhyay, R., Duflo, E., Pande, R., and Topalova, P. 2009. "Powerful Women: Does Exposure Reduce Bias?" *Quarterly Journal of Economics* 124(4): 1497–1540.

Beaman, L., Duflo, E., Pande, R., and Topalova, P. 2012. "Female Leadership Raises Aspirations and Educational Attainment for Girls: A Policy Experiment in India." *Science* 355: 582–6.

Beath, A., Christa, F., and Enikopolov, R. 2013. "Empowering Women through Development Aid: Evidence from a Field Experiment in Afghanistan." *American Political Science Review*, 107: 540–57. doi:10.1017/S0003055413000270.

Besley, T, Folke, O., Persson, T., and Rickne, J. 2013. "Gender Quotas and the Crisis of the Mediocre Man: Theory and Evidence from Sweden." Mimeo.

Bhalotra, S. and Clots-Figueras, I. 2014. "Health and the Political Agency of Women." *American Economic Journal: Economic Policy* 6(2): 164–97.

Bhalotra, S., Clots-Figueras, I., and Iyer, L. 2014. "Path-Breakers: How Does Women's Political Participation Respond to Electoral Success?" mimeo.

Bhavnani, R. 2009. "Do Electoral Quotas Work After They Are Withdrawn? Evidence from a Natural Experiment in India." *American Political Science Review* 103 (1): 23–35.

Boisjoly, J., Duncan, G., Kremer, M., Levy, D., and Eccles, J. 2006. "Empathy or Antipathy? The Consequences of Racially and Socially Diverse Peers on Attitudes and Behaviors." *American Economic Review*, 96: 1890–1906.

Brollo, F. and Troiano, U. 2016. "What Happens When a Woman Wins an Election? Evidence from Close Races in Brazil." *Journal of Development Economics* 122(Sept.): 28–45.

Campa, P. 2012. "Gender Quotas, Female Politicians and Public Expenditures: Quasi-Experimental Evidence." Working Paper, Stockholm University.

Card, D., Ibarrán, P., Regalia, F., Rosas, D., and Soares, Y. 2011. "The Labor Market Impacts of Youth Training in the Dominican Republic." *Journal of Labor Economics*, 29(2): 267–300.

Chaaban, J, and Cunningham, W. 2011. "Measuring the Economic Gain of Investing in Girls. The Girl Effect Dividend." Policy Research Working Paper 5753. World Bank.

Chattopadhyay, R. and Duflo, E. 2004. "Women as Policy Makers: Evidence from a Randomized Policy Experiment in India," *Econometrica, Econometric Society* 72(5): 1409–43.

Clots-Figueras, I. 2011. "Women in Politics: Evidence from the Indian States." *Journal of Public Economics* 95: 664–90.

2012. "Are Female Leaders Good for Education? Evidence from India." *American Economic Journal: Applied Economics* 4(1): 212–44.

Coate, S. and Loury, G. C. 1993. "Will Affirmative-Action Policies Eliminate Negative Stereotypes?" *The American Economic Review* 83(5): 1220–40.

DeLisi, M., Kosloski, A., Sween, M., et al. 2010. "Murder by numbers: Monetary costs imposed by a sample of homicide offenders."

The Journal of Forensic Psychiatry & Psychology 21, 501–13. doi:10.1080/ 14789940903564388.

de Mel, S., McKenzie, D., and Woodruff, C. 2009. "Are Women More Credit Constrained? Experimental Evidence on Gender and Microenterprise Returns." *American Economic Journal: Applied Economics* 1(3): 1–32.

Deininger, K., Goyal, A., and Nagarajan, H. 2013. "Women's Inheritance Rights and Intergenerational Transmission of Resources in India." *Journal of Human Resources* 48(1): 114–41.

Dhaliwal, I, Duflo, E., Glennester, R., and Tulloch, C. 2012. "Comparative Cost-Effectiveness Analysis to Inform Policy in Developing Countries. A General Framework with Applications for Education." Abdul Latif Jameel Poverty Action Lab (J-PAL), MIT.

Doepke, M., Tertilt, M., and Voena, A. 2012. "The Economics and Politics of Women's Rights." *Annual Review of Economics* 4: 339–372.

Duflo, E. 2003. "Grandmothers and Granddaughters: Old Age Pension and Intra-household Allocation in South Africa." *World Bank Economic Review* 17(1), 1–25.

2012. "Women Empowerment and Economic Development." *Journal of Economic Literature* 50(4): 1051–79.

Duflo, E., Dupas, P., and Kremer, M. 2012. "Education, HIV, and Early Fertility. Experimental Evidence from Kenya." Mimeo.

Eggers, A. 2011. "Is Female Political Participation Self-Reinforcing? Evidence from French Municipal Politics." Mimeograph.

Fafchamps, M., McKenzie, D., Quinn, S., and Woodruff, C. 2014. "Microenterprise Growth and The Flypaper Effect: Evidence from a Randomized Experiment in Ghana." *Journal of Development Economics, Elsevier* 106(C): 211–26.

Fearon, J. and Hoeffler, A. 2014. "Beyond Civil War: The Costs of Interpersonal Violence and the Next Round of MDGs." Paper prepared for the Copenhagen Consensus.

Field E. 2003. "Fertility Responses to Urban Land Titling Programs: The Roles of Ownership Security and the Distribution of Household Asset." Unpublished manuscript, Harvard University.

Field, E. and Ambrus, A. 2008. "Early Marriage, Age of Menarche, and Female Schooling Attainment in Bangladesh." *Journal of Political Economy* 116(5): 881–930.

Field, E., Jayachandran, S., and Pande, R. 2010. "Do Traditional Institutions Constrain Female Entrepreneurship? A Field Experiment on Business Training in India." *American Economic Review* 100(2): 125–9.

Gagliarducci, S. and Paserman, D. 2012. "Gender Interactions within Hierarchies: Evidence from the Political Arena." *Review of Economic Studies* 79(3): 1021–52.

Ghani, E., Kerr, W. R., and O'Connell, S. D. 2014. "Political Reservations and Women's Entrepreneurship in India." *Journal of Development Economics* 108 (May 2014): 138–53.

International Labour Organization. (2012). *Global Employment Trends for Women*. Geneva: Author.

Iyer, L., Mani, A., Mishra, P., and Topalova, P. 2012. "The Power of Political Voice: Women's Political Representation and Crime in India." *American Economic Journal: Applied Economics* 4(4): 165–93.

Jensen, R., 2012. "Do Labor Market Opportunities Affect Young Women's Work and Family Decisions? Experimental Evidence from India." *The Quarterly Journal of Economics* 127(2): 753–92.

Jensen, R. and Thornton, R. 2003. "Early Female Marriage in the Developing World." *Gender and Development* 11(2): 9–19.

Karlan, D. and Valdivia, M. 2011. "Teaching Entrepreneurship: Impact of Business Training on Microfinance Clients and Institutions." *Review of Economics and Statistics* 93(2): 510–527.

Karlan, D. and Zinman, J. 2011. "Microfinance in Theory and Practice. Using Randomized Credit Scoring for Impact Evaluation." *Science* 332(6035): 1278–84.

Knight, J. B. and Sabot, R. H. 1990. *Education, Productivity, and Inequality*. Washington, DC: Oxford University Press.

Behrman, J. R. with Kohler, H.-P. 2014. "Population and Demography: Assessment Paper," Copenhagen Consensus Project: Post-2015 Consensus Copenhagen, Denmark: Copenhagen Consensus Project.

Luke, N. and Munshi, K. 2011. "Women as Agents of Change: Female Income and Mobility in India." *Journal of Development Economics* 94(1): 1–17.

Lundberg, S. J., Pollak, R. A., and Wales, T. J. 1997. "Do Husbands and Wives Pool Their Resources? Evidence from the United Kingdom Child Benefit." *Journal of Human Resources* 32(3), 1132–51.

MacMillan, R. 2000. Adolescent victimization and income deficits in adulthood: Rethinking the costs of criminal violence from a life-course perspective, *Criminology* 38: 553–88. doi:10.1111/j.1745-9125.2000.tb00899.

Malhotra A., Warner, A., McGonagle, A., and Lee-Rife, S. 2011. *Solutions to End Child Marriage, What the Evidence Shows*. Washington, DC: International Center for Research on Women.

Miguel, E. and Kremer, M. 2004, "Worms: Identifying Impacts on Education and Health in the Presence of Treatment Externalities." *Econometrica* 72: 159–217.

National Alliance to End Sexual Violence. 2010 2010 Survey of Rape Crisis Centers.

Pande, R. and Ford, D. 2011. "Gender Quotas and Female Leadership: A Review," Background paper for the World Development Report on Gender.

Pronyk, P. M., Hargreaves, J. R., Kim, et al. 2006. "Effect of a structural intervention for the prevention of intimate-partner violence and HIV in rural South Africa: a cluster randomised trial." *The Lancet* 368(9551): 1973–1983. DOI: 10.1016/S0140–6736(06)69744–4

Psacharopoulos, G. 2014. *Benefits and Costs of the Education Targets for the Post-2015 Development Agenda*. Copenhagen Consensus.

Psacharopoulos, G. and Patrinos, H. 2002. "Returns to Investment in Education: A Further Update."*Education Economics* 12(2): 111–34.

Roy, S. 2014. "Empowering Women: Inheritance Rights and Female Education in India." Mimeo.

Schultz, T. P. (2002). Why Governments Should Invest More to Educate Girls. *World Development* 30(2): 207–25.

Sekhon, J. S. and Titiunik, R. 2012. "When Natural Experiments Are Neither Natural Nor Experiments." *American Political Science Review* 106 (1): 35–57.

Svensson, J. 2005. "Eight Questions about Corruption." *Journal of Economic Perspectives* 19(5): 19–42.

Thomas, D. 1990. "Intra-household resource allocation: an inferential approach." *Journal of Human Resources* 25(4) 635–64.

United Nations. 2013a. "Promote gender equality and empower women." Fact sheet.

2013b. "We Can End Poverty." Fact Sheet. http://www.un.org/millenniumgoals/pdf/Goal_3_fs.pdf.

United Nations, Department of Economic and Social Affairs, Population Division. 2013. "World Marriage Data 2012" (POP/DB/Marr/Rev2012).

United Nations, High Level Panel. 2014. "A New Global Partnership."

World Bank. 2014a. *Voice and Agency: Empowering Women and Girls for Shared Prosperity*. Washington, DC: World Bank.

2014b. *World Development Indicators 2014*. Washington, DC: World Bank.

World Health Organization. (2013). "Global and Regional Estimates of Violence against Women: Prevalence and Health Effects of Intimate Partner Violence and Non-Partner Sexual Violence." http://www.povertyactionlab.org/.

Alternative Perspective

ELISSA BRAUNSTEIN

Summary

In this perspective I identify and discuss the chapter's methodological problems and evidentiary gaps with the intent of improving its evaluative power. Methodologically, I use a gender-aware analysis to identify the challenges of conducting benefit-cost analysis based on microexperimental evidence. I then argue the case for including macroeconomic perspectives and evidence, drawing from the research on gender equality and growth.

Beginning with methodological issues, as the author points out, the key strength of randomized controlled trials is their ability to test policy changes very specifically and directly. But the reliability of BCRs from such trials must be evaluated with an awareness of their weaknesses as well as strengths.

Many assumptions have to be made about prices. From a gender equality perspective, the question of price is particularly confounding because using market prices and incomes to estimate benefits and costs incorporates value into project evaluation in ways that can disadvantage women. Using just market prices to estimate the cost of gender discrimination biases BCRs downward.

A related issue is the invisibility of nonmarket work, much of it unpaid care work performed by women and girls. However, this is also a productive activity and has been valued as a substantial contributor to overall GDP. Also, attributing women's lack of lack of economic participation to insufficient training or information ignores socially determined constraints, especially the traditional sexual division of labor. Other policy routes may therefore be needed, for example, rural electrification, which can allow women to reallocate their household work in transformative ways.

A weakness of relying on controlled trials is that public externalities are missed because of the small scale. Ultimately, if we want to grapple with development's big questions, we have to venture into the seemingly less well-defined world of macro-economics. Macroeconomic approaches afford insights into lots of important dynamics that are simply inaccessible using randomized trials. There is also the practical argument about engaging with the widely cited instrumental case for gender equality: that gender equality is good for economic growth.

That gender inequality is bad for economic growth is one of the more compelling policy arguments proffered by development professionals these days, and a number of empirical studies have tried to estimate just how much gender discrimination costs in terms of sacrificed growth. It has been estimated that up to 20 percent of the difference in growth rates between East Asia and sub-Saharan Africa between 1960 and 1992 can be attributed to inequality in education and employment.

A paper by Joyce Jacobson for an earlier Copenhagen Consensus exercise estimated global GDP loss due to gender inequality in employment to be between 7 and 16 percent. Approximating costs of interventions can be more difficult. However, for MDG3 (promote gender equality and women's empowerment), the UN estimated a cost of 1.1 percent of GDP in low-income countries, although this rose to 3.2 percent for mainstreaming gender equality activities under other goals.

There are two main points to conclude with. First, benefit cost evaluations of policies for gender equality must be gender-aware in the sense of incorporating how gender structures, many of which exist outside the market sphere, shape choice and opportunity in economically significant ways. Second, restricting evidence to a limited sampling of microexperimental studies misses a large macroliterature on gender, one whose incorporation would greatly improve the scale and scope aspects of the BCRs.

19.2 Alternative Perspective

JOYCE P. JACOBSEN

Summary

Clots-Figueras addresses all of the relevant post-2015 goals and reports on the most recent relevant experimental results having to do with explicit benefit-cost ratios (BCRs) for this gender-related research. However, the evidence base is restricted to experimental papers. This perspective suggests different views regarding how to measure and assess evidence regarding BCRs. This includes addressing the question of what elements are preconditions and what events are actually more likely to occur if economic situations for women are improved.

The chapter ably demonstrates the advantages and limitations of benefit-cost analysis. It raises important questions such as whether the BCR should be seen as a lower bound because of the large, unmeasured spillover effects. For gender-related outcomes in particular, it is unclear what the range of effects may be and whether they are all desirable. Increasing women's participation in the labor force, for example, is not necessarily an end in itself and may have other outcomes, some of which could be undesirable.

Project-specific BCRs may also not scale up to society-wide policies. For example, educating too many people to fill the number of higher-level jobs available or providing microfinance to a start-up in an already crowded market may not be beneficial. On the other hand, small-scale studies could also underestimate the larger societal impact of policies. For example, a more educated population may lead to more efficient institutions and more efficient interactions with others.

There are, however, other options. For instance, take a set of countries (or a pair of countries) that have different levels of social spending on a particular matter of interest, such as women's healthcare. We can then compare the different outcomes for such standard indicators as maternal mortality, infant mortality, and other health outcomes for both women and others (especially children). Combined with calculations of the monetary value of a DALY, this can then lead to a BCR calculation.

Some of the most interesting historical examples involve two neighboring countries, often with a common cultural heritage, that then separate in terms of their social policy at some critical juncture. The division of Germany after WWII is a case in point; reunification showed how re-equilibration then occurred. Countries in different locations but with a common cultural background – Australia, the United States, and the UK, for example – provide other useful comparisons.

Economic development and women's equality almost always occur in near tandem, with more developed countries also having higher levels of gender. But cause and effect are difficult to assign. Clots-Figueras makes the case for women receiving full political rights as a prerequisite for other positive economic changes, but are legal changes necessary for women to benefit? It may be more difficult to argue also that political representation quotas are necessary because most highly developed countries have reached that state without them.

Arguing that a policy should be implemented because it has a sufficiently high BCR ignores the question of who bears the costs and who reaps the benefits. It may be preferable in issues such as gender equality to argue in favor of their inherent morality rather than in purely economic terms.

In conclusion, although more work remains to be done in calculating and considering BCRs for gender-related issues, the chapter takes a crucial first step in the right direction.

Benefits and Costs of the Food and Nutrition Targets for the Post-2015 Development Agenda

CHAPTER 20

SUSAN HORTON AND JOHN HODDINOTT

Introduction

Nutrition has always been a key development indicator. Good nutrition allows for healthy growth and development of children, and inadequate nutrition is a major contributing factor to child mortality. Good nutrition is also important for cognitive development and, hence, educational success, both of which are important determinants of labor productivity and hence economic growth. Good nutrition also implies balance – neither undernutrition nor overnutrition.

In what follows we will first briefly review the evolution of nutrition goals, from the Millennium Development Goals (MDGs) to 2015, to the World Health Organization targets to 2025, and the Sustainable Development Goals (SDGs) to 2030. We then comment briefly on the SDG target for nutrition and provide an economic perspective on the goal (using Hoddinott et al., 2013), suggesting that the benefit-cost ratio of nutrition investments is very attractive.

The Evolution of the Nutrition Goals

Stunting – low height for age – is an excellent nutrition indicator to include in the SDGs. It improves on the earlier nutrition indicator used in the MDGs. MDG 1 had two quantitative targets and one qualitative: halving the poverty rate, halving the number "hungry," and a more aspirational goal regarding access to employment. "Hunger," in turn, was defined in terms of the number of children who were underweight (using the WHO Child Growth Standards), hence the specific goal was to halve the proportion of children underweight over the period 1990 to 2015.

Over the decade or so since the MDGs were set, our understanding of undernutrition and its measurement has advanced further. Underweight (weight for age) is a composite measure, which aggregates two different aspects of undernutrition, namely weight for height (or wasting, a measure of current nutritional status) and height for age (or stunting, a measure of long-run nutritional status). The underweight goal has served its purpose to focus attention on nutrition. Going forward we can improve on the original MDG target in two ways. First, stunting is a better indicator than underweight. And second, in a world with some regions with growing population, a goal of halving the *proportion* who are hungry is a weaker goal (easier to achieve) than one of halving the current *number* who are hungry.

Just to illustrate why stunting is a better indicator than underweight, imagine a child who is born and grows up in early childhood consuming a diet largely consisting of starchy staples, and whose mother faced the same diet during her pregnancy. Such a diet is devoid of the variety of foods needed to provide the nutrients required for healthy growth. This child is likely to end up stunted by age two (short for his/her age), after which catch-up in height is more difficult. This child may also be (according to Barker, 1992) "programmed" for a diet of scarcity and more vulnerable to obesity if faced with high-fat and high-added-sugar foods. The MDG goal (halving underweight) will incorrectly categorize this child as of normal weight, whereas the SDG target (stunting) will correctly categorize this child as suffering from long-run undernutrition. Lutter et al. (2011) demonstrate that using the underweight goal for Latin America would have suggested in 2008 that all 13 countries were on track to meet MDG 1 (expressed in terms of underweight); however, if stunting had been used instead of underweight, 5 of the 13 countries would not be on track to meet the goal.

Sustainable Development Goal 2 ("End hunger, achieve food security, and improved nutrition and promote sustainable agriculture") contains a mix of lofty (but hard to measure) goals (relating to hunger, food security, and sustainable increases in agricultural productivity) and two more measurable goals (achieve the WHO goals for stunting and wasting). The World Health Organization (WHO) nutrition goals for 2025 (WHO, 2014), as adopted by the World Health Assembly, are to

- Reduce by 40 percent the number of children under 5 who are stunted.
- Achieve a 50 percent reduction in the rate of anemia in women of reproductive age.
- Achieve a 30 percent reduction in the rate of infants born with low birth weight.
- Ensure that there is no increase in the rate of children who are overweight.
- Increase to at least 50 percent the rate of exclusive breastfeeding in the first six months.
- Reduce and maintain childhood wasting to less than 5 percent.

Advantages and Disadvantages of the Stunting Goal

Some Advantages of the Stunting Goal

- Child growth depends on dietary intake (quality and quantity) for the first 1000 days, i.e., for the mother during pregnancy and for the child during the first two years of life.
- Growth also depends on health status and is affected by improvements in sanitation and reduced infection.
- Growth also is affected by quality of care, and children who have both better nutrition/health and care do better than those with only one of these inputs.
- Hence growth is a good indicator of the quality of the early life environment.

- Growth is readily measurable (although it relies on reasonably good age data) and is less invasive than nutrition indicators, which require samples of bodily fluids.
- Child height at age two is a good predictor of achieved adult height.
- Achieved adult height is associated with wages: from a survey of eight high-income countries (Gao and Smyth, 2010), the median increase of hourly wages per centimeter of additional height was 0.55 percent; and from a survey of eight low- and middle-income countries, the median was 4.5 percent (Horton and Steckel, 2013).
- Achieved adult height also tracks economic development quite well (Figures 20.1, 20.2, and 20.3 from Horton and Steckel, 2013, which show that height tracks the economic "takeoff" for a range of countries).

Some Disadvantages

- Height deficits in children cannot be overcome in one generation: even with excellent nutrition and the best health environment, the mother's own achieved height can limit the height of her offspring, i.e., heights do not adjust instantaneously to improved environments. One can imagine that there is survival value in mothers not giving birth to children who are considerably larger than the mothers themselves were at birth.
- Height is a measure of long-term nutritional status, and it is helpful to interpret in conjunction with information on weight for height.
- Some children have normal height but are thin for their height (wasted) because of famine or near-famine conditions: wasting is more closely linked with immediate mortality outcomes than stunting.
- Likewise, children may have normal height but be obese.
- Height for age in adolescents can be somewhat difficult to interpret: the adolescent growth spurt typically occurs later in poorer countries; however, this is not an issue when setting an under-five stunting target.

Finally, although there is merit in recalibrating the WHO goal given the SDG goal (it seems a little unambitious for the SDG goal to simply lengthen

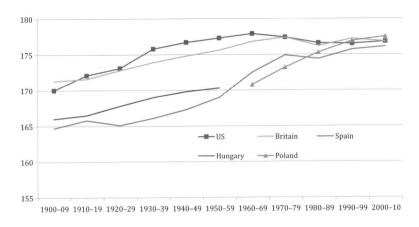

Figure 20.1 *Trends in adult male height (in cm), representative countries from North America and Northern, Southern, and Eastern Europe, 1900–2000*

Source: Horton, S. and R. H. Steckel. (2013). Malnutrition: global economic losses attributable to malnutrition 1900–2000 and projections to 2050. In B. Lomborg (ed.) *How Much Have Global Problems Cost the World?* Cambridge: Cambridge University Press.

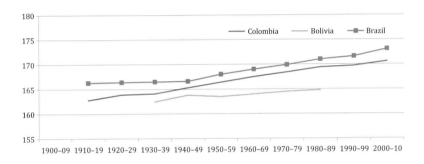

Figure 20.2 *Trends in adult male height (in cm), representative countries from South America, 1900–2000*

Source: Horton, S. and R. H. Steckel. (2013). Malnutrition: global economic losses attributable to malnutrition 1900–2000 and projections to 2050. In B. Lomborg (ed.) *How Much Have Global Problems Cost the World?* Cambridge: Cambridge University Press.

the time horizon from 2025 to 2030, without also increasing the target reduction), the WHO goal (a 40 percent drop in the number over 15 years) is very ambitious considering that the MDG goal was a 50 percent drop in the proportion over 25 years, and that between 1997 and 2012 only five countries (Nepal, Bangladesh, Lesotho, Vietnam, and Ethiopia) achieved annual reductions in stunting of 1.2 percentage points per year or more (Headey and Hoddinott, 2014). According to UNICEF (2014), there were 169 million stunted children in 2010, hence the 2025 goal would be to reduce this to 101 million.

An Economic Perspective on the Stunting Goal

A few studies have made estimates of the contribution of stunting to GDP, of which one (Hoddinott et al., 2013) calculates the benefit-cost ratio of nutrition interventions aimed at

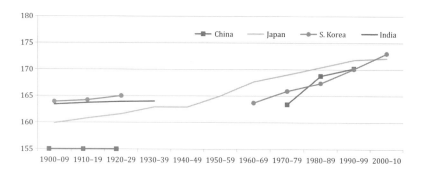

Figure 20.3 *Trends in adult male height (in cm), representative countries from Asia, 1900–2000*

Source: Horton, S. and R. H. Steckel. (2013). Malnutrition: global economic losses attributable to malnutrition 1900–2000 and projections to 2050. In B. Lomborg (ed.) *How Much Have Global Problems Cost the World?* Cambridge: Cambridge University Press.

reducing stunting. Hoddinott et al. (2013) point out the channels through which height can affect future income. There is a direct effect on wages (taller individuals may earn more, more so in low- and middle-income countries, where physical productivity matters in some manual occupations). There are also indirect effects through improved cognition and hence wages (individuals with higher cognitive scores earn more and via their increased schooling achievement also earn more). There are also potentially increased health costs associated with chronic disease in adulthood, for which undernutrition in childhood can be a risk factor.

Hoddinott et al. (2013) take advantage of longitudinal data on approximately 1450 individuals in Guatemala who were followed up in adulthood, two to three decades after they participated in a controlled trial of a nutrition supplement in childhood. A detailed resurvey of these individuals obtained data on their hourly earnings, hours worked, marital status, migration patterns, household consumption, and other variables. Those individuals who were not stunted at three years of age were found to have household consumption 66 percent higher in adulthood, using econometric methods to control for other confounding variables. This is taken as an estimate of the returns to better nutrition (avoiding stunting). (Hoddinott et al., 2013, apply 90 percent of 66 percent, i.e., a 59.4 percent increase, in their model, just to be a little conservative).

Hoddinott et al. (2013) compare these returns to the cost of improving nutrition, using costs from an evidence-based package of interventions (Bhutta et al., 2013). The intervention package is expected (using an epidemiological model) to reduce stunting by 20 percent. (The other 80 percent reduction requires changes to the underlying determinants of nutrition, for example, increased agricultural production, increased empowerment of women, investments in sanitation, etc., which tend to be more costly than direct nutrition interventions). Hoddinott et al. (2013) model the application of the package of direct nutrition interventions in 17 countries with a high burden of stunting (nine countries in Africa and the Middle East, five in South Asia, and three in East Asia, whose combined population in 2012 exceeded 2.5 billion).

The costs are calculated for a cohort of children born in 2015, who receive the interventions up until age two, who enter the labor market at age 21, and for whom the benefits are modeled until they reach age 36.[1] The dollar value of the benefits is based on current per capita income, projected growth rates of GNP, and the 59.4 percent benefit

---

[1] Beyond this point, future benefits start to be less significant due to discounting, and this also allows for early mortality of some of the population. We model the future benefits, and benefit cost ratios out to ages 50 and 60 in a sensitivity analysis presented in Table 20.2.

Table 20.1 Benefit-cost ratio per child for nutrition investment in 17 countries

Goal: 40% stunting reduction	3% discount rate			5% discount rate		
Country	PV Benefit	PV Cost	B:C ratio	PV Benefit	PV Cost	B:C ratio
Indonesia	8884	94.83	93.7	4522	94.83	47.7
Philippines	8152	94.83	86	4150	94.83	43.8
India	7358	97.11	75.8	3745	97.11	38.6
Vietnam	6583	94.83	69.4	3351	94.83	35.3
Pakistan	5519	97.11	56.8	2810	97.11	28.9
Yemen	5449	97.11	56.1	2774	97.11	28.6
Nigeria	4928	102.99	47.8	2508	102.99	24.4
Sudan	4632	102.5	45.2	2358	102.5	23
Bangladesh	**3408**	**97.11**	**35.1**	**1735**	**97.11**	**17.9**
Burma	3274	97.11	33.7	1667	97.11	17.2
Kenya	3070	102.5	30	1563	102.5	15.2
Tanzania	2945	102.5	28.7	1499	102.5	14.6
Uganda	2613	102.5	25.5	1330	102.5	13
Nepal	2461	97.11	25.3	1253	97.11	12.9
Ethiopia	2138	102.5	20.9	1088	102.5	10.6
Madagascar	1918	102.99	19.3	1012	102.99	9.8
DRC	713	102.5	7	359	102.5	3.5

Source: Hoddinott, J., H. Alderman, J. R. Behrman, L. Haddad, and S. Horton. The economic rationale for investing in stunting. *Maternal and Child Nutrition* 9(S2): 69–82, 2013.

from improved nutrition. Costs and benefits are discounted at 5 percent (and for sensitivity analysis also at 3 percent. In Figure 20.4, we show the future benefit for a country similar to Bangladesh (the country with the median benefit-cost ratio), comparing future labor market outcomes for a child who was not stunted, with those for a child who was. When these benefits are discounted back to 2010 (the year when the child was born), these give the values (PV Benefit) in Table 20.1, which can be compared to the costs of a nutrition intervention occurring in the child's first year of life, costing around $100/child in each of the 17 countries.

The benefit-cost ratios calculated range from 3.5:1 (Democratic Republic of the Congo) to 42.7 (Indonesia) when a 5 percent discount rate is used (Figure 20.5). The variations depend on the country's current level of income, projected growth rate, the current rate of stunting, and other parameters. Countries that are growing faster and/or have

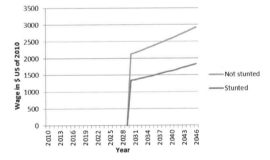

Figure 20.4 *Wage path for children born in 2010 who are not stunted, compared to those stunted*

Note: This example assumes growth of per capita GDP in real terms of 2 percent per annum over the 36 years considered, in a hypothetical country similar to Bangladesh.

higher incomes have higher benefit-cost ratios, because the absolute dollar value of the benefits (due to higher wages) are greater, while there is less variation in costs of the nutrition intervention.

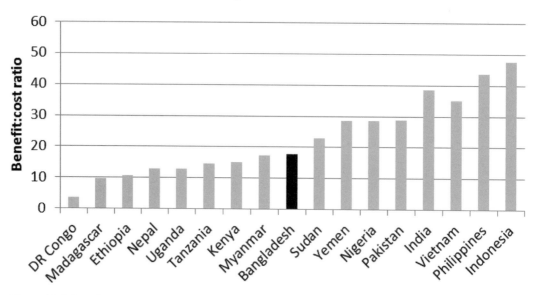

Figure 20.5 *Benefit-cost ratio for nutrition investments, 17 countries*

Source: Author, based on Hoddinott et al. (2013).

Table 20.1 summarizes the estimates for the 17 countries. The total cost will depend on the number of children in each country.

Since the publication of Hoddinott et al. (2013), there have been two updates of these calculations: one for a wider set of countries (International Food Policy Research Institute, 2014) and one specifically for African countries (Hoddinott, 2016). These calculations follow the same method described earlier but differ in terms of the period of time over which they are calculated, the baseline data on per capita income, and the percentage change in income attributable to the reduction in stunting. Although these alternative calculations change the reported benefit-cost ratios, these changes are marginal. The median benefit-cost ratio reported in International Food Policy Research Institute (2014) is 16 and for the 15 African countries reported in Hoddinott (2016), the benefit-cost ratio is 15.8. These newer calculations provide further evidence that the benefits of investing in actions to reduce stunting significantly outweigh the costs.

Would the Bhutta et al. (2013) investment package be sufficient to achieve a 40 percent (or greater) reduction in numbers stunted between 2010 and 2030? For Bangladesh, the median country in terms of benefit-cost ratio, the stunting rate in 1990 was 63.4 percent, which fell to 41.4 percent in 2010 (UNICEF, 2014), i.e., a 35 percent (22.0 percentage points) reduction in stunting. If the Bhutta et al. (2013) investment package caused a 20 percent reduction from 41.4 percent and the same trend reduction of 35 percent (from 1990 to 2010) continued for another 20 years, this should be enough to reduce the proportion of stunting by close to 50 percent between 2010 and 2030. Bangladesh had 6.334 million stunted children in 2010 (41.4 percent of 15.3 million children under 5). In 2025, the number of children under five is projected to be 14.2 million, and if the proportion stunted falls to 20.7 percent (half of 41.4 percent), then there would be 2.9 million stunted children in 2025, which achieves the WHO goal. This is, however, very much a preliminary estimate, which would require a more detailed analysis to substantiate.

Table 20.2 Benefit-cost ratio per child for nutrition investments in 17 countries for individuals working to age 50 or 60

	Benefits to age 50		Benefits to age 60	
	3%	5%	3%	5%
DRC	12.3	4.7	15.4	4.9
Madagascar	34.2	13.1	42.7	13.5
Ethiopia	37.0	14.1	46.2	14.6
Nepal	44.9	17.2	56.1	17.7
Uganda	45.2	17.3	56.4	17.8
Tanzania	51.0	19.5	63.6	20.1
Burma	59.8	22.8	74.6	23.5
Kenya	60.0	22.9	74.9	23.6
Bangladesh	62.2	23.8	77.7	24.5
Sudan	80.2	30.6	100.0	31.5
Nigeria	84.9	32.4	105.9	33.4
Yemen	99.5	38.0	124.2	39.2
Pakistan	100.8	38.5	125.8	39.7
Vietnam	123.1	47.0	153.7	48.5
India	134.4	51.3	167.7	52.9
Philippines	152.5	58.2	190.3	60.0
Indonesia	166.2	63.5	207.4	65.4

Can we generalize this informal estimate to other countries? Bangladesh is an unusual case, in that it has a trend rate of reduction in stunting (even without adding nutrition interventions) that is higher than the average for low- and lower-middle-income countries. Clearly the biggest concern regarding numbers of stunted children will be what happens in sub-Saharan African countries where the underlying trends are currently in the wrong direction as proportions of children stunted are decreasing slowly, but absolute numbers stunted are increasing because numbers of children under 5 are increasing.

Sensitivity Analysis: Modeling Benefits of Longer Time in Workforce

The results presented in Table 20.1 assume that individuals work only until the age of 36 or that the benefits of improved nutrition stop at age 36.

Under this conservative assumption the benefit-cost ratios are generally large and justify interventions to reduce stunting.

Table 20.2 summarizes the results when this assumption is relaxed. The methodology is the same as described earlier, except that the benefits, in terms of the increase in income, are assumed to continue until either age 50 or 60. If this is the case (and at this time, we do not have evidence that these benefits would continue), unsurprisingly the benefits and benefit-cost ratios are larger than in Table 20.1. For Bangladesh, the median country, the benefit-cost ratios, when benefits up to age 50 are included, are 23.8 and 62.2 for the 5 percent and 3 percent discount rates, respectively. For the optimistic scenario of working career to age 60, the corresponding benefit-cost ratios are 24.5 and 77.7. Note that we have not factored in premature mortality, so that the results to ages 50 and 60 are somewhat on the optimistic side.

Conclusions: A Stunting Goal?

Stunting is a better goal than underweight. It is an excellent measure of the health, diet, and care provided to children during the 1000 days from conception to age two. Although it is not quite as predictive of mortality as underweight, it is much more predictive of economic outcomes (cognitive scores, education, and wages). Stunting data need to be complemented with additional information provided about the extremes in weight for height, namely wasting in countries facing short-term crises, and overweight/obesity in all countries, even the low- and middle-income ones.

Economic models suggest that the returns to investments in nutrition have high benefit-cost ratios, and that this should be a top development priority. A very rough estimate suggests that reducing numbers stunted by 40 percent by 2030 globally would be a "stretch" goal – optimistic, but possibly achievable with strong effort. A higher target might prove problematic unless trends in sub-Saharan Africa change.

References

Barker, D. J. P. (1992). *The Fetal and Infant Origins of Adult Disease*. Chichester, West Sussex: BMJ Books, Wiley-Blackwell.

Bhutta, Z. A., J. K. Das, A. Rizvi, et al. (2013). Evidence based interventions for improving maternal and child nutrition: what can be done and at what cost? *Lancet* **382** (9890): 452–77.

Gao, W. and R. Smyth, (2010). Health human capital, height and wages in China: *Journal of Development Studies* **46**, 466–84.

Headey, D. and J. Hoddinott, (2014). Understanding the Rapid Reduction of Undernutrition in Nepal, 2001–2011. IFPRI Discussion paper 01384, Washington, DC: International Food Policy Research Institute.

Hoddinott, J. (2016). The economics of reducing malnutrition in sub-Saharan Africa. Working Paper. Global Panel on Agriculture and Food Systems for Nutrition.

Hoddinott, J., H. Alderman, J. R. Behrman, L. Haddad, and S. Horton. (2013). The economic rationale for investing in stunting. *Maternal and Child Nutrition* **9**(S2): 69–82.

Horton, S. and R. H. Steckel. (2013). Malnutrition: global economic losses attributable to malnutrition 1900–2000 and projections to 2050. In B. Lomborg (ed.) *How Much Have Global Problems Cost the World?* Cambridge: Cambridge University Press.

International Food Policy Research Institute. (2014). *Global Nutrition Report 2014: Actions and Accountability to Accelerate the World's Progress on Nutrition*. Washington, DC: Author.

Lutter, C. K., C. M. Chaparro, and S. Muñoz. (2011). Progress towards Millennium Development Goal 1 in Latin America and the Caribbean: the importance of the choice of indicator for undernutrition. *Bulletin of the World Health Organization* **89**:22–30.

Open Working Group (2014). Proposal of the Open Working Group for Sustainable Development Goals, July 19, 2014. Available at http://sustainabledevelopment.un.org/focussdgs.html (accessed October 5, 2014).

UNICEF. (2014). Child Nutrition interactive dashboard. Available at http://data.unicef.org/resources/2013/webapps/nutrition (accessed October 5, 2014).

World Health Organization (WHO) (2014). *Introduction: Global Nutrition Targets Policy Brief Series*. Geneva: WHO. Available at www.who.int/nutrition/topics/globaltargets_policybrief_overview.pdf (accessed October 6, 2014).

Benefits and Costs of the Population and Demography Targets for the Post-2015 Development Agenda

HANS-PETER KOHLER AND JERE R. BEHRMAN

Background

Prioritizing the Post-2015 UN Development Agenda on Population and Demography requires a recognition that national demographic trajectories are currently more diverse than in the middle and late twentieth century. Wealthy countries of Europe, Asia, and the Americas face rapid population aging, while Africa and some countries in Asia prepare for the largest cohort of young people the world has ever seen. And many of the world's poorest countries, particularly in sub-Saharan Africa, continue to face premature mortality, high fertility, and often unmet need for contraception.

The Report of the Global Thematic Consultation on Population Dynamics (UNFPA, UNDESA, UN-HABITAT, IOM, 2013; thereafter GTC-PD Report) highlights three central aspects of how population dynamics affect the post-2015 development agenda:

1. Population dynamics are at the center of the main development challenges of the twenty-first century and must therefore be addressed in the post-2015 development agenda.
2. Mega population trends – population growth, population aging, migration, and urbanization – present both important developmental challenges and opportunities that have direct and indirect implications for social, economic, and environmental development.
3. Demography is not destiny. Rights-based and gender-responsive policies can address and harness population dynamics.

The GTC-PD Report then groups the specific policy options in four thematic priority areas: high fertility and population growth, low fertility and

population aging, migration and human mobility, and urbanization. Closely related recommendations were adopted as part of the International Conference on Population and Development (ICPD) Beyond 2014 Global Report (UNFPA, 2014), which is the culmination of a landmark UN review of progress, gaps, challenges and emerging issues in relation to the ICPD Programme of Action. These two reports are important because they are likely to shape the international agenda on population.

The goal of this chapter is to discuss the post-2015 development agenda in the area of Population and Demography, focusing primarily on aspects of population size, age structure, and geographic distribution.[1,2] It is important also to highlight that "population quality," including human capital such as health and education, is an important further aspect of population dynamics that is essential for addressing the challenges of future population changes and for realizing the benefits of population dynamics for social, economic, and environmental development (Behrman and Kohler, 2014).

Thematic Priority 1: High Fertility and Population Growth

It is important to recognize that a significant part of twenty-first-century population growth will result

---

[1] For a related discussion of future policy priorities in the area of population quantity, quality, and mobility, see Behrman and Kohler (2014).

[2] The other priority areas emphasized in the GTC-PD Report are economic development and income security, population data and projections, and development cooperation and partnerships.

from ongoing expansions of life expectancy and from the unfolding of population momentum. In the former case, future population growth is therefore the "by-product" of important successes in improving individual and population health as part of past development strategies, and in the latter case, future population growth is an ongoing implication of past high fertility that has resulted in a "youth bulge" and large number of young adults who will enter or are still in primary reproductive ages. In both of these cases, development strategies will have to focus on accommodating population growth, including through migration, urbanization, and investments in human capital/health and on reaping potential benefits from changing age structures and expanding life expectancies ("demographic dividends").

Nevertheless, a significant part of twenty-first-century population growth will be in countries that continue to have relatively high levels of fertility while having experienced significant declines in child and adult mortality. For example, a report prepared for the 2012 World Economic Forum (Global Agenda Council on Population Growth, 2012), identified 58 high-fertility countries, defined as countries with net reproduction rates (NRRs) of more than 1.5, that have intrinsic population growth rates of 1.4 percent or higher.[3]

These are concentrated in Africa, where 39 out of the 55 countries have high fertility, but also exist in Asia (9 countries), Oceania (6 countries), and Latin America (4 countries). Almost two-thirds of these high-fertility countries are classified by the United Nations as least developed, and 38 out of the total of 48 countries that are classified as least developed have high fertility. Despite having currently only about 18 percent of the world population, high-fertility countries account today for about 38 percent of the 78 million persons that are added annually to the world population. After 2060, world population is projected to grow exclusively as a result of population growth in the current high-fertility countries. During the twenty-first century, therefore, the current high-fertility countries will be the major contributors to continued world population growth.

UN Global Consultation Priorities

The GTC-PD Report states the following priorities in the area of high fertility and population growth:

1. Accelerate implementation of universal access to quality, accessible, affordable, and comprehensive sexual and reproductive information, education, services, and supplies across the life cycle.
2. Eliminate all forms of gender-based violence against women and girls.
3. Eliminate early and forced marriage.

Priorities/Targets with High Benefit-Cost Ratios

We propose for the post-2015 development agenda a continuation of the current Millennium Development Goal 5 (MDG 5), "Improve Maternal Health," including the SRH-related priority/target of:

- Post-2015 Development Priority 1a: Achieving universal access to sexual and reproductive health (SRH) information, education, and services by 2030.

The benefit-cost ratios of expanding access to SHR programs are likely to be large (Table 21.1). In addition we propose a stronger focus on unmet need for modern contraception. Unmet need was included in MDG 5 as an indicator, but recent evidence suggests that it should be elevated to an explicit target. For example, during 2003–12, the number of women wanting to avoid pregnancy increased substantially, from 716 million (54 percent) of 1,321 million in 2003, to 827 million (57 percent) of 1,448 million in 2008, to 867 million (57 percent) of 1,520 million in 2012 (Darroch and Singh, 2013). Due to increases in the use of

---

[3] A net reproduction rates (NRR) of more than 1.5 means that more than 1.5 daughters are born to women given 2010 fertility and mortality levels. This implies that the next generation is 50 percent larger than the current generation, and at constant fertility and mortality levels, a NRR of 1.5 implies a long-term annual population growth rate of about 1.4 percent. The intrinsic growth rate is the population growth rate that would prevail in the long term if current patterns of fertility and mortality were to prevail in a population and the population is closed to migration.

Table 21.1 Summary of costs, benefits, and benefit-cost ratios for voluntary family planning programs

Annual net benefits and costs (3% discount rate)		Annual benefits	Annual costs of satisfying unmet need in developing countries	BCR
Benefit component:	Assumptions	Billion USD	Billion USD	
Reduced infant and maternal mortality	Low (DALY = 1K)	110	3.6	30
	High (DALY = 5K)	180		50
Income growth (including life cycle, distributional, and intergenerational benefits)	Low	216	3.6	60
	High	360		100
Total, family planning programs (sum)	*Low*	*326*	*3.6*	*90*
	High	*470*		*150*

See Appendix of the online version of this chapter (Kohler and Behrman 2014) and Kohler (2013) for details of these benefit-cost calculations.

modern contraception, the overall proportion of women with unmet need decreased from 29 percent (210 million) in 2003, to 26 percent (222 million) in 2012. However, the absolute number increased, and unmet need continued still to be very high in 2012 (Figure 21.1), especially in sub-Saharan Africa (53 million [60 percent] of 89 million), south Asia (83 million [34 percent] of 246 million), and western Asia (14 million [50 percent] of 27 million) (Darroch and Singh, 2013).

Because of this importance, we propose to elevate unmet need to an explicit priority, for instance along the following lines:

- Post-2015 Development Priority 1b: Eliminate unmet need for modern contraception by 2040

The implementation of these priorities is likely to have particularly high returns among vulnerable populations, including adolescents and poor individuals, who are often most affected by limited access to SHR information and services, and youth, who present a large and growing faction of the population in many low- and middle-income countries.

These priorities are supported by evidence that (a) reduced fertility in high-fertility contexts results in improved child outcomes and more rapid economic development, and (b) voluntary family planning programs can make important contributions toward reducing fertility (for a review, see Kohler, 2013).

Ongoing information deficits about contraceptive technologies and the benefits of reduced fertility, low status and limited autonomy of women, and inadequate health systems in many high-fertility contexts imply "market failures" and "policy failures" resulting in insufficient market provision and governmental subsidization of many family planning programs. Policies that improve access to voluntary family planning programs and related SRH information, education and services therefore have large benefit-cost ratios (Table 21.1) and should be high priorities in the post-2015 development agenda, especially when combined with programs that promote investments in health and other human capital in early childhood. A detailed discussion of the benefit-cost ratios for the expansion of family planning programs is provided in the Appendix of the online version of this chapter (Kohler and Behrman, 2014) and in Kohler (2013).

This importance of SHR information, education and services is consistent with ICPD's emphasis that sexual and reproductive health and rights (SRHR) constitute a basic human right and are a prerequisite for sustainable development (UNFPA, 2014; United Nations, 1996). And while our benefit-cost analyses necessarily take a somewhat narrow focus on population growth, we agree with this broader importance of SRHR.

However, fertility decline during the demographic transition is not only due to family planning programs and related SRH services. Economic development, urbanization, increased education, and labor force participation (particularly for women) have been important drivers in the past and are likely to remain important drivers of fertility trends in the future.

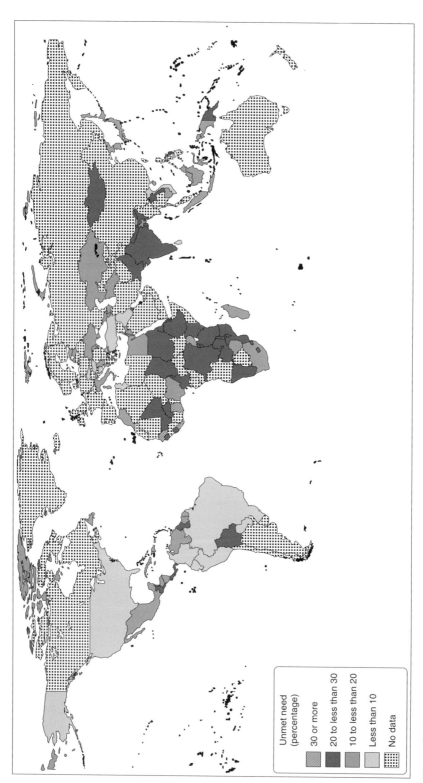

Figure 21.1 *Percentage of women with an unmet need for family planning (any method) among those ages 15–49 who are married or in a union: Most recent data available*

Source: Population Division of the Department of Economic and Social Affairs of the United Nations Secretariat (2013). World Contraceptive Patterns 2013. New York: United Nations.

Unmet need
(percentage)

30 or more
20 to less than 30
10 to less than 20
Less than 10
No data

Because the benefits of reduced fertility are critically related to the ability of populations to benefit from reduced population growth and the resulting age-structure changes during the demographic transitions, policies targeting the priority area of high fertility and population growth need to be implemented as part of a range of social policies that support sustainable development. For example, in low- and middle-income countries that have experienced the onset of significant fertility declines and are currently or will soon experience large increases in the working-age share of their population, institutions and policies should therefore be adopted to permit exploitation of the "demographic dividend" (Bloom et al., 2002) through higher economic growth.

Investment in human capital across the life-course, including increasing access to, enrollment in, and quality of formal schooling, is an essential component of population-related development strategies (Section 6). Other authors cover goals that cover such areas.

Indicators

We propose a continuation of the following existing MDG 5 indicators as part of the post-2015 development agenda. We also suggest including a differentiation of these indicators by age, gender (where applicable), rural/urban, and major race/ethnic group to draw attention to within-country differentials in the attainment of important development priorities.

- Maternal mortality ratio (MDG 5a)
- Proportion of births attended by skilled health personnel (MDG 5a)
- Access to SRH services (MDG 5b)
- Contraceptive prevalence rate (MDG 5b)
- Adolescent birth rate (MDG 5b)
- Antenatal care coverage (MDG 5b; four visits)
- Unmet need for family planning (MDG 5b)

Discussion

Current UN projections suggest that the global population will grow 32 percent to reach 9.5 billion by 2050. The response needs to be twofold.

On the one hand, a significant part of the growth will come from population momentum (with relatively large number of individuals at reproductive ages) and expected further increases in longevity. This population growth thus results from past "successes," and policy responses will need to focus on (1) accommodating additional population growth through urbanization, migration, and increases in population density; (2) increasing investments in health and human capital; and (3) institutional reforms that will facilitate the realization of potential demographic dividends.

On the other hand, poor reproductive health outcomes and relatively rapid population growth remain an important concern in a number of low-income countries. International and national spending devoted to family planning, however, has declined significantly in recent years. Recent research has revised our understanding of the interactions between population growth and economic development, as well as the effects of voluntary family planning programs in terms of reduced fertility, improved reproductive health outcomes, and other life cycle and intergenerational consequences. We argue that an ongoing investment in and expansion of SRH information, education, and services should be a high-priority component of development policies in the next decades, with benefit-cost ratios likely to be high. It is important that these policies are implemented in a human rights–based framework.

The GTC-PD Report also highlights the elimination of gender-based violence, although the overall effect of these policies on population dynamics is probably relatively small. The report also highlights the elimination of early and forced marriage as important policies for addressing population dynamics, and we believe that policies aimed at the expansion of schooling for girls can achieve this aim cost-effectively.

Thematic Priority 2: Low Fertility and Population Aging

Populations are aging in high-income and increasingly also in middle-income and even low-income countries. As a result of continued progress in reducing mortality (including at old and oldest ages) and decades of low – sometimes very low – fertility, many high-income countries face very rapid population aging in the next decades. Old-age dependency ratios are therefore going to increase significantly in most high-income countries, and it is becoming a policy challenge in many middle-income countries (Beard et al., 2012).

Population aging implies that the median age of the population increases, as does the fraction of the population above, say, age 65.[4] Population aging in high-income countries occurs in societies with well-developed social institutions, including extensive intergenerational transfer schemes, the sustainability of which is importantly affected by changes in the population age structure. Population aging potentially also affects productivity, innovation, and social, economic, and psychological well-being.

UN Global Consultation Priorities

The GTC-PD Report states the following priorities in the area of low fertility and population aging:

1. Eliminate discrimination based on age in order to ensure that people of all ages are able to contribute to society.
2. Provide increased coverage and adequate levels of social protection, including pensions and health care.
3. Develop appropriate technologies and infrastructure to accommodate the needs of older persons and persons with disabilities.
4. Provide special support measures for older women. Promote policies that make it easier for people in caregiving roles to combine and share work and domestic responsibilities.

Priorities with High Benefit-Cost Ratios

To consider policy options and targets, it is important first to recognize that population aging is a consequence of past "successes" in social, economic, and human development. In terms of population dynamics alone, increases in fertility rates in low-fertility countries are the primary demographic

mechanisms that can affect rates of population aging. The effect of increases in fertility is, however, long term, and few empirically supported policy options exist for doing so (Dahl et al., 2013; Kohler et al., 2006; Luci-Greulich and Thévenon, 2013; Salles et al., 2010). Current evidence suggests that policies and institutional reforms that increase gender equality and the compatibility of child-rearing with labor force participation are most promising in terms stabilizing and/or moderately increasing fertility levels in high-income countries with very low total fertility rate (TFR) levels (Luci-Greulich and Thévenon, 2013; Myrskylä et al., 2009), but even in the presence of such policies, below-replacement fertility is likely to persist in many high-income and middle-income countries.

Migration is an important adjustment mechanism through which the effects of population aging on the size and quality of the labor force can be managed. However, migration is generally not able to stop or even reverse the general trend toward increasing population aging in middle- and high-income countries during the twenty-first century (UN Population Division, 2000).

The most promising policy options in the area of low fertility and population aging should be focused on accommodating aging populations in social, economic, and environmental development and creating institutional environments where possible negative consequences of population aging are lessened.

In this context, a large body of research has emphasized the benefits of the elimination of incentives for early retirement (e.g., National Research Council, 2012; Wise, 2010). A key policy priority for addressing the fiscal and economic consequences of population aging with a potentially very high benefit-cost ratio therefore is as follows:

- Post-2015 Development Priority 2: Public pension systems should eliminate incentives for retiring at specific ages and be designed to be

---

[4] However, it is important to note that the average remaining life expectancy can increase in aging populations, and old-age dependency ratios that are adjusted for gains in life expectancy increase considerably less than old-age dependency measures calculated based on fixed ages (conventionally age 65; Sanderson and Scherbov, 2008).

actuarially neutral (possibly taking individual characteristics that are fixed long before retirement age) into account.[5] To address the inherent inequality resulting in pensions systems from differential life expectancies, pension systems should also be based on expected years of remaining life.

Although the benefit-cost ratios for pension reforms along the preceding line are likely to be high, specific calculations are beyond the scope of this chapter. The benefits, although probably substantial (National Research Council, 2012; Wise, 2010), depend critically on the specifics of national pension systems and the details of the proposed pension reform within a national context. The assessment of benefits is further complicated, as issues related to health care and health insurance reform are often closely tied to reforms of pension systems. Although benefits are difficult to evaluate, the estimation of costs of pension reforms is even more complex. Specifically, the primary costs are those of an institutional reform and associated legal changes, both of which are very difficult to assess in general (e.g., see Clements et al., 2013).

Despite this limited evidence, we believe that these costs are relatively small compared to the benefits resulting from the elimination of incentives for early retirement.

Other reviews of the macroeconomic implications of population aging, including the fiscal implications on pension and related intergenerational transfer systems, have come to similar conclusions that the benefits of pension and related reforms are high, while a specific quantification of benefits and costs is challenging. For instance, a U.S. National Research Committee assessing the macroeconomic consequences of population aging recently concluded (National Research Council, 2012): "While population aging is likely to result in a larger fraction of national output being spent on consumption by older persons, this does not pose an insurmountable challenge provided that sensible policies are implemented with enough lead time to allow companies and households to respond."

In addition to the preceding priority of pension reform, other promising policy priorities in this area include the following:

1. Social safety nets and health and pension systems should be untied from formal labor market participation, to reduce distortions and benefit the poorer members of society, who tend to work in informal employment or home production that is not covered by formal-sector benefits.

2. Renewed efforts to assess formal and informal means of making education over the life cycle more effective through transparent and open institutions (rather than institutions captured by groups of employers or employees) may yield high rates of return.

3. Promote investments in adult health and human capital, especially in contexts where "healthy aging" can facilitate higher labor force participation and productivity at older ages (see also Jamison et al., 2014; WHO, 2013).

4. Institutions and legal restrictions should be adapted to accommodate child-rearing that occurs outside of two-parent households, when parents are older and more educated, and when parents are often jointly active in the labor market.

5. Promote more effective market provision of care of elderly, disabled, and vulnerable populations, and improve access to insurance markets enabling individuals to insure against caretaking responsibilities and caretaking needs.

There are also several policy options that would have fairly low benefit-cost ratios. For example,

---

[5] Actuarial neutrality is a marginal concept, relating to the effect of working an additional year. It implies that the present value of accrued pension benefits for working an additional year is the same as in the year before (meaning that benefits increase only by the additional entitlement earned in that year). Conversely, retiring a year earlier should reduce the pension benefit both by the entitlement that would have been earned during the year and by an amount to reflect the longer duration for which the pension must be paid. In contrast, actuarial fairness of a pension system requires that the present value of lifetime contributions equals the present value of lifetime benefits (Queisser and Whitehouse, 2006). Actuarial fairness thus relates to the entire lifetime of contributions and benefits. A pension system can be actuarially fair but not neutral, and vice versa. For a detailed discussion of actuarial neutrality and fairness see Queisser and Whitehouse (2006).

the benefit-cost ratios for policies to increase fertility through generous parental leave, child benefit, and related social programs in low-fertility settings are likely to be fairly low. For example, in a recent review of the expansion of Norwegian maternal leave, the authors concluded, "Taken together, our findings suggest the generous extensions to paid leave were costly, had no measurable effect on outcomes [such as children's school outcomes, parental earnings and participation in the labor market] and regressive redistribution properties" (Dahl et al., 2013).

In contrast to the weak evidence for the expansion of maternal leave policies, there is some recent evidence that the expansion of day-care facilities has contributed to increases in fertility (or, at least, a slowing down of fertility decline; Bauernschuster et al., 2014; Luci-Greulich and Thévenon, 2013; Rindfuss et al., 2004). Increasing access to early child care is therefore a potentially promising option for policy makers concerned about very low levels of fertility in high-income countries. However, policies are often not integrated and can have conflicting outcomes. The lack of well-documented benefits of many policies that aim at increasing fertility in high-income, low-fertility countries leads us to conclude that the benefit-cost ratios of such policies are low and most likely below one. Possible exceptions are the expansion of early childhood education and high-quality day care, where several studies have indicated sizable benefit-cost ratios in high-income countries. Heckman et al. (2010), for example, estimate a benefit-cost ratio of 7–12 for the HighScope Perry Preschool Program using a 3 percent discount rate. Benefit-cost ratios may even be higher in low-income countries, for which Psacharopoulos (2014) estimate benefit-cost ratios of up to 37.

Indicators and Targets

Possible measurable targets to evaluate the preceding priorities in the area of low fertility and population aging include the following:

- To make pension systems more actuarially neutral, eliminate age-based eligibility criteria for retirement (indicators could include the implicit

Social Security tax[6] developed by the international Social Security Project; Wise, 2010).
- Reduce inequalities in pension benefits by basing retirement benefits on expected years of remaining life given fixed characteristics.
- In low- and middle-income countries, whose population will have rapidly growing numbers of persons at older ages, develop or expand health and pension systems that are untied from formal labor market participation.
- Improve cognitive abilities among adults ages 50–60 by 25 percent by 2050 (using some standardized testing).
- Reduce activities of daily living (ADL)-disabilities among adults ages 50–60 and 60–70 by 25 percent by 2050.
- Expand availability of private and/or public day care for children at 2 to 5 years of age to 90 percent, including the provision of subsidized day care for children in poor households.

[6] The implicit Social Security tax reflects the fact that the wage compensation for working an additional year consists of two components: the first is wage earnings, and the second is the "increase" in the expected present discounted value of promised future Social Security benefits. If the difference between these two components is positive, then the benefits of a person who works for an additional year, and thus forgoes one year of benefits, would be increased to offset the fact that they are received for one fewer years. This is true, for example, for the typical worker in the United States: if a worker forgoes claiming benefits at the earliest possible age (62) and works another year, benefits in subsequent years are increased by 6.67 percent to account for the fact that benefits will be received for one fewer year. In many other countries, however, the accrual is significantly negative. This is largely a consequence of not increasing benefits enough if the age of benefit receipt is delayed. In this case, benefits are not actuarially neutral, and the gain in wage earnings is partially, or even mostly, offset by a loss in future Social Security benefits. The ratio of this loss to wage earnings (after tax) is called the Social Security implicit tax on earnings. In many countries, this tax can be 80 percent or more at certain ages. To provide a simple summary of the country-specific incentives for early retirement, Wise (2010) sums the implicit tax rates on continued work beginning at age 55 or at an early retirement age – when a person is first eligible for Social Security benefits – and running through age 69. This measure, which Wise (2010) calls the "tax force to retire" or "implicit Social Security tax" varies from 1.6 in the United States to 9.2 in Italy.

Discussion

From the narrow perspective on population dynamics that this chapter addresses, there do not seem to be policies and/or interventions with high benefit-cost ratios that can significantly affect or reverse these broad trends toward persistent low fertility and increasingly older populations. Indeed, these consequences of the unfolding demographic transition should importantly frame – rather than be the target of – future development policies. These patterns have already been a long-standing reality in many high-income countries, and several middle-income countries, including countries in Latin America and South Asia, will experience the most significant and rapid population aging in the next half-century.

The policy challenge in the next decades will be adjust to this reality of low fertility and longer lives and develop social, economic, and policy contexts that are sustainable with these demographic trends. In this context, we have outlined some of the more promising policy options earlier.

We disagree with some of the implications of the policy aim (2) in the GTC-PD Report that states: "Provide increased coverage and adequate levels of social protection, including pensions and health care." Specifically, pension systems provide incentives for individuals to retire relatively early, even if they are healthy with fairly long life expectancies (Wise, 2010). This early retirement contributes to rapidly increasing dependency burdens and potentially unsustainable pensions and transfer systems. There is also some evidence that relatively early retirement results in reduced well-being through declines in cognitive abilities, higher levels of depression, and sometimes worse overall health (Rohwedder and Willis, 2010; Sahlgren, 2013). Hence, an important development target in aging societies with extensive social transfer systems in the next decades will be to reduce incentives for early retirement, which may mean that at "young old ages" the eligibility for public pensions is made more restrictive, and incentives for individuals to remain in the labor force are strengthened.

Thematic Priority 3: Migration and Human Mobility

As a result of the differential timing of the demographic transition, population growth will continue to differ significantly between regions and types of economies. These differences primarily reflect differences in fertility and mortality rates, but they are also affected some by international migration. In 2010, the global stock of migrants (defined as people living in a country other than the one in which they were born) is estimated to have been 214 million. Although this number is large – 3.4 times the population of France – it represents just 3.1 percent of the world population. Of course, migrants are not distributed equally across types of countries or regions (Figure 21.2a), with almost 60 percent of the total living in developed countries. Focusing on flow rather than stock data, recent estimates suggest that the largest population movements occur between South and West Asia, from Latin to North America, and within Africa (Abel and Sander, 2014), and that significant migration flows occur both within and across regions defined by economic development (Figure 21.2b).

And if the relatively high economic growth rates of developing countries on average in recent decades compared to the developed countries continues, both push and pull factors would seem to lead to an increasing share of international migrants in developing countries.

The age distribution of migrants tends to be different from that of their destination populations. Globally, people born in other countries tend to represent relatively large shares of the prime working-age population (people 20 to 64 years old) and people 65 and over (Table 21.2). But there are striking differences between more- and less-developed regions, in both the shares of foreign-born inhabitants and their age patterns. In more-developed regions, migrants represent 12.8 percent of the 20–64 segment of the population (19 percent in Northern America and 21 percent in Oceania), 4.8 percent of the population under the age of 20, and 8.5 percent of the population 65 and older. In less-developed regions, the largest percentage of

Table 21.2 International migrant stock as percentage of total population, by age range, 2010

Region	International migrant stock as a percentage of the total population by age		
	0–19	20–64	65+
World	1.3	4.0	4.7
More developed regions	4.8	12.8	8.5
Less developed regions	0.9	1.8	2.4
Africa	1.0	2.8	2.3
Asia	0.9	1.7	2.3
Europe	4.9	11.5	8.1
Latin America and the Caribbean	0.8	1.5	2.3
Northern America	5.2	18.6	12.8
Oceania	5.9	20.8	27.5

Source: UN Population Division (2010).

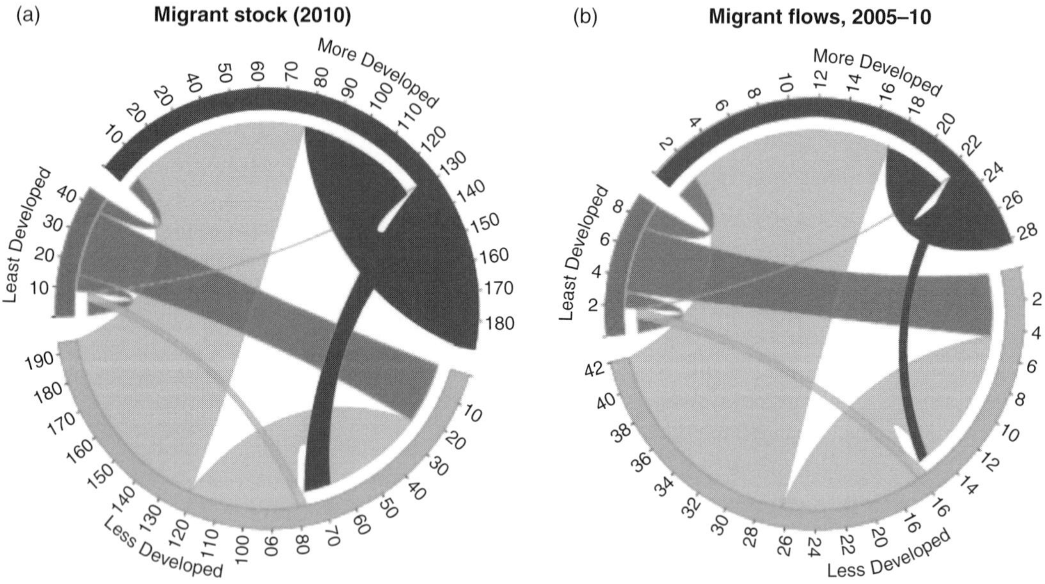

Figure 21.2 *Migration stock and flow across regions defined by economic development, late 2000s*

Notes: The direction of the flow is encoded by both the origin country's color and a gap between the flow and the destination country's segment. The volume of the movement is indicated by the width of the flow. Tick marks on the circle segments show the number of migrants.

Source: Abel and Sander (2014), Quantifying global international migration flows. Science 343(6178): 1520–1522. doi:10.1126/science.1248676. Reprinted with permission from AAAS.

migrants is in the 65 and over group (2.4 percent); migrants represent just 0.9 percent of people under the age of 20 and 1.8 percent of people 20 to 64 years old. Absolute numbers still amount to over 40 percent of total migrants, however.

UN Global Consultation Priorities

The GTC-PD Report states the following priorities in the area of migration and human mobility:

1. Eliminate policies that create barriers for migrants to access their human rights, in particular in the case of migrant children and families.
2. Respect equal treatment with regard to employment, wages, working conditions, and social protection and other social benefits, including health care; and implement measures to regulate the work of recruitment agencies to ensure the protection of migrant workers, especially domestic workers, and to lower costs of migration.
3. Reinforce and establish bilateral, regional, and global partnerships on migration to address vulnerability of migrants and to promote the realization of the full development potential of migration.
4. Promote the preservation and portability of Social Security entitlements, recognition of educational qualifications, and development of skills to better match labor supply and demand within and between countries through comprehensive bilateral, regional, and multilateral mechanisms.
5. Ensure that migration is mainstreamed in national and sectoral development policies, in regional and global development agendas and development agencies through the strengthening of policy and institutional coherence at all levels of multistakeholder engagement.
6. Engage within existing international frameworks for instance UNFCCC[7] and its National Adaptation Plans of Action, and within a post-Hyogo framework,[8] to address climate change–related movements as well as factoring migration into efforts in relation to disaster risk reduction.

Priorities with High Benefit-Cost Ratios

If workers are much more productive in one country than in another, restrictions on immigration lead to large efficiency losses. For example, Kennan (2012) quantifies these losses, using a model in which efficiency differences are labor-augmenting, and free trade in product markets leads to factor price equalization so that wages measured in efficiency units of labor are equalized across countries. He estimates that the gains from removing immigration restrictions within a simple static model of migration costs are about as large as the gains from a growth miracle that more than doubles income levels in developing countries.

Mukand (2012) examines the effect of movement by half of the developing world's workforce to developing countries if migration closes a quarter of the migrants' productivity gap. He estimates that migrants' average income would rise by $7,000, increasing global output by 30 percent. Pritchett (2007) estimates that even a modest easing of restrictions could produce high returns: a 3 percent increase in the labor force in developed countries through migration would yield annual benefits larger than those from eliminating remaining trade barriers. A survey of the literature on the impact of immigration on domestic wages finds that few studies report a negative impact (Blau and Kahn, 2012). D'Amuri and Peri (2014) find that immigration encourages nonmigrants in Western Europe to take on more complex work. Recent work has also reduced concerns about a potential "brain drain" from developing countries, in part because emigration increases the returns to human capital investments and thus induces increased investments. In addition, recent research on the relationship between migration and development has also emphasized the positive – and often very significant – contributions of remittances on migrant-sending countries (Kapur and McHale, 2012).

---

[7] United Nations Framework Convention on Climate Change.
[8] The post-Hyogo framework is the current UN Post-2015 Framework for Disaster Risk Reduction.

From a global perspective, liberalizing international migration in the developed countries would produce considerable output gains benefiting poorer people in developing countries. Thus, migration liberalization is likely to be a major "win–win" option on the global agenda. Of course, some people will lose out from competition with migrants' labor, and adjustment costs will be incurred. We therefore propose the following policy priority that is likely to have a high – although difficult to quantify – benefit-cost ratio:

- Post-2015 Development Priority 3: Reduce barriers to migration within low- and middle-income countries as well as between low- and middle-income countries and high-income countries.

Anderson and Winters (2009) use a computable general equilibrium model and estimate benefit-cost ratios of reducing barriers to migration of 112–336 globally (using a 3 percent discount rate; the benefit-cost ratios are 45–137 with a 6 percent discount rate) and 229–838 for developing countries (using a 3 percent discount rate; the benefit-cost ratios are 100–299 with a 6 percent discount rate). Nevertheless, these benefit-cost considerations do not include the costs of achieving migration reform and a reduction in the barriers to migration. Anderson and Winters (2009) thus conclude that reducing migration barriers is clearly an extremely high payoff activity, "if only the political will to bring about a successful conclusion to the Doha round can be found." But the Doha negotiations have stalled, and migration reform in the United States continues to be postponed, suggesting that the costs of achieving this political will might be substantial (or are at least perceived to be substantial).[9]

Consistent with the with this and other studies, we conclude that the benefits of reducing barriers to migration within low- and middle-income countries as well as between low- and middle-income countries and high-income countries are likely to be substantial. Benefits are likely to be incurred by migrants and nonmigrants and in both receiving and sending countries. But the history of migration reform also suggests that the process of achieving this aim is challenging.

In addition, the following policy priorities are closely related to reducing barriers to migration, and we consider them as important targets for the post-2015 development agenda:

1. Receiving countries should develop migration policies that are better informed by their demographic, economic, and social needs.
2. Criteria for any restrictions on migration should be rationalized. They should be based on well-defined efficiency and distributional criteria, not family connections.
3. Frameworks should be created that allow for more transitory migration between countries and improved monitoring of transitory movements across countries and regions that affect the transmission of infectious diseases.

Indicators and Targets

Possible measurable targets for liberalizing international migration include the following:

1. Countries should agree to increase their annual immigration caps by double their annual per capita income growth in the previous quinquennium.
2. Special treatment of potential immigrants based on family connections should be phased out by reducing the share of immigrants in the total due to family connections by 10 percent per year.

The first of these would lead to focus of immigration into countries that have growing labor demands and capacity for absorbing immigrants and adjusting employment for existing citizens of such countries. The second would phase out immigration based on family connections, but in absolute numbers more slowly in countries with more rapidly growing absorption capacities if the first target is adopted as well.

---

[9] In addition to the large uncertainties regarding the costs of migration reform, commentaries written as part of the Copenhagen Consensus Project on the benefit-cost assessments for reducing the barriers to migration also highlight that the empirical estimates of the gains of migration might be overestimated in these analyses; see, for instance, Rosenzweig (2004) and Deardorff (2009).

Discussion

The studies summarized earlier estimate that the benefits from liberalization of international migration are likely to be considerable. Good estimates of the resource costs from doing so are not available, but they are likely to be much smaller than the estimated gains, so the benefit-cost ratios are likely to be high. We support the priorities of the GTC-PD Report given earlier. But what seems of primary importance to obtain these potential substantial global gains is widespread recognition that increased international migration is likely to have gains that, if undertaken at a moderate pace to allow internal adjustments, will be shared by citizens of both recipient and origin countries.

Thematic Priority 4: Urbanization

The global population will continue to urbanize rapidly during the next decades, particularly in low- and middle-income countries (UN Population Division, 2012). Recent changes have been dramatic. In 1950, there were more than two rural residents for every urban resident. By 2010, there were slightly more urban than rural residents. By 2050, there are projected to be more than twice as many urban as rural residents, and by 2100, there will be more than five times as many.

There are considerable differences in urbanization across major regions. In 1950, Europe had the most urban inhabitants, somewhat more than Asia, and Africa had a very small urban population, with only Oceania among the regions included having a smaller urban population. By 2010, the Asian urban population had expanded to almost four times the European level, and the African urban population had expanded beyond the North American level. But the *percentage* of the population that was urban was relatively low for Africa (39 percent) and Asia (44 percent), in comparison with Oceania (71 percent), Europe (73 percent), and particularly Latin America and the Caribbean (79 percent) and North America (82 percent). Projections for 2010–2100 are for the urban populations

of Asia and Africa, to account for more than 80 percent of the world's city-dwellers by the end of the twenty-first century. Rural populations are projected to decline in all regions except Africa, where numbers living in the countryside are projected to increase by 59 percent.

Megacities (cities with more than 10 million people) have been growing very quickly. In 1970, the world had just two megacities (Tokyo and New York), with a combined population of 40 million. By 2011, the number of megacities had increased to 23 (13 in Asia, 4 in Latin America, and 2 each in Africa, Europe, and North America), with a total population of 359 million. By 2025, the number of megacities is projected to increase to 37, with a total population of 630 million. Most of these megacities are projected to be in Asia (22), with a few of the larger ones in the Americas (6 in Latin America, 3 in North America) and some of the smaller ones in Europe and Africa. The populations of many of these megacities are projected to be on the order of magnitude of the populations of many countries.

UN Global Consultation Priorities

The GTC-PD Report states the following priorities in the area of urbanization.

1. Develop national development policies and plans backed up by reliable and evidence-based data that foster balanced urban, rural, and regional development and guide population and economic growth in ways that protect natural environments, are socially inclusive, and are economically productive.
2. Enable and support city governments to prepare, implement, and monitor participatory city development plans that promote sustainable cities and resilient populations by accommodating a growing number of urban residents, including the poor, and ensure affordable access to land, housing, water, sanitation, energy, ICT, and transport as well as health, education, and other essential services.
3. Minimize the environmental impact of cities by creating incentives to manage urban sprawl without hastening rural agricultural land

conversion, avoiding encroachment of settlements in environmentally vulnerable areas, and promoting planning for dense cities with higher energy efficiency.

4. Establish national incentives programs that embrace technological innovation and creativity of urban populations, especially in the green economy, and which empower growing urban populations with economic opportunity, including through business development. Enhance the economic, social, and cultural amenities of smaller and medium-sized cities to create incentives for people to move/migrate to them.

5. Improve the quality of life of half of their country's slum dwellers by 2030, including assurance of secure land tenure, durable housing, basic sanitation, potable water, better health services, and adequate living space.

Discussion

Meaningful global benefit-cost ratios for changes to promote better urbanization are difficult to estimate because of the quite varying conditions among countries for what are basically national and subnational policies and regulations. Likewise establishing meaningful global targets is very challenging and not likely to be feasible. Selected interventions are likely to have high benefit-cost ratios, depending on particular contexts. These have the potential to make urbanization more efficient and more equitable by achieving balance between functions for which there are considerable economies of scale such as transportation and communication network and functions for which decentralization is likely to lead to the best responses to heterogeneous local conditions and preferences.

Population Quality: A Key Aspect of the Development Agenda on Population and Demography in the Twenty-First Century

Population quality – including health, education, and other forms of human capital – is an important

dimension of the development agenda (Behrman and Kohler, 2014). The GTC-PD Report does emphasize dimensions of population quality, and important aspects are captured by authors of other chapters. And although this chapter tries to evaluate policy options and targets related to population quantity, our discussion would be incomplete if we did not highlight the importance of population quality and some promising policies in this area.

Education and Schooling

Education should be broadly defined to include all acquisition of knowledge rather than limited to formal schooling. The highest social rates of return to investments in human capital are probably not from increased formal schooling. In most societies, subsidies for formal schooling are much higher at higher schooling levels, the beneficiaries of which come primarily from middle- or upper-income households. From the point of view of pro-poor concerns about distribution, shifting toward a more targeted subsidy system would seem to be justified, although the transition to such a system might be difficult because of the vested interests of the middle- and upper-income classes in the current system.

Programs to increase parental knowledge about the importance of and means of stimulating their children, particularly in the early years of life, are likely to yield high private and social rates of return and benefit particularly children from poorer families. The limited evidence suggests that the rates of return to such preschool investments are likely to be high (Engle et al., 2007, 2011; Hoddinott, Alderman, et al., 2013, Hoddinott, Behrman, et al., 2013; Psacharopoulos, 2014; Victora et al., 2008).

Preschool programs for children three to five years old are likely to have high social rates of return. Moreover, expansion of such programs is likely to benefit primarily children from poorer families. Benefit-cost estimates of reducing the gap between preschool enrollment for children from the highest income quintile and other quintiles based on data from more than 70 developing countries are well over 1 (Engle et al., 2011).

Studies for the United States also indicate high rates of return to preschool children from poor families (Heckman, 2006).

More than 100 million girls, most of them in low- and middle-income countries, have never been enrolled in school. Increased incentives for enrollment of girls at all levels of schooling are likely to yield high social rates of return and benefit members of poorer families.

Increased incentives for boys to progress through school on time are likely to yield fairly high social returns and benefit poorer families, as among students enrolled in school, boys tend to lag on average behind girls in almost all countries, particularly those from poor families (see, for example Grant and Behrman, 2010).

Private schooling has expanded rapidly in recent years (among poor households in rural South Asia, for example). Looking forward, it will be important to craft schooling policies that are neutral with regard to school ownership rather than favoring public ownership. Some recent studies suggest substantial promise for performance-based incentive systems, albeit with some qualifications concerning the types of behaviors that are induced to improve test scores (see, for example Behrman et al. ,forthcoming; Muralidharan and Sundararaman, 2011; Thorne-Lyman et al., 2010).

Social returns to more general education (learning how to learn) and to education over the life cycle are likely to increase in an aging and rapidly changing world.

Health and Nutrition

Human capital is multifaceted. It is not simply about education; there are likely to be important human capital investments in health and nutrition.

Nutritional investments are likely to yield high social rates of return, with beneficiaries concentrated among poorer families. Particularly important are macronutrients during pregnancy and just after birth in contexts in which women and children tend to be undernourished, and micronutrients such as iron and iodine where they exist are inadequate. Such investments are particularly important in South Asia, in a number of countries in sub-Saharan Africa, and in individual countries or regions within countries elsewhere (such as Guatemala). Recent estimates suggest high rates of return to investing in nutrition, particularly in early life (Adair et al., 2009; Behrman et al., 2009; Hoddinott, Alderman, et al., 2013, Hoddinott, Behrman, et al., 2013; Hoddinott, Maluccio et al., 2008; Victora et al., 2008, 2010).

Investments in adult health and human capital may yield significant returns, especially in contexts where "healthy aging" can facilitate higher labor force participation and productivity at older ages. Currently or in the near future, the most rapidly growing age groups in some relatively poor countries, including countries in sub-Saharan Africa, will include adults over the age of 40, many of whom who are prematurely old and limited by chronic conditions and disabilities that might be treated with current knowledge.

Prevention of common chronic diseases through behavioral changes (for example, stopping smoking); regulatory changes (for example, requiring that nutritional information be provided and restricting the use of certain ingredients, such as salt and trans fats); and structural changes (such as creating walkable neighborhoods) may yield important returns by maintaining the health and human capital of aging workforces and populations in many countries. Rapidly aging populations may mean that such changes yield high social rates of returns.

Health systems in low- and middle-income countries and international public and private agencies need to be reoriented to the changing realities of disease composition (the growing importance of noncommunicable diseases and accidents relative to traditional communicable diseases). Doing so is likely to result in efficiency gains and be somewhat pro-poor, given the relatively high incidence of diseases, including the "diseases of development," among poorer members of societies.

Social safety nets and health and pension systems should be untied from formal labor market participation, to reduce distortions and benefit the poorer members of society, who tend to work in informal employment that is not covered by formal-sector benefits.

Table 21.3 Approximate benefit-cost ratios for key policy priorities in the area of population and demography (not including priorities in the area of population quality, many of which have high benefit-cost ratios and are discussed as part of other chapters)

Priority	Approximate benefit-cost ratio (BCR)
Priorities with high benefit-cost ratios	
1. Achieving *universal access to sexual and reproductive health (SRH) services* by 2030, and *eliminating unmet need for modern contraception by 2040* (Section 2)	$> 90^a$
2. *Reducing barriers to migration* within low- and middle-income countries, as well as between low- and middle-income countries and high-income countries (Section 4)	$> 45^b$
Priorities with probably high, but difficult to quantify, benefit-cost ratios	
3. *Elimination of age-based eligibility criteria for retirement*, and the development of public pension systems that are based on expected years of remaining life given fixed characteristics (Section 3)	*high*, but difficult to quantify
4. Programs facilitating *more efficient and more equitable urbanization* (Section 5)	*high*, but difficult to quantify
Priorities with relatively low benefit-cost ratios	
5. Maintenance and expansion of public pension eligibility at "relatively young old ages" (Section 3)	*low*, but difficult to quantify
6. Family policies aimed at *increasing low fertility in high-income countries* (with the exception of the expansion of early childhood education and high-quality day care) (Section 3)	*low*, and most likely < 1 due to the limited effects of most policy interventions, but difficult to quantify in general

Notes: [a]See Appendix of the online version of this chapter (Kohler and Behrman, 2014) and Kohler (2013) for details of benefit-cost calculations.
[b]Based on Anderson and Winters (2009); the cost entering these benefit-cost calculation do not include the political and institutional costs of migration reform.

Discussion: Prioritization of Targets and Policies

Broadly speaking, we support the general policy recommendations in the GTC-PD Report, including the need to address and harness population dynamics through human rights-based and gender-responsive policies. Nevertheless, our chapter highlights several specific priorities for targets and policies that differ in emphasis from the presentation in that report.

Table 21.3 summaries the key findings of our discussion. Within population and demography, the priorities that have the highest benefit-cost ratios are

- Achieving universal access to sexual and reproductive health (SRH) services by 2030, and

eliminating unmet need for modern contraception by 2040.

- A reduction of barriers to migration within low- and middle-income countries, as well as between low- and middle-income countries and high-income countries.

There are also several priorities for which benefit-cost ratios are likely to be substantial, despite large uncertainties regarding their estimation. These priorities with probably high, but difficult to quantify, benefit-cost ratios include

- Elimination of age-based eligibility criteria for retirement, and the development of public pension systems that are based on expected years of remaining life given fixed characteristics.

- Selected interventions, dependent on particular contexts, that make more efficient and more equitable the inevitable urbanization by achieving balance between functions for which there are considerable economies of scale such as transportation and communication network and functions for which decentralization is likely to lead to the best responses to heterogeneous local conditions and preferences.

Policies with relatively low benefit-cost ratios include

- Maintenance and expansion of public pension eligibility at "relatively young old ages."
- Family policies aimed at increasing low fertility in high-income countries (with the exception of the expansion of early childhood education and high-quality day care).

We also highlight that "population quality" (or human capital), including aspects such as health and education, is an important further aspect of population dynamics that is essential for addressing the challenges of future population changes, for promoting gender equality and human rights, and for realizing the benefits of population dynamics for social, economic, and environmental development.

Recent years have heightened the relevance for understanding population quantity, quality, and mobility in a globalized world, and global migration in particular has been catapulted into the headlines. Although the 2016 migrant/refugee crisis in Europe may turn out to be relatively transitory, this event points to the importance for the longer run of rethinking international migrant movements. As discussed in this chapter, there are strong arguments from a long-run economic perspective to rethink and readjust regulations concerning international migration, with long-term benefits probably offsetting considerably the short-term transition costs.

To realize these potential economic gains, however, countries need immigration policies that are forward looking, allow economic migration in addition to refugee migration, and facilitate a rapid integration of migration into labor markets – a task that is likely to be challenging if migration flows increase very rapidly, as has been the case in Germany and several other countries during the current migration crisis. In addition, increased migration and mobility occurring as part of overall globalization, not just the current migration crisis, have renewed concerns about the global spread of new infectious diseases, such as SARS, Ebola, or Zika, with possible profound implications for population dynamics through their effects on health, mortality, and fertility. These headline-grabbing global diseases have not changed the basic aspect of the global epidemiological transition that predicts continued shifts of the global burden of disease toward noncommunicable diseases, as has been highlighted in this chapter and some related literatures (e.g., Behrman and Kohler, 2014), along with possibly policy responses to shifting disease burdens in both developing and developed countries. Developing mechanisms for resilience to such new epidemics, and maintaining this resilience despite an overall shift of disease burden toward noncommunicable diseases will therefore be important in the post-2015 development agenda.

References

Abel, G. J. and Sander, N. (2014). Quantifying global international migration flows. *Science* 343 (6178): 1520–2. doi:10.1126/science.1248676.

Adair, L. S., Martorell, R., Stein, A. D., et al. (2009). Size at birth, weight gain in infancy and childhood, and adult blood pressure in 5 low- and middle-income-country cohorts: when does weight gain matter? *American Journal of Clinical Nutrition* 89(5): 1383–92. doi:10.3945/ajcn.2008.27139.

Anderson, K. and Winters, A. L. (2009). The challenge of reducing international trade and migration barriers. In: Lomborg, B. (ed.), *Global Crises, Global Solutions*, 2nd ed., Cambridge, MA: Cambridge University Press, 451–503.

Bauernschuster, S., Hener, T., and Rainer, H. (2014). Children of a (policy) revolution: The introduction of universal child care and its effect on fertility. CESifo Working Paper Series No. 4776, URL: http://ssrn.com/abstract= 2439616.

Beard, J., Biggs, S., Bloom, D., et al. (2012). Global population ageing: Peril or promise? PGDA Working Paper No. 89 (Global Agenda Council on Ageing Society), URL: www.hsph.harvard.edu/pgda/working.htm.

Behrman, J. R., Calderon, M. C., Preston, S., Hoddinott, J., Martorell, R., and Stein, A. D. (2009). Nutritional supplementation of girls influences the growth of their children: prospective study in Guatemala. *American Journal of Clinical Nutrition* 90: 1372–1379.

Behrman, J. R. and Kohler, H.-P. (2014). Population quantity, quality, and mobility. In: Fardoust, S. and Behrman, J. R. (eds.), *Towards a Better Global Economy: Policy Implications for Global Citizens in the 21st Century*, Oxford, UK: Oxford University Press, forthcoming. Working paper version is available at www.gcf.ch/?page_id=5811.

Blau, F. D. and Kahn, L. M. (2012). Immigration and the distribution of incomes. NBER Working Paper #18515, URL: www.nber.org/papers/w18515.

Bloom, D. E., Canning, D., and Sevilla, J. (2002). *The Demographic Dividend: A New Perspective on the Economic Consequences of Population Change*. Santa Monica, CA: RAND Corporation.

Canning, D. (2012). Copenhagen consensus perspective paper on "Infectious Disease." Copenhagen Consensus Project 2012, URL: www.copenhagenconsensus.com.

Clements, B. J., Coady, D., Eich, F., et al. (2013). The challenge of public pension reform in advanced and emerging economies. International Monetary Fund, IMF Occasional Papers #275, URL: http://econpapers.repec.org/repec:imf:imfocp:275.

Dahl, G. B., Løken, K. V., Mogstad, M., and Salvanes, K. V. (2013). What is the case for paid maternity leave? NBER Working Paper #19595, URL: www.nber.org/papers/w19595.

D'Amuri, F. and Peri, G. (2014). Immigration, jobs, and employment protection: Evidence from Europe before and during the great recession. *Journal of the European Economic Association* 12(2): 432–464. doi:10.1111/jeea.12040.

Darroch, J. E. and Singh, S. (2013). Trends in contraceptive need and use in developing countries in 2003, 2008, and 2012: an analysis of national surveys. *Lancet* 381(9879): 1756–62. doi:10.1016/S0140-6736(13)60597-8.

Deardorff, A. V. (2009). Alternative perspective: The challenge of reducing international trade and migration barriers. In: Lomborg, B. (ed.), *Global Crises, Global Solutions*, 2nd ed., Cambridge: Cambridge University Press, 504–10.

Engle, P. L., Black, M. M., Behrman, et al. (2007). Strategies to avoid the loss of developmental potential in more than 200 million children in the developing world. *Lancet* 369(9557): 229–42. doi:10.1016/S0140-6736(07)60112-3.

Engle, P. L., Fernald, L. C. H., Alderman, H., et al. (2011). Strategies for reducing inequalities and improving developmental outcomes for young children in low-income and middle-income countries. *Lancet* 378(9799): 1339–53. doi:10.1016/S0140-6736(11)60889-1.

Global Agenda Council on Population Growth (2012). *Seven billion and growing: A 21st century perspective on population*. Geneva, Switzerland: World Economic Forum.

Grant, M. J. and Behrman, J. R. (2010). Gender gaps in educational attainment in less developed countries. *Population and Development Review* 36(1): 71–89. doi:10.1111/j. 1728–4457.2010.00318.x.

Heckman, J. J. (2006). Skill formation and the economics of investing in disadvantaged children. *Science* 312(5782): 1900–02.

Heckman, J. J., Moon, S. H., Pinto, R., Savelyev, P. A., and Yavitz, A. (2010). The rate of return to the HighScope Perry preschool program. *Journal of Public Economics* 94(1–2): 114–28. doi:10.1016/j.jpubeco.2009.11.001.

Hoddinott, J., Alderman, H., Behrman, J. R., Haddad, L. and Horton, S. (2013a). The economic rationale for investing in stunting reduction. *Maternal and Child Nutrition* 9(Suppl. 2): 69–82. doi:10.1111/mcn.12080.

Hoddinott, J., Behrman, J. R., Maluccio, J. A., et al. (2013b). Adult consequences of growth failure in early childhood. *American Journal of Clinical Nutrition* 98(5): 1170–78. doi:10.3945/ajcn.113.064584.

Hoddinott, J., Maluccio, J. A., Behrman, J. R., Flores, R. and Martorell, R. (2008). Effect of a nutrition intervention during early childhood on economic productivity in Guatemalan adults. *Lancet* 371 (9610): 411–16. doi:10.1016/S0140-6736(08) 60205-6.

Jamison, D. T. et al. (2014). Post-2015 Copenhagen Consensus: Health. Copenhagen Consensus Project, Post-2015 Development Goals.

Kapur, D. and McHale, J. (2012). Economic effects of emigration on sending countries. In: Rosenblum, M. R. and Tichenor, D. J. (eds.), *Oxford Handbook of the Politics of International Migration*, Oxford, UK: Oxford University Press, Chapter 6, 131–52.

Kennan, J. (2012). Open borders. NBER Working Paper #18307, URL: www.nber.org/papers/w18307.

Kohler, H.-P. (2013). Population growth. In: Lomborg, B. (ed.), *Global Problems, Smart Solutions*, Cambridge: Cambridge University Press. Working paper version available at http://repository.upenn.edu/psc_working_papers/34.

Kohler, Hans-Peter and Behrman, Jere R. (2014). Population and Demography: Benefits and Costs of the Population and Demography Targets for the Post-2015 Development Agenda. Copenhagen Consensus Project: Post-2015 Consensus. URL: www.copenhagenconsensus.com/post-2015-consensus/populationanddemography.

Kohler, H.-P., Billari, F. C. and Ortega, J. A. (2006). Low fertility in Europe: causes, implications and policy options. In: Harris, F. R. (ed.), *The Baby Bust: Who Will Do the Work? Who Will Pay the Taxes?* Lanham, MD: Rowman & Littlefield Publishers, 48–109. URL: http://books.google.com/books?id=75alsu8U9QAC&pg=PA48.

Lee, R. D. and Mason, A. (2011). Generational economics in a changing world. *Population and Development Review* 37: 115–42. doi:10.1111/j.1728-4457.2011.00380.x.

Luci-Greulich, A. and Thévenon, O. (2013). The impact of family policies on fertility trends in developed countries. *European Journal of Population* 29(4): 387–416. doi:10.1007/s10680–013–9295–4.

Malhotra, A., Warner, A., McGonagle, A. and Lee-Rife, S. (2011). *Solutions to end child marriage: What the evidence shows*, Washington, DC: International Center for Research on Women (ICRW), URL: www.icrw.org/files/publications/Solutions-to-End-Child-Marriage.pdf.

Martin, P. (2004). Migration. In: Lomborg, B. (ed.), *Global Crises, Global Solutions*, Cambridge: Cambridge University Press, 443–73.

Mukand, S. (2012). International migration, politics and culture: The case for greater labour mobility. Chatham House Policy Paper, URL: www.chathamhouse.org/publications/papers/view/186357.

Muralidharan, K. and Sundararaman, V. (2011). Teacher opinions on performance pay: Evidence from India. *Economics of Education Review* 30(3): 394–403. doi:10.1016/j.econedurev.2011.02.001.

Myrskylä, M., Kohler, H.-P., and Billari, F. C. (2009). Advances in development reverse fertility declines. *Nature* 460(7256): 741–3. doi:10.1038/nature08230.

National Research Council (1986). *Population Growth and Economic Development: Policy Questions*. Washington, DC: National Academy Press.

——— (2012). *Aging and the Macroeconomy. Long-Term Implications of an Older Population*. Washington, DC: National Academy Press. National Research Council (NRC): Committee on the Long-Run Macroeconomic Effects of the Aging U.S. Population, Board on Mathematical Sciences and their Applications, Division on Engineering and Physical Sciences, Committee on Population, Division of Behavioral and Social Sciences and Education.

Pritchett, L. (2007). *Let Their People Come: Breaking the Deadlock in International Labor Mobility*. Washington, DC: Center for Global Development, Brookings Institution Press.

Psacharopoulos, G. (2014). Education assessment paper: Benefits and costs of the education targets for the post-2015 development agenda. Copenhagen Consensus Project, Post-2015 Development Goals, URL: www.copenhagenconsensus.com//publication/post-2015-consensus-education-assessment-psacharopoulos.

Queisser, M. and Whitehouse, E. R. (2006). Neutral or Fair? Actuarial Concepts and Pension-System Design. OECD Social, Employment and Migration Working Papers #40. doi:10.1787/1815199x. URL: www.oecd-ilibrary.org/social-issues-migration-health/neutral-or-fair_351382456457.

Rindfuss, R. R., Guilkey, D., Morgan, P. S., Kravdal, Ø., and Guzzo, K. B. (2004). Child care availability and fertility in Norway: Pro-natalist effects. Paper presented at the annual meeting of the Population Association of America, Boston, MA, April 1–3, 2004 URL: http://paa2004.princeton.edu.

Rohwedder, S. and Willis, R. J. (2010). Mental retirement. *Journal of Economic Perspectives* 24(1): 119–138. doi:10.1257/jep.24.1.119.

Rosenzweig, M. (2004). Migration: Alternative perspectives. In: Lomborg, B. (ed.), *Global Crises, Global Solutions*, Cambridge: Cambridge University Press, 478–88.

Sahlgren, G. H. (2013). *Work longer, live healthier: The relationship between economic activity, health and government policy*. London: Institute of Economic Affairs. doi:10.2139/ssrn.2267408. Institute of Economic Affairs (IEA) Discussion Paper No. 46.

Salles, A., Rossier, C. and Brachet, S. (2010). Understanding the long term effects of family policies on fertility: The diffusion of different family models in France and Germany. *Demographic Research* 22: 1057–96. doi:10.4054/DemRes.2010.22.34.

Sanderson, W. and Scherbov, S. (2008). Rethinking age and aging. *Population Bulletin* 63(4): 1–16.

Thorne-Lyman, A. L., Valpiani, N., Sun, K., et al. (2010). Household dietary diversity and food expenditures are closely linked in rural Bangladesh, increasing the risk of malnutrition due to the financial crisis. *Journal of Nutrition* 140(1): 182S–188S. doi:10.3945/jn.109.110809.

UN Population Division (2000). *Replacement Migration: Is It a Solution to Declining and Ageing Populations?* New York: Population Division, Department of Economic and Social Affairs, United Nations.

— (2009). What would it take to accelerate fertility decline in the least developed countries? UN Population Division Policy Brief No. 2009/1, URL: www.un.org/esa/population/publications/UNPD_policybriefs/UNPD_policy_brief1.pdf.

— (2010). World Population Prospects, the 2010 revision: Standard (median) forecasts. United Nations, Department of Economic and Social Affairs, Population Division, URL: http://esa.un.org/unpd/wpp/.

— (2012). *World Urbanization Prospects: The 2011 Revision*. New York: Population Division, Department of Economic and Social Affairs, United Nations.

UNFPA (2014). *ICPD Beyond 2014 Global Report*. New York: United Nations. URL: www.unfpa.org/public/home/sitemap/ICPDReport.

UNFPA, UNDESA, UN-HABITAT, IOM (2013). Population Dynamics in the Post-2015 Development Agenda: Report of the Global Thematic Consultation on Population Dynamics. United Nations. URL: www.worldwewant2015.org/file/313464/download/340868.

United Nations (1996). *Programme of Action Adopted at the International Conference on Population and Development, Cairo*. New York: United Nations.

Victora, C. G., Adair, L., Fall, C., et al. (2008). Maternal and child undernutrition: consequences for adult health and human capital. *Lancet* 371(9609): 340–357. doi:10.1016/S0140-6736(07)61692-4.

Victora, C. G., de Onis, M., Hallal, P. C., Blössner, M. and Shrimpton, R. (2010). Worldwide timing of growth faltering: revisiting implications for interventions. *Pediatrics* 125(3): e473–80. doi:10.1542/peds.2009-1519.

Walker, J.-A. (2013). Why ending child marriage needs to be an education goal: The case for improved coordination between ending child marriage and girls' education movements in West Africa. Center for Universal Education, URL: www.brookings.edu/~/media/Research/Files/Reports/2013/12/improving percent20learning%20outcomes%20girls%20africa/walker_girls_education.pdf.

WHO (2013). *Health in the Post-2015 Development Agenda: Report of the Global Thematic Consultation on Population Dynamics*. WHO and United Nations, URL: www.worldwewant2015.org/health.

Wise, D. A. (2010). Facilitating longer working lives: International evidence on why and how. *Demography* 47(1): S131–49. doi:10.1353/dem.2010.0000.

21.1 Alternative Perspective

DAVID CANNING

Summary

The chapter covers a wide range of issues, and there is a lack of detail in some of the arguments. We have to think of priorities across as well as within issues, and this chapter puts forward five thematic priorities.

There is a fundamental issue of applying benefit-cost analysis to reducing fertility because this takes no account of the well-being of those potentially born. This is probably an insoluble philosophical problem, but we also have the more mundane issue that people like to have children, and this benefit is not included in the analysis. People value children, and the proper place for decision making should be at the household level. I would prefer to see targets based on access to family planning rather than contraceptive use. On the benefit of maternal and child health, much of the benefit of family planning comes from better birth spacing and timing, rather than number of births. Births before the mother is 18 or less than 36 months after the previous birth are very high risk to both mother and child.

The largest impact of family planning appears to be through rising per capita income, which I do not see as a measure of welfare. National income accounting does not, for example, include leisure time. Similarly, the value to parents of having children does not appear in the national income accounts.

When families make decisions, there is a strong case for giving more power to women, particularly in male-dominated societies, as husbands almost always want more children than their wives, but it is the wives who bear the costs of higher fertility.

Improvement in healthy life span has contributed as much as economic growth to improvements in human welfare since 1960. The problem of an aging population is that it can lead to a rise in the old age dependency ratio. But this does not have to be so. If the old save for their retirement needs, including healthcare, they are not dependent. A simple way to achieve this is to force savings out of earnings into private accounts to meet retirement needs, supplemented by a basic pension to avoid poverty. In this way, there are only minimal transfers between generations, which means the age dependency issue is not really a problem. Population aging is incompatible with the current institutions and work and pension arrangements in many countries. We have to change the institutions and pension systems.

I agree with the chapter's emphasis on migration as a potential source of large welfare gains. The most difficult challenge to migration is the fear of changes in the receiving country's political economy due to migration. A simple way of allowing migration would be for countries to merge and remove national borders, which is essentially the approach of the European Union. However, large countries have more heterogeneous populations, and it is more difficult to provide public goods to heterogeneous populations. Nevertheless, to realize the overall benefits, workers who compete with migrants need to be compensated. On the issue of family connections, I disagree with the authors; there are enormous welfare gains from allowing migration due to family connections.

My view on urbanization is that at the individual level, welfare seems to be higher in cities than in rural areas. This is true not only in terms of income but also health. However, there seems to be little or no effect on economic growth, and we should therefore be agnostic on the issue of encouraging or discouraging urbanization.

On the issue of population quality, I agree with the view that subsidies should be targeted at early education in kindergarten and primary school, rather than tertiary education, on the grounds that returns at the earlier levels may be higher, and focusing on these levels will tend to help poorer families and encourage equality. I also agree with the emphasis on health as a factor that has a high benefit-cost ratio both in itself and in terms of its effects on physical and cognitive ability and worker productivity.

In terms of overall priorities, migration and pension reform have very little direct resource cost and make efficiency gains by changing institutions or rules. The problem is that there are winners as well as losers, so mechanisms are needed to achieve the gains in ways that are politically acceptable. Family planning has very high benefit-cost ratios and would benefit the poor. I would prioritize this over amelioration of urbanization because it is difficult to think that the various location-specific interventions needed would exceed these values.

21.2 Alternative Perspective

GREGORY CASEY AND ODED GALOR

Summary

In all facets of life, people must make decisions about how to allocate scarce resources. Potential parents must decide how many children to have and how much to invest in the future of each child. This decision is known as the "quantity-quality" trade-off. At the most fundamental level, when individuals invest more in the human capital of each child and have fewer children, they raise the future per capita earnings power of the next generation. Developing countries have high rates of fertility, which place a great burden on governments and aid agencies hoping to alleviate poverty and deprivation. In these settings, policies inducing parents to have fewer children and invest more in the education of each child will have positive effects beyond those captured by short-term cost-benefit analysis.

Rich countries face the opposite problem, of falling fertility and rising numbers of older dependents. Countries can make up the shortfall in public revenue by encouraging high skill immigration, which has positive effects also on sending countries by raising the return to human capital accumulation.

For much of human history, differences in per capita income across the globe were negligible because increases in productivity were used to support larger populations. This negative feedback loop between productivity and population, as described by Malthus, began to unravel at the turn of the nineteenth century in parts of Western Europe. Fertility began to lag behind increases in productivity, leading to higher living standards. Eventually, fertility rates began to fall as incomes continued to rise. This process led to a rapid increase in the living standards of Western Europe and its offshoots as well as a corresponding rise in the degree of global inequality. Understanding this demographic transition is essential for devising policies to help spur economic and demographic change in developing countries.

Having fewer children but investing more in their education produces a more educated workforce, drives up living standards, and increases technological progress. Meanwhile, increased technological progress raises the return to human capital investment, inducing parents to substitute toward child quality. This relationship between fertility and economic growth is the basis of Unified Growth Theory. The rising importance of human capital also lowers the return to child labor and increases the earning power of women, reinforcing this pattern. Understanding these links, therefore, provides important insights into the most effective ways to influence fertility and growth through public policies.

For developing countries to become rich, resources need to be devoted to increasing income per person rather than supporting larger and larger populations. Policies that lower the cost or raise the benefits of investing in child quality relative to having more children will generate a positive feedback cycle between higher levels of human capital and further economic development. Lowering the cost of education is a commonly suggested policy, but standard benefit-cost analysis will underestimate total benefits, which will unfold slowly as fertility and economic structure adapt.

Developed countries may attempt to boost fertility to help support an aging population, but risk undoing the positive effects that increased child quality investment and female labor force participation have had on economic growth. Increased immigration of high-skilled individuals provides another, and more immediate, way to generate tax revenues needed to support retirees.

The various components of the post-2015 development agenda interact in complex ways. For example, increasing the returns to education will help reduce fertility rates, while increasing access to contraceptives will help increase the investments parents make in schooling. These factors have a positive effect on gender equality, which can itself affect future schooling and fertility decisions.

Policies that raise the return to education in developing countries have positive implications well beyond the already substantial effects identified by standard cost-benefit calculations. For developed countries, increased skilled migration helps to raise public revenues without undoing the positive effects of low fertility and high educational standards.

Benefits and Costs of Two Science and Technology Targets for the Post-2015 Development Agenda

KEITH E. MASKUS

Introduction

In its deliberations regarding development of the Sustainable Development Goals (SDGs), the United Nations (UN) working group considered various issues involving science and technology (S&T) initiatives. In general, the working group viewed technology development and transfer as a way to "strengthen and enhance means of implementation and global partnership for sustainable development." The inclusion of S&T to help achieve SDG is sensible because access to, and effective implementation of, knowledge and technical information are fundamentally important sources of economic growth (Keller, 2004). They are equally central in meeting public needs, such as adaptation to climate change, water safety, and public health (Maskus and Okediji, 2014). Thus, S&T initiatives speak both to economic development and sustainability, making them a suitable candidate for inclusion in the SDG in some form.

Unfortunately, most of the cases in which technology was listed in the UN working documents involved broad aspirations, rather than clearly articulated targets. This lack of policy specificity is unsurprising because technology transfer and investments in research and development (R&D) are largely private decisions, although significant expenditures are also undertaken by public authorities and their grantees. In this context, such words as *promote* and *encourage* are appropriate in this area because the primary objectives may simply be to improve market and governance conditions to induce firms to disseminate technologies and undertake R&D programs that are conducive to economic and social development. Such exhortations are difficult to assess numerically, however.

Because of this limited information, this chapter articulates specific objectives that both facilitate the broad objectives of the SDG and are amenable to reasonable cost-benefit calculations. I select two cross-cutting objectives that, if achieved, could offer strong facilitation to technology diffusion, access to knowledge, and growth of technological capacities in developing countries.

The first objective is to increase the ratio of R&D spending over GDP to specific targets in developing and emerging economies. This idea was mentioned in a midterm working group document, though without articulating specific targets.[1] I analyze the notion that policies might be implemented to expand the R&D/GDP ratio to 0.5 percent in developing nations, and 1.5 percent in emerging nations, by 2030. The policies involve expanding R&D tax credits to achieve 50 percent of the incremental R&D and direct government expenditures to accomplish the other 50 percent. Economic benefits include spillover learning from expanded R&D investments and gains from additional innovations that may be induced. Costs include efficiency losses from attracting resources from other uses, financing costs, and administrative and compliance costs. The calculations suggest that the benefits from these policies generally exceed the costs, but the benefit-cost ratio falls below 1.4 unless there are implausibly high estimates of induced-innovation gains in the future.

The second objective is to establish 10-year visas permitting free mobility of skilled (technical and managerial) labor among countries participating in "innovation zones." The idea is to increase

[1] United Nations Development Program, *TST Issues Brief: Science, Technology and Innovation, Knowledge-sharing, and Capacity-building*, October 2014.

technology diffusion, efficiency, and learning among enterprises within such zones. Quantification of the associated costs and benefits is particularly speculative, given the scarcity of relevant studies of what would be a radically new initiative. To implement the idea, I consider potential effects within two suggestive zones: one that is North–South in orientation and one that is South–South. Both focus on such arrangements within the Western Hemisphere, with the North comprising Canada and the United States and the South comprising the rest of the Americas. Here the suggestion is far more positive: the benefit-cost ratio of a tightly limited North–South agreement exceeds 13 under conservative parameter estimates. The bulk of this net gain comes from large income increases for the skilled workers and associated remittances. Even netting out these impacts, however, the benefit-cost ratio within the hemisphere is around four. An innovation zone among the developing economies would result in far smaller flows but still would generate a benefit-cost ratio over seven.

Benefits and Costs of National R&D Targets

Background

It is often argued that expanding national investments in R&D is important for economic development and growth (Griffith, 2000; Romer, 1990). Such investments generate new and lower-cost ways of producing goods and services, facilitate innovation of new products, and support higher real wages and human capital. Consumer gains through higher quality and new product varieties are significant sources of welfare growth (Aghion and Howitt, 1998). Firms with R&D laboratories are more likely to experience productivity gains from acquiring advanced international technologies (Keller, 2004).

Although important, these factors are not enough to justify government intervention to subsidize R&D, for the benefits may accrue to those undertaking the private investments. Rather, the case for government support rests on market failure: private firms are not able to fully appropriate the productivity returns to R&D. Instead, some of the increased knowledge and know-how generate higher productivity for other firms, which may not have to pay for these gains. Similarly, because it is difficult to exclude others from using knowledge, there may be consumer gains that cannot be captured as income to innovators.

Many studies have demonstrated that the social returns to R&D, accounting for these spillovers, are higher than the private returns, implying that the market by itself supports a suboptimal level of investment (Griffith, 2000). Basic scientific research, for example, may support numerous market applications but have little direct economic return (Nelson, 2005). These problems offer the basic justification for national public intervention. Moreover, some of these external gains cross borders, meaning that the gains to the investing economy are lower than global gains (Eaton and Kortum, 1996; Keller, 2004). In this sense, knowledge is a global public good, especially where it supports innovation in technologies relevant for meeting social needs, implying that some forms of international support or coordination are required for optimal provision (Maskus, 2006).

The idea of raising the ratio of R&D expenditures in GDP in developing and emerging economies reflects the view that such investments generate sufficient spillover gains as to justify the costs of policy interventions. Indeed, public policy among technologically advanced economies has stimulated productivity and growth, albeit with a mixed record (Griffith, 2000; Rodriguez-Pose and Crescenzi, 2006; Westmore, 2013). Bloom et al. (2002) found that R&D tax credits in 19 OECD countries over 1979–97 were effective, in that a 10 percent fall in the cost of R&D stimulated nearly a 10 percent rise in expenditures in the long run. Gonzalez and Pazo (2008) noted that public subsidies to R&D expand investments by small and medium-sized enterprises (SMEs) and that there is little evidence that public R&D crowds out the induced private expenditure. Similarly, Kohler et al. (2012) found that tax incentives in recent years have generally stimulated additional R&D, though the type of incentive mattered.

Although R&D subsidies in the OECD may induce more expenditures, this does not necessarily

Table 22.1 Basic figures on R&D ratios

	RD/GDP ratio current %	RD/GDP ratio current min	RD/GDP ratio current max	Annual ratio growth rate %	2030 expected RD ratio %	2030 target RD ratio	Target ratio growth rate %
DCs (26)	0.19	0.02	0.40	3.7	0.30	0.75	19.7
DCs (26)	0.19	0.02	0.40	3.7	0.30	0.5	11.0
ECs no China (35)	0.83	0.41	1.15	2.8	1.18	2.0	9.4
ECs no China (35)	0.83	0.41	1.15	2.8	1.18	1.5	5.4
China	1.69	1.69	1.69	9.5	4.10	3.0	5.2
MDCs (28)	2.61	1.25	4.54	1.3	3.12	3.5	1.0

Source: Author's calculations using data from World Development Indicators. RD/GDP ratio is the within-group GNI-weighted average over 2008–10 or most recent (using 2012 GNI at ATLAS method); annual growth rate refers to percentage growth of weighted RD/GDP ratio from 2000–10 or closest years available. Sample sizes in parentheses depend on available R&D data.

mean that there are positive effects on third-party spillovers, productivity, and competitiveness, the ultimate targets. In this context, welfare analyses of specific R&D support policies, which attempt to set spillover gains against program costs, are scarce and rather reserved. Lester (2012), for example, computed that a basic R&D tax credit in Canada for smaller firms generates a net benefit but that extended credits and direct assistance incur costs greater than welfare gains. Russo (2004) calculated that the Canadian incremental R&D tax credit supports substantial net benefits but that comprehensive tax credits do not. Goolsbee (1998) speculated that government funding of R&D in the United States has in large part just pushed up the wages of scientists and engineers, who are in inelastic supply, without achieving much innovation. There appear to be no studies of these basic policy questions in any developing or emerging countries.

Current Situation

To assess the policies that may be required to raise R&D/GDP ratios, it is important first to note some recent figures. Thus, I present in Table 22.1 basic data, taken from the World Bank's World Development Indicators (WDI), showing the share of R&D in GDP and growth in that ratio, in a sample of 26 developing countries (DCs), 35 emerging countries (ECs), China, and, for

perspective, 18 developed (MDCs) countries. The DC sample is small due to limited data availability, but it does cover such major economies as Colombia, Egypt, Indonesia, and Thailand. I exclude countries defined by the World Bank to be low-income because their current ratios are so low there is virtually no likelihood they would rise to significant levels within 15 years.

As shown in Table 22.1, the most recent GNI-weighted R&D ratio among the developing countries is 0.19, with considerable variability among them. The ratio grew about 3.7 percent annually from 2000–2010, which is notable relative growth in R&D. If that growth were to continue linearly, by 2030 the group of DCs would achieve a ratio of 0.3. Among the emerging countries, excluding China, the most recent weighted R&D ratio is 0.83, reflecting growth of 2.8 percent per year. Again, it is noteworthy that existing conditions induced this relatively rapid growth, which, if it continues, would place the ECs as a group at a ratio of 1.18 by 2030.

China is a special case. By itself, the 2010 R&D ratio was 1.69, far higher than the other ECs and higher than many nations in the developed sample. China's ratio rose 9.5 percent per year, astonishing in light of the rapid GDP growth it accompanied. Were that growth to continue, China's ratio would reach 4.1 in 2030. Finally, the group of developed economies displays R&D ratios ranging from

1.25 to 4.54, with a weighted average of 2.61. This ratio grew the slowest among the groups because they are closest to the technological frontier, which tends to diminish returns to R&D.

This data review suggests several relevant elements for the analysis. First, I assume as a baseline that each group's R&D/GDP ratio will rise at its historical trend and achieve the "2030 expected ratio" levels within 15 years without further policy interventions. Thus, the cost-benefit analysis focuses on attempts to raise the ratios incrementally above these levels, with policies increasing growth rates above existing trends. Second, for both DCs and ECs it makes sense to define a moderate objective for the R&D ratio. I analyze the goal of raising the 2030 ratio among DCs from 0.3 percent to 0.5 percent (along a linear path), requiring an 11.0 percent annual growth rate. The analogous target for the ECs would be a ratio of 1.5 percent of GDP, with a corresponding growth rate of 5.4 percent per annum.[2] These are substantial increases and would require more than marginal changes in incentive packages. Third, there seems little reason to hold China and the developed countries to additional growth in their R&D ratios. Thus, I focus the benefit-cost analysis here on the targets noted for the DCs and ECs.

Model and Assumptions

Note that there are many policy instruments that governments could use to raise R&D spending, and it would be impossible to consider all of them, especially in light of limited data. Thus, I focus on a combination of two policies, assumed to operate independently. These come from considering the breakdown of R&D into government research expenditures and business-enterprise research investments. This split is available for a small number of DCs and ECs using World Bank and OECD data, which consistently find that essentially 50 percent of R&D expenditures are public and 50 percent are made by businesses. I therefore posit that any increase in R&D toward an annual target is split evenly between public and private sources. The associated policies are, first, direct government grants to R&D and, second, an R&D tax credit sufficient to achieve the enterprise

target. I assume in the basic scenarios that these policies work equally across countries within each group and that no program impacts spill over into effects in other country groups. In subsequent calculations I do account for cross-border global externalities.

I modify a partial-equilibrium model of R&D costs and benefits from Lester (2012), which was developed for Canadian policy. I assume the incremental policy initiatives begin in 2015 and have effects in 2016 through 2030, for a 15-year horizon. Specifically, I compute for each year from 2016 to 2030 a target level of real R&D expenditures that would achieve the requisite linear growth in the R&D/GDP ratio for given constant growth rates in real GDP. These GDP growth rates are set at 5 percent for DCs and 3.5 percent for ECs, which seem reasonable for the next 15-year period.[3]

In essence, the model identifies and computes the following benefits and costs, keeping in mind that achieving the R&D targets is not, in itself, a welfare benefit. There are three cost elements. First is the efficiency loss imposed on the economy by subsidizing the use of capital and skilled labor into R&D activities that would not otherwise exist. Second is the marginal efficiency burden of the fiscal cost of paying for the increased public expenditures and the lost tax revenues of the tax credit, accounting for the spillover changes in GDP. Third is the cost to the government of administering the programs and enterprises of complying with it. I assume these various costs last during the 15-year life of the program but no further.

There are essentially two domestic benefits. One is the spillover productivity gains to the economy, which depend on how much take-up there is in the program and the extent of output growth in firms benefiting from the externality. I assume that these productivity-related external gains exist through the length of the program but then revert to zero because there is no further incremental R&D

---

[2] In the original report I consider more ambitious targets as well; see Maskus (2014). The results in terms of benefit-cost ratios are similar in both scenarios for both DCs and ECs.

[3] Selection of GDP growth rates has little impact on benefit-cost ratios.

created. A second is the possibility that these spillovers will generate additional domestic innovation from reverse engineering, demonstration effects, and learning by doing in laboratories, resulting in further cost reductions. Because these dynamic gains can continue in the longer term, I permit them to continue for an additional ten years beyond the program.

More broadly, expanded R&D expenditures have the additional benefit that new knowledge supports external consumer gains in the home economy, such as improved health status from new medicines. Moreover, these benefits can cross borders, procuring greater consumer gains and lower production costs in foreign locations. The extent of such international gains is much debated in the literature. Spillovers may be impeded by distance, inadequate economic and social infrastructure, poor absorptive capacities, and intellectual property rights. Nevertheless, greater R&D expenditures in DCs and ECs should support some increase in global usage gains, and I include a rough calculation later.

The table in Appendix 1 lists the model equations and shows the parameter values chosen for the benefit-cost analysis. These assumptions are fully explained in the original report (Maskus, 2014). I initially determine the target levels of incremental real (PPP-adjusted) R&D expenditures for each year of the program required to reach the target R&D/GDP ratio by 2030. Key parameters include the direct spillover from the incremental R&D investments into lower costs and higher productivity, the effective subsidization of R&D from the tax credits, the marginal excess burden of taxes needed to finance the subsidies and public R&D, and the welfare gains from directly and indirectly inducing more innovation, including international spillovers. Most parameters are changed in different cases to capture the potential range of impacts.

Results

Table 22.2 presents the calculations of benefits and costs, discounted to net present value (NPV) for DCs, using discount rates of 3 percent and 5 percent, of raising the target R&D ratio to

0.5 percent by 2030. Columns are labeled by number to indicate various scenarios in the partial-equilibrium setup. The first column contains the results for a benchmark set of parameter values. Program benefits, discounted at 3 percent, amount to $18.7 billion, while costs sum to $17.2 billion, yielding a benefit-cost (B/C) ratio of 1.09 for the case where induced innovation ends with the program (i.e., the 15-year period). Adding 10 more years of the strictly domestic induced innovation gains at 1 percent would raise the B/C ratio to 1.13 (see the "B/C 25" entry). Note that discounting by 5 percent reduces the NPV of both benefits and costs but has little impact on the B/C ratio.

Columns 2 through 7 consider changes in parameters for the basic scenarios, some that raise benefits and some that raise costs.[4] For example, increasing the private spillover rate ("e private") from 0.6 to 0.8 raises the B/C ratio marginally from 1.09 to 1.12 (column 2), while raising the marginal excess burden of taxes actually reduces the B-C ratio to below 1.0 (column 3). The most favorable primary scenarios are in columns 5 through 7, where the induced innovation benefit rate is raised from 0.01 to 0.04. In these cases the B/C ratio is around 1.2 over 15 years and 1.4 over 25 years.

Table 22.3 repeats this analysis for the group of emerging countries, assuming policies achieve an increase in the R&D ratio to 1.5 percent of GDP. Because the model and parameters used are the same, it is not surprising that the primary difference is just in the much larger scale of benefits and costs. However, the conclusion about benefits versus costs remains the same: the ratio peaks at 1.41, depending on model circumstances.

To summarize these basic computations, expanding the R&D share in GDP above and beyond what it is likely to attain automatically both generates welfare benefits and incurs economic and budgetary costs. Thus, although the most positive cases do support a ratio of domestic benefits to costs solidly above unity, the program does not

---

[4] The final two columns are discussed after the basic scenarios.

Table 22.2 Computations of discounted benefit-cost ratios for incremental R&D targets in developing countries: Raise RD/GDP ratio to 0.5 percent by 2030 (benefits and costs in $b)

Parameter	1	2	3	4	5	6	7		8	9
e private	0.6	0.8	0.6	0.6	0.6	0.6	0.6		0.6	0.6
e public	0.8	0.8	0.8	0.8	0.8	0.8	0.8		0.8	0.8
s weighted	0.6	0.7	0.6	0.6	0.6	0.6	0.6		0.6	0.6
Burden	0.2	0.2	0.3	0.2	0.2	0.2	0.2		0.2	0.2
Fixed cost	0.01	0.01	0.01	0.005	0.01	0.005	0.005		0.005	0.005
Innovation	0.01	0.01	0.01	0.01	0.04	0.04	0.04		0.18	0.30
Tax rate	0.25	0.25	0.25	0.25	0.25	0.25	0.2		0.25	0.25
Disc at 3%	NPV	NPV	NPV	NPV	NPV	NPV	NPV		NPV	NPV
Ben 15	18.7	23.4	18.7	18.7	20.8	20.8	20.8	Ben 40	45.9	64.4
Cost 15	17.2	20.9	21.4	16.9	17.1	16.8	16.8	Cost 40	16.8	16.8
B/C 15	1.09	1.12	0.88	1.11	1.22	1.24	1.24	B/C 40	2.73	3.86
Ben 25	19.5	24.1	19.5	19.5	23.8	23.8	23.8			
Cost 25	17.2	20.9	21.4	16.9	17.1	16.8	16.8			
B/C 25	1.13	1.12	0.91	1.15	1.39	1.42	1.41			
Disc at 5%	NPV	NPV	NPV	NPV	NPV	NPV	NPV		NPV	NPV
Ben 15	15.4	19.2	15.4	15.4	17.1	17.1	17.1	Ben 40	31.9	43.3
Cost 15	14.1	17.1	17.5	13.9	14.1	13.8	13.8	Cost 40	13.8	13.8
B/C 15	1.09	1.12	0.88	1.11	1.22	1.24	1.24	B/C 40	2.32	3.16
Ben 25	15.9	19.7	15.9	15.9	19.1	19.1	19.1			
Cost 25	14.1	17.1	17.5	13.9	14.1	13.8	13.8			
B/C 25	1.12	1.15	0.91	1.15	1.36	1.39	1.38			

Source: Author's calculations, which assume a 5 percent annual real GDP growth rate. R&D target is assumed to be achieved by a tax credit to private investors for 50 percent of increment and direct government expenditure for remaining 50 percent.

seem to rise beyond this range. If, therefore, a primary goal of programs to raise the relative share of R&D in the DCs and ECs is to expand domestic productivity, there do not seem be sufficiently large net benefits available to qualify as strong or phenomenal investments. Such countries would be better advised to invest in human capital and governance to establish solid frameworks within which knowledge spillovers from access to international technologies are optimized.

This pessimistic conclusion is offset considerably, however, if there are large usage spillovers, as shown in the final two columns of Tables 22.2 and 22.3. In Table 22.2, for example, column

8 shows that over 40 years the additional domestic and international consumer gains from an 18 percent spillover rate would procure discounted program benefits of between $32 billion and $46 billion, using the different discount factors. At the same time, program costs would not change much because they are modeled to end in year 15. These assumptions then generate notably larger B/C ratios of between 2.3 and 2.7. With the larger 30 percent spillover rate the B/C ratio would rise to between 3.2 and 3.9, marking the program as potentially quite successful. In Table 22.3, where the large emerging countries would expand their R&D ratios aggressively to 1.5 percent of GDP

Table 22.3 Computations of discounted benefit-cost ratios for incremental R&D targets in emerging countries: Raise RD/GDP ratio to 1.5 percent by 2030 (benefits and costs in $b)

Parameter	1	2	3	4	5	6	7		8	9
e private	0.6	0.8	0.6	0.6	0.6	0.6	0.6		0.6	0.6
e public	0.8	0.8	0.8	0.8	0.8	0.8	0.8		0.8	0.8
s weighted	0.6	0.7	0.6	0.6	0.6	0.6	0.6		0.6	0.6
Burden	0.2	0.2	0.3	0.2	0.2	0.2	0.2		0.2	0.2
Fixed cost	0.01	0.01	0.01	0.005	0.01	0.005	0.005		0.005	0.005
Innovation	0.01	0.01	0.01	0.01	0.04	0.04	0.04		0.18	0.30
Tax rate	0.25	0.25	0.25	0.25	0.25	0.25	0.2		0.25	0.25
Disc at 3%	NPV	NPV	NPV	NPV	NPV	NPV	NPV		NPV	NPV
Ben 15	143.7	179.2	143.7	143.7	159.6	159.6	159.6	Ben 40	347.2	486.5
Cost 15	132.2	159.9	163.8	129.5	131.4	128.7	129.1	Cost 40	128.6	127.8
B/C 15	1.09	1.12	0.88	1.11	1.22	1.24	1.24	B/C 40	2.70	3.81
Ben 25	149.2	184.8	149.2	149.2	181.9	181.9	181.9			
Cost 25	132.2	159.9	163.8	129.5	131.4	128.7	129.1			
B/C 25	1.13	1.16	0.91	1.15	1.38	1.41	1.41			
Disc at 5%	NPV	NPV	NPV	NPV	NPV	NPV	NPV		NPV	NPV
Ben 15	118.2	147.4	118.2	118.2	131.3	131.3	131.3	Ben 40	242.7	328.6
Cost 15	108.7	131.5	134.7	106.5	108.0	105.8	106.1	Cost 40	105.8	105.2
B/C 15	1.09	1.12	0.88	1.11	1.22	1.24	1.24	B/C 40	2.29	3.12
Ben 25	121.9	151.2	121.9	121.9	146.4	146.4	146.4			
Cost 25	108.7	131.5	134.7	106.5	108.0	105.8	106.1			
B/C 25	1.12	1.15	0.91	1.14	1.35	1.38	1.38			

Source: Author's calculations, which assume a 3.5 percent annual real GDP growth rate. R&D target is assumed to be achieved by a tax credit to private investors for 50 percent of increment and direct government expenditure for remaining 50 percent.

by 2030, the available benefits would mount to between $243 billion and $487 billion, albeit with similar B/C ratios.

To conclude, assessments of policies to generate higher R&D ratios in developing and emerging countries depend a great deal on program goals and likely outcomes. In discussing science and technology as a sustainable development goal, the UN emphasized expanding the access of poor countries to international knowledge. In this context the basic computations seem most relevant. Growing the intensity of domestic R&D expenditures would not appear to be an objective with a large net payoff. However, if such programs could

procure significant external consumer gains across borders, R&D programs could accomplish notable net benefits. This latter point must be tempered by reality, however: there is scarce evidence in the literature or history of such external gains from DCs and ECs.

Benefits and Costs of Expanded International Skilled-Labor Mobility

Many international economists argue that one policy that would greatly increase global efficiency and welfare, while raising incomes in the developing world, is significant relaxations of barriers to cross-border immigration and emigration, including temporary movements of labor (van der Mensbrugghe and Roland-Holst, 2009; Walmsley and Winters, 2005). In the words of Clemens (2011), the world is leaving "trillion dollar bills on the sidewalk." Indeed, the welfare gains from removing international mobility barriers, as calculated by various simulation models, are staggering, ranging from 67 percent to 147 percent of global GDP (Hamilton and Whalley, 1984; Iregui, 2005; Klein and Ventura, 2007; Moses and Letnes, 2004). In comparison, the potential gains from removing all remaining barriers to merchandise trade amount to perhaps 1 percent of world GDP (Anderson and Martin, 2005; Gourinchas and Jeanne, 2006; Hertel and Keeney, 2006).

The reason for this large gap in welfare impacts is that there are big differences between wages in high-income countries and low-income countries. Accordingly, even partial liberalization of legal migration could attract large flows of labor, moving workers from low-productivity locations to high-productivity locations. Moreover, much of these income gains would be sent back to origin countries as remittances, generating net income gains in both sending and receiving countries. This is not the case for trade liberalization, which only increases productivity on the margin. To put this in basic welfare terms, labor migration generates "rectangles" of income gains, while trade liberalization achieves smaller "triangles" of efficiency increases.[5] Labor migration also affects native wages in both source and host countries, which is accounted for in the following calculations.

The focus here is marginal changes in the temporary mobility of skilled managerial and technical workers (MTWs). Such flows have the basic effects discussed earlier but also raise two kinds of welfare externalities to account for. Fiscal externalities refer to the possibility that public investments in the education of workers in the source nation are lost when they move abroad and that these workers' departure diminishes the remaining tax base. Productivity externalities refer to the possibility that the presence of technically skilled workers in an economy may generate more

efficiency in other workers and firms through innovation, learning, and the attraction of high-technology foreign direct investment (FDI). The extent to which these impacts exist is much debated, but little answered, in the empirical literature. They are at the heart of concerns in developing countries about "brain drain." I incorporate these possibilities into the analysis as well.

Current Situation

It is impossible to find consistent and systematic data on international flows of skilled managerial and technical workers, particularly on a bilateral basis. Thus, I use the limited available evidence to build a bilateral matrix of stocks of such migrants within the Western Hemisphere, the area on which this analysis is focused. I then use this matrix to construct an assessment of changes in temporary skilled labor flows.

The initial step is to use the database put together by Docquier, Lohest, and Marfouk (2007; hereafter DLM).[6] These figures list for all source countries estimates of the stocks of educated labor (those with at least some tertiary education) that were born in those sources, residing legally in each OECD economy, including Mexico, in census years 1990 and 2000.[7] That is, the database estimates the stocks of foreign-born immigrants and permanent residents, from each origin, with higher education. From this database I calculate such stocks in 2000 for the following sources: Argentina (ARG), Brazil (BRA), Chile (CHL), Mexico (MEX), Canada (CAN), and the United States (USA), along with aggregates for Central America (CAM), the Caribbean (CAR), and the rest of South America (SAM). Because only Canada, Mexico, and the United States are destinations in the data, I made assumptions about what relative migration would look like in other

---

[5] Of course, both can result in dynamic gains over time, which does not change the basic message. For more details, see Maskus (2014).

[6] Available at www.abdeslammarfouk.com/dlm-database .html.

[7] All data used here refer to legal migration.

directions, based on distance and the share of tertiary-educated workers (taken from the World Bank's World Development Indicators [WDI]) in the source nations.[8] This procedure enabled computation of bilateral stocks of tertiary migrants in 2000. However, because not all tertiary-educated workers are managerial and technical workers, I adjust the stocks based on estimates of the share of MTWs in tertiary-educated workers in each source. Finally, to update these estimates to 2010, I incorporated data from the United Nations on the bilateral stocks of foreign-born legal migrants.[9] These figures refer to all migrants, regardless of educational status. Applying 2000 bilateral shares of tertiary education among migrants, and the proportion of MTWs, I then computed 2010 bilateral migrant stocks.

The 2010 estimates are provided in Table 22.4, which may be read from left to right to note source to destination. In the aggregated areas the intra-area migrant stocks are positive because people do move from, say, Ecuador to Colombia. Canada and the United States are large net destination countries. By these calculations the United States hosted over 1.9 million MTWs in 2010. The Caribbean sends large numbers of skilled workers to Canada and the United States but relatively few to other Latin American locations. There were nearly 705,000 in-migrants from Mexico into the United States in 2010, making Mexico the largest source. Among the emerging regions, Mexico and Argentina absorb the most MTWs. The United States supplies by far the largest volume of such skilled workers to Mexico, pointing out the two-way nature of this trade. There are also proximity effects: Chile is the largest source of Argentine in-migrants.

Innovation Zones: The Idea

The policies posited to increase temporary MTW migration are straightforward. Specifically, I consider a joint decision by countries in the Western Hemisphere to increase their availability of work visas by particular percentages of their total in-migrant MTW stocks in 2010, with the visas available to eligible skilled workers from anywhere among participant nations. This is the essential idea of an "innovation zone" in which skilled workers with visas would be permitted to circulate freely and work for a lengthy period, say 10 years, among countries in the zone. Workers wishing to get such a visa must demonstrate that they have appropriate credentials and an offer of an employed position in one of a designated set of management or scientific and technical fields or that a recognized commercial or academic organization sponsors them for this treatment. Visa grantees would be permitted to bring immediate family members with them to make such circulation attractive.

Two types of visa relaxations are considered in the analysis: a one-time, 5 percent increase that is implemented immediately, with economic effects working out in the impact year and then being sustained through 2030, and a 20 percent increase phased in over five years. More broadly, I consider two types of innovation zones. One is North–South, including the United States and Canada on the one hand and the Latin American and Caribbean countries and regions on the other. The second is a South–South arrangement, involving just the emerging and developing countries of Latin America and the Caribbean. Following this analysis I offer a rough guess about the potential impacts of extending free labor circulation worldwide in a "global innovation zone."

Model and Assumptions

I put together a partial-equilibrium model of the MTW flows that would ensue from the visa policy changes and offer an assessment of the welfare benefits and costs. I assume that the policy interventions are permanent but consider just the impacts of visas issued from 2016 through 2030. In this context, note that a visa issued in 2030 would be valid for ten years, so I consider the economic effects through 2040.

---

[8] Details of such assumptions are available on request.

[9] United Nations, Population Division, Department of Economic and Social Affairs, *Trends in International Migrant Stock: Migrants by Destination and Origin, 2010*, at http://esa.un.org/MigOrigin/.

Table 22.4 Estimates of intra-Americas bilateral migrant stocks of managerial and technical workers, 2010

Origin	Destination									TOTAL
	CAR	MEX	CAM	ARG	BRA	CHL	SAM	CAN	USA	
CAR	12,870	450	1,255	77	12	57	2,486	56,361	369,138	442,707
MEX	629	–	3,737	678	229	760	3,155	13,582	704,815	727,586
CAM	277	2,015	11,563	15	26	43	158	10,218	142,167	166,483
ARG	720	2,476	454	–	6,938	21,540	20,956	5,804	48,253	107,140
BRA	330	740	268	7,292	–	2,927	16,294	5,782	81,989	115,622
CHL	652	1,243	681	65,937	6,089	–	8,292	10,166	30,130	123,189
SAM	2,813	3,785	533	58,395	6,323	10,373	38,870	26,576	188,247	335,917
CAN	2,433	1,816	552	282	302	881	1,350	–	382,787	390,403
USA	30,211	125,147	4,889	1,762	2,551	2,848	7,199	136,944	–	311,550
TOTAL	50,935	137,673	23,933	134,437	22,471	39,429	98,761	265,433	1,947,527	2,720,599

Notes: CAR = Caribbean, MEX = Mexico, CAM = Central America, excluding Mexico, ARG = Argentina, BRA = Brazil, CHL = Chile, SAM = other South America, CAN = Canada, USA = United States.
Source: Computed by author from sources detailed in text.

The model is presented in Appendix 2, along with parameter values and ranges.[10] I assume that the visas are increased by 5 percent (or 20 percent phased in over time) of each country's estimated initial MTW inward stock and that the demand for them arises across source countries (including Canada and the United States) in proportion to their initial shares. I assume further that wage changes and tax collections in each source and destination country are based on this initial bilateral mobility, which is problematic, for it does not capture the possibility of intercountry mobility across zone members of MTWs during visa duration. However, this additional within-visa mobility would almost surely raise benefits more than it would raise costs, meaning the basic B/C ratios are likely biased downward.

I assume that the visas are fully taken up, whether by individuals or employees of corporations or universities. Thus, in each country or region both inward and outward skilled-labor movements go up. This has impacts on wages of nonmigrant MTWs, depending on labor-demand elasticities, estimates of which I take from the literature. In fact, changes in these parameters make virtually no difference in the implied welfare estimates, and I keep them fixed in all policy simulations.

Following is the list of benefits and costs that I compute. The largest benefit is the real income gain to those who become mobile within the region. I calculate the wage gains to be the difference between destination and source wages, adjusted for the inherent productivity differential, which is a key parameter. To be conservative I choose a low value (0.2) and a high value (0.5) for it. This means that a mover from, say, Brazil to Canada gains just 20 percent or 50 percent of the wage gap between those countries. Regarding these international wage gaps, some difficult questions need to be addressed. First, it is unreasonable to imagine that skilled workers moving from a high-wage location to a low-wage location would agree to be paid less than their existing Canadian salaries. Thus, I make the asymmetric assumption that such movements are not accompanied by any wage (productivity) loss. Second, it makes little sense to suppose that the wage gap between

sources and destinations would remain the same over time, given that low-wage developing countries are likely to grow faster than high-wage developed countries over the next 15 years. Thus, I permit a 2 percent wage catch-up between low-wage sources and high-wage destinations per year.

Third, the distribution of the gains to mobility depends on the degree to which real wage increases are remitted as income payments back to the source countries. The most recent microdata surveys suggest that about 70 percent of high-skilled migrants from developing countries send remittances home and that the average annual remittance is around $5,000 (Gibson and McKenzie, 2010). Within the model these figures imply a remittance rate of 0.32, which I take to be the high estimate, using 0.2 at the low end. Note that the size of remittances does not affect the overall within-zone welfare calculations, but does help determine the distribution of gains and losses between countries.

An element that does matter for welfare is the "fiscal externality" of labor mobility, which is at the heart of the brain drain (BD) controversy (Gibson and McKenzie, 2011). Popular understanding of BD points to the loss of tax revenues in origin nations as highly skilled workers migrate abroad and to the loss of human capital. Regarding taxes, I follow the U.S. tradition of taxation at destination for all countries. That is, the United States taxes the incomes of even temporary in-migrants, such as those on H-1B visas. I also assume that remittances are taxed as gross income at the destination and that source countries choose not to engage in double taxation and therefore leave remittances untaxed. Next, tax-revenue changes per se are not welfare impacts. Rather, the welfare effects depend on how changes in taxes affect real productivity, whether through impacts on infrastructure or factor supplies. Although there are numerous ways to approach this question, the most neutral is to figure that where a country loses (gains) tax revenues on labor incomes it must increase (reduce) the revenues collected otherwise to replace them. These

[10] See Maskus (2014) for a full description of the model.

changes then reduce (raise) economic welfare via the marginal excess tax burden imposed on the economy, as noted in the model equations.

The other component of potential brain drain is the loss of human capital, which itself may have spillover productivity effects. Specifically, a loss of human capital could reduce the productivity of remaining workers. Similarly, emigration of health professionals could lower health status by reducing the supply of doctors and nurses. Moreover, it may be that remaining workers are of lower quality than those who departed, or that there simply are not enough MTWs to meet local needs. Several observations must be made here. First, extensive empirical analysis has failed to find evidence of significant human-capital externalities (Clemens, 2011). Next, although it is intuitive that net BD should be the outcome of skilled labor movements, more recent theory suggests that the opposite idea, of an endogenous "brain gain," is perhaps more likely. Specifically, the opportunity to move abroad for higher wages and better working conditions can induce more young people to invest in schooling, resulting in a higher home stock of educated labor (Mountford, 1997). Note that the proposal considered in the present analysis relates to brain circulation rather than potential brain drain through permanent emigration.

Given these factors, I am skeptical about the conclusion of any brain drain or brain gain human capital externalities. Nonetheless, the issue continues to drive policy concerns about skilled-worker emigration (United Nations Conference on Trade and Development [UNCTAD], 2012). Thus, in supplementary calculations of the North–South innovation zone I add a cost factor roughly attempting to capture these potential externalities. I do this by raising for developing countries the marginal excess burden of the tax loss on gross outward MTW movements by 50 percent (e.g., from 0.2 to 0.3).

A potentially more relevant factor is the possibility of technological spillovers and dynamic innovation effects, which is supported by empirical literature. Circulating business travelers have a positive and causal impact on patenting in the United States by firms in destination countries

(Hovhannisyan and Keller, 2012). FDI is, to a great extent, the process of transferring advanced technologies to advantageous production locations, in large part by movement of skilled managers and engineers among facilities. Finally, there are significant productivity spillovers from inward FDI and technology licensing (Keller, 2010).[11] Calculating such spillovers from temporary labor mobility is quite difficult. In this context I make a series of assumptions, all designed to be conservative about the magnitude of such effects, which are discussed in Maskus (2014). These assumptions together imply that for each $1 billion in wages earned by MTW visa recipients in the North–South case, there is a spillover real GDP gain at the destination of $15 million, with a smaller impact in the South–South case.[12]

It is possible to envision another source of GDP gains that would be spread across the innovation zone. Openness to trade seems to be pro-growth, and trade liberalization generates dynamic gains significantly greater than static models would predict, due to greater product variety and innovation (Broda and Weinstein, 2006; Rutherford and Tarr, 2002; Wacziarg and Welch, 2008). In principle, greater openness to mobility of skilled labor should have a similar effect, particularly because foreign-born technical workers are disproportionately involved in innovation (Hunt and Gauthier-Loiselle, 2010; Kerr, 2013; Stuen et al., 2012). Despite such findings, there is no clear evidence on which to base a computation of a growth dividend. Thus, I simply note the possibility that induced growth could add significantly to program benefits without adding specific estimates.

---

[11] It is worth noting that because these kinds of positive learning effects are stronger in countries with an established capacity to undertake R&D, there likely is an important complementarity between the R&D targets analyzed earlier and innovation zones. That is, a joint policy of increasing R&D and issuing more MTW circulation visas could have technology benefits greater than the sum of the individual projects.

[12] More generally, such spillovers could occur anywhere within the zone, depending on where the movers work and transfer their knowledge gained.

Results

The initial scenario I consider is an innovation zone among the countries of the Western Hemisphere (excluding Cuba), permitting a 5 percent increase in bilateral flows of MTWs in proportion to their initial shares. For comparison purposes, this visa relaxation would translate into about 136,000 workers circulating in the region, with the largest share going to the United States at 97,000 workers. This may be compared to the current cap in the United States of 65,000 H-1B visas, so it is a significant rise. This increase is assumed to be implemented in 2015 and have full effects, beginning in 2016 and lasting through 2040. Note that the idea is for these flows to continue through time, whether through extended visas or new workers as older visas expire, so the program benefits and costs could be expected to continue well beyond that time frame.

The results for a set of medium parameter estimates are given in Table 22.5. Participating countries and members are arrayed on the left-hand side and various welfare impacts by country are in the columns. Note first that there are large gains in income to the MTW movers, around $16.3 billion when discounted at 3 percent. About $3.2 billion would be remitted back to source countries. The implied economic efficiency gains are small in both source and destination locations, and they have no effective impact on the welfare calculations. Source countries lose about $2.2 billion in welfare due to lower tax collections on outflows, but destinations, including the developing economies, gain in the aggregate around $2.8 billion. Most of the developing countries in fact suffer net losses from these fiscal externalities. The technology spillovers in destinations are small, estimated at $1.6 billion over 25 years. This reflects both the limited amount of mobility modeled and the modest spillover parameters.

It is clear that total program benefits far exceed costs for all countries with the exception of Canada. Among developing nations the ratios range from 5.9 in Chile to over 47 in Central America. For the developing countries this presentation of large net gains is misleading, for the great bulk comes from income gains to workers who

leave. These should be considered gains to the workers, not the source countries, though in this case the latter do benefit from remittances. These are included in the "net impact source" column, where the gains for developing countries are up to $1.1 billion in Mexico. The impact in Chile is small because only 6,000 workers leave that country, and because its MTW wage is already high, the income gains do not support significant remittances.

The final column lists benefit-cost ratios when the gains to movers (and therefore remittances as well) are excluded to focus on the fiscal and technological externalities. Here the absence of remittance income means that the B/C ratios are below unity for Brazil and Chile, though Mexico and Argentina sustain significant net benefits.

As for the overall program ratios, the appropriate figure is 9.5, placing skilled labor visas within an innovation zone nearly in the "phenomenal" range. Again, however, this large net benefit is largely due to moving workers enjoying higher real wages abroad. Taking them out achieves a program B/C ratio of 2.0, which is still noteworthy.

Three further calculations with this basic model should be mentioned. First, using the high parameter estimates, implying greater induced innovation and spillovers, more than doubles the program B/C ratio, from 9.5 to 21.3. This reinforces the idea that an ability to absorb and improve technological information arriving through labor mobility is important to garner net benefits. Second, accounting for the potential negative human-capital externalities from brain drain, which requires a higher marginal excess tax burden in southern countries, reduces the B/C ratios for those countries, and the overall program ratio falls from 9.5 to 8.2 using medium parameter values. Finally, the available net benefits from establishing a limited South–South innovation zone are considerably lower, though the B/C ratio remains above unity, at 2.9. This suggests that to establish considerable efficiency and spillover gains in the region the inclusion of Canada and the United States is paramount.

To gain a sense of the maximum program effects available, consider a 20 percent increase in bilateral MTW visas, phased in over time, and including Canada and the United States. This situation

Table 22.5 Computations of discounted benefit-cost ratios for North–South Western Hemisphere Innovation Zone: 5 percent increase in visas for managerial and technical workers, ten-year duration (medium parameter values)

Parameter values: $\delta = 0.2$, $\rho = 0.2$, $i_{ns} = .06$, $i_{ss} = .04$

Benefits and costs ($m)		Inc gains out-movers	Remit to source	Eff cost source	Tax loss source	Net impact source	Eff gain destination	Tax gain destination	Spill gain destination	Net impact destination	Total benefits	Total costs	B/C ratio	Without movers B/C ratio
		A	B	C	D	B+C+D	E	F	G	E+F+G	A+E+F+G	D		
disc 3%	CAR	4,024.0	804.8	−14.8	−161.4	628.6	0.1	70.6	144.9	215.6	4,239.6	−161.4	26.3	1.3
	MEX	6,780.3	1,356.1	−10.6	−272.5	1,073.0	0.3	271.1	537.0	808.4	7,588.7	−272.5	27.9	3.0
	CAM	1,581.0	316.2	−0.4	−33.7	282.1	0.0	14.1	29.5	43.6	1,624.6	−33.7	48.2	1.3
	ARG	591.8	118.4	−0.3	−27.7	90.4	0.3	62.3	85.9	148.6	740.4	−27.7	26.8	5.4
	BRA	812.1	162.4	−0.1	−47.4	114.9	0.0	13.6	17.8	31.3	843.4	−47.4	17.8	0.7
	CHL	343.8	68.8	−1.4	−65.1	2.3	0.1	20.1	20.6	40.8	384.6	−65.1	5.9	0.6
	SAM	2,073.6	414.7	−1.2	−114.6	298.9	0.1	36.9	73.0	110.0	2,183.5	−114.6	19.1	1.0
	CAN	114.1	0.0	−12.1	−801.3	−813.4	4.0	378.2	157.5	539.6	653.7	−801.3	0.8	0.7
	USA	0.0	0.0	−0.9	−6,56.6	−657.5	26.4	1,892.1	557.6	2,476.1	2,476.1	−656.6	3.8	3.8
	TOTAL	1,6320.7	3,241.3	−41.9	−2,180.2	1,019.2	31.4	2,758.8	1,623.8	4,414.0	20,734.6	−2,180.2	9.5	2.0
		Inc gains out-movers	Remit to source	Eff cost source	Tax loss source	Net impact source	Eff gain dest	Tax gain dest	Spill gain dest	Net impact destination	Total benefits	Total costs	B/C ratio	Without movers B/C ratio
disc 5%	CAR	3,383.0	676.6	−12.2	−133.2	531.2	0.1	58.3	119.5	177.9	3,560.9	−133.2	26.7	1.3
	MEX	5,700.2	1,140.0	−8.8	−224.8	906.4	0.2	223.7	443.1	667.0	6,367.2	−224.8	28.3	3.0
	CAM	1,329.1	265.8	−0.3	−27.8	237.7	0.0	11.6	24.3	35.9	1,365.1	−27.8	49.0	1.3
	ARG	497.5	99.5	−0.3	−22.8	76.4	0.3	51.4	70.9	122.6	620.1	−22.8	27.2	5.4
	BRA	682.7	136.5	−0.1	−39.1	97.4	0.0	11.2	14.7	25.8	708.5	−39.1	18.1	0.7
	CHL	289.0	57.8	−1.2	−53.7	2.9	0.1	16.6	17.0	33.7	322.7	−53.7	6.0	0.6
	SAM	1,743.2	348.6	−1.0	−94.6	253.1	0.1	30.4	60.2	90.7	1,834.0	−94.6	19.4	1.0
	CAN	95.9	0.0	−10.0	−661.1	−671.1	3.3	312.0	129.9	445.2	541.2	−661.1	0.8	0.7
	USA	0.0	0.0	−0.8	−541.8	−542.5	21.8	1,561.1	460.1	2,043.0	2,043.0	−541.8	3.8	3.8
	TOTAL	13,720.8	2,725.0	−34.6	−1,798.9	891.5	25.9	2,276.3	1,339.8	3,642.0	17,362.7	−1,798.9	9.7	2.0

involves far larger increases in within-hemisphere circulation of MTWs. With every annual increase in mobility the impacts on source and destination labor markers are calculated, and the database is updated for the following year. Despite the permanence of the policy I compute impacts only through 2040.

Results are in Table 22.6 and rely on the high parameter values. Not shown are the total increases in within-zone mobility, which amount to over 500,000 MTW visas across the hemisphere. Whatever the political feasibility of such a policy, it would generate very large income growth for circulating professionals, who would gain an NPV of over $158 billion in income over the 25-year period, discounted at 3 percent. This increase would result in over $63 billion in additional remittances under the assumptions here. Again, efficiency costs in sources and efficiency gains in destinations are small in relation to total program effects. Welfare impacts associated with tax changes (fiscal externalities) are considerably larger, with a loss in sources of $8.7 billion, which is more than offset by gains in destination countries of over $14.6 billion.

The potential gains in GDP from spillovers into local TFP growth also would be considerably larger in this case. Discounted at 3 percent, such effects would amount to $6.9 billion in additional real GDP. Note that about three-fourths of this increase would go to Mexico, Canada, and the United States, where the cross-border circulation and associated learning and network economies would be greatest. Nonetheless, there would be notable gains in the Caribbean, South America, and Argentina as well.

This larger visa program expands both costs and benefits, resulting in an overall B/C ratio of around 21, with large net gains in the developing countries. To be sure, the bulk of these net benefits come from wage increases earned by circulating workers who get to practice their professions in higher-wage areas. However, there are additional net gains arising from expanded tax revenues and spillover productivity gains from greater circulation of skilled workers.

To summarize this model, even a modest increase in MTW visas within a Western Hemisphere innovation zone, especially one including Canada and the United States, would generate large net benefits for its participants. Most of these gains would go to the workers themselves, however, and how they would be split among countries and regions would depend on remittances and tax policy. The gains from technological spillovers are small in relation to the full program effects and, from a political-economy standpoint, may not warrant the political costs of such a change. They are real, however, and offer a net benefit in knowledge acquisition to participant countries. Moreover, if these impacts were to induce further within-zone innovation increases, a possibility not considered here, the net gains would be correspondingly larger.

These rough calculations should be treated with caution, though I believe they are a reasonable guide to the kinds of essentially static outcomes one could anticipate with expanded MTW visa circulation. It is difficult to know whether these computed effects are underestimates or overestimates of what might ensue from innovation zones. In my view, the net gains are likely understated for at least two reasons. First, there is a complementarity between the mobility of skilled workers and the volumes of technology flows through trade, FDI and licensing. In that sense, a positive response of technology flows to expanded visas would markedly increase the spillover benefits over time. Second, as discussed earlier, there may be a growth dividend associated with greater MTW mobility, in line with what has been experienced from openness to trade and FDI.

We might also speculate on what effects could emerge from a global innovation zone, which would be an agreement among all WTO members to increase their visa allocations and permit free circulation within those visa periods. Building a database for analyzing this idea would be challenging given the limited information available about bilateral mobility patterns. As a simple benchmark, however, consider that the Western Hemisphere constitutes about one-third of world GDP, though it has a somewhat smaller portion of global managerial and technical workers. In that context, it would not be out of line to anticipate a scale of benefits and costs that would more than double their levels here.

Table 22.6 Computations of discounted benefit-cost ratios for North–South Western Hemisphere Innovation Zone: 20 percent increase in visas for managerial and technical workers phased in over five years, ten-year duration (high parameter values)

Parameter values: $\delta = 0.5$, $\rho = 0.32$, $i_{ns} = .06$, $i_{ss} = .04$

Benefits and costs ($m)		Inc gains out-movers	Remit to source	Eff cost source	Tax loss source	Net impact source	Eff gain destination	Tax gain destination	Spill gain destination	Net impact destination	Total benefits	Total costs	B/C ratio	Without movers B/C ratio
		A	B	C	D	B+C+D	E	F	G	E+F+G	A+E+F+G	D		
disc 3%	CAR	39078.3	15699.9	-225.6	-643.6	14830.7	2.1	281.8	579.4	863.3	39941.7	-643.6	62.1	1.3
	MEX	65846.5	26454.2	-162.1	-1086.4	25205.7	4.1	1081.8	2144.2	3230.2	69076.7	-1086.4	63.6	3.0
	CAM	15353.7	6168.4	-5.4	-134.5	6028.6	0.1	56.1	117.6	173.7	15527.4	-134.5	115.5	1.3
	ARG	5747.4	2309.0	-4.6	-110.3	2194.1	5.2	248.4	342.6	596.3	6343.7	-110.3	57.5	5.4
	BRA	7886.4	3168.4	-1.3	-188.9	2978.2	0.0	55.8	75.6	131.5	8017.9	-188.9	42.4	0.7
	CHL	3338.7	1341.4	-21.8	-259.4	1060.1	1.6	90.1	90.5	182.2	3520.9	-259.4	13.6	0.7
	SAM	20137.2	8090.2	-18.1	-456.9	7615.2	1.1	149.2	297.9	448.2	20585.4	-456.9	45.1	1.0
	CAN	1107.9	0.0	-184.9	-3194.7	-3379.6	61.0	1770.0	1626.6	3457.6	4565.6	-3194.7	1.4	1.1
	USA	0.0	0.0	-14.4	-2617.9	-2632.3	402.8	10854.6	1616.2	12873.7	12873.7	-2617.9	4.9	4.9
	TOTAL	158496.0	63231.5	-638.4	-8692.6	53900.5	478.2	14587.9	6890.7	21956.8	180452.8	-8692.6	20.8	2.5
disc 5%	CAR	34325.3	13578.8	-193.7	-556.7	12828.5	1.8	243.8	501.1	746.7	35072.0	-556.7	63.0	1.3
	MEX	57837.7	22880.2	-139.2	-939.6	21801.4	3.6	935.7	1854.5	2793.8	60631.5	-939.6	64.5	3.0
	CAM	13486.3	5335.1	-4.6	-116.3	5214.1	0.1	48.5	101.7	150.3	13636.5	-116.3	117.2	1.3
	ARG	5048.3	1997.1	-4.0	-95.4	1897.7	4.5	214.9	296.4	515.7	5564.0	-95.4	58.3	5.4
	BRA	6927.2	2740.3	-1.1	-163.4	2575.8	0.0	48.3	65.4	113.8	7040.9	-163.4	43.1	0.7
	CHL	2932.6	1160.1	-18.8	-224.4	917.0	1.4	77.9	78.3	157.5	3090.2	-224.4	13.8	0.7
	SAM	17687.9	6997.2	-15.5	-395.2	6586.5	1.0	129.0	257.6	387.6	18075.6	-395.2	45.7	1.0
	CAN	973.2	0.0	-158.7	-2763.1	-2921.8	52.4	1530.8	1406.9	2990.1	3963.3	-2763.1	1.4	1.1
	USA	0.0	0.0	-12.4	-2264.2	-2276.6	345.8	9388.2	1397.9	11131.9	11131.9	-2264.2	4.9	4.9
	TOTAL	139218.5	54688.8	-548.1	-7518.2	46622.5	410.6	12617.0	5959.7	18987.3	158205.8	-7518.2	21.0	2.5

Concluding Remarks

This chapter has considered two potential ideas for expanding the access of developing countries to advanced global technologies and technical information. The first was for developing and emerging countries to implement policies that would raise the share of R&D in GDP to targeted levels by 2030. Under the assumptions of the model there would be notable benefits available in terms of knowledge and learning externalities. However, these gains would be largely offset by increases in costs of financing the expansion (or diversion) of resources into R&D. The B/C ratio rarely exceeds about 1.4 in the most optimistic scenarios, ranking this suggestion rather low in comparison with other potential sustainable development goals. Thus, emerging and developing countries likely would be better advised to focus on other forms of gaining better access.

The second idea presents a more attractive alternative, which is to form innovation zones among participant countries, within which technical and professional workers could circulate and work freely for up to ten years. Even a modest, one-time expansion of visas within a North–South Western Hemisphere innovation zone would offer a large B/C ratio, ranging between 9.5 and 20.8. An aggressive (20 percent) visa expansion over five years would establish a far larger scale of benefits and costs, but retain a similar B/C ratio. Most of these gains come from higher salaries earned by workers, who may be expected to send more remittances home. The spillover productivity gains that could emerge from brain circulation are smaller but still quite significant. Excluding the direct income gains to movers, these visa increases still may be expected to generate benefit-cost ratios of about 2, with large net benefits to the more open developing countries, such as the Caribbean, Mexico, and Argentina.

There remains much we do not know about how circulatory patterns and endogenous responses in terms of growth in FDI, transfer of R&D facilities, and establishment of research networks that would emerge within innovation zones. Given the significant responsiveness of technology flows to expanded movements of managerial and engineering labor that has been found in the literature,

I suspect these endogenous effects could be large. Certainly, they are worth further study.

Appendix 1

Equations for Partial Equilibrium Model of R&D Policies

This simple PE model is slightly adapted from that in Lester (2012), who performed a benefit-cost analysis of two Canadian policies: an R&D tax credit and a "contribution funding" program with extensive reporting requirements. As noted in the text, I assume that DCs and ECs, as groups, implement an R&D tax credit to encourage 50 percent of the required incremental gain in real R&D spending and offer direct grants as government expenditure for the other 50 percent.

Variable and parameter list:

	Variable or parameter	Range
I	Target real R&D by year	Varies by year
e_p	Spillover parameter from private R&D	0.6, 0.8
e_g	Spillover parameter from public R&D	0.8
ε	Absolute value of R&D price elasticity	1.0
s_p	Effective subsidy rate to private R&D	0.2, 0.4
s_g	Effective subsidy rate to public R&D	1.0
c	Marginal program compliance cost	0.008
a	Marginal program administrative cost	0.0015
i	Domestic innovation productivity gains	0.01, 0.04
i'	Global innovation usage gains	0.18, 0.30
b	Marginal excess tax burden	0.2, 0.3
t	Marginal effective tax rate on GDP	0.2, 0.25
f	Fixed cost parameter to firms	0.005, 0.01
g	Fixed cost parameter to government	0.005

Model equations:

Weighted subsidy rate:	$s = 0.5 * s_p + 0.5 * s_g$
Spillover benefits private:	$L = (I * e_p * \varepsilon(s - c))/(1 + (s - c)) * \varepsilon$
Spillover benefits public:	$L = (I * e_g * \varepsilon(s - c))/(1 + (s - c)) * \varepsilon$
Induced innovation benefits:	$D = i * I$ or $D = I' * I$
Efficiency loss:	$P = (I/(1 + (s - c) * \varepsilon)) * [(s - c) + 0.5 (s\text{-}c)^2 * \varepsilon - (s + a) * (1 + (s - c) * \varepsilon]$
Financing costs:	$B = b * (s * I + A - t * (L + P))$
Fixed costs to firms:	$F = f * I$
Administration costs:	$A = g * I$
Welfare impact:	$W = L + D + P - B - F - A$

Appendix 2

Equations for Partial Equilibrium Model of Innovation Zones

This basic model is designed to capture the effects of relaxations in skilled-labor visas on behalf of managerial and technically skilled workers, permitting free work circulation within the region for ten years, which may be renewed though the visa levels remain higher permanently. The policy considered is for countries to raise their skilled-labor visas by 5 percent of existing inward PTW migrant stocks, allocated across the bilateral source shares of those stocks. This is done in year 0 (2015) and has immediate economic effects beginning in 2016.

Model equations:

Initial MTW labor forces:	M_s^0, M_d^0
Growth in bilateral labor flows:	$E_{sd} = \alpha_{sd} * v * M_d^0$
Total outward movers:	$E_s = \sum_d E_{sd}$
Total inward movers:	$E_d = \sum_s E_{ds}$
Wage change at source:	$W_s^1 = W_s^0(1 - \eta_s * (E_s/L_s))$
Wage change at destination:	$W_d^1 = W_d^0(1 + \eta_d * (E_d/L_d))$
Income gain to movers:	$\Delta Y_{st} = \delta * \sum_d (E_{sd} * (W_d^1 - W_s^0) * (1-\theta)^t)$
	if $W_d^0 > W_s^0$
	0 otherwise
Bilateral remittances:	$\Delta R_{dst} = \rho * \Delta Y_{sdt}$
Efficiency loss source:	$B = 0.5 * Es(W_s^0 - W_s^1)$

Variable and parameter list:

Variable or parameter		Range
M_d	Initial PTW migrants in destination	Varies by country
$L_d,$ L_s	Initial PTW labor force in destination, source	Varies by country
v	Percentage expansion of PTW circulation visas	.05 1-year
α_{sd}	Share of bilateral PTW flows from s to d	Varies by flow
η_d, η_s	Elasticity of labor demand in d, s	(–0.25, –0.35)
δ	Productivity differential	0.2, 0.5
ρ	Remittance rate	0.2, 0.32
θ	Wage catch-up per year	0.02
t_s, t_d	Average effective income tax rate in s, d	(0.15, 0.15)
b_s, b_d	Marginal excess tax burden in s, d	(0.2, 0.2)
i_{NN}	North–North productivity spillover	0.015
i_{NS}	North–South productivity spillover	0.03, 0.06
i_{SN}	South–North productivity spillover	0.0075
i_{SS}	South–South productivity spillover	0.02, 0.04
i	Domestic innovation productivity gains	0.04
i'	Global innovation usage gains	0.09

Efficiency gain destination:	$D = 0.5 * E_d(W_d^0 - W_d^1)$
Fiscal externality source:	$Z_s = -bt_s W_s^0 E_s$
	Assume no double taxation of R
Fiscal externality destination:	$Z_d = bt_d \delta W_d^1 E_d$
	if $W_d^1 > W_s^0$
	$Z_d = bt_d W_s^0 E_d$
	otherwise
Spillover GDP N-N:	$I_d = i_{NN} W_s^0 E_{ds}$
	USA to CAN and CAN to USA
Spillover GDP N-S:	$I_d = i_{NS} \sum_s W_s^0 E_{ds}$
	USA or CAN to others
Spillover GDP S-N:	$I_d = i_{SN} \delta \sum_s W_d^1 E_{ds}$
	Others to USA or CAN

Spillover GDP S-S:
$$I_d = i_{SS}\delta\sum_s W_d^1 E_{ds}$$

Others if $W_d^1 > W_s^0$

$$I_d = i_{SS}\sum_s W_s^0 E_{ds}$$

Others if not

Induced innovation benefits:

$$N = i * I_d \text{ or } N = i^* * I_d$$

Gain to movers: $\quad W_m = \Delta Y_{st} - \Delta R_{st}$

Welfare change source: $\quad W_s = \Delta R_{st} - B + Z_s - H$

Welfare change destination: $\quad W_d = D + Z_d + I_d + N$

Global welfare impact: $\quad W = W_m + W_s + W_d$

References

Aghion, Philippe and Peter Howitt. 1998. *Endogenous Growth Theory*. Cambridge: MIT Press.

Anderson, Kym and Will Martin. 2005. Agricultural Trade Reform and the Doha Development Agenda. *The World Economy* 28: 1301–27.

Bloom, Nick, Rachel Griffith and John Van Reenen. 2002. Do R&D Tax Credits Work? Evidence from a Panel of Countries, 1979–1997. *Journal of Public Economics* 85: 1–31.

Broda, Christian and David E. Weinstein. 2006. Globalization and the Gains from Variety. *Quarterly Journal of Economics* 121: 541–85.

Clemens, Michael A. 2011. Economics and Emigration: Trillion-Dollar Bills on the Sidewalk? *Journal of Economic Perspectives* 25: 83–106.

Docquier, Frederic, Olivier Lohest, and Abdeslam Marfouk. 2007. Brain Drain in Developing Countries. *World Bank Economic Review* 21: 193–218.

Eaton, Jonathan and Samuel J. Kortum. 1996. Trade in Ideas: Patenting and Productivity in the OECD. *Journal of International Economics* 40: 251–78.

Gibson, John and David McKenzie. 2010. The Economic Consequences of "Brain Drain" of the Best and Brightest: Microeconomic Evidence from Five Countries. World Bank, Policy Research Paper 5394.

2011. Eight Questions about the Brain Drain. *Journal of Economic Perspectives* 25: 107–128.

Gonzalez, Xulia and Consuelo Pazo. 2008. Do Public Subsidies Stimulate Private R&D Spending? *Research Policy* 37: 371–389.

Goolsbee, Austan. 1998. Does Government R&D Policy Mainly Benefit Scientists and Engineers? *American Economic Review: Papers and Proceedings* 88: 298–302.

Gourinchas, Pierre-Olivier and Olivier Jeanne. 2006. The Elusive Gains from International Financial Integration. *Review of Economic Studies* 73: 715–41.

Griffith, Rachel. 2000. How Important is Business R&D for Economic Growth and Should the Government Subsidize It? The Institute for Fiscal Studies, Briefing Note no.12.

Hamilton, Bob and John Whalley. 1984. Efficiency and Distributional Implications of Global Restrictions on Labour Mobility. *Journal of Development Economics* 14: 61–75.

Hertel, Thomas and Roman Keeney. 2006. What Is at Stake: The Relative Importance of Import Barriers, Export Subsidies, and Domestic Support. In *Agricultural Trade Reform and the Doha Development Agenda*, ed. Kym Anderson and William Martin (Washington, DC: World Bank).

Hovhannisyan, Nune and Wolf Keller. 2012. International Business Travel: An Engine of Innovation? Center for Economic Policy and Research Working Paper 7829.

Hunt, Jennifer and Marjolaine Gauthier-Loiselle. 2010. How Much Does Immigration Boost Innovation? *American Economic Journal: Macroeconomics* 2: 31–56.

Iregui, Ana Maria. 2005. Efficiency Gains from the Elimination of Global Restrictions on Labour Mobility. In *Poverty, International Migration and Asylum*, ed. George J. Borjas and Jeff Crisp (New York: Palgrave-Macmillan).

Keller, Wolfgang. 2004. International Technology Diffusion. *Journal of Economic Literature* 42: 752–82.

2010. International Trade, Foreign Direct Investment, and Technology Spillovers. In *Handbook of the Economics of Innovation*, ed. Bronwyn Hall and Nathan Rosenberg (Amsterdam: Elsevier-North Holland).

Kerr, William R. 2013. U.S. High-Skilled Immigration, Innovation, and Entrepreneurship: Empirical Approaches and Evidence. Harvard Business School Working Paper, No. 14-017.

Klein, Paul and Gustavo Ventura. 2007. TFP Differences and the Aggregate Effects of Labor

Mobility in the Long Run. *The B.E. Journal of Macroeconomics* 7: Article 10.

Kohler, Christian, Philippe Laredo, and Christian Rammer. 2012. *The Impact and Effectiveness of Fiscal Incentives for R&D.* Manchester Institute of Innovation Research.

Lester, John. 2012. Benefit-Cost Analysis of R&D Support Programs. *Canadian Tax Journal* 60: 793–836.

Maskus, Keith E. 2006. Information as a Global Public Good. In *Expert Series Number Six: Knowledge.* (Stockholm: Task Force on Global Public Goods).

2014. Benefits and Costs of the Science and Technology Targets for the Post-2015 Development Agenda. Copenhagen Consensus Center, working paper.

Maskus, Keith E. and Ruth L. Okediji. 2014. Legal and Economic Perspectives on International Technology Transfer in Environmentally Sound Technologies. In *Intellectual Property Rights: Legal and Economic Challenges for Development*, ed. M. Cimoli, G. Dosi, K. E. Maskus, R. L. Okediji, J. H. Reichman, and J. E. Stiglitz (Oxford: Oxford University Press).

Moses, Jonathon W. and Bjorn Letnes. 2004. The Economic Costs to International Labor Restrictions: Revisiting the Empirical Discussion. *World Development* 32: 1609–26.

Mountford, Alexander. 1997. Can a Brain Drain Be Good for Growth in the Source Economy? *Journal of Development Economics* 53: 287–303.

Nelson, Richard R. 2005. Linkages between the Market Economy and the Scientific Commons. In *International Public Goods and Transfer of Technology under a Globalized Intellectual Property Regime*, ed. Keith E. Maskus and Jerome H. Reichman (Cambridge: Cambridge University Press).

Rodriguez-Pose, Andres and Riccardo Crescenzi. 2006. R&D Spillovers, Innovation Systems and the Genesis of Regional Growth in Europe. Bruges European Economic Research Papers 5.

Romer, Paul M. 1990. Endogenous Technological Change. *Journal of Political Economy* 98: S71–102.

Russo, Benjamin. 2004. A Cost-Benefit Analysis of R&D Tax Incentives. *Canadian Journal of Economics* 37: 313–35.

Rutherford, Thomas F. and David G. Tarr. 2002. Trade Liberalization, Product Variety and Growth in a Small Open Economy: A Quantitative Assessment. *Journal of International Economics* 56: 247–52.

Stuen, Eric, Ahmed Mushfiq Mobarak, and Keith E. Maskus. 2012. Skilled Immigration and Innovation: Evidence from Enrollment Fluctuations in U.S. Doctoral Programs. *Economic Journal* 122: 1143–76.

United Nations Conference on Trade and Development (UNCTAD). 2012. *Least Developed Countries Report 2012: Harnessing Remittances and Diaspora Knowledge to Build Productive Capacities* (Geneva: UNCTAD).

Van der Mensbrugghe, Dominique and David Roland-Holst. 2009. Global Economic Prospects for Increasing Developing-Country Migration into Developed Countries. United Nations Development Programme Human Development Research Paper 2009/50.

Wacziarg, Romain and Karen Horn Welch. 2008. Trade Liberalization and Growth: New Evidence. *World Bank Economic Review* 22: 187–231.

Walmsley, Terrie L. and L. Alan Winters. 2005. Relaxing the Restrictions on the Temporary Movement of Natural Persons: A Simulation Analysis. *Journal of Economic Integration* 20: 688–726.

Westmore, Ben. 2013. R&D, Patenting and Growth: The Role of Public Policy. OECD Economics Department Working Papers, no. 1047, OECD Publishing.

22.1 Alternative Perspective

KAMAL SAGGI

Summary

Saggi finds that the Maskus chapter provides a clear and convincing analysis of his chosen policy initiatives and there is little he disagrees with. Productivity is perhaps the most important determinant of a country's living standards in the long run. It can either continue producing the same with fewer resources or invest in R&D that delivers new or better products. In principle, developing countries could use the fruits of foreign R&D, but in practice conducting domestic R&D can facilitate exchange of technology by lowering transaction costs as new knowledge and technological change accumulates.

To the extent that intellectual property rights in developing countries have been strengthened by ratification of the TRIPS agreement, incentives for R&D should have been strengthened worldwide. Numbers of patent applications have indeed grown rapidly, particularly in Asia and most especially in China, which now takes the global lead in patent numbers. This nicely mirrors the observed increase in R&D expenditures, but of course tells us nothing about the quality of the output or its economic value. Maskus's proposals, taken together, could help to boost the quality of R&D output.

Because inventors can extract only a fraction of the value of their innovation and because R&D generates so many unforeseen externalities, it seems clear that market forces will tend to fund too little R&D. This makes a case for encouraging more, but policies are likely to produce more benefits if they increase research rather than development, which is likely to produce fewer spillovers.

The author's views on the large welfare gains possible by allowing free movement of labor are correct. The case is the same as for capital: to allow all factors of production to be employed most efficiently by allowing them to move freely throughout the world. Loosening the constraint on international labor mobility allows the world economy to narrow the gap between the marginal products of labor in different locations and thereby increase world output. To set against this is the fact that source countries may lose out from the "brain drain." This cannot be ignored because, although human capital externalities are difficult to quantify, this does not mean they are unimportant.

In addition to Maskus's two proposals, Saggi suggests FDI as another potentially fruitful area for government policy. Trade between subsidiaries and the headquarters of multinational companies may account for one-third of world trade, and foreign direct investment is now the dominant channel through which firms serve customers in foreign markets. Given the importance of multinationals, initiatives aimed at encouraging the international flow of technology must take the incentives of such firms into account. FDI is becoming more important in developing countries, which now have one-third of the total global stock. Whereas mergers and acquisitions are common in industrialized countries, FDI in developing countries is more likely to involve construction of new production facilities. Both types, however, carry the potential for technology transfer.

More and more R&D is being conducted abroad, so already helping economies to grow. Given the overwhelming importance of FDI to R&D and technology transfer and the scarcity of resources in developing countries, it might be easier for such countries to secure productivity gains by encouraging FDI to their local economies and having multinationals invest in R&D as opposed to doing it entirely on their own. Increased labor mobility will be difficult to achieve, despite the large benefits it can produce, but encouraging FDI may be a much easier way for developing countries to increase their R&D and increase their participation in global production networks.

419

22.2 Alternative Perspective

PAMELA SMITH

Summary

The *technology transfer* goals under consideration by the UN Open Working Group include general and technology-specific targets, as well as goals that are foundational to technology transfers that occur through trade and foreign direct investment. The ultimate goal of these targets is to promote sustainable economic development.

Pamela J. Smith reviews the technology transfer proposals of Keith E. Maskus and then offers a broader perspective on policy options.

Maskus proposes two policies that have the potential for increasing technology transfers to developing countries. The first is to increase the ratio of *R&D spending* as a percentage of GDP in developing countries. Maskus calculates benefit-cost ratios for developing and emerging countries corresponding with a range of R&D spending scenarios. He concludes that the proposed policies do not qualify as "strong or phenomenal" priorities for the UN agenda. Smith agrees with this conclusion and that developing countries would benefit more from investing in policies that yield a higher benefit-cost ratio.

The second policy is to establish "*innovation zones.*" This would involve offering ten-year visas that permit free mobility of skilled labor among participants in the zones. Maskus calculates benefit-cost ratios for countries that are the source and destination of migrating skilled labor within a North–South zone and South–South zone. He concludes that the proposed policy qualifies as a "phenomenal" priority for the UN agenda. Smith agrees that the technology transfers that would occur within an innovation zone are economically significant, but adds the caveat that benefits and costs vary considerably across source and destination countries of the migrants.

In Smith's assessment, the Maskus analysis is conservative so as not to overestimate the effects of the policies. Smith also notes two intentional omissions. The first is the omission of *international spillovers* in the analysis of the R&D spending policy. The second is the omission of *human capital spillovers* in the analysis of innovation zones. Smith discusses the implications of these omissions, yet concludes that these omissions do not change the basic conclusion regarding the economic significance of the policies and their priority in the UN agenda.

Smith offers broader perspectives from the literature on policy options that support economic development through technology transfers. Smith begins by considering the *channels* for technology transfers including: trade, foreign direct investment, licensing, and labor movements. Second, Smith considers the *developing country conditions* that support technology transfers via these means. The most basic of these conditions are the ability to absorb technologies and adapt them to meet domestic needs. Third, Smith discusses the arguments for *government intervention* to support technology transfers. The basic argument is that the role of government is to create incentives for private actors to generate the socially optimal levels of technology transfers. Fourth, Smith discusses *appropriate policies* to support technology transfers. She highlights findings in the literature on "technology ladders," which suggest an evolution of conditions for technology transfers that roughly correspond with the level of development of countries.

Finally, Smith revisits the Maskus proposals from the broader literature perspective. From this vantage point, she regards the *R&D spending policy* as a "national policy" that targets a basic condition in developing countries needed to absorb and adapt inward flows of technology – the local R&D infrastructure. She concludes that this policy is likely to be most effective for middle-income developing countries that have an existing R&D sector and are at the duplicative imitation or creative imitation stages. Alternatively, she regards the *innovation zone policy* as an "international policy" that supports the circulation of high-skilled labor and whose beneficiaries depend on the size of the zone and its participants. She concludes that this policy is likely to be most effective for middle-income developing countries that would experience inflows of skilled labor, and for low-income developing countries that would receive remittances from labor that has outmigrated. She views these two general policies as superior to technology-specific policies that would likely be less effective at supporting technology transfers and ultimately economic development.

Global Benefits and Costs of Achieving Universal Coverage of Basic Water and Sanitation Services as part of the 2030 Agenda for Sustainable Development

GUY HUTTON*

Glossary

BCR	Benefit-Cost Ratio
DALY	Disability-Adjusted Life-Year
DHS	Demographic and Health Survey
GDP	Gross Domestic Product
JMP	Joint Monitoring Programme
MDG	Millennium Development Goal
MICS	Multiple Indicator Cluster Survey
OD	Open Defecation
ODF	Open Defecation Free
SDG	Sustainable Development Goal
UN	United Nations
UNICEF	United Nations Children's Fund
WASH	Drinking-water, sanitation, and hygiene
WHO	World Health Organization

Introduction

In September 2015, heads of state from all around the world adopted the 2030 Agenda for Sustainable Development, an ambitious plan of action for "people, planet and prosperity," with 17 Sustainable Development Goals (SDGs) and 169 targets. Building on the UN Millennium Declaration and its eight Millennium Development Goals (MDGs; 2000–2015), the 2030 Agenda expands the MDG focus on poverty reduction to cover all aspects of sustainable development in all countries of the world, calling for peace and partnership and the need to leave no one behind. Water is covered as a single issue in Sustainable Development Goal 6, as well as other SDGs such as disaster risk reduction, education, health, nutrition, and gender (UN-Water, 2016a).

Six targets are included in the water goal. Targets 6.1 and 6.2 build on the MDG targets on drinking water and basic sanitation, providing continuity while expanding their scope and refining definitions. Targets 6.3 to 6.6 address the broader water context that was not explicitly included in the MDG framework, such as water quality and wastewater management, water scarcity and use efficiency, integrated water resources management, and the protection and restoration of water-related ecosystems.

Although global costing and cost-benefit studies have been previously conducted (Hutton, 2012; Hutton and Varughese, 2016), and a more recent study examined the approximate costs of an overall water goal (UNU and UNOSD, 2013; UN-Water, 2016b), a new study is required to understand the overall economic returns on expanding and sustainably operating WASH services according to the new service definitions and target dates, as well as the extent to which additional financing can be sourced. Given the large set of development priorities under discussion, and a proliferation from 21 global targets under the MDGs to 169 global targets under the SDGs, and an expansion from 60 to 230 proposed indicators to monitor, there is a risk the next set of goals will be less smart and not maximize the potential impact of the next 15 years. With this in mind, this chapter provides an evidence base with which to compare different WASH targets and world regions by benefit-cost ratio.

* The author was with the World Bank when this chapter was written and is now with UNICEF.

Methods

Aims

The work covered here is part of a larger costing study being conducted by the World Bank in collaboration with United Nations agencies and other partners (Hutton and Varughese, 2016). The aims of this larger study were to estimate global, regional, and country-level costs, benefits, and financing options of safely managed drinking-water supply and sanitation interventions to meet the proposed WASH Targets 6.1 and 6.2. However, as it was conducted earlier, not included in the present study were safely managed water supply and sanitation (a higher standard than "basic") nor basic hygiene (handwashing with soap and water). Neither this study nor the larger study included institutional WASH access such as in schools and healthcare facilities. The specific targets and definitions of indicators proposed essentially include the universal coverage of households with basic WASH services by 2030, with faster acceleration of access for the population groups currently with lowest access. Once the underlying coverage data sets are available, targets that provide a greater proportion of the overall population with more advanced WASH services will be estimated. This chapter provides benefit-cost ratios for basic WASH services.

The Estimation Model

The methods and assumptions are fully described in Hutton and Varughese (2016). A model was constructed using Microsoft Excel©, consisting of one major "input-output" worksheet that calculates costs and benefits of WASH interventions at country, regional, and global levels. This worksheet links to databases on unit costs, coverage, health, and economic variables assembled for each country. As the data were assembled from global databases, the worksheet allows for countries themselves at a later date to change country-specific inputs to remodel the outputs.

The basis of all the calculations are two key statistics, one on population numbers over the study period and the other WASH service coverage in the year 2015 under different service definitions. The model moves populations from lower to higher service levels, calculating the costs and benefits of doing so. This is done for each wealth quintile[1] separately, accelerating coverage at a faster rate to those populations with lower coverage.

Countries and World Regions Included

The quantitative model is run at country level and the results aggregated to give the regional and global totals or averages, weighted by country population size. Countries classified by the World Bank as high-income countries are excluded from the study, except Equatorial Guinea, which was included, as it has below 50 percent sanitation coverage, and Russia, which has coverage closer to 90 percent sanitation coverage but due to its population size still has an important number of child deaths attributed to poor WASH. The majority of countries excluded are high-income countries (see Appendix 1). Several upper-middle-income countries were omitted (Hungary, Western Sahara, Palestine, and several small-island states) due to lack of mortality data from the most recent burden of disease study from WHO (Prüss-Üstun, Bartram, et al., 2014). This leaves a total of 140 countries included in the study. In this current study, results are only presented by MDG region (see Appendix 1)[2] and globally.

Population Estimates

Population size for rural and urban areas was sourced from UN statistics for the latest year (2012) and UN projected estimates to 2030 by urban and rural areas. The countries included represent 6.12 billion (84 percent) of the world's projected 7.3 billion population in 2015, and 7.15 billion (85 percent) of the world's projected

---

[1] Wealth quintiles are created when populations are split by five equal groups according to their wealth level, which is approximated by a household asset index from survey data.
[2] (1) Caucasus and Central Asia (CCA), (2) North Africa (N Africa), (3) Sub-Saharan Africa (SSA), (4) Latin America and the Caribbean (LAC), (5) Eastern Asia (E Asia), (6) Southern Asia (S Asia), (7) South-eastern Asia (SE Asia), (8) Western Asia (W Asia), and (9) Oceania.

Table 23.1 Population (000s) included in study by world region (years 2015 and 2030)

MDG Region	2015	2030
Latin America and the Caribbean	601,160	685,434
Sub-Saharan Africa	987,655	1,421,913
Northern Africa	176,847	210,325
Western Asia	173,001	216,244
Caucasus and Central Asia	83,078	94,555
South Asia	1,793,616	2,085,479
South-East Asia	626,984	715,713
Eastern Asia	1,429,665	1,483,404
Oceania	2,367	2,767
Developed countries	247,304	229,667
World	**6,121,677**	**7,145,501**

8.4 billion population in 2030.[3] In 2015 43 percent of the population in these countries will live in urban areas, rising to 56 percent in 2030. Table 23.1 shows the population distribution of included countries across MDG regions in 2015 compared with 2030.

It is recognized that a single "rural" versus "urban" breakdown does not reflect the global diversity of settlement types and densities. However, as this present study draws on the only global database of drinking water, sanitation and hand-washing coverage – provided by the Joint Monitoring Programme – the study is limited by the singular rural/urban distinction of the JMP's data sets (WHO and UNICEF, 2014). Instead, this study explores the potential for cost variation in different technology options, which provide lower and upper estimates for costs. For the health impact analysis, populations are disaggregated into three age groups (0–4 years, 5–14 years, and 15+ years) due to the differential information available for these groups on disease incidence.

Service Definitions and Data Sources

The WASH targets in SDG 6 include universal access to safely managed WASH services.

- Target 6.1: By 2030, achieve universal and equitable access to safe and affordable drinking water for all.

- Target 6.2: By 2030, achieve access to adequate and equitable sanitation and hygiene for all and end open defecation, paying special attention to the needs of women and girls and those in vulnerable situations.

Targets need concrete definitions to conduct an economic analysis and to monitor them consistently over time. Given that safely managed services represent a higher service definition than "improved" water supply and sanitation in MDG target 7C, this study focused on assessing the economic returns of lower service levels. The Joint Monitoring Programme has termed the lower service levels as "basic," which are similar (but not identical) to the MDG definitions.

Eliminating open defecation is a necessary milestone on the way to everyone having basic sanitation. Open defecation is when excreta of adults or children (a) are deposited (directly or after being covered by a layer of earth) in the bush, a field, a beach, or other open area; (b) are discharged into a drainage channel, river, sea, or other water body; or (c) are wrapped in temporary material and discarded (WHO and UNICEF, 2006). Note, however, that if sewage is flushed from a toilet to a drain that leads directly to canal, river, or open water body without treatment first, it is currently classified by the Joint Monitoring Programme as "improved" sanitation. Hence (b) listed earlier does not apply, although from an environmental standpoint it is effectively open defecation.

- Indicator used for current study: Percentage of population practicing open defecation. Two other proposed indicators are not used due to current lack of global data.[4]
- Data source: JMP currently compiles and reports data on open defecation by rural and urban areas, with defecation practice recorded at the overall

---

[3] These figures do not take into account the fact that some countries will have graduated to high income level by 2030 and hence will no longer be classified as a developing country.

[4] These include (1) percentage of households in which no one practices open defecation, and (2) percentage of children under five whose stools are hygienically disposed of.

household level.[5] The latest estimates (2012) were projected by JMP to 2015 using current trends.

- Incremental costs: given that this target does not require "improved" sanitation (or "basic" under the new terminology), lower cost options have been selected to meet this target. Hence the calculations assume that the lowest cost options are used to end open defecation – which includes a private traditional latrine in rural areas and private or communal toilets in urban areas. However, note that latrine options with lower capital cost may not last as long as a more expensive option – hence the cost advantage is not so great when considering annual equivalent costs (including renovation or replacement).

Basic drinking water at home. Drinking water is water used by humans for drinking, cooking, food preparation, personal hygiene, or similar purposes (WHO and UNICEF, 2006). Households are considered to have a "basic" drinking water service when they use water from a household piped water supply; a protected community source such as a well, spring, and borehole; or collected rainwater. In terms of water source type, the previous definition of "improved" water is the same as "basic" water, except that the latter requires that the total collection time is 30 minutes or less for a round-trip. This definition varies from the MDG definition in that the latter did not include criteria for collection time.

- Indicator used for current study: Percentage of population using a protected community source or piped water with a total collection time of 30 minutes or less for a round-trip, including queuing.
- Data source: JMP currently compiles and reports data on use of improved sources by urban and rural areas, but with no consideration of the time to source. Hence, using the same data sets that report time to source, an adjustment has been made by JMP to generate the numbers on this indicator. The latest estimates (2012) were projected by JMP 2015 using current trends.
- Incremental costs: this involves estimating the full costs of providing access to a basic source within a 30-minute round-trip to households

currently without access. Basic sources include protected wells and springs sources either available at community or private household level. For estimating costs, the majority of unserved populations are assumed to be supplied by a protected community borehole/tubewell (50 percent of unserved) or a protected dug well (50 percent of unserved).

Basic sanitation at home. To be counted as "basic" sanitation, facilities must effectively separate excreta from human contact and ensure that excreta do not reenter the immediate environment. The same quality of sanitation facility types as the MDG Target 7c are considered.

- Indicator used for current study: Percentage of population using a basic sanitation facility.
- Data source: JMP currently compiles and reports data on use of improved facility that is owned and used by the household, with rural and urban breakdowns. Use of an improved facility of a neighbor is excluded from the current estimate. The latest estimates (2012) were projected by the JMP 2015 using current trends.
- Incremental costs: this involves estimating the full costs of providing access to basic sanitation to households currently without access. For the costing exercise, the mix of basic facilities assumed to be used by households includes a pour-flush pit latrine (50 percent of unserved) and a dry pit latrine (50 percent of unserved) in rural areas, and a flush toilet to septic tank (50 percent of unserved) and any type of pit latrine (50 percent of unserved) in urban areas.

Progressive elimination of inequalities in access. Future indicators will be disaggregated on the following four dimensions.

1. Income level: by income or wealth quintiles
2. Geographical setting: urban versus rural areas
3. Type of urban settlement: slums versus formal urban settlements
4. Population group: disadvantaged groups versus the general population

[5] If the respondent answers that any adult household members are practicing open defecation, then the entire household is classified as practicing open defecation.

Due to current data constraints, disaggregation in the present study will be made for the first two of these: wealth quintiles and urban/rural area.

Coverage for New Population (Population Growth)

The total population of the 140 countries included in this study is predicted to grow from 6.12 billion in 2015 to 7.15 billion in 2030. Therefore, a coverage assumption is needed for this additional global population of 1 billion. Assuming household sizes stay roughly the same, additions to the population will need to be covered by new dwellings. However, the challenge lies in estimating the incremental costs of investing in improved drinking-water systems and sanitation facilities that are paid for in new dwellings, given that these facilities are difficult to separate from the infrastructure costs of the new dwelling itself. Given the lack of cost data on the additional cost of WASH facilities in new dwellings, the same unit costs are used as for "adding" WASH services to dwellings currently without them.

Cost Estimation

The total intervention cost consists of all resources required to put in place, operate, and maintain a WASH service. The terminology of IRC's WASH-Cost project is used here for investment costs (Capital expenditure = "CapEx"), major maintenance costs (Capital maintenance expenditure = "CapManEx") and regular recurrent costs (Operating expenditure = "OpEx"; Fonseca, Franceys, et al., 2010). CapEx ideally includes planning and supervision, hardware, construction and house alteration, protection of water sources, education, and behavior change. CapManEx ideally includes maintenance of hardware, replacement of parts, and renovation or rehabilitation when required. OpEx ideally includes operating materials to provide a service, regulation, ongoing protection and monitoring of water sources, water treatment and distribution, and continuous education activities. For this study, emptying of septic tanks and latrines is considered as capital maintenance as it is more likely to happen every few years as opposed to every year.

Further disaggregation of costs is possible, but cost data are limited and hence only these three categories are were used.[6] "Direct expenditures" used in IRC's WASHCost are included as software costs in the categories. Due to lack of unit cost data on some cost components, software costs for initial program delivery including behavior change are added as 10 percent of the CapEx, and CapManEx is estimated at 30 percent of the CapEx every five years for hardware maintenance, while for safe excreta management the emptying and treatment of septic tanks and pit latrines is considered an additional cost.

In presenting cost estimates, a distinction is made between serving the unserved and sustaining services to the served:

1. Incremental costs of extending WASH services: the capital costs of extending access to basic WASH for those currently not having access.
2. Costs of sustaining WASH services: these include the costs of maintaining, renovating and replacing WASH services for all populations with any WASH facility.

These two estimates are aggregated to estimate total costs of both extending and sustaining WASH services to the target populations. To meet coverage targets in the post-2015 proposals, the cost-benefit analysis presented in this chapter focuses on the economic returns of extending access to the unserved (including all cost categories).

Cost data were obtained through an extensive search of the peer-reviewed published literature as well as gray literature (project documents, agency reports) sourced from contacts and the internet. In addition, cost data available were sent to experts in the 40 countries with the highest number of unserved populations for verification and request to provide latest country-based estimates. Basic classification of the technology types are according to service definitions earlier. The studies obtained, the countries they were conducted in, and what

---

[6] For example, IRC's WASHCost project distinguished between: (1) capital expenditure, (2) operational costs, (3) capital maintenance, (4) direct support costs, (5) indirect support costs, and (6) loan interest.

Table 23.2 High- and low-cost scenarios for technology options for unserved populations

Location	Low-cost scenario	Baseline scenario	High-cost scenario
Basic Water			
All	100% dug well	50% borehole or tubewell and 50% dug well	100% borehole or tubewell
Basic Sanitation			
Rural	100% dry pit	50% pour-flush to pit and 50% dry pit	100% pour flush to pit
Urban	100% any pit latrine	50% septic tank or sewerage with treatment (according to current coverage) and 50% any pit latrine	100% septic tank or sewerage

service definitions their data covered will be provided in a future report version. Cost data were available for at least one service definition for at least half the countries. The methodology used by the Disease Control Priorities project (Edition 3) was used to obtain costs in U.S. dollars in the baseline year, as follows:

- Step 1: data are tabulated in local currency for the year in which they were collected.
- Step 2: costs are updated to 2015 prices using the GDP deflator for that country.[7]
- Step 3: costs are converted to U.S. dollars using the exchange rate from mid-2014.

For countries without data for a given service type and level, data were extrapolated from a neighboring country with similar economic development level for which data were available. The price observed in the country with data was adjusted for difference in price levels, using GDP per capita expressed at Purchasing Power.[8]

Given that cost data between different studies even in the same country can be highly variable, and the major data source being agency reports as opposed to peer-reviewed journals, the results of a global costing exercise are highly uncertain. One major source of uncertainty is the quality and representativeness of the cost data sets obtained, given they were extrapolated from single settings to an entire country or to a neighboring country. It therefore required a judgment call on which data most likely represented the average context in each country. A second set of uncertainties relate to what level of service the unit costs refer to, given there are many subtle differences in technologies and management approaches that determine the

eventual unit costs. A third uncertainty relates to the expected duration of hardware. Often, due to poor maintenance and lack of spare parts, the actual life span will vary from the expected (engineered) life span. To deal with the latter, this present study opted to use a theoretical engineered life span, using the same assumption of length of life per technology type.[9] In order to provide a service for the entire life span, capital maintenance costs required to sustain the services were included. A fourth uncertainty is the present value of future costs, which is calculated using a baseline discount rate of 3 percent. A final set of uncertainties relate to an uncertain future: population growth and migration being different from those projected and the impact of a variable and changing climate on the populations access to WASH services thus requiring WASH services to be more resilient. There is limited experience with climate adaptation in the WASH sector, and guidelines on optimal technology options for climate resilience do not yet exist.

This present study explores uncertainty in discount rate, value of prevented deaths, and differences between income groups. In the baseline analysis, a mix of technologies are assumed to be adopted by populations, shown in Table 23.2. A future publication will examine variations in technology mix,

---

[7] For the years 2013–5 without data, the GDP deflator for 2012 is used.

[8] For example, if the unit cost is US$ 30 in the source country (Country A), with a GDP at purchasing power of $1000, then the extrapolated unit cost to Country B with a GDP at purchasing power of $500 would be US$ 15.

[9] Borehole/tubewell: 20 years; dug well: 10 years; septic tank: 20 years; pit latrine: 8 years.

Table 23.3 Benefits of drinking water supply, sanitation, and handwashing

Benefit	Water	Sanitation
Included benefits		
Health	• Averted cases of diarrheal disease • Averted cases of malnutrition-related diseases	• Averted cases of helminths
Health economic	• Costs related to diseases such as healthcare, lost productivity, and premature mortality	
Time value	• Travel and waiting time averted when water supply and sanitation access is improved	
Excluded benefits		
Other health	• Dehydration from lack of access to water	• Dehydration from not drinking due to poor latrine access (especially women) • Less flood-related health impacts
Reuse of nutrients		• Use of human faeces or sludge as soil conditioner and fertilizer in agriculture
Energy		• Use of human (and animal) waste as input to biogas digester leading to fuel cost savings and income opportunities
Education	• Improved educational levels due to higher school enrollment, attendance, and completion rates • Impact of averted childhood malnutrition on education	
Water treatment		• Less household time spent treating drinking water, including boiling
Water security		• Safe reuse of treated wastewater in agriculture
Environment		• Improved quality of water supply available from surface and groundwater, and related savings
Leisure and quality of life/intangibles	• Leisure and nonuse values of water resources • Reduced effort of associated with water hauling and gender impacts	• Safety, privacy, dignity, comfort, status, prestige, aesthetics, gender impacts
Reduced access fees		• Reduced payment of for toilets with entry fee
Property	• Rise in value of property	
Income	• Increased incomes due to more tourist income and business opportunities	

differences in duration of the life of technologies, and low and high unit cost estimates.

Benefit Estimation

Benefit Overview

A large range of economic and social benefits can result from improved WASH services. Table 23.3 presents the main ones, indicating those that have been included and excluded in this study. As is evident from the table, more benefits have been excluded than included.

Although many of these benefits have previously been evaluated in context-specific studies, evidence is lacking from sufficient countries to enable a credible global assessment.

The economic value of benefits is the sum of financial transactions, hypothetical or actual cash savings, as well as an imputed value for nonmarket benefits, where resources are used in more productive or welfare-enhancing activities as a result of the WASH intervention. Economic values exclude transfer payments such as taxes and subsidies. Once these benefits included in Table 23.3 are

Table 23.4 Relative risk reductions in health impacts for WASH interventions

Intervention	Reduction in diarrheal disease (and consequent diseases) compared to unimproved facility	Reduction in helminths compared to no or unimproved facility
Water supply		
Improved community water source	34%	0%
Basic piped water	45%	0%
Piped water, high quality	79%	0%
Sanitation		
Improved on-site sanitation, no formal excreta management (100% coverage)	28%	50%
Improved sanitation with formal excreta management (100% coverage)	69%	100%

Source: Column 2 - Water and sanitation (Wolf, Prüss-Üstun, et al., 2014); Column 3 – assumption.

aggregated, they reflect a lower bound on the overall societal benefit or utility gained from implementing an intervention. It is a lower bound because several benefits of WASH services are excluded from the monetary estimates. However, it should be understood that economic values do not necessarily reflect the direct financial impact. For example, the cash impact on the household is influenced by employment opportunities and availability of subsidized healthcare, while the budget impact on a line ministry depends on cost recovery policies (e.g., on healthcare). Economic figures therefore do not allow the private sector to accurately assess the market potential for providing a drinking water or sanitation service – which instead requires willingness to pay or tariff studies. As a purely financial analysis will undervalue water and sanitation services, the purpose of this study is to estimate the overall costs and benefits to society – thus informing overall debates on the "right" level of coverage, resource allocation, and technology choice for different populations.

Health Benefit Estimation

Over recent decades, compelling evidence has been gathered that significant and beneficial health impacts are associated with improvements in access to safe drinking-water, basic sanitation, and handwashing facilities (Freeman, Stocks, et al., 2014; Wolf, Prüss-Üstun, et al., 2014). The routes of pathogens to affect health via the medium of water are many and diverse. Five different routes of infection for water-related diseases are distinguished: waterborne diseases (e.g., cholera, typhoid), water-washed diseases (e.g., trachoma), water-based diseases (e.g., schistosomiasis), water-related vector-borne diseases (e.g., malaria, filariasis, and dengue), and water-dispersed infections (e.g., legionellosis). Although a full analysis of improved water and sanitation services would consider pathogens using all these pathways, the present study focuses on waterborne and water-washed diseases. At the household level, it is the transmission of these diseases that is most closely associated with poor water supply and sanitation. Moreover, waterborne and water-washed diseases are responsible for the greatest proportion of WASH-related disease burden. For the purpose of estimating health benefits from improving WASH, populations are classified into different starting WASH service points, which relate to a given health risk, shown in Table 23.4.

In terms of burden of disease, the most significant waterborne and water-washed disease is infectious diarrhea. Infectious diarrhea includes cholera, salmonellosis, shigellosis, amoebiasis, and other protozoal and viral intestinal infections. These are transmitted by water, person-to-person contact, animal-to-human contact, and foodborne, droplet, and aerosol routes. As infectious diarrhea is responsible for a major share of the estimated global burden of disease resulting from poor access to water supply and sanitation (Prüss-Üstun, Bartram, et al., 2014), and as there are data for all regions on its incidence rates and deaths, this analysis estimates the reduction in diarrhea incidence rates and premature mortality from diarrhea. In addition, given that environmental risk factors are estimated to account for 50 percent of undernutrition in the developing world, diseases with higher incidence or case fatality due to malnutrition are also included using a method previously applied at country (Hutton, Rodriguez, et al., 2014) and global levels (Hutton, 2012). In this approach, a proportion of cases of respiratory infection and malaria in children 0–5 years old are attributed to poor water supply and sanitation, based on very severe and moderately severe malnutrition rates and determined by region-specific attribution factors estimated by Fishman et al. (Fishman, Caulfield, et al., 2004). Case fatality is also predicted to be affected by WASH interventions, given that malnourished children are more likely to die when they suffer from respiratory infection, malaria, measles, and other infections.

Economic benefits related to health impacts of improved WASH services include three main ones, as previously evaluated (Hutton, 2012):

1. Savings related to seeking less healthcare. Healthcare savings are estimated as a function of treatment seeking rates, medical practices, and unit costs of medical services. Medical practices include the types of treatment given for a disease and the rate of in-patient admission. All these variables fluctuate by disease and country. In addition, patients and their carers incur other treatment-seeking costs such as travel costs.

2. Savings related to productive time losses from disease. Productivity losses are estimated based on disease rates, the number of days absent from productive activities, and the unit value of productive time. Given the extensive surveying required to estimate actual financial losses from lost productive time, an economic value is given instead to time based on the sick person's age using proxies. For adults too sick to carry out normal activities, their time is valued at 30 percent of the average GDP per capita converted to an hourly rate. For children of school age, and for carers spending time

tending sick infants (0–5 years old), their time is valued at 15 percent of the average GDP per capita converted to an hourly rate. Men's and women's time are given the same value.

3. Savings related to reductions in premature mortality. Mortality is valued using the human capital approach. The human capital approach estimates the total present value of future earnings of productive adults, hence considering their future life expectancy. The GDP per capita is used to reflect the economic contribution of the average member of society. To promote equality within policies influenced by cost-benefit analysis, all people within the same country are given the same value, irrespective of age and wealth quintile.

Table 23.5 shows the data values, or ranges, for each health variable used in the analysis.

In the health benefit calculations, results are presented by income quintile using two variables for which data are available by income quintile for most countries, namely WASH coverage and under-five deaths. The latter variable is used to approximate distribution of deaths and morbidity from WASH-related diseases. All other variables for the health economic estimates are based on averages across the entire population. Although the results give an indication of the differences between income quintiles for health economic benefits, it is not known whether true rates would be lower or higher had all the input variables been available by income quintile. The reason for this uncertainty is that other variables could be either higher or lower for poorer people than the nonpoor (e.g., healthcare seeking, healthcare unit costs, impact on work productivity or income), hence with unknown direction of overall cost.

Time Benefit Estimation

Table 23.6 shows the values and data sources for time savings due to closer physical access and less waiting time for water sources and sanitation facilities at home or in the community. For water supply, two round-trips are assumed per household to fulfill their needs for household water supply (min. 20 liters per person per day). Households gaining access to basic improved water supply

Table 23.5 Variables, data sources, and values for health economic benefits, for the example of diarrheal diseases

Benefit by sector	Variable	Data source	Data values
Healthcare costs of disease	Unit cost per treatment	WHO regional unit cost data	Cost per outpatient visit and cost per inpatient day varies by country (Source: WHO CHOICE)
	Number of cases of diarrheal disease	DHS, MICS	Two-week prevalence varies by country, from 3% to 36%
	Visits or days per case	Previous study	One outpatient visit per case seeking care (includes return visits) Av. 5 days for hospitalized cases
	Hospitalization rate Transport cost per visit	Previous study Assumptions	10% of ambulatory cases are hospitalized US$ 0.50 per visit for outpatient and US$ 1.00 per visit for inpatient (includes accompanying persons)
Welfare gained due to days lost from work avoided	Days off work/ episode	Expert opinion	One-day average per episode of diarrhea, five days for ALRI and malaria
	Number of people of working age	UN statistics	Variable by country
	Opportunity cost of time	World Bank data	30% of hourly monetary income, using GDP per capita as the proxy for time value
Welfare gained due to school absenteeism avoided	Absent days/episode	Expert opinion	One-day average per episode of diarrhea, five days for ALRI and malaria
	Number of school-age children (5–14)	UN statistics	Variable by country
	Opportunity cost of time of student	World Bank data	15% of hourly monetary income, using GDP per capita as the proxy for time value
Welfare gained to parents due to less child illness	Days sick	Expert opinion	One-day average per episode of diarrhea, five days for ALRI and malaria
	Number of young children (0–4)	UN statistics	Variable by country
	Opportunity cost of time of carer	World Bank data	15% of hourly monetary income, using GDP per capita to proxy time value

Table 23.6 Variables, data sources, and values for "convenience" time savings

		Access time	
Variable	Data source	Urban areas	Rural areas
Water supply (baseline = distant water source)			
Unimproved source Improved source Household piped water	Expert opinion and evidence review[1]	40 minutes round-trip 20 minutes round-trip Less than 5 minutes round-trip	60 minutes round-trip 20 minutes round-trip Less than 5 minutes round-trip
Sanitation (baseline = open defecation)			
Open defecation Basic (private) sanitation	Expert opinion, studies from Southeast Asia[2]	15 minutes travel time round-trip 5 minutes travel and waiting time round-trip	20 minutes travel time round-trip 5 minutes travel and waiting time round-trip

[1] See reviewed studies (Hutton and Haller, 2004).
[2] From a survey of >5,000 households conducted in six Southeast Asian studies, a single round-trip to place of open defecation was found to require up to 15 minutes in urban areas and from up to 20 minutes in rural areas, varying by country (Hutton, Rodriguez, et al., 2014).

Table 23.7 Total population to serve from 2015 to 2030 to reach universal access to basic services (million)

MDG Region	Drinking water Urban	Rural	Total	Sanitation Urban	Rural	Total
Latin America and the Caribbean	114	19	133	157	40	197
Sub-Saharan Africa	417	521	939	493	639	1,132
Northern Africa	34	15	49	34	16	50
Western Asia	44	19	63	45	20	65
Caucasus and Central Asia	11	12	23	10	6	16
South Asia	345	239	584	473	632	1,305
South-East Asia	189	65	254	159	117	276
Eastern Asia	240	0	240	329	50	379
Oceania	0	0	1	0	0	0
Developed countries	2	0	2	20	7	27
World	**1,396**	**892**	**2,287**	**1,721**	**1,727**	**3,448**

reduces round-trip times from 40 to 20 minutes in urban areas and from 60 to 20 minutes in rural areas. The time saving is a combination of closer access and higher number of water points, leading to less queuing time. For sanitation, in the baseline only one trip per day is assumed for defecation.

Sensitivity Analysis

One-way sensitivity analysis was performed on the value of death, substituting a cost per DALY of US $1,000 and US$5,000 in all countries instead of the value of life using the human capital approach. Also, the economic benefits from preventing premature death were estimated using the value-of-a-statistical life instead of the human capital approach. The value of life of US$2 million was extrapolated to countries based on the difference in GDP per capita in the United States and the target countries, using purchasing power parity values.

Results

Baseline Results

Populations Served

This report presents benefit-cost ratios for basic water and sanitation services for rural and urban areas, by MDG region.[10] The results are presented in this section using the human capital approach to value premature mortality at 3 percent discount rate, while Appendix 2 presents at 5 percent discount rate. The results using DALY rates to value premature mortality are presented in the sensitivity analysis (for 3 percent discount rate) and in Appendix 2 for 5 percent discount rate.

Based on the new indicator definitions for basic water and sanitation, by 2030 a total of 2.3 billion additional people will need to be covered with basic water, and 3.5 billion additional people will need to be covered with basic sanitation (see Table 23.7). For water supply, over 900 million of the unserved reside in sub-Saharan Africa, while for sanitation over 1 billion of the unserved reside in each of sub-Saharan Africa and South Asia.

Overall Results

Table 23.8 shows the annual costs and benefits for ending open defecation and providing universal access to basic water and basic sanitation. For ending open defecation, only rural figures are

[10] A later World Bank–UN report will present a fuller set of results that also includes the costs of reaching and maintaining the proposed WASH targets and the options for financing. In addition, hygiene measures (handwashing) and advanced water supply and sanitation will be assessed.

Table 23.8 Annual costs and benefits to meet and sustain universal access (100 percent coverage), focusing on the projected unserved population in 2015 (US$ billions)

Intervention	DALY value	3% Discount			5% Discount		
		Benefit	Cost	BCR	Benefit	Cost	BCR
Eliminate open defecation	1000	81	14	5.8	73	12	6.0
(rural only)	5000	99	14	7.1	87	12	7.3
Universal access to basic	1000	50	15	3.3	40	13	3.3
drinking water at home	5000	66	15	4.4	54	13	4.2
Universal access to basic	1000	94	33	2.9	81	28	2.9
sanitation at home	5000	107	33	3.3	90	28	3.2

BCR is the amount of times the benefits exceed the costs of an intervention. Note: The annual costs (at 5 percent discount rate) are different from the Hutton and Varughese (2016) estimate, as the latter included only capital costs.

presented, while for the basic service rural and urban figures are aggregated. The BCR of ending open defecation is approximately 5.7 at a DALY value of US$1,000 and approximately 6.9 at a DALY value of US$5,000. At a discount rate of 3 percent, the benefits vary from US$ 80 billion to US$100 billion per year, at DALY values of US$1,000 and US$5,000, respectively. The annual cost – inclusive of capital and operating costs – of ending open defecation over a 15-year period from 2015–2030 is between US$12 billion and US$14 billion.

The BCR of providing basic water is 3.3 at a DALY value of US$1,000, under both 5 percent and 3 percent discount rates. When a DALY has a value of US$ 5,000, the BCR varies from 4.2 to 4.4 under 5 percent and 3 percent discount rates, respectively. The benefits of basic water vary from US$54 billion to US$66 billion per year, at DALY values of US$1,000 and US$5,000, respectively.[11] The annual cost – inclusive of capital and operating costs – of providing basic water supply over a 15-year period from 2015–2030 is approximately US$14 billion, assuming a phased increase in coverage.

The BCR of providing basic sanitation is 2.9 at a DALY value of US$1,000, under both 5 percent and 3 percent discount rates, respectively. When a DALY has a value of US$5,000, the BCR increases to 3.2 and 3.3, under 5 percent and 3 percent discount rates, respectively. The benefits of basic sanitation vary from US$80 billion to US$90 billion per year, at DALY values of US$1,000 and US$5,000, respectively. The annual cost –

inclusive of capital and operating costs – of providing basic sanitation supply over a 15-year period from 2015–2030 varies from US$28 billion to US$33 billion, at 5 percent and 3 percent discount rates, respectively.

The number of deaths averted from basic water supply is expected to be 34 percent of the 500,000 annual deaths, or 170,000 saved lives per year, while for basic sanitation it is expected that 28 percent of the 280,000 annual deaths, or 80,000 saved lives per year. In addition to these averted deaths, there will be additional averted deaths from indirect pathways that are attributed to poor WASH (acute lower respiratory infection, measles, malaria, and others), which is potentially as many as 100,000 per year.

Water Supply

In the following sections, the benefit-cost ratios are presented using the human capital approach to value-prevented deaths. Overall, this methodology gives slightly higher ratios than using the DALY methodology using US$5,000 per DALY averted. However, there is significant variation between regions in the differences between methodologies,

[11] Note that the estimated benefits are the same under 3 percent and 5 percent discount rate as the health and access time benefits are estimated as a present value in the current year, while costs vary under 3 percent and 5 percent discount rate because annualization formula for capital items is dependent on the discount rate.

Table 23.9 Benefit-cost ratios for basic water supply in urban areas, by income quintile (3 percent discount rate)

MDG Region	Q5 (richest)	Q4	Q3	Q2	Q1 (poorest)	Total
Latin America and the Caribbean	2.9	3.1	2.9	3.0	3.1	3.0
Sub-Saharan Africa	2.6	2.9	3.1	3.5	3.5	3.2
Northern Africa	2.3	2.4	2.4	2.5	2.7	2.5
Western Asia	2.6	2.6	2.6	2.7	2.7	2.6
Caucasus and Central Asia	3.1	3.0	3.2	3.2	3.3	3.1
South Asia	1.8	2.2	2.1	2.3	2.4	2.2
South-East Asia	2.4	2.7	2.4	2.5	2.9	2.6
Eastern Asia	5.0	5.4	5.0	5.4	6.2	5.4
Oceania	1.9	1.9	2.2	2.6	3.0	2.3
Developed countries	2.4	2.2	2.4	2.3	2.3	2.4
World	**3.1**	**3.4**	**3.2**	**3.5**	**3.8**	**3.4**

Table 23.10 Benefit-cost ratios for basic water supply in rural areas, by income quintile (3 percent discount rate)

MDG Region	Q5 (richest)	Q4	Q3	Q2	Q1 (poorest)	Total
Latin America and the Caribbean	4.7	5.5	6.7	8.1	10.2	8.2
Sub-Saharan Africa	6.2	6.8	7.2	7.9	8.0	7.3
Northern Africa	8.9	9.1	9.5	9.8	10.4	9.7
Western Asia	6.0	5.6	5.9	5.8	6.4	6.0
Caucasus and Central Asia	9.6	9.1	9.7	9.4	10.1	9.6
South Asia	3.6	4.0	4.4	4.8	5.1	4.5
South-East Asia	6.6	8.4	9.6	9.6	9.8	9.3
Eastern Asia	20.1	20.1	22.1	19.7	11.9	15.9
Oceania	5.1	5.0	5.7	6.8	8.2	6.6
Developed countries	–	–	–	–	15.9	15.9
World	**5.6**	**6.2**	**6.6**	**7.2**	**7.6**	**6.8**

given that the HCA values prevented death based on a country's GDP per capita, whereas the DALY methodology applies the same value across the world.[12]

In urban areas, the benefit-cost ratio for basic water varies between regions 2.2 (South Asia) to 5.4 (Eastern Asia), with a global ratio of 3.4. Ratios are in general higher for poorer populations (see Table 23.9). At 5 percent discount rate, the global benefit-cost ratio reduces from 3.4 to 3.1. Using the value-of-statistical-life, the global BCR increases to 3.6 at a discount rate of 3 percent.

In rural areas, the benefit-cost ratio for basic water varies between regions 4.5 (South Asia) to 16 (Eastern Asia), with a global ratio of 6.8. Again, ratios are higher for poorer populations (see Table 23.10). At 5 percent discount rate, the global benefit-cost ratio reduces from 6.8 to 5.7. Using the value-of-statistical-life, the global BCR increases to 7.3 at a discount rate of 3 percent.

[12] Hence, low-income countries will have a higher BCR under the DALY methodology, whereas middle-income and developed countries in the analysis will have a higher BCR under the HCA methodology.

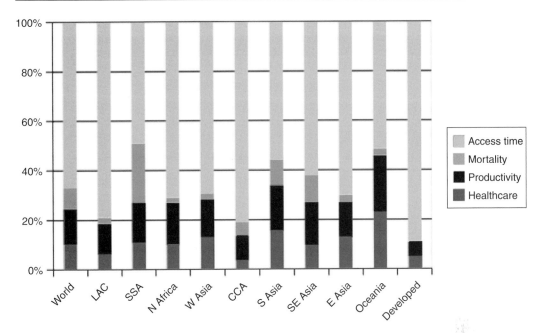

Figure 23.1 *Benefit breakdown for delivering universal access to basic water supply in urban areas*

Figure 23.1 shows the breakdown for different benefits of delivering universal access to basic water supply in urban areas. Globally, the economic value of saved access time accounts for close to 70 percent of the benefits, while healthcare, health-related productivity, and averted mortality each account for between 8 percent and 14 percent of the total. Similar proportions were found for rural areas as for urban areas. Across regions there are some differences, such as higher proportion accounted for mortality reduction in sub-Saharan Africa. In both sub-Saharan Africa and South Asia, health benefits accounted for close to 50 percent of total benefits.

Sanitation

In urban areas, the benefit-cost ratio for basic sanitation varies between regions 1.2 (sub-Saharan Africa) to 5.7 (Oceania), with a global ratio of 2.5. Ratios are marginally higher for poorer populations (see Table 23.11). At 5 percent discount rate, the global benefit-cost ratio reduces from 2.5 to 2.3. Using value-of-statistical-life, the global BCR increases to 3.0 at a discount rate of 3 percent.

In rural areas, the benefit-cost ratio for basic sanitation varies between regions 3.8 (sub-Saharan Africa) to 47 (Oceania), with a global ratio of 5.2. The BCR is higher for the bottom quintile at 5.8 compared to the highest quintile at 4.6 (see Table 23.12). At 5 percent discount rate, the global benefit-cost ratio reduces from 5.2 to 4.8. Using value-of-statistical-life, the global BCR increases to 5.9 at a discount rate of 3 percent.

To eliminate open defecation, simpler sanitation options are feasible. However, these options have a shorter life span and require continued software to motivate communities to remain ODF and repair or replace or their latrine when it stops functioning. When the life span of a simple or traditional latrine is assumed to be one year only, the benefit-cost ratio is 6.0 globally, varying from 3.9 (sub-Saharan Africa) to 33 (Oceania; see Table 23.13). The results are highly sensitive to the assumptions of how long the hardware and software will last – if these are increased to 2 years then the benefit-cost ratios are double those values in Table 23.13. At 5 percent

Table 23.11 Benefit-cost ratios for basic sanitation in urban areas, by income quintile (3 percent discount rate)

MDG Region	Q5 (richest)	Q4	Q3	Q2	Q1 (poorest)	Total
Latin America and the Caribbean	3.2	3.3	3.3	3.3	3.4	3.3
Sub-Saharan Africa	1.1	1.1	1.2	1.2	1.2	1.2
Northern Africa	2.1	2.1	2.2	2.2	2.3	2.2
Western Asia	3.0	3.0	3.0	3.1	3.1	3.0
Caucasus and Central Asia	3.3	3.2	3.3	3.4	3.4	3.3
South Asia	2.6	2.7	2.9	3.0	3.1	2.9
South-East Asia	2.4	2.5	2.5	2.6	2.7	2.5
Eastern Asia	3.8	3.9	3.9	4.1	4.4	4.0
Oceania	5.3	5.3	5.6	6.0	6.1	5.7
Developed countries	3.4	3.4	3.4	3.5	3.7	3.5
World	**2.4**	**2.5**	**2.5**	**2.5**	**2.7**	**2.5**

Table 23.12 Benefit-cost ratios for basic sanitation in rural areas, by income quintile (3 percent discount rate)

MDG Region	Q5 (richest)	Q4	Q3	Q2	Q1 (poorest)	Total
Latin America and the Caribbean	6.9	7.5	7.9	8.2	8.6	8.1
Sub-Saharan Africa	3.8	3.6	3.7	3.9	3.9	3.8
Northern Africa	5.4	5.6	5.8	5.9	6.0	5.8
Western Asia	6.6	6.6	6.8	7.3	8.0	7.3
Caucasus and Central Asia	19.0	19.4	19.5	19.8	21.3	19.9
South Asia	4.9	5.1	5.4	5.7	5.9	5.5
South-East Asia	16.5	18.0	18.0	18.0	17.8	17.8
Eastern Asia	2.9	3.0	3.2	3.2	23.5	12.9
Oceania	44.9	44.9	46.8	50.2	48.1	47.2
Developed countries	33.2	33.3	33.3	33.5	33.8	33.4
World	**4.6**	**4.6**	**5.0**	**5.3**	**5.8**	**5.2**

discount rate, the global benefit-cost ratio stays the same at 6.0. Using the value-of-statistical-life, the global BCR increases to 6.5, at a discount rate of 3 percent.

Figure 23.2 shows the breakdown for different benefits of delivering universal access to basic sanitation in urban areas. Globally, the access time accounts for over 70 percent of the benefits, while mortality accounts for a little over 20 percent and both healthcare and health-related productivity each account for less than 5 percent. Similar proportions were found for rural areas as for urban areas. Across regions there are some differences, such as higher proportion accounted for access time in developed countries.

Sensitivity Analysis

The results of the analyses where premature mortality is converted to DALYs lost and valued at US$1,000 and US$5,000 per DALY across all countries is presented in Table 23.14 and Table 23.15, respectively. Globally the benefit-cost ratios are lower than the main baseline results

Table 23.13 Benefit-cost ratios for eliminating open defecation in rural areas, by income quintile (3 percent discount rate)

MDG Region	Q5 (richest)	Q4	Q3	Q2	Q1 (poorest)	Total
Latin America and the Caribbean	9.1	9.9	10.3	10.6	11.0	10.5
Sub-Saharan Africa	3.6	3.7	3.9	4.1	4.2	3.9
Northern Africa	5.9	6.2	6.4	6.5	6.7	6.4
Western Asia	7.8	7.8	8.0	8.6	9.5	8.6
Caucasus and Central Asia	15.5	15.7	15.9	16.1	16.8	16.1
South Asia	6.0	6.3	6.7	7.0	7.3	6.7
South-East Asia	13.7	14.2	14.4	14.5	14.9	14.2
Eastern Asia	4.2	4.3	4.5	4.5	21.2	13.5
Oceania	31.6	31.6	32.8	35.2	33.3	32.7
Developed countries	22.2	22.3	22.3	22.4	22.6	22.4
World	**5.1**	**5.4**	**5.9**	**6.3**	**6.8**	**6.0**

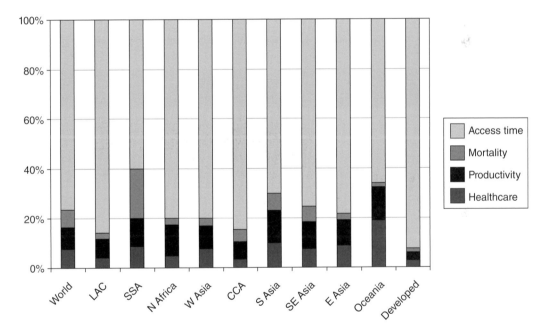

Figure 23.2 *Benefit breakdown for delivering universal access to basic sanitation in urban areas*

(using the human capital approach) when valued at US$1,000 (Table 23.14) and slightly higher than the baseline when valued at US$5,000 (Table 23.15). The overall benefit-cost ratios (in Table 23.8) are closer to the urban BCRs in Tables 23.14 and 23.15 because the costs are heavily weighted toward urban areas where the

intervention costs are estimated to be about twice the costs in rural areas. Although the difference in DALY value is five times, the impact on benefit-cost ratios is not that significant because the majority of benefit comes from time savings. The same tables are presented at a discount rate of 5 percent in Appendix 2.

Table 23.14 Benefit-cost ratios when premature mortality is valued at US$1,000 per DALY averted (3 percent discount rate)

MDG Region	Basic Water		Basic Sanitation		ODF
	Urban	Rural	Urban	Rural	Rural
Latin America and the Caribbean	3.0	8.0	3.3	8.0	10.4
Sub-Saharan Africa	2.1	4.5	0.9	2.7	3.7
Northern Africa	2.4	9.5	2.2	5.8	6.4
Western Asia	2.6	5.8	3.0	7.2	8.5
Caucasus and Central Asia	2.9	9.0	3.2	19.6	15.9
South Asia	2.0	4.2	2.8	5.3	6.4
South-East Asia	2.4	8.8	2.5	17.2	13.8
Eastern Asia	5.3	14.4	4.0	12.7	13.4
Oceania	2.3	6.5	5.7	46.9	32.5
Developed	2.3	15.8	3.5	33.4	22.3
World	**3.1**	**5.1**	**2.4**	**4.5**	**5.8**

Table 23.15 Benefit-cost ratios when premature mortality is valued at US$5,000 per DALY averted (3 percent discount rate)

MDG Region	Basic Water		Basic Sanitation		ODF
	Urban	Rural	Urban	Rural	Rural
Latin America and the Caribbean	3.0	8.2	3.3	8.1	10.5
Sub-Saharan Africa	4.0	8.6	1.3	4.0	5.5
Northern Africa	2.5	9.9	2.2	5.9	6.4
Western Asia	2.7	6.5	3.0	7.6	8.9
Caucasus and Central Asia	3.0	9.5	3.3	20.0	16.2
South Asia	2.9	5.8	3.2	6.2	7.5
South-East Asia	2.6	9.5	2.5	17.8	14.3
Eastern Asia	5.4	14.8	4.0	12.8	13.5
Oceania	2.5	7.0	5.8	49.3	34.1
Developed	2.4	15.8	3.5	33.4	22.3
World	**3.7**	**7.9**	**2.6**	**5.6**	**7.1**

Overall Findings

In summary, the main findings are as follows:

1. Water supply and sanitation give significant economic returns to society. However, several impacts were excluded due to difficulty in monetizing benefits (see Table 23.3), such as environmental benefits and the greater privacy and dignity associated with improved sanitation.

In addition, indirect health impacts including health externalities of communicable diseases were not fully accounted for. Hence if all the benefits could be monetized, the benefit-cost ratios would be significantly higher than those presented.

2. Higher benefit-cost ratios in lower income quintiles, accounted for by the higher health impacts in these population groups (due to worse

baseline situation, hence higher capacity to benefit). This is an interesting finding – and one compelling reason to serve the poorest first.

3. Higher benefit-cost ratios in rural areas than urban areas, accounted for by lower unit costs and higher capacity to benefit from health and access time savings.

4. Higher benefit-cost ratios for water supply than for sanitation. Overall, water supply has higher ratios than in previous global cost-benefit studies (Hutton, 2012), due to developments in the underlying evidence (see conclusions for more comments).

5. The decrease in benefit-cost ratio when using a higher discount rate (of 5 percent instead of 3 percent) is only marginal in most cases because both costs and benefits are (almost) equally incurred in future years.

Conclusions

This study has confirmed that drinking water supply and sanitation both generate high economic returns to society, with returns exceeding costs for all interventions at both 3 percent and 5 percent discount rates. The study showed that economic returns varied between different regions of the world. This variation is partly expected due to different relative price levels of water and sanitation services and different capacity to benefit (such as existing disease rates). The variation is also likely to be due to weak data for some regions and countries (e.g., unit costs of services for Central Asia, Oceania, North Africa, Western Asia, and developed countries). Furthermore, the assumptions on time savings may be less applicable for some regions where there have been no studies on time savings. On the other hand, the most data were available for costs and benefits for countries with the highest numbers of unserved population. Despite the variation, economic returns remain above unity for all regions and interventions.

The results vary compared to previous global studies. The main variance is for water supply, where the benefit-cost ratios presented in this study are at least twice as high compared with the most recent global study. This is partly due to higher health benefits, resulting from an updated meta-analysis on the health impact of basic water supply (34 percent instead of 18 percent reduction in diarrheal disease). It is also due to an updated unit cost database, which has lower unit costs than used in previous studies. A third reason is that in this study some populations receive a lower cost technology (divided between borehole and dug well) than in the previous study, which assumed only borehole. The benefit-cost ratios are also marginally lower for sanitation, comparing the global BCR of 5.5 in the previous study with 3.4 (urban) and 6.8 (rural) in the present study.

Appendix 1

Table 23.16 Countries included and excluded in study, by MDG region

MDG Region	Included	Excluded
LAC	Argentina, Belize, Bolivia, Brazil, Colombia, Costa Rica, Cuba, Dominica, Dominican Republic, Ecuador, El Salvador, Grenada, Guatemala, Guyana, Haiti, Honduras, Jamaica, Mexico, Nicaragua, Panama, Paraguay, Peru, Saint Lucia, Saint Vincent and the Grenadines, Suriname, Trinidad and Tobago, Venezuela	Anguilla, Antigua and Barbuda, Aruba, Bahamas, Barbados, British Virgin Islands, Cayman Islands, Chile, Falkland Islands (Malvinas), French Guiana, Guadeloupe, Martinique, Montserrat, Caribbean Netherlands, Puerto Rico, Saint Kitts and Nevis, United States Virgin Islands, Uruguay, Turks and Caicos Islands
SSA	Angola, Benin, Botswana, Burkina Faso, Burundi, Cameroon, Cape Verde, Central African Republic, Chad, Comoros, Congo, Côte d'Ivoire, Democratic Republic of the Congo, Djibouti, Equatorial Guinea, Eritrea, Ethiopia, Gabon, Gambia, Ghana, Guinea, Guinea-Bissau, Kenya, Lesotho, Liberia, Madagascar, Malawi, Mali, Mauritania, Mauritius, Mozambique, Namibia, Niger, Nigeria, Rwanda, Sao Tome and Principe, Senegal, Seychelles, Sierra Leone, Somalia, South Africa, South Sudan, Sudan, Swaziland, Togo, Uganda, United Republic of Tanzania, Zambia, Zimbabwe	Mayotte, Réunion
Northern Africa	Algeria, Egypt, Libya, Morocco, Tunisia	Western Sahara
Western Asia	Iraq, Jordan, Lebanon, Syrian, Arab, Republic Turkey, Yemen,	Bahrain, Kuwait, State of Palestine, Oman, Qatar, Saudi Arabia, United Arab Emirates
Caucasus and Central Asia	Armenia, Azerbaijan, Georgia, Kazakhstan, Kyrgyzstan, Tajikistan, Turkmenistan, Uzbekistan	
South Asia	Afghanistan, Bangladesh, Bhutan, India, Iran (Islamic Republic of), Maldives, Nepal, Pakistan, Sri Lanka	
South-East Asia	Cambodia, Indonesia, Lao People's Democratic Republic, Malaysia, Myanmar, Philippines, Thailand, Timor-Leste, Viet Nam	Brunei Darussalam, Singapore
Eastern Asia	China, Dem. People's Republic of Korea, Mongolia	Hong Kong (China), Macao (China), Republic of Korea
Oceania	Cook Islands, Fiji, Kiribati, Marshall Islands, Micronesia (Fed. States of), Nauru, Niue, Palau, Papua New Guinea, Samoa, Solomon Islands, Tonga, Tuvalu, Vanuatu	American Samoa, French Polynesia, Guam, New Caledonia, Northern Mariana Islands, Tokelau
Developed (upper-middle income)	Albania, Belarus, Bosnia and Herzegovina, Bulgaria, Republic of Moldova, Romania, Russian Federation, Serbia, TFYR Macedonia, Ukraine	Hungary
Developed (high income)		Andorra, Australia, Austria, Belgium, Bermuda, Canada, Channel Islands, Croatia, Cyprus, Czech Republic, Denmark, Estonia, Faroe Islands, Finland, France, Germany, Greece, Greenland, Iceland, Ireland, Isle of Man, Israel, Italy, Japan, Latvia, Liechtenstein, Lithuania, Luxembourg, Malta, Monaco, Montenegro, Netherlands, New Zealand, Norway, Poland, Portugal, San Marino, Slovakia, Slovenia, Spain, Sweden, Switzerland, United Kingdom, United States of America

Appendix 2

Results using DALY values for premature death at 5 percent discount rate (Tables 23.17 and 23.18)

Table 23.17 Benefit-cost ratios when premature mortality is valued at US$1,000 per DALY averted (5 percent discount rate)

MDG Region	Basic Water		Basic Sanitation		ODF
	Urban	Rural	Urban	Rural	Rural
Latin America and the Caribbean	2.9	7.8	3.3	8.1	10.2
Sub-Saharan Africa	1.9	4.3	0.9	2.6	3.6
Northern Africa	2.4	9.3	2.2	5.8	6.3
Western Asia	2.5	5.7	3.0	7.3	8.3
Caucasus and Central Asia	2.8	8.8	3.3	19.7	15.6
South Asia	1.9	4.1	2.8	5.2	6.3
South-East Asia	2.3	8.6	2.5	17.3	13.6
Eastern Asia	5.1	14.1	4.0	12.8	13.2
Oceania	2.2	6.4	5.7	47.1	31.9
Developed	2.3	15.5	3.6	33.6	22.0
World	**2.9**	**4.8**	**2.4**	**4.5**	**6.0**

Table 23.18 Benefit-cost ratios when premature mortality is valued at US$5,000 per DALY averted (5 percent discount rate)

MDG Region	Basic Water		Basic Sanitation		ODF
	Urban	Rural	Urban	Rural	Rural
Latin America and the Caribbean	2.9	8.0	3.3	8.2	10.3
Sub-Saharan Africa	3.5	7.6	1.2	3.8	5.1
Northern Africa	2.4	9.6	2.2	5.9	6.3
Western Asia	2.6	6.2	3.0	7.6	8.6
Caucasus and Central Asia	2.9	9.2	3.3	20.1	15.9
South Asia	2.6	5.4	3.1	6.0	7.2
South-East Asia	2.5	9.2	2.6	17.8	14.0
Eastern Asia	5.2	14.4	4.0	12.9	13.3
Oceania	2.4	6.8	5.8	49.1	33.2
Developed	2.3	15.5	3.6	33.6	22.0
World	**3.4**	**7.1**	**2.6**	**5.4**	**7.3**

References

Fishman, S., L. Caulfield, et al. (2004). Childhood and Maternal Underweight. In *Comparative Quantification of Health Risks: Global and Regional Burden of Disease Due to Selected Major Risk Factors, Volume 2*, ed. M. Ezzati, A. Rodgers, A. Lopez, and C. Murray. Geneva: World Health Organization.

Fonseca, C., R. Franceys, et al. (2010). *Life-Cycle Costs Approach. Glossary and Cost Components*. WASHCost Briefing Note 1. IRC The Hague: IRC International Water and Sanitation Centre.

Freeman, M., M. Stocks, et al. (2014). "Hygiene and health: systematic review of handwashing practices worldwide and update of health effects." *Tropical Medicine and International Health* 19(8): 906–16.

Hutton, G. (2012). *Global Costs and Benefits of Drinking-Water Supply and Sanitation Interventions to Reach the MDG Target and Universal Coverage*. Report No. WHO/HSE/WSH/12.01. Geneva: World Health Organization.

Hutton, G. and L. Haller (2004). *Evaluation of the Non-Health Costs and Benefits of water and Sanitation Improvements at Global Level*. Geneva: World Health Organization. WHO/SDE/WSH/04.04.

Hutton, G., U.-P. Rodriguez, et al. (2014). "Economic efficiency of sanitation interventions in Southeast Asia." *Journal of Water, Sanitation and Hygiene in Development* 4(1): 23–36.

Hutton, G. and Varughese, M. (2016). *Costs of Meeting the 2030 Sustainable Development Agenda Targets on Drinking Water, Sanitation and Hygiene*. Washington, DC: World Bank, Water and Sanitation Program.

Prüss-Üstun, A., J. Bartram, et al. (2014). "Burden of diarrheal disease from inadequate water,
sanitation and hygiene in low- and middle-income countries: a retrospective analysis of data from 145 countries." *Tropical Medicine and International Health* 19(8): 894–905.

UNU and UNOSD (2013). *Water for Sustainability: Framing Water within the Post-2015 Development Agenda*. Hamilton, Ontario, Canada: United Nations University Institute for Water, Environment and Health; UN Office of Sustainable Development; Stockholm Environment Institute. United Nations University, Canada.

UN-Water (2016a). *Water and Sanitation Interlinkages across the 2030 Agenda for Sustainable Development*. Geneva: UN-Water.

(2016b). *Means of Implementation: A Focus on Sustainable Development Goals 6 and 17*. Geneva: UN-Water.

WHO and UNICEF (2006). *Meeting the MDG Drinking Water and Sanitation Target. The Urban and Rural Challenge of the Decade*, Geneva: WHO/UNICEF Joint Monitoring Programme for Water Supply and Sanitation. WHO and New York: UNICEF.

(2013). *Post 2015 WASH Targets and Indicators*, WHO/UNICEF Joint Monitoring Programme for Water Supply and Sanitation. Geneva: WHO and New York: UNICEF. In collaboration with the Water Supply and Sanitation Collaborative Council, Geneva.

(2014). *Progress on Drinking Water and Sanitation*. 2014 Update, WHO/UNICEF Joint Monitoring Programme for Water Supply and Sanitation. Geneva: WHO and New York: UNICEF.

Wolf, J., A. Prüss-Üstun, et al. (2014). "Assessing the impact of drinking-water and sanitation on diarrhoeal disease in low- and middle-income countries: a systematic review and regression analysis." *Tropical Medicine and International Health* 8(19).

Alternative Perspective

DALE WHITTINGTON

Summary

Guy Hutton's chapter is part of a series of publications from the WHO and World Bank that suggest the benefits of water and sanitation interventions in developing countries are an order of magnitude or more higher than the costs of improved services. However, I challenge this finding on a number of grounds, particularly related to the assumptions made in the economic analysis.

The benefit-cost analysis rests on two assumptions, that each person's well-being is to count, and count according to their own valuation, and that this is also the valuation placed on the change by society. The challenge is to learn about individuals' preferences and measure the strength of these in monetary terms, either via the willingness to pay (WTP) for the outcome or the willingness to accept (WTA) compensation to forego the change.

Some experts are reluctant to measure benefits in terms of expressed preferences because they believe that people do not fully understand either the benefit or the causal relationship between hygiene and health. They are thus inclined to substitute their own assessment of the benefits into the benefit-cost calculation, which creates a challenge for BCA. In simple terms, if the benefit-cost ratio of a WASH intervention is 10:1, or even 20:1 as suggested in the chapter, why don't individuals rush to adopt these interventions?

The reasonableness of the benefit estimate depends largely on the accuracy of the estimates of time saving, which is what delivers the greatest benefit. Consider one of the sources of time savings – not walking to an open defecation site. If we assume a rural household of two adults and three children, the monthly benefits estimated in the chapter would be about US$5 per month, but would everyone actually change their behavior? In practice, in rural India, there is evidence that many people prefer to practice open defecation, which means that the benefit in the chapter must be considered highly speculative and subject to a high level of uncertainty.

A similar argument applies to the benefits of avoided mortality. The human capital approach has no theoretical justification; a WTP figure would give a much lower benefit, particularly in poor communities, but some experts are uncomfortable with this. The substitution of expert judgment gives the appearance of greater certainty in the benefit estimates and, in many situations, inflates the economic benefits.

There are other concerns. It seems unlikely, for example, that the usage of new WASH facilities would actually be 100 percent. It is also assumed that the costs of water and sanitation interventions vary directly with GDP, whereas many of the components involving materials or skilled services do not. I also have concerns that, in the baseline case, the costs may have been discounted at 8 percent, and the benefits at only 3 percent.

Although the author does a sensitivity analysis for individual factors, this does not give an accurate picture of the overall uncertainty. For example, four key parameters are needed to estimate the benefits of mortality reduction, but none is known with much certainty for a specific location where the new WASH intervention is to occur. The final result depends on the product of four uncertain parameters.

To summarize, I am not arguing in this review of the chapter that WASH interventions will fail a cost-benefit test. In fact, I believe that carefully done cost-benefit analyses will show that many WASH interventions will be economically attractive investments. But the analysis needs to be done.

Summary

Both the UN Panel of Eminent Persons and the Open Working Group for Sustainable Development Goals struggled with how to frame goals for the broader water resources management challenge. It is easy to agree that water resources should be used more efficiently, but that does not necessarily mean minimizing water use. Most water problems are essentially local, and tailored local solutions must be developed. These must also recognize that water is a renewable resource; after use by humans, each molecule of water reenters the natural hydrological cycle.

All this means that it does not make economic sense to present an average benefit-cost ratio for investment in water infrastructure such as dams. Some projects make good economic sense, while others do not. One approach to providing a figure for comparison with other options under consideration in this project would be to use a baseline of some of the most economically attractive dams in the world and assume that the BCR for others would be lower. Using this approach, we find that even the large multipurpose dam in the Blue Nile gorge in Ethiopia – one of the most attractive places in the world for hydropower generation – has a much lower benefit-cost ratio than smaller-scale WASH interventions.

Health policy interventions (e.g., vaccination, malaria, HIV-AIDS, hospital care) consistently dominate the Copenhagen Consensus rankings, whereas these are generally at the bottom of the list of development priorities in low-income countries. Similarly, they are not at the top of the priority list for many households in developing countries. I suggest there are five systemic reasons why the Copenhagen Consensus process overlooks the economic importance of large-scale infrastructure projects.

First, analysts underestimate the costs of targeted health and social interventions, in part because they implicitly assume that infrastructure is in place to enable the efficient delivery of health services. Ex post cost-benefit analysis of infrastructure projects often reveals cost overruns, and analysts responsible for the appraisal of large water resources projects have long been aware of this issue. More ex post cost-benefit analysis of targeted health and social policy interventions is needed to temper overly optimistic cost estimates.

Second, analysts overestimate the benefits of targeted health interventions, in part because arbitrary assumptions are made about the value of mortality risk reductions. In practice, poor households place a surprisingly low value on reduced mortality risk. Because the value of lives saved often dominates the benefits, this can inflate the apparent attractiveness of health projects, whereas this is a less important part of the benefits of infrastructure projects.

The third reason is the difference in the planning horizon, which is much longer for infrastructure projects and hence makes proper comparison difficult. Fourth, projects such as dams can often get private-sector funding and may fall outside the scope of international aid, and finally, the Nobel Panel appears to demand very high-quality evidence, often only available from randomized trials where strong causal links have been demonstrated.

There are also a number of additional challenges in the analysis of large-scale water resource projects. Because the use of water is so all-pervasive, it is rarely possible to include all the economic benefits of improved water service. It is also difficult to account for both the positive and negative impacts of reduced hydrological variability, particularly as water resources cross administrative and political boundaries. Finally, the causal links between investments in water infrastructure and economic growth run in both directions.

This discussion raises the question of what can be done to improve the Copenhagen Consensus Project's approach. I have two suggestions. First, sector specialists should be asked to provide more evidence from ex post cost-benefit analyses to support the findings from their ex ante studies. The second is to divide sector policy proposals into short- and long-range interventions, using some necessarily arbitrary threshold (e.g., ten years) that would separate large-scale infrastructure projects from the "simple" delivery of health and social services. The Nobel Panel could rank proposals in each category separately, making a judgment on the fraction of total funding to be allocated to each.

Benefits and Costs of the Poverty Targets for the Post-2015 Development Agenda

CHAPTER 24

JOHN GIBSON

Introduction

The first Sustainable Development Goal (SDG) is to "end poverty in all its forms everywhere," and the first target under this goal is that by 2030 the world should have eradicated extreme poverty for all people everywhere, currently measured as people living on less than $1.25 a day. In contrast to the Millennium Development Goals (MDGs), this adoption of zero targets is a common theme within the SDGs (for example, the zero hunger target). However, such targets are both highly unlikely to be met and an inefficient use of global resources.

In this chapter I discuss two sets of reasons why there is unlikely to be zero poverty, or zero hunger, by 2030. The first reasons relate to measurement problems with zero targets; despite being attractive rallying cries for activists, they create difficulty for the statistical measurement of human progress. The targets relate to the lower tail of distributions so statistics on living standards have to reliably measure not just means and totals but also variances. The main source of empirical data for monitoring progress is household surveys, which developed primarily to provide mean weights for consumer price indexes and later to aid in calculation of national accounts. Common designs used for those tasks overstate variances and mix together chronic and transient welfare components. Consequently, it will be difficult to detect the achievement of zero poverty or zero hunger with the existing approach to surveys. Moreover, as countries escape from mass poverty, the remaining poverty becomes more sensitive to inequality, and the design of household surveys is increasingly ill-suited to measuring inequality in a more affluent and more urban world.

The second set of reasons relates to qualitative differences between past and future problems. The role of one-off institutional reforms in East Asia whose effects are unlikely to be replicated elsewhere; the characteristics of rice as an ideal food for the poor, which gives East Asia another advantage in poverty reduction makes poverty reduction elsewhere more challenging, and the fact that as countries escape from mass poverty the nature of poverty changes, with the poor becoming less like the majority in terms of location, ethnicity, caste, or religion. Each of these factors is likely to make poverty reduction going forward much harder than it was for the two decades from 1990.

The perspective taken here is that of someone involved in designing, implementing, and analyzing surveys for measuring poverty at country level, in countries that vary widely in the success they have had to date in reducing poverty and in their capacity to undertake basic socioeconomic measurement and analysis. From this point of view, too many targets adopted as part of the SDGs appear to be unhinged from the reality of statistical measurement in poor countries. Some SDG participants may have been unduly confident in existing data and in the abilities of governments and the UN to deliver even basic statistical measurement and reporting. The failure of the UN to publish a *Handbook on Poverty Statistics*, which has remained in draft form for the last nine years following a process begun in 1997, is an example of this lack of capacity. This inability of the UN to be competent even to publish a handbook – let alone to monitor ever more complex development goals – is despite the clear evidence of the need to improve the quality of data on poverty and hunger via more harmonized survey methodology (De Weerdt et al., 2016).

The rest of this chapter first gives a brief history of the long intellectual road to a zero poverty target, followed by a review of global poverty reduction over the last three decades. I then focus on measurement problems and estimation of the costs and benefits of developing human capital. The penultimate section discusses factors that made the achievement of the MDG poverty goals easier than what is likely for the SDGs going forward. The final section considers one way of valuing the benefits of poverty reduction, in terms of increased human capital, and reports on a limited cost-benefit comparison for eliminating extreme poverty. Additionally, I provide qualitative assessments of other SDG targets related to poverty reduction proposed by various bodies involved in the goal-setting process such as the High Level Panel and Open Working Group.

The Intellectual Road to Zero Poverty Targets

The modern literature on measuring poverty dates to the late nineteenth century, in the work of Charles Booth and Seebohm Rowntree, but there has been an explosion of poverty measurement in the last two decades prompted by the growing availability of household survey data. For example, the global poverty counts by Chen and Ravallion (2013) rely on a household survey database of almost 900 surveys from 125 low- and middle-income countries fielded between 1979 and 2011. Yet in this century of research, the main output is measures of poverty in its own terms but not in broadly economic terms that let trade-offs be considered, where the costs and benefits of reducing poverty are balanced against each other. Instead, modern studies typically report the incidence, depth, and severity of poverty using unified measures due to Foster, Greer, and Thorbecke (1984). These measures tell one the proportion of a population who are below the poverty line, how far below the line they are on average, and the inequality among the poor that is revealed by poverty statistics that put more weight on those furthest below the line. More rarely, poverty measurement is given a time dimension; for a given poverty line

and a given distribution of income or consumption below that line, how many years would it take at a constant and uniform growth rate for everyone to escape poverty (Morduch, 1998)?

Among these typical ways to measure poverty, only the depth of poverty statistic that gives the average proportionate shortfall from the poverty line can be interpreted in monetary terms. If an all-seeing, all-knowing government perfectly targeted transfers to the poor, giving them just enough to close poverty gaps, and if such transfers had no administrative cost, created no disincentive effects, and the information for perfect targeting was freely available, then the sum of all the poverty gaps might be interpreted as a measure of the total cost of poverty. Indeed, Clunies-Ross and Huq (2014) use this approach to calculate a global poverty gap of $82 billion, for $1.25 per day poverty (in 2005 PPP terms). An implicit cost-benefit argument is also made by these authors, who argue that social protection systems could be used to eradicate poverty because the required transfers are equivalent to just two-thirds of official development assistance.

Yet this way of measuring the cost of poverty is neither conceptually sensible nor practically useful. At the conceptual level it is tautological – the cost of being poor is just that you are poor – when in fact there are likely effects of poverty on education, health, life expectancy, capacity for innovation, and perhaps even macroeconomic performance that are ignored. At the practical level, perfectly targeted transfers amount to marginal tax rates of 100 percent because every dollar of extra income earned by a poor person reduces their transfers received by the same amount. Moreover, transfers are administratively costly, and targeting is neither perfect nor costless.

The work of researchers in measuring poverty in its own terms rather than allowing for trade-offs may reflect a normative view that poverty is such a bad thing that it should be eradicated irrespective of costs. If so, such a judgment is a relatively recent way of thinking. Ravallion (2011) uses textual analysis to examine changing views of poverty over three centuries; at the beginning of this period (and in earlier times) there was an acceptance of the inevitability of poverty, with some prominent thinkers even arguing for its necessity to spur economic activity.

However, beginning in what Ravallion terms the "first Poverty Enlightenment" of the late eighteenth century there is growing discussion of the ideas that poverty is not the result of some natural ordering, and that a minimum acceptable standard of living should be available for all members of society. A similar timing for this shift in thought is given in Alfred Marshall's discussion of the mid-eighteenth-century French Physiocrats. In his *Principles of Economics*, Marshall (1920, p. 626) notes they had a great indirect influence on neoclassical economics because of their motivations:

> ... [t]he chief motive of their study was not, as it had been with most of their predecessors, to increase the riches of merchants and fill the exchequers of kings; it was to diminish the suffering and degradation that was caused by extreme poverty.

Perhaps if Mercantilism had stayed the dominant school of thought, the "optimal poverty" to most "increase the riches of merchants" might have been calculated. But instead, the neoclassical school dominates, although such cost-benefit calculus has not extended to poverty. Instead, many people would consider that poverty reduction is human development, and as such it is not something to be traded off against progress on other fronts. This sort of thinking is also consistent with the adoption of zero targets, such as under the SDGs. However, a zero target of completely eliminating extreme poverty by 2030 probably will not be met, and efforts to do so may well distract from the more urgent tasks of doing a better job of monitoring what poverty reduction actually does occur.

The Record on Global Poverty Reduction

The record on global poverty reduction over the last three decades is summarized in many papers by Shaohua Chen and Martin Ravallion (2001, 2010, 2013). These studies rely on a survey database that has grown over time. Apart from the Middle East and North Africa, who contribute little to global poverty counts, the surveys now cover more than three-quarters of the population of each region and 90 percent of the developing world. The trends in the head count poverty rate (the percentage of the population below the $1.25 PPP 2005 poverty line) for East Asia and the Pacific (EAP), South Asia, and sub-Saharan Africa are shown in Figure 24.1. The other regions of the world contribute less than 4 percent to global poverty and so are ignored here. The source of the figure is Chen and Ravallion (2013), who present the estimates for every three years from 1981 until 2008, and Olinto and Uematsu (2013), who provide the estimates for 2010.

It is useful to begin the discussion from 1987, when the poverty rates for these regions were all within one percentage point of each other. The other difference from the original source is that China is divided out from the rest of EAP – typically in the global poverty counts the reporting combines China with the rest of East Asia and the Pacific. Such reporting obscures the fact that other parts of East Asia have been just as successful as China, with more continual poverty reduction (e.g., compare 1987 to 1993 in the figure) and so moves the question from "what is special about China" to "what is special about East Asia."

The trend annual rates of decline in the head count poverty rate in Figure 24.1 are –7.5 percent for China, –6.1 percent for the rest of East Asia and the Pacific, and –2.3 percent for South Asia. All three trends are precisely estimated, with robust t-statistics that vary from 5.9 to 12.6. In contrast, the trend rate of decline in poverty rates for sub-Saharan Africa is just –0.008 and would be insignificantly different from zero were it not for the observation in 2010. Allow for the moment the possibility that there is something fundamentally different about the rate of poverty reduction in East Asia compared with in sub-Saharan Africa. In 1987, 48 percent of the poor were living in EAP (including China), and only 15 percent were in sub-Saharan Africa, but by 2010 these proportions had largely reversed; just 22 percent of the poor were in EAP, and 35 percent of the poor were in sub-Saharan Africa. The great success of East Asia in reducing poverty becomes less and less relevant to global poverty counts going forward, because

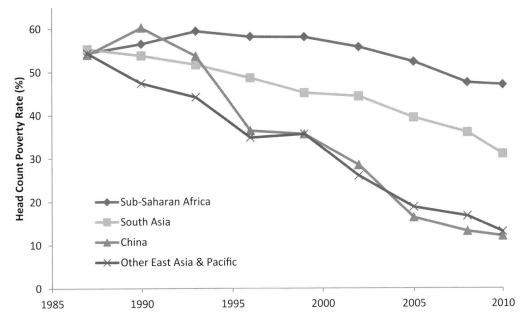

Figure 24.1 *The uneven escape from extreme poverty around the world: Africa lagging*

Source: Chen and Ravallion (2013) and Olinto and Uematsu (2013).

few of the poor will be found there, while the evident lack of success in sub-Saharan Africa increasingly matters to the likelihood of meeting global poverty targets. Moreover, several favorable factors that contributed to poverty reduction in East Asia are much weaker elsewhere, as discussed in Section 5 of this chapter.

Problems in Monitoring Progress to Zero Poverty

In order to reliably monitor progress toward the SDG poverty targets, and to focus attention on the countries where progress is slowest, poverty must be measured consistently over time and space. One view of the growing survey evidence base noted in Section 3 is that the statistical foundations for measuring progress toward poverty targets are getting firmer over time because more countries have ever more surveys. However, the opposite may be true, with several factors suggesting that measures of poverty and inequality may become less reliable

over time. Some surveys are poorly designed to measure living standards and poverty in an era of rising affluence and urban transition (World Bank, 2014). In addition, a problem for measurement is posed by zero targets because standard survey approaches yield some unknown mixture of chronic and transient welfare components, and the SDG targets give no allowance for measured poverty or hunger that is above zero, in part because it captures transitory variations in living standards.

Zero Targets and the Importance of Estimated Variances in Living Standards

The zero targets for the SDG poverty and hunger goals relate to the proportion of the population living below acceptable thresholds – poverty lines in one case and dietary energy standards in the other. These goals involve the lower tail of distributions, so statistics on living standards have to reliably measure not just means and totals but also variances, which most household surveys cannot do.

The data workhorse for poverty analysis is a Household Consumption Expenditure Survey (HCES).[1] Income surveys are widely used for poverty analysis in rich countries (and bring their own problems that are discussed later), but for developing regions only Latin America relies more on income surveys than on HCES. Despite differences, most HCES are designed to capture a snapshot of the living standard of the members of a household who eat meals from a common pot that the householders themselves have cooked from ingredients that they acquired by either purchase, receiving as a gift or payment, or self-production.

In order to keep the reporting burden manageable, a household will typically be part of the survey for only a short period of time such as a week, fortnight, or month. Their consumption activities during that reference period may be reported by recall – usually from an interview that takes place in the one and only visit to the household – or may be recorded with a diary that will typically involve interviewers making revisits for short, adjacent, periods (e.g., every second day) to check on their diary-keeping. For example, Dupriez et al. (2014) survey statistics offices in 100 low- and middle-income countries to obtain metadata on their food consumption surveys and find 40 percent of these surveys use the diary method, with the median diary-keeping survey having the interviewers make five visits to the household in two weeks.

A problem then is how to interpret this "snapshot" from having a record of the household's consumption over just a week, fortnight, or month when often what is wanted is a longer run record of welfare. For example, base weights for a Consumer Price Index typically refer to an average across the year because there will be seasonal variation in the importance of many commodities (e.g., heating oil in the winter, ice cream in the summer). One common approach to this issue is to split the HCES sample into subsamples, each of which is seen in a different month of the year. When all the subsamples are combined, it is as if a synthetic household had been seen for the full year. This is perfectly fine for means and totals – which the household surveys were originally designed to measure – but not for variances. For

example, Gibson et al. (2003) have benchmark data from year-long expenditure diaries in urban China – an infeasible method of data collection in most places and becoming so in China – and use these data to compare with what shorter reporting periods would show. A monthly reference period, and surveying one-twelfth of the sample every month to create a synthetic annual mean, gave the same mean annual expenditures as the year-long diary, but variance-based measures were greatly exaggerated; the standard deviation was twice as high and the poverty head count and Gini inequality measures inflated by 50–65 percent. The variance-based measures are overstated when short reference period data are combined into a synthetic annual total because many short-term shocks tend to cancel out over time.

Although these reference period issues affect poverty measurement, they are especially clear in hunger measurement because the global agency in charge of this – the Food and Agriculture Organization (FAO) – has explicitly chosen to measure chronic hunger on an annual basis. In contrast, the time period over which poverty (and inequality) is measured varies across countries with little concern about adjusting to a common reference period basis (Gibson et al., 2001). The reason why the FAO only measures annual hunger is that they rely on country averages of dietary energy per person from aggregate Food Balance Sheets, which are calculated annually. In order to distribute these country-level totals across the population, the FAO uses adjusted estimates of the interhousehold variance in calories, from household surveys. Specifically, they dampen variances because the snapshot of usual diet given by the short reference periods for surveys causes what FAO considers to be excess variability (Cafiero, 2014).

How big is the overstatement of hunger due to the excess variance in short reference period survey data? The example in Figure 24.2 suggests

[1] I use the generic term HCES to refer to a range of household survey efforts to capture total household consumption expenditures, which includes budget surveys, income and expenditure surveys, living standards surveys, and others. Gibson (2006) discusses the comparative strengths of each type of survey for poverty analysis.

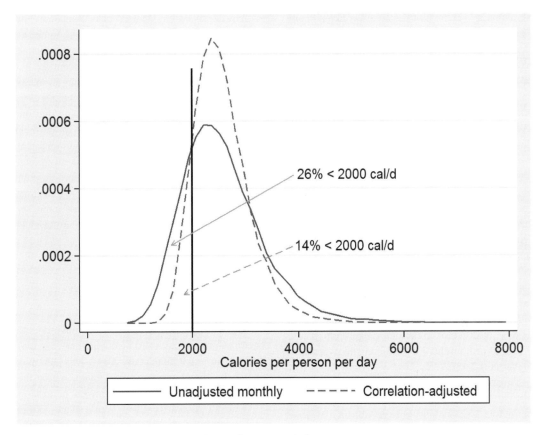

Figure 24.2 *Overstated hunger from short reference period surveys*

that survey estimates of the hunger rate (based here on the population having less than 2000 calories per person per day) are almost doubled. The distribution of per capita calories in these data are based on detailed monthly surveys from Myanmar, and in the unadjusted estimates it appears that 26 percent of the population get less than 2000 calories per day (Gibson, 2016). But in the adjusted estimates, which account for partially reversed shocks over the year, the hunger rate falls to just 14 percent once the excess variance is corrected

The basis for adjusting the variances in Figure 24.2 (to get a less spread out distribution) is that the Myanmar survey revisited households six months later, with the consumption recall then repeated for this second period.[2] This lets one estimate correlations between values of a living standards indicator for the same households in separate periods. These correlations are implicitly

assumed to be 1.0 if short reference period survey data are treated as equivalent to annual data. If the correlations are, say, 0.7, monthly reference period surveys overstate annual variances by 40 percent, and by 80 percent if the correlations are as low as 0.5. The correlation-based method almost exactly replicates what benchmark annual data show, for variance-based statistics such as inequality and poverty indices (Gibson et al., 2003). For the example of Myanmar, the correlation in per capita calories, six months apart, was just 0.45, and so using a single recall period (even if it is a month long) greatly overstates chronic hunger because it includes shocks that are partially reversed in the rest of the year. Notably in the results for

[2] In the Dupriez et al. (2014) metadata survey of statistics offices, only two of 100 HCES had this feature.

Myanmar, the correlations were lower in per capita terms than in household terms because household size also fluctuates over the course of the year, were lower for urban people, and were no different in rural irrigated regions than in the seasonal dry zone. These features suggest that these low correlations reflect various demographic and economic shocks rather than being primarily due to seasonal fluctuations (Gibson, 2016).

Another way to think about the excess variance in short reference period survey data is that this excess variance shows low autocorrelations in outcomes of interest. For any variable with a low autocorrelation, taking a single snapshot – as in a typical survey – will tend to mismeasure the long-run average, whereas repeated observations will give a better estimate. McKenzie (2012) reports autocorrelations from surveys with repeat visits (excluding diary-keeping surveys with revisits for very short, adjacent, periods); for household income these autocorrelations range from 0.2 to 0.5, and for household expenditures they are a bit higher at 0.2 to 0.7.

Consequently, the typical survey approach that just takes a snapshot of the living standards of the household will include a large transient welfare component in any calculated hunger or poverty estimates. In the example from Myanmar, the 26 percent hunger rate using the unadjusted monthly data can be thought of as showing a 14 percent chronic hunger rate and a 12 percent transitory hunger rate. Using a similar method, but for poverty rates, Gibson (2001) found that the poverty measured by a survey in Papua New Guinea with a two-week reference period was split equally between chronic and transient components. Because the SDGs aim to completely eliminate chronic hunger (and poverty), they have no allowance for measured hunger or poverty rates that are above zero due to picking up transitory variation from short-reference period surveys.

This point is also made by an older literature that compares using household income with using expenditures as welfare indicators for poverty analysis. The high transitory component in measured income blurs a poverty profile, so it less clearly shows characteristics of the long-term poor, by mixing households with low permanent incomes

with those having temporary shocks to income. For example, Slesnick (1993) reports a high homeownership rate of 30 percent for the income poor in the United States (compared to just 15 percent for the consumption poor) and low food budget shares (which imply higher welfare under Engel's Law). These patterns go against the expectation that the poor have few assets and devote most of their budgets to necessities like food but are consistent with the idea that the income poor at any given point in time will be a mixture of the chronic poor and the nonpoor who suffered a negative transitory income shock. Zero targets do not leave scope for nonzero poverty due to people who experience transitory shocks.

Rising Inequality Sensitivity of Poverty Highlights Survey Problems

As countries become less poor, the poverty rate becomes more sensitive to inequality and less sensitive to growth (Olinto et al., 2014). This pattern is shown by the experience of Vietnam, where the head count poverty rate fell from 64 percent in 1993 to 17 percent in 2008 (World Bank, 2012) and was down to about 5 percent by 2010.[3] Figure 24.3 shows this progress (using the left axis) and also what happened to the sensitivity to growth and inequality (using the right axis). When the poverty rate was high, the elasticity with respect to inequality was just over half the elasticity with respect to growth, but as the poverty rate fell, the relative size of the inequality elasticity rose to almost three times that of the growth elasticity.[4] Another way to show the fall in growth-sensitivity is to consider the growth rate in mean consumption needed to achieve a one percentage point fall in the head count poverty rate; when the poverty rate was high in 2002, a growth rate of 1.6 percent per annum was sufficient to drop the poverty rate by a percentage point, but by 2010 it took an

---

[3] The uncertainty for 2010 is because the survey living standards indicator was revised then, to reflect Vietnam's rising affluence.

[4] These elasticities are calculated from a Beta Lorenz curve, using the *Povcal* software of Chen et al. (2000).

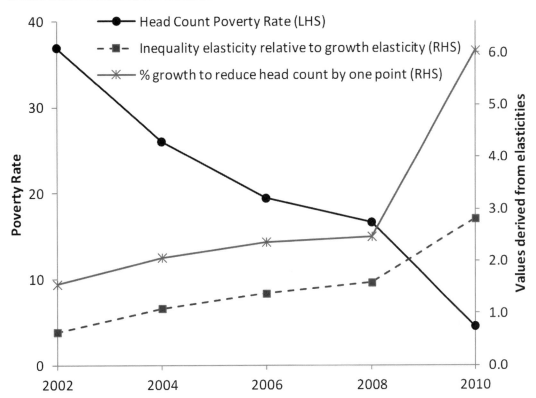

Figure 24.3 *Declining effectiveness of growth in reducing poverty as poverty falls, Vietnam, 2002–2010*

Source: Author's calculations from VHLSS data.

annual growth rate of 6 percent to achieve the same drop in the poverty rate.

That poverty rates become more inequality-sensitive and less growth sensitive as countries prosper matters to policy makers and practitioners. The policy problem is that reducing inequality so as to eradicate poverty can create distributional conflicts and may be viewed as a zero-sum game. In contrast, economic growth is positive-sum, with growth-oriented policies subject to fewer rent-seeking losses than occur with attempts at redistribution. The practitioner problem is that surveys may be doing a poor job of measuring inequality. However, less attention is paid to this problem than to debates about discrepancies in the growth record told with surveys versus with national accounts (Deaton, 2005). Even studies that doubt the survey-based record of average progress rely on the survey estimates of inequality (Pinkovskiy and

Sala-i-Martin, 2009). Yet there are several reasons to increasingly doubt the inequality data from the surveys.

Problems in Surveying Food Consumption

One reason why HCES do an increasingly poor job of measuring inequality is that they misallocate effort, paying too little attention to capturing income-elastic consumption that becomes more important with rising affluence. For example, the food modules of HCES are organized according to lists of ingredients such as rice, wheat flour, maize flour, and so forth. Asking about ingredients makes sense for people who prepare their own meals, and thus made sense at baseline of the MDGs (1990) when most of the poor were still rural and likely ate together as a family. But this approach makes far less sense for urban people who obtain food independent of other family members, in the form of prepared meals, whether as street foods, in restaurants, or purchased to heat and eat at home. Yet these meals are largely missed. In the Dupriez et al. (2014) metadata study, the average number of groups in the food list for recall surveys is 110 but just three of these are for meals and other forms of food eaten away from home, and most studies do not report quantities for these.

By ignoring eating out, policy makers may get distracted by dead-end debates, such as one in India about seemingly rising undernutrition during the recent era of rapid economic growth (Smith, 2015) and a similar one in China that showed meat consumption to be almost static despite a rapid increase in supply and income (Ma, Huang, Fuller, and Rozelle, 2006).

Meals out are highly income elastic, and their budget share rises with rising affluence, and they become the most important category of food expenditure. One would not know this from looking at HCES questionnaires with their many questions on ingredients and few on meals. Figure 24.4 reports trends in the share of total food expenditure on eating out, for urban China and national Vietnam, showing the crossover between grains for home consumption and eating out.

The other problem for surveying food consumption is independent eating, or more broadly the issue of surveying urban family members who may only sleep together but not work and eat together as they did in the countryside. In a survey experiment in Tanzania, Beegle et al. (2012) compare two types of HCES diary surveys; in one, each adult records their own commodity acquisitions, while in the other, one respondent keeps a diary on behalf of the whole household. For rural households, there is no difference in the consumption recorded with one type of diary or the other. But urban households report 29 percent lower consumption, if surveyed with a household-level diary rather than having each adult keeping a diary.

Problems in Measuring Housing Services

The other form of poorly measured consumption whose high income elasticity makes it of growing importance is housing. With rising affluence,

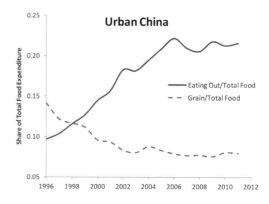

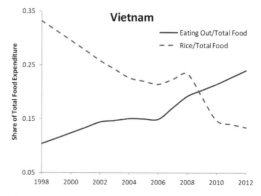

Figure 24.4 *Changing Importance of ingredients and eating out in household food consumption*

housing eventually becomes the largest household budget item; for example, 44 percent of a U.S. cost-of-living index is housing (Jolliffe, 2006). Ideally, surveys would enable consumption of housing services to be calculated for both renters and owner-occupiers, taking account of temporal and regional differences. While most household surveys ask for actual rents paid, in many developing countries renters are a small minority, so it is hard to extrapolate from rents paid by these renters to impute rents for the owner-occupiers.

Indeed, some surveys do such a poor job that consumption of housing services is dropped from analyses (Deaton and Dupriez, 2011). An equivalent treatment is to assume that housing has a constant budget share so that this form of consumption can be imputed as a simple ratio to the value of consumption in the parts of the budget that are better measured by surveys. For example, poverty measurement in Vietnam from the 1990s

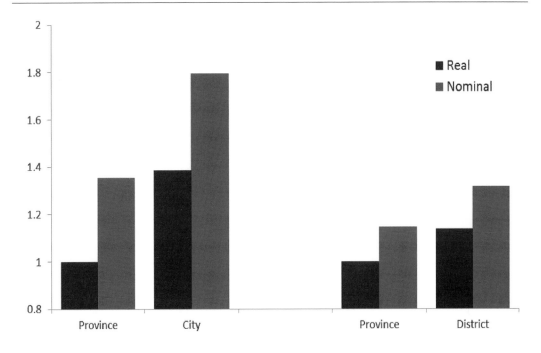

Theil Index (Real, Province-level = 1)   Gini Index (Real, Province-level = 1)

Figure 24.5 *Overstated spatial inequality in China's GDP per capita, 2010*

though 2008 treated consumption of housing as a constant proportion of other nonfood consumption so housing was an unchanged 6 percent of the total budget (World Bank, 2012). When this assumption was dropped, and the estimated value of housing consumption was derived by applying the rent-to-value ratio of renters to the dwelling values that owner-occupiers reported, the average share of housing in household budgets rose to 15 percent. Moreover, housing was estimated to be 27 percent of the budget for people in the richest quintile and just 8 percent for the poorest quintile, suggesting that the assumption about constant housing shares had greatly understated inequality.

Treating housing as a fixed ratio to other forms of consumption also ignores the implications of the Balassa-Samuelson effect, that prices of nontraded goods are higher in richer areas. Housing is the quintessential nontraded good, so it is expected that richer areas will have higher housing prices, and that these spatial price differentials will grow over time as an economy urbanizes and becomes richer. So if housing consumption and prices are poorly measured (or not measured at all) what is interpreted as rising inequality may just be increasing spatial price differences. For example, Li and Gibson (2014) construct a spatial price index for urban China and find nominal incomes outside Beijing need to be inflated 33 percent to put them on a comparable cost-of-living basis, even allowing just housing costs to differ between Beijing and other cities.

Figure 24.5 shows what happens to measured inequality if no account is taken of this spatial variation in the cost of living. The overstated inequality is not as great if inequality is measured with the Gini index, where not deflating for spatial cost of living differences cases an upward bias in the Gini coefficient of 15–16 percent.[5]

---

[5] In Figure 24.5, both the Theil and the Gini have been scaled to equal 1 for real inequality at provincial level.

Taking an average of the two inequality measures, approximately one-quarter of apparent spatial inequality in China disappears once account is taken of cost of living differences coming just from house prices. It will especially be true for China, because of the absence of housing markets under central planning, but probably is true more generally throughout rapidly urbanizing Asia, that the spatial cost of living differentials from urban housing markets are likely to have grown from a low base.

The Recent Past May Not Be a Good Guide to the Future

Even if progress toward zero poverty by 2030 is measured accurately and precisely, at least three features of poverty reduction make past progress in the MDG era too sunny a guide to what can be expected in future: the role of one-off institutional reforms in East Asia, whose effects are unlikely to be repeated; the characteristics of rice as an ideal food for the poor, which gives East Asia another advantage in poverty reduction; and the changing nature of poverty as countries escape mass poverty. Each of these factors is likely to make poverty reduction going forward much harder than it was for the two decades from 1990.

What Was Special about East Asia?

Many of the countries in East Asia can be described as highly capable states, with long histories of centralized government activity and social organization, but who recently followed misguided policy. China before Deng Xiaoping's reforms and Vietnam before *Doi Moi* are good examples, but Cambodia under the Khmer Rouge, Myanmar under the generals, and phases of despotic rule in Indonesia, Philippines, and Thailand can also be described in these terms. The contrast between North and South Korea is perhaps the starkest example of how misguided policies and institutions can stymie the escape from mass poverty. In contrast, many poor people elsewhere live in countries that have always had very limited state capacity. It is easier for highly capable states to stop

doing the wrong thing than for weak states to start doing the plethora of right things needed across the economic and political spectrum. Hence, one-off institutional reforms in East Asia may have triggered an escape from mass poverty that is simply not replicable, so poverty reduction elsewhere will be harder than it was in East Asia.

The Household Responsibility System in China, adopted after the abandonment of collective farming, is good illustration. It solved the monitoring problem by letting peasants once again become the residual claimant so that they had every incentive to apply optimal levels of effort and no need to divert resources to monitoring. While land under the HRS was still owned by the village, it was contracted out to individual households who had control rights over cultivation decisions and who could keep all of their output after they delivered a certain quota of grain to the state and made payment to village authorities for rent, taxes, and contributions to the public welfare fund.

Between 1979 and 1984, when the Household Responsibility System went from being used in almost no villages to being used in almost all villages, agricultural productivity increased tremendously. Figure 24.6 shows trends in Total Factor Productivity (TFP) for the three main crops of rice, wheat, and maize, based on Jin et al. (2002). For this six-year period of institutional change, the trend annual rate of productivity increase was 8.4 percent for rice, 10.7 percent for maize, and 12.2 percent for wheat; this rapid rise in output relative to the weighted sum of inputs stands in stark contrast to the prereform period where TFP had stagnated over much of the communal farming era. Productivity growth in African agriculture is also low, but there is no single thing that African governments can do (or stop doing) that will raise TFP in the remarkable way that China experienced by abandoning collective farming.

Rural China was overwhelmingly poor at the time of the HRS reforms; Ravallion and Chen (2007) estimate that 76 percent of the rural population was below the poverty line in 1980. Yet by 1985, when the HRS had been fully adopted, the rural poverty rate was less than one-third of this level, at just 23 percent. It is not overstating the case to argue that the abandonment of collective

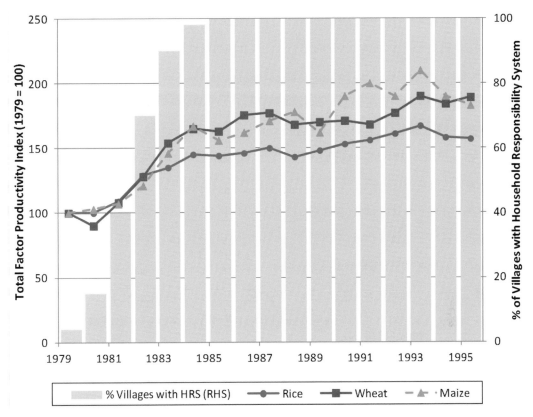

Figure 24.6 *Agricultural productivity jumps after household responsibility system reforms in China*

Source: Jin et al. (2002).

farming in China is the greatest antipoverty policy change in history. This one-off institutional reform, which has some parallels elsewhere in East Asia (e.g., the *Doi Moi* reform in Vietnam), had impacts that are unlikely to be replicated by any future reforms in countries where most of the poor now live.

A further feature of the institutional reforms in East Asia was their positive impacts on reducing inequality; this matters because as shown in Section 4, once countries escape mass poverty, the scope for further poverty reduction depends more on inequality than on growth. Again using China to illustrate, Figure 24.7 shows how one form of inequality – that between areas – fell sharply during the HRS reform period. The figure shows the (weighted) coefficient of variation in provincial GDP per capita, but the pattern is the

same if inequality is measured with the Gini coefficient or Theil index.[6]

The key thing to note from this example is that the shared prosperity occurred because the government stopped following (some) misguided policies, which also raised productivity. In the countries where the poor are now concentrated, the trade-offs between equity and efficiency are likely to be rather more difficult to deal with.

[6] The coefficient of variation is: $CoV = \sqrt{\sum_{j=1}^{m} (p_j/P)(y_{wj} - \mu)^2}/\mu$ where $m = 30$ provinces, p_j and P are the jth province's and the overall population, μ and y_{wj} are the jth province's and the overall population-weighted mean GDP per capita. The corrected resident population series developed by Li and Gibson (2013) is used in the calculations.

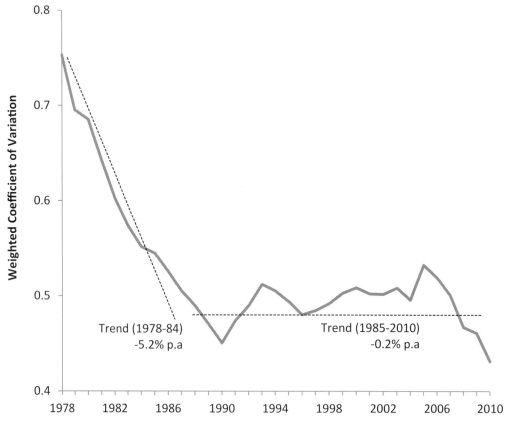

Figure 24.7 *Falling inequality as China abandoned collective farming*

NB: t-statistic for 1985–2010 trend is 0.8 and t-statistic for 1978–84 trend is 34.2.

The Role of Rice

Another key advantage for East Asia is from food; rice is more important in the diets of the poor in East Asia than in South Asia, and more important again than in sub-Saharan Africa. In East Asia, rice provides almost 60 percent of calories in the diets of the poor.[7] In contrast, for South Asia rice gives just over one-third of the calories for the poor and is not much more important than wheat, which provides one-quarter of calories.[8] What is special about rice as a food for the poor is its negative income elasticity and different long-run price trend than the other two major staples – maize and wheat. Timmer (2014) notes that rice has been an inferior good at the global level since the mid-1990s, and it was earlier shown to be an inferior

good in East Asia from the 1980s (Ito et al., 1989). In terms of price trends, the long-run rate of decline in rice prices is twice that of maize and ten times faster than the fall in wheat prices.[9] Thus, "even if

[7] This average, of 58 percent of calories, is based on cost-of-basic-needs (CBN) poverty line food baskets if available, and otherwise from reports on the composition of the diet broken down by income groups and/or sector. The calculation only covers rice as an ingredient, rather than the rice eaten as purchased meals and other ready-to-eat foods.

[8] The comparison uses World Bank developing country groups and is restricted to countries with populations greater than 5 million (but excludes North Korea).

[9] Timmer (2009) reports rice prices declined at –0.53 percent per annum over 1900–2008, conditional on prices of maize and wheat. For the other two staples, the conditional trend rates of decline were –0.27 percent (maize) and –0.05 percent (wheat).

maize and wheat prices remained stable in real terms, rice prices would be lower by more than 40 percent after a century" (Timmer, 2009, p. 26).

There is some debate about whether low food prices are good or bad for the poor, with dispute due especially to general equilibrium effects on wages (Jacoby, 2013). But most studies see high food prices as poverty-increasing because there are many more net buyers than net sellers. Thus, simulations that multiply agricultural incomes and household food spending by relative food price rises typically find net effects of higher poverty (de Hoyos and Medvedev, 2011), even with wage changes counted (Ivanic and Martin, 2008).[10] The effects of long-run falls in staple food prices in spurring poverty reduction will likely be even more important in future because the poor urbanize faster than developing country populations as a whole (Ravallion, Chen, and Sangraula, 2007), and the urban poor unambiguously benefit from lower grain prices (Wright, 2014).

The tendency for rice prices to fall faster than prices of other staples reflects features of rice, which make it close to a perfect food for the poor. As people escape poverty they quickly switch from rice and consume more income-elastic cereal products like bread, and also dairy, fats, and meats.[11] Rising consumption of these other foods does not raise indirect demand for rice, which is rarely used for animal feed. In contrast, a "food versus feed" competition arises with other staples as middle-class demand expands – in terms of the animals eaten by the middle class (Yotopoulos, 1985). Thus, people escaping poverty in countries where wheat or maize is the main source of calories may put pressure on prices of these staples because those crops also feed animals. In these countries, rising staples prices due to middle-class demand may trap some of the poor below the rapidly rising poverty line.

A further (tragically misguided) pressure on food prices is biofuels policy. Wright (2014) shows how these shift the output of calories from the food market (with low demand elasticities) to the price-elastic market for motor vehicle fuels, causing large price rises in the first market, little price change in the second market, and massive global wealth transfers from (poor) consumers to

(rich) farmers. While maize (and oilseeds) is a primary feedstock for biofuels, there is no direct biofuel demand for rice, which provided a further advantage for the escape from mass poverty in East Asia compared to other regions.

Changing Composition and Stubborn Persistence of Poverty

When a country is mired in mass poverty, the average poor person has characteristics that will not be dissimilar to the average person. But with the escape from mass poverty the poor increasingly begin to differ from the mainstream and therefore also from the decision makers. The same policies and interventions that worked for the majority may not work as well for these minorities, and there also may be less political will to eradicate poverty if the poor are increasingly different from the mainstream decision makers.

Consider the example of Vietnam, which has successfully escaped from mass poverty. When poverty was first measured, in 1993, four-fifths of the poor were either from the majority Kinh group or were Hoa (Chinese), and the remaining one-fifth were from ethnic minority groups (Figure 24.8a). But by 2010 the composition of the poor had greatly changed, with ethnic minority groups almost one-half of the total poor. The reason for this shift in composition is that the poverty rate for the Kinh/Hoa majority fell from over 50 percent to around 10 percent, but for ethnic minority groups the head count poverty rate never fell below 50 percent (Figure 24.8b).

---

[10] One of the few developing countries that may gain, in the aggregate, from higher prices of a food staple is Vietnam (Ivanic and Martin, 2008), but even there gains are more concentrated than losses, so higher rice prices make most households worse off (Linh and Glewwe, 2011).

[11] For example, in Indonesia the poorest 40 percent in rural areas increased rice consumption by about 1 percent per year over four decades to 2006, the next two quintiles had static consumption, and consumption of the richest rural quintile fell by about 1 percent per year (Timmer, 2014). For the poorest urban quintile, rice consumption was almost static, and demand fell monotonically for each richer quintile, with a fall of 1.6 percent per year for the richest quintile.

(a)
Composition of the Poor

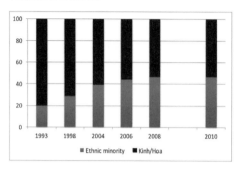

(b)
Poverty Rates

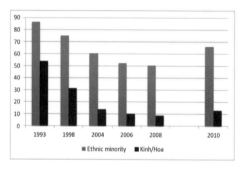

Figure 24.8 *Changing composition of poverty as countries escape mass poverty, Vietnam, 1993–2010*

Source: World Bank (2012).

The point of Figure 24.8 is that the poverty reduction that is yet to occur in Vietnam will need to be quite different to the poverty reduction that has already occurred. The factors that prevent ethnic minorities from participating in the general escape from poverty made by the majority will need to be dealt with, and the task is much harder. In this respect Vietnam is not atypical; for example, the analysis of poverty trends in India by Panagariya and Mukim (2014) shows that the head count poverty rate of scheduled castes and scheduled tribes was 32 percent above the all-group poverty rate in 1983, but by 2009/10 these minority groups (comprising one-quarter of India's population) had a poverty rate 44 percent above the average.

Moreover, a characteristic of many poverty-stricken ethnic minority groups is their higher fertility and younger age structure. For example, the 2001 census for India reveals a total fertility rate for the scheduled castes of 15 percent above the all-group fertility rate and for scheduled tribes of 25 percent above the all-group rate (Bose, 2001). In China, this factor is exacerbated by the exceptions to the one-child policy granted to ethnic minorities.

These structural gaps may take generations to close because they appear in early life in the form of schooling achievement gaps. For example, surveys of primary schools in rural China (Shaanxi, Gansu, and Qinghai provinces) show non-Han minority students whose mother tongue is not Mandarin score more than 0.6 standard deviations below Han students in standardized exams (Yang et al., 2013). These achievement gaps will lead to lower educational attainment, worse occupational outcomes, lower relative incomes, and a persistence of poverty among these minority group members. In getting to zero poverty, countries like Vietnam, China, and India will have to solve minority disadvantage problems that are still unresolved even in rich countries.

A Limited Cost-Benefit Analysis

Eliminating Extreme Poverty

To allow for a cost-benefit evaluation of zero targets for poverty, the cost of poverty can be calculated as change in the value of a country's human capital stock. The lifetime labor income approach of Jorgenson and Fraumeni (1989, 1992) measures human capital embodied in people and is based on the discounted present value of expected future labor incomes generated over the working life. This method uses time series of cross-sectional labor force surveys (or censuses), life tables to measure survival probabilities, and assumptions about future discount rates and growth rates in income.

A cross-country comparison of human capital for 16 OECD countries using this approach shows the stock of human capital is worth about five times the value of produced capital, and 8 to 16 times the value of GDP (Liu, 2013). This approach has also been applied to the long run history of Britain, for human capital estimates back to 1760 (Kunnas, 2016). Conditions in Britain in the eighteenth century were worse than in today's developing countries, with average life expectancy below 40 years (in comparison, a developing country like Vietnam had life expectancy already over 70 years at baseline for the MDGs in 1990). Moreover, the economic structure of eighteenth-century Britain was like today's poor countries, with more than 70 percent of the population in the countryside and three-quarters of the rural population involved in agriculture.

A person age a years with a certain level of education has expected earnings n years in the future that are assumed to be the current earnings of people of the same education and gender who are $a + n$ years old, adjusted for the expected rate of growth in real incomes. The present value of lifetime labor income for an individual is just their current annual labor income plus the present value of their expected lifetime income in the next period (this expectation also takes account of survival probabilities and unemployment risk at each age). Thus, by backward recursion from an assumed retirement age of 65, it is possible to calculate the present value of lifetime income at each age and to aggregate across cohorts to produce a national total value of human capital at a given point in time. The required formula is

$$H_a^t = W_a^t Y_a^t + S_{a,a+1}^t H_{a+1}^t (1 + g)/(1 + i)$$

H_a^t = per capita human capital; the present value of lifetime labor income, of individuals age a at time t;

W = employment rate;

Y = per capita current annual labor income of employed individuals;

$S_{a,a+1}$ = probability of surviving one more year from age a;

g = annual growth rate in real income;

i = discount rate.

To adapt this method to valuing poverty, an additional stratum for cohorts is needed – poverty status. Thus, separately for poor and nonpoor males and females, with different levels of educational qualifications, age-earnings profiles are estimated for Vietnam for every two years from 2002–2012. The use of Vietnam as an example is because of the credible estimates of the mortality due to poverty here (Banerjee and Duflo, 2010). Specifically, the five-year mortality rate of people who had been extremely poor or very poor (below PPP$2/day at baseline) was 1 percent, while for those on $2–$4 per day it was just 0.6 percent. These imply annual survival probabilities of 97.5 percent and 98.0 percent for the poor and nonpoor age 45+ years. The other assumptions are of an annual (real) discount rate of 0.03 and real income growth rate of 0.05. Cohorts are defined by four levels of completed education: no qualifications, primary, junior secondary, and senior secondary and above. Age-earnings profiles are estimated for paid employees and assumed to hold for the relevant working-age population of each cohort. The results are all reported in terms of December 2012 Dong, based on using the monthly CPI for Vietnam.[12]

Figure 24.9 shows estimated lifetime labor income for the four educational groups, within cohorts defined by gender and poverty status. These show the economic value of a person of a particular age and a particular type – in other words, you are the capitalized value of what you are expected to earn between now and retirement, after allowing for risks of unemployment and death. Thus, young, well-educated, nonpoor, males are worth over 3.5 billion dong (US$170,000) in the labor market while young, poor, unqualified, males are worth less than 1 billion dong. Old people are always worth less because they have fewer years remaining of expected earnings to be capitalized. Adding up these estimates across all ages and cohorts, and weighting by the (changing) size of each group in Vietnam, gives the aggregate value of human capital in each year.

In 2002 human capital in Vietnam was worth 22,667 trillion dong, and by 2012 this had increased to 63,049 trillion (all in December 2012 prices). This increase is equivalent to two trillion U.S. dollars at market exchange rates. Almost half

---

[12] The results for the value of human capital in Vietnam are from joint unpublished research with Dr. Trinh Le.

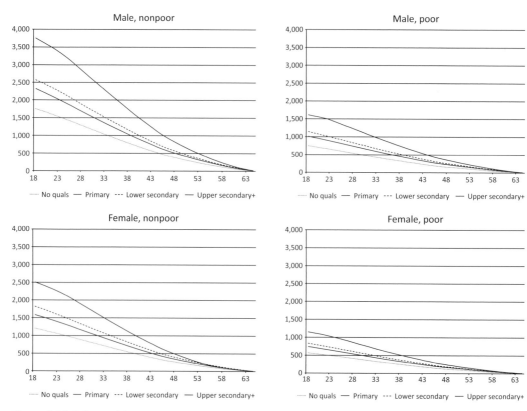

Figure 24.9 *Lifetime labor income by gender and poverty status, 2012 (million VN dong, in December 2012 prices)*

the increase was from labor market improvement, in terms of higher real wages and employment rates. The rise in the working-age population accounted for 18 percent of the human capital change, and poverty reduction accounted for 8 percent. Another one-quarter of the total increase in the value of human capital reflects interactions between these various factors.

These estimates of the baseline value of human capital are compared with a hypothetical case of zero extreme poverty. The "no poverty" value of aggregate human capital rises from 26,450 trillion dong in 2002 to 63,883 trillion dong in 2012. The gap between the baseline value of human capital and the no-poverty value gets proportionately smaller over time. In 2002, eradicating extreme poverty would have raised the aggregate value of human capital in Vietnam by 16.7 percent but by 2012 by just 1.3 percent.

How do these human capital benefits of poverty reduction compare with costs? Some simple, back-of-envelope, calculations are made here. The sum of poverty gaps is a lower bound to the cost of eliminating extreme poverty by means of perfectly targeted transfers. The present value of perpetual transfers at the level needed to close the poverty gaps are calculated, using a discount rate of 0.03 to match what is used in the human capital calculations. The calculated costs are presented in the first two columns of Table 24.1.

The estimated benefit of eradicating extreme poverty is based on the gap between the baseline human capital estimates and the no-poverty estimates. These capitalized values already take account of future income streams, so no further discounting is needed. Therefore, a comparison of the change in human capital – the marginal benefit of eradicating extreme poverty – and the cost of

Table 24.1 Comparison of monetary costs and benefits of eradicating extreme poverty in Vietnam (with benefits measured in terms of human capital)

Year	Hypothetical Costs of Eliminating Extreme Poverty With Transfers		Benefits of Eliminating Extreme Poverty and Benefit-Cost Ratio			
	Sum of the poverty gaps (trillion dong)	Present value of perpetual transfers (trillion dong)	Human Capital (trillion dong)			Benefit-to-Cost Ratio*
			Baseline	No Poverty	Change	
2002	18.2	606.4	22667	26450	3783	6.2
2004	13.6	452.5	25953	28444	2491	5.5
2006	10.9	364.8	33857	36168	2311	6.3
2008	11.5	383.2	37975	40180	2205	5.8
2010	3.4	112.6	55772	56748	976	8.7

Source: Author's calculations derived from joint unpublished research with Dr. Trinh Le.

* This benefit-to-cost ratio assumes that transfers are perfectly targeted; have no administrative, informational, and incentive cost; and also that the marginal cost of public funds needed for making the transfers is zero. These are clearly unrealistic assumptions.

perpetual transfers should yield a valid benefit to cost ratio. The figures in the last column of Table 24.1 suggest that this ratio ranges from 6 to 9, although further considerations need to be taken into account before drawing inferences from this.

First, transfers are not costless. A large literature estimates what is known as the "marginal cost of funds" – the fact that to raise a dollar of tax revenue (in order to make an antipoverty transfer or to fund any public spending) it costs the economy more than a dollar because of the deadweight losses caused by the tax system (Allgood and Snow, 1998). In a simulation analysis for 38 African countries, Warlters and Auriol (2005) suggest that the marginal cost of public funds ranges from 1.1 to 1.3.

In addition to the marginal cost of funds, one should allow for the administrative costs of making transfers. There is also the likelihood of targeting errors, and any informational cost of targeting. Putting these all together, the estimates of the present value of perpetual transfers in Table 24.1 should perhaps be raised by at least 50 percent. After making this adjustment, the benefit to cost ratios would be in the range of 4 to 6 rather than the 6 to 9 range as shown in the table. Moreover, Vietnam had one of the most successful records of economic growth and poverty reduction in the last two decades. Therefore, any extrapolating

from these estimates to other developing countries should add some discount for the fact that most of those other countries are unlikely to be as successful as Vietnam, and so the benefit-to-cost ratio elsewhere may be even lower. On balance, it seems that the target of eliminating extreme poverty should be place in the "Fair" category.

Other Poverty-Related SDG Targets

Social Protection

The High Level Panel suggested a target of "cover *x* percent of people who are poor and vulnerable with social protection systems" and the Open Working Group suggests that the social protection should include floors. An important aspect of the current enthusiasm for social protection programs is the hope that they can help to promote people out of poverty (Hashemi and Umaira, 2011). But there are grounds for doubting some of the mechanisms behind the promoting-out-of-poverty idea. Kraay and McKenzie (2014) show that evidence for poverty traps (the idea that poverty begets poverty) is quite weak. Long periods of stagnant incomes are rare, both for countries and for households, so being "stuck" in a low-level equilibrium is unlikely. Various claimed causal mechanisms for poverty traps also lack credible evidence.

One reputed basis for poverty traps is nutritional efficiency wages – the poor are too hungry to be able to work themselves out of poverty – but Subramanian and Deaton (1996) show that calories are too cheap for their lack to trap someone in poverty. Another claim is occupational poverty traps – the poor choose occupations and businesses with low entry costs (Dercon and Krishnan, 1996), but borrowing constraints and lumpy production technology keep them trapped earning at subsistence levels. However, the evidence from studies of microenterprises in Mexico (McKenzie and Woodruff, 2006) and Sri Lanka (de Mel, McKenzie, and Woodruff, 2009b) is that these enterprises can begin with a range of different starting capital levels, and those starting with a low level of capital are not necessarily trapped using a particular production technology that limits their scope for growth. In other words, stories about nonconvexities that lead to poverty traps are just that – stories.

Notwithstanding the lack of credible evidence for some of the background mechanisms, many conditional cash transfers (CCTs) aim to break intergenerational links to poor human capital for children. What is not given enough consideration, however, is that there may be various unobservable factors that limit the productivity of the parents, and thus limit the real income available for spending on children. These unobservable factors also may directly limit the development of the children, rather than the limitations coming just through lack of income. It is impossible for observational studies to show causal effects of household resource limitations on children's human capital, no matter how strong may be the empirical correlation between income and child outcomes. But analysis of a randomized program that gave large subsidies (equivalent to two-thirds of average income) gives grounds for caution; Jacob et al. (2014) found no effects of these transfers on children's schooling outcomes, or their subsequent criminal activity or health. This lack of effect from transfers contrasts with the results from observational studies in the same setting, where CCTs are associated with large changes in children's outcomes.

There are also grounds for concern about conditionality. When social protection benefits are targeted to groups that are perceived to be socially needy, individual members of those groups may have an incentive to continue the behavior that causes them to be viewed as needy. For example, in Brazil's *Bolsa Alimentacao*, an evaluation showed that children exposed to the program gained significantly less weight per month than similar children (Morris et al., 2004). The authors of the evaluation concluded that the failure of one of the target outcomes (children's weight) to respond positively to the program may have been due to a perception that benefits would be discontinued if the child started to grow well. That is, conditionality seemed to perpetuate the circumstances that the transfers were trying to overcome.

It is also the case that social protection programs create long-term fiscal obligations, and the burden of these may harm future economic growth. It is typical to see the fiscal costs of transfer programs reported as flow measures; for example, the International Labour Office suggest that the costs of a complete social protection package in low- and middle-income countries ranges from 4–11 percent of GDP per annum (Hagemejer, 2009). More sophisticated analyses are starting to forecast costs using lifetime simulations. For example, in New Zealand the lifetime cost of future fiscal liabilities for the cohort of current welfare beneficiaries was estimated by actuaries as equivalent to 59 percent of GDP (Bennett, 2012). This actuarial analysis also showed a large gap between the programs with the most policy attention and the ones that were the big drivers of future costs (McBride and Greenfield, 2013). In general, the costly programs were the ones that expanded in a passive, demand-driven, way so that large future fiscal liabilities were created with not much attention paid to them.

For the countries that have not yet created these fiscal burdens, they should carefully consider the incidence of the taxes needed to fund such transfer programs. In a world with increasing competition for skilled workers (Kapur and McHale, 2005), relying on highly progressive taxes to fund social transfers may be unwise. The developing countries with such taxes already suffer heavy fiscal losses from the emigration of highly skilled workers (Gibson and McKenzie, 2012), and it is likely that intercountry competition for such workers will intensify in future given uneven population aging trends. The funding of expanded social protection programs may therefore by quite vulnerable, and international targets that encourage such expansion may be unhelpful.

Taking all of these considerations into account, the best that can be said about the social protection target is that the ratio of benefits to costs remains uncertain. If this target had to be consigned to a particular evaluation category, it would most likely be "Poor," given the many unintended consequences that may result.

Disaster Resilience

The target proposed by the Open Working Group is to "build resilience of the poor and reduce by x percent deaths and economic losses related to disasters." Because deaths and losses due to disasters are bad things, the goal of reducing these losses seems like a good thing. But like all good things, it is best in moderation. In fact, economics has a standard for exactly how much moderation is needed: the socially efficient standard is to reduce the risk from disasters only to the point where the marginal cost per life saved is the same as for other risk-reducing activities (Viscusi, 2000). The target as stated has nothing about an efficiency standard, in terms of the level of death and loss reduction expected per dollar invested into disaster resilience, so it should be considered as poorly specified. If this target was adopted, it would likely lead to overinvestment in disaster-mitigation activities, at the cost of underinvestment in other risk-reducing activities.

Disasters are costly, and all else the same, we would like that they did less damage and took fewer lives. But just how costly they are is not very clear because the estimates available typically use different methods, with quite big discrepancies between them. Some variation in estimates is also due to the multiple dimensions of impacts from natural disasters and the large redistributive effects; these make it hard to determine whether the various published cost estimates correspond to net welfare impacts (Hallegatte and Przyluski, 2010). Notwithstanding these comparability issues, when a development target specifies reducing losses from a particular

type of risk and does not put it in a framework of efficient overall risk reduction, there is a high likelihood that costly distortions will result.

By enshrining a target of reducing deaths related to a particular type of risk – disasters in this case – while not dealing with other risks, it will almost surely guarantee that countries will misallocate their risk mitigation and risk-bearing efforts. Society often spends too much to reduce some risks (and not enough to reduce others) because of political influences and errors in judgment about risk (Viscusi and Hamilton, 1999). These inefficiencies cost lives, which is ironic because proponents of the disasters target are probably motivated by a desire to save lives. Stricter disaster mitigation standards may have the perverse effect of creating such large social losses that they cause an *increase* in expected mortality. The reason for this paradox is that excessive disaster risk standards will reduce incomes because "too many" resources are spent on trying to prevent losses from disasters. This wasteful overinvestment in reducing loss from a particular risk provides a lower return than if the money was spent in other ways, and so lowers incomes. At lower incomes, people engage in more risky activities (Lutter, Morrall, and Viscusi, 1999). Therefore, in general, undertaking an inefficiently excessive risk reduction effort may, paradoxically, increase the expected number of deaths through this income pathway (Gerdtham, 2002).

Apart from making this logical point, about a poorly specified development target, no evaluation is attempted here. Fundamentally the costs and benefits of this target are unknowable because an evaluation of disaster resilience has to use endogenous damage functions and there is no clear basis on which these can be identified. These damage functions would apply if, say, attempts at protection against disasters by forming seawalls for defense against tsunami or stop banks for flood protection, lead to increased land use in the at-risk zone, and that greater land use then causes losses to increase. In conclusion, this post-2015 target should be considered as "Poor" because it is poorly specified, and if followed closely, it would likely result in inefficient patterns of risk reduction.

Economic Rights

The target proposed by the Open Working Group is to "ensure equality of economic opportunity for all women and men, including secure rights to own land, property and other productive assets and access to financial services for all women and men," while the High Level Panel suggest a target of increasing the proportion of the population with secure rights to land, property, and other assets. These can broadly be considered as targeting "economic rights" with a special focus on equalizing rights for men and women. Although there is nothing egregious about this target, the motivation for the gender-focus may reflect an outdated reading of the evidence.

The evidence from agriculture is that there seems to be a gender bias in access to productive assets and inputs, and/or in the returns to entrepreneurial and labor effort. For example, a longitudinal study of coffee producers in Papua New Guinea found returns to men's own-account coffee production up to twice the returns to women's work on coffee (Overfield, 1998). Women reacted to this by allocating more time to the cash-earning activities that they had more control over, especially vegetable production and marketing, even though net returns to the household were lower from vegetables than they were from coffee. Female labor is the binding constraint in this environment (also seen from marriage market institutions of bride price rather than dowry), and unequal access to inputs that skews female labor allocation harmed overall household production efficiency (Overfield and Fleming, 2001). Similarly, in Burkina Faso, household output could potentially have been 10–20 percent higher if inputs were reallocated across the plots controlled by men and women (Udry et al., 1995). These authors also note how policy interventions aiming to reduce this apparent inefficiency might be thwarted by changes in male labor supply and changes in bargaining in the marriage market. Another result comes from Benin; female rice farmers are discriminated against with regard to irrigation scheme membership and access to land and equipment, resulting in significant negative impacts on their productivity and income, despite women appearing

to be equally as technically efficient as men (Kinkingninhoun-Mêdagbé et al., 2010).[13]

Yet it is unclear if gender inequalities in access to productive inputs (including finance) cause the same inefficiencies in other sectors of the economy. Because agriculture declines with development while these other sectors become more important, targets for the post-2015 period should probably pay less attention to the evidence from agriculture and more attention to evidence from other parts of the economy. This nonagricultural evidence is much more recent and so may not have influenced the perceptions of participants in the debates about the post-2015 agenda. The other feature of this new evidence is that it tends to be more rigorously identified than the earlier evidence from agriculture, which was exclusively based on observational studies. Some of the most credible evidence comes from the randomized allocation of grants to microenterprise owners, which overcomes some of the problems of previous studies caused by endogeneity of input choices. In Sri Lanka, these grants resulted in large, sustained increases in income for male owners but no increase in income for female owners (de Mel, McKenzie, and Woodruff, 2009a). In urban Ghana, where cash and in-kind grants were randomly given to male- and female-owned microenterprises (Fafchamps et al., 2014), this additional capital caused no gain in profits for female-owned subsistence enterprises (although there were some effects for the larger enterprises run by women). These results suggest that capital alone may not be enough to grow subsistence enterprises owned by women, and that even with equal access to inputs for male and female entrepreneurs, there may not be the changes in outputs or profits that might be expected, based on the prior results in the agricultural sector.

It is also unclear how countries would monitor the percentage of their population with secure rights to land, property, other assets, and financial services. Most property rights are not binary

[13] An earlier review found that it seems to be a general feature of farming in low-income countries that males and females are equally as technically efficient (Quisumbing, 1996).

variables but instead vary in strength. That subtlety would be hard to capture in an easily comparable indicator over time and space. Although there is a large literature on access to finance, and one could use surveys to monitor whether men or women have higher rates of bank account ownership, technological change is quickly undermining such indicators. In many developing countries, all that will be needed to access financial services in the future is a mobile phone. Given these difficulties, one could imagine that monitoring of this proposed post-2015 target might be based on an indicator that measured formalization of informal businesses and employment because promoting formalization is also a goal that has emerged from other parts of the post-2015 dialogue. Yet the evidence is that most informal firms appear not to benefit from formalizing and that it is unclear whether there is a public rationale for trying to formalize subsistence enterprises (Bruhm and McKenzie, 2014). Thus, if some variant of this "economic rights" target is adopted, it quite likely will be used to support a formalization drive that is probably unnecessary. Perhaps the best categorization of this target is "Uncertain" because the evidence does not show consistent patterns, and also because this rating may give policy makers grounds for pause before they embark on misguided efforts to promote formalization when the evidence to support such policies is weak at best.

Full Employment

The target proposed by the Open Working Group is to "achieve full and productive employment for all, including women and young people." There is no similar target proposed by the High Level Panel. Yet without any further consideration of what full employment means, this is an empty target because there is no clear basis for what is to be monitored.

The typical notion used by economists for "full employment" is the nonaccelerating inflation rate of unemployment (NAIRU). The NAIRU corresponds to a level of unemployment that, if policy makers attempted to lower it further (e.g., by stimulatory monetary policy), the rate of inflation would rise. It is difficult to see how a post-2015

target could accommodate this complexity because the NAIRU is well above zero. Moreover, there are further complications. First, the NAIRU varies over time; for example, estimates for the United States suggest that the NAIRU has varied between 4.8 percent and 6.5 percent over the last couple of decades.[14] Second, these variations in the NAIRU may have systematic causes, such as productivity shocks, demographic change, trade policy, and changes in the efficiency of job matching (Ball and Mankiw, 2002). None of these factors would be expected to stay constant during a 15-year period that corresponds to the length of time that the post-2015 target might be on the books. Therefore, adherence to this target would potentially distort the flexibility of macroeconomic policy around the world for a long time.

It is also likely that this full-employment target would be used by some policy makers and interest groups to argue for greater employment protection provisions. Yet the economic evidence is that employment protection regulations are costly for the overall economy and often end up hurting the very workers they are designed to protect. In terms of economy-wide effects, Besley and Burgess (2004) studied variation in pro-worker employment regulation in India, and found that states with such a bias had increased urban poverty and lowered output, employment, investment, and productivity in formal manufacturing. These regulations also increased the size of the informal sector (hence, potentially working against the aims of the formalization target discussed under the "economic rights" section earlier).

There is also evidence that these type of employment protection regulations tend to hurt vulnerable workers. Leonardi and Pica (2013) exploit a natural experiment from a reform in Italy that raised the cost for employers of dismissing workers from

---

[14] The Philadelphia Federal Research Bank provides a spreadsheet with "real time" estimates of the NAIRU calculated by their economists, available here: www.philadelphiafed.org/research-and-data/real-time-center/greenbook-data/nairu-dataset.cfm. These estimates vary quarter by quarter, but also by forecast vintage; there may be different estimates of the NAIRU for the same quarter, as understanding about the state of the business cycle and the available productive capacity of the economy varies over time.

small firms. Theory predicts that offered wages will be lower if employers demand compensation for higher expected future firing costs (Lazear, 1990), and the empirical results support this; roughly two-thirds of the expected increase in firing costs is translated onto lower wages. The effects are concentrated on the entry wage of newly hired workers, who lose up to 6 percent of their wage upon hire by a small firm after the reform, with the negative effects especially marked for young, blue-collar, workers with low bargaining power.

The evidence suggests that a "full employment" target would be difficult to monitor because there is a lot of complexity as to what full employment means. Such a target also would likely cause a number of perverse, costly, and unintended consequences in the labor market and more broadly. As such, this proposed target falls into the "Poor" category.

Conclusions

The last 30 years have seen huge progress in reducing extreme poverty in many parts of the world, but there are several reasons to doubt that the zero poverty goal under the SDGs will be reached in time. First, there are compositional effects that likely will be a drag on progress: at the global level the evident success of East Asia in escaping from mass poverty becomes ever less relevant over time because few of the poor are left in East Asia, while the much slower escape from poverty in sub-Saharan Africa increasingly matters because that is where the largest number of the poor now are. Moreover, the success of East Asia in realizing rapid poverty reduction is not easily repeated elsewhere.

Compositional effects also come into play at the micro level; with the escape from mass poverty, the remaining poor increasingly come from ethnic or religious minorities. Even in rich countries it has proven difficult to overcome the structural disadvantages that prevent some groups from sharing in the prosperity enjoyed by others. The declining marginal value of poverty reduction – in terms of the contribution to aggregate human capital – as

countries escape from mass poverty is also apparent from the example of Vietnam.

Finally, after the escape from mass poverty, it is increasingly inequality rather than growth that matters for further poverty reduction. There may be more risk of distributional conflict when the main poverty fighting policy is to dampen inequality compared to when growth-oriented policies were the best option. Moreover, the heightened sensitivity of poverty to inequality makes measuring increasingly difficult. The survey designs that do a reasonable job of capturing average living standards for a poor and rural population may do a poor job of measuring inequality in an increasingly affluent and urban population. Indeed, a missed opportunity of the SDGs was to make policy makers more cognizant of these measurement difficulties and to push for improvements in monitoring the poverty reduction actually occurring without the distraction from perhaps unlikely zero targets.

References

Allgood, S., and Snow, A. (1998). The marginal cost of raising tax revenue and redistributing income. *Journal of Political Economy*, *106*(6), 1246–73.

Ball, L., and Mankiw, G. (2002). The NAIRU in theory and practice. *Journal of Economic Perspectives*, *16*(4), 115–36.

Banerjee, A., and Duflo, E. (2010). Aging and Death under a Dollar a Day. In D. Wise (ed.) *Research Findings in the Economics of Aging* (pp. 169–203). Chicago: University of Chicago Press.

Beegle, K., De Weerdt, J., Friedman, J., and Gibson, J. (2012). Methods of household consumption measurement through surveys: experimental results from Tanzania. *Journal of Development Economics*, *98*(1), 3–18.

Benjamin, D., Brandt, L., and Giles, J. (2005). The evolution of income inequality in rural China. *Economic Development and Cultural Change*, *53*(4), 769–824.

Bennett, P. (2012). Investment approach refocuses entire welfare system. Ministry of Social Development, Wellington, New Zealand. www.msd.govt.nz/about-msd-and-our-work/

newsroom/media-releases/2012/valuation-report.html.

Besley, T., and Burgess, R. (2004). Can labor regulation hinder economic performance? Evidence from India. *The Quarterly Journal of Economics*, *119*(1), 91–134.

Bose, A. (2001). *Population of India: 2001 Census Results and Methodology*. Delhi: BR Publishing Corporation, Distributed by BRPC (India).

Bruhn, M., and McKenzie, D. (2014). Entry regulation and the formalization of microenterprises in developing countries. *The World Bank Research Observer*, *29*(2), 186–201.

Cafiero C. 2014. Advances in hunger measurement: traditional FAO methods and recent innovations. *FAO Statistics Division Working Paper Series* No. 14–04.

Chen, S., Datt, G., and Ravallion, M. (2000). *POVCAL: A Program for Calculating Poverty Measures from Grouped Data*. Development Research Group. Washington, DC: The World Bank.

Chen, S., and Ravallion, M. (2001). How did the world's poorest fare in the 1990s? *Review of Income and Wealth*, *47*(3), 283–300.

(2010). The developing world is poorer than we thought, but no less successful in the fight against poverty. *The Quarterly Journal of Economics*, *125*(4), 1577–1625.

(2013). More relatively-poor people in a less absolutely-poor world. *Review of Income and Wealth*, *59*(1), 1–28.

Clunies-Ross, A., and Huq, M. (2014). *The Universal Social Safety-Net and the Attack on World Poverty: Pressing Need, Manageable Cost, Practical Possibilities, Favourable Spillovers*. New York: Routledge.

Deaton, A. (2005). Measuring poverty in a growing world (or measuring growth in a poor world). *Review of Economics and Statistics*, *87*(1), 1–19.

Deaton, A., and Dupriez, O. (2011). Purchasing power parity exchange rates for the global poor. *American Economic Journal: Applied Economics*, *3*(2), 137–66.

de Hoyos, R., and Medvedev, D. (2011). Poverty effects of higher food prices: a global perspective. *Review of Development Economics*, *15*(3), 387–402.

de Mel, S., McKenzie, D., and Woodruff, C. (2009b). Innovative Firms or Innovative Owners? Determinants of Innovation in Micro, Small, and Medium Enterprises. *IZA Discussion Paper* No. 3962, Institute for the Study of Labor.

(2009a). Are women more credit constrained? Experimental evidence on gender and microenterprise returns. *American Economic Journal: Applied Economics*, *1*(3), 1–32.

Dercon, S., and Krishnan, P. (1996). Income portfolios in rural Ethiopia and Tanzania: choices and constraints. *The Journal of Development Studies*, *32*(6), 850–75.

De Weerdt, J., Beegle, K., Friedman, J., and Gibson, J. (2016). The challenge of measuring hunger through survey. *Economic Development and Cultural Change*, *64*(4), 727–58.

Dupriez, O., Smith, L., and Troubat, N. (2014). *Assessment of the Reliability and Relevance of the Food Data Collected in National Household Consumption and Expenditure Surveys*. FAO, IHSN and World Bank accessed 6 April 2014: www.ihsn.org/home/node/34.

Fafchamps, M., McKenzie, D., Quinn, S., and Woodruff, C. (2014). Microenterprise growth and the flypaper effect: evidence from a randomized experiment in Ghana. *Journal of Development Economics*, *106*(1), 211–26.

Foster, J., Greer, J., and Thorbecke, E. (1984). A class of decomposable poverty measures. *Econometrica*, 761–66.

Gerdtham, U.-G. (2002). Do life-saving regulations save lives? *Journal of Risk and Uncertainty*, *24*(3), 231–49.

Gibson, J. (2001). Measuring chronic poverty without a panel. *Journal of Development Economics*, *65*(2), 243–66.

(2006). Statistical Tools and Estimation Methods for Poverty Measures Based on Cross-Sectional Household Surveys. In G. Kamanou (ed.) *United Nations Handbook of Poverty Statistics* (pp. 128–205). New York: United Nations Statistics Division.

(2016). Measuring Chronic Hunger from Diet Snapshots: Why "Bottom up" Survey Counts and "Top down" FAO Estimates Will Never Meet. *Working Paper* 16/07, Department of Economics, University of Waikato.

Gibson, J., and McKenzie, D. (2012). The economic consequences of "brain drain" of the best and brightest: microeconomic evidence from five countries. *The Economic Journal*, *122*(560), 339–75.

Gibson, J., Rozelle, S., and Huang, J. (2001). Why is income inequality so low in China compared to other countries? The effect of household survey methods. *Economics Letters*, 71(3): 329–333.

(2003). Improving estimates of inequality and poverty from urban China's Household Income and Expenditure survey. *Review of Income and Wealth*, 49(1): 53–68.

Hagemejer, K. (2009). Rights-Based Approach to Social Security Coverage Expansion. In R. Holzmann, D. Robalino, and N. Takayama (eds.), *Closing the Coverage Gap: The Role of Social Pensions and Other Retirement Income Transfers* (pp. 57–72). Washington, DC: The World Bank.

Hallegatte, S., and Przyluski, V. (2010). *The Economics of Natural Disasters: Concepts and Methods.* World Bank. https://openknowledge .worldbank.org/handle/10986/3991 License: Creative Commons Attribution CC BY 3.0.

Hashemi, S., and Umaira, W. (2011). New pathways for the poorest: the graduation model from BRAC. *CSP Research Report* No. 10, Centre for Social Protection and Institute for Development Studies, University of Sussex.

Ito, S., Peterson, E., and Grant, W. (1989). Rice in Asia: is it becoming an inferior good? *American Journal of Agricultural Economics*, 71(1), 32–42.

Ivanic, M., and Martin, W. (2008). Implications of higher global food prices for poverty in low-income countries. *Agricultural Economics*, 39(s1), 405–16.

Jacob, B., Kapustin, M., and Ludwig, J. (2014). Human capital effects of anti-poverty programs: Evidence from a randomized housing voucher lottery. *Working Paper* No. w20164, National Bureau of Economic Research.

Jacoby, H. (2013). Food prices, wages, and welfare in rural India. *Policy Research Working Paper* No. 6412, The World Bank.

Jin, S., Huang, J., Hu, R., and Rozelle, S. (2002). The creation and spread of technology and total factor productivity in China's agriculture. *American Journal of Agricultural Economics*, 84(4), 916–30.

Jolliffe, D. (2006). Poverty, prices, and place: how sensitive is the spatial distribution of poverty to cost-of-living adjustments? *Economic Inquiry*, 44(2), 296–310.

Jorgenson, D., and Fraumeni, B. (1989). The Accumulation of Human and Non-Human Capital, 1948–1984. In R. E. Lipsey and H. S. Tice (eds.), *The Measurement of Savings, Investment, and Wealth*. Chicago: The University of Chicago Press.

(1992). Investment in education and U.S. economic growth. *Scandinavian Journal of Economics*, 94(*Supp*), 51–70.

Kapur, D., and McHale, J. (2005). *Give Us Your Best and Brightest: The Global Hunt for Talent and Its Impact on the Developing World.* Washington, DC: Center for Global Development.

Kinkingninhoun-Mêdagbé, F., Diagne, A., Simtowe, F., Agboh-Noameshie, A., and Adégbola, P. (2010). Gender discrimination and its impact on income, productivity, and technical efficiency: evidence from Benin. *Agriculture and Human Values*, 27(1), 57–69.

Kraay, A., and McKenzie, D. (2014). Do Poverty Traps Exist? *Policy Research Working Paper*, No. 6835, The World Bank.

Kunnas, J. (2016). Human capital in Britain, 1760–2009. *Scandinavian Economic History Review*, 1–24.

Lazear, E. (1990). Job security provisions and employment. *Quarterly Journal of Economics*, 105(3), 699–726.

Leonardi, M., and Pica, G. (2013). Who pays for it? The heterogeneous wage effects of employment protection legislation. *The Economic Journal*, 123(573), 1236–78.

Li, C., and Gibson, J. (2013). Rising Regional Inequality in China: Fact or Artifact? *World Development*, 47(1), 16–29.

(2014). Spatial price differences and inequality in the People's Republic of China: housing market evidence. *Asian Development Review*, 31(1), 92–120.

Lin, J. (1987). The household responsibility system reform in China: a peasant's institutional choice. *American Journal of Agricultural Economics*, 69(2), 410–15.

Linh, V., and Glewwe, P. (2011). Impacts of rising food prices on poverty and welfare in Vietnam. *Journal of Agricultural and Resource Economics*, 36(1), 14–27.

Liu, G. (2013). Measuring the Stock of Human Capital for International and Inter-temporal Comparisons. In *Measuring Economic Sustainability and Progress*. Chicago: University of Chicago Press. www.nber.org/ chapters/c12832.pdf.

Lutter, R., Morrall, J., and Viscusi, W. K. (1999). The cost-per-life-saved cutoff for safety-enhancing regulations. *Economic Inquiry*, *37*(4), 599–608.

Ma, H., Huang, J., Fuller, F., and Rozelle, S. (2006). Getting rich and eating out: consumption of food away from home in urban China. *Canadian Journal of Agricultural Economics*, *54*(1), 101–19.

Marshall, A. (1890). *Principles of Economics* (8th ed., 1920), London: Macmillan; reprinted by Prometheus Books.

McBride, B., and Greenfield, A. (2013). Actuarial valuation of the New Zealand welfare system. Presentation at the Actuaries Summit, Sydney, May 2013. www.actuaries.asn.au/Library/Events/SUM/2013/3d-GreenfieldMcBride.pdf.

McKenzie, D. 2012. Beyond baseline and follow-up: The case for more T in experiments. *Journal of Development Economics*, *99*(2): 210–221.

McKenzie, D., and Woodruff, C. (2006). Do entry costs provide an empirical basis for poverty traps? Evidence from Mexican microenterprises. *Economic Development and Cultural Change*, *55*(1), 3–42.

Morduch, J. (1998). Poverty, economic growth, and average exit time. *Economics Letters*, *59*(3), 385–90.

Morris, S., Olinto, P., Flores, R., Nilson, E., and Figueiro, A. (2004). Conditional cash transfers are associated with a small reduction in the rate of weight gain of preschool children in northeast Brazil. *The Journal of Nutrition*, *134*(9), 2336–41.

Olinto, P., Ibarra, G., and Saavedra-Chanduvi, J. (2014). Accelerating poverty reduction in a less poor world. *Policy Research Working Paper* No. 6855, The World Bank.

Olinto, P., and Uematsu, H. (2013). The state of the poor: where are the poor and where are they poorest? *World Bank Poverty and Equity Department*.

Overfield, D. (1998). An investigation of the household economy: coffee production and gender relations in Papua New Guinea. *Journal of Development Studies*, *34*(1), 52–70.

Overfield, D., and Fleming, E. (2001). A note on the influence of gender relations on the technical efficiency of smallholder coffee production in Papua New Guinea. *Journal of Agricultural Economics*, *52*(1), 153–56.

Panagariya, A., and Mukim, M. (2014). A comprehensive analysis of poverty in India. *Asian Development Review*, *31*(1), 1–52.

Pinkovskiy, M., and Sala-i-Martin, X. (2009). Parametric estimations of the world distribution of income. *Working Paper* No. w15433, National Bureau of Economic Research.

Quisumbing, A. (1996). Male-female differences in agricultural productivity: methodological issues and empirical evidence. *World Development*, *24*(10), 1579–95.

Ravallion, M. (2011). The two poverty enlightenments: Historical insights from digitized books spanning three centuries. *Policy Research Working Paper* No. 5549, The World Bank.

(2016). *The Economics of Poverty: History, Measurement, and Policy*, New York: Oxford University Press.

Ravallion, M., and Chen, S. (2007). China's (uneven) progress against poverty. *Journal of Development Economics*, *87*(1), 1–42.

Ravallion, M., Chen, S., and Sangraula, P. (2007). New evidence on the urbanization of global poverty. *Population and Development Review*, *33*(4), 667–701.

Slesnick, D. (1993). Gaining ground: poverty in the postwar United States. *Journal of Political Economy*, *101*(1), 1–38.

Smith, L. C. (2015). The great Indian calorie debate: explaining rising undernourishment during India's rapid economic growth. *Food Policy*, *50*(1), 53–67.

Subramanian, S., and Deaton, A. (1996). The demand for food and calories. *Journal of Political Economy*, *104*(1), 133–62.

Timmer, C. P. (2009). Rice price formation in the short run and the long run: The role of market structure in explaining volatility. *Working Paper* No. 172, Center for Global Development, Washington DC.

(2014). Food security in Asia and the Pacific: The rapidly changing role of rice. *Asia & The Pacific Policy Studies*, *1*(1), 73–90.

Udry, C., Hoddinott, J., Alderman, H., and Haddad, L. (1995). Gender differentials in farm productivity: implications for household efficiency and agricultural policy. *Food Policy*, *20*(5), 407–23.

Viscusi, W. K. (2000). Risk equity. *Journal of Legal Studies*, *29*(2), 843–71.

Viscusi, W. K., and Hamilton, J. (1999). Are risk regulators rational? Evidence from hazardous waste cleanup decisions. *American Economic Review*, *89*(4), 1010–27.

Warlters, M., and Auriol, E. (2005). The marginal cost of public funds in Africa. *Policy Research Working Paper* No. 3679, The World Bank.

Wen, G. (1993). Total factor productivity change in China's farming sector: 1952–1989. *Economic Development and Cultural Change*, *42*(1), 1–41.

World Bank (2012). *Well Begun, Not Yet Done: Vietnam's Remarkable Progress on Poverty Reduction and the Emerging Challenges*. Hanoi: World Bank.

  (2014). *A Measured Approach to Ending Poverty and Boosting Shared Prosperity: Concepts, Data, and the Twin Goals*. Washington, DC: World Bank. doi:10.1596/978-1-4648-0361-1.

Wright, B. (2014). Global biofuels: key to the puzzle of grain market behavior. *The Journal of Economic Perspectives*, *28*(1), 73–97.

Yang, Y., Wang, H., Zhang, L., et al. (2013). The Han-minority achievement gap, language and returns to schools in Rural China. *Working Paper* No. 258, Rural Education Action Project, Stanford University.

Yixin, C. (2010). Under the Same Maoist Sky: Accounting for Death Rate Discrepancies in Anhui and Jiangxi. In K. Manning and F. Wemheuer (eds), *Eating Bitterness: New Perspectives on China's Great Leap Forward and Famine* (pp. 197–225). Vancouver: UBC Press.

Yotopoulos, P. (1985). Middle-income classes and food crises: The "new" food-feed competition. *Economic Development and Cultural Change*, *33*(3), 463–83.

24.1 Alternative Perspective

GUARAV DATT

Summary

This chapter offers some reflections on the components of SDG1, dealing with poverty, noting first its huge scope. Ending poverty can justifiably be seen as an overarching aim of all development efforts, and hence one can hardly object to SDG1 as an aspirational goal for "the future we want."

The target on eradication of extreme poverty (SDG1.1) is similar to that set by the World Bank. However, the latter calls for reduction to a minimal, low target (3 percent). The conceptual argument has to do with the notion of "frictional" poverty – the idea that at any given point in time, there may always be an irreducible lower bound to poverty given that economic systems are constantly in the process of adjusting to shocks of one kind or another, and even the most comprehensive social protection system is unlikely to guarantee that no one ever falls below the poverty line. This is conceptually sounder, and the post-2015 target should be aligned with this.

However, the 3 percent is a global target, which raises the uncomfortable possibility that it could be reached with many smaller countries still having much higher levels of extreme poverty. This is a very real possibility, given that there are 17 countries with a projected poverty incidence of 30 percent or higher (15 in sub-Saharan Africa) in 2030, by which time the global incidence is projected to have reached 4.8 percent, based on growth data from national accounts.

There is also an issue of Purchasing Power Parities. The $1.25 per day figure is set in terms of 2005 PPPs, but a new set became available in 2011. These are controversial, but there is agreement is that the new PPPs entail a large downward revision relative to the 2005 PPPs if extrapolated to 2011 using relative rates of inflation. This is not a trivial issue, as the use of the new PPPs *without a recalibration of the 2005 $1.25 poverty standard* could imply a reduction of the incidence of extreme poverty by more than half. There is no agreement on which set of figures should be used, but the debate argues for some flexibility in the post-2015 target. The threshold of extreme poverty should be reviewed with each methodologically-sound revision of purchasing-power parity exchange rates.

SDG1.2 is to halve the incidence of "poverty in all its dimensions." Rather than seeing poverty purely in terms of income or consumption, this focuses attention on specific capability failures relating to health, education, shelter, and access to basic amenities. These may be the result both of market failures and government failures, particularly in relation to public goods and how markets function. This calls for the use of a composite index such as the Multidimensional Poverty Index. However, it is difficult to judge whether halving is an under- or overambitious target without settling how what is proposed to be halved is measured.

Regarding the remaining three targets, social protection, social exclusion, and resilience against shocks overlap with other goals and are difficult to separate. They should therefore probably not be seen as independent components of the overall poverty goal. Nevertheless, on the issue of resilience to shocks, there is a case for augmenting the targets to include the vulnerable as well as just the poor. The poor are a subset of the vulnerable, but the vulnerable could include many nonpoor who are nonetheless vulnerable to poverty in that they could be consigned to the ranks of the poor if hit by a negative shock.

24.2 Alternative Perspective

VALERIE KOZEL

Summary

The Copenhagen Consensus Center's initiative to sponsor "hard-nosed" assessments of the economic costs and benefits of proposed goals and targets, along with the strengths and weaknesses of data and methodologies to monitor progress, is providing welcome contributions to ongoing discussions. The chapter from John Gibson raises three questions: Do the proposed poverty targets strike the right balance between breadth, idealism, and realism? Is it appropriate to focus solely on extreme poverty ($1.25 a day)? and Are data and monitoring methodologies sufficiently robust and well-specified to carry the debate forward?

The proposed post-2015 Sustainable Development Goals are a broader and more ambitious set of development goals than the previous MDGs. The call to eradicate poverty "in all its forms everywhere" is very ambitious. None but the most idealistic believe that this goal – or the other SDG zero-goals – are possible to achieve. Gibson points out some of the underlying features of rapid poverty reduction in the past that are not likely to carry forward into the future. There is one important additional factor that may slow the pace of future poverty reduction: as policies and programs become more narrowly targeted and concentrate on groups that have been socially excluded or are discriminated against, they may not have widespread political support.

Although the proposed targets have been criticized as being too ambitious, others argue that the $1.25 a day poverty line is not ambitious enough and has no relevance for middle- and upper-income countries. By this reckoning, a set of (higher-order) goals is needed that better capture the rising aspirations that all countries have for the well-being of their citizens. We take the view that

"stretch" goals have an essential role in post-2015 SDG discussions.

Reducing global poverty, as defined using a truly global standard that reflects standards that apply in all countries, would be an additional such goal to put alongside the proposed zero target for extreme poverty. Taking out the billion people in extreme poverty, and the billion who are prosperous by global standards, leaves five billion who are poor by standards of rich countries but not poor by the standards of the very poorest countries. The short answer to the question of whether the $1.25 a day target is the only one that matters is "of course not."

Although we have learned a lot about what it takes to reduce poverty, we still struggle – and endlessly debate – how best to measure poverty and monitor progress. The chapter does a nice job of describing current problems with poverty data and measurement methodologies and notes – correctly – that measurement problems are likely to worsen over time. Changes in consumption patterns affect the poor as well as the more affluent and must be reflected in surveys.

Although there is clearly merit in harmonization to enable global comparability, different methodologies also reflect the cultures and needs of individual countries. National governments are much more interested in making consistent comparisons over time than modifying their systems to comply with global standards. Nevertheless, it is also important to update poverty monitoring systems on a regular basis, particularly as countries become more affluent and economies are more globally integrated. Doing it right – constructing comprehensive measures of household welfare, adjusting for regional cost of living differences, updating poverty lines – is essential for robust poverty monitoring, both at the national level as well as for global poverty monitoring.

Good Governance and the Sustainable Development Goals

Assessing Governance Targets*

MARY E. HILDERBRAND

Introduction

Governance and institutions have been among the focal themes of planning for the post-2015 global agenda. The High Level Panel on the Post-2015 Development Agenda named building "peace and effective, open and accountable institutions for all" as one of "five big, transformative shifts" that its members saw as necessary for a new global development agenda (United Nations, 2013). The Secretary-General's report on the post-2015 agenda laid out six "essential elements" for integrating the numerous potential goals and targets: dignity (ending poverty and fighting inequalities); people (human development); prosperity (economic development); planet (environmental protection and climate change); partnership (global solidarity); and *justice (promoting "safe and peaceful societies, and strong institutions"*; United Nations, 2014b, italics mine). Thus, in contrast with the Millennium Development Goals (MDGs), the quality of governance and institutions is given a prominent place on the new global agenda.

The focus on governance comes from two different perspectives. Some assessments of performance on the existing goals have blamed poor governance when results were disappointing, suggesting that improving governance is essential for making further progress (or sustaining progress) in areas such as poverty reduction, health, education, and water and sanitation. This view, then, sees governance and institutions as necessary means to get results on other development goals. Another perspective is that "good governance," especially components such as participation, transparency, inclusiveness, and access to justice, is a part of development itself; thus, good governance is seen

as a development goal to be pursued for its own sake, not just as a means to enable economic development. Both perspectives are reflected in the United Nations (UN) statements on the post-2015 agenda.

Setting goals and targets for governance and institutions is difficult, and there are many problems and challenges associated with doing so. Whereas there is broad agreement that "good governance" (however that is defined) is preferable to poor governance, there is considerable disagreement over whether establishing specific goals and targets will lead to meaningful improvements in governance. If the motivation is based on the argument that governance is necessary to reach other goals, what do we actually know about the relationship between governance and development? If improving governance is important – whether as ends or means – is including it in the development goals likely to elicit the desired improvements? Setting targets implies being able to measure progress. Can we do that? Do we know how to get, or support, good governance? What are the difficulties and the potential unintended consequences?

This chapter is one of a series focusing on benefit-cost analysis of proposed targets in different sectors, in order to contribute to the discussion with realistic analysis of targets in terms of their likely costs and benefits. As noted earlier, the

---

* This chapter was written for the Copenhagen Consensus Center. It was written prior to the adoption of the Sustainable Development Goals (SDGs). The proposed goals for governance and institutions as described here were officially adopted as part of the SDGs. Throughout the chapter I refer to the SDGs as the "post-2015 agenda."

Box 25.1 Open working group proposals for sustainable development goals: Goal 16

Goal 16: Promote peaceful and inclusive societies for sustainable development, provide access to justice for all and build effective, accountable, and inclusive institutions at all levels.

16.1   Significantly reduce all forms of violence and related death rates everywhere

16.2   End abuse, exploitation, trafficking, and all forms of violence and torture against children

16.3   Promote the rule of law at the national and international levels, and ensure equal access to justice for all

16.4   By 2030 significantly reduce illicit financial and arms flows, strengthen recovery and return of stolen assets, and combat all forms of organized crime

16.5   Substantially reduce corruption and bribery in all its forms

16.6   Develop effective, accountable, and transparent institutions at all levels

16.7   Ensure responsive, inclusive, participatory, and representative decision making at all levels

16.8   Broaden and strengthen the participation of developing countries in the institutions of global governance

16.9   By 2030 provide legal identity for all including birth registration

16.10 Ensure public access to information and protect fundamental freedoms, in accordance with national legislation and international agreements

16.a   Strengthen relevant national institutions, including through international cooperation, for building capacities at all levels, in particular in developing countries, for preventing violence and combating terrorism and crime

16.b   Promote and enforce nondiscriminatory laws and policies for sustainable development

Source: United Nations, 2014a. Italics mine.

proposal to introduce governance targets raises fundamental questions that need to be addressed prior to that of economic costs and benefits. Furthermore, costs and benefits with regard to governance reforms are less amenable to being measured than in other areas, and only general estimations are possible, at best. Thus, this chapter will first address several prior issues: the global governance agenda, measurement and data issues, the relationship between governance and development, and the record of governance reform efforts. Then it will assess a subset of proposed targets, with attention to benefit and costs, as well as other criteria, including a number of problems and risks.

The range of targets proposed by the Open Working Group on Sustainable Development Goals is broad and includes substantially distinct dimensions of governance.[1] (Box 25.1 includes a full list of these targets.) This chapter will not address the whole range, but will focus on a subset of dimensions that are central to most views of governance: effective, accountable, transparent, and inclusive institutions.[2] Although this narrows the scope considerably, it still involves multiple dimensions of governance and institutions. The analysis, then, necessarily remains at a fairly general level.

The analysis of this chapter leads to a conclusion that, however desirable the broad governance goals are, there are many reasons to be cautious about setting across-the-board targets in the area of governance as part of the post-2015 agenda. The relationship between governance and development is not entirely clear, efforts at promoting governance reform have had mixed and generally disappointing results, and expectations or targets for reform have often created incentives for surface reforms that do not actually improve governance.

Nevertheless, the broad aspirations expressed in the proposed goals can provide an opportunity for countries, political leaders, and civil society to work domestically to further define the goals, set

---

[1] The Open Working Group was set up as a result of the Rio +20 conference and outcome with the purpose of developing a set of sustainable development goals for consideration by the General Assembly. These goals were intended from the outset to be integrated into the post-2015 UN development agenda (United Nations, 2014a, p. 1).

[2] Not addressing the goals regarding peace, justice, and international governance is not meant to imply that they are less important. But they involve different sets of institutional concerns and would need to be assessed separately.

priorities, and define more concrete targets within countries that can help them move toward better governance. The analysis here provides some guidance about the nature of more or less workable targets for governance and institutions. Targets will be most workable if they are

- Focused on functions that are important to improve, rather than predetermining particular institutional forms.
- Sufficiently specific that they provide some guidance for practice and allow meaningful assessment of improvement. The preference should be for disaggregation of problems to be solved and goals to be reached, rather than for broad, composite targets and measures.
- Flexible enough at the international level for countries to set their own priorities and approaches to improving governance and institutions. More of the choices of targets and approaches should be at the national level than the international.
- Probably multiple, to reflect the multidimensionality of governance and institutions. Dashboards of indicators that allow tracking where performance has improved or not are one approach, but with a spare number of indicators.

Some Definitional Matters

The term *governance* is widely used, but there is little agreement on its definition. One set of definitions refers to how public authority is exercised and decisions made. A second definition makes a distinction between "government" and "governance," using the latter to refer to the idea that addressing contemporary policy problems is broader than just government and defining it as how government, the private sector, and civil society work together to get things done. In the world of international development practice, "governance" is frequently used as part of a normative construct, "good governance" (or its absence), to refer to a set of characteristics that are seen as desirable: rule of law, transparency, participation, accountability, and effectiveness.

These differences are significant in that they mean there is disagreement about what the focus of governance efforts should be, what should be measured, and why. For the purposes of this chapter, and reflecting the focus of the discussions regarding potential targets, I will use the terms generally to refer to the various dimensions that are often referred to as good (or less good) governance. I will use *governance* and *institutions*, and *governance reform* and *institutional reform*, interchangeably.

Governance on the Development Agenda

Although the lack of governance targets in the MDGs might give the impression that governance has been a neglected area in development during this period, that is hardly the case. Rather, governance and institutions have been central to the work of development assistance agencies, international financial institutions (IFIs), and regional development banks over the past couple of decades. In a summary of the magnitude of governance efforts, Andrews found that almost half of World Bank projects supported institutional reforms in 2011, and that a quarter of the Bank's project spending in the years 2006–2011 supported activities in public administration, law, and justice, and significantly more if institutional content in other areas was included. Similarly, public-sector reforms were central to bilateral donor and regional development banks' efforts; for example, they were involved in half the projects of the UK's DFID and of the Asian and African Development Banks (Andrews, 2013a, p. 6). Reform efforts are widespread around the world, and they seem to have become ongoing, permanent processes in many places.

Several trends converged to bring us to the current concern with governance. First, thinking about development began to change in the mid to late 1990s to put a new emphasis on institutions, as promised economic growth did not materialize in many countries that had introduced and sustained stabilization and structural adjustment reform efforts during the 1980s and early 1990s.[3] Work

---

[3] This followed the period in the 1980s and early 1990s in which the "Washington consensus," with its attention on getting macroeconomic policies right and allowing market

in institutional economics highlighted institutional barriers to growth. (See Clague, 1997.) Effective states began to be seen as essential for properly functioning markets, as well as for social and human development. Analysts increasingly turned their attention away from downsizing the state to building its capability to fulfill its roles, as well as reorienting the state away from production and control and toward regulation and facilitation of private-sector-led development.

In the context of globalization, work on international competitiveness also began to call attention to the quality of institutions. Porter led the way in analyzing the conditions under which countries could effectively compete in the global market, focusing on the strength or weakness of such institutions as rule of law, strength of judicial and legal institutions, levels of corruption, and quality of bureaucracy, primarily for their effects on the willingness of investors to risk investment in a particular environment, but also for the effects on transaction costs and therefore overall cost competitiveness (Porter, 1990).

A second trend came out of public-sector reforms in developed countries. During the 1980s and '90s, a number of countries were experimenting with ways to cut costs and improve performance. A new approach of setting goals and targets, holding managers and organizations responsible for meeting them, and demanding results as a basis for both managers' job success and for future budgets became widespread among developed countries. Legislatures, concerned about cutting costs and showing results to taxpayers and constituents, pushed the increasing attention to results. Public-sector reforms reflecting the ideas of New Public Management were introduced, most notably in New Zealand, Australia, the United Kingdom, and the United States, but increasingly in other developed countries as well.

The performance/results movement described earlier and the concern with accountability for providing results for money were extended into the development assistance arena. IFIs and regional development banks, concerned about the viability of loans, began to ask borrowing countries not just for policy reforms, but also for efforts on governance, including in particular strengthening financial

institutions and accountability. Bilateral donors, with legislatures wanting to make sure that development assistance funds produced results, also began to demand efforts on governance. In addition, donors' doubts about the effectiveness of aid led some to focus support on countries with sufficiently strong governance to give some confidence that aid money could produce the desired results.

Although the attention to governance was initially driven by donors' and IFIs' concern with accountability for the money they provided, it evolved into something much larger. Research that showed connections between various aspects of institutions and economic growth, and evidence that poor governance – including corruption – hinders development became the basis for an active and quickly expanding governance agenda for developing countries.

From a different angle, a new focus on poverty alleviation and pro-poor growth by the World Bank and many other donors during the 1990s fueled the mushrooming of the governance agenda into a wider range of issues, including decentralization and more open participation by citizens, communities, and civil society organizations. For example, the Poverty Reduction Strategy Papers that highly indebted countries were asked to develop and commit to in order to receive debt relief included a plethora of governance expectations. (See Grindle, 2004.)

While the impact of donor pressures and the donors' leading role in shaping thinking about development was a major cause of the new attention to institutions, it was not the only source. Some political leaders, in some cases in the context of newly democratic political systems, undertook public-sector and other institutional reforms out of a desire to make things work better. Singapore, though not democratic, became a model of strong

forces to operate freely, dominated mainstream development thinking. Under that thinking, there was little attention to institutions, apart from some reference to the importance of rule of law and economic freedom. The attitude toward the public sector emphasized downsizing, streamlining, privatizing, and liberalizing. The main concern was to get the state out of the way of the private sector and to cut and rationalize bloated bureaucracies and reduce their drain on government budgets.

institutions making a difference for development. Mexico and Indonesia are example of countries with newly democratic systems that undertook reforms (with mixed success); in both countries those reforms were influenced by international actors and thinking, but it can be argued that the desire for them came largely out of a local desire for improvement and a need to be responsive to citizens.

Issues in Measurement

A major challenge for both analysis and policy relating to governance and institutions is the problem of measurement. Quality of institutions and changes in governance are not generally things that can be counted, or measured directly, and identifying indicators that are meaningful and capture the complexity is difficult. Furthermore, even for potential indicators, data are unevenly available, inconsistent, and often unreliable.

Among the most widely used measurements are the World Bank's Worldwide Governance Indicators (WGIs), introduced in 1996. They provide data on six dimensions of governance: voice and accountability, political stability and absence of violence, government effectiveness, regulatory quality, rule of law, and control of corruption. This has been one of the most comprehensive sets of data in terms of its substantive and international coverage. The measurements are based on statistical aggregation of multiple surveys on each of the dimensions and are mostly perception-based data. (See Kaufmann, Kraay, and Mastruzzi, 2008.)[4] Another similar measure is the Quality of Government from the University of Gothenburg (Teorell, Dahlström, and Dahlberg, 2011).

Other major governance data sets include Transparency International's Corruption Perceptions Index (CPI) and the Freedom House data on political freedom and freedom of the press. These and many other sources of governance data are similar to the WGIs in that they are primarily perception based and provide a single score and (usually) a ranking compared to other countries. Some rely on surveys of citizens and others on experts' assessments of a particular dimension. There are also a few measures that try to get more objective data on citizens' actual experience with government and institutions, generally through surveys that ask about experience rather than perception.[5] One exception is the World Bank's Doing Business Report, which collects data more directly on countries' processes for starting and conducting a business.

With increasing interest in a wider range of governance dimensions and with also growing pressure to find ways to measure changes in governance, whether for academic or policy purposes, there has been an explosion of indicators and attempts to construct indices and gather data on a wide range of governance dimensions. The World Bank's "Actionable Governance Indicators Data" web portal pulls together 26 different sets of data.[6] At least some of those represent attempts to go beyond the very aggregated measures and to break down large categories of governance into more specific indicators. Nevertheless, many are still limited in timeframe and country coverage.

There have been extensive critiques of both the WGIs and the CPI. (See, for example, Arndt and Oman, 2006; Galtung, 2005; Pollitt, 2011; Stanig, 2014.) One major concern is the weakness of the underlying data as subjective and not very reliable. Cross-country and longitudinal comparisons have to be done with great care: the WGIs are not finely tuned measures, and small differences or changes cannot be used for comparison. Furthermore, some measures, such as the CPI, have limitations for comparison across either time or countries, due to variation in how data are collected and how the survey instruments are designed from year to year. And, how people answer survey questions, even ones asking about actual experience, may vary from place to place and under different conditions (Galtung, 2005).

Indices that combine several different measures and put them into one summary measure are

---

[4] Current data and explanations are available online at http://info.worldbank.org/governance/wgi/index.aspx#home.

[5] An example is surveys that ask people how many times during a year they have had to pay a bribe for particular services or to particular types of officials.

[6] www.agidata.org.

effective in getting attention to issues, as they are visible and seemingly easy to understand. But they are less useful as a measure of what is actually being done because what is happening to the various components is obscured. Pollitt notes that each dimension of governance in the WGIs, for instance, includes data on a wide range of indicators, combining inputs, process, and outcomes and covering some policy sectors, but not all (Pollitt, 2011, pp. 450–451).

On the other hand, single, narrowly defined indicators do not capture the multidimensionality of governance. Stanig et al., advocate the use of a "dashboard" rather than a single indicator, with measurements for several indicators of a dimension of governance. They have applied this to capacity for governance innovation (Stanig and Kayser, 2013) and governance at transnational, national, and city levels, including administrative capacity and strength of civil society (Anheier, Stanig, and Kayser, 2013).[7] Although dashboards are likely to be much more informative about governance performance, and a more useful and meaningful guide for policy than indices or single indicators alone, they are less easily comparable across countries. They may also risk repeating the problem of the unmanageable number of expectations that have characterized the governance agenda during the past two decades, especially if externally imposed.

Governance and Development: The Debate about the Evidence

The global governance agenda relied substantially on research findings from the late 1990s and early 2000s. Perhaps most prominent was the work by Acemoglu, Johnson, and Robinson, whose historical analysis concluded that institutional factors explained differences in levels of development, and particularly that security of property rights was the most important single factor behind variation in wealth of countries (2001).

Less popularly known but influential within the development field were a series of cross-national analyses that tested the relationship between various institutions and economic growth and found positive relationships. Knack and Keefer found

that protection of property rights was critical for economic growth and that poor institutions in terms of rule of law, risk of expropriation, and contract repudiation prevented poor countries from catching up (Knack and Keefer, 1995, 1997). Mauro found that corruption was negatively correlated with economic growth (1995). Evans and Rauch found a positive relationship between merit-based civil service and economic growth (1999). Kaufmann and Kraay found a correlation between levels of income and the six broad indicators of governance in the WGIs (2003). Others had similar findings with a variety of governance indicators.[8] The general conclusions drawn from this body of work were that institutions matter for development and that improvements in institutions will contribute to, and indeed are a prerequisite for, economic development.

These conclusions are not universally accepted. First, claims that the findings are more than correlations but demonstrate causal links have been questioned. Khan noted the lack of data over sufficient periods of time, but also argued that the inclusion of high-income countries in the samples skews the findings. His analysis of the effects of property rights, with the high-income countries removed, finds no significant difference between developing countries with high and low rates of economic growth (Khan, 2007). Similarly, a study of African countries that corrected for per capita income found no effect of the governance indicators on growth (Sachs et al., 2004).

Second, the direction of causality may be the opposite of what is assumed; good governance seems to be a result of economic development, perhaps more than the reverse (Goldsmith, 2007; Khan, 2007). Goldsmith noted that cross-national econometric analysis may exaggerate the relationship between governance and development, including both potentially being the result of other factors such as human capital development and endogeneity of institutions, making it difficult to

---

[7] For other discussions of and examples of the dashboard approach, see Andrews, 2014.

[8] For summaries of the research, see Burki and Perry, 1998, pp. 17–19; Khan, 2007, pp. 7–16; and Williams et al., 2009, pp. 6–8. Khan and Williams also include critiques.

test the effect of institutions independently (2007). The studies also primarily looked at relationships between institutional measures and levels of income, not rates of growth, so are less relevant to effects on economic growth in the short term (Rodrik, 2006).

Third, the view that governance changes are required as a prerequisite for development is seen as ignoring historical evidence to the contrary. Chang's historical analysis of the timing of governance reforms and economic development spurts shows that in many developed countries, periods of substantial economic growth preceded the kind of reforms now being urged on developing countries (2002). Goldsmith, comparing four current and historical cases, found that economic growth can occur even with fairly "objectionable" institutional conditions and that "good" institutions do not necessarily lead to economic growth (2007).

Finally, Grindle argues that, not only is the current governance agenda enormous and unmanageable, but there is also not strong enough evidence about the effect of particular governance reforms to be able to easily prioritize and narrow the agenda (2004 and 2007). In a critique of "institutional fundamentalism," Rodrik concluded: "the cross-national literature has been unable to establish a strong causal link between any particular design feature of institutions and economic growth. We know that growth happens when investors feel secure, but we have no idea what specific institutional blueprints will make them feel more secure in a given context. The literature gives us no hint as to what the right levers are" (2006, p. 979).

We know, then, that there is a correlation between governance and income levels, and that wealthy countries have better governance on average. We can predict that economic development, and higher levels of income, are likely to lead to better governance. But we do not have a very good understanding of, or very clear evidence on, the other side of the equation – of how and whether improving governance will lead to economic development.

Governance Reform Efforts

More recently, a series of studies have analyzed governance reform efforts, utilizing the rich data provided by the multitude of institutional reforms over the past couple of decades. These studies have sought to understand the effects of institutional reform efforts on development generally and on the quality of governance more specifically, as well as under what conditions institutional reform may be effective. A number of these look at efforts to improve government effectiveness, transparency, and accountability, so their findings are particularly relevant. Overall, their findings with regard to the results of governance reform efforts are not very encouraging.

A 2011 evaluation looking at 80 countries receiving World Bank public-sector reform support found overall that 39 percent of countries saw improvements in governance while 25 percent worsened, and the rates were similar for countries that were not receiving World Bank support.[9] Although 83 percent of the projects were rated as having had satisfactory outcomes, country-level analysis showed that only 47 percent achieved their objectives. Furthermore, there was variation across reform sectors, with public financial management outcomes being somewhat more positive than civil service and administration, where 75 percent of the countries getting support had seen no change in outcomes, and anticorruption efforts, for which the objectives were not achieved in 70 percent of countries. Regarding the latter, the report concludes: "The relatively limited results suggest that the Bank has not yet found a way to make interventions to reduce corruption more effective" (Independent Evaluation Group [IEG], 2011, pp. 67–75).

Andrews conducted a broader analysis, looking at government effectiveness and utilizing the WGIs, with similar findings. Of 145 countries that had introduced institutional reforms with World Bank or other donor agency support between 1998 and 2008, government effectiveness improved in half the countries and worsened in half. Analysis using Quality of Government data found that 70 percent of reforming countries had declines in quality of government. From these and a review of a range

[9] As measured by the World Bank's Country Policy and Institutional Assessment.

of other studies of institutional reform efforts, the author concluded overall that 40–60 percent of reforming countries do not show improved indicators of government effectiveness following reforms (Andrews, 2013a, pp. 14–21; see also pp. 18–28).

Analyses of transparency and accountability initiatives (TAIs), defined to emphasize citizen-led initiatives, find mixed results. An assessment of the quite varied literature on this topic concludes:

> [U]nder some conditions, some TAIs create opportunities for citizens and states to interact constructively, contributing to five kinds of outcomes:
>
> – better budget utilization
> – improved service delivery
> – greater state responsiveness to citizens' needs
> – the creation of spaces for citizen engagement
> – the empowerment of local voices" (McGee and Gaventa, 2011, p. 16).[10]

The authors caution, however, that available evidence of impact is uneven and that the evidence is insufficient to draw conclusions about overall trends (McGee and Gaventa, 2011, p. 19). A major conclusion is that the context is extremely important in affecting outcomes.

Similarly, Kosack and Fung's analysis of 16 random control experiments on transparency in service delivery found that 11 of the 16 reported some positive effect. They also found that the context played a large role in the outcome and that initiatives that took account of the context were more likely to be successful (Kosack and Fung, 2014).[11]

Initiatives that seek to increase participation have also been a major focus of governance efforts. Several studies have looked across large numbers of cases, and they conclude that, despite the enthusiasm for and large investments in participatory efforts, the evidence in support of them is weak. They uniformly reported not finding causal relationships between either development or governance outcomes and participation-oriented initiatives. (See Gaventa and Barrett, 2010; Mansuri and Rao, 2004 and 2013; Rocha Menocal and Sharma, 2008.) Similarly, there is a "paucity of research and evidence about what works and under what conditions" (O'Neil, Foresti, and Hudson, 2007, p. vi).

These studies did find positive effects at an intermediate level of efforts to increase social accountability and empower citizens, including greater citizen awareness, more accountability of local officials, some empowerment of marginalized groups, and improved government attention to communities that led to improved delivery of health, education, and other public services. These positive effects are important. But the authors were cautious regarding questions of sustainability, limits to scaling up, and risk of capture of programs, among other concerns. (See Gaventa and Barrett, 2010; Mansuri and Rao, 2013; Rocha Menocal, and Sharma, 2008.)[12]

Summarizing Conclusions about Governance and Development

In summary, there is little clear evidence of direct causal links between governance improvement and broad development outcomes, such as economic growth and poverty reduction. The evidence that most often points to such causal relationships comes from cross-national analysis, which has been questioned. Individual case studies show mixed results. Thus, the evidence does not support expecting that improvements in governance will lead to better economic outcomes, or seeing such improvements as prerequisites for economic development. This is not to conclude that there is no relationship between governance and development, simply that it is more nuanced that the cross-national studies suggest, and that we do not have very strong, generalizable evidence on those nuances. Caution is therefore warranted regarding

---

[10] See also their summary of the studies and findings (McGee and Gaventa, 2011, pp. 16–18), as well as McGee and Gaventa, 2010.

[11] A case study set in Uganda is cited by many authors as evidence for the power of information and transparency to improve budget utilization and service delivery (Reinikka and Svensson, 2004). A reanalysis of that case, however, finds that, although it lends some support to the importance of transparency, other factors were important in getting the results, and the role of transparency "should not be overestimated" (Hubbard, 2007).

[12] For a comprehensive and current review of the empirical evidence about citizen participation, see J-PAL, 2013.

the assumption of broad causal relationships and the justification of policies based on them.

If the concern with governance is not just as a means to other development "goods," but as an end in itself, the lack of clear evidence between governance and development is not relevant. But the question of whether interventions actually make a difference in improving governance is. The results here are mixed. Large-scale reviews of experiences with governance reform efforts provide evidence that such interventions sometimes have positive effects for outcomes, but they also do not provide clear evidence of direct causal links with economic development or governance outcomes. There is more evidence for intermediate effects that may have a longer-term effect on development, but that is difficult to show.

One conclusion that comes up consistently is the importance of context in shaping outcomes and the necessity to take context into account in designing and implementing initiatives. There is limited guidance, though, about what elements of context are most significant. Although the more recent studies have increasingly tried to go beyond the question of whether there is a linkage between specific governance reforms and development outcomes to address questions of the conditions under which they work or not, and what makes a difference in terms of policy design and implementation, more research is needed on the conditions under which governance reforms are likely to be successful.

Reforming Governance

The mixed but often disappointing results of the large investments in governance reform have led both academics and donor agencies to try to understand why reforms so often fail and under what conditions they are more likely to work. "Political will" of top leadership, along with "country ownership," are often cited as key factors, and lack of political will is often blamed for poor reform performance. These are indeed important factors, but they are necessary, not sufficient conditions, and as explanations they tend to obscure the political complexities surrounding such reforms.

A common theme in recent research about institutional reform experiences, especially those that are sponsored by donors, is the blueprint nature of many of the reforms and the failure to contextualize them. (See, for example, Andrews, 2013a; O'Neill, Foresti, and Hudson, 2007; Pritchett and Woolcock, 2004; Rodrik, 2006.)

Andrews argues further that typical governance reform initiatives create incentives for political leaders to adopt certain institutional forms that make the country look good, whether or not these lead to stronger institutions that meet the needs in the country. This is especially the case with situations where access to international financing or other kinds of recognition depends on checking particular institutional boxes. He argues that more effective institutional reform comes from identifying the problem that needs to be solved and developing institutional solutions, probably in an incremental way and growing out of the existing institutional context (Andrews, 2013a).

Despite the tendency to talk about these reforms as if they are technical, changes in institutions and organizations are deeply political. Because institutional reforms involve changing how things are done within societies, organizations, and political systems, they can rarely be successfully done by fiat by a handful of experts at the top. Some governance efforts may be primarily inside government and involve bureaucratic politics and changes in not only formal but also informal relationships and procedures. Such reforms have to involve the participation of a wide range of officials and staff at different levels. Many governance reforms go further and may alter, or seek to alter, how states and societies (or components in each) interact. Thus, they are deeply embedded in questions of political power and political and social conflict. They are complex, and efforts to implement them will require broad participation, negotiation, and adjustments if they are to work. (See Pritchett and Woolcock, 2004.)

This analysis implies that those individuals and organizations supporting reforms internationally should take care not to set requirements, or targets, that push best-practice solutions on countries and that create incentives for reforms on the surface that do not actually mean better governance in the country.

Issues in Setting Governance Targets

Establishing goals, setting targets, and measuring progress toward the targets are integral to the performance management, or results-oriented management, approach. Within public management, goals and targets are seen as a way to get public agencies away from being inward looking and focused too much on process, control, and rules and to get them to pay more attention to the goals of the organizations, programs, or policies. Within development projects, it can also focus attention on what the project is supposed to be accomplishing and set standards for evaluation.

When utilized within an organization or program by skilled managers who are committed to the idea and to the goals, who communicate all the way through the organization, and who organize the people and effort around the goals, a goal orientation can be powerful. It can both transform the organizational culture and make the organization or program much more effective in doing its work and accomplishing its goals.

The risks are well known. Defining goals that can be measured (either directly or indirectly), and identifying indicators that accurately represent those goals are critical. If targets are associated with a system of rewards and penalties, then they are likely to serve as strong incentives. If the targets or how they are measured do not accurately get at what is intended, the incentives they create may lead to effort that diverges from the goals. Furthermore, even if targets and measurement match the goals, there are various ways that people can "cheat" in how things are counted, which may lead to meeting the targets but not actually reaching the intended outcome. (See Hood, 2006.)

The MDGs were an effort to apply a results-oriented approach to get results in development. Although there was progress in some areas, it was uneven globally and within countries, and some targets were not reached. Many observers see the results as positive, if somewhat disappointing; others are critical of the attempt to set global development targets. Easterly declared it "a success in global consciousness-raising, but a failure in using that consciousness for its stated objectives," that is, a failure in using targets to elicit development (Easterly, 2009). Of course, much of the discussion for the post-2015 agenda has to do with how to correct some of the problems regarding the earlier targets, including the unevenness of results.

If there is disagreement regarding using targets for other areas of development, there is much more intense debate with regard to governance performance. The arguments in favor of doing so are based largely on the power of measurement and targets as incentives, and the expectation that they will lead to action and results. In addition, if targets are set for other development goals (with the incentives to focus on them) and not for governance, then governance may be neglected. Because setting targets and being able to assess improvement in performance requires measurement, developing better indicators and measurements for governance is a key preoccupation of those who favor a results orientation.

On the other hand, those who argue against setting targets in governance point to the difficulty (or even impossibility) of measuring some or all of the dimensions of governance and institutions, the risks of cheating and distortions as a result, and the less than impressive results of two decades of investment in governance reform by the international development community.

There are daunting challenges for using targets for governance and many pitfalls to be avoided. Some come from the risks of targeting in any context; some come from the particular difficulties of measurement, weakness of data, and difficulty of identifying appropriate indicators in the governance context. As discussed earlier, the kinds of things that are being measured – such as effectiveness, transparency, accountability – for the most part cannot be counted or measured directly. So they either have subjective, perception-based estimates or, alternatively, indicators that are proxies, or both. There are real risks of getting targets wrong. There are also real risks of government officials finding ways to meet goals in ways that are window-dressing rather than real reform. There is the risk that goals that can be measured more easily are likely to be identified, targeted and given priority, while those that are harder to measure may get less attention.[13]

Setting the same targets for all countries assumes that they are relevant for all countries. That is a more problematic assumption for governance than it is for health, education, or water and sanitation. The challenges facing countries with different levels of institutional development and very different institutional makeup are unlikely to be the same. In addition, there may be trade-offs between governance goals, at least in the short run (for instance, between effectiveness and goals that may constrain state power, such as transparency or participation), and how those are chosen and prioritized may vary.

The risk of the approach leading to efforts to meet the targets but not actually accomplish meaningful reform or improvement in governance is greatest where reform is complex, unclear, very political, and not amenable to measurement. There is reason to believe that setting targets and measuring progress toward them is not likely to be an effective approach in such areas. (See Foresti and Wild, 2014.) For example, despite the importance of citizen participation, that is one dimension of governance that seems especially unsuited for using targets to get results.

In the MDGs, targets were set at a global level, rather than just a national level, so that progress toward the goals was measured globally. That meant that progress could be recorded on the basis of good performance in just a few large countries, while many other smaller ones lagged behind. Governance is particularly unsuited to measurement at the global level, given the diverse nature of the challenges and the weakness of measures that can be reliably used across countries.

One of the main problems with a results orientation and the use of performance measurement and systems of goals and targets has been that the expectations have often been set by someone outside and thus lack legitimacy within the relevant community – whether an organization, a program, or a country. If they are seen as a tool for accountability to someone else, such as a donor or an IFI, rather than as an internally determined tool for accomplishing goals that a country or organization considers priorities, they are unlikely to be effective.

The implication for practice, and for the specific issue of the post-2015 agenda, is that if governance targets are going to be adopted, they need to be done so with a judicious hand, with care, with many caveats, and with a great deal of room for flexibility.

Types of Targets

There are several different ways of categorizing targets: (1) output, process, outcome; (2) form vs. function; and (3) breadth. These are important because they are connected with different incentives and different advantages and disadvantages.

1. *Outcome vs. output or process.* The standard approach in public management and in evaluation to thinking about targets is to distinguish between those that measure inputs, outputs (activities of the organization or program), and outcomes or impacts (effects in terms of the larger purpose). Inputs and outputs are typically things that can be counted (money and activities). They are valuable for knowing whether an organization or program is efficient and whether it is doing its work. There can also be targets that focus on process – on how the work is done.

Outcomes tend to be more difficult to measure than outputs and even more difficult to attribute to the work of the organization or program. Yet outcome measures are critical for knowing whether the purposes are being accomplished, and they create incentives to focus on results. The performance management movement in recent years has focused primarily but not exclusively, on outcome measures and targets. The MDGs were explicitly outcome measures, and the call for post-2015 goals is also expressed in terms of outcome targets.

Nevertheless, despite the general preference to use outcome measures, they are not always a good fit in the governance area, and it can be difficult to think of targets in terms of outcomes. In addition, there will be disagreement about what are or are

---

[13] For example, in reform efforts that try to improve customer service, speed is often privileged over the quality of service because the former can be easily targeted and measured.

not outcomes. With regard to transparency, for instance, if transparency is seen as a value in its own right, then an increase in it may be seen as an outcome. But if transparency is a means to better other goals, such as greater accountability, less corruption, or more effective citizen engagement, then transparency goals would be appropriately seen as process goals, and the outcomes would need to be expressed in terms of other governance ends. But, as the evidence connecting measures to improve transparency and those other ends is not clear, that remains problematic. (See Bergh et al., 2012; McGee and Gaventa, 2011.)

2. *Form vs. function.* A more recent approach to governance targets differentiates between targets that focus on "form" and those that focus on improvement in performance of particular "functions." (See Andrews, 2013a; Chapman, 2014; Foresti and Wild, 2014.) This reflects the critique of typical approaches to governance and institutional reform that ask countries to put in place particular institutions that are preidentified as solutions to governance problems, i.e., the "form" approach. So "function" targets do not specify how to reach a particular goal, but ideally will help identify key functions that are important to strengthen.

Targets expressed as "forms" may involve, for example, adopting international standards for particular processes or certain institutional approaches to solving problems, such as anticorruption commissions for controlling corruption or passing Freedom of Information laws to increase citizens' access to government information. Experience has shown that such targets create incentives for adoption of an institutional reform, but not for implementing reforms or for finding meaningful solutions to problems (Andrews, 2013a). There is a high risk of "rituals of reform," rather than real improvement (Goldfinch, 2006).

"Function" targets focus on improving performance on key functions that are important for development and for citizens. Ideally, these will be outcome measures, but they could also be assessments of outputs (which are ways of measuring implementation). These will necessarily be quite specifically defined, and it is critical to make sure that targets involve measures of important functions and ones that are directly affected by the quality of governance and institutions. There is a risk of selecting targets and indicators that are too narrow; it may be important to choose multiple targets or ones that are important in multiple dimensions. Examples of function targets, in a range of areas, include birth registration, keeping citizens safe (for instance, in terms of road safety or crime rates), food security, capacity utilization of ports for management of necessary trade functions.[14] Improving particular areas of service provision and quality in health and education can also be considered function targets.[15]

3. *Breadth.* Finally, targets can be quite different in scope, or breadth. Some targets may be very broadly defined; others may be quite specific and narrow. Targets, then, can be expressed in terms of broad governance dimensions, such as greater transparency, reduction in corruption, higher levels of participation, or greater effectiveness or efficiency. These make sense intuitively, as they are articulations of key elements of "good governance." These are the kind of outcomes that the WGIs and Corruption Perception Index are designed to get at. The difficulty with them, however, is that what they include or exclude is not clear, they are very difficult to measure in a way that one can have confidence in, and the data that we have for measuring them are not very satisfactory.

Assessing Governance Targets

Assessing governance targets involves a series of considerations: the type of target and the

---

[14] These are among targets proposed and discussed by Matt Andrews. See http://matthewandrews.typepad.com/the_limits_of_institution/, 4/24/14, 4/23/14, 12/29/13.

[15] Where improvement of sectoral institutions matches other proposed Sustainable Development Goals, targets that are intended to elicit improvements in those institutions would most appropriately be included as part of the targets under those goals, rather than under governance generally. (See the related argument for using transparency and accountability as cross-cutting governance principles across other goals, rather than focusing on them as separate governance issues; Bergh et al., 2012, pp. 10–11.)

accompanying advantages and risks; availability and quality of data; potential benefits; costs; and potential problems.

Cost-Benefit Analysis and Governance

There are challenges for using cost-benefit analysis for governance. There has been little work in this area. The problems of measurement and data are significant limitations, although Johnsøn, who looked at cost-benefit analysis in relation to anti-corruption efforts, argues that these are less constraining than the "underdevelopment and underutilization" of evaluation methods in governance (Johnsøn, 2014, p. 1).[16]

Neither benefits nor costs can be easily quantified or monetized. For some specific anticorruption measures, it is possible to estimate amounts of money that could be saved by reducing certain kinds of corruption and to measure the costs of particular measures to get those savings. And some reforms in financial management have direct financial benefits that can be quantified. But with measures to increase transparency or participation, for instance, it is not clear what the direct benefits will be, if any, and indirect benefits are especially difficult to measure. (See Johnsøn, 2014, pp. 8–14, for a discussion of measuring and monetizing benefits.)

With costs, it is possible to analyze what kinds of direct costs would be likely to be incurred in an effort to reach the target, *given a particular approach to doing so*. As cost is often not considered as a particular criterion, it seems likely that costs of such reforms tend to be underestimated. Targets that involve adopting particular forms may not involve very much cost, especially if it just means passing a law. But even those may involve setting up a new organizational unit.[17] Actual implementation of many institutional reforms involves a range of costs: possibly investing in information systems (including hardware and software, networking capabilities, and maintaining and updating them), perhaps hiring new staff, certainly training or retraining staff, perhaps raising salaries. There will be other administrative and coordination costs. Reforms that involve changes not just at the center but at local and other subnational levels

throughout a country may require substantial administrative, coordination, personnel, and capacity development costs. Furthermore, there are less direct costs, having to do with the disruption in regular work and the time it takes to learn and to adjust to new systems of doing things.

One of the most significant limitations to applying cost-benefit analysis across countries is that costs, as well as benefits, of implementing particular reforms or approaches will vary in different contexts. Therefore, even with specific approaches and mechanisms to be evaluated, it would be hard to generalize beyond a particular country context. Cost-benefit analysis is also difficult to apply to broadly defined, complex goals and reforms. (Johnsøn, 2014, pp. 18–21). Thus, the assessment of proposed governance targets for the post-2015 agenda in terms of costs and benefits can be done only at a very general level, to suggest the sorts of potential costs and benefits that might be expected.

Financial or economic costs of particular interventions are not the only factor to be considered in assessing targets. It is also necessary to consider other potential risks, problems, and limitations. These relate to a variety of factors: the likelihood that measures to meet the target can be implemented and have the expected results, the importance of the measure, the incentives created, the clarity of the measure, the quality of the data, and the administrative and political challenges.

Assessing Proposed Targets

In this section, I attempt to assess the proposed targets from the Open Working Group (OWG), as noted earlier, that related most directly to the governance dimensions considered in this chapter –

---

[16] See also the work by Olken, in which he uses a randomized field experiment methodology to compare two approaches to reducing corruption – increasing government audits and increasing community participation in monitoring. After finding that increasing audits was more effective, he then did a cost-benefit analysis and found that the audit approach had a positive cost-benefit ratio. He discussed the choices made in terms of valuing costs and benefits (Olken, 2007, pp. 240–3).

[17] Although frequently in such situations they would not be adequately funded or staffed.

effectiveness, transparency, accountability, and participation. This included five subgoals from the entire set of governance goals:[18]

16.5   Substantially reduce corruption and bribery in all its forms

16.6   Develop effective, accountable, and transparent institutions at all levels

16.7   Ensure responsive, inclusive, participatory, and representative decision making at all levels

16.9   Provide legal identity for all including birth registration

16.10 Ensure public access to information and protect fundamental freedoms, in accordance with national legislation and international agreements

Table 25.1 assesses those proposals in terms of the type of target; potential benefits and costs; and problems, limitations, and risks. The assessments are subjective and preliminary but reflect my best judgment. For the most part, the utility of this exercise is less to conclude that a particular target is better than another, but more to indicate that particular kinds of targets are likely to be more helpful and more productive of good results than others, and to suggest considerations that need to be taken into account.

Of the five targets considered, all but one are very broad in scope (for example, "develop effective, accountable, and transparent institutional at all levels"). Several – including the example just cited – include multiple targets, so would have to be broken down into component parts with indicators for each. It does seem that the lessons about the need for institutional reform to move away from an emphasis on adopting particular forms have been heeded, with some exceptions, as most of the broadly defined targets are stated in terms of governance outcomes. Nevertheless, available measures and likely indicators do not always support focusing on outcomes, especially with regard to participation and access to information.

With the very broadly defined targets, it is impossible to estimate costs even in a general way because there is no way to know what measures would or would not be taken toward the target. Any estimation of benefits has to rely on linkages with broad development outcomes, for which the evidence is weak or lacking, or on the value of the governance dimension itself (such as transparency or participation), which is impossible to estimate or generalize about. So assessing such broad targets is difficult. The question will be how to operationalize them in terms of the kinds of indicators – whether composite governance indicators that purport to give an overall view of governance quality, or perhaps a set of more narrowly defined indicators that get at some separate aspects of the governance dimension.

The target of "providing legal identity to all, including registering all children at birth" is different from the other goals. It is clear, is concrete, and could serve as an incentive for action. It has several advantages as a target: it requires considerable organizational and administrative capacity to accomplish, including reaching throughout the entire country. That capacity, once built, could have spin-off effects for other work that the government needs to be able to accomplish that required similar capacity. Making sure all citizens have a legal identity also helps the government reach citizens for other programs. In addition, legal identity for citizens supports their ability to claim their rights and is an element of other dimensions of governance, including participation, inclusiveness, and rule of law. Therefore, although a narrow function, it catches several dimensions and can serve as an indicator across governance more broadly. (See Andrews, 2013b.[19]) On the other hand, its narrowness contrasts so greatly with others that it begs to be accompanied by other similarly concrete and narrowly defined goals.

---

[18] The Open Working Group targets from Goal 16 that are not included relate to other parts of the goal-set, not considered directly in this chapter, including promoting peaceful and inclusive societies, providing access to justice for all, and ensuring participation of developing countries in global governance.

[19] To my knowledge, it is Andrews who made this proposal originally and has laid out a case for civil registration, and specifically registration of births, as a potentially valuable target (2013b).

Table 23.1 Assessment of proposed governance targets

Proposed targets[a]	Indicators[b]	Possible data sources[b]	Type of target	Benefits	Cost	Problems, risks, limitations	Overall assessment
16.5 Substantially reduce corruption and bribery in all its forms	Perception of level of corruption; Number of births paid	TI corruption barometers TI CPI TI bribery index	Broad governance outcome	Could reduce cost of doing business; increase funds available for public services and other public uses; reduce cost for poor of interacting with state.	Uncertain. Depend on what has to be done.	Very broadly stated. To take on all forms of corruption would be a very big agenda. Likely to be significant resistance; may be hard to implement politically.	Cost-benefit uncertain, because we can expect benefits but do not know the costs. Good in that it focuses on outcomes, not just adoption of particular institutional forms. Perhaps too big to be manageable.
16.6 Develop effective, and accountable, and transparent institutions at all levels	Level and change in effectiveness, accountability, and transparency, at central and subnational levels of government.	WGI scores for effectiveness and for voice and accountability; TI corruption barometers; subnational data (To measure as one target rather than separately would require a single composite governance indicator)	Mixed, but intended to be broad governance outcome. Would need better measures.	Governance benefits – government would likely be better at getting things done. Citizens would benefit from better government/ governance. But benefits of improved governance on development outcomes uncertain.	Uncertain – depends on what is done.	Target so broad that it is not clear what is measured. Obscures what has improved and what has not. (Applies to the scores for effectiveness, transparency, and accountability separately; a single composite score would be even more obscuring.)	Uncertain cost-benefit. May be suggestive of quality of governance, but not sufficient as target by itself. Important set of goals for governance, but would have to be operationalized more specifically to be workable as target.
16.7 Ensure responsive, inclusive, participatory and representative decision making at all levels	Citizen or NGO participation in monitoring of public services Opportunities for participation in policy formulation and implementation Responsiveness of government at central and local levels to citizen demands	Surveys CIRI Human rights data Freedom House	Broad governance outcome and process. But available data are about conditions for participation, not outcomes.	Opportunities to participate may be seen as a development value; government policies and programs may be more effective as a result. But economic development benefits uncertain.	Uncertain. May involve developing and managing new systems or mechanisms for participation and decision-making. May also require capacity development at community level for citizen participation	Extremely difficult to measure. May be significant political and/or bureaucratic resistance.	Uncertain cost-benefit. Very broadly stated target and hard to measure. Meaningful participation may be less amenable to use of targets than some other areas of governance.

(cont.)

Table 25.1 (*cont.*)

Proposed targets[a]	Indicators[b]	Possible data sources[b]	Type of target	Benefits	Cost	Problems, risks, limitations	Overall assessment
16.9 By 2030 provide legal identity for all, including birth registration	% of children registered at birth % of population with legal identify documents	Administrative records, surveys	Specific function; output and outcome	Indicates gov't capacity to manage a basic process throughout its territory and for all groups. Building that capacity is important support for other gov't programs. Also gives people legal standing and helps them claim rights (Andrews, 2013b).	Moderate- administrative costs of implementing; IT systems and costs of storing and managing data; training and supervision costs; coordination with clinics and local authorities. Communities that have been repressed (as opposed to excluded) may be threatened by it.	Very narrowly defined. Requires strong systems of information and document management, and ability to coordinate. In some countries that would be a major capacity building effort. Reaching marginalized and remote communities could be difficult in some countries. Requires a certain trust in the government.	Very good as target for government effectiveness and possibly inclusiveness. Benefits (direct and indirect) likely to outweigh costs. More specific. Outcomes to measure more objectively. Significant benefits across dimensions of governance, and helps support gov't effectiveness in other areas. May need to be complemented by other specific targets.
16.10 Ensure public access to information...	Adoption of Freedom of Information acts in Adoption of data policy Implementation of above policies Score on Open Budget Index	Surveys Government records Open Budget Index	Mixed – Fairly broad governance outcome. But likely indicators are partly form and partly more specific function.	Information access is supposed to help accountability and also enable citizen participation. In reality, benefits are uncertain.	Relatively low, although making information easily available in usable and meaningful ways takes considerable effort and organization.	Stated very broadly, so not clear what information is important. If legislation is weak, then implementation of that legislation may not mean much.	Fair. Too broad, but has some advantages. Depends on how operationalized. As stated, it implies measurement of implementation, rather than just adoption, which is more meaningful but more difficult.

(*cont.*)

Table 25.1 *(cont.)*

Proposed targets[a]	Indicators[b]	Possible data sources[b]	Type of target	Benefits	Cost	Problems, risks, limitations	Overall assessment
16.10 (cont.) ...and protect fundamental freedoms in accordance with national legislation and international agreements	Level and change in measures of freedom of speech, of the press, of political choice.	CIRI Freedom House	Broad governance outcomes	More open societies give people more opportunity to be fully capable citizens, enable participation. Press freedom is seen as helpful in anticorruption efforts. Linkages to improved economic performance uncertain.	Fairly low cost in immediate financial terms. Uncertain whether openness leads to demands for services from citizens or greater accountability that might make government more efficient. So long-term costs uncertain.	Depending on context, may be politically unattractive to powerful. Easy for political leaders to say they are doing it and not actually make any change. So important to have measures that are independent of government.	Cost-benefit uncertain, but in freedoms are indeed a value, probably a positive cost-benefit ratio, if implemented. However, broad as a target, and very political. Uncertain whether it would have that much effect as a target. Selecting a key part of it, such as freedom of the press, would be more meaningful.

[a] United Nations, 2014a.
[b] Draws on related work by Foresti and Wild, 2014.

General Points from Assessment

Broadly stated governance goals are aspirational but not very helpful as real targets that affect behavior and performance, and the available measures and data to use for such general goals have limitations. Operationalizing the goals in practice means one of two alternatives: using composite measures that give a general indication of performance on that dimension (and improving those measures) or coming up with more specific targets. The general goals and measures could potentially be used alongside more specific measures but cannot be relied on for very clear-cut indications of change over time or comparison across countries. Disaggregating large categories into more specific goals for which targets and measurement can be meaningful will be more likely to be helpful.

Some areas of governance are more amenable to using targets and indicators than others, related to the availability of good indicators and measurement, as well as the complexity and political nature of reforms involved. Government effectiveness and anticorruption are two areas in which targets are more likely to be possible. In the former, indicators that related to the accomplishment of important functions can be identified; targets expressed in the terms of those indicators can create positive, effective incentives. In anticorruption, at least some measurement – while still problematic – is possible, and targets that involve reducing particular types of corruption may yield results. In contrast, targets for increasing participation are unlikely to be effective and more likely to lead to window-dressing to meet goals, but without actually improving governance. Transparency is somewhere in the middle; finding ways to target improvement in transparency in particular functions may be possible.

Although outcome targets are generally preferred over output and process targets, they are not necessarily best with regard to governance and institutions. It seems easier to come up with potential outcome measures for institutional effectiveness then for either transparency or participation. Effectiveness is about doing things, so one can identify things that need to be done and see whether they are accomplished or not. Transparency, though, is really about "how" things are done; so targets that are about improving the process are more typical. In anticorruption efforts, there are potential outcome measures, such as reductions in bribery or other types of corruption; the challenges have to do with the nature of the data and the relative invisibility of what one is trying to measure.

In general, it is not effective to set goals that involve the adoption of particular institutional *forms*. A particular institutional approach that works in one setting may not work in another setting, and it may not address the important problems. Requiring certain forms makes it easy for officials to check a box that something has been done without necessarily making any improvement in institutional performance. Rather, goals that target strengthening particular functions have a much better chance of creating positive incentives to carry out meaningful reform in important areas. This leaves flexibility for leaders and officials in different places to develop solutions that work in their contexts.

Cost-benefit analysis as an approach for assessing the selection of targets is less productive in the area of governance than in other development areas, for several reasons. These include the inherent difficulty of quantifying and measuring benefits, as well as the very general nature of proposed targets. It is only with a particular set of actions that costs can be seriously estimated. Thus, when a particular reform or institutional mechanism, or a set of alternative solutions is specified, cost-benefit analysis (or cost-effectiveness analysis) becomes directly relevant and more useful. Furthermore, costs and benefits vary significantly across countries. Cost-benefit analysis will primarily be a valuable tool at the national level in making decisions about which institutional reforms to adopt.

Concrete indicators in areas where government effort and capacity are important for citizens and for the economy might be similarly useful to the birth registration target. Increasing transparency and access to information in key areas, perhaps especially budget formulation and implementation, may also be promising. Anticorruption targets that sort out specific areas of corruption and set targets

Conclusions

Goal 16, with its all-encompassing targets for governance and institutions as part of the global sustainable development agenda, lays out an ambitious agenda for transforming governance across the world. These are admirable aspirations and – indeed – a clear expression of "The World We Want" (UNDG, 2013). The analysis in this chapter, however, suggests that that it is a leap to go from agreeing that these are what we would like to see in governance and being able to say with confidence that such targets can effectively lead to more effective, transparent, accountable, and inclusive governance. There are reasons to be cautious about setting targets for governance as part of the 2015 agenda. It is critical to avoid the post-2015 goals being just an extension of the global governance agenda of the past two decades, with its multitude of goals, large investments, and disappointing results.

Whereas the chapter argues that the proposed targets' breadth does not allow them to be used very effectively as guides for policy or action, the broad aspirations expressed in them can provide an opportunity for political leaders and civil society to work in their own countries to set priorities and define more concrete targets that can help them to move toward better governance. To the extent that these operate to motivate such national commitment, they may be extremely valuable.

The analysis provides some guidance for developing governance and institutional targets that may be workable. They should be focused on functions that are important for government and citizens; sufficiently specific and concrete to allow meaningful assessment of improvement; probably multiple, to reflect the multidimensionality of governance, but not too numerous. They should not predetermine exact institutional forms to be adopted.

People and countries will disagree about what and how to prioritize institutional reform. Countries at different levels of institutional development and with different configurations of strengths and weaknesses will have different challenges and therefore different priorities, even assuming that improved governance is a shared agenda. Flexibility needs to be built into a system of goals and targets to allow countries to figure out institutional solutions that fit their priorities, problems, and contexts and that work for them.

Although the evidence linking broad governance dimensions and broad development outcomes such as growth and poverty reduction is not clear, within sectors such as education and health, the improvement of institutions such as delivery systems and accountability are more closely connected to potential improvements in sectoral outcomes. An argument can be made for building attention to governance into goals and targets for particular development sectors, rather than (or in addition to) broad stand-alone governance goals.

As others have noted in relation to the MDGs and the post-2015 agenda, it is important to invest (both globally and within countries) in data collection for relevant indicators and in building the capacity and prominence of statistical agencies. For governance, it is not just the difficulty of measurement, but also the lack of reliable data, that acts as a major constraint for assessing performance. It is especially important for countries to have information available that is usable for them in making decisions. And citizens and civil society groups need information (as well as access to that information) in order to hold government accountable and to have the ability to participate effectively in public life. Thus, the capacity to produce and use data becomes in itself an important factor for good governance.

References

Acemoglu, Daron, Simon Johnson, and James A. Robinson, 2001. "The Colonial Origins of Comparative Development: An Empirical Investigation." *American Economic Review* 91 (5): 1369–401.

Andrews, Matt, 2010. "Good Government Means Different Things in Different Countries," *Governance* 23 (1): 7–35.

2013a. *The Limits of Institutional Reform in Development: Changing Rules for Realistic Solutions*. Cambridge: Cambridge University Press.

2013b. http://matthewandrews.typepad.com/the_limits_of_institution/2013/11/more-on-registration-as-a-governance-indicator.html.

2014. *An Ends-Means Approach to looking at Governance*. CID Working Paper No. 281. Cambridge, MA: Center for International Development, Harvard University.

Anheier, Helmut K., Piero Stanig, and Mark Kayser, 2013. "Introducing a New Generation of Governance Indicators." In *The Governance Report 2013*. Oxford: Oxford University Press, pp. 117–48.

Arndt, Christiane, and Charles Oman, 2006. *Uses and Abuses of Governance Indicators*. Paris: OECD Development Center.

Bergh, Gina et al., 2012. *Building Governance into a Post-2015 Framework: Exploring Transparency and Accountability as an Entry Point*. London: Overseas Development Institute.

Bertucci, Guido, and Allan Rosenbaum, 2007. *Implementing the Millennium Development Goals: Challenges and Responses for Public Administration*. Department of Economic and Social Affairs. Division for Public Administration and Development Management. New York: United Nations.

Burki, Shahid Javed, and Guillermo E. Perry, 1998. *Beyond the Washington Consensus: Institutions Matter*. Washington, DC: World Bank.

Chang, Ha-Joon, 2002. *Kicking Away the Ladder: Development Strategy in Historical Perspective*. London: Anthem Press.

Chapman, Peter, 2014. "Function, not Form: Defining Targets for Justice in the Post-2015 Development Agenda." *Global Policy Journal* blog. Mar 4: 1–4.

Clague, Christopher et al., 1997. "Institutions and Economic Performance: Property Rights and Contract Enforcement." In Christopher Clague, ed., *Institutions and Economic Development: Growth and Governance in Less-Developed and Post-Socialist Countries*. Baltimore, MD: Johns Hopkins University Press, 67–90.

Dahlberg, Stefan et al., 2013. *The Quality of Government Expert Survey 2008–2011: A Report*. Goteborg: Quality of Government Institute, University of Gothenburg.

Doornbos, Martin, 2003. "'Good Governance': The Metamorphosis of a Policy Metaphor." *Journal of International Affairs* (57) 1: 3–17.

Earle, Lucy, and Zoe Scott, 2010. *Assessing the Evidence of the Impact of Governance on Development Outcomes and Poverty Reduction*. GSDRC Issues Paper. Birmingham: Governance and Social Development Resource Center, International Development Department, University of Birmingham.

Easterly, William, 2009. "It's Over: The Tragedy of the Millennium Development Goals." www.huffingtonpost.com/william-easterly/its-over-the-tragedy-of-t_b_226120.html.

Evans, Peter B., and James E. Rauch, 1999. "Bureaucracy and Growth: A Cross-National Analysis of the Effects of 'Weberian' State Structures on Economic Growth." *American Sociological Review* 64: 748–65.

Foresti, Marta, and Leni Wild, 2014. *Governance Targets and Indicators for Post 2015: An Initial Assessment*. London: Overseas Development Institute.

Galtung, Fredrik, 2005. *Measuring the Immeasurable: Boundaries and Functions of (Macro) Corruption Indices*. London: Tiri.

Gaventa, John, and Gregory Barrett, 2010. *So What Difference Does it Make? Mapping the Outcomes of Citizen Engagement*. IDS Working Paper 347. Brighton: Institute of Development Studies.

Goldfinch, Shaun, 2006. "Rituals of Reform, Policy Transfer, and the National University Corporation Reforms of Japan." *Governance* 19 (4): 585–604.

Goldfinch, Shaun, Karl Kerouen, Jr., and Paulina Pospieszna, 2012. "Flying Blind? Evidence for Good Governance Public Management Reform Agendas, Implementation and Outcomes in Low Income Countries." *Public Administration and Development* 33: 50–61.

Goldsmith, Arthur A., 2007. "Is Governance Reform a Catalyst for Development?" *Governance* 20 (2): 165–88.

Grindle, Merilee S., 2004. "Good Enough Governance: Poverty Reduction and Reform in Developing Countries." *Governance* 17 (4): 525–48.

2007. "Good Enough Governance Revisited." *Development Policy Review* 25 (5): 553–74.

Hood, Christopher, 2006. "Gaming in Targetworld: The Targets Approach to Managing British Public Services." *Public Administration Review* 66 (4): 515–21.

Hubbard, Paul, 2007. *Putting the Power of Transparency in Context: Information's Role in Reducing Corruption in Uganda's Education Sector.* Washington, DC: Center for Global Development.

Hyden, Goren, Julius Court, and Ken Mease, 2003. *The Bureaucracy and Governance in 16 Developing Countries.* World Governance Survey Discussion Paper 7. London: Overseas Development Institute.

Independent Evaluation Group (IEG), 2011. *IEG Annual Report 2011: Results and Performance of the World Bank Group.* Washington, DC: Independent Evaluation Group, the World Bank Group.

Jann, Werner, 2007. "Public Administration under Pressure – the Search for New Forms of Public Governance." In Guido Bertucci and Allan Rosenbaum, eds., *Implementing the Millennium Development Goals: Challenges and Responses for Public Administration.* Department of Economic and Social Affairs, Division for Public Administration and Development Management. New York: United Nations.

Johnsøn, Jesper, 2014. *Cost-effectiveness and Cost-Benefit Analysis of Governance and Anti-Corruption Activities.* Bergen, Norway: Anti-Corruption Resource Center.

J-PAL, 2013. *Governance Review Paper.* Cambridge, MA: The Abdul Latif Jameel Poverty Action Lab.

Kaufmann, Daniel, and Aart Kraay, 2003. *Growth without Governance.* Policy Research Working Paper 2928. Washington, DC: World Bank.

Kaufmann, Daniel, Aart Kraay, and Massimo Mastruzzi. 2008. *Governance Matters.* Washington, DC: World Bank.

Kaufmann, Daniel, Aart Kraay, and Pablo Zoido-Lobaton. 1999. *Governance Matters.* Policy Research Working Paper 2196. Washington: World Bank.

Khan, Mushtaq, 2007. *Governance, Economic Growth and Development since the 1960s.* DESA Working Paper No 54. ST/ESA/2007/WDP/54. New York: United Nations Division of Economic and Social Affairs.

Knack, Stephen, and Philip Keefer, 1995. "Institutions and Economic Performance: Cross-Country Tests Using Alternative Institutional Measures." *Economics and Politics* 7 (3): 207–227.

1997. "Why Don't Poor Countries Catch Up? A Cross-National Test of an Institutional Explanation." *Economic Inquiry* 35(3): 590–602.

Kosack, Stephen, and Archon Fung, 2014. "Does Transparency Improve Governance?" *Annual Review of Political Science* 17: 65–87.

Mansuri, Ghazala, and Vijayendra Rao, 2004. "Community-Based and -Driven Development: A Critical Review." *World Bank Research Observer* 19 (1): 1–39.

2013. *Localizing Development: Does Participation Work?* World Bank Policy Research Report. Washington, DC: The World Bank.

Mauro, Paolo, 1995. "Corruption and Growth." *Quarterly Journal of Economics* 110: 681–712.

McGee, Rosemary, and John Gaventa, 2010. *Synthesis Report: Review of Impact and Effectiveness of Transparency and Accountability Initiatives.* Brighton: Institute of Development Studies.

McGee, Rosie, and John Gaventa, 2011. *Shifting Power? Assessing the Impact of Transparency and Accountability Initiatives.* IDS Working Paper (383). Brighton: Institute of Development Studies.

Olken, Benjamin A., 2007. "Monitoring Corruption: Evidence from a Field Experiment in Indonesia." *Journal of Political Economy* 115 (2): 200–49.

O'Neil, Tammie, Marta Foresti, and Alan Hudson, 2007. *Evaluation of Citizens' Voice and Accountability: Review of the Literature and Donor Approaches.* London: DFID.

Pollitt, Christopher, 2011. "'Moderation in All Things': International Comparisons of Governance Quality." *Financial Accountability & Management* 27 (4): 437–57.

Porter, Michael, 1990. *The Competitive Advantage of Nations.* New York: Free Press.

Pritchett, Lant, and Michael Woolcock, 2004. "Solutions When *the* Solution is the Problem: Arraying the Disarray in Development." *World Development* (32) 4: 191–212.

Reinikka, Ritva, and Jakob Svensson, 2004. "Local Capture: Evidence from a Central Government

Transfer Program in Uganda." *Quarterly Journal of Economics* 119 (2): 679–706.

Rocha Menocal, Alina, and Bhavna Sharma, 2008. *Joint Evaluation of Citizens' Voice and Accountability: Synthesis Report*. London: DFID.

Rodrik, Dani, 2006. "Goodbye Washington Consensus, Hello Washington Confusion? A Review of the World Bank's Economic Growth in the 1990s: Learning from a Decade of Reform." *Journal of Economic Literature* 44 (4): 973–987.

Sachs, Jeffrey D. et al., 2004. "Ending Africa's Poverty Trap." *Brookings Papers on Economic Activity* 1: 117–240.

Sen, Amartya, 1999. *Development as Freedom*. Oxford: Oxford University Press.

Stanig, Piero, 2014. "Governance Indicators." In *The Governance Report 2014*. Oxford: Oxford University Press, pp. 111–149.

Stanig, Piero, and Mark A. Kayser, 2013. "Governance Indicators: Some Proposals." In Helmut K. Anheier and Regina A. List, eds., *Governance Challenges and Innovations: Financial and Fiscal Governance*. Oxford: Oxford University Press, pp. 189–220.

Tangri, Roger, and Andrew M. Mwenda, 2006. "Politics, Donors, and the Ineffectiveness of Anti-Corruption Institutions in Uganda." *Journal of Modern African Studies* 44 (1): 101–124.

Teorell, Jan, Carl Dahlström, and Stefan Dahlberg, 2011. *The QoG Expert Survey Dataset*. Goteborg: University of Gothenburg,

The Quality of Government Institute. www.qog.pol.gu.se.

Transparency International, 2009. *The Anti-Corruption Plain Language Guide*. Berlin: Transparency International.

United Nations, 2013. *A New Global Partnership: Eradicate Poverty and Transform Economies through Sustainable Development*. Report of the High-Level Panel of Eminent Persons on the Post-2015 Development Agenda. New York: United Nations.

2014a. *Open Working Group Proposal for Sustainable Development Goals*. New York: Department of Economic and Social Affairs. Division for Sustainable Development.

2014b. *The Road to Dignity by 2030: Ending Poverty, Transforming All Lives, and Protecting the Planet*. Synthesis Report of the Secretary-General on the Post-2015 Agenda. New York: United Nations.

United Nations Development Group (UNDG), 2013. *A Million Voices: The World We Want*. New York: UNDG Millennium Development Goals Task Force. www.undp.org/content/undp/en/home/librarypage/mdg/a-million-voices–the-world-we-want.html.

Williams, Gareth et al., 2009. "Politics and Growth." *Development Policy Review* 27(1): 5–31.

World Bank, 2002. *Building Institutions for Markets. World Development Report 2002*. Oxford: Oxford University Press.

25.1 Alternative Perspective

AART KRAAY

Summary

Hilderbrand raises a number of concerns about possible SDGs in the area of governance, which can be summarized as:

- Governance is difficult to define.
- Governance is difficult to measure.
- The effect of good governance on development outcomes is not well documented.
- The effectiveness of aid-financed interventions to promote good governance are not clear.

Although these points are all valid, I argue that they do not make governance targets either infeasible or undesirable. My argument is simply that there were similarly serious challenges to the MDG to "eradicate extreme poverty," but this did not stop it being adopted and becoming a highly visible "flagship" MDG. Allowing the perfect to be the enemy of the good risks missing the opportunity to have a governance SDG that renews international emphasis on the importance of good governance, both as intrinsically desirable and as a means to achieving other development goals.

Definitions: Despite the conceptual and definitional challenges, the international community operationalized the goal of eliminating extreme poverty by setting three specific targets: to halve the proportion of people living on less than $1.25 per day, to achieve "full and productive employment and decent work for all," and to halve the proportion of people suffering from hunger. A similar case can be made regarding governance. Despite the profusion of definitions, it is possible to identify a few common themes that are amenable to measurement. Most of them emphasize the importance of a capable state, operating under the rule of law, which is able to provide an array of public goods and be held accountable for failure to deliver them.

Measurement: Agreeing to define "extreme poverty" in terms of the proportion of people living on less than $1.25 a day raises immense practical measurement challenges. Measuring governance similarly poses a wide range of practical challenges. The first important one is to strike an appropriate balance between subjective measures of perception of governance quality and corresponding objective measures. Despite the pejorative labelling of "soft" data in the case of surveys, both types of data can play an important role. Perceptions matter, as people will not, for example use the police or court services properly if they see them as corrupt. In contrast, "hard" indicators of laws or regulations on corrupt practices may not be useful without knowing how well they are enforced. The second important issue is to acknowledge and quantify measurement error in governance indices.

Links to Development: Although the empirical evidence linking good governance with development is not yet fully conclusive, there was similarly little hard evidence for a causal link from high poverty to subsequent reduced growth. However, this did not prevent poverty reduction goals being set. Both the poverty MDG, and a possible governance SDG, may be seen as aspirational targets. When viewed as an aspirational target, it should be broad and ambitious.

Links to Aid: Hilderbrand also discusses the very mixed evidence on the efficacy of aid in promoting governance reforms. However, similar lack of strong evidence at the time between aid and growth – the main source of poverty reduction – did not prevent adoption of the poverty reduction target. It is also true that, for both poverty and governance – some barriers to progress represent domestic policy failures, which could be corrected without the need for international aid.

A governance SDG is an opportunity to set a challenge for developed and developing countries alike to work toward a broad aspirational goal.

Alternative Perspective

MATT ANDREWS

Summary

I start from a position of skepticism of the value of having post-2015 goals at all and even more of including governance in such a set. Global-level statistics on the MDGs appear quite accurate, and progress in some areas is used to support the argument for such global goals. However, there is great variation at the national level, with one study, for example, showing that about 50 percent of countries are on track to meet extreme poverty, gender, child mortality, and water goals, but less than 30 percent are on track to meet hunger, maternal mortality, and HIV/AIDS goals.

I draw several key lessons when considering this kind of evidence. First, higher growth countries did better in meeting MDG targets than lower growth countries, which could suggest that the development community should focus on fostering economic growth instead of promoting a new set of targets. MDG success is contextual and deeply affected by a country's social and economic situation. Second, progress has been greatest in areas where measured performance captures (mostly) logistical improvements. Building more schools and laying water pipes are largely technical exercises. Progress on sanitation issues, on the other hand, has arguably been slower because the logistical component involves more complex political and social interactions.

A third lesson is that because targets focus on parts of the development process that can be seen and quickly assessed and not on the harder to see (and to do) and longer to achieve parts, there are likely to be large gaps between form and function (where performance only looks better). Many of the best-performing MDG countries now have many schools and high enrollment rates in schools, for instance, but also experience severe shortages of teachers and textbooks and major gaps between enrollment and achievement. There are also gaps within countries between rural and urban areas: the fourth lesson is that goals and targets can bias performance to easier concentrated urban areas, creating a gap between performance in these locations and the more distributed local, rural settings.

A final lesson is that targets encourage promises – of budgetary priorities in particular – that often do not lead to actual follow-through, creating an execution gap that is not easily closed.

All this suggests that indicators are not as effective as many might believe. We know, for instance, that governance indicators are very sensitive to factors that have nothing to do with governance and governance reform (like a country's wealth or its growth rate). Governance indicators are also heavily influenced by signals of change and by logistical manifestations of change; for instance, composite indicators like the WGIs actually rise and fall on the basis of reform signals, which are often used to deflect attention from poor reform performance. The message is simply that targets and indicators don't work terribly well when one is dealing with complex challenges.

Deep and lasting change occurs because of contextual pressures in specific countries, rather than global targets. China and India, for example, are developing without the aid of indicators or global targets; much like Western European nations, the United States, Japan, and South Korea did.

If governance indicators must be included in the post-2015 agenda, I would start by focusing on closing the gaps between meeting targets and actual achievement. I would allow choice in the governance agendas and targets, assessing progress with reforms in a set of key areas appropriate to a given country. However, this may only capture "process" improvements, so there is also a need to include governance ends into the indicators, including public safety, electricity access, education and health care provision, employment and inflation rates, and the mobility of citizens. Governance is not really an end in itself; governance processes matter mostly because they influence the degree to which governments meet citizen needs.

Conclusion

IDENTIFYING PHENOMENAL DEVELOPMENT TARGETS

Finn Kydland, Tom Schelling, and Nancy Stokey

Over the next 15 years the Global Goal targets examined in the research section of this book will help to direct somewhere in the region of $2.5 trillion[1] to be spent on development assistance, as well as countless trillions in national budgets. As the members of the Eminent Panel that examined the research and made recommendations on the proposed targets, particularly in terms of value-for-money, we believe that it is important that those making funding decisions have access to information on costs and benefits.

A natural political inclination is to promise all good things to everyone. This, in no small part, is how the United Nations ended up with 169 targets. All are well-intentioned.

However, the analyses presented in this book demonstrate that some of the targets are less worthwhile, producing only a little more than $1 in social benefits per dollar spent, while others produce much higher social returns. After careful consideration and engagement with the research authors, we selected the 19 targets that we expect to produce the greatest benefits.

The analyses suggest that if the United Nations (UN) concentrates on these top 19 targets, it could achieve $20 to $40 in social benefits per dollar spent. In contrast, allocating it evenly across all 169 targets would reduce the figure to less than $10.

Targets that will help people directly through health benefits are worth championing. As we read about in Chapter 13, tuberculosis (TB) is a "hidden" disease. More than two billion people carry the bacterium that causes it. About 10 percent of those people will develop TB at some point, and about 1.5 million people each year die from TB. But treatment is inexpensive and, in most cases, highly effective. Spending a dollar on diagnosis and treatment is a low-cost way to give many more years of productive life to many people. Ebola and Zika may receive the headlines, but TB is a much bigger problem, and one that we recommend receives high priority.

Reducing childhood malnutrition, described in Chapter 20, is another excellent target. A good diet allows children's brains and muscles to develop better, producing lifelong benefits. Well-nourished children stay in school longer, learn more, and end up being much more productive members of society. The available evidence suggests that providing better nutrition for 68 million children each year would produce over $40 in long-term social benefits for every dollar spent.

There are excellent targets that would help the planet as well. As readers learned in Chapter 7, governments around the world still subsidize the use of fossil fuels to the tune of more than $500 billion each year. Cutting these subsidies would reduce pollution and free up resources for investments in health, education, and infrastructure.

Research from Chapter 2 shows that protecting coral reefs turns out to be a surprisingly efficient target as well. There are benefits in terms of biodiversity, but healthy reefs also produce more tangible and immediate benefits. They increase fish stocks – benefitting both fishermen and consumers – and attract visitors who explore

---

[1] Copenhagen Consensus calculations, 2015, unpublished.

Box C.1 The phenomenal development targets

People

Lower Chronic Child Malnutrition by 40 Percent

Providing nutritional supplements, deworming, and improving the balance of diet for 0- to 2-year-olds will cost $11bn and prevent 68m children from being malnourished every year.

Halve Malaria Infection

Distributing long-lasting insecticide treated bed-nets and delaying resistance to the malaria drug artemisinin will cost $0.6bn, prevent 100m cases of malaria and save 440,000 lives per year.

Reduce Tuberculosis Deaths by 90 Percent

Massively scaling up detection and treatment of tuberculosis will cost $8bn and save up to an additional 1.3m lives per year.

Cut Early Death from Chronic Disease by One-Third

Raising the price of tobacco, administering aspirin and preventative therapy for heart disease, reducing salt intake, and providing low-cost blood pressure medicine will cost $9bn and save 5m lives per year.

Avoid 1.1 Million HIV Infections through Circumcision

Circumcising 90 percent of HIV-negative men in the five worst-affected countries will cost $35m annually and avert 1.1m infections by 2030 with the preventive benefit increasing over time.

Reduce Newborn Mortality by 70 Percent

Protecting expecting mothers from disease, having skilled medical staff support their deliveries, and ensuring high-quality postnatal care will cost $14bn and prevent 2m newborn deaths per year.

Increase Immunization to Reduce Child Deaths by 25 Percent

Expanding immunization coverage to include protection from forms of influenza, pneumonia, and diarrheal disease will cost $1bn and save 1m children per year.

Make Family Planning Available to Everyone

Allowing women to decide if, when, and how often they become pregnant will cost $3.6bn per year and cut maternal deaths by 150,000, while providing a demographic dividend.

Eliminate Violence against Women and Girls

Right now, every year 305 million women are domestically abused, costing the world $4.4 trillion in damages.

Planet

Phase out Fossil Fuel Subsidies

Removing fossil fuel subsidies will cost less than $37bn per year, lower carbon emissions, and free up $548bn in government revenue to spend on, for example, health, infrastructure, and education.

Halve Coral Reef Loss

Protecting marine habitats will cost $3bn per year but will prevent the loss of 3m hectares of coral reef, providing natural fishing hatcheries and boosting tourism.

(cont.)

Box C.1 *(cont.)*

Tax Pollution Damage from Energy

Air pollution is the world's biggest environmental killer, causing more than 7m annual deaths. Taxes proportional to the damage from air pollution and CO_2 will reduce environmental impacts efficiently.

Cut Indoor Air Pollution by 20 Percent

Providing more clean cookstoves will cost $11bn and prevent 1.3m deaths per year from indoor air pollution.

Prosperity

Reduce Trade Restrictions (Full Doha)

Achieving more free trade (e.g., the Doha round) would make each person in the developing world $1,000 richer per year by 2030, lifting 160m people out of extreme poverty at a cost of $20bn per year.

Improve Gender Equality in Ownership, Business, and Politics

Ensuring women can own and inherit property, perform basic business needs like signing a contract. and be represented in parliament will empower women.

Boost Agricultural Yield Growth by 40 Percent

Investing an extra $2.5bn per year in agricultural R&D to boost yields will reduce food prices for poor people, mean 80m fewer people go hungry, and provide benefits worth $84bn per year.

Increase Girls' Education by Two Years

Ensuring girls receive more education will increase their future wages, improve their health, reduce their risk of violence, and start a virtuous cycle for the next generations.

Achieve Universal Primary Education in Sub-Saharan Africa

At a cost of $9bn per year, this target will ensure 30m more kids per year attend primary school

Triple Preschool in Sub-Saharan Africa

Preschool instills within children a lifelong desire to learn. Ensuring preschool coverage rises from 18 percent to 59 percent will cost up to $6bn and will give that experience to at least 30m more children per year

their beauties – benefitting everyone working in the tourist industry, as well as the tourists themselves.

Perhaps the most important, overarching problem facing the world is poverty. One in ten people in the world survive on less than $1.90 a day.[2] Poverty is the ultimate source of many other problems. The immediate result is high rates of infant mortality, as well as poor cognitive skills and reduced productive capacity among surviving children. The ultimate result is a cycle of poverty.

Better nutrition and better schools will help alleviate poverty, and both deserve attention. But there is one target that promises to be incredibly effective: lowering barriers to international trade (Chapter 9). The historical evidence on this point is compelling. In China, South Korea, India, Chile, and many other countries, reducing trade restrictions

[2] World Bank. Poverty and Shared Prosperity 2016. Available at: www.worldbank.org/en/publication/poverty-and-shared-prosperity.

has lifted incomes, reduced poverty, and triggered decades of rapid income growth.

Poverty reduction was the first item in the UN's list of Millennium Development Goals, and the numerical target was achieved. Why? Income growth in China was a big part of the story. And how did the Chinese achieve that remarkable feat? Most evidence suggests that international trade was a key ingredient. Trade produces immediate benefits by opening up markets, but it also facilitates the flow of ideas and technologies, producing even greater benefits over a longer horizon. As the research shows, a successful Doha free trade agreement could lift 160 million people out of extreme poverty.

Our list of phenomenal targets will not solve all the world's problems, but neither could any list under realistic budgets.

What our list can do is to help the UN, governments, and donors to make its choices like a savvy shopper with limited funds. Prioritizing good targets will vastly increase the benefits to people around the world, as well as generations to come. Governments should forgo the temptation to spread limited resources thinly across a broad set of projects with widely varying potential. Instead, when it comes to implementation, they should focus on the smartest development goals.

HOW TO IMPLEMENT THE GLOBAL GOALS, KNOWING WHAT DOES A LOT OF GOOD AND WHAT DOESN'T

Bjorn Lomborg

The research and findings in this book show the targets that would achieve a lot of good for every dollar spent, those that give fair returns, and those that barely do as much good as they would cost. It is now up to us to use this knowledge.

Many of the descriptions of the Global Goals or the SDGs focused on words like *transformative, universal*, and *balanced*. Although well-meaning, this is not the right criteria. The dramatic reduction in poverty in the last 25 years is an unparalleled

good, but it was incremental, not transformative. Even more important, it wasn't an outcome of deliberate, transformative policies. Likewise, a successful free trade agreement would be phenomenally positive but not transformational.

Conversely, many deliberately transformational policies have more than a whiff of social engineering – the radical agrarian socialism in Cambodia in the late 1970s joins a host of similar historical examples that were definitely transformative but not desirable.

Although the sentiment that the SDGs should be universal – applied equally to developed and developing countries – is psychologically understandable, tackling malaria and lifting people above a dollar a day is simply not something that applies equally to poor and rich countries alike. And when preference is given to targets that are "balanced," in an attempt to do one thing that addresses economic, social and environmental concerns all at once, such apparent aesthetical symmetry may seem appealing, but it is likely to be a guide to bad targets. Trade tackles poverty, artemisinin drugs tackle malaria, and emission targets tackle air pollution. We shouldn't intentionally try to make every target work on every ill.

Perhaps the most important realization of the Global Goals is that having 169 targets mean having no priorities. An uncomfortable reality is that most targets and even some goals ought to go. The MDGs were a success exactly because they did not promise to deal with everything, but promised – at heart – just seven simple and obvious, big-picture targets.

We are now past the point where any pruning can take place – in public, at least. But that does not mean that governments, donors, and the UN itself are going to give equal weight to all the targets when it comes to implementation. Behind closed doors, everyone acknowledges that 169 targets are too many and that some need to come before others.

The risk now is that, in the absence of a foundation for smart decision making, targets end up being prioritized in a process that is skewed by the media and advocacy groups toward those with the best public relations – the cutest animals, the

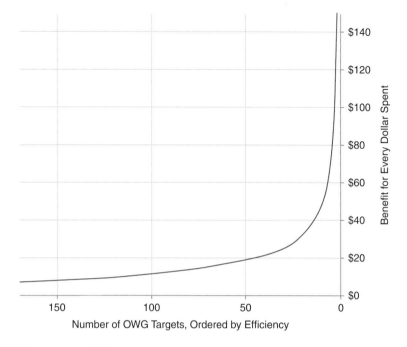

Figure C.1 *Efficiency of prioritizing targets*

scariest scenarios, the most touching pictures of crying babies. We can and should do better.

It is useful to look at the impact of these choices in Figure C.1. This uses the best estimates from the Copenhagen Consensus researchers on the efficiency of each of the 169 targets.

Given that many of the official targets are obtuse and very broad, it is important to recognize that these are only approximate estimates. But with 169 targets, it is likely that if some have been overestimated, others have been underestimated, and the full impact is certainly preserved in the order-of-magnitude in the argument.

Out the *x*-axis we have placed all targets according to their efficiency. Thus, all the way to the right, closest to zero is the most effective target, followed by the next-most effective target all the way to the least effective at number 169 at the far left.

We can now look at the efficiency of a dollar spent equally across targets. If we implemented all 169 targets, we can look to the farthest left and see that a dollar spent will deliver benefits of $7.

What this means, of course, is that one billion dollars spent across all targets would deliver $7 billion in benefits. This is not bad. It is a consequence of spending some money on really great targets like contraception and free trade, most on mediocre targets, and some on poor targets.

If we cut away the least-effective targets and pick just the 100 most-effective targets, the average benefit for every dollar will have risen to $12.

Reduce this to just the 40 top targets, and the average benefit will be $21. By reducing the number of targets by about three-quarters, we can triple the benefits.

And if we zero in on the 19 best targets like the list of those selected by the eminent economists earlier, this would be the equivalent to doing $32 of social good for every dollar spent – more than four times more efficient than spreading the spending across all 169 targets. Each billion dollars now has a return of $32 billion.

It is clear that picking the low-hanging fruit or the very effective targets first will do much more good than spraying money around.

SOCIAL, ECONOMIC AND ENVIRONMENTAL BENEFITS FOR EVERY DOLLAR SPENT

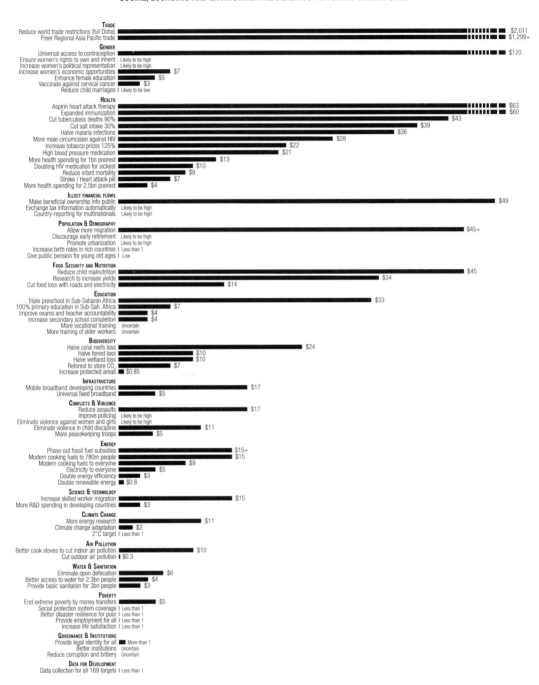

Figure C.2 *Social, economic, and environmental benefits for every dollar spent*

It is important to remember that this is not just a question of economic efficiency and theoretical neatness. If spending across the 169 targets can help save one life, the same spending on the top 19 can save more than four lives.

Prioritizing the smartest targets is an opportunity to leave the world much better than what could come out of spending across all 169 targets.

Yet, prioritizing is hard. It involves saying no to many deserving and well-intentioned causes. But it's important to realize that not prioritizing does not make priorities go away. It simply means that we do less than we could have done.

Perhaps the most eloquent statement on the need for priorities comes from Apple founder Steve Jobs:

> People think focus means saying yes to the thing you've got to focus on. But that's not what it means at all. It means saying no to the hundred other good ideas that there are. You have to pick carefully. I'm actually as proud of the things we haven't done as the things I have done. Innovation is saying no to 1,000 things.[3]

Imagine if donors, following this research, could manage to take the focus away from just one bad target and put it onto one phenomenal one.

Given that such targets will shape the spending of billions of dollars, and a phenomenal target can do $25+ more good for each dollar spent, we can end up helping the world with hundreds of billions of dollars more good. Shifting the entire $2.5 trillion of development aid could potentially make the world more than $62 trillion better off in terms of environmental, social and economic benefits.

Prioritizing the SDGs essentially leverages the world's $2.5 trillion development budget and the countless trillions in national budgets around the world. Even making a small shift in the way we implement these could do amazing good. Ensuring this shift could be the best thing that any of us could help to achieve in the next decade and a half.

[3] Forbes. Steve Jobs: Get Rid of the Crappy Stuff 2011. Available at: www.forbes.com/sites/carminegallo/2011/05/16/steve-jobs-get-rid-of-the-crappy-stuff/#7758e83a563a.

Index

AAP. *See* ambient air pollution
abuse. *See* child abuse
accountability mechanisms
  DFID, xxv–xxvi, 477
  IFF and, 185
  USAID, xxv–xxvi
Achilles Heel (Baker), 189
ACS. *See* American Cancer Society
ACTs. *See* artemisinin combination therapy
actuarial neutrality, 381
adaptation investment, in climate change strategies, 60
administrative data, 94
adult education, 125
adult height, 368. *See also* stunting
Affordable Medicines Facility-malaria (AMFm) pilot, 291
Africa. *See also* sub-Saharan Africa
  education development in, 119
  GDP in, 174
  malaria in, estimated benefit-cost ratios for, 289
African Development Bank, 174
AFTA. *See* ASEAN free trade agreement
aging, 220. *See also* population aging
agriculture. *See also* post-harvest losses
  fossil fuel use and, 158
  on-farm technologies, 323
  rice production and consumption, 457–459
  trade reform as influence on, 207–208
Aichi Targets, 38–47
  carbon stocks
    conservation of, 46–47
    estimation of, 46
  CBA of, 39–41
    assessment of, 41–42
    for coral reef losses, reduction of, 44–45, 50
    for forest losses, reduction of, 42–44
    for protected area losses, reduction of, 45–46
    for wetlands losses, reduction of, 43–44, 50
  CBD and, 38
  investment costs, 42
  strategic goals, 42
  UNEP and, 38
aid, international
  expansion of, xxv–xxvi
  MDG's and, xxv–xxvi
air pollution. *See also* ambient air pollution; emissions;
    household air pollution

deaths from, 13
  GBD Project, 13
    IER model, 13
    YLL, 18, 24
  global health effects, 13–16
  low-carbon technologies for, 55–56, 59–60, 66,
    146
  PM2.5 target range for
    IER model, 13
    RR information on, 13
  targets for
    through air quality improvement, 16
    domains of, 16
    for reduction in health effects, 16
    for reduction in sources of, 16
    selected, 16
    zero, 16
alcohol use, violence and, 80
Alliance for Affordable Internet, 321
ambient air pollution (AAP)
  CBA, 22–32
    cost ratios in, 28–32
    for emissions, 29–30
    with ICS, 29–32
    regional, 29–32
    targets in, 22–25
  control options for, costs of, 26–29
    through energy subsidies, 26–28
    through fuel quality, 27–28
    through road vehicle technologies, 28–29,
      32
    with solid fuels, 27–28
    through solid waste management, 27–28, 31
    through taxation policies, 27
  exposure rates, by region, 13–14
  health effects of, 22–27
    annual, estimation of, 25
    costs of, 27
    monetized values of, 24–27
  from solid fuel use, 13, 15
  targets for, 16
    CBA of, 22–25
    regional, 25
American Cancer Society (ACS), 245
AMFm pilot. *See* Affordable Medicines Facility-malaria pilot
AMLD. *See* Anti Money Laundering Directive

Andrews, Matt, 499–500
antenatal care, infant mortality and, 270–271
Anti Money Laundering Directive (AMLD), 177,
    180
anti-malarial drugs. *See also* malaria
    ACTs, 287–290
        affordability of, 291
        AMFm pilot, 291
    artemisinin resistance, 287–288
antiretroviral therapy (ART), 277–278
APEC. *See* Asia Pacific Economic Cooperation
ART. *See* antiretroviral therapy
artemisinin combination therapy (ACTs), 287–290
    affordability of, 291
    AMFm pilot, 291
artemisinin resistance, 287–288
ASEAN free trade agreement (AFTA), 197
Asia Pacific Economic Cooperation (APEC), 197,
    200
Asia-Pacific region, trade reform in, 199–200, 205
    under AFTA, 197
aspirin therapy, 236
assault, 69
    rape and, 74–75, 343–344

bad data, costs of, 99–100
Baker, Raymond, 189
Ban Ki-Moon, 7
bank account ownership, by women, 349–351
Barrett, Christopher, 337–338
BECCS. *See* bio-energy with carbon capture storage
beneficial ownership, transparency in, 182, 184
benefit-cost ratios
    for AAP strategies, 28–32
    for civil war violence, 80
    for education development, 121
        estimation methods in, 122–123
        evidence of, 123–124
        by level of schooling, 129, 131
        for primary schooling, 130
        rate of return in, 122, 124–125, 133–136
        by region, 124, 129–130
    for family planning, 377
    for gender equality, 360
    for HAP strategies, 21–24
    for healthcare system development, 219
        methodology for, 220–227
        premature mortality, 220–221, 224
        for proposed targets, 226
        for SDG, 221–222
        sensitivity analysis of, 225
    for HIV reduction strategies
        with ART, 278–281
        findings for, 280
        life years gained in, 280
        limitations in, 281
        with MMC, 278–281
    for HPV prevention strategies, 248–250

    for IFF, 182–183, 185
    in infant mortality reduction strategies, 273
    for international migration, 385–386, 405–413
        assessment of, 406–408
        assumptions about, 407–410
        computations of, 412, 414
        model for, 407–410
        results of, 411–413
    for malaria, estimates in, 288–290
        in Africa, 289
        per life year gained, 290
    for nutrition, 373
        stunting and, 369–373
    for OD, 437
    for population aging, 380–382
    for population demographics, 390
    for population growth, 376–379
    for R&D, 400–405
        assessment of, 401–402
        assumptions in, 402–403
        computations of, 404–405
        models in, 402–403
        results of, 403–405
    for TB, 258–259
    of trade liberalization, 201
    of trade reform, 201, 203–205
    for water sanitation interventions, 432–436
        for OD elimination strategies, 437
        for populations served, 432
        for sanitation safety, by region, 435–436
        for universal access to sanitation, 433
        for water supply safety, by region, 433–435
bilateral trade, 217
biodiversity
    AICHI Targets for, 38–47
    CBD and, 38
    development goals
        background of, 38–41
        costs and benefits of, 47
bio-energy with carbon capture storage (BECCS), 56
Blomberg, S. Brock, 89
Booth, Charles, 447
Brander, Luke, 50–51
Braunstein, Elissa, 364–365
broadband technology, 295–300
    access networks for, 301
    affordability of, 297–298
    availability of, 297
    CBA of, 305–309, 314
        assessment methodology for, 302–304, 309
        benefits of, measurement of, 300–301, 303
        costs of, measurement of, 301–305
        reverse causality hypothesis, 300–301
        robustness checks in, 308
        as scenario-dependent, 306, 314
        sensitivity analysis in, 307–308
        targets for, 303–304
    defined, 296–297

broadband technology (cont.)
  digital divide in, 296
  government infrastructure for, 311–312
  investment projects for, 311
  in LDCs, 320–321
  measurement of, 296–298
  network deployment costs, 311–312
  quality of, 297
  state aid as funding, 311
    in EU, 315
  universal penetration of, 305–307, 313
  wireless technology, 307
    spectrum management of, 310
business ownership, by women, 349–351

Cameron, David, 6
cancer. *See* cervical cancer
Canning, David, 395–396
carbon capture storage (CCS), 55–56
  BECCS, 56
carbon pricing, 66
carbon stocks
  conservation of, 46–47
  estimation of, 46
Cardamone, Tom, 191
cardiovascular disease (CVD), 233
  aspirin therapy, 236
  population salt reduction strategies, 236–237
  secondary prevention of, 237–238
Casey, Gregory, 397–398
CBA. *See* cost-benefit analysis
CBD. *See* Convention on Biological Diversity
CCS. *See* carbon capture storage
censuses, 112–113
  costs of, 91, 96–98
  population, 95–97
cervical cancer, 244–246
  incidence rates of, 244
  Pap test/smear for, 245–246
  prevention of, 244–245, 251
  screening for, 245–246
CGE models. *See* computable general equilibrium models
child abuse, 69–73
  forced early marriage as, 73
  sexual abuse as, 73
    costs of, 73
child marriage, 73
  incidence rates for, 345
childbirth
  care after, 270
  care during, 270
children. *See also* infant mortality
  malnutrition among, 332
  obesity in, 367–368, 374
  stunting in, reduction goals for, 367–374
    advantages of, 368–370
    benefit-cost ratio for, 369–373

disadvantages of, 368–369
  economic perspective on, 369–373
underweight in, 367–368
violence against, 69–73
  homicide, 70–71
  interpersonal, 69–70
  non-fatal, 71–72
China
  coal in, 147–148
  HRS in, 456–457
  poverty deficits in, xxvi
  zero poverty in, 456–460
circumcision. *See* male medical circumcision
civil war violence, 79–83
  annual changes for, 82
  cost-benefit ratio for, 80
  percentage of countries with, 82–83
  reduction of, 79–81
  targets for, 81–83
climate change
  CBA for, 57–60
    emission intensity targets, 58
    global carbon emission targets, 57–58
    summary of, 61
  energy technology issues, 55–56
    adaptation investment, 60
    BECCS, 56
    CCS, 55–56
    for emissions reduction, 57
    GDP investment in, 58–60
  Green Climate Fund, 57
  from greenhouse gases, 207
  IPCC, 54–55
  Kaya Identity, 57–58
  under Kyoto Protocol, 57
  overview of, 54
  post-2015 development agenda on, 56–57
    target recommendations for, 60–61
coal
  in China, 147–148
  HAP from, 14–15
  in India, 147–148
computable general equilibrium (CGE) models, 198
contraception, 357
contractual agreements, women and, 349–351
Convention on Biological Diversity (CBD), 38
  Aichi Targets and, 38
cooking fuels, modern access to, 150, 159–160
cookstoves, 37
  HAP from, 15–16
    ICS, 20
    improvements in, fuel savings from, 20
    LPG, 20
Copenhagen Consensus
  CBA by, xxiv–xxv
  development targets under, 5–6

RethinkHIV campaign, 5–6
coral reefs, loss of, 44–45, 50
Core Welfare Indicator Questionnaire (CWIQ), 96–98,
    106–107, 110
corporate tax evasion, 172
Corruption Perception Index (CPI), 479
cost-benefit analysis (CBA). *See also* benefit-cost ratios
    for AAP, 22–32
        cost ratios in, 28–32
        for emissions, 29–30
        with ICS, 29–32
        regional factors, 29–32
        targets in, 22–25
    of Aichi Targets, 39–41
        assessment of, 41–42
        for coral reef losses, reduction of, 44–45
        for forest losses, reduction of, 42–44
        for protected area losses, reduction of, 45–46
        for wetlands losses, reduction of, 43–44
    of broadband technology, 305–309, 314
        assessment methodology for, 302–304, 309
        benefits of, measurement of, 300–301, 303
        costs of, measurement of, 301–305
        reverse causality hypothesis, 300–301
        robustness checks in, 308
        as scenario-dependent, 306, 314
        sensitivity analysis in, 307–308
        targets for, 303–304
    for climate change, 57–60
        emission intensity targets, 58
        global carbon emission targets, 57–58
        summary of, 61
    by Copenhagen Consensus, xxiv–xxv
    development stakeholders' use of, xxvii–xxx
    of education development, 120–123
    function and purpose of, xxiv–xxv
    of gender equality
        child marriage and, reduction of, 345–349
        reduction in violence against girls and women, 343–345,
            347
    governance and, 487
    for HAP, 16–24
        cost-ratios in, 21–24
        for global benefits, 21–22
        for health effects, 17–20
        targets in, 16–17
    for healthcare system development, 219
    of ICT, 299–309, 312
    for IFF, 171, 179–185
        in UK, 180–183
    of MDGs, xxvii–xxx
    for PHL, 333–334
        cost allocations in, 334
        investment scenarios in, 334
    of SDGs, xxvii–xxx
    of zero poverty targets, 460–468
        for disaster resilience, 465

    for economic rights, 466–467
    elimination strategies in, 460–463
    for full employment, 467–468
    for social protection, 463–465
    in Vietnam, 461–463
CPI. *See* Corruption Perception Index
CVD. *See* cardiovascular disease
CWIQ. *See* Core Welfare Indicator Questionnaire

DALY values. *See* Disability Adjusted Life Year values
data collection
    administrative, 94
    bad data, costs of, 99–100
    behavioural effects of, 91
    censuses, 112–113
        costs of, 91, 96–98
        population, 95–97
    costs of, 91, 94
        of censuses, 91, 96–98
        of monitoring, 91
        opportunity, 91
        for pre-2015 development agenda, 92–94
    CWIQ, 96–98, 106–107, 110
    DHS, 95–96, 106, 114
    good data, benefits of, 99
    LSMS, 95, 106–107, 110–111
    MDG indicators, 103–105
    methodology for, 94–96
        minimum requirements in, 96
    MICS, 96, 107
    monitoring of
        costs of, 91
        development approaches to, 92
    post-2015 development agenda for, 93
        benefits of, 100–101
        costs of, 100–101, 108
    pre-2015 development agenda for, 92–94
        costs of, 108–109
        in large countries, 109
        in medium countries, 108–109
        in small countries, 108
    quality of, 92–93, 99
    results of, 96–98
    revolution in, 92
    surveys, 94–96
        health, 95–96. *See also* Demographic and Health
            Surveys
        household, 93–94
        indicator list by information access type, 95
        in sub-Saharan Africa, 93–94
Datt, Guarav, 473
DDA. *See* Doha Development Agenda
deforestation, 42–44
    AICHI Targets for, 38–47
    development goals, 38–41
Demographic and Health Surveys (DHS), 95–96, 106, 114
demographics. *See* population demographics

Demombynes, Gabriel, 118
Deng Xiaoping, 456
Denmark, HIV/AIDS projects in, 6
Department for International Development (DFID),
    xxv–xxvi, 477
development. *See also* Millennium Development Goals;
    Sustainable Development Goals; targets
    efficiency of. *See* Millennium Development Goals;
        Sustainable Development Goals
    governance and, 480–483
        institutional fundamentalism and, 481
        reform efforts, 481–483
        TAIs, 482
    institutional, 485, 493
    international, 118, 477, 484
development targets. *See* targets
DFID. *See* Department for International Development
DFID, accountability mechanisms, xxv–xxvi, 477
DHS. *See* Demographic and Health Surveys
diabetes, 220, 231–233, 251
diffusion, of technology, 297
digital divide, 296
digital inclusion, social acceptance through, 295
Disability Adjusted Life Year (DALY) values, 9, 150
    estimation of, 229
    in healthcare system development, 219–225
    infant mortality and, 273
    with malaria, 289–290
    for NCD, 237
    TB and, 258–259
    for water sanitation interventions, 433, 436–438, 441
        for premature mortality, 441
disease. *See* non-communicable disease; vaccines; water-
        borne disease
Doha Development Agenda (DDA), 192, 197
    economic consequences of, 198–199
    environmental impact of, 207
    net benefits of, 203–204
    trade reform under, 208–209
domestic violence, 73, 75
drinking water, safe, 340–341, 425, 428. *See also* water-
        borne disease
    benefit-cost ratios for, by region, 433–435
drug resistance
    to artemisinin, 287–288
    to TB
        MDR, 255–258
        XDR, 255
drug trafficking, 67, 172

early childhood education. *See* pre-school education
East Asia. *See also* China
    zero poverty targets in, 456–460
        composition of, 459–460
        persistence of, 459–460
        rice production and consumption, 457–459
economic growth and development

CGE models, 198
    as development target, 503
    energy production as influence on, 148
        Feedback Hypothesis, 148
        Growth Hypothesis, 148
        Neutrality Hypothesis, 148
    IFF and, 174
    trade and, 194–196
    Unified Growth Theory and, 397
ecosystems
    coral reefs, 44–45, 50
    failures of, 44
    forests, loss of, 42–44
    Marine Trophic Index, 44
    protected areas, loss of, 45–46
    wetlands, losses of, 43–44, 50
education, development of
    adult, 125
    benefit-cost ratios for, 121
        estimation methods in, 122–123
        evidence of, 123–124
        by level of schooling, 129, 131
        for primary schooling, 130
        rate of return in, 122, 124–125, 133–136
        by region, 124, 129–130
    CBA of, 120–123
    costs of, 131–132
        in sub-Saharan Africa, 132
    cultural influences on, 119
    externalities for, 130–131
    finance for, 125
        lack of, 119
    historical perspectives on, 119
        in Africa, 119
    literary influences on, 125
    of mothers, 131
    in OECD countries, 124
    political climate of country as influence on, 119
    population quality and, 388–389
    post-2015 development agenda for, 119–132
        assessment of, 128–131
        goals of, 120
        targets in, 133–135
    poverty as influence on, 119
    pre-school, 123, 127
        enrollment ratio, 131
        in sub-Saharan Africa, 129–131
    primary, 126, 128
        benefit-cost ratios of, 130
        in sub-Saharan Africa, 129–130
    private investment in, 124
    quality of, 124–125, 127–128
        PISA scores, 128
    secondary, 125, 127
    in sub-Saharan Africa
        costs of, 132
        pre-school, 129–131

primary schooling in, 129–130
tertiary, 127–128
vocational, 125
for women, 356–358
World Bank and, 119, 123–124
EIA 2013. *See* International Energy Outlook 2013
electricity, universal access to, 149–150
emissions, reduction of
  AAP and, CBA for, 29–30
  climate change and
    CBA for, 57–58, 61
    energy technology for, 57
  global carbon targets, 57–58
  intensity targets, 58
  through road-vehicle technology, 28–29, 32
employment, gender equality in, 339–345
empowerment, by gender
  through education, 339
  through employment, 339–345
  through reduction of violence against girls and women and,
    343–345
energy, production and use of
  access to, inequality in, 162
  benefits and costs of, 151, 161
  coal
    in China, 147–148
    HAP from, 14–15
    in India, 147–148
  for cooking fuels, modern access to, 150, 159–160
  current trends in, 144–146
  economic growth and development and, 148
    Feedback Hypothesis, 148
    Growth Hypothesis, 148
    Neutrality Hypothesis, 148
  efficiency measures, 144
    gap in, 151–152
    global improvement strategies, 150–154
    in LDCs, 151
  EIA 2013, 144–146
  elasticity of, 145
  energy ladder hypothesis, 144
  environmental policies and, 148–149
  in EU, 157–158
    in Germany, 157
    in Norway, 158
    renewable energies, 155
    in Sweden, 158
    under Treaty of Lisbon, 157
    in UK, 157–158
  global systems, 143
    SE4ALL, 143–144
  hydro, 155
  IEA and, 152–154, 157
  LNG, 146–147
    fracking, 147
    technology for, 147
  modern access to, 149

  for cooking fuels, 150
  universal, 150
  through universal electrification, 149–150
  nuclear power, 147
  in OECD countries, 153–154
  post-2015 development agenda, target recommendations
    for, 161–162
  poverty, 143
  R&D in, 160–161
  renewable, 143
    doubling shares of, 154–156
    in EU, 155
    IRENA, 155
    R&D for, 161
  shale gas, 143, 146–147
  solar, 154–155
  in sub-Saharan Africa, 143
  subsidies, 155
    AAP and, control of, 26–28
    for fossil fuels, 156–159
    phasing out of, 156–157
  sustainability, SE4ALL program, 143–144
  wind, 154–155
energy ladder hypothesis, 144
energy technology, for climate change, 55–56
  adaptation investment, 60
  BECCS, 56
  CCS, 55–56
  for emissions reduction, 57
  GDP investment in, 58–60
enterprise, technology and, 399–400, 402
environmental justice, 66
environmental policies
  DDA as influence on, 207
  as development target, 502–503
  energy production and, 148–149
  global, 206–207
  healthcare system development and, 227
  trade reform as influence on, 206–207
EPI. *See* Expanded Program on Immunization
epidemiology, 35
European Union (EU)
  broadband technology in, state aid for, 315
  energy production and use in, 157–158
    in Germany, 157
    in Norway, 158
    for renewable energies, 155
    in Sweden, 158
    under Treaty of Lisbon, 157
    in UK, 157–158
Expanded Program on Immunization (EPI), 245
extensively drug-resistant TB (XDR-TB), 255

family planning, 357
  benefit-cost ratios for, 377
FAO. *See* Food and Agriculture Organization
FATF. *See* Financial Action Task Force

Feedback Hypothesis, 148
feed-in-tariffs (FITs), 155
female genital mutilation (FGM), 69–70, 73
  reduction strategies, 80
fertility
  global rates for, 227
  net reproduction rate and, 376
  population aging and, 379–383
    benefit-cost ratios, 380–382
    indicators for, 382
    migration as factor in, 380
    policy reforms and, 381
    targets for, 382
    UN global consultation priorities, 380
  population growth and, 375–379
    benefit-cost ratio targets, 376–379
    indicators for, 379
    by region, 376
    UN global consultation priorities, 376–377
  Unified Growth Theory and, 397
FGM. See female genital mutilation
finance. See also illicit financial flows
  for education development, 125
    lack of, 119
  microfinance, 159
  money laundering
    under AMLD, 177, 180
    IFF and, 171–172
  regulation of, 312
Financial Action Task Force (FATF), 177, 189
financial flows. See illicit financial flows
Fischer, Carolyn, 66
FITs. See feed-in-tariffs
Food and Agriculture Organization (FAO), 8
food losses, 322
  zero food waste and, 323
food prices, global, 331
food security. See also malnutrition; nutrition
  future projections about, 8
  nutrition and, 337–338
  producer surplus, 333
forests, losses of, 42–44
fossil fuels
  in agricultural sector, 158
  coal
    in China, 147–148
    HAP from, 14–15
    in India, 147–148
  energy subsidies for, 156, 158–159
    phasing out of, 156–157
fracking, 147
fuels. See solid fuels; specific fuel sources
Fukushima nuclear accident, 147
full employment, 467–468
  NAIRU, 467

Galor, Oded, 397–398
GAVI. See Global Alliance of Vaccines and Immunization

GBD 2010 Project. See Global Burden of Disease 2010
    Project
GDP. See gross domestic product
gender
  empowerment
    through education, 339
    through employment, 339–345
    through reduction of violence against girls and women
      and, 343–345
  HAP exposure rates by, 17
  violence, 73, 75. See also intimate-partner violence;
      women
gender equality
  in bank account ownership, 349–351
  benefit-cost ratios for, 360
  for business ownership, 349–351
  CBA of
    of child marriage, reduction of, 345–349
    of violence against girls and women, reduction of,
      343–345, 347
  in contractual agreements, 349–351
  through economic opportunities, 351–357
  MDG for, 339–341
    through education, 339, 356–358
    through employment, 339–345
    through maternal health, 339
    safe water access and, 340–341
    sanitation safety and, 340–341
  policy recommendations for, 357–360
  through political representation, 351–357
  post-2015 development agenda for, 341
  through property rights, 349–351
  through sexual and reproductive health, for women,
      357
gender violence, 73, 75
General Agreement on Tariffs and Trade (GATT),
    193
Germany, energy production and use in, 157
Gleave, Madeleine, 170
Glewwe, Paul, 141
Global Alliance of Vaccines and Immunization (GAVI),
    245
Global Burden of Disease (GBD) 2010 Project, 13
  YLL, 18, 24
global energy systems, 143
  SE4ALL, 143–144
global environmental policies, 206–207
global warming, 5, 157. See also Kyoto Protocol
  greenhouse gases and, 143
good data, benefits of, 99
governance
  CBA and, 487
  defined, 477
  development and, 480–483
    institutional fundamentalism and, 481
    reform efforts, 481–483
    TAIs, 482
  IFF as influence on, 175

IFIs and, 477–479
inclusiveness and, 475, 488
institutional perspectives on, 475–476
in MDGs, 477–479, 485
measurement issues, 479–480
  CPI, 479
  WGI, 479–480
Open Working Group Proposals for, 476, 487–488
as SDG, 475–476
targets for, 484–491
  assessment of, 486–493
  breadth of, 486
  form and function of, 486
  outcome and output measurements, 485–486
taxation and, 175
Washington Consensus on, 477–478
Green Climate Fund, 57
greenhouse gases
  climate change from, 207
  global warming, 143
  Kyoto Protocol on, 35
  reduction of, 157, 207
  stabilization of, 55–56
gross domestic product (GDP)
  in Africa, 174
  IFF and, 174
Growth Hypothesis, 148

handwashing, 428
HAP. See household air pollution
HCES. See Household Consumption Expenditure Survey
health. See sexual health
health delivery systems
  NCDs and, 240
  population quality and, 389
healthcare systems, development of. See also antenatal care;
        universal healthcare; women's health
  access to, 227
  aging and, 220
  benefit-cost ratios for, 219
    methodology for, 220–227
    premature mortality, 220–221, 224
    for proposed targets, 226
    for SDG, 221–222
    sensitivity analysis of, 225
  CBA for, 219
  DALY and, 219–225
  disability and, reduction strategies for, 219–220
  environmental hazards, 227
  global fertility, 227
  government spending on, 221
  in LMICs, 219–220
  mortality
    adult, reduction of, 219
    child, reduction of, 219
    premature, 220–221, 223–224, 227–228
  universal, 227
Heckman, James, 125

high blood pressure. See hypertension
high fertility. See fertility
High-Level Panel of Eminent Person (HLPEP), 266
HIV/AIDS treatment, 3
  ART, 277–278
    cost-benefit ratio for, 278–281
    implementation challenges for, 281
  in Denmark, 6
  goals of, 282
  MMC, 278
    cost-benefit ratio for, 278–281
    implementation challenges for, 281–282
  RethinkHIV campaign, 5–6, 281
HLPEP. See High-Level Panel of Eminent Person
Hoekman, Bernard, 216
Holland, Mike, 35–36
homicide, 68–69
  against children, 70–71
  costs of, 68–69, 75
  against women, costs of, 75
household air pollution (HAP)
  CBA for, 16–24
    cost-ratios in, 21–24
    for global benefits, 21–22
    for health effects, 17–20
    targets in, 16–17
  from coal use, 14–15
  control options, costs of, 20–21
    unit cost estimations, 21
  from cookstoves, 15–16
    ICS, 20
    improvements in, fuel savings from, 20
    LPG, 20
  exposure rates
    by gender, 17
    by pollution source, 17–18
    by region, 14–16
  health effects of, 18
    annual, estimation of, 19
    CBA for, 17–20
    cost of, 20
    monetized values of, 18–20
  non-health benefits, 19–20
    cooking time improvements, value of, 20
    solid fuel savings value, 20
  from solid fuel use, 13–15
  targets for, 16
Household Consumption Expenditure Survey (HCES), 450,
        453–454
Household Responsibility System (HRS), 456–457
household surveys, 93–94
HPV. See human papilloma virus
HRS. See Household Responsibility System
human capital
  loss of, through international migration, 410
  population quality and, 389
  spillovers, 420
  zero poverty targets and, 461–462

human immunodeficiency virus (HIV), in sub-Saharan
　　Africa, 277
　　ART treatment, 277–278
　　　cost-benefit ratio for, 278–281
　　　implementation challenges for,
　　　　281
　　benefit-cost ratio for, in reduction strategies
　　　with ART, 278–281
　　　findings for, 280
　　　life years gained in, 280
　　　limitations in, 281
　　　with MMC, 278–281
　　global focus on, 277
　　MMC as treatment for, 278
　　　cost-benefit ratio for, 278–281
　　　implementation challenges for,
　　　　281–282
　　treatment strategies, 3
　　　with ART, 277–281
　　　in Denmark, 6
　　　goals of, 282
　　　with MMC, 278–281
　　　RethinkHIV campaign, 5–6, 281
human mobility, 175
　　fiscal externality of, 409
　　population demographics and,
　　　383–387
　　　benefit-cost ratios for, 385–386
　　　indicators for, 386
　　　regional, by age range, 384
　　　targets for, 386
　　　UN global consultation priorities, 385
human papilloma virus (HPV), 244
　　benefit-cost ratio comparisons, 248–250
　　direct health gains, as development target,
　　　246–247
　　externalities as factor in, 247–248
　　productivity gains
　　　behavior-related, 247
　　　care-related, 247
　　　outcome-related, 247
　　RRP, 248
　　vaccination, 244–245
　　　barriers to, 251
　　　coverage costs of, 248, 251
　　　direct health gains of, 246–247
　　　EPI, 245
　　　GAVI, 245
　　　healthcare cost savings, 247
human trafficking, 172, 476
hunger. *See also* food security
　　at-risk projections, 332
　　defined, 367
　　nutrition goals and, 367
hydro energy, 155
hypertension, 233–234
　　management strategies, 236–238
　　stroke and, 233

IADB. *See* Inter-American Development Bank
ICS. *See* improved biomass and coal cookstoves
ICT. *See* information communication technologies
IEA. *See* International Energy Agency
IER model. *See* integrated PM2.5 exposure response model
IFF. *See* illicit financial flows
IFIs. *See* international financial institutions
illicit financial flows (IFF)
　　accountability mechanisms and, 185
　　benefit-cost ratios for, 182–183, 185
　　categories of, 172
　　CBA for, 171, 179–185
　　　in UK, 180–183
　　components of, 171–172
　　definition of, 172
　　development impacts of, 173–176
　　　for economic growth, 174
　　　for income distribution, 174–176
　　　for social development, 174
　　GDP influenced by, 174
　　governance influenced by, 175
　　IMF response to, 173
　　inequality and, 173
　　money laundering and, 171–172
　　proposed targets, 176–179
　　　beneficial ownership, 177, 180–182
　　　future recommendations for, 186
　　　for tax information exchange, 177–178
　　　trade misinvoicing, 178–179, 191
　　　zero targets, 177
　　in SDG, 173
　　state legitimacy and, 172
　　tax evasion and, 171–172
　　　multinational, 171
　　tax systems and, 174–175
　　theft of state assets, 171–172
　　trade mispricing and, 174
　　transparency and, 191
　　World Bank response to, 173
IMF. *See* International Monetary Fund
immunization. *See* vaccines
IMPACT. *See* International Model for Policy Analysis of
　　Agricultural Commodity and Trade
improved biomass and coal cookstoves (ICS), 20
inclusiveness, 295
　　governance and, 475, 488
income distribution development, 174–176
　　inequality in, 174–175
India
　　coal in, 147–148
　　poverty deficits in, xxvi
　　TRAI in, 302
inequality, 1
　　to energy access, 162
　　human social mobility and, 175
　　IFF and, 173
　　income, 174–175
　　poverty and, 192, 446–447, 449–453

infant mortality
   antenatal care and, 270–271
   benefit-cost ratio, in reduction strategies, 273
   childbirth and
      care after, 270
      care during, 270
   for children under five, 266–267
   cost effectiveness of, 270–273
      for essential health services, 272
   by country, 275–276
   DALY and, 273
   defined, 266
   global trends in, 266–267
      projections for, 266–270
   HLPEP and, 266
   income per capita as factor in, 270
   interventions, 270–273
   malaria prevention, 271
   regional distribution of, by age group, 268
      country-specific estimates, 271
   targets for, 270–273
information communication technologies (ICT). *See also*
         broadband technology
   CBA of, 299–309, 312
   expansion of services, 312
   importance of, 295
   institutional framework for, 308–312
      competition authorities in, 311
      through infrastructure sharing, 305–307
      policy interventions, 309–311
      regulatory interventions, 309–311
   international organizations' role in, 312
   ITU and, 295
      targets for, 298–299
   MDGs for, 295
   network deployment regulations, 310–311
   in OECD countries, 297–298
   post-2015 development agenda, 295
      proposed targets for, 299–300
   price comparisons of, 298
   revolution in, 194, 209
   SDGs for, 295–300, 312
innovation zones, 399–400, 407
   establishment of, 420
   human capital spillovers, 420
   partial equilibrium model of, 416
   types of, 407
insecticide-treated bed nets
   LLITNs, 287–288
   subsidies for, 288
institutional development, 485, 493. *See also* Millennium
         Development Goals; Sustainable Development Goals
institutional fundamentalism, 481
integrated PM2.5 exposure response (IER) model, 13
intensity targets, for emissions reductions, 58
Inter-American Development Bank (IADB), 5
Intergovernmental Panel on Climate Change (IPCC), 54–55,
   325

international development, 118, 477, 484. *See also*
         Millennium Development Goals; Sustainable
         Development Goals
International Energy Agency (IEA), 152–154, 157
International Energy Outlook (EIA) 2013, 144–146
international financial institutions (IFIs), 477–479
international migration. *See* migration
International Model for Policy Analysis of Agricultural
         Commodity and Trade (IMPACT), 324–326, 331–333
International Monetary Fund (IMF), 173
International Renewable Energy Agency (IRENA), 155
international spillovers, 420
International Telecommunications Union (ITU), 295
   targets for, 298–299
international trade barriers, 192–198
   arguments for reduction of, 193–198
   dynamic economic gains, 194–196
   labor market interventions, 193
   static economic gains, 193–194
interpersonal violence, 68–70
   costs of, 69–70
   decline of, 67–68
intimate-partner violence (IPV)
   costs of, 76
   interventions for, 344
   against women, 73, 75
IPCC. *See* Intergovernmental Panel on Climate Change
IPV. *See* intimate-partner violence
IRENA. *See* International Renewable Energy Agency
ITU. *See* International Telecommunications Union

Jacobsen, Joyce P., 366
Japan, nuclear power in, 147
Jerven, Morten, 8
Jeuland, Marc, 37
Johnston, Deborah, 117
justice systems
   access to, 475–476
   environmental, 66
   in post-2015 development agenda, 475
   violence and, institutional responses to, 80

Kar, Dev, 191
Kaya Identity, 57–58
Koutroumpis, Pantelis, 320–321
Kozel, Valerie, 474
Kraay, Aart, 497–498
Krafft, Caroline, 141
Kyoto Protocol, 35
   climate change under, 57

labour markets
   benefit-cost ratios for, international migration in, 405–413
      assessment of, 406–408
      assumptions about, 407–410
      computations of, 412, 414
      model for, 407–410
      results of, 411–413

labour markets (cont.)
    fiscal externality of, 409
    managerial and technical workers, 408
Least Developed Countries (LDCs), 2
    broadband technology in, 320–321
    energy efficiency measures in, 151
legitimacy, of states, 172
liberalization of trade, 193, 195
    in Asia-Pacific region, 199–200
    benefit-cost ratio of, 201
life expectancy, 380
liquified natural gas (LNG), 146–147
    fracking, 147
    technology for, 147
literacy rates, 2
Living Standards Measurement Study (LSMS), 95, 106–107,
        110–111
LLITNs. See long-lasting insecticide-treated bed nets
LMICs. See low and middle income countries
LNG. See liquified natural gas
Lomborg, Bjorn, 179
long-lasting insecticide-treated bed nets (LLITNs),
        287–288
Low, Patrick, 217–218
low and middle income countries (LMICs), 219–220
    NCDs in, 231
    TB in, 255
low fertility. See fertility
low height. See stunting
low-carbon technologies, 55–56, 59–60, 66, 146
low-sulfur diesel, 28
LPG cookstoves, 20
LSMS. See Living Standards Measurement Study

malaria, control of
    ACTs, 287–290
        affordability of, 291
        AMFm pilot, 291
    benefit-cost ratios, estimates in, 288–290
        in Africa, 289
        per life year gained, 290
    challenges to, 290–291
        diagnostic, 290–291
    DALY and, 289–290
    incidence rates for, 287
    insecticide-treated bed nets and
        LLITNs, 287–288
        subsidies for, 288
    intervention and reduction strategies for
        artemisinin resistance and, 287–288
        combinations of, 289
        infant mortality and, 271
        through MFTs, 287
        public policy considerations in, 291
    RDTs for, 291
    WWARN and, 288
male medical circumcision (MMC), 278

malnutrition
    among children, 332
    hunger and, 207
managerial and technical workers, 408
Manning, Richard, 98
Marine Trophic Index, 44
marriage. See child marriage
Marshall, Alfred, 448
maternal health
    cost effectiveness of, 272
    mortality and, 339, 357
McVittie, Alistair, 52–53
MDGs. See Millennium Development Goals
MDR-TB. See multi-drug resistant TB
megacities, 387
Mendelsohn, Robert, 64–65
methodology
    in broadband technology assessment, 302–304, 309
    for data collection, 94–96
        minimum requirements in, 96
    for healthcare system development, 220–227
    for PHL, 324–326
        data in, 326–333
        through grouped logistic regression, 324
        IMPACT, 324–326, 331–333
        infrastructural variables, 326–328, 331
        results of, 326–333
    in water sanitation interventions, 423–432
        excluded countries in, 440
MFTs. See multiple first-line therapies
microfinance, 159, 344
MICS. See multiple indicator cluster survey
migration, international, 204–205
    benefit-cost ratios for, in labor markets, 405–413
        assessment of, 406–408
        assumptions about, 407–410
        computations of, 412, 414
        model for, 407–410
        results of, 411–413
    human capital losses through, 410
    liberalization of, 386
    of managerial and technical workers, 408
    population aging and, 380
    population demographics and, 383–387
        benefit-cost ratios for, 385–386
        indicators for, 386
        regional, by age range, 384
        targets for, 386
        UN global consultation priorities, 385
    reform of, costs of, 386
Millennium Development Goals (MDGs), 2–9. See also
        post-2015 development agenda; pre-2015
        development agenda; specific goals
    for biodiversity, 38–41. See also Aichi Targets
    CBA of, xxvii–xxx
    for data collection, 103–105
    for deforestation, 38–41. See also Aichi Targets

development targets, 3–4
    under Copenhagen Consensus, 5–6
    in future, 6–7
    prioritizing of, 4–9
    expansion of international aid as, xxv–xxvi
    for gender equality, 339–341
        through education, 339, 356–358
        through employment, 339–345
        through maternal health, 339
        safe water access and, 340–341
        sanitation safety and, 340–341
    governance in, 477–479, 485
    HIV/AIDS treatment, 3
    for ICT, 295
    numerical targets in, adoption of, xxv
    for nutrition, 367–368
    SDGs compared to, xxiv–xxvii
    universal concept of development through, xxvi–xxvii
MMC. *See* male medical circumcision
mobility. *See* human mobility
money laundering
    under AMLD, 177, 180
    IFF and, 171–172
morbidity, valuation of
    with AAP, 26
    with HAP, 19
Morris, Adele, 168–169
mortality. *See also* infant mortality
    adult, 219
    child, 219
    life expectancy and, 220
    maternal, 339, 357
    premature, 220–221, 223–224
        from non-communicable disease, 225–227
        reduction strategies, 227–228
        technological progress and, 228
        water sanitation interventions and, 441
    reduction of, 219
    valuation of
        with AAP, 26
        with HAP, 19
    YLL, 18, 24
mosquitoes. *See also* malaria
    insecticide-treated bed nets
        LLITNs, 287–288
        subsidies for, 288
Moss, Todd, 170
mothers, education of, 131
multi-drug resistant TB (MDR-TB), 255–258
multiple first-line therapies (MFTs), for malaria, 287
multiple indicator cluster survey (MICS), 96, 107

NAIRU. *See* non-accelerating inflation rate of employment
natural gas. *See* liquified natural gas
natural habitats, 42–43
NCD. *See* non-communicable disease
neonatal mortality. *See* infant mortality

net reproduction rate, 376
Neutrality Hypothesis, 148
non-accelerating inflation rate of employment (NAIRU), 467
non-communicable disease (NCD), 225–227
    CVD, 233
        aspirin therapy, 236
        population salt reduction strategies, 236–237
        secondary prevention of, 237–238
    DALY for, 237
    global incidence rates for, 231
    health delivery systems and, 240
    health goals, 232
    hypertension, 233–234
        management strategies, 236–238
    indicators for, 231–234
        WHO framework for, 231–232
    intervention strategies for, 234–235
        complexity of, 240
        results of, 239–240
    in LMICs, 231
    mortality rates of, WHO estimates of, 234
    overview of, 240–241
    quality of care for, 240
    risk-taking behaviors for, 240
    targets for, 231–234
    tobacco use, 234
        taxation of, 235–236
    WHO and, 239–240
        framework for indicators of, 231–232
        premature mortality rate estimates, 234–235
non-fatal violence, against children, 71–72
non-tariff measures (NTMs), 216
Norway, energy production and use in, 158
NTMs. *See* non-tariff measures
nuclear power, 147
nutrition goals
    benefit-cost ratio for, 373
        for stunting reduction, 369–373
    evolution of, 367–368
    food security and, 337–338
    hunger and, 367
    malnutrition, 207
    MDG, 367–368
    obesity and, 367–368, 374
    population quality and, 389
    purpose and function of, 367
    SDG, 367–368
    sensitivity analysis of, 373
    stunting, reduction of, 367–374
        advantages of, 368–370
        benefit-cost ratio for, 369–373
        disadvantages of, 368–369
        economic perspective on, 369–373
    WHO guidelines, 368

obesity, 367–368, 374
OD. *See* open defecation

OECD countries. *See* Organisation for Economic Co-operation and Development countries
on-farm technologies, 323
open defecation (OD), 424–425
  benefit-cost ratios for, 437
Open Working Group Proposals, on governance, 476, 487–488
Orazem, Peter, 142
Organisation for Economic Co-operation and Development (OECD) countries
  education development and, 124
  energy and production use in, 153–154
  ICT in, 297–298
  R&D in, 400–401
  taxation policy standards, 178
Overseas Development Aid, 191

Pap test/smear, 245–246
PHL. *See* post-harvest losses
PISA scores. *See* Programme for International Student Assessment scores
PM2.5 target range, for air pollution. *See also* ambient air pollution; household air pollution
  IER model, 13
  RR information, 13
political representation, gender equality through, 351–357
pollution. *See* air pollution; ambient air pollution; household air pollution
population aging
  life expectancy and, 380
  low fertility and, 379–383
    benefit-cost ratios, 380–382
    indicators for, 382
    migration as factor in, 380
    policy reforms and, 381
    targets for, 382
    UN global consultation priorities, 380
  social effects of, 380
population censuses, 95–97
population demographics. *See also* population aging
  benefit-cost ratios for, 390
  development of, 375
  human mobility and, 383–387
  migration as factor in, 383–387
    benefit-cost ratios for, 385–386
    indicators for, 386
    regional, by age range, 384
    targets for, 386
    UN global consultation priorities, 385
  public policy on, 390–391
  targets for, prioritization of, 390–391
  urbanization and, 387–388
    in megacities, 387
    UN global consultation priorities, 387–388
population growth, 375–379
  benefit-cost ratio targets, 376–379
  indicators for, 379

  by region, 376
  UN global consultation priorities, 376–377
  water sanitation interventions and, 426
population quality, 375, 388–389
  education and, 388–389
  health delivery systems and, 389
  human capital and, 389
  nutrition and, 389
population salt reduction, 236–237
Positive Parenting Program (Triple P), 80
post-2015 development agenda, MDG
  on climate change, 56–57. *See also* air pollution
    target recommendations for, 60–61
  for data collection, 93
    benefits of, 100–101
    costs of, 100–101, 108
  for education, 119–132
    assessment of, 128–131
    goals of, 120
    targets in, 133–135
  for energy production and use, 161–162
  food security and, 337–338
  for gender equality, 341
  for ICT, 295
    proposed targets for, 299–300
  justice in, 475
  for TB control interventions, 255–256
post-harvest losses (PHL), 322–324
  annual growth rates and, 325
  CBA for, 333–334
    cost allocations in, 334
    investment scenarios in, 334
  economic losses from, 323
  food losses and, 322
    zero food waste and, 323
  as global policy, 322
  infrastructure for, 323–324
  methodology for, 324–326
    data in, 326–333
    through grouped logistic regression, 324
    IMPACT, 324–326, 331–333
    infrastructural variables, 326–328, 331
    results of, 326–333
  in sub-Saharan Africa, 323
  technology for, 323–324
    adoption of, 323
    investment in, 330–331
    on-farm, 323
poverty, reduction of. *See also* zero poverty targets
  educational development influenced by, 119
  energy, 143
  global rates, 1
  inequality and, 192, 446–447, 449–453
  record on, 448–449
  statistics on, 446–448
  surveys on, 446
    inequality in, 452–453
  trade reform as influence on, 205–206

poverty deficits
   in China, xxvi
   in India, xxvi
poverty targets. *See also* zero poverty targets
   USAID, xxv–xxvi
   World Bank, xxv–xxvi
PPP. *See* purchasing power parity
pre-2015 development agenda, MDG
   for data collection, 92–94
      costs of, 108–109
      in large countries, 109
      in medium countries, 108–109
      in small countries, 108
   on data collection, 92–94
premature mortality, 220–221, 223–224
   from NCDs, 234–235
   from non-communicable disease, 225–227
   reduction strategies, 227–228
   technological progress and, 228
   water sanitation interventions and, 441
pre-school education, 123, 127
   enrollment ratio, 131
   in sub-Saharan Africa, 129–131
price volatility, domestic markets influenced by,
      200–202
primary education, 126, 128
   benefit-cost ratios of, 130
   in sub-Saharan Africa, 129–130
Principles of Economics (Marshall), 448
priority setting, of MDG targets, 4–9
productivity, technology and, 295–296, 300
Programme for International Student Assessment (PISA)
      scores, 128
property rights, for women, 349–351
protected areas, loss of, 45–46

quality of care, for NCDs, 240

rape, 74–75, 343–344
rapid diagnostic tests (RDTs), 291
R&D. *See* research and development
RDTs. *See* rapid diagnostic tests
recurrent respiratory papillomatosis (RRP), 248
reforestation programs, 47
relative risk (RR) information, 13
renewable energy, 143
   doubling shares of, 154–156
   in EU, 155
   IRENA, 155
   R&D for, 161
renewable portfolio standards (RPS), 155
representation. *See* political representation
reproduction. *See also* family planning; fertility
   as human right, 377
   net reproductive rate, 376
research and development (R&D), 399
   benefit-cost ratios for, 400–405

      assessment of, 401–402
      assumptions in, 402–403
      computations of, 404–405
      models in, 402–403
      results of, 403–405
   in energy production and use, 160–161
      for renewable energy, 161
   international spillovers and, 420
   national investments in, expansion of, 400–401
   in OECD countries, 400–401
   partial equilibrium model of, 415
   system approaches to, 160–161
   technological spillovers and, 410
RethinkHIV campaign, 5–6, 281
Reuter, Peter, 189–190
reverse causality hypothesis, 300–301
rice production and consumption, 457–459
rights. *See* property rights
Rowntree, Seebohm, 447
RPS. *See* renewable portfolio standards
RR information. *See* relative risk information
RRP. *See* recurrent respiratory papillomatosis

safe drinking water. *See* drinking water
Saggi, Kamal, 419
Sandefur, Justin, 118
sanitation, safety goals for, 340–341. *See also* water
      sanitation interventions
   in homes, 425
Sanusi, Lamido, 175
science and technology. *See also* research and development
   innovation zones for, 399–400, 407
      establishment of, 420
      human capital spillovers, 420
      partial equilibrium model of, 416
      types of, 407
   SDGs for, 399–400
SDGs. *See* Sustainable Development Goals
SE4ALL. *See* Sustainable Energy for All Initiative
secondary education, 125, 127
sensitivity analysis
   of broadband technology, 307–308
   of healthcare system development, 225
   of nutrition goals, 373
   of water sanitation interventions, 432, 436–438
sexual health
   as human right, 377
   for women, 357
sexual violence
   assault and rape, 74–75, 343–344
   child abuse as, 73
   costs of, 76
shale gas, 143, 146–147
Smith, Pamela, 420–421
smoking. *See* tobacco use
Soares, Rodrigo R., 90
social protections, 463–465

social security tax, 382
solar energy, 154–155
solid fuels. *See also* fossil fuels; *specific fuel sources*
    AAP from, 13, 15
        costs of control options, 27–28
    HAP from, 13–15
solid waste management, AAP and, 27–28, 31
state legitimacy. *See* legitimacy
statistics. *See also* data collection
    on poverty, 446–448
stroke, 233
stunting reduction, goals for, 367–374
    advantages of, 368–370
    benefit-cost ratio for, 369–373
    disadvantages of, 368–369
    economic perspective on, 369–373
sub-Saharan Africa. *See also* human immunodeficiency virus
    educational development in
        costs of, 132
        pre-school, 129–131
        primary schooling in, 129–130
    energy production and use in, 143
    PHL in, 323
    surveys in, 93–94
subsidies
    energy, 155
        AAP and, control of, 26–28
        for fossil fuels, 156–159
    tax, 193
surveys, 94–96
    HCES and, 450, 453–454
    health, 95–96. *See also* Demographic and Health Surveys
    household, 93–94
        HCES, 450, 453–454
    indicator list by information access type, 95
    in sub-Saharan Africa, 93–94
    on zero poverty targets, 446
        for food consumption, 453–454
        for housing services, 454–456
        inequality in, 452–453
Sustainable Development Goals (SDGs). *See also* Aichi
    Targets; *specific goals*
    CBA of, xxvii–xxx
    costs of, 7
    development of, xxv–xxvii
    energy sustainability, 143–144
    function and purpose of, xxiv
    governance, 475–476
    for healthcare system development, 221–222
    for ICT, 295–300, 312
    IFF in, 173
    MDGs compared to, xxiv–xxvii
    for nutrition, 367–368
    for science and technology, 399–400
    universal concept of development through, xxvi–xxvii
Sustainable Energy for All Initiative (SE4ALL),
    143–144
Sweden, energy production and use in, 158

TAIs. *See* transparency and accountability
    initiatives
targets, development, 3–4. *See also* poverty targets; zero
    targets
    for AAP, 16
        CBA of, 22–25
        regional factors in, 25
    for air pollution
        through air quality improvement, 16
        domains of, 16
        for reduction in health effects, 16
        for reduction in sources of, 16
        selected, 16
        zero, 16
    for broadband technology, 303–304
    in CBA
        for AAP, 22–25
        for HAP, 16–17
    under Copenhagen Consensus, 5–6
    education development, post-2015 development agenda
        for, 119–135
    for emissions reduction
        global, 57–58
        intensity targets, 58
    in future, 6–7
    for governance, 484–491
        assessment of, 486–493
        breadth of targets, 486
        form and function of targets, 486
        outcome and output measurements of targets,
          485–486
    identification of, 8, 504
        for economic growth, 503
        for environmental issues, 502–503
        for humans, 502
    IFF, 176–179
        beneficial ownership, 177, 180–182
        future recommendations for, 186
        for tax information exchange, 177–178
        trade misinvoicing, 178–179, 191
        zero targets, 177
    implementation of, 507
    for international migration, 386
    for NCDs, 231–234
    numerical, adoption of, xxv
    for population aging, 382
    for population demographics, 390–391
    for population growth, 376–379
    prioritizing of, 4–9
    violence and, interventions against, 84–85
        for civil war violence, 81–83
tariffs
    FITs, 155
    foreign, 196
    under GATT, 193
    NTMs, 216
    revenue losses from, 202
    size of, 196

tax evasion
  corporate, 172
  IFF and, 171–172
    multinational, 171
tax information exchange, 177–178
taxation policies
  for AAP, 27
  governance and, 175
  IFF and, 174–175
  OECD standards for, 178
  for tobacco use, 235–236
  trade and, 193
TB. *See* tuberculosis
technological spillovers, 410
technology. *See also* broadband technology; science and
    technology
  adoption of, 320, 323, 334
  CCS, 55–56
    BECSSS, 56
  diffusion of, 297
  enterprise and, 399–400, 402
  for LNG, 147
  low-carbon, 55–56, 59–60, 66, 146
  for PHL, 323–324
    adoption of, 323
    investment in, 330–331
    on-farm, 323
  premature mortality influenced by, 228
  productivity and, 295–296, 300
  R&D for
    in energy production and use, 160–161
    system approaches to, 160–161
  road vehicle, 28–29, 32
  social inclusion through, 295
technology transfer, 420
Telecom Regulatory Authority of India (TRIA), 302
tertiary education, 127–128
TFA. *See* Trade Facilitation Agreement
theft of state assets, 171–172
tobacco use, 234
  taxation of, 235–236
TPP. *See* Trans-Pacific Partnership
trade. *See also* trade reform
  under AFTA, 197
  aid for, 191
  bilateral, 217
  under DDA, 192, 197, 208–209
    economic consequences of, 198–199
    environmental impact of, 207
    net benefits of, 203–204
    reform, 208–209
  economic growth and, 194–196
  under GATT, 193
  ICT revolution, 194, 209
  IFF and, 178–179
  international barriers to, 192–198
    arguments for reduction of, 193–198
    dynamic economic gains, 194–196

    labor market interventions, 193
    static economic gains, 193–194
  international migration and, 204–205
  liberalization of, 193, 195
    in Asia-Pacific region, 199–200
    benefit-cost ratio of, 201
    price volatility and, domestic markets influenced by,
      200–202
  tariffs and, 193
    foreign, 196
    revenue losses for, from trade reform, 202
    size of, 196
  tax subsidies and, 193
  taxation policies and, 193
  under TFA, 216
  under TPP, 192, 197, 199–200
  WTO and, 192
Trade Facilitation Agreement (TFA), 216
trade misinvoicing, 178–179, 191
trade mispricing, 174
trade reform
  agricultural policy influenced by, 207–208
  in Asia-Pacific region, 199–200, 205
  benefit-cost ratio of, 201, 203–205
  DDA and, 208–209
  economic costs of, 202–208
  environmental benefits of, 204
  environmental policy influenced by, 206–207
    global, 206–207
  malnutrition and, 207
  net benefits of, 203–205
  poverty alleviation through, 205–206
  social benefits of, 204
  tariff revenue losses from, 202
trafficking. *See* drug trafficking; human trafficking
Trans-Pacific Partnership (TPP), 192, 197
  APEC and, 197
transparency
  in beneficial ownership, 182, 184
  IFF and, 191
transparency and accountability initiatives (TAIs), 482
Treaty of Lisbon, 157
TRIA. *See* Telecom Regulatory Authority of India
Triple P. *See* Positive Parenting Program
tuberculosis (TB)
  benefit-cost ratio for, 258–259
  control interventions for
    cost effectiveness of, 256–258
    under post-2015 development agenda, 255–256
    through screening, 257
    through treatment, 257
  DALY and, 258–259
  global funding for, lack of, 255
  incidence rates for, 255
  in LMICs, 255
  MDR, 255–258
  stages of, 255
  XDR, 255

UK. *See* United Kingdom
ultra-low sulfur diesel (ULSD), 30–31
UN. *See* United Nations
underweight, in children, 367–368
UNECE. *See* United Nations; United Nations Economic
    Commission for Europe
UNEP. *See* United Nations
UNFCCC. *See* United Nations
Unified Growth Theory, 397
United Kingdom (UK)
    AMLD in, 177, 180
    energy production and use in, 157–158
    IFF in, CBA for, 180–183
United Nations (UN). *See also* Millennium Development
        Goals; Sustainable Development Goals
    FAO, 8
    global goals, 1–2
    on international migration, global consultation priorities
        for, 385
    LDCs and, as development category, 2
    population aging and, global consultation priorities for,
        380
    population growth and, global consultation priorities for,
        376–377
    UNEP, 38
    UNFCCC, 54–55
    universal norms and targets and, development of, xxiv
    urbanization and, global consultation priorities, 387–388
United Nations Economic Commission for Europe (UNECE),
    35
United Nations Environment Programme (UNEP). *See*
    United Nations
United Nations Framework Convention on Climate Change
    (UNFCCC). *See* United Nations
universal broadband penetration, 305–307, 313
universal healthcare, 227
universities. *See* tertiary education
urbanization, 387–388
    in megacities, 387
    UN global consultation priorities, 387–388
USAID
    accountability mechanisms, xxv–xxvi
    extreme poverty targets for, xxv–xxvi

vaccines, for HPV, 244–245
    barriers to, 251
    coverage costs of, 248, 251
    direct health gains of, 246–247
    EPI, 245
    GAVI, 245
    healthcare cost savings, 247
Vietnam, zero poverty targets in, 461–463
violence
    alcohol use as factor in, 80
    assault as, 69
    child abuse, 69–73
        forced early marriage as, 73
        sexual, 73

against children, 69–73. *See also* child abuse
    homicide, 70–71
    interpersonal, 69–70
    non-fatal, 71–72
civil war, 79–83
    annual changes for, 82
    benefit-cost ratio for, 80
    percentage of countries with, 82–83
    reduction of, 79–81
    targets for, 81–83
collective, 68–70
    costs of, 69–70
cost-benefit ratio for, 84–85
    for civil war violence, 80
domestic, 73, 75
gender, 73, 75
by global region, 69
homicide, 68–69
    against children, 70–71
    costs of, 68–69, 75
    against women, costs of, 75
international development approaches to, 68
interpersonal, 68–70
    costs of, 69–70
    decline of, 67–68
intervention targets, 84–85
    for civil war violence, 81–83
IPV
    costs of, 76
    interventions for, 344
    against women, 73, 75
justice systems' response to, 80
rates of, 67
reduction strategies
    for civil war violence, 79–81
    through improved judicial performance, 78–79
    international aid programs, 78–79
    return on investment in, 79–81
    sectoral shares of development assistance, 78
sexual
    assault and rape, 74–75
    child abuse as, 73
    costs of, 76
against women, 67, 73–78
    FGM, 69–70, 73, 75–78, 80
    homicide, costs of, 75
    IPV, 73, 75, 344
    rape, 74–75, 343–344
    sexual assault and rape, 74–75
vocational education, 125

WASH project. *See* water sanitation interventions
Washington Consensus, 477–478
water sanitation interventions
    access to, 425–426
    aims of, 423
    benefit estimation of, 428–431
        data sources in, 431

for economic benefits, 428–429
    for health benefits, 429–431
    relative risk reductions, 429
    time benefits, 430–431
benefit-cost ratios for, 432–436
    for OD elimination strategies, 437
    for populations served, 432
    for sanitation safety, by region, 435–436
    for universal access to sanitation, 433
    for water supply safety, by region, 433–435
cost estimation of, 426–427
    high and low scenarios, 427
DALY values, 433, 436–438, 441
    for premature mortality, 441
estimation models, 423–426
    data sources in, 424–426
    population growth in, 426
    for population size, 423–424
    by region, 423
    service definitions in, 424–426
through handwashing, 428
methodological approach to, 423–432
    excluded countries in, 440
OD and, elimination strategies for, 424–425
    benefit-cost ratios for, 437
for safe drinking water, 425, 428
    benefit-cost ratios for, by region, 433–435
sensitivity analysis of, 432, 436–438
water-borne disease, 225, 429–430
wetlands, loss, 43–44, 50
WGIs. See Worldwide Governance Indicators
Whittington, Dale, 443–445
WHO. See World Health Organization
wind energy, 154–155
wireless technology, 307
    spectrum management of, 310
women. See also gender; gender equality; maternal health;
        mothers
    bank account ownership by, 349–351
    business ownership by, 349–351
    contractual agreements by, legality of, 349–351
    education for, 356–358
    forced early marriage of, 73
    political representation and, equal access to, 351–357
    property rights for, 349–351
    rights of, national income as factor in, 350
    violence against, 67, 73–78
        FGM, 69–70, 73, 75–78, 80
        homicide, costs of, 75
        IPV, 73, 75, 344
        sexual assault and rape, 74–75, 343–344
women's health
    cervical cancer, 244–246
        incidence rates of, 244
        Pap test/smear for, 245–246

prevention of, 244–245, 251
        screening for, 245–246
    family planning, 357
    maternal, cost effectiveness of, 272
    reproductive health, 357
    sexual health, 357
World Bank
    education strategies, 119, 123–124
    extreme poverty targets for, xxv–xxvi
    IFF and, 173
World Energy Council, 143
World Health Organization (WHO)
    EPI, 245
    NCD and, 239–240
        framework for indicators of, 231–232
        premature mortality rate estimates, 234–235
    nutrition goals, 368
World Trade Organization (WTO), 192
World Wide Antimalarial Resistance Network (WWARN),
    288
Worldwide Governance Indicators (WGIs), 479–480
WTO. See World Trade Organization
WWARN. See World Wide Antimalarial Resistance
    Network

XDR-TB. See extensively drug-resistant TB

years of life lost (YLL), 18, 24

zero food waste, 323
zero poverty targets
    CBA of, 460–468
        for disaster resilience, 465
        for economic rights, 466–467
        elimination strategies in, 460–463
        for full employment, 467–468
        for social protection, 463–465
        in Vietnam, 461–463
    in East Asia, 456–460
        composition of poverty, 459–460
        persistence of poverty, 459–460
        rice production and consumption, 457–459
    human capital and, 461–463
    surveys for, 446
        for food consumption, 453–454
        for housing services, 454–456
        inequality in, 452–453
zero targets
    for air pollution, 16
    HCES and, 450, 453–454
    historical development of, 447–448
        first Poverty Enlightenment, 448
    for IFF, 177
    monitoring of, 449–456
    variances in living standards and, 449–452